The Book of

Mysteries of the Unexplained

Publications International, Ltd.

ISBN: 978-1-64558-941-9

Manufactured in U.S.A.

8 7 6 5 4 3 2 1

Let's get social!

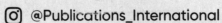 @Publications_International

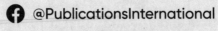 @PublicationsInternational

www.pilbooks.com

Contents

✳   ✳   ✳   ✳

The Curse of King Tut's Tomb✦ A Superior Haunting:
The Edmund Fitzgerald✦ Who Wants to Be a Billionaire?✦
Underground Cities✦ What's Going on Down There?✦ Hey,
It's the Freemasons!✦ The Philadelphia Experiment✦ The
Intergalactic Journey of Scientology✦ The Mystery of the
700-Year-Old Piper✦ In Mushrooms We Trust✦ The Library
of the Muses✦ The Mound Builders: Myth Making in Early
America✦ The Mystery of Easter Island✦ Shhh! It's a Secret
Society✦ The Mystery of Montauk✦ The Secret of the Stones✦
The Anasazi✦ Lily Dale, New York—U.S. Headquarters of
the Spiritualism Movement✦ Ghosts of Higher Education✦
The Ghosts of Chicago's Old Town Tatu✦ Chicago's Oriental
Theatre Is Never Completely Empty✦ The Haunted Destroyer✦
Myrtles Plantation: A Blast From the Past✦ The Sad Fate of
British Airship R101✦ The Curse of Griffith Park✦ Rogues'
Hollow✦ The Smurl Incident✦ St. Louis Cemetery Is Number
One Among Spirits✦ Some Guests Stay Forever at the
Chelsea✦ Tombstone Shadows✦ An Eternal Seaside Retreat:
Cape May's Ghosts✦ Fort Delaware Prison Hosts Ghosts
Through the Ages✦ Atchison, Kansas: A True Ghost Town✦
Capitol Ghosts in Raleigh, North Carolina✦ Who Founded
The Mafia?✦ Conneaut Lake Park✦ The Maudlin Spirits of the
Mounds Theater✦ The Paranormal at Paramount Studios✦ The
Lost Colony of Roanoke✦ Sandstone Gateway to Heaven✦ The
Seven Wonders of the Ancient World✦ Coming to America✦
Ghost Towns of the Ancients✦ George's Food and Drink:
Serving Food, Wine, and Spirits✦ North Carolina's Train of
Terror✦ Did You Hear About What They Saw?✦ The Last
Run of the Montreal Express✦ The Glowing Coed✦ Ghosts of
Harpers Ferry✦ Sunday Best Photoshoot

Chapter 1

They Did What?

Nostradamus: Seer of Visions

Nostradamus was born in December 1503 in Saint-Rémy-de-Provence, a small town in southern France. Little is known about his childhood except that he came from a very large family and that he may have been educated by his maternal great-grandfather. In his teens, Nostradamus entered the University of Avignon but was only there for about a year before the school was forced to close its doors due to an outbreak of the plague. He later became a successful apothecary and even created a pill that could supposedly protect against the plague.

✳ ✳ ✳ ✳

Looking to the Future

IT IS BELIEVED that some time in the 1540s, Nostradamus began taking an interest in the occult, particularly in ways to predict the future. His preferred method was scrying: gazing into a bowl of water or a mirror and waiting for visions to appear.

Nostradamus published a highly successful almanac for the year 1550, which included some of his prophecies and predictions. This almanac was so successful that Nostradamus wrote more, perhaps even several a year, until his death in 1566. Even so, it was a single book that caused the most controversy, both when it was released and even today.

Les Prophéties

In addition to creating his almanacs, Nostradamus also began compiling his previously unpublished prophecies into one massive volume. Released in 1555, *Les Prophéties* (*The Prophecies*) would become one of the most controversial and perplexing books ever written. The book contained hundreds of quatrains (four-line stanzas or poems), but Nostradamus worried that some might see his prophecies as demonic, so he encoded them to obscure their true meanings. Nostradamus did everything from playing with the syntax of the quatrains to switching between French, Greek, Latin, and other languages.

When the book was first released, some people did think that Nostradamus was in league with the devil. Others simply thought he was insane and that his quatrains were nothing more than the ramblings of a delusional man. As time went on, though, people started looking to Nostradamus's prophecies to see if they were coming true. It became a common practice that after a major event in history, people would pull out a copy of *Les Prophéties* to see if they could find a hidden reference to it buried in one of Nostradamus's quatrains. It is a practice that has continued to this day.

One of the interesting and frustrating things about Nostradamus's *Les Prophéties* is that due to the printing procedures in his time, no two editions of his book were ever alike. Not only were there differences in spelling or punctuation, but entire words and phrases were often changed, especially when translated from French to English. Presently, there are more than 200 editions of *Les Prophéties* in print, all of which have subtle differences in the text. So it's not surprising that people from all over the world have looked into their version and found references to the French Revolution, Napoleon, the rise of Hitler, the JFK assassination, even the Apollo moon landing. But of all the messages reportedly hidden in Nostradamus's quatrains, the most talked about recently are those relating to the terrorist attacks on September 11, 2001.

Soon after the Twin Towers fell, an e-mail started making the rounds, which claimed that Nostradamus had predicted the events and quoted the following quatrain as proof:

In the City of God there will be a great thunder,

Two Brothers torn apart by Chaos,

While the fortress endures,

The great leader will succumb,

The third big war will begin when the big city is burning

—Nostradamus, 1654

Anyone reading the above can clearly see that Nostradamus is describing September 11, the Twin Towers ("Two Brothers") falling, and the start of World War III. Pretty chilling, except Nostradamus never wrote it. It's nothing more than an internet hoax that spread like wildfire. It's a pretty bad hoax, too. First, Nostradamus wrote quatrains, which have four lines. This one has five. Also, consider that the date Nostradamus supposedly penned this—1654—was almost 90 years after he died. Nostradamus might have been able to see the future, but there's no mention of him being able to write from beyond the grave.

However, others believe Nostradamus did indeed pen a quatrain that predicted September 11. It is quatrain I.87, which when translated reads:

Volcanic fire from the center of the earth

Will cause tremors around the new city;

Two great rocks will make war for a long time

Then Arethusa will redden a new river.

Those who believe this quatrain predicted September 11 believe that the "new city" is a thinly-veiled reference to New York City. They further state that Nostradamus would often use rocks to refer to religious beliefs and that the third stanza refers to the religious differences between the United States and the terrorists. Skeptic James Randi, however, believes that the "new city" referred to is Naples, not New York. So who's right? No one is really sure, so for now, the debate continues... at least until the next major catastrophe hits and people go scrambling to see what Nostradamus had to say about it.

The Clairvoyant Crime-Buster

Before there were TV shows like Ghost Whisperer *and* Medium, *which make the idea of solving crimes through ESP seem almost commonplace, there was psychic detective Arthur Price Roberts. And his work was accomplished in the early 1900s, when high-tech aids like electronic surveillance and DNA identification were still only far-fetched dreams. Police in those times often used psychics to help solve many cases.*

✳ ✳ ✳ ✳

"I See Dead People"

A MODEST MAN BORN in Wales in 1866, Roberts deliberately avoided a formal education because he believed too much learning could stifle his unusual abilities. He moved to Milwaukee, Wisconsin, as a young man where, ironically, the man who never learned to read was nicknamed "Doc."

One of his earliest well-known cases involved a baffling missing person incident in Peshtigo, a small town about 160 miles north of Milwaukee. A man named Duncan McGregor had gone missing in July 1905, leaving no clue as to his whereabouts. The police searched for him for months, and finally his desperate wife decided to go to the psychic detective who had already made a name for himself in Milwaukee. She didn't even have to explain the situation to Roberts; he knew immediately upon meeting her who she was.

Roberts meditated on the vanished husband, then sadly had to tell Mrs. McGregor that he'd been murdered and that his body was in the Peshtigo River, caught near the bottom in a pile of timber. Roberts proved correct in every detail.

Mystery of the Mad Bombers

Roberts solved numerous documented cases. He helped a Chicago man find his brother who had traveled to Albuquerque and had not been heard from for months; Roberts predicted that the brother's body would be found in a certain spot in Devil's Canyon, and it was. After coming up with new evidence for an 11th hour pardon, Roberts saved a Chicago man named Ignatz Potz, who had been condemned to die for a murder he didn't commit. But his most famous coup came in 1935 when he correctly predicted that the city of Milwaukee would be hit by six large dynamite explosions, losing a town hall, banks, and police stations. People snickered; such mayhem was unheard of in Milwaukee. Roberts made his prediction on October 18 of that year. In little more than a week, the Milwaukee area entered a time of terror.

First, a town hall in the outlying community of Shorewood was blasted, killing two children and wounding many other people. A few weeks later, the mad bombers hit two banks and two police stations. Federal agents descended upon the city, and several local officers were assigned to work solely on solving the bombings. Finally, the police went to Roberts to learn what was coming next. Roberts told them one more blast was in the works, that it would be south of the Menomonee River, and that it would be the final bomb. Police took him at his word and blanketed the area with officers and sharpshooters. And sure enough, on November 4, a garage in the predicted area blew to smithereens in an explosion that could be heard as far as eight miles away. The two terrorists, young men 18 and 21 years old, had been hard at work in the shed assembling 50 pounds of dynamite when their plan literally backfired. Few people argued with Roberts's abilities after that.

His Final Fortune

Roberts's eeriest prediction, however, may have been that of his own death. In November 1939, he told a group of assembled friends that he would be leaving this world on January 2, 1940. And he did, passing quietly in his own home on that exact date. Many of his most amazing accomplishments will probably never be known because a lot of his work was done secretly for various law enforcement agencies. But "Doc" Roberts had an undeniable gift, and he died secure in the knowledge that he had used it to help others as best he could.

H. H. Holmes: Serial Killer at the World's Fair

H. H. Holmes has secured a place in history as one of the cruelest, most horrifyingly prolific killers the world has ever seen. From his headquarters at a Chicago hotel, Holmes slaughtered at least 27 people starting in the early 1890s. Many filmmakers, scholars, and authors have tried to understand the mind of the madman Holmes. Here is an overview of the twisted, convoluted details of the real-life "Doctor Death."

✳ ✳ ✳ ✳

Troubled Child

BORN IN MAY 1860, Herman Webster Mudgett was a highly intelligent child and did well in school, but he was constantly in trouble. As a teen, he became abusive to animals and small children—a classic characteristic of serial killers.

Fascinated with bones, skeletons, and the human body, Mudgett decided to pursue a degree in medicine, which seemed a natural fit. He changed his name to H. H. Holmes, married Clara Lovering, and with her inheritance, enrolled in medical school in Burlington, Vermont.

Swindler, Liar, Cheat

In medical school, Holmes was able to be around skeletons, cadavers, and fresh corpses all the time, which suited him just fine. Very soon, however, it was obvious that Holmes wasn't in the medical field for humanitarian reasons. Ever the swindler, Holmes came up with a scheme whereby he'd take insurance policies out on family members he didn't actually have. He would steal cadavers from the school, make them look as if they'd had an accident, then identify the bodies as those of his family members to collect the insurance money. Some of these frauds brought in $10,000 or more per body.

When authorities became suspicious of all these dead "family members," Holmes abandoned Clara and their newborn baby. Where he went after that is a little murky, as the next six or so years of Holmes's life are not well documented. But by the mid-1880s, Holmes was back on the radar as a charming, intelligent, bold-faced liar and thief with murderous intentions. This time, his mark was Chicago. The city would become the site of Holmes's biggest, deadliest swindle of all.

The Roots of a Murderous Plan

If you lived in Chicago in the late 1800s, you were likely consumed with thoughts of the World's Fair. Officially known as the World's Columbian Exposition of 1893, the colossal event had most of the Midwest working for its success. It was to be the event that would make America a superstar country and make Chicago one of the country's A-list cities. The Great Fire of 1871 had demolished the town; the World's Fair vowed to bring it back in a big way.

It was during the years of preparation for the big fair that Holmes began his path of murder. With so many people flooding the city every day looking to nab one of the thousands of new jobs in the area, Chicago was experiencing a population boom that made it very easy to lose track of people. Holmes recognized this as an opportunity to lure women into his clutches while most people had their focus elsewhere.

He married his second wife, Myrtle, in 1885, even though he had never actually divorced Clara. While Myrtle lived in suburban Wilmette, Holmes took a place in Chicago, and the couple lived apart for most of their marriage. Holmes needed to be in the city because he was working at a drugstore in Chicago's Englewood neighborhood. He worked for the elderly Mrs. Holdens, a kind woman who was happy to have such an attractive young doctor help out at her busy store. When Mrs. Holden disappeared without a trace in 1887 and Holmes purchased the store, no one suspected a thing.

Holmes (who now had full access to a well-stocked drugstore with countless medical tools, chemicals, and medicines) purchased a vacant lot across the street from the drugstore and began construction on a house with a strange floor plan he'd designed himself. The three-story house would have 60 rooms, more than 50 doors placed in an odd fashion throughout the structure, trap doors, secret passageways, windowless rooms, and chutes that led down to a deep basement. Holmes hired and fired construction crews on a regular basis, and it was said that his swindler's streak got him out of paying for most (or perhaps all) of the materials and labor used to create what would later be known as the "Murder Castle."

Death: Up & Running

As construction of the "castle" wrapped up, Holmes made plans for several of his employees. The bookkeeper Holmes had at the store around 1890 was Ned Connor, a man who had come to Chicago with his lovely wife, Julia, and their baby daughter, Pearl. Holmes found Julia irresistible and quickly put the make on her, firing Ned so his wife could take his place. It is believed that as his new bookkeeper, Julia was possibly an accomplice in the fraudulent actions at the drugstore, which eased Holmes's mind and allowed him to concentrate on his new building.

Advertised as a lodging for World's Fair tourists, the building opened in 1892. Holmes placed ads in the newspaper to rent rooms, but also listed fake classifieds, calling for females interested in working for a start-up company. He also placed ads for marriage, posing as a successful businessman in need of a wife. Any woman who answered these fake ads was interviewed by Holmes, was told to keep everything a secret, and was instructed to withdraw all funds from her bank account in order to start a new life with him as his worker, wife, or whatever role he had offered. Holmes was a brilliant liar and quite the charmer, and naive 19th-century women fell for it. Once they passed Holmes's tests, these women became his prisoners, doomed to meet their grisly ends.

Gas pipes were secretly installed throughout the house with nozzles that piped noxious fumes into the rooms. Holmes would turn on the gas so that the victim du jour would drop to the floor unconscious. While she was out cold, Holmes would usually rape her, then send the girl down to the basement via the chute. Once there, he would perform experiments on her at his dissection table or torture her with various equipment.

He reportedly listened to the screams of the victims from an adjacent room.

Once he had brutalized the unfortunate soul, he would dump her body into a vat of lime acid to completely destroy the evidence. Other times, he sold bones and organs to contacts in the medical field. Holmes murdered at least 22 people in his home, mostly women, though every once in awhile a worried male neighbor or a concerned relative looking for a missing young woman would get too suspicious for Holmes's liking and go missing themselves.

While the "Murder Castle" was in operation, Holmes continued to marry various women and carry out insurance fraud and other deviant acts. After the World's Fair ended, creditors put pressure on him again, and Holmes knew it was time to flee. He traveled across the United States and Canada, scamming and murdering along the way. Strange as it seems, when Holmes was finally caught and brought to justice, it wasn't initially for homicide; a horse-swindling scheme he attempted to pull off with longtime partner in fraud Ben Pietzel was what gave authorities enough evidence to arrest Holmes. When they searched Holmes's Chicago dwelling, their investigation turned up a lot more than they anticipated.

The End of "Doctor Death"

Over the years, one detective had been hot on Holmes's trail. Detective Frank Geyer, a veteran Pinkerton detective, had done his best to follow this creepy man whose identity changed with the weather. Geyer had traced many of the missing World's Fair women back to Holmes's lodging house and had discovered trails that pointed to his fraudulent activities. In 1895, Holmes entered a guilty plea for the horse-fraud case, and Geyer took that opportunity to expand the investigation. He was particularly interested in the whereabouts of three children—Howard, Nellie, and Alice Pietzel, children of Holmes's now murdered accomplice, Ben Pietzel.

Geyer traced the children—and then Holmes—by following his mail. When his search took him to Canada, Geyer knocked on doors all over Toronto to track down Holmes. Finally, he found a house where Holmes had allegedly stayed with several children in tow. Buried in a shallow grave in the backyard were the bodies of the two Pietzel girls. The boy was found several months later in an oven in an Indianapolis home.

When the evidence was brought back to court, Geyer got full clearance to investigate every dark nook and cranny of Holmes's house and business, and one of America's most chilling stories of murder and crime officially broke. As detectives and police officers uncovered layer after layer of hideous evidence, the public became more and more frightened—and fascinated. The *Chicago Tribune* published the floor plan of the "Murder Castle," tourists flocked to ogle the building, and tabloids ran horrifying descriptions of what had happened to the victims inside, events both real and embellished. Then, in August 1895, Holmes's house of horrors burnt to the ground.

While all that took place, inside his heavily guarded cell, Herman Webster Mudgett confessed to his crimes. He officially confessed to 27 murders, six attempted murders, and a whole lot of fraud. What he didn't confess to, however, were any feelings of remorse. Holmes claimed at times to be possessed by the devil, though depending on the day, he'd also claim to be innocent of any wrongdoing whatsoever. All told, estimates of his victims may have hit the 200 mark. Just because he confessed to 27 murders doesn't mean that's what his final tally was—indeed, with the kind of liar Holmes was, it's pretty certain that the number isn't accurate at all.

Holmes was executed by hanging in 1896. He was buried in a coffin lined with cement, topped with more cement, and buried in a double grave—instructions he gave in his last will and testament so that "no one could dig him back up." Was he ready to rest eternally after a life of such monstrosity? Or was he afraid that someone would conduct experiments on him as he had done to so many hapless victims? Whatever the case, the monster who destroyed so many lives had finally been stopped.

Psychic Detectives

When the corpse just can't be found, the murderer remains unknown, and the weapon has been stashed in some secret corner, criminal investigations hit a stalemate and law enforcement agencies may tap their secret weapons—individuals who find things through some unconventional methods.

✳ ✳ ✳ ✳

"Reading" the Ripper: Robert James Lees

WHEN THE PSYCHOTIC murderer known as Jack the Ripper terrorized London in the 1880s, the detectives of Scotland Yard consulted a psychic named Robert James Lees who said he had glimpsed the killer's face in several visions. Lees also claimed he had correctly forecasted at least three of the well-publicized murders of women. The Ripper wrote a sarcastic note to detectives stating that they would still never catch him. Indeed, the killer proved right in this prediction.

Feeling Their Vibes: Florence Sternfels

As a psychometrist—a psychic who gathers impressions by handling material objects—Florence Sternfels was successful enough to charge a dollar for readings in Edgewater, New Jersey, in the early 20th century. Born in 1891, Sternfels believed that her gift was a natural ability rather than a supernatural one, so she never billed police for her help in solving crimes. Some of her best "hits" included preventing a man from blowing up an army base with dynamite, finding two missing boys alive in Philadelphia, and leading police to the body of a murdered young woman. She worked with police as far away as Europe to solve tough cases but lived quietly in New Jersey until her death in 1965.

The Dutch Grocer's Gift: Gerard Croiset

Born in the Netherlands in 1909, Gerard Croiset nurtured a growing psychic ability from age six. In 1935, he joined a Spiritualist group, began to hone his talents, and within two years had set up shop as a psychic and healer. After a touring lecturer discovered his abilities in 1945, Croiset began assisting law enforcement agencies around the world, traveling as far as Japan and Australia. He specialized in finding missing children but also helped authorities locate lost papers and artifacts. At the same time, Croiset ran a popular clinic for psychic healing that treated both humans and animals. His son, Gerard Croiset, Jr., was also a professional psychic and parapsychologist.

Accidental Psychic: Peter Hurkos

As one of the most famous psychic detectives of the 20th century, Peter Hurkos did his best work by picking up vibes from victims' clothing. Born in the Netherlands in 1911, Hurkos lived an ordinary life as a house painter until a fall required him to undergo brain surgery at age 30. The operation seemed to trigger his latent psychic powers, and he was almost immediately able to mentally retrieve information about people and "read" the history of objects by handling them.

Hurkos assisted in the Boston Strangler investigation in the early 1960s, and in 1969, he was brought in to help solve the grisly murders executed by Charles Manson. He gave police many accurate details including the name Charlie, a description of Manson, and that the murders were ritual slayings.

The TV Screen Mind of Dorothy Allison

New Jersey housewife Dorothy Allison broke into the world of clairvoyant crime solving when she dreamed about a missing local boy as if seeing it on television. In her dream, the five-year-old boy was stuck in some kind of pipe. When she called police, she also described the child's clothing, including the odd fact that he was wearing his shoes on the opposite feet.

When Allison underwent hypnosis to learn more details, she added that the boy's surroundings involved a fenced school and a factory. She was proven correct on all accounts when the boy's body was found about two months after he went missing, floating close to a pipe in a pond near a school and a factory with his little shoes still tied onto the wrong feet.

Allison, who began having psychic experiences as a child, considered her gift a blessing and never asked for pay. One of her more famous cases was that of missing heiress Patty Hearst in 1974. Although Allison was unable to find her, every prediction she made about the young woman came true, including the fact that she had dyed her hair red.

Like a Bolt Out of the Blue: John Catchings

While at a Texas barbeque on an overcast July 4, 1969, a bolt of lightning hit 22-year-old John Catchings. He survived but said the electric blast opened him to his life's calling as a psychic. He then followed in the footsteps of his mother, Bertie, who earned her living giving "readings."

Catchings often helped police solve puzzling cases but became famous after helping police find a missing, 32-year-old Houston nurse named Gail Lorke. She vanished in late October 1982, after her husband, Steven, claimed she had stayed home from work because she was sick.

Because Catchings worked by holding objects that belonged to victims, Lorke's sister, who was suspicious of Steven, went to Catchings with a photo of Gail and her belt. Allegedly, Catchings saw that Lorke had indeed been murdered by her husband and left under a heap of refuse that included parts of an old, wooden fence. He also gave police several other key details.

Detectives were able to use the information to get Steven Lorke to confess his crime.

Among many other successes, Catchings also helped police find the body of Mike Dickens in 1980 after telling them the young man would be found buried in a creek bed near a shoe and other rubbish, including old tires and boards. Police discovered the body there just as Catchings had described it.

Fame from Fortunes: Irene Hughes

In 2008, famed investigative psychic Irene Hughes claimed a career tally of more than 2,000 police cases on her website. Born around 1920 (sources vary) in rural Tennessee, Hughes shocked her church congregation at age four when she shouted out that the minister would soon leave them. She was right and kept on making predictions, advised by a Japanese "spirit guide" named Kaygee. After World War II, Hughes moved to Chicago to take a job as a newspaper reporter. She financed her trip by betting on a few horse races using her psychic abilities! She gained fame in 1967 when she correctly prophesied Chicago's terrible blizzard and that the Cardinals would win the World Series. By 1968, she was advising Howard Hughes and correctly predicted his death in 1976.

Hughes's more famous predictions included the death of North Vietnamese premier Ho Chi Minh in 1969 (although she was off by a week), the circumstances of Ted Kennedy's Chappaquiddick fiasco, and that Jacqueline Kennedy would marry someone with the characteristics of her eventual second husband, Aristotle Onassis. Hughes operated out of a luxurious office on Chicago's Michigan Avenue and commanded as much as $500 an hour from her many eager clients. She hosted radio and TV shows, wrote three books, and in the 1980s and '90s, wrote a much-read column of New Year's predictions for the *National Enquirer*. She died in 2012 in a retirement home in Beecher, Illinois.

True Tales of Being Buried Alive

Generally, burial is something that happens after death. Whether by accident, intent, or diabolical design, there are some who settled down for a "dirt nap" a little prematurely.

✳ ✳ ✳ ✳

David Blaine

ON APRIL 5, 1999, before an estimated crowd of 75,000 on Manhattan's Upper West Side, magician David Blaine undertook his "Buried Alive" stunt, voluntarily going six feet under, albeit with a small air tube. Placed inside a transparent plastic coffin with a mere six inches of headroom and two inches on either side, the illusionist was lowered into his burial pit. Next, a three-ton water-filled tank was lowered on top of his tomb. The magician ate nothing during his stunt and reportedly only sipped two to three tablespoons of water per day—a fasting schedule likely designed to keep bodily wastes to a minimum. After seven days of self-entombment, Blaine popped out, none the worse for wear. Many believed that the magician had somehow left his tomb and returned only when it was time to emerge. However, these naysayers couldn't explain why he'd been visible the entire time and how witnesses saw him move on a number of occasions. Blaine called it a "test of endurance of…the human body and mind…." Even famous debunker and fellow magic man James Randi praised him.

Barbara Jane Mackle

Could there be anything more horrifying than a forced burial? Emory University student Barbara Jane Mackle suffered through such an ordeal and miraculously lived to tell the tale. Abducted from a motel room on December 17, 1968, the 20-year-old daughter of business mogul Robert Mackle was whisked off to a remote location and buried under 18 inches of earth. Her coffinlike box was sparsely equipped with food, water, a pair of vent tubes, and a light. After receiving their

$500,000 ransom, the kidnappers informed the FBI of the girl's location. Some 80 hours after Mackle entered her underground prison, she was discovered in a wooded area roughly 20 miles northeast of Atlanta. Her light source had failed just a few hours after her burial, and she was severely dehydrated, but otherwise the young woman was in good condition. Both kidnappers were eventually apprehended.

School Bus Kidnapping and Live Burial

A notably bizarre burial occurred in 1976 when an entire school bus filled with children was hijacked in Chowchilla, California. The driver and 26 children were removed from the bus, placed into vans, and driven a hundred miles to a quarry in the town of Livermore. There they were forced into a moving van buried several feet below ground. Limited survival supplies and minimal air vents welcomed them into a pitch-black, claustrophobic hell. After 12 long hours, the students feverishly started looking for ways out. Fashioning a crude ladder out of old mattresses, the bus driver and a group of boys climbed to the top of the moving van where they had originally entered. Using a wooden beam, they were able to slowly pry off the heavy, metal lid that separated them from sweet freedom. After 16 hours below ground, they emerged. Despite their harrowing experience, all survived. A ransom note was eventually traced back to Frederick Woods, the quarry owner's son. He and accomplices Richard and James Schoenfeld were convicted and sentenced to life in prison.

Toltecs

The Toltecs, a pre-Columbian Native American people, practiced a ceremony called "Burial of the Warrior." During this rite of passage, a young man would enter a forest and bury himself in a shallow grave for a full day. In a modern-day incarnation of the ritualistic practice, people voluntarily go underground claiming that burial beneath Mother Earth is a way of returning to the womb. Breathing strategies and duration of burial are left unknown until the moment of truth.

Howard Hughes: The Paragon of Paranoia

The sad condition of reclusive mogul Howard Hughes in his last years is well known—he became a bearded, emaciated, germophobe hiding in his Las Vegas hotel room. But the actual details of Hughes's strange life are even more shocking. Money definitely did not seem to buy him happiness.

✳ ✳ ✳ ✳

A Golden Youth

BORN IN HOUSTON, Texas, in 1905, to an overprotective mother and an entrepreneur father who made a fortune from inventing a special drill bit, Howard Hughes moved to California shortly after his mother died when he was 17. There he was exposed to the Hollywood film industry through his screenwriter uncle, Rupert Hughes. When his father died two years later, Howard inherited nearly a million dollars while still in his teens. Through shrewd investments he managed to parlay that into a serious fortune, which gave him the means to pursue his interest in films that had been ignited by Uncle Rupert.

Hughes became the darling of Hollywood beauty queens. He produced several successful films, including *Scarface* and *Hell's Angels* (which cost him nearly $4 million of his own money). Next, he turned his imaginative talents to aviation. He formed his own aircraft company, built many planes himself, and broke a variety of world records. He even won a Congressional Gold Medal in 1939 for his achievements in aviation.

But his life took a drastic turn in 1946, when he suffered injuries in a plane crash that led to a lifelong addiction to painkillers. He also downed several seaplanes and was involved in a few auto accidents—perhaps these mishaps planted the idea that the world was out to get him, and the safest way to avoid more accidents was to stay at home.

Evolving Into a Hermit

Hughes married movie starlet Jean Peters in 1957, but they spent little time together and later divorced. He eventually moved to Las Vegas and bought the Desert Inn so he could turn its penthouse into his personal safe house.

In 1968, *Fortune* magazine named Howard Hughes the richest man in America, with an estimated wealth of $1 billion. But his personal eccentricities mounted almost as quickly as his fortune. Hughes was afraid of outside contamination of all sorts, from unseen bacteria to city water systems to entire ethnic groups. He was even afraid of children. He also burned his clothes if he found out that someone he knew had an illness.

Dangerously Decrepit

Biographer Michael Drosnin provided shocking details about Hughes's lifestyle: He spent most of his time naked, his matted hair hanging shoulder-length and his nails so long they curled over. Hughes even stored his own urine in glass jars. His home was choked with old newspapers and used tissues, and he sometimes wore empty tissue boxes as shoes. Hughes was obsessive, however, about organizing the memos that he scribbled on hundreds of yellow pads.

Hughes usually ate just one meal per day, and he sometimes subsisted on dessert alone. His dental hygiene was abysmal—his teeth literally rotted in his mouth. When he finally died from heart failure in 1976, the formerly robust, 6'4" man weighed only 90 pounds. He had grown too weak to handle his codeine syringe and had turned himself into a human pincushion, with five broken hypodermic needles embedded in his arms.

He Couldn't Take It with Him

Howard Hughes died without a will, although he had kept his aides in line for nearly two decades by dangling the promise of a fat windfall upon his death. In the end, his giant estate was inherited by some cousins. Hughes left another legacy—his long list of achievements. He built the first communication satellite—the kind used today to link the far corners of the world. His Hughes Aircraft Company greatly advanced modern aviation. And he produced award-winning movies. However, the full extent of his influence on the world will probably never be known.

The Lizzie Borden Murder Mystery

Most people know the rhyme that begins, "Lizzie Borden took an axe and gave her mother 40 whacks…" In reality, approximately 20 hatchet chops cut down Abby Borden, but no matter the number, Lizzie's stepmother was very much dead on that sultry August morning in 1892. Lizzie's father, Andrew, was killed about an hour later. His life was cut short by about a dozen hatchet chops to the head.

✳ ✳ ✳ ✳

Andrew Borden, an American "Scrooge"

ANDREW JACKSON BORDEN had been one of the richest men in Fall River, Massachusetts, with a net worth of nearly half a million dollars. In 1892, that was enormous wealth. Andrew was a shrewd businessman: At the time of his death, he was the president of the Union Savings Bank and director of another bank plus several profitable cotton mills.

Despite his wealth, Andrew was miserly. Though some of his neighbors' homes had running hot water, the three-story Borden home had just two cold-water taps, and there was no water available above the first floor. The Bordens' only latrine was in the cellar, so they generally used chamber pots that were either dumped onto the lawn behind the house or emptied into the cellar toilet. And, although most wealthy people used gas lighting, the Bordens lit their house with inexpensive kerosene lamps.

Worst of all, for many years, Andrew was an undertaker who offered some of the lowest prices in town. He worked on the bodies in the basement of the Borden home, and allegedly, he bent the knees of the deceased—and in some cases, cut off their feet—to fit the bodies into smaller, less expensive coffins in order to increase his business.

So, despite the brutality of Andrew's murder, it seems few people mourned his loss. The question wasn't why he was killed, but who did it.

Lizzie vs. William

In 1997, when psychic Jane Doherty visited the murder site, she uncovered several clues about the Lizzie Borden case. Doherty felt that the real murderer was someone named "Willie." There is no real evidence to support this claim, but some say Andrew had an illegitimate son named William, who may have spent time as an inmate in an insane asylum. His constant companion was reportedly his hatchet, which he talked to as though it were a friend. Also, at least one witness reportedly saw William at the Borden house on the day of the murders. William was supposedly there to challenge Andrew about his new will.

Was William the killer? A few years after the murders, William took poison and then hung himself in the woods. Near his swinging body, he'd reportedly left his hatchet on the ground. So with William dead and Lizzie already acquitted, the Borden murder case was put to rest.

Lizzie's Forbidden Romance

One of the most curious explanations for the murder involves the Bordens' servant Bridget Sullivan. Her participation has always raised questions. Like the other members of the Borden household, Bridget had suffered from apparent food poisoning the night before the murders. She claimed to have been ill in the backyard of the Borden home.

During the time Abby was being murdered, Bridget was apparently washing windows in the back of the house. Later, when Andrew was killed, Bridget was resting in her room upstairs. Why didn't she hear two people being butchered?

According to some theories, Lizzie and Bridget had been romantically involved. In this version of the story, their relationship was discovered shortly before the murders. Around this same time, Andrew was reportedly rewriting his will. His wife was now "Mrs. Borden," to Lizzie, not "Mother," as Lizzie had called her stepmother for many years. The reason for the estrangement was never clear.

Lizzie also had a strange relationship with her father and had given him her high school ring, as though he were her sweetheart. He wore the ring on his pinky finger and was buried with it.

Just a day before the murders, Lizzie had been attempting to purchase prussic acid—a deadly poison—and the family came down with "food poisoning" that night. Some speculate that Bridget was Lizzie's accomplice in the murders and helped clean up the blood afterward.

This theory was bolstered when, a few years after the murders, Lizzie became involved with actress Nance O'Neil. For two years, Lizzie and the statuesque actress were inseparable. This prompted Emma Borden, Lizzie's sister, to move out of their home. At the time, the rift between the sisters sparked rumors that either Lizzie or Emma might reveal more about the other's role in the 1892 murders. However, neither of them said anything new about the killings.

Whodunit?

Most people believe that Lizzie was the killer. She was the only one accused of the crime, with good reason. Lizzie appeared to be the only one in the house at the time, other than Bridget. She showed no signs of grief when the murders were discovered. During questioning, Lizzie changed her story several times. The evidence was entirely circumstantial, but it was compelling enough to go to trial.

Ultimately, the jury accepted her attorney's closing argument, that the murders were "morally and physically impossible for this young woman defendant." In other words, Lizzie had to be innocent because she was petite and well bred. In 19th-century New England, that seemed like a logical and persuasive defense. Lizzie went free, and no one else was charged with the crimes.

But Lizzie wasn't the only one with motive, means, and opportunity. The most likely suspects were family members, working alone or with other relatives. Only a few had solid alibis, and—like Lizzie—many changed their stories during police questioning. But there was never enough evidence to officially accuse anyone other than Lizzie.

So whether or not Lizzie Borden "took an ax" and killed her parents, she's the one best remembered for the crime.

Lizzie Borden Bed & Breakfast

The Borden house has been sold several times over the years, but today it is a bed-and-breakfast—the main draw, of course, being the building's macabre history. The Victorian residence has been restored to reflect the details of the Borden home at the time of the murders, including the couch on which Andrew lay, his skull hideously smashed.

As a guest, you can stay in one of six rooms, even the one in which Abby was murdered. Then, after a good night's sleep, you'll be treated to a breakfast reminiscent of the one the Bordens had on their final morning in 1892. That is, if you got to sleep at all. (They say the place is haunted.)

As with all good morbid attractions, the proprietors at the Lizzie Borden B&B don't take themselves too seriously.

History's Maddest Rulers

We all complain about our nation's leadership from time to time, but check out these crazy rulers and their devilish deeds.

✳ ✳ ✳ ✳

Vlad the Impaler

EVERYONE HAS HEARD of the infamous Count Dracula. Half man, half bat, this beastly hybrid lived to drink human blood. But not everyone knows that novelist Bram Stoker's inspiration for the evil madman came from an actual person who was much worse than he's been portrayed. Vlad III Dracula (1431–1476) governed Wallachia, a Hungarian principality that later merged with neighbors Transylvania and Moldavia to form Romania. To say that Dracula ruled with an iron fist barely scratches the surface—an "iron stake" is more accurate. During his six-year reign of terror, it is believed that Dracula murdered as many as 40,000 people whom he considered enemies. Most of these unfortunates met their end by impalement, hence Dracula's ominous moniker. With a sharpened stake as wide as a man's arm, his victims were often pierced from the anus to the mouth, not through the heart as Hollywood legend implies. The madman often blinded, strangled, decapitated, hanged, boiled, burned, or skinned his victims. Once, a concubine hoping to spare her life claimed that she was carrying Dracula's child. When he discovered she was lying, he had her womb cut open and remarked, "Let the world see where I have been."

Idi Amin Dada

To the eye, Ugandan president Idi Amin Dada (1925–2003) was a deceptive contradiction. Viewed as a cartoonlike character by the press (*Time* dubbed him a "killer and clown, big-hearted buffoon and strutting martinet"), the former major general nevertheless found a way to kill an estimated 300,000 people while in power. Many of his victims were killed to squelch the ruler's paranoid fears of being overthrown. Others were eliminated simply for his own ghoulish pleasure. Known as the "butcher of Uganda," Dada reportedly kept severed heads in his refrigerator and may have eaten some of his victims. And allegedly, when Dada learned that his second wife was pregnant with another man's child, he had her dismembered. After the atrocity, he ordered her remains stitched together so he could show her corpse to their children.

Justin II

In the final days of his reign, Byzantine Emperor Justin II (c. 520–578) descended into an overwhelming insanity that was only briefly punctuated by moments of lucidity. Accounts tell of a daft ruler who went mad after a nervous breakdown. Monitored closely by attendants, the emperor sometimes needed to be restrained lest he commit undue harm upon himself or others. The crazed ruler would often lunge at his attendants in an attempt to bite them, and reports suggest that he actually devoured a number of his faithful servants during his reign.

King George III

Great Britain's King George III (1738–1820) suffered recurring bouts of dementia during his reign. Believed to be suffering the ill effects of porphyria, a blood disorder that can produce psychotic symptoms, the king often acted in an outlandish manner. Fits of gloom and melancholy often alternated with excited periods where the king would talk incessantly and act strangely. During one such bout, George III reportedly spoke nonsense for a period lasting some 58 hours. But whether or not the king was insane, his "caregivers" were a bit suspect as well, at least by today's standards. Doctors often tried bleeding him to remove bad substances. When this failed, another doctor decided to draw the poison out of his brain by cutting small holes in his forehead. The king was also confined to a straightjacket, denied heat in the winter, and fed chemical agents that did nothing more than make him vomit. King George III eventually went blind and died in a back room of Windsor Castle. Such a tale begs the obvious question: Who was really mad here?

Vitellius

If an unquenchable bloodlust is the hallmark of a true madman, Roman emperor Aulus Vitellius Germanicus Augustus (AD 15–69) ranks near the top. Simply known as Vitellius, he took perverse joy in watching his victims squirm. His actions sound like something lifted from a Stephen King novel, yet they are reportedly true. Consider this: On impulse, and purely for his own amusement, Vitellius would summon personal friends and acquaintances to his court, then order them killed, or do the deed himself. On one occasion, two sons begging for their father's life were executed beside him. At another time, Vitellius gave a glass of poisoned water to a thirsty man stricken with fever and watched in utter glee as it took effect. Psychological tortures also factored heavily into this madman's repertoire. The ruler once issued a reprieve to a subject who was to be executed. As the man praised the emperor for his mercy, Vitellius ordered him killed in his presence saying that he wished to "feast [on] his eyes." His motives for such loathing are shrouded in mystery, but in the end, Vitellius was tortured, killed, and thrown in the Tigris River by the leader of an opposing faction.

Caligula

The famed Caligula (Gaius Caesar Augustus Germanicus) (AD 12–41) served as emperor of Rome from AD 37 until his death. During that time, he reputedly engaged in long-term incestuous trysts with his sisters; forced losers of an oratory competition to erase their wax tablets with their tongues; ordered men's heads shaved (due to his own insecurity over his baldness); bestowed a consulship and priesthood upon his favorite horse; and ordered spectators to fight lions and tigers to the death during a shortage of criminals. In AD 41, Caligula was stabbed to death by his own Praetorian guards.

Don't Try This at Home: Body Modification Artists

Ever wish you looked different? Maybe you'd like to be a little taller or have a smaller nose. The following people wanted more than that. Read on to learn about a few of the more devoted individuals in the world of body modification.

✳ ✳ ✳ ✳

Dennis Avner, aka Stalking Cat

ONE OF THE more publicly known body modification artists, Stalking Cat underwent numerous surgeries to transform himself into a tiger. Believing that resembling his totem animal was the destiny set forth by his Native American heritage, Avner began his lifelong project at age 23 with full-body cat-stripe tattoos. He had his hairline altered and silicone injections added to his lips; he got facial implants in order to thread whiskers through his cheeks, as well as implants to alter the shape of his brow and forehead; he had his upper lip split and his ears surgically pointed; and his teeth were filed and capped to be pointy and fanglike. Stalking Cat was a computer programmer, who also made appearances on television shows to show off his odd obsession. Stalking Cat passed away in 2012.

Paul Lawrence, aka The Enigma

As a youth, Paul Lawrence studied piano, flute, and dance. But as a teenager, he decided swallowing swords was more fun, and thus began his career in the sideshow industry as The Enigma. Lawrence's entire body is covered with tattoos of interlocking puzzle pieces of a greenish-blue hue. He's had nubby horns implanted in his forehead and sports a long goatee. Some of his sideshow work includes music, some of it involves sword swallowing, but all of it is quite puzzling.

Isobel Varley, aka The Painted Lady

Proving you don't have to be young to be wild, in 2000, Isobel Varley was noted by *The Guinness Book of Records* as being "The World's Most Tattooed Senior Woman." Varley didn't start getting inked until she was 49 years old, making her a media darling in the world of tattoo artists and aficionados. Varley made special appearances at conventions, often appeared in newspapers and magazines, and had been featured on television shows all over the world. The Painted Lady passed away in 2015.

Eric Sprague, aka Lizardman

It's hard to say which aspect of Lizardman is most alarming: his split tongue; his green, scaly, tattooed face; or his bumpy brow and tattooed eyelids. Or maybe it's how well he articulates the reasons why he's done all this in the first place. Sprague began his transformation into Lizardman during college, after becoming interested in body-based performance art. He chose the lizard because he thought it would look good and age well. Lizardman (who has undergone more than 700 hours of tattooing) performs sideshow acts that involve suspension, drilling, sword-swallowing, and fire manipulation.

Your Name Here

If you have a really strong stomach, a lot of money, and a rather dark sense of humor, you too could join the body-modification subculture. People who aren't yet household names like the artists listed above are busy doing incredibly strange things to their bodies every day, such as ear-pointing and stretching, castration, tooth extraction, even amputations. Some claim it's a spiritual thing, some do it for sexual reasons, and some of them do it for reasons they'll never share. Whatever the case, extreme body modification is incredibly dangerous unless you have a qualified, trained professional helping out with sterile equipment and the proper tools. Don't try it at home—or anywhere—unless you're ready to make serious body alterations you can't take back.

Thomas Tresham Ties Triangles Together

Nothing prompts a person to build a bizarre, triangular stone lodge in the middle of nowhere quite like religious persecution. At least, that's how Sir Thomas Tresham felt back in 1593 when he began work on what would become the mysterious Rushton Triangular Lodge, a structure that he hoped would be much more than a place to hang his hat.

✳ ✳ ✳ ✳

But Why?

A<small>T THE END</small> of the 16th century, life wasn't much fun for Catholics living in England, as Tresham could attest. As a devout Catholic, he'd spent 15 years in prison—his faith had made him a criminal in the eyes of the law. Once he was a free man, Tresham figured he'd better keep his mouth shut about his religion, but that didn't keep him from professing his faith in other ways.

Tresham decided to build a secretly Catholic monument near Rushton that would encode messages to keep it safe from Protestant adversaries. The bricks and mortar of his lodge would showcase aspects of his faith without betraying his freedom. The man stuck to his plan so diligently that the details of Rushton Triangular Lodge are downright weird.

The Rule of Three

To represent the Holy Trinity, Tresham designed the building with only three walls. The structure is itself a perfect equilateral triangle, its walls meeting at 60-degree angles. Glorifying the Holy Trinity via the rule of three is repeated (and repeated and repeated) throughout the whole building. Check this out:

✳ Each of the three walls is 33.3 feet.

✳ Each floor of the three-story building has three windows.

* Each wall has three gables. Each gable is 3 feet by 3 feet with three-sided pinnacles.

* There are nine gargoyles (three sets of three).

* Friezes run along the walls on each side of the building,containing a phrase in Latin—each phrase contains exactly 33 letters.

* And though the main room on each floor is hexagonal in shape, if you draw three bisecting lines through a hexagon, you get six more equilateral triangles.

* And if all those threes are making you a little dizzy, just wait—Tresham was far from content with a few triangular tricks. The building's ornaments were where Tresham spared no expense to work in secret codes for the glory of the Lord.

Gables, and Windows, and Math, Oh My!

Two of the gables of Tresham's lodge are inscribed with dates. One of the dates is 1641, one is 1626. Indeed, Tresham carved future dates into the side of the building for a reason. If you subtract 1593 (the year he started building) from 1626, you get 33. Subtract 1593 from 1641, and you get 48. Both numbers are divisible by three—no big surprise there—but there's something more. If you add the *anno domani* (commonly known as "AD") you get the years of Jesus' death and the Virgin Mary's death, respectively. The second gable shows the dates 3898 BC and 3509 BC, dates that are said to be the years of the Great Flood and the call of Abraham.

The windows provided another place for Tresham to work in his code magic. The three windows on the first floor are in the shape of a Gothic trefoil, a vaguely triangular-shape Christian symbol that also happened to be the Tresham family crest. The trefoil-shape is carried through to the basement windows as well, all of which are, of course, repeated in threes.

Double Entendres

As mentioned before, there were three 33-character-long inscriptions on the Rushton Lodge, one on each side. The inscriptions and their respective translations read as follows:

* "Aperiatur terra & germinet salvatorem" means "Let the earth open and let them bring forth a Savior."

* "Quis seperabit nos a charitate Christi" means "Who shall separate us from the love of Christ."

* "Consideravi opera tua domine at expavi" means "I have considered your works and am sorely afraid."

In addition, if you inspect all the waterspouts at Tresham's place, you'll find a letter above each one. Together, they create an acronym for the first three letters of a Latin mass. An inscription above the main door to the lodge reads *Tres Testiminium Dant*, which means "these three bear witness." But Tresham's wife is said to have called him "Tres" for short; knowing that, one might interpret this as: "Tresham bears witness," which was certainly the point of all this obsessive building.

Even More Hidden Meaning?

Tresham got away with his secretly Catholic building—though it certainly raised a few eyebrows. In fact, the building (which is now maintained as a historical site by the English Heritage organization) is still a source of much discussion. Some people don't think Tresham was über-Catholic at all, that all those numbers and all that funky math were rooted in black magic.

Either way, the building is a great example of the era's love of allegory—using something to represent something else entirely. After the Triangular Lodge was done, Tresham started *another* building full of secret codes and mysterious math called Lyveden New Bield but died before it was finished. It still sits in England exactly as it was left, half-built and full of its own mystery.

The Collyer Brothers: Pack Rats Extraordinaire

It all started out so well. The Collyer boys were born into a fairly prominent New York family: Homer in 1881 and Langley in 1885. Their father, Herman, was a doctor; their mother was an educated woman who worked occasionally as an opera singer. Both boys attended Columbia University and earned degrees in law and engineering, respectively.

In 1909, the family broke apart when Dr. Collyer left for unknown reasons. Homer, Langley, and their mother stayed in the family house at 2078 Fifth Avenue, smack in the middle of Harlem, which at the time was an affluent white neighborhood. But as the neighborhood changed, so did the boys. When their mother died in 1929, the boys were left to fend for themselves, and that's when things got really bizarre.

What's Up with the Quirky Neighbors?

THE COLLYER BOYS weren't very good with details like paying bills, so they had no telephone, electricity, or running water in the house. Paranoid about burglars, the eccentric brothers boarded up all the windows in the house and put iron gates over the doors. Kerosene lamps lit the house, and a kerosene stove provided nominal heat during the frigid New York winters. Water was retrieved from a pump at a nearby park—but only under the cover of darkness. This is also when they did their junk collecting.

In 1933, Homer went blind, and he would later be crippled by a battle with rheumatism. Langley prescribed his ailing brother a treatment: He was to eat 100 oranges per week, supplemented with a few peanut butter sandwiches for good measure. It's no surprise that Homer never regained his eyesight.

On top of all the reclusiveness, home remedies, and water fetching, the Collyer brothers were constantly hoarding. Individuals who suffer from this "pack rat syndrome" (also known as syllogomania) save everything. This is never done in a neat, organized way—one of the hallmarks of a compulsive hoarder is a totally chaotic, stuffed-to-the-rafters home. Hoarders have so many possessions that they are usually rendered incapable of carrying out basic living functions like washing dishes or cleaning the house.

Such was the case with Homer and Langley. Hoping that one day his brother would regain his eyesight, for several decades, Langley saved every New York newspaper he could find—by the end he had several tons of newspapers. The brothers also amassed a collection that included sewing machines, baby carriages, rusted car parts, chandeliers, mannequins, old bicycles, thousands of books, and five pianos. If one of the two happened upon something, it went into the house, piled on top of everything else. Over the years, they created a palace of junk.

Knock, Knock

In 1942, after the Collyers had neglected to pay their mortgage for some time, the bank set eviction proceedings in motion, and a cleanup crew was sent to 2078 Fifth Avenue. They were met by an irate Langley, and the police were summoned.

The police eventually entered the fortress but not without a struggle. All entrances to the house were blocked with what the officers identified as "refuse" and "garbage" that was "neck-deep." When they finally found Langley, he wrote a check for the remainder of the mortgage and sent the authorities on their merry way. For the next five years, the Collyer brothers lived in an increasingly hermitlike manner, and sightings of the eccentric men became less frequent.

Then in 1947, the police received a phone call from a man identifying himself as Charles Smith, who claimed there was a dead body in the Collyer house. When police arrived, they found it more impenetrable than before. The only way into the house was through an upper-story window, and even then, gaining access involved removing huge chunks of junk and throwing them to the street below.

When one of the officers finally got inside the cavernous house, he went through the labyrinthine rooms searching for the source of a nasty odor. Between several piles of trash, the officer found Homer. Police reports stated that he'd died from a combination of malnutrition and cardiac arrest and had only been dead for a few hours. Langley, however, was nowhere to be found.

A manhunt was deployed in New York, but most people figured Langley was still inside the house, waiting to catch one of the officials with his homemade booby traps. As it turned out, they were right—sort of. Langley was indeed in the house, but he wasn't about to catch anyone. His body was found about ten feet from his brother's and had been providing lunch for the neighborhood rats for a couple of weeks by the time he was found. It appeared that Langley was trying to bring food to Homer when he was caught in one of his own traps.

The Numbers

In the end, more than 100 tons of junk were removed from the Collyer house. That's more than 200,000 pounds of shoes, medical equipment, suitcases, phonebooks, tapestries, newspapers, animal parts, etc.

The house was razed, and Collyer Brothers Park now stands in its place. Over the years, the obsessive brothers have been the subject of several books and plays, and even a comic book, though no one's made a movie of their lives just yet.

The Ghost of the Sausage Vat Murder

The story of Louisa Luetgert, the murdered wife of "Sausage King" Adolph Luetgert, is a gruesome tale of betrayal, death, and a lingering specter. It is also one of the greatest stories in Chicago lore. According to legend, each year on the anniversary of her death, Louisa appears on the corner of Hermitage Avenue where it once crossed Diversey Parkway. But her ghost not only haunts her old neighborhood; allegedly, she also coaxed her treacherous husband into an early grave.

✳   ✳   ✳   ✳

Land of Opportunity

ADOLPH LUETGERT WAS born in Germany and came to America after the Civil War. He arrived in Chicago around 1865 and worked in tanneries for several years before opening his first business—a liquor store—in 1872. Luetgert married his first wife, Caroline Roepke, that same year. She gave birth to two boys, only one of whom survived childhood. Just two months after Caroline died in November 1877, Luetgert quickly remarried a much younger woman, Louisa Bicknese, and moved to the northwest side of the city. As a gift, he gave her an unusual gold ring that had her initials inscribed inside the band. Little did Luetgert know that this ring would prove to be his downfall.

Trouble for the "Sausage King"

In 1892, Luetgert built a sausage factory at the southwest corner of Hermitage and Diversey. But just a year later, sausage sales declined due to an economic depression. Luetgert had put his life's savings into the factory, along with plenty of borrowed money, so when his business suffered, creditors started coming after him.

Instead of trying to reorganize his finances, however, Luetgert answered a newspaper ad posted by an English millionaire who made a deal with him to buy out the majority of the sausage business. The Englishman proved to be a conman, and Luetgert ended up losing even more money in the deal. Luetgert eventually laid off many of his workers, but a few remained as he attempted to keep the factory out of the hands of creditors for as long as possible.

Luetgert's business losses took a terrible toll on his marriage. Friends and neighbors frequently heard the Luetgerts arguing, and things became so bad that Luetgert eventually started sleeping in his office at the factory. He carried on with several mistresses and even became involved with a household servant who was related to his wife. When Louisa found out about his involvement with her relative, she became enraged.

Luetgert soon gave the neighbors even more to gossip about. One night, during another shouting match with Louisa, he allegedly took his wife by the throat and began choking her. After noticing alarmed neighbors watching him through the parlor window, Luetgert reportedly calmed down and released his wife before she collapsed. A few days later, Luetgert was seen chasing his wife down the street, shouting at her and waving a revolver.

Vanishing Louisa

Louisa disappeared on May 1, 1897. When questioned about it days later, Luetgert stated that Louisa had left him and was possibly staying with her sister or another man. When Louisa's brother, Dietrich Bicknese, asked Luetgert why he had not informed the police of Louisa's disappearance, the sausage maker told him that he'd hired a private investigator to find her because he didn't trust the police.

When Bicknese informed the police of his sister's disappearance, Captain Herman Schuettler and his men began to search for Louisa. They questioned neighbors and relatives, who detailed the couple's violent arguments. Schuettler summoned Luetgert to the precinct house on a couple of occasions and each time pressed him about his wife's disappearance. Luetgert stated that he did not report Louisa's disappearance because he could not afford the disgrace and scandal.

During the investigation, a young German girl named Emma Schimke told police that she had passed by the factory with her sister at about 10:30 PM on May 1 and remembered seeing Luetgert leading his wife down the alleyway behind the factory.

Police also questioned employees of the sausage factory. Frank Bialk, a night watchman at the plant, told police that when he arrived for work on May 1, he found a fire going in one of the boilers. He said Luetgert asked him to keep the fire going and then sent him on a couple of trivial errands while Luetgert stayed in the basement. When Bialk returned to the factory, he went back to the boiler fire and heard Luetgert finishing his work at around 3:00 AM.

Later that morning, Bialk saw a sticky, gluelike substance on the floor near the vat. He noticed that it seemed to contain bits of bone, but he thought nothing of it. After all, Luetgert used all sorts of waste meats to make his sausage, so he assumed that's what it was.

On May 3, Luetgert asked another employee, Frank Odorofsky, to clean the basement and told him to keep quiet about it. Odorofsky put the slimy substance into a barrel, and scattered it near the railroad tracks as Luetgert had requested.

A Gruesome Discovery

On May 15, the police search was narrowed to the factory basement and a vat that was two-thirds full of a brownish, brackish liquid. Using gunnysacks as filters, officers drained the greasy paste from the vat and began poking through the residue with sticks. Officer Walter Dean found several bone fragments and two gold rings—one a heavy gold band engraved with the initials "L. L."

Luetgert, proclaiming his innocence, was questioned again shortly after the search and was subsequently arrested for the murder of his wife several days later. Despite the fact that Louisa's body was never found and there was no real evidence to link her husband to the crime, the police and prosecutors believed they had a solid case against Luetgert. He was indicted for Louisa's murder, and the details of the crime shocked the city. Even though he had been charged with boiling Louisa's body, rumors circulated that she had actually been ground up into sausage that was sold to local butcher shops and restaurants. Not surprisingly, sausage sales dropped dramatically in Chicago in 1897.

Hounded to the Grave?

Luetgert's trial ended in a hung jury on October 21. The judge threw out the case, and so prosecutors decided to try the whole thing over again. A second trial was held in 1898, and this time Luetgert was convicted and sentenced to a life term at Joliet Prison.

While in prison, Luetgert continued to maintain his innocence and was placed in charge of meats in the cold-storage warehouse. Officials described him as a model prisoner. But by 1899, Luetgert began to speak less and less and often quarreled with other convicts. He soon became a shadow of his former, blustering self, fighting for no reason and often babbling incoherently in his cell at night. But was he talking to himself or to someone else?

Legend has it that Luetgert claimed Louisa haunted him in his jail cell, intent on having revenge for her murder. Was she really haunting him, or was the ghost just a figment of his rapidly deteriorating mind? Based on the fact that neighbors also reported seeing Louisa's ghost, one has to wonder if she did indeed drive Luetgert insane.

Luetgert died in 1900, likely from heart trouble. The coroner who conducted the autopsy also reported that his liver was greatly enlarged and in such a condition of degeneration that "mental strain would have caused his death at any time."

Perhaps Louisa really did visit him after all.

The Ghost of Louisa Luetgert

Regardless of who killed Louisa, her spirit reportedly did not rest in peace. Soon after Luetgert was sent to prison, neighbors swore they saw Louisa's ghost inside her former home, wearing a white dress and leaning against the fireplace mantel.

The sausage factory stood empty for years, looming over the neighborhood as a grim reminder of the horrors that had taken place there. Eventually, the Library Bureau Company purchased the factory for a workshop and storehouse for library furniture and office supplies. During renovations, they discarded the infamous vats in the basement.

On June 26, 1904, the old factory caught on fire. Despite the damage done to the building's interior, the Library Bureau reopened its facilities in the former sausage factory. In 1907, a contracting mason purchased the old Luetgert house and moved it from behind the factory to another lot in the neighborhood, hoping to dispel the grim memories—and ghost—attached to it.

Hermitage Avenue no longer intersects with Diversey, and by the 1990s, the crumbling factory stood empty. But in the late '90s, around the 100th anniversary of Louisa's death, the former sausage factory was converted into condominiums and a brand-new neighborhood sprang up to replace the aging homes that remained from the days of the Luetgerts. Fashionable brick homes and apartments appeared around the old factory, and rundown taverns were replaced with coffee shops.

But one thing has not changed. Legend has it that each year on May 1, the anniversary of her death, the ghost of Louisa can still be spotted walking down Hermitage Avenue near the old sausage factory, reliving her final moments on this earth.

Jeffrey Dahmer: "The Milwaukee Monster"

The Oxford Apartments in Milwaukee are gone. The seedy complex at 924 North 25th Street was torn down in 1992 to prevent the site from becoming a ghoulish tourist attraction. But the empty lot still attracts visitors hoping to see a remnant of Apartment 213 and "The Milwaukee Monster." The small one-bedroom apartment was reputed to be tidy, clean, and home to charming serial killer Jeffrey Dahmer, his pet fish, and his collection of dismembered corpses.

✳ ✳ ✳ ✳

Once Upon a Time

JEFFREY DAHMER WAS born in Milwaukee on May 21, 1960, and his family later moved to Ohio. He attended Ohio State University for one semester, then enlisted in the army in 1979. After being discharged for chronic drunkenness, he eventually moved back to Wisconsin, where he lived with his grandmother.

According to his parents, Dahmer started off as a sweet boy but became increasingly withdrawn during adolescence. They noticed his preoccupation with death, but they dismissed it. Friends knew he liked to dissect roadkill. Once he even impaled a dog's head on a stick. Another time, when his father noticed foul smells coming from the garage, Jeffrey told his dad he was using acid to strip the flesh from animal carcasses. Later, his stepmother realized that he might have been cleaning human bones.

There's a First Time for Everything

Dahmer committed his first murder in June 1978, at age 18. While still living with his parents in Ohio, he picked up a young male hitchhiker. The two had sex, then Dahmer beat the man to death, dismembered his body, and buried him in the woods. Later, Dahmer exhumed the body, crushed the bones with a mallet, and scattered them throughout the woods. His next three victims were all men Dahmer met at gay bars and brought back to a hotel or to his grandmother's house, where he seduced, drugged, and strangled them before sexually assaulting their corpses and cutting them up.

Bad Moves

In September 1988, Dahmer's grandmother kicked him out because he and his friends were too loud and drank too much. The day after he moved into his own apartment, Dahmer was arrested for fondling, drugging, and propositioning a 13-year-old Laotian boy. He was sentenced to a year in prison but was released after ten months. No one knew that he had already murdered four men.

After being released on probation for the assault, Dahmer moved back in with his grandmother. But as a stipulation of his early release, he had to find his own apartment. In May 1990, Dahmer moved to his now infamous home at the Oxford Apartments.

Modus Operandi

Living on his own, Dahmer stepped up his killing spree. Between May and July 1991, he killed an average of one person each week, until he had committed a total of 17 known murders. With few exceptions, the victims were poor, gay, nonwhite men. He would meet them in gay bars or bathhouses, drug them, strangle them, have sex with them, and then dismember them with an electric saw. He saved some parts to eat, and some skulls he cleaned and kept as trophies. He even experimented with creating "zombies" by drilling holes into his victims' heads and injecting acid into their brains while they were still alive. For the most part, he was unsuccessful, as only one man survived for more than a few hours.

On May 27, 1991, a 14-year-old Laotian boy escaped Dahmer's apartment and ran into the streets, half-naked, drugged, and groggy. Neighbors called the police. Horribly, they escorted the boy back to Dahmer's apartment. Sweet-spoken Dahmer convinced the police that it was merely a lover's spat and that the boy was an adult. The police left without doing a background check on Dahmer. If they had, they would have discovered that he was a convicted child molester still on probation. After the police left, the boy, who was the brother of the boy Dahmer had been imprisoned for molesting, became his latest victim. The next week, when neighbors saw reports of a missing boy who looked like Dahmer's "boyfriend," they contacted the police and FBI but were told that he was an adult and with his lover.

The One that Got Away

Tracy Edwards was the lucky one. On July 22, police saw him running down the street with a handcuff on his wrist and stopped him for questioning. Edwards said a man was trying to kill him. He led the police back to Dahmer's apartment, where they found a human head in the refrigerator, an array of skulls in the closet, a barrel of miscellaneous body parts, a pot full of hands and penises, a box of stray bones, a freezer full of entrails, and snapshots of mutilated bodies in various stages of decay arranged in sexual poses. The police arrested Dahmer on the spot, ending his 13-year killing spree.

Crazy Like a Fox

At his trial, Dahmer's lawyer tried to convince the jury that his client was insane, emphasizing the heinousness of the crimes. Still, Dahmer was found sane and guilty of all 15 charges against him and was sentenced to 936 years in prison, which amounted to 15 consecutive life sentences.

And So We Come to the End

Dahmer was fairly infamous when he entered the Columbia Correctional Institute in Portage. He was kept out of the main prison population to protect him from other inmates. Even so, on November 28, 1994, he was assigned to a work detail with two convicted killers: Jesse Anderson and Christopher Scarver. When the guards checked in on them after a while, Anderson and Dahmer were dead; Dahmer's skull had been crushed.

Ghastly Medieval Torture Devices

The following devices, designed to maim, torture, and kill, prove that mankind has far to go in its quest for civility.

❋ ❋ ❋ ❋

The Rack

DURING MEDIEVAL TIMES, being interrogated meant experiencing excruciating pain as one's body was stretched on the infamous Rack. The operating premise was diabolically simple. Victims laid on their backs with arms extended while

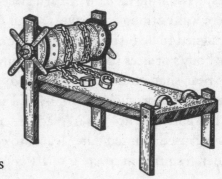

straps anchored the hands and feet to opposite ends of the table. The torture began when the operator rotated rollers at each end in opposing directions. At the very least, severe joint dislocations occurred. At worst, limbs were ripped clean off and death would result. Even when the tortured victim was subsequently released, they'd often be incapable of standing erect since muscle fibers stretched beyond a certain point lose their ability to contract.

The Iron Maiden

The Iron Maiden torture device differs wildly from the popular heavy metal band of the same name, even if both could ultimately make one's ears bleed. Insidious in its intent, the 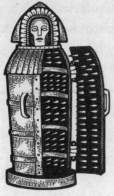 sarcophagus-shape instrument opened to allow the victim to step inside. Once there, protruding spikes on the front and back halves would spear the occupant as the door was closed. Agonies were prolonged because spikes were strategically positioned to find the eyes, chest, and back but not vital organs. As a result, death occurred only after the victim had bled out, an agonizing process that could sometimes last for days.

The Pear

Despite sharing its name with a sweet fruit, there was nothing at all sweet about the Pear. Designed to be inserted in the most sensitive of the body's orifices (i.e., mouth, rectum, vagina), the pear-shape torture tool was used as a punishment for those who had committed sexual sins or blasphemy. Once put in place, a screw mechanism caused pointed outer leaves to expand ever wider, resulting in severe internal mutilation.

The Tongue Tearer

Self-explanatory in name, the Tongue Tearer worked precisely as advertised. Resembling a wire cutter with an eye bolt passing through its end grips, a victim's mouth was forced open as the Tongue Tearer was employed. After finding purchase on its slippery quarry, the eye bolt at the opposite end of the device was tightened, ever so slowly, until the tongue became completely detached from the horrified victim's mouth.

The Lead Sprinkler

With its innocuous sounding name, one might expect to find this item gracing a formal garden, not doing the devil's handiwork in a dank dungeon. Shaped like a maraca, the Lead Sprinkler held molten lead inside a perforated spherical head. The torturer would simply hold the device over the victim and give it a shake.

Mysterious Marilyn

Marilyn Monroe's life story has been exposed and analyzed countless times. The problem is that each version seems to contradict the others, making it difficult to sort out even the simplest details of her complicated life. Read on to discover some myths and truths about the intriguing, contradictory, misunderstood film star who still fascinates us today.

✳ ✳ ✳ ✳

THE ICONIC FILM star whose work includes classics such as *How to Marry a Millionaire* and *Some Like It Hot* continues to be the subject of intense scrutiny. But despite all of the books and movies made about Marilyn Monroe, misconceptions about her life abound, including the following:

Myth: Marilyn was illegitimate.

Fact: According to Marilyn's birth certificate, her mother's estranged husband, Martin Edward Mortensen, was her father, but Marilyn herself never believed this. Her mother, Gladys, left Mortensen after several months of marriage and proceeded to have a series of affairs, most notably with Stanley Gifford, an employee at the film lab where she worked. Mortensen, who had never met Marilyn, always claimed he was her real father. After his death in 1981, a copy of Marilyn's birth certificate was found in his effects, and it is now widely believed that he was telling the truth.

Myth: Marilyn was born blonde.

Fact: Marilyn Monroe's natural hair color was brown. In 1946, she was offered a job modeling for a series of Lustre Cream shampoo ads on the condition that she trade her flowing brunette curls for a straightened blonde hairstyle. It is said that she strongly resisted coloring her hair but ultimately relented under pressure. She was 20 years old at the time and would remain a blonde for the rest of her life.

Myth: Marilyn personified the dumb blonde.

Fact: Marilyn Monroe rose to stardom playing the "dumb blonde" and was considered a master of this Hollywood archetype. But was she actually featherbrained? She definitely played up that image for the public, but her private pursuits were surprisingly intellectual. She wasn't interested in vapid romance novels; instead, she was often observed on her movie sets absorbed in classic works such as Thomas Payne's *The Rights of Man*. Her library was filled with titles by Willa Cather, Dorothy Parker, and Carson McCullers, among many other notable authors. In one famous photograph, she is sitting in front of her book collection reading a copy of *Poetry and Prose: Heinrich Heine*.

Marilyn also took her work as an actress very seriously and insisted that every take be perfect, which often resulted in her being perceived as difficult to work with. Her 1955 departure from Hollywood to study with Lee Strasberg at the Actors Studio in New York City was a bold attempt to take control of her career. She even went so far as to start her own production company, which enabled her to reject any director or script of which she did not approve.

Myth: Marilyn committed suicide.

Fact: On August 5, 1962, Marilyn was found dead in her home in Brentwood, California. The Los Angeles County coroner's office classified her death as "probable suicide," but many people, especially those closest to her, never believed it. During the summer of 1962, things were looking up for Marilyn. She had just achieved a publicity coup with a cover story in *Life* magazine. Her contract with 20th Century Fox studios had been successfully renegotiated, and several projects were in the works, including a film version of the Broadway musical *A Tree Grows in Brooklyn*. She was busy planning renovations of her new house, the first she had ever purchased (albeit with the help of her ex-husband Joe DiMaggio).

To those who knew her well, it simply did not make sense that she would take her own life, and there are even conspiracy theorists who claim that President John F. Kennedy had a hand in her death. But given the fact that her long-term addiction to sleeping pills had led to near-overdoses in the past, the most logical explanation is that her death was an accident.

Time Travelers

Hold on to your hat—you're in for a wild, mind-blowing ride back and forth through the realms of time!

✳   ✳   ✳   ✳

IN 2013, MANY people didn't believe President Obama when he claimed that he often fired guns on the skeet shooting range at Camp David. But others believed that Obama had actually come close to revealing the "real" truth: that he has been working for the CIA for more than 30 years, and that he had personally used the CIA's top secret "jump room" to visit Mars on several occasions as a young man. This is probably not the wildest conspiracy theory about a president that's ever circulated, but it's certainly in the top tier.

However, there's at least one witness who claims to have known the future president in his Mars-hopping days: a Seattle attorney named Andrew Basiago, who also only claims to have been to Mars himself as an Earth ambassador to a Martian civilization in the early 1980s.

But by then, Basiago says, he was an old hand with the CIA: some years before, when he was only 12, he was a participant in a top secret initiative called "Project Pegasus," an elite force that used "radiant energy" principles discovered in the papers of inventor Nikola Tesla to travel through time.

Basiago claims that he traveled through time using eight different technologies as a boy, but mainly using a teleporter that consisted of two "elliptical booms" that stood eight feet tall, positioned about ten feet apart and separated by a curtain of "radiant energy." Participants would jump through the curtain and enter a "vortal tunnel" that took them through time and space. By jumping though, Basiago claims to have attended Ford's Theatre on the night Abraham Lincoln was shot more than once—often enough that on a few occasions, he saw himself, on other trips, among the crowd. Oddly, though this would imply that each "jump" took him to the same "timeline," he says that every time he attended the theatre, the events of the night came off slightly differently, as though he were going to different "timelines" on each trip.

But Lincoln's assassination wasn't the only historic event Basiago claims to have attended. In 1972, he says, he used a "plasma confinement chamber" in East Hanover, New Jersey, to travel back to 1863 to see the Gettysburg Address. Basiago even claims that photographic evidence of this exists; In the foreground of the one photograph of Lincoln at Gettysburg that exists stands a young boy in oversized men's shows, standing casually outside of the crowd in the background. Basiago says that the boy is him.

Basiago told his story over the course of several appearances on Coast to Coast AM, a radio program where conspiracies, UFOs, hauntings, and other strange phenomena are discussed during late night broadcasts. The online forums on which listeners discuss the topics spoken about on the show once brought forth the story of another alleged time traveler:

the story of John Titor, who began posting on the forum in 2000 and claimed to be a time traveler from 2036. Physicists tried to drill him on the mathematics and theories behind time travel, and he seemed to pass every test.

Titor claimed that he was a soldier based in Tampa who was visiting year 2000 for personal reasons—perhaps to collect old family photos that had been destroyed by his time. He even posted schematics showing the devices he used to travel in time, and many at the time became convinced that he was telling the truth.

However, the stories he told about the future of the United States failed to come to pass. In 2001, he claimed that unrest in America surrounding the 2004 presidential election would gradually build up until it became a full-on Civil War, broadly defined as a war between urban and rural parts of the country eventually splitting the United States into five regions. In 2011, he claimed, he was a young teenage soldier for a group called The Fighting Diamondbacks fighting for the rural armies. But the war, he said, would end in 2015 when Russia launched a nuclear assault destroying most American cities, killing as many as half of the people in the country and creating a "new" America in which Omaha, Nebraska served as the nation's capital. Titor said there was an upside to this: in many ways, he said, the world was better with half of the people gone.

Titor's odd story found a lot of supporters when it was first posted, and the events of September 11, 2001 convinced many people that World War III was, in fact, at hand. However, the 2004 election came and went without anything happening in the United States that could ever reasonably be called a civil war breaking out. There was still no such war going in 2008, either, by which time Titor claimed that the war would be fully raging and undeniable.

Fans of Coast to Coast AM are certainly not the only people who claim to have traveled through time, though, and some of the supposed time travelers have far more bona fide military credentials than Titor, who eventually disappeared from the forums. In 1935, Sir Victor Goddard, an air marshall in the Royal Air Force, claimed that he flew into a strange storm while flying his plane above an airfield in Scotland. The turbulence was so bad that he nearly crashed, and he emerged from the storm to find that the landscape beneath him now contained strange-looking aircraft in hangars that weren't there before, all attended by officers wearing blue uniforms instead of the brown ones the RAF normally used.

Four years later, the RAF officially changed the uniforms from brown to blue and began using planes like the ones he had seen after the "storm."

This wasn't Goddard's only brush with the unknown. A decade later, he overheard an officer telling of a dream he'd had in which Air Marshall Goddard had died in a wreck when the plane he was flying in iced over and crashed on a beach. That night, Goddard's plane did, indeed, ice over, and an emergency landing was forced on a beach. Though the dream had ended with Goddard dead, Goddard, having had a sort of early warning, kept his cool and brought the plane safely down. The dream he overheard may very well have saved his life.

Confederates South of the Equator

"Confederados," they call them in Brazil: Southerners who fled farther south, into the tropics, after losing the Civil War.

✳   ✳   ✳   ✳

IN THE SOUTHERN Brazilian state of São Paulo, there survives a town named Americana where the great-great-grandchildren of Confederate rebels speak in a Georgia drawl with a Portuguese accent. They are descendants of the "Confederados", a group of Southerners who settled in Brazil after the Civil War ended.

Every year, a diminishing number of offspring reunite for the Festa Confederada, a celebration of Dixie culture. They serve deep-fried chicken, fly the Confederate flag, dress in antebellum fashion, and downplay the issue of slavery.

Fleeing the South

In the post-Civil War upheaval, a Confederate migration found tens of thousands of people escaping to Europe, Mexico, and beyond. While the 2,500 who settled in Mexico ultimately saw their hopes dashed and were forced to return to the United States, the 9,000 who continued "way, way down South" to Brazil found a dependable protector in its emperor, Dom Pedro II. He wanted the Southerners to bring state-of-the-art cotton-farming know-how to his country.

Pedro was gradually phasing out slavery in Brazil. His daughter, Princess Isabel, would end the institution with the stroke of a pen, ushering in the Golden Law of abolition in 1888. But with a few exceptions, the Confederados didn't appear to have brought all the practices of their antebellum plantations to the tropics. A recent study by Brazilian researcher Alcides Gussi was able to find evidence of only 66 slaves owned by four families of Confederados in Brazil. Many of the immigrants were too poor to own slaves, and the rest relied largely on cheap local labor.

A New Home

By the end of the 1860s, Southerners were steaming for Brazil from the ports of New Orleans, Charleston, Newport News, Baltimore, and Galveston to settle in towns such as Americana and nearby Santa Bárbara D'Oeste. "My grandfather came from Texas and built his house in the middle of a forest," 86-year-old Maria Weissinger told the *Atlanta Journal-Constitution* in 2003. The new land was fertile but rife with insects that carried deadly tropical diseases. Many refugees gave up and returned to the Reconstruction South, but about two in five stayed in their adopted homeland.

Weakened Roots

After nearly 150 years, most of the Confederados have been absorbed into the populations of big cities, but in the industrial town of Americana, traces of the South survive, kept alive in part by a group called the Fraternity of American Descendents. Multiple generations in, the lines between Confederados and Brazilians have become more blurred than ever. Many of the observant Confederados in Americana no longer speak English, but many continue to travel to a cemetery in nearby Santa Bárbara D'Oeste, where the graves tell the stories of their families' fading Confederate roots. In 1972, the cemetery was visited by one settler's great-niece: Rosalyn Carter, wife of future president Jimmy Carter, then governor of Georgia.

Aesop: Was the Fantastic Fabler a Fable Himself?

Aesop's tales of talking animals—the industrious ant and the irresponsible grasshopper, or the fast but arrogant rabbit and the plodding but persistent tortoise—have been a staple of traditional folklore for centuries. But as it turns out, Aesop himself may have been as much a fable as his famous tales.

✳   ✳   ✳   ✳

I T'S FUN TO tell Aesop's tales—especially since many of them take the air out of someone else's inflated ego or show the comic consequences of someone else's bad behavior. And with talking animals to boot! What's not to love?

Who Was Aesop?

By various traditions, Aesop (620–560 BC?) was a slave from Phrygia (central Turkey), Thrace (northern Greece), Sardis (western Turkey), or Ethiopia (horn of Africa), who was brought to the Greek island of Samos in the early 6th century BC and was eventually set free because of his wit and wisdom.

What we actually know of his life may be as fictional as his stories. Aesop's first official biography wasn't composed until the 14th century, and it was composed for the purposes of entertainment—not history. In it, Aesop appears as an unsightly, ungainly, and clever rogue who is always undermining and outwitting his master with his clever use of language. In one instance, when his master Xanthus has given precise directions for fixing "a lentil soup" for a special dinner party, Aesop fixes one boiled lentil and then avoids punishment by forcing the embarrassed Xanthus to admit that Aesop was only following his directions. In this version, Aesop the fabler is a subversive figure who turns the tables on the powerful—a trickster as common to folklore around the world as animal stories.

Later biographies frame Aesop as a serious moral teacher and take most of the fun out of him. He becomes, after meritoriously winning freedom, a famous personality of the court of the Lydian King Croesus in Sardis (modern Sart, Turkey). Besides amazing the king and all the wisest men of the day, Aesop traveled about Greece instructing the powerful with his fables.

Even Aesop's death became a fable with as pointed a moral as any of his tales. He was framed and executed by dishonest men at Delphi (a famous Greek shrine) when he refused to distribute some of Croesus's gold (which the king had sent to the shrine as a gift) because of the men's greed. However, ensuing disasters forced the guilty to fess up, and so the "the blood of Aesop" became a proverb for dishonest deeds that eventually come to light and come home to roost.

So, Was There an Aesop?

Well, perhaps. The Greeks and Romans certainly thought there was. But, as with Homer, the famous bard who traditionally composed the *Iliad* and *Odyssey*, whether the author created the works or the works created the author is open for debate. Just as Demodocus, the blind bard who appears in Book Eight of the *Odyssey*, may have suggested the tradition that Homer was blind, so too the sly and satirical characters of the fables may have helped to create the character that became Aesop. In any case, both Aesop's fables and Aesop's life make for "fabulous" reading.

Rasputin: Depraved Sex Freak or Maligned Holy Man?

We know this much: Grigori Yefimovich Rasputin, a barely literate Russian peasant, grew close to the last tsaritsa—close enough to cost him his life. Incredibly lurid stories ricocheted off the walls of the Winter Palace: drunken satyr, faith healer, master manipulator. What's true? And why does Rasputin fascinate us even today?

✳ ✳ ✳ ✳

THE RASPUTIN SAGA began on January 22, 1869, in the grubby peasant village of Pokrovskoe, Russia. Baby Rasputin was born on the day of the Orthodox saint Grigori, and was thus named after him. There wasn't much to distinguish little Grigori from tens of millions of Russian peasant kids, and he grew up a rowdy drunk. He married a peasant woman named Praskovia, who hung back in Pokrovskoe raising their five kids in Rasputin's general absence.

At 28, Rasputin was born again, rural Russian style. He sobered up—a small miracle in itself—and wandered between monasteries seeking knowledge. Evidently, he fell in with the khlysti—a secretive, heretical Eastern Orthodox sect swirling with rumors of orgies, flagellation, and the like. He gained a mystical aura, and his behavior reflected a sincere spiritual search.

In 1903, he wandered to the capital, St. Petersburg, where he impressed the local Orthodox clergy. Word spread. The ruling Romanov family soon heard of Rasputin.

The Romanovs held a powerful yet precarious position. Ethnically, they were more German than Russian, a hot-button topic for the bona fide Slavs they ruled. Greedy flatterers and brutal infighters made the corridors of power a steep slope with weak rock and loose mud: As you climbed, your prestige and influence grew—but woe to you if you slipped (or were pushed). In that event, the rest would step aside and let you fall—caring only to get out of your way. This was no safe place for a naive peasant—however spiritually inclined. Even the Romanovs lived in fear, for tsars tended to die violent deaths. They ruled a dirt-poor population that was seething with resentment. Tsaryevich ("tsar's son") Alexei, the heir apparent, was a fragile hemophiliac who could bleed out from a skinned knee, aptly symbolic of the blood in the political water in St. Petersburg in those final days of the last tsar, Nikolai II.

As the tsaritsa worried over gravely ill Alexei in 1906, she thought of Rasputin and his healing reputation. He answered her summons in person, blessed Alexei with an Orthodox ikon and left. Alexei improved, and Tsaritsa Aleksandra was hooked on Rasputin. She consulted him often, promoted him to her friends, and pulled him onto that treacherous slope of imperial favor. For his final ten years, Rasputin became a polarizing figure as he grew more influential. His small covey of upper-crust supporters (mostly female) hung on his every word, even as a growing legion of nobles, peasants, and clergy saw in Rasputin all that was wrong with the monarchy.

What few ask now is: What was Rasputin thinking? What was he feeling? His swift rise from muddy fields to the royal palace gave him an understandable ego trip. He was a peasant but not an idiot; he realized his rise would earn him jealous enemies. The sheer fury of their hatred seems to have surprised, frightened, and saddened him, for he wasn't a hateful man. He certainly felt duty-bound to the tsaritsa, whose unwavering favor deflected most of his enemies' blows. Rasputin's internal spiritual struggle (against sin, toward holiness) registers authentic, at least until his last year or so of life—but he made regular visits to prostitutes long before that. Defenders claim that he was only steeling himself against sexual temptation; you can imagine what his enemies said.

Life worsened for Rasputin in 1914, when he was stabbed by a former prostitute. He survived, but the experience shook him. After recuperating, he abandoned any restraint he'd ever exercised. Rasputin better acquainted himself with the bottoms of liquor bottles—and those of his visitors. Most likely he expected death and gave in to natural human desires: Cartoons portrayed him as a cancer infecting the monarchy, especially after Russia went to war with Germany. Military setbacks left Russians with much to mourn and resent. A wave of mandatory patriotism swept Russia, focusing discontent upon the royal family's Germanic ties. In the end, clergy and nobility agreed with the media: down with Rasputin.

A Plot, a Death, and a Prediction

Led by a fabulously rich libertine named Felix Yusupov, a group of Rasputin's enemies lured him to a meeting on December 29, 1916. The popular story is that he scarfed a bunch of poisoned food and wine, somehow didn't die, was shot, got up, was beaten and shot some more, then was finally tied up and thrown alive through the ice of a frozen river. What is sure: Rasputin was shot, bound, and dumped into freezing water to die. Whether or not he was still alive when dumped and whether or not he actually partook of the cyanide munchies, he was found with at least one fatal bullet wound.

The tsaritsa buried her advisor on royal property. After the Romanovs fell, a mob dug up Rasputin and burned his corpse. To our knowledge, nothing remains of him.

Rasputin had predicted that if he were slain by the nobility, the Russian monarchy wouldn't long survive him. His prophecy came true: Less than a year after his death, the Russian Revolution deposed the tsar. The Reds would soon murder the entire royal family; had they captured Rasputin, it's hard to imagine him being spared. For the "Mad Monk" who was neither mad nor monastic, the muddy road of life had dead-ended in the treacherous forest of imperial favor.

The Amazons: Man-Eaters of the Ancient World

They were the ultimate feminists—powerful, independent women who formed female-only societies that had no use for men beyond procreation. They were the epitome of girl power, fierce mounted warriors who often emasculated the best male fighters from other societies. They were the Amazons—man-eaters of the ancient world.

✳ ✳ ✳ ✳

THE ANCIENT GREEKS were enthralled by the Amazons. Greek writers, like today's Hollywood gossip columnists, relished lurid tales of love affairs between Amazon queens and their Greek boy toys. Others wrote of epic battles between Amazon warriors and the greatest heroes of Greek mythology.

Given their prominent place in Greek lore, the story of the Amazons has generally been considered the stuff of legend. But recent archeological finds suggest that a race of these warrior über-women actually did exist.

The Amazons According to the Greeks

History's first mention of the Amazons is found in Homer's *Iliad*, written in the 7th or 8th century BC. Homer told of a group of women he called *Antianeira* ("those who fight like men"), who fought on the side of Troy against the Greeks. They were led by Penthesilea, who fought Achilles and was slain by him. According to some accounts, Achilles fell in love with her immediately afterward. Achilles was highly skilled in the art of warfare, but it seems he was sorely lacking in the intricacies of courtship.

From then on, the Amazons became forever linked with the ancient Greeks. Their very name is believed to derive from the Greek *a-mazos*, meaning "without a breast." This referred to the Amazon practice of removing the right breast of their young girls so that they would be unencumbered in the use of the bow and spear. Somewhat draconian, yes, but no one could accuse the Amazons of being anything less than hard-core. This may have made Greek, Roman, and European artists a bit squeamish because their depictions of Amazons showed them with two breasts, though the right breast was often covered or hidden.

According to Greek mythology, the Amazons were the offspring of Ares, god of war, who was the son of the mightiest of the Greek gods, Zeus. Though the Amazons may have had Greek roots, they didn't want anything to do with them. Like young adults eager to move from their parents' homes, the Amazons established their realm in a land called Pontus in modern-day northeastern Turkey, where they founded several important cities, including Smyrna.

The Greeks paint a picture of the Amazons as a female-dominated society of man-haters that banned men from living among them. In an odd dichotomy between chastity and promiscuity, sexual encounters with men were taboo except for once a year when the Amazons would choose male partners from the neighboring Gargareans strictly for the purposes of procreation. Female babies were kept; males were killed or sent back with their fathers. Females were raised to do everything a man could do—and to do it better.

Soap Opera Encounters with Greek Heroes

The Greeks and the Amazons interacted in a turbulent love-hate relationship resembling something from a Hollywood soap opera. Hercules, as one of his labors, had to obtain the girdle of the Amazon queen Hippolyte. He was accompanied in his task by Theseus, who stole Hippolyte's sister Antiope.

This led to on-going warfare between the Greeks and Amazons as well as several trysts between members of the two societies. One account has Theseus and Antiope falling in love, with her dying by his side during a battle against the Amazons. Another account has Theseus and Hippolyte becoming lovers. Stories of Hercules have him alternately wooing and warring with various Amazonian women.

Jason and the Argonauts met the Amazons on the island of Lemnos. Completely unaware of the true nature of the island's inhabitants, Jason queried the Amazons as to the where-abouts of their men. They told him their men were all killed in an earlier invasion. What the Argonauts didn't realize was that the Amazons themselves were the killers. The Amazons, anticipating another opportunity for manslaughter, invited the Argonauts to stay and become their husbands. But Jason and the boys, perhaps intimidated by the appearance of the Amazons in full battle dress, graciously declined and hightailed it off the island.

More than Myth?

The Greek historian Herodotus perhaps provides the best connection of the Greeks to what may be the true race of Amazons. Writing in the 5th century BC, Herodotus chronicles a group of warrior women who were defeated in battle by the Greeks. These Androktones ("killers of men"), as he called them, were put on a prison ship, where they happily went about killing the all-male Greek crew. Hellcats on land but hopeless on water, the women drifted to the north shores of the Black Sea to the land of the Scythians, a nomadic people of Iranian descent.

Here, says Herodotus, they intermarried with the Scythian men on the condition that they be allowed to keep their tra-ditional warrior customs. They added a heartwarming social tenet that no woman could wed until she had killed a man in battle. Together, they migrated northeast across the Russian steppes, eventually evolving into the Sarmatian culture, which featured a prominent role for women hunting and fighting by the sides of their husbands. The men may have given their wives the loving pet name *ha-mazan*, the Iranian word for "warrior."

Though the Amazons are still mostly perceived as myth, recent archeological discoveries lend credence to Herodotus's account and help elevate the Amazons from the pages of Greek legend to historical fact. Excavations of Sarmatian burial grounds found the majority of those interred there were heavily armed women, all of whom got the very best spots in the site.

Identities Lost: The Druids and the Picts

What do you know about the Druids? How about the Picts? Chances are, what you know (or think you know) is wrong. These two "lost" peoples are saddled with serious cases of mistaken identity.

❋ ❋ ❋ ❋

MOST CONTEMPORARY PERCEPTIONS of the Druids and Picts tend to be derived from legend and lore. As such, our conceptions of these peoples range from erroneous and unlikely to just plain foolish. Let's start with the Druids. They are often credited with the building of Stonehenge, the great stone megalith believed to be their sacred temple, as well as their arena for savage human sacrifice rituals. True or False?

False. First of all, Stonehenge was built around 2000 BC –1,400 years before the Druids emerged. Second, though we know admittedly little of Druidic practice, it seemed to be traditional and conservative. The Druids did have specific divinity-related beliefs, but it is not known whether they actually carried out human sacrifices.

What about the Picts? Although often reduced to a mythical race of magical fairies, the Picts actually ruled Scotland before the Scots. So who were the Druids and the Picts?

The Druids—The Priestly Class

As the priestly class of Celtic society, the Druids served as the Celts' spiritual leaders—repositories of knowledge about the world and the universe, as well as authorities on Celtic history, law, religion, and culture. In short, they were the preservers of the Celtic way of life.

The Druids provided the Celts with a connection to their gods, the universe, and the natural order. They preached of the power and authority of the deities and taught the immortality of the soul and reincarnation. They were experts in astronomy and the natural world. They also had an innate connection to all things living: They preferred holding great rituals among natural shrines provided by the forests, springs, and groves. To become a Druid, one had to survive extensive training. Druid wannabes and Druid-trained minstrels and bards had to endure as many as 20 years of oral education and memorization.

More Powerful than Celtic Chieftains

In terms of power, the Druids took a backseat to no one. Even the Celtic chieftains, well-versed in power politics, recognized the overarching authority of the Druids. Celtic society had well-defined power and social structures and territories and property rights. The Druids were deemed the ultimate arbiters in all matters relating to such. If there was a legal or financial dispute between two parties, it was unequivocally settled in special Druid-presided courts. Armed conflicts were immediately ended by Druid rulings. Their word was final.

In the end, however, there were two forces to which even the Druids had to succumb—the Romans and Christianity. With the Roman invasion of Britain in AD 43, Emperor Claudius decreed that Druidism throughout the Roman Empire was to be outlawed. The Romans destroyed the last vestiges of official Druidism in Britain with the annihilation of the Druid stronghold of Anglesey in AD 61. Surviving Druids fled to unconquered Ireland and Scotland, only to become completely marginalized by the influence of Christianity within a few centuries.

Stripped of power and status, the Druids of ancient Celtic society disappeared. They morphed into wandering poets and storytellers with no connection to their once illustrious past.

The Picts—The Painted People

The Picts were, in simplest terms, the people who inhabited ancient Scotland before the Scots. Their origins are unknown, but some scholars believe that the Picts were descendants of the Caledonians or other Iron Age tribes who invaded Britain.

No one knows what the Picts called themselves; the origin of their name comes from other sources and probably derives from the Pictish custom of tattooing or painting their bodies. The Irish called them Cruithni, meaning "the people of the designs." The Romans called them Picti, which is Latin for "painted people"; however, the Romans probably used the term as a general moniker for all the untamed peoples living north of Hadrian's Wall.

A Second-Hand History

The Picts themselves left no written records. All descriptions of their history and culture come from second-hand accounts. The earliest of these is a Roman account from AD 297 stating that the Picti and the Hiberni (Irish) were already well-established enemies of the Britons to the south.

The Picts were also well-established enemies of each other. Before the arrival of the Romans, the Picts spent most of their time fighting amongst themselves. The threat posed by the Roman conquest of Britain forced the squabbling Pict kingdoms to come together and eventually evolve into the nation-state of Pictland. The united Picts were strong enough not only to resist conquest by the Romans, but also to launch periodic raids on Roman-occupied Britain.

Having defied the Romans, the Picts later succumbed to a more benevolent invasion launched by Irish Christian missionaries. Arriving in Pictland in the late 6th century, they succeeded in converting the polytheistic Pict elite within two decades. Much of the written history of the Picts comes from the Irish Christian annals. If not for the writings of the Romans and the Irish missionaries, we might not have knowledge of the Picts today.

Despite the existence of an established Pict state, Pictland disappeared with the changing of its name to the Kingdom of Alba in AD 843, a move signifying the rise of the Gaels as the dominant people in Scotland. By the 11th century, virtually all vestiges of them had vanished.

Cleopatra: Stranger Than Fiction

In his work, Antony and Cleopatra, *the immortal William Shakespeare gave the Egyptian queen the following line: "Be it known that we, the greatest, are misthought." These "misthoughts" could be the myths, untruths, and fallacies that seem to surround Cleopatra. Though movies and the media tend to focus on these misconceptions, the true stories are equally fascinating.*

✳   ✳   ✳   ✳

MYTH: Cleopatra was Egyptian.

FACT: Cleopatra may have been the queen of Egypt, but she was actually Greek. Her family had called Egypt home for hundreds of years, but their lineage was linked to a general in Alexander the Great's army named Ptolemy who came from Macedonia.

MYTH: Cleopatra was a vision of beauty.

FACT: Beauty, of course, is in the eye of the beholder. In ancient times, there were no cameras, but a person of Cleopatra's stature and wealth could have their likeness sculpted. If the image on an ancient Roman coin is believed to be accurate, then Cleopatra was endowed with a large, hooked nose and was as cheeky as a chipmunk.

MYTH: Cleopatra dissolved a pearl earring in a glass of vinegar and drank it. As the story goes, upon meeting Marc Antony, Cleopatra held a series of lavish feasts. On the eve of the final gala, Cleopatra bet Antony that she could arrange for the costliest meal in the world. As the banquet came to a close, she supposedly removed an enormous pearl from her ear, dropped it into a goblet of wine vinegar, then drank it down, with Antony admitting defeat.

FACT: Scientifically speaking, calcium carbonate—the mineral of which pearls are composed—will dissolve in an acid such as vinegar. However, based on the description of the pearl in question, it is likely that the short dip in vinegar resulted in nothing more than a soggy gem, as it would have taken a very long time for that amount of calcium carbonate to dissolve.

MYTH: Julius Caesar allowed Cleopatra to remain queen of Egypt because he loved her.

FACT: Though not married, Cleopatra did bear Caesar a son, Caesarion. However, that was hardly reason enough to hand over an entire country to her. Most likely, Caesar felt that any male ruler would pose a formidable threat to his empire, whereas Cleopatra was a safer alternative to rule Egypt.

MYTH: Cleopatra died from the bite of an asp after learning of Marc Antony's death.

FACT: It's unknown exactly how or why Cleopatra committed suicide. According to legend, after hearing of the death of her lover, she had two poisonous asps brought to her in a basket of figs. The person who found the expired Cleopatra noted two small marks on her arm, but the snakes in question were never located. Cleopatra may very well have been distraught about her lover's demise, but it is more likely that rumors she was about to be captured, chained, and exhibited in the streets of Rome drove her to suicide.

Pancho Villa: The Man with Two Faces

Hero or criminal? You decide.

THE MAN THE world knew as Pancho Villa led a contradictory life that caused some to venerate him as a saint and others to loathe him as a fiend. Certainly, Pancho Villa was a man of bold action with an uncanny sense of destiny whose exploits— whether actual or mythical, inherently good or evil—have become the stuff of legend. Even in his own time, he was celebrated as a living folk hero by Mexicans and Americans alike. In fact, film companies sent crews to revolutionary Mexico to chronicle his exploits—a circumstance that pleased the wily Villa, if for no other reason than the gold the directors brought with them. Journalists, novelists, friends, and enemies all conspired to create the image of a man whose true nature remained elusive. To the present day, the name of Francisco "Pancho" Villa continues to inspire both admiration and scorn with equal fervor... depending on whom you ask.

General Pancho Villa: Hero of the People

Pancho Villa was born Doroteo Arango in Durango, Mexico, either in 1877 or 1879. As the son of a peasant family working for a hacienda owner, he realized that he would eventually inherit his father's debt and work the land until the day he died. At age 16, however, Doroteo returned home to find his sister fending off the lecherous advances of a local don. Unable to countenance the dishonoring of his beloved sister, Villa obtained a pistol, shot and killed the offending "gentleman," and escaped to the hills. For nearly ten years, he lived as a bandit, robbing from the rich and giving to the poor men who joined him. With the start of the Mexican Revolution, Villa came down from the mountains to form an army in support of the populist platform espoused by Francisco Madero.

Pancho Villa: Esteemed General

As a general, Villa staged bold cavalry charges that over-whelmed his opponents even at great risk to his own life. General Villa was very popular with the ladies (purportedly marrying 26 times) and loved to dance. However, he did not drink and once famously choked on a dram of brandy offered him by fellow revolutionary General Emiliano Zapata. As the Mexican Revolution ground through a series of corrupt leaders, Villa remained true to his populist ideology.

When his political rival, Venustiano Carranza, came to power, Villa became a wanted man again, this time in both Mexico and the United States. As in his youth, he took to the mountains, evading capture for several years until, weary of life on the run, he surrendered in 1920. Villa purchased a former hacienda known as La Purísima Concepción de El Canutillo and moved there with about 400 of his soldiers and their families. Rather than become like the wealthy landowners he despised, however, Villa used the hacienda to form an agricultural community that soon swelled to approximately 2,000 men, women, and chil-dren who received an education and shared in the profits.

Pancho Villa: Murderous Thug

When American President Woodrow Wilson chose to sup-port the presidency of Villa's rival Venustiano Carranza, Villa retaliated. On January 11, 1916, Villa and a group of his men stopped a train in Santa Ysabel, Mexico, and brutally killed 18 Texas businessmen. Murder and banditry were nothing new to Villa; as a young man he had made his living stealing cattle and was a murderer before he reached 20. As a revolutionary general, he ordered executions for specious reasons, robbed herds of cattle to sell north of the border, and shot merchants who refused to take the money he had printed for his army. His cattle thieving incensed powerful newspaper magnate William Randolph Hearst who conducted a long-term smear campaign against the bandit, which, among other things, led to the criminalization of marijuana in the United States.

Pancho Villa's greatest moment of infamy, however, came at 2:30 AM on March 9, 1916, when he led a band of 500 horse-mounted followers against the 13th U.S. Cavalry and then into Columbus, New Mexico, where the bandits killed indiscriminately and destroyed property. When the Villistas departed at 7:00 AM, 14 American soldiers, 10 civilians, and scores of bandits lay dead. President Wilson ordered Brigadier General John J. Pershing to lead a punitive cavalry expedition into Mexico to capture Villa but multiple, costly attempts to corner the cunning outlaw proved fruitless. Soon, the nuisance of Pancho Villa was replaced in the national consciousness by the United States' entry into the war raging in Europe.

The End of the Man, the Start of the Legend

Pancho Villa was assassinated by unknown persons while visiting the village of Parral in 1923. After Villa's death, one of his officers allegedly opened his tomb in Parral and removed his head to sell to a Chicago millionaire who collected skulls. Villa's body was later moved to Mexico City and interred in the Tomb of the Illustrious, but many believe that it was simply a headless decoy and his true resting place remains in Northern Mexico. Thus, even the final resting place of Villa's body has become obscured by speculation and doubt.

The Bloody Countess

In the early 1600s, villagers in the Carpathian region of Hungary whispered amongst themselves about a vampire living in the local castle. The villain, however, was no supernatural monster, but a purely human one. An investigation brought to light the brutal atrocities of Countess Elizabeth Bathory, who was accused of torturing hundreds of young girls to death and even bathing in their blood.

❋   ❋   ❋   ❋

The Best Sort of People

Elizabeth Bathory (born Erzsébet Báthory in 1560) was the daughter of one of the oldest and most influential bloodlines in Hungary. Her wedding in 1575 to Ferenc Nadasdy was enough of an event to warrant written approval and an expensive gift from the Holy Roman Emperor himself.

Of course, there were rumors that a streak of insanity ran in Elizabeth's family; some rumors hint that she may have been related to Vlad the Impaler. However, nobles of the time were given wide latitude when it came to eccentric behavior.

Ferenc would go on to become one of the greatest Hungarian military heroes of the age. He was a battle-hardened man, but even so, his own wife made him nervous. He was aware that she treated the servants even more harshly than he did—and he had no reservations when it came to punishing the help. He was known to place flaming oil-covered wicks between the toes of lazy servants. But Elizabeth's punishments far exceeded even this brutality. Ferenc saw evidence of this when he discovered a servant who had been covered with honey and tied to a tree to be ravaged by ants as punishment for stealing food. Still, Ferenc spent a great deal of time away at war, and someone had to manage his castle. Elizabeth took on the task willingly; in turn, he turned a deaf ear to complaints about her activities.

From Punishment to Atrocity

Initially, Elizabeth's punishments may have been no more harsh than those imposed by her contemporaries. However, with her husband's lengthy absences and eventual death, Elizabeth found that she had virtually no restrictions on her behavior. A series of lovers of both sexes occupied some of her time. She also dabbled in black magic, though this was not uncommon in an age when paganism and Christianity were contending for supremacy. She spent hours doing nothing more than gazing into a wraparound mirror of her own design, crafted to hold her upright so that she would not tire as she examined her own reflection. The exacting fashion of the day required Elizabeth, always a vain woman, to constantly worry over the angle of her collar or the style of her hair. She had a small army of body servants constantly by her side to help maintain her appearance. They were often required to attend to their mistress in the nude as an expression of subservience. If they failed in their duties, Elizabeth would strike out, pummeling them into the ground. On one notable occasion, a servant pulled too hard when combing Elizabeth's hair; Elizabeth struck the offender in the face hard enough to cause the girl's blood to spray and cover the countess. Initially furious, Elizabeth discovered she liked the sensation, believing her skin was softer, smoother, and more translucent after the experience.

A Taste for Blood

The incident led to the legends, which cannot be confirmed, that Elizabeth Bathory took to bathing in the blood of virgins to maintain her youthful appearance. One rumor has her inviting 60 peasant girls for a banquet, only to lock them in a room and slaughter them one at a time, letting their blood run over her body. Though that incident may be apocryphal, it is certain that the countess began torturing girls without restraint. Aided by two trustworthy servants who recruited a never-ending supply of hopeful girls from the poor families of the area, she would beat her victims with a club until they were scarcely recognizable. When her arms grew tired, she had her two assistants continue the punishment as she watched. She had a spiked iron cage specially built and would place a girl within it, shaking the cage as the individual bounced from side to side and was impaled over and over on the spikes. She drove pins into lips and breasts, held flames to pubic regions, and once pulled a victim's mouth open so forcefully that the girl's cheeks split. Perhaps most chillingly, allegations of vampirism and cannibalism arose when Elizabeth began biting her victims, tearing off the flesh with her bare teeth. On one occasion, too sick to rise from her bed, the countess demanded that a peasant girl be brought to her. She roused herself long enough to bite chunks from the girl's face, shoulders, and nipples. Elizabeth's chambers had to be covered with fresh cinders daily to prevent the countess from slipping on the bloody floor.

Justice for the Countess

Eventually, even the cloak of nobility couldn't hide Elizabeth's atrocities. The situation was compounded by the fact that she got sloppy, killing in such numbers that the local clergy refused to perform any more burials. Thereafter, she would throw bodies to the wolves in full view of local villagers, who naturally complained to the authorities. The final straw was when Elizabeth began to prey on the minor aristocracy as well as the peasants; the disappearance of people of higher birth could not be tolerated. The king decided that something had to be done, and in January 1611, a trial was held. Elizabeth was not allowed to testify, but her assistants were compelled to—condemning themselves to death in the process—and they provided eyewitness accounts of the terrible practices of the countess. Especially damning was the discovery of a list, in Elizabeth's own handwriting, describing more than 600 people she had tortured to death.

Elizabeth Bathory was convicted of perpetrating "horrifying cruelties" and was sentenced to be walled up alive in her own castle. She survived for nearly four years but was finally discovered dead on August 21, 1614, by one of her guards who had risked a peek through a tiny food slot. The countess was unrepentant to the end.

D. B. Cooper: Man of Mystery

D. B. Cooper is perhaps the most famous criminal alias since Jack the Ripper. Although the fate of the infamous hijacker remains a mystery, the origins of the nom de crime "D. B. Cooper" is a matter that's easier to solve.

✳ ✳ ✳ ✳

The Crime

AT PORTLAND (OREGON) International Airport the night before Thanksgiving in 1971, a man in a business suit, reportedly in his mid-40s, boarded Northwest Orient Airlines flight 305 bound for Seattle, Washington. He had booked his seat under the name Dan Cooper. Once the flight was airborne, Cooper informed a flight attendant that his briefcase contained an explosive device. In the days before thorough baggage inspection was standard procedure at airports, this was a viable threat. The flight attendant relayed the information to the pilots, who immediately put the plane into a holding pattern so that Cooper could communicate his demands to FBI agents on the ground.

When the Boeing 727 landed at Seattle–Tacoma Airport, the other passengers were released in exchange for $200,000 in unmarked $20 bills and two sets of parachutes. FBI agents photographed each bill before handing over the ransom and then scrambled a fighter plane to follow the passenger craft when Cooper demanded that it take off for Mexico City via Reno, Nevada. At 10,000 feet, Cooper lowered the aft stairs of the aircraft and, with the ransom money strapped to his chest, parachuted into the night, still dressed in his business suit. The pilot noted the area as being near the Lewis River, 25 miles north of Portland, somewhere over the Cascade Mountains.

The mysterious hijacker was never seen again. The FBI found a number of fingerprints on the plane that didn't match those of the other passengers or members of the crew, but the only real clue that Cooper left behind was his necktie. On February 10, 1980, an eight-year-old boy found $5,800 in decaying $20 bills along the Columbia River, just a few miles northwest of Vancouver, Washington. The serial numbers matched those included in the ransom. Other than that, not a single note of the ransom money has turned up in circulation.

Origins of the Name

The FBI launched a massive hunt for the man who had hijacked Flight 305. This included checking the rap sheets of every known felon with the name Dan Cooper, just in case the hijacker had been stupid enough to use his real name. When Portland agents interviewed a man by the name of D. B. Cooper, the story was picked up by a local reporter. This D. B. Cooper was cleared of any involvement in the case, but the alias stuck and was adopted by the national media.

Who Was Dan Cooper?

Countless books, TV shows, and even a movie have attempted to answer this question. The FBI has investigated some 10,000 people, dozens of whom had at some point confessed to family or friends that they were the real D. B. Cooper. In October 2007, the FBI announced that it had finally obtained a partial DNA profile of Cooper with evidence lifted from the tie he left on the plane. This has helped rule out many of those suspected of (or who have confessed to) the hijacking.

The author of one book about the case, a retired FBI agent, offered a $100,000 reward for just one of the bills from the ransom money. He's never had to pay out. Officially, the FBI does not believe that Cooper survived the jump. However, no evidence of his body or the bright yellow and red parachute he used to make the jump has ever been found. On December 31, 2007, more than 36 years after the man forever known as D. B.

Cooper disappeared into the night sky, the FBI revived the case by publishing never-before-seen sketches of the hijacker and appealing for new witnesses.

Jack the Ripper

Between 1888 and 1891, he brutally murdered at least five women in London's East End. But was there really a connection between Jack the Ripper and the British royal family?

THE SERIAL KILLER known as Jack the Ripper is one of history's most famous murderers. He breathed terror into the gas-lit streets and foggy back alleys of the Whitechapel area of London and became renowned the world over. Despite the countless books and movies detailing his story, however, his identity and motives remain shrouded in mystery. One of the most popular theories, espoused by the 2001 movie *From Hell* (starring Johnny Depp), links the killer to the British royal family.

The Crimes

Five murders are definitively attributed to Jack the Ripper, and he has variously been connected to at least six other unsolved slayings in the London area. The body of the first victim, 43-year-old Mary Ann Nichols, was discovered on the morning of August 31, 1888. Nichols's throat had been cut and her abdomen mutilated. The subsequent murders, which took place over a three-year period, grew in brutality. The killer removed the uterus of his second victim, Annie Chapman; part of the womb and left kidney of Catherine Eddowes; and the heart of Mary Kelly. All of his victims were prostitutes.

The Name

A man claiming to be the murderer sent a letter (dated September 25, 1888) to the Central News Agency, which passed it on to the Metropolitan Police. The letter included the line, "I am down on whores and I shant quit ripping them till I do get buckled." It was signed, "Yours truly, Jack the Ripper." A later postcard included the same sign-off. When police went public with details, the name "Jack the Ripper" stuck.

The Suspects

Officers from the Metropolitan Police and Scotland Yard had four main suspects: a poor Polish resident of Whitechapel by the name of Kosminski, a barrister who committed suicide in December 1888, a Russian-born thief, and an American doctor who fled to the States in November 1888 while on bail for gross indecency. Since there was little or no evidence against any of these men, the case spawned many conspiracy theories, the most popular of which links the killings to the royal family.

The Royal Conspiracy

The heir to the British throne was Prince Albert Victor, grandson of Queen Victoria and son of the man who would later become King Edward VII. The prince, popularly known as Eddy, had a penchant for hanging around in the East End, and rumors abounded that he had a daughter, Alice, out of wedlock with a shop girl named Annie Crook. To prevent major embarrassment to the Crown, Eddy sought assistance from Queen Victoria's physician, Dr. William Gull, who institutionalized Annie to keep her quiet. However, her friends, including Mary Kelly, also knew the identity of Alice's father, so Dr. Gull created the persona of Jack the Ripper and brutally silenced them one by one. A variation on this theory has Dr. Gull acting without the knowledge of the prince, instead driven by madness resulting from a stroke he suffered in 1887.

Royal involvement would certainly explain why the police were unable to uncover the identity of the Ripper or to even settle on a prime suspect. There *was* a shop girl named Annie Crook who had an illegitimate daughter named Alice, but there is nothing to connect her to either the prince or the murdered prostitutes. In fact, there is no evidence to suggest that the murdered women knew one another. Until the identity of Jack the Ripper is settled beyond doubt, these and other conspiracy theories will likely persist.

Stealing History

Move over, Indiana Jones—the theft of priceless artifacts has been going on for centuries.

✳ ✳ ✳ ✳

IT'S LIKE SOMETHING out of a James Bond movie: An international collector pays big bucks to organized criminals to steal priceless antiquities and smuggle them over international borders. National treasures have been purloined for centuries—taken to distant lands to bring prestige and value to museums, treasuries, and private collections.

A Thief in the Night

Sometimes, looters go straight to the source. Since the days of the earliest pharaohs, Egyptian rulers lived in fear of tomb robbers and went to great lengths to protect the possessions they intended to take into the hereafter.

But thieves were not always cloaked peasants who dug into pyramids in the dark of night; sometimes even Egyptian kings entered the graves of their predecessors to "borrow" goodies for use in the afterlife. King Tutankhamen's tomb included a second inner coffin, four miniature coffins, and some gold bands that had been removed from the tomb of his older brother, Smenkare. The tomb of Pharaoh Pinudjem I included "recycled" sarcophagi from the tomb of Thothmosis I, Egypt's ruler from three dynasties earlier.

More recently, archaeological sites in the western United States have suffered a rash of thefts by shovel-toting bandits intent on digging up Native and Central American artifacts to sell in thriving legitimate and gray-market art and collectibles markets. In 2003, for instance, one Vanderbilt University professor worked with Guatemalan police, villagers, and even local drug lords to track down a stolen 1,200-year-old monument to a Mayan king.

Museums Robbed and Looted

Museum robberies have become a huge problem, especially for institutions that cannot afford state-of-the-art security systems. In 2001, for example, Russia's Culture Ministry stated that, on average, one Russian museum was victimized by theft each month. In Iraq in April 2003, during the chaos of the U.S.-led invasion of Iraq, some 170,000 items were looted or destroyed in the Iraqi National Museum; many of these artifacts subsequently made their way into private hands. Authorities are slowly stirring themselves to crack down on a burgeoning traffic in stolen artifacts. In 2005, an Italian court sentenced a Roman antiquities dealer to ten years in prison for receiving and exporting stolen artifacts. The dealer's company sold 110 items through the prestigious auction house Sotheby's and sold another 96 artifacts to ten museums around the world before the operation was shut down.

Government Theft

Conquest and colonization have provided other supply sources for collections. The Israelite temple in Jerusalem was looted by invading armies at least twice: by Babylonian King Nebuchadnezzar around 586 BC, and again by Roman Emperor Vespasian in AD 70. In 480 BC, when the Persian army sacked Athens, artifacts in the wooden Acropolis temple were carted off to Persepolis as war booty, and during his 1798–99 expedition to Egypt, Napoleon's army uncovered one of the most famous spoils of war, the Rosetta Stone—which was in turn captured by Britain in 1801. Equally famous are the "Elgin Marbles," relief statues from Greece's Parthenon that were brought to London's British Museum in 1816 by the British ambassador to Turkey.

During World War II, the Nazi regime took the pastime of art collecting to a new level. Thousands of priceless paintings, drawings, and sculptures were removed from museums in France and Russia at the behest of senior Nazi leaders. After Europe was liberated in 1945, many works of art were recovered, but others, such as Russia's fabled Amber Room panels, were never recovered at all.

Chapter 2

Did You See That?

Nessie: Shock in the Loch

The legend of Nessie, the purported inhabitant of Scotland's Loch Ness, dates back to the year 565 when a roving Christian missionary named St. Columba is said to have rebuked a huge water monster to save the life of a swimmer. Rumors persisted from that time on, but it wasn't until the 20th century that the creature became internationally famous.

✳ ✳ ✳ ✳

Monster Ahoy

IN 1933, ONE witness said he saw the creature three times; that same year, a vacationing couple claimed they saw a large creature with flippers and a long neck slither across the road and then heard it splash into the lake. These incidents made news around the world, and the hunt for Nessie was on. Sightings multiplied and became more and more difficult to explain away. In 1971, a priest named Father Gregory Brusey saw a speedy long-necked creature cruising through the loch. One investigator estimates that more than 3,000 people have seen Nessie. The witnesses come from every walk of life, including teachers, doctors, police officers, and scientists.

Monster Media Madness

As technology has advanced, Nessie has been hunted with more sophisticated equipment, often with disappointing results. In 1934, a doctor snapped the famous "Surgeon's

Photo," which showed a dinosaurlike head atop a long neck sticking out of the water. It has since been proven a hoax and what was thought to be Nessie was actually a picture of a toy submarine. Many other photos have been taken, but all are inconclusive.

Since 1934, numerous expeditions have been mounted in search of Nessie. Scuba divers and even submarines have scoured the lake to no avail because the amount of peat in the water makes visibility extremely poor.

In 2003, the British Broadcasting Corporation undertook a massive satellite-assisted sonar sweep of the entire lake, but again with no results. And in 2007, cameras were given to 50,000 people attending a concert on the lake's shore in hopes that someone might get lucky and snap a shot of Nessie. But apparently she doesn't like rock music—Nessie was a no-show.

The Ness-essary Debate

Theories about Nessie's true nature abound. One of the most popular ideas, thanks to the oft-reported long neck, flippers, and bulbous body, is that Nessie is a surviving plesiosaur—a marine reptile thought to have gone extinct 65 million years ago. Critics insist that even if a cold-blooded reptile could exist in the lake's frigid waters, Loch Ness is not large enough to support a breeding population of them. Other theories suggest that Nessie is a giant eel, a string of seals or otters swimming in formation, floating logs, a porpoise, or a huge sturgeon.

Locals have hinted that the creature is actually a demon. Stories of devil worship and mysterious rituals in the area have gone hand in hand with rumors of bodies found floating in the loch. In the early 1900s, famed occultist Aleister Crowley owned a home on the lake's southern shore where he held "black masses" and conducted other ceremonies that may have aimed to "raise" monsters. And for centuries, Scots have repeated folktales of the kelpie, or water horse, a creature that can shape-shift in order to lure the unwary into the water.

Whatever the truth about Nessie, she has made quite a splash as a tourist attraction. Every year thousands of people try their luck at spotting and recording the world's most famous monster.

Mythical Creatures

From the time man first began telling tales around the campfire, every human culture has described creatures with characteristics quite different from run-of-the-mill animals. The legends of horses and snakes with wings, behemoths with horns in odd places, or other conglomerations live on to tease us with questions of their existence.

✳ ✳ ✳ ✳

Dragons: Real Scorchers

ONE OF THE oldest and most universal mythical creatures is the dragon. Huge, winged lizards or serpents with greenish scales and flaming breath are found in tales from ancient China to medieval Europe.

In China, the dragon originally represented the rising sun, happiness, and fertility. Sumerians included dragons in their religious art as early as 4000 BC. The ancient Greeks called their dragon *Draco* and pictured it as a massive, winged snake emitting light and squeezing victims to death in its coils. In the British Isles, dragons were associated with the legendary King Arthur and St. George, and though it is generally accepted that dragons do not exist, some think ancient man's glimpses of giant sea snakes may have inspired dragon myths.

People Acting Fishy: Mermaids and Mermen

The ancient Babylonians worshipped a half-human/half-fish creature named Oannes who gave them the gift of civilization. Some think that mermaids spotted at sea by lonesome sailors are nothing more than manatees—large flat-tailed mammals. But rumors and stories persist.

Unicorns: Creatures That Make a Point

Variations of the unicorn, a horse with a single, long horn growing out of its forehead, appear in myths worldwide. It is possible that a similar, actual creature may have appeared at one time to inspire these myths. In the 1800s, a French woman grew a single, ten-inch horn from her forehead. A wax casting of the horn is preserved in Philadelphia's Mütter Museum. More recently, in 2003, a 95-year-old Chinese woman began growing a similar horn. By May 2007, it was five inches long. These are called cutaneous (skin-related) horns and, if possible in humans, could also logically occur in other large mammals. Unicorns are usually portrayed as snow white, gentle, noble creatures—each with a very long, twisted horn that comes to a sharp point.

Pegasus: Cloud Galloper

Greek legend has it that when Poseidon, god of the sea, got together with Medusa, the gorgon with the snake-infested hair, their offspring was Pegasus, a great white horse with wings. Pegasus became the mount of the hero Bellerophon, and together they slew the bizarre Chimera (a fire-breathing monster with the head of a lion, body of a goat, and tail of a snake). Pride in the great deed made Bellerophon think he could ride Pegasus to Mt. Olympus, home of the gods, so he sprang away for the heavens. But the mortal Bellerophon was thrown back to Earth by Zeus, who kept the winged horse for himself. There is a constellation named for Pegasus.

Cyclops: Keeping an Eye Out

They were not pretty, according to Greek legend. The small group of grotesque, one-eyed giants called Cyclopes (in the plural) was warlike and given to eating human flesh. Their one skill was an astonishing talent for creating weapons for the gods, such as swords and arrows. Could such people ever have existed? Humans inflicted with an endocrine disorder known as gigantism have been known to reach a height of eight feet, and very rarely humans may also be born with a birth defect that gives them a single eye, so perhaps this monster has roots in a long-forgotten, actual human being.

Having a Lot of Faun

Very similar to goat-man creatures called satyrs but not at all related to baby deer (fawns), fauns looked like men from the navel up, except for the goat horns sprouting from their temples. They also bounded about on goat legs and hooves. Fathered by the Greek god Faunus, fauns protected the natural world, especially fields and woods. They were also similar in appearance to Pan, Greek god of nature, who gave us the word panic for the fright he could inspire by blowing on his magical conch shell. Mr. Tumnus from C. S. Lewis's *The Lion, the Witch, and the Wardrobe* was a faun.

Centaurs: When Horse and Rider are Truly One

A skilled rider will often appear as one with his or her galloping steed, so it isn't hard to see how ancient Greeks may have envisioned a creature that was humanlike from the trunk up but with the legs and body of a stallion—it makes for truly seamless horsemanship. Centaurs were meat-eating revelers who loved to drink, according to Greek legend, except for one gentle man-horse named Chiron known for his wisdom and teaching abilities. Chiron lives on as the centaur constellation Sagittarius, and centaurs are still seen on the coats of arms of many old European families.

Trolls: Mammoth Mountain Men

Although the descriptions of these ugly, manlike beings vary from country to country, trolls originated in Scandinavian lands, where they were said to be gigantic, grotesque humanoids who lived in the hills or mountains, mined ore, and became wondrous metalsmiths. Trolls could turn to stone if caught in the sun, and Norway's ancient rock pillars are said to be evidence of this belief. But perhaps legends of trolls are based on a few individuals with a disorder that would not have been understood in ancient times. A rare hormonal disorder called gigantism causes excessive growth of the long bones, and, thus, greatly increased height.

Griffins: In the Cat-Bird Seat?

Depictions of these folk monsters can be found in artwork from ancient Egypt and other cradles of civilization as early as 3300 BC. Mainly a lion-eagle combo, griffins featured a lion's body and an eagle's wings, head, and legs. But they also sported big ears and fierce, ruby-colored eyes. Griffins often guarded rich treasure troves and viciously defended their turf with their sharp beaks and talons. They have survived in modern fantasy fiction, including Lewis Carroll's *Alice's Adventures in Wonderland*.

Fairies: Not Always Tinkerbell

Fairies, also known as wood nymphs, sprites, pixies, and many other names in cultures around the world, are usually thought of as attractive little spirit beings, proportioned like humans and charmingly dressed in wildflowers and acorns. In modern times, they are often depicted as sweet little beings with translucent wings who spread sparkles with their wands. But in medieval times, the *fée* or *fay*, as they were called in Old French or English, could be naughty or nice.

One Irish tradition maintains that fairies often stole babies, substituting an old, wrinkled fairy or even a bundled log in place of the infant. Some European folk traditions believed fairies were descended from an old, superior race of humanoid creatures, and others thought they were fallen angels that had landed in woods or meadows. Shakespeare's play, *A Midsummer Night's Dream*, with its royal fairies Oberon and Titania, helped popularize the notion of fairies as small, magical people living in their own kingdom among humans. And folk belief worldwide still insists that these little people must be treated respectfully and given offerings and gifts to keep them from pulling nasty tricks on their human neighbors.

White House Ghosts

The colonial-style mansion at 1600 Pennsylvania Avenue may be America's most famous address, as well as one of the most haunted. Day and night, visitors have seen spirits that include presidents William Henry Harrison, Andrew Jackson, and Abraham Lincoln. The spirits of these men are almost as powerful today as when they ruled America.

✳ ✳ ✳ ✳

William Henry Harrison Feels a Little Blue

WILLIAM HENRY HARRISON was the first American president to die in office. While giving his inauguration speech on an icy, windy March 4, 1841, Harrison caught a cold that quickly turned to pneumonia.

There are stories about Harrison, half-conscious with fever, wandering the corridors of the White House, looking for a quiet room in which to rest. Unfortunately, there was no escape from the demands of his office…nor from the doctors whose treatments likely killed him. While Harrison's lungs filled with fluid and fever wracked his body, his doctors bled him, then treated him with mustard, laxatives, ipecac, rhubarb, and mercury. It is speculated that the president died not from the "ordinary winter cold" that he'd contracted, but from the care of his doctors. William Henry Harrison died April 4, 1841, just one month after taking office—but rumors have it that his spirit lingers on.

Harrison's translucent ghost is seen throughout the White House, but especially in the residential areas. His skin is pale blue, and his breathing makes an ominous rattling noise. He appears to be looking for something and walks through closed doors. Some believe that he's looking for rest or a cure for his illness. Others say he's searching for his office, so he can complete his term as president.

Andrew Jackson Likes the Ladies

If you'd prefer to see a happier ghost, look for Andrew Jackson. He's probably in the Queen's Bedroom where his bed is displayed. But Jackson may not necessarily be looking for his old bed—in life he was quite the ladies' man and, today, the Queen's Bedroom is reserved for female guests of honor.

Mary Todd Lincoln frequently complained about the ghost of Andrew Jackson cursing and stomping in the corridors of the White House. When she left the presidential estate, Jackson stopped complaining.

Visitors may simply sense Jackson's presence in the Queen's Bedroom or feel a bone-chilling breeze when they're around his bed. Others have reported that Jackson's ghost climbs under the covers, sending guests shrieking out of the room. But Jackson isn't the only president who haunts this room.

Two Wartime Leaders Meet

During World War II, the Queen's Bedroom was called the Rose Room, and it wasn't reserved for women. While visiting the White House during the war, Winston Churchill strolled into the Rose Room completely naked and smoking a cigar after taking a bath. It was then that he encountered the ghost of Abraham Lincoln standing in front of the fireplace with one hand on the mantle, staring down at the hearth. Always a quick wit, Churchill said, "Good evening, Mr. President. You seem to have me at a disadvantage."

According to Churchill, Lincoln smiled at him then vanished. Churchill refused to stay in that room again, but Lincoln wasn't finished surprising guests.

Lincoln Wakes Up the Queen

When Queen Wilhelmina of The Netherlands stayed in the Queen's Bedroom in 1945, she was hoping to get a good night's sleep. Instead, she was awakened by noisy footsteps in the corridor outside her room. Annoyed, she waited for the person to return to his room, but he stopped at her door and knocked loudly, several times. When the queen finally opened her door, she was face to face with the specter of Abraham Lincoln. She said that he looked a bit pale but very much alive and was dressed in travel clothes, including a top hat and coat. The queen gasped, and Lincoln vanished.

Lincoln's ghost may be the most solid-looking and "real" spirit at the White House, and hundreds of people have encountered it. Strangely enough, Lincoln, who seemed to be in touch with "the other side" even before he died, claimed he once saw his own apparition and talked about it often.

Abraham Lincoln Sees His Own Ghost

The morning after Abraham Lincoln was first elected president, he had a premonition about his death. He saw two reflections of himself in a mirror. One image was how he usually appeared, fit and healthy. In the other reflection, his face was pale and ghostly. Lincoln and his wife believed it predicted that he wouldn't complete his second term in office.

Later, Lincoln saw his own funeral in a dream. He said that he was in the White House, but it was strangely quiet and filled with mourners. Walking through the halls, he entered the East Room, where, to his horror, he saw a body wrapped in funeral vestments and surrounded by soldiers.

He said he approached one of the soldiers to find out what had happened. "Who is dead in the White House?" Lincoln demanded in his dream. "The president," the soldier replied. "He was killed by an assassin!"

A few days later, that fateful day when he attended Ford Theatre for the last time, President Lincoln called a meeting of his cabinet members. He told them that they would have important news the following morning. He also explained that he'd had a strange dream...one that he'd had twice before. He saw himself alone and adrift in a boat without oars. That was all he said, and the cabinet members left the president's office with a very uneasy feeling. The following morning, they received news that the president had been assassinated.

Lincoln Never Leaves

Lincoln's apparition has been seen clearly by hundreds of people, including Eleanor Roosevelt's maid, who saw Abe sitting on a bed, removing his boots. Franklin Roosevelt's valet ran out of the White House after encountering Lincoln's spirit. Calvin Coolidge's wife saw Lincoln's face reflected in a window in the Yellow Oval Room.

President Lincoln has been seen in many places in the White House but most frequently in the Lincoln Bedroom. Although the late president's bed is now in this room, during his lifetime, it was the cabinet room in which he signed the Emancipation Proclamation.

Ghosts of Presidents' Families and Foes

Abigail Adams used to hang laundry on clotheslines in the White House's East Room. Her ghost appears there regularly in a cap and wrapped in a shawl. She's usually carrying laundry or checking to see if her laundry is dry.

Dorothea "Dolley" Madison defends the Rose Garden that she designed and planted. When Woodrow Wilson's second wife, Edith, ordered gardeners to dig up the garden for new plants, Dolley's apparition appeared and allegedly insisted that no one was going to touch her garden. The landscaping ceased, and Dolley's roses remain exactly as they were when the Madisons lived in the White House in the early 1800s.

Abraham Lincoln's son Willie died in February 1862 after a brief illness. Soon after, the First Lady began holding séances in the White House to communicate with him. The president was equally obsessed with his son's death and had his coffin reopened at least twice, just to look at him. Willie's apparition has been seen at the White House regularly since then, most often appearing in the second-floor bedrooms where his presence was witnessed by Lyndon Johnson's daughter Lynda.

However, Lynda's bedroom may have been haunted by other spirits as well. Harry Truman's mother died in that room, and Lynda used to report unexplained footsteps in the bedroom. Sometimes, her phone would ring in the middle of the night and, when she answered, no one was on the line.

Also on the second floor, people have heard the ghost of Frances Cleveland crying, perhaps reliving a time when her husband, Grover, was diagnosed with cancer.

One very out-of-place spirit appears to be a British soldier from around 1814 when the White House was besieged and burned during the War of 1812. The uniformed soldier looks lost and is holding a torch. When he realizes that he's been spotted, he looks alarmed and vanishes.

The White House's Oldest Ghost

David Burns may be the oldest ghost at the White House. He donated the land on which the house was built. One day, Franklin Roosevelt heard his name being called, and when he replied, the voice said that he was Mr. Burns.

FDR's valet, Cesar Carrera, told a similar story. Carrera was in the Yellow Oval Room when he heard a soft, distant voice say, "I'm Mr. Burns." When Carrera looked, no one was there.

Later, during the Truman years, a guard at the White House also heard a soft voice announce himself as Mr. Burns. The guard expected to see Truman's Secretary of State, James Byrnes, but no one appeared. What's more, the guard checked the roster and learned that Byrnes hadn't been in the building at all that day.

The White House may be America's most haunted public building. Ghosts are seen there, day and night. On the White House's website, staff members talk about their regular ghostly encounters. In the words of Harry Truman, the White House is haunted, "sure as shooting."

The Windy City's Famous Phantom: Resurrection Mary

Most big cities have their share of ghost stories, and Chicago is no different. But beyond the tales of haunted houses, spirit-infested graveyards, and spooky theaters, there is one Chicago legend that stands out among the rest. It's the story of a beautiful female phantom, a hitchhiking ghost that nearly everyone in the Windy City has heard of. Her name is "Resurrection Mary" and she is Chicago's most famous ghost.

✳   ✳   ✳   ✳

The Girl by the Side of the Road

THE STORY OF Resurrection Mary begins in the mid-1930s, when drivers began reporting a ghostly young woman on the road near the gates of Resurrection Cemetery, located on Archer Avenue in Chicago's southwestern suburbs. Some drivers claimed that she was looking for a ride, but others reported that she actually attempted to jump onto the running boards of their automobiles as they drove past.

A short time later, the reports took another, more mysterious turn. The unusual incidents moved away from the cemetery and began to center around the Oh Henry Ballroom (known today as Willowbrook Ballroom), located a few miles south of the graveyard on Archer Avenue. Many claimed to see the young woman on the road near the ballroom and sometimes inside the dancehall itself. Young men claimed that they met the girl at a dance, spent the evening with her, then offered her a ride home at closing time. Her vague directions always led them north along Archer Avenue until they reached the gates of Resurrection Cemetery—where the girl would inexplicably vanish from the car! Some drivers even claimed to accidentally run over the girl outside the cemetery. When they went to her aid, her body was always gone. Others said that their automobiles actually passed through the young woman before she disappeared through the cemetery gates.

Police and local newspapers began hearing similar stories from frightened and frazzled drivers who had encountered the mysterious young woman. These first-hand accounts created the legend of "Resurrection Mary," as she came to be known.

Will the Real Resurrection Mary Please Stand Up?

One version of the story says that Resurrection Mary was a young woman who died on Archer Avenue in the early 1930s. On a cold winter's night, Mary spent the evening dancing at the Oh Henry Ballroom, but after an argument with her boyfriend, she decided to walk home. She was killed when a passing car slid on the ice and struck her.

According to the story, Mary was buried in Resurrection Cemetery, and since that time, she has been spotted along Archer Avenue. Many believe that she may be returning to her eternal resting place after one last dance. This legend has been told countless times over the years and there may actually be some elements of truth to it—although, there may be more than one "Resurrection Mary" haunting Archer Avenue.

One of the prime candidates for Mary's real-life identity was a young Polish girl named Mary Bregovy. Mary loved to dance, especially at the Oh Henry Ballroom, and was killed one night in March 1934 after spending the evening at the ballroom and then downtown at some of the late-night clubs. She was killed along Wacker Drive in Chicago when the car that she was riding in collided with an elevated train support.

Bregovy's parents buried her in Resurrection Cemetery, and then, a short time later, a cemetery caretaker spotted her supposed ghost walking through the graveyard. Stranger still, passing motorists on Archer Avenue soon began telling stories of her apparition trying to hitch rides as they passed the cemetery's front gates. For this reason, many believe that the ghost stories of Mary Bregovy may have given birth to the legend of Resurrection Mary.

However, she may not be the only one. As encounters with Mary have been passed along over the years, many descriptions of the phantom have varied. Mary Bregovy had bobbed, light-brown hair, but some reports describe Resurrection Mary as having long blonde hair. Who could this ghost be?

It's possible that this may be a young woman named Mary Miskowski, who was killed along Archer Avenue in October 1930. According to sources, she also loved to dance at the Oh Henry Ballroom and at some of the local nightspots. Many people who knew her in life believed that she might be the ghostly hitchhiker reported in the southwestern suburbs.

In the end, we may never know Resurrection Mary's true identity. But there's no denying that sightings of her have been backed up with credible eyewitness accounts. In these real, first-person reports, witnesses give specific places, dates, and times for their encounters with Mary—encounters that remain unexplained to this day. Besides that, Mary is one of the few ghosts to ever leave physical evidence behind!

The Gates of Resurrection Cemetery

On August 10, 1976, around 10:30 PM, a man driving past Resurrection Cemetery noticed a young girl wearing a white dress standing inside the cemetery gates. She was holding on to the bars of the gate, looking out toward the road. Thinking that she was locked in the cemetery, the man stopped at a nearby police station and alerted an officer to the young woman's predicament. An officer responded to the call, but when he arrived at the cemetery, the girl was gone. He called out with his loudspeaker and looked for her with his spotlight, but nobody was there. However, when he walked up to the gates for a closer inspection, he saw something very unusual. It looked as though someone had pulled two of the green-colored bronze bars with such intensity that handprints were seared into the metal. The bars were blackened and burned at precisely the spot where a small woman's hands would have been.

When word got out about the handprints, people from all over the area came to see them. Cemetery officials denied that anything supernatural had occurred, and they later claimed that the marks were created when a truck accidentally backed into the gates and a workman had tried to heat them up and bend them back. It was a convenient explanation but one that failed to explain the indentations that appeared to be left by small fingers and were plainly visible in the metal.

Cemetery officials were disturbed by this new publicity, so, in an attempt to dispel the crowds of curiosity-seekers, they tried to remove the marks with a blowtorch. However, this made them even more noticeable, so they cut out the bars with plans to straighten or replace them.

But removing the bars only made things worse as people wondered what the cemetery had to hide. Local officials were so embarrassed that the bars were put back into place, straightened, and then left alone so that the burned areas would oxidize and eventually match the other bars. However, the blackened areas of the bars did not oxidize, and the twisted handprints remained obvious until the late 1990s when the bars were finally removed. At great expense, Resurrection Cemetery replaced the entire front gates and the notorious bars were gone for good.

A Broken Spirit Lingers On

Sightings of Resurrection Mary aren't as frequent as in years past, but they do still continue. Even though a good portion of the encounters can be explained by the fact that Mary has become such a part of Chicago lore that nearly everyone has heard of her, some of the sightings seem to be authentic. So whether you believe in her or not, Mary is still seen walking along Archer Avenue, people still claim to pick her up during the cold winter months, and she continues to be the Windy City's most famous ghost.

Fireball in the Sky

While playing football on the afternoon of September 12, 1952, a group of boys in Flatwoods, West Virginia, saw a large fireball fly over their heads. The object seemed to stop near the hillside property of Bailey Fisher. Some thought the object was a UFO, but others said it was just a meteor. They decided to investigate.

Darkness was falling as the boys made their way toward the hill, so they stopped at the home of Kathleen May to borrow a flashlight. Seeing how excited the boys were, May, her two sons, and their friend, Eugene Lemon, decided to join them. The group set off to find out exactly what had landed on the hill.

✳ ✳ ✳ ✳

Walking Through the Darkness

As they neared the top of the hill, the group smelled a strange odor that reminded them of burning metal. Continuing on, some members of the group thought they saw an object that resembled a spaceship. Shining their flashlights in front of them, the group was startled when something not of this world moved out from behind a nearby tree.

The Encounter

The description of what is now known as the Flatwoods Monster is almost beyond belief. It stood around 12 feet tall and had a round, reddish face from which two large holes were visible. Looming up from behind the creature's head was a large pointed hood. The creature, which appeared to be made of a dark metal, had no arms or legs and seemed to float through the air. Looking back, the witnesses believe what they saw was a protective suit or perhaps a robot rather than a monster.

When a flashlight beam hit the creature, its "eyes" lit up and it began floating toward the group while making a strange hissing noise. The horrible stench was now overpowering and some in the group immediately felt nauseous. Because she was at the head of the group, Kathleen May had the best view of the monster. She later stated that as the creature was moving toward her, it squirted or dripped a strange fluid on her that resembled oil but had an unusual odor to it.

Terrified beyond belief, the group fled down the hillside and back to the May house, where they telephoned Sheriff Robert Carr, who responded with his deputy, Burnell Long. After talking with the group, they gathered some men and went to the Fisher property to investigate. But they only found a gummy residue and what appeared to be skid marks on the ground. There was no monster and no spaceship. However, the group did report that the heavy stench of what smelled like burning metal was still in the air.

The Aftermath

A. Lee Stewart, a member of the of the search party and copublisher of the *Braxton Democrat*, knew a good story when he saw one, so he sent the tale over the news wire, and almost immediately, people were asking Kathleen May for interviews. On September 19, 1952, May and Stewart discussed the

Flatwoods Monster on the TV show *We the People*. For the show, an artist sketched the creature based on May's description, but he took some liberties, and the resulting sketch was so outrageous that people started saying the whole thing was a hoax.

Slowly, though, others came forward to admit that they too had seen a strange craft flying through the sky near Flatwoods on September 12. One witness described it as roughly the size of a single-car garage. He said that he lost sight of the craft when it appeared to land on a nearby hill.

Since that night in 1952, the Flatwoods Monster has never been seen again, leaving many people to wonder what exactly those people encountered. A monster? An alien from another world? Or perhaps nothing more than a giant owl? One thing is for sure: There were far too many witnesses to deny that they stumbled upon something strange that night.

The Bell Witch of Tennessee

There is perhaps no haunting in America that resonates quite like the event that occurred on the farm of John Bell in rural Tennessee. The story stands unique in the annals of folklore as one of the rare cases in which a spirit not only injured the residents of a haunted house but also caused the death of one of them! For this reason, even though the haunting occurred in the early 1800s, it has not yet been forgotten.

＊　＊　＊　＊

THE STORY OF the Bell Witch will be forever linked to the small town of Adams in northwestern Tennessee. In 1804, John Bell, his wife, Lucy, and their six children came to the region from North Carolina. He purchased 1,000 acres of land on the Red River, and the Bell family settled quite comfortably into the community. John Bell was well liked, as was Lucy, who often opened her home to travelers.

Bumps in the Night

The Bell haunting began in 1817 after John Bell and his son Drew spotted odd creatures in the woods near their farm. When they shot at the strange beasts, they vanished. Soon after, a series of weird knocking, scraping, and scratching sounds began on the exterior of the house and then at the front door. Shortly thereafter, the sounds moved inside and seemed to emanate from the bedroom belonging to the Bell sons.

This continued for weeks, and before long, the irritating sounds were heard all over the house. They continued from room to room, stopping when everyone was awake and starting again when they all went back to bed.

The Bells also heard what sounded like a dog pawing at the wooden floor or chains being dragged through the house. They even heard thumps and thuds, as though furniture was being overturned. These sounds were frightening, but not as terrifying as the noises that followed—the smacking of lips, gurgling, gulping, and choking—sounds seemingly made by a human. The nerves of the Bell family were starting to unravel as the sounds became a nightly occurrence.

The Coming of the Witch

The disembodied sounds were followed by unseen hands. Items in the house were broken and blankets were yanked from the beds. Hair was pulled and the children were slapped and poked, causing them to cry in pain. The Bells' daughter Betsy was once slapped so hard that her cheeks stayed bright red for hours.

Whatever the cause of this unseen force, most of its violent outbursts were directed at Betsy. She would often run screaming from her room in terror as the unseen hands prodded, pinched, and poked her. Strangely, the force became even crueler to her whenever she entertained her young suitor, Joshua Gardner, at the house. Desperately seeking answers, John Bell enlisted the help of some of his neighbors to investigate.

Even in the presence of these witnesses, the strange sounds continued, chairs overturned, and objects flew about the room. The neighbors formed an investigative committee, determined to find a cause for the terrifying events. Regardless, the household was in chaos. Word began to spread of the strange happenings, and friends and strangers came to the farm to witness it for themselves. Dozens of people heard the banging and rapping sounds and chunks of rock and wood were thrown at curious guests by unseen hands.

Investigations and Setbacks

As the investigative committee searched for answers, they set up experiments, tried to communicate with the force, and kept a close eye on the events that took place. They set up overnight vigils, but the attacks only increased in intensity. Betsy was treated brutally and began to have sensations that the breath was being sucked out of her body. She was scratched and her flesh bled as though she was being pierced with invisible pins and needles. She also suffered fainting spells and often blacked out for 30 to 40 minutes at a time.

Soon, a raspy whistling sound was audible, as if someone was trying to speak. It progressed until the force began to talk in a weak whisper. The voice of the force told them that it was a spirit whose rest had been disturbed, and it made many claims as to its origins, from being an ancient spirit to the ghost of a murdered peddler.

The excitement in the community grew as word spread that the spirit was communicating. People came from far and wide to hear the unexplained voice. Hundreds of people witnessed the activity caused by the witch. There were those who came to the Bell farm intent on either driving out the witch or proving that the entire affair was a hoax. But without fail, each of them left the farm confessing that the unusual events were beyond their understanding.

A Strange Affliction

John Bell began to complain of a curious numbness in his mouth that caused his tongue to swell so greatly that he was unable to eat or drink for days at a time. As the haunting progressed, he began to suffer other inexplicable symptoms, most notably bizarre facial tics that rendered him unable to talk or eat and often made him lose consciousness. These odd seizures lasted from a few hours to a week, and they increased in severity as time wore on.

No one knows why John Bell was targeted by the spirit, but from the beginning, the witch made it clear that it would torment him for the rest of his life. Bell was also physically abused by the witch and many witnesses recalled him being slapped by unseen hands or crying out in pain as he was stabbed with invisible pins. Bell's doctor was helpless when it came to finding a cure for his ailments. The witch laughed at his efforts and declared that no medicine could cure him.

Some believe the reason for Bell's suffering was revealed one night when the spirit claimed to belong to Kate Batts, an eccentric neighbor who had disliked Bell because of some bad business dealings in the past. Whether the spirit was Batts is unknown, but people began calling the witch Kate.

The Death of John Bell

By 1820, John Bell's physical condition had worsened. His facial jerks and twitches continued, as did the swelling of his tongue and the seizures that left him nearly paralyzed for hours or days at a time. In late October, he suffered another fit and took to his bed. He would never leave the house again. As Bell writhed in pain, Kate remained nearby, laughing and cursing at the dying man.

On the morning of December 19, 1820, Lucy checked on her husband who appeared to be sleeping soundly. An hour later, she returned to the bedroom and realized that he was in a stupor. When John, Jr., went to get his father's medicine, he discovered that all of his father's prescriptions had vanished. In place of them was a small vial that contained a dark-colored liquid. No one knew what had happened to the medicines or what was in the vial.

Suddenly, Kate's voice took over the room. She claimed that she had poisoned Bell with the contents of the dark vial and that he would never rise from his bed again. The mysterious liquid was tested on a family cat, and the animal was dead in seconds.

John Bell never did recover. On December 20, he took one last shuddering breath and died. Laughter filled the house as the witch stated that she hoped John Bell would burn in hell.

Bell was laid to rest in a small cemetery, a short distance from the family home. As mourners left the cemetery, the voice of Kate returned, echoing loudly in the cold morning air. She cheered the death of the man she hated so much.

This ended the most terrifying chapter of a haunting that left an indelible mark in the annals of supernatural history. But the Bell Witch was not finished—at least not quite yet.

The Broken Engagement

After the funeral, the activities of the witch seemed to subside, but she was not totally gone. Kate remained with the family throughout the winter and spring of 1821, but she was not quite as vicious as she had been, not even to Betsy, around whom her activities continued to be centered.

During the haunting, it was clear that Betsy would be punished as long as she allowed herself to be courted by Joshua Gardner. But Betsy and Joshua refused to give in to Kate's wishes. In fact, on Easter Sunday 1821, the couple became engaged, much to the delight of their family and friends. But their joy would not last long as the antics of the witch returned with horrific force. Realizing that the witch would never leave her alone as long as she stayed with Joshua, Betsy broke off the engagement and never saw him again.

The Return of the Witch

In the summer of 1821, the witch left the Bell family, promising to return in seven years. In 1828, she came back and announced her return in the same manner as when the original haunting first began—scratching and other eerie sounds, objects moving, and blankets pulled from the beds.

The Bells decided to ignore the activity, and, if spoken to by the spirit, they ignored it as well. In this way, they hoped the visitation might end quickly. And so it did—the witch left the house after a few weeks.

Insight Into the Future?

However, much of the activity during the witch's 1828 visit took place at the home of John Bell, Jr., who had built a house on land that he had inherited from his father. The witch allegedly made several accurate predictions about the future, including the Civil War, the end of slavery, the rise of the United States as a world power, and the coming of World Wars I and II. She even predicted the end of the world, stating that the world would end with the temperature of the planet rising so high that it would become uninhabitable.

Kate stayed with John Bell, Jr., for several months. Before she left, she promised to return again in 107 years, which would have meant a resurgence of supernatural actvity in 1935. Though there is no record that she ever did so, there are some that maintain that the Bell Witch has never left Adams, Tennessee. Strange events still occur where the old Bell farm stood. Old Kate is still talked about today and you'd have to travel far to find someone who does not believe that something very strange occurred there in the early 1800s.

What was it exactly? No one knows for sure, but there's no question that it made an indelible mark on American history.

Monsters Across America

Dracula, Frankenstein, the Wolf Man—these are the monsters who strike fear into the hearts of children—the same ones that parents chase away and tell their kids there's no such thing as monsters. But are they wrong?

✳ ✳ ✳ ✳

Dover Demon

FOR TWO DAYS in 1977, the town of Dover, Massachusetts, was under attack from a bizarre creature that seemed to be from another world. The first encounter with the beast—nicknamed the Dover Demon—occurred on the evening of April 21. Bill Bartlett was out for a drive with some friends when they saw something strange climbing on a stone wall. The creature appeared to be only about three feet tall but had a giant, oversize head with large, orange eyes. The rest of the body was tan and hairless with long, thin arms and legs.

Several hours later, the same creature was spotted by 15-year-old John Baxter, who watched it scurry up a hillside. The following day, a couple reported seeing the Demon, too. When authorities asked for a description, the couple's matched the ones given by the other witnesses except for one difference: The creature the couple encountered appeared to have glowing green eyes. Despite repeated attempts to locate it, the creature was never seen again.

Momo

In the early 1970s, reports came flooding in of a strange creature roaming the woods near the small town of Louisiana, Missouri. Standing nearly seven feet tall, Momo (short for Missouri Monster) was completely covered in black fur with glowing orange eyes. The first major report came in July 1971 when Joan Mills and Mary Ryan claimed to have been harassed by a "half ape, half man" creature that made bizarre noises at them as they passed it on Highway 79. Even though the creature didn't make physical contact with them, both women believed it would have harmed them had it been given the chance. That seemed to be confirmed the following year when, on July 11, 1972, brothers Terry and Wally Harrison spotted a giant, hairy beast carrying a dead dog. The boys screamed, alerting family members, who caught a glimpse of the creature before it disappeared into the woods. Sightings continued for a couple of weeks, but Momo hasn't been seen since.

Lawndale Thunderbird

If you're ever in Lawndale, Illinois, keep an eye out for giant birds lest they sneak up on you and whisk you away. That's what almost happened in 1977 when Lawndale residents noticed two large black birds with white-banded necks and 10- to 12-foot wingspans flying overhead. The birds, though enormous, seemed harmless enough. That is, until they swooped down and one of them reportedly tried to take off with ten-year-old Marlon Lowe while he played in his yard. The boy was not seriously injured, but the thunderbird did manage to lift the terrified boy several feet off the ground and carry him for nearly 40 feet before dropping him. Over the next few weeks, the birds were seen flying over various houses and fields in nearby towns, but, thankfully, they did not attack anyone else. And though they appear to have left Lawndale for good, reports of thunderbird sightings continue across the United States. The most recent one was on September 25, 2001, in South Greensburg, Pennsylvania.

Ohio Bridge Trolls

In May 1955, a man driving along the Miami River near Loveland, Ohio, came across a frightening sight. Huddled under a darkened bridge were several bald-headed creatures, each three to four feet tall. Spellbound, the man pulled over and watched the creatures, which he said had webbed hands and feet. Though they made no sound, the man said the creatures appeared to be communicating with each other and did not notice him watching them. However, when one of the creatures held up a wand or rod that began emitting showers of sparks, the man quickly left.

He drove straight to the local police station, which dispatched a car to the bridge. A search of the area turned up nothing, and, to this day, there have been no more reported sightings of these strange creatures.

Maryland's Goatman

Think goats are cute and fuzzy little creatures? If so, a trip through Prince George's County in Maryland just might change your mind. Since the 1950s, people have reported horrifying encounters with a creature known only as the Goatman. From afar, many claim to have mistaken the Goatman for a human being. But as he draws nearer, his cloven feet become visible, as do the horns growing out of his head. If that's not enough to make you turn and run, reports as recent as 2006 state that the Goatman now carries an ax with him.

Gatormen

The swamplands of Florida are filled with alligators, but most of them don't have human faces. Since the 1700s, tales of strange half-man, half-alligator creatures have circulated throughout the area. Gatormen are described as having the face, neck, chest, and arms of a man and the midsection, back legs, and tail of an alligator. Unlike most other monsters and strange beasts, Gatormen reportedly prefer to travel and hunt in packs and even appear to have their own verbal language. What's more, recent sightings have them traveling outside the state of Florida and taking up residence in the swamplands of Louisiana and swimming around a remote Texas swamp in 2001.

Skunk Ape

Since the 1960s, a creature has been spotted in the Florida Everglades that many call Bigfoot's stinky cousin: the skunk ape. The beast is said to closely resemble Bigfoot with one minor difference—it smells like rotten eggs. In late 2000, Sarasota police received an anonymous letter from a woman who complained that an escaped animal was roaming near her home at night. Included with the letter were two close-up photographs of the creature—a large beast that resembled an orangutan standing behind some palmetto leaves, baring its teeth.

Lizard Man

At around 2:00 AM on June 29, 1988, Christopher Davis got a flat tire on a back road near the Scape Ore Swamp in South Carolina. Just as the teen finished changing the tire, he was suddenly attacked by a seven-foot-tall creature with scaly green skin and glowing red eyes. Davis was able to get back into his car and drive away but not before the Lizard Man managed to climb onto the roof and claw at it, trying to get inside. As he drove, Davis could see the creature had three claws on each of its "hands." Eventually, the creature fell from the car and Davis was able to escape. A search of the scene later that day turned up nothing. Despite numerous subsequent sightings, the creature has yet to be apprehended.

Devil Monkeys

Far and away, some of the strangest creatures said to be roaming the countryside are the Devil Monkeys. Take an adult kangaroo, stick a monkey or baboon head on top, and you've got yourself a Devil Monkey. By most accounts, these creatures can cover hundreds of feet in just a few quick hops. They're nothing to tangle with, either. Although Devil Monkeys have traditionally stuck to attacking livestock and the occasional family pet, some  reports have them attempting to claw their way into people's homes. Originally spotted in Virginia in the 1950s, Devil Monkeys have now been spotted all across the United States. On a related note, in May 2001, residents of New Delhi, India, were sent into a panic when a four-foot-tall half-monkey, half-human creature began attacking them as they slept.

Beware of Cries from the Bridge

Bridges provide us with a way to get from one place to another. But when that other place is the afterlife, a crybaby bridge is born. Located throughout the United States, crybaby bridges are said to mark locations where a baby died. And, according to legend, if you're brave enough to wait patiently on the bridge, you'll actually hear the baby cry. Here are some of the most popular crybaby bridges across the United States.

✻ ✻ ✻ ✻

Middletown, New Jersey

COOPER ROAD IS a lonely stretch of road that wanders through the backwoods of Middletown. Stay on this road long enough and you will eventually come to the crybaby bridge under which a baby is said to have drowned. If you want to hear the baby cry, just position your vehicle in the middle of the bridge and wait. But make sure you don't turn your car off or you won't be able to start it again.

Monmouth, Illinois

It's a case of "the more the scarier" for this crybaby bridge in western Illinois. According to legend, an entire busload of small children drove off the bridge when the driver lost control. It is said that if you go to the bridge at night, turn off your car's engine, and put your vehicle in neutral, you'll hear cries from the dead children. Shortly thereafter, ghostly hands will push your car across the bridge and back onto the road, leaving tiny handprints on the back of your car.

Concord, North Carolina

Just outside of Concord is a bridge on Poplar Tent Road that locals refer to as Sally's Bridge. According to local lore, a young woman named Sally was driving home with her baby when she lost control of her car, skidded across the bridge, and crashed. The baby was ejected from the vehicle and fell into the water. Panic-stricken, Sally dove into the water to try to save her child, but sadly both mother and child drowned. Today, legend has it that Sally's ghost will bang on your car, desperately trying to find someone to help save her dying child.

Upper Marlboro, Maryland

The story associated with this crybaby bridge says that a young, single woman became pregnant. Embarrassed and afraid of being disowned, she somehow managed to conceal her pregnancy from her family and friends. When the baby was born, the woman waited until nightfall, walked out to the bridge, then threw the baby from the bridge into the water below. Legend has it that if you go out to the bridge at night, you'll hear the baby crying.

Cable, Ohio

Far and away, the state of Ohio harbors the most crybaby bridges, each with its own unique spin on the classic crybaby bridge story. For example, legend has it that on a cold November night in the tiny town of Cable, a deeply depressed woman bundled up her newborn baby and walked onto a bridge that crossed over some railroad tracks. She waited patiently until she heard the sound of a distant train whistle. With the baby still in her arms, the woman jumped in front of the oncoming train just as it reached the bridge. Both were killed instantly.

If you visit this bridge, be forewarned—especially when it's close to midnight. Unlucky travelers crossing the bridge at that time have reported that their cars suddenly stalled. When they tried to restart the engines, they heard the sound of a distant train whistle, which seemed to signal the start of a bizarre and ghostly flashback. As the whistle got closer, motorists reported hearing a baby crying. Then, just when it sounded as though the train was right next to the bridge, they heard a woman scream…and then everything went silent. Only then were they able to start their cars again.

The Champion of American Lake Monsters

In 1609, French explorer Samuel de Champlain was astonished to see a thick, eight- to ten-foot-tall creature in the waters between present-day Vermont and New York. His subsequent report set in motion the legend of Champ, the "monster" in Lake Champlain.

✳ ✳ ✳ ✳

Eerie Encounters

EVEN BEFORE CHAMPLAIN'S visit, Champ was known to Native Americans as Chaousarou. Over time, Champ has become one of North America's most famous lake monsters. News stories of its existence were frequent enough that in 1873, showman P. T. Barnum offered $50,000 for the creature, dead or alive. That same year, Champ almost sank a steamboat, and in the 1880s, a number of people, including a sheriff, glimpsed it splashing playfully offshore. It is generally described as dark in color (olive green, gray, or brown) with a serpentlike body.

Sightings have continued into modern times, and witnesses have compiled some film evidence that is difficult to ignore. In 1977, a woman named Sandra Mansi photographed a long-necked creature poking its head out of the water near St. Albans, Vermont, close to the Canadian border. She estimated the animal was 10 to 15 feet long and told an investigator that its skin looked "slimy" and similar to that of an eel. Mansi presented her photo and story at a 1981 conference held at Lake Champlain. Although she had misplaced the negative by then, subsequent analyses of the photo have generally failed to find any evidence that it was manipulated.

In September 2002, a researcher named Dennis Hall, who headed a lake monster investigation group known as Champ Quest, videotaped what looked like three creatures undulating through the water near Ferrisburgh, Vermont. Hall claimed that he saw unidentifiable animals in Lake Champlain on 19 separate occasions.

In 2006, two fishermen captured digital video footage of what appeared to be parts of a very large animal swimming in the lake. The images were thoroughly examined under the direction of ABC News technicians, and though the creature on the video could not be proved to be Champ, the team could find nothing to disprove it, either.

Champ or Chump?

As the sixth-largest freshwater lake in the United States (and stretching about six miles into Quebec, Canada), Lake Champlain provides ample habitat and nourishment for a good-size water cryptid, or unknown animal. The lake plunges as deep as 400 feet in spots and covers 490 square miles.

Skeptics offer the usual explanations for Champ sightings: large sturgeons, floating logs or water plants, otters, or an optical illusion caused by sunlight and shadow. Others think Champ could be a remnant of a species of primitive whale called a zeuglodon or an ancient marine reptile known as a plesiosaur, both believed by biologists to be long extinct. But until uncontestable images of the creature's entire body are produced, this argument will undoubtedly continue.

Champ does claim one rare, official nod to the probability of its existence: Legislation by both the states of New York and Vermont proclaim that Champ is a protected—though unknown—species and make it illegal to harm the creature in any way. Now someone just needs to find Champ to tell it that it's safe to come out!

The Kecksburg Incident

Did visitors from outer space really once land in a western Pennsylvania thicket?

❋   ❋   ❋   ❋

Dropping in for a Visit

ON DECEMBER 9, 1965, an unidentified flying object (UFO) streaked through the late-afternoon sky and landed in Kecksburg—a rural Pennsylvania community about 40 miles southeast of Pittsburgh. This much is not disputed. However, specific accounts vary widely from person to person. Even after closely examining the facts, many people remain undecided about exactly what happened. "Roswell" type incidents—ultra-mysterious in nature and reeking of a governmental cover-up—have an uncanny way of causing confusion.

Trajectory-Interruptus

A meteor on a collision course with Earth will generally "bounce" as it enters the atmosphere. This occurs due to friction, which forcefully slows the average space rock from 6 to 45 miles per second to a few hundred miles per hour, the speed at which it strikes Earth and officially becomes a meteorite. According to the official explanation offered by the U.S. Air Force, it was a meteorite that landed in Kecksburg. However, witnesses reported that the object completed back and forth maneuvers before landing at a very low speed—moves that an un-powered chunk of earthbound rock simply cannot perform. Strike one against the meteor theory.

An Acorn-Shape Meteorite?

When a meteor manages to pierce Earth's atmosphere, it has the physical properties of exactly what it is: a space rock. That is to say, it will generally be unevenly shaped, rough, and dark-ish in color, much like rocks found on Earth. But at Kecksburg, eyewitnesses reported seeing something far, far different. The unusual object they described was bronze to golden in color, acorn-shape, and as large as a Volkswagen Beetle automobile. Unless the universe has started to produce uniformly shaped and colored meteorites, the official explanation seems highly unlikely. Strike two for the meteor theory.

Markedly Different

Then there's the baffling issue of markings. A meteorite can be chock-full of holes, cracks, and other such surface imperfections. It can also vary somewhat in color. But it should never, ever have markings that seem intelligently designed. Witnesses at Kecksburg describe intricate writings similar to Egyptian hieroglyphics located near the base of the object. A cursory examination of space rocks at any natural history museum reveals that such a thing doesn't occur naturally. Strike three for the meteor theory. Logically following such a trail, could an unnatural force have been responsible for the item witnessed at Kecksburg? At least one man thought so.

Reportis Rigor Mortis

Just after the Kecksburg UFO landed, reporter John Murphy arrived at the scene. Like any seasoned pro, the newsman immediately snapped photos and gathered eyewitness accounts of the event. Strangely, FBI agents arrived, cordoned off the area, and confiscated all but one roll of his film. Undaunted, Murphy assembled a radio documentary entitled *Object in the Woods* to describe his experience. Just before the special was to air, the reporter received an unexpected visit by two men. According to a fellow employee, a dark-suited pair identified themselves as government agents and subsequently confiscated a portion of Murphy's audiotapes.

A week later, a clearly perturbed Murphy aired a watered-down version of his documentary. In it, he claimed that certain interviewees requested their accounts be removed for fear of retribution at the hands of police, military, and government officials. In 1969, John Murphy was struck dead by an unidentified car while crossing the street.

Resurrected by Robert Stack

In all likelihood the Kecksburg incident would have remained dormant and under-explored had it not been for the television show *Unsolved Mysteries*. In a 1990 segment, narrator Robert Stack took an in-depth look at what occurred in Kecksburg, feeding a firestorm of interest that eventually brought forth two new witnesses. The first, a U.S. Air Force officer stationed at Lockbourne AFB (near Columbus, Ohio), claimed to have seen a flatbed truck carrying a mysterious object as it arrived on base on December 10, 1965. The military man told of a tarpaulin-covered conical object that he couldn't identify and a "shoot to kill" order given to him for anyone who ventured too close. He was told that the truck was bound for Wright–Patterson AFB in Dayton, Ohio, an installation that's alleged to contain downed flying saucers. The other witness was a building con-tractor who claimed to have delivered 6,500 special bricks to a hanger inside Wright–Patterson AFB on December 12, 1965. Curious, he peeked inside the hanger and saw a "bell-shaped" device, 12-feet high, surrounded by several men wearing anti-radiation style suits. Upon leaving, he was told that he had just witnessed an object that would become "common knowledge" in the next 20 years.

Will We Ever Know the Truth?

Like Roswell before it, we will probably never know for cer-tain what occurred in western Pennsylvania back in 1965. The more that's learned about the case, the more confus-ing and contradictory it becomes. For instance, the official 1965 meteorite explanation contains more holes than Bonnie and Clyde's death car, and other explanations, such as orbiting space debris (from past U.S. and Russian missions) reenter-ing Earth's atmosphere, seem equally preposterous. In 2005, as the result of a new investigation launched by the Sci-Fi Television Network, NASA asserted that the object was a Russian satellite. According to a NASA spokesperson, docu-ments of this investigation were somehow misplaced in the

1990s. Mysteriously, this finding directly contradicts the official air force version that nothing at all was found at the Kecksburg site. It also runs counter to a 2003 report made by NASA's own Nicholas L. Johnson, Chief Scientist for Orbital Debris. That document shows no missing satellites at the time of the incident. This includes a missing Russian Venus Probe (since accounted for)—the very item that was once considered a prime crash candidate.

Brave New World

These days, visitors to Kecksburg will be hard-pressed to find any trace of the encounter—perhaps that's how it should be. Since speculation comes to an abrupt halt whenever a concrete answer is provided, Kecksburg's reputation as "Roswell of the East" looks secure, at least for the foreseeable future. But if one longs for proof that something mysterious occurred there, they need look no further than the backyard of the Kecksburg Volunteer Fire Department. There, in all of its acorn-shape glory, stands an full-scale mock-up of the spacecraft reportedly found in this peaceful town on December 9, 1965. There too rests the mystery, intrigue, and romance that have accompanied this alleged space traveler for more than 40 years.

Monster of the Chesapeake

Chesapeake Bay, a 200-mile intrusion of the Atlantic Ocean into Virginia and Maryland, is 12 miles wide at its mouth, allowing plenty of room for strange saltwater creatures to slither on in. Encounters with giant, serpentine beasts up and down the Eastern seaboard were reported during the 1800s, but sightings of Chessie, a huge, snakelike creature with a football-shape head and flippers began to escalate in the 1960s.

✱ ✱ ✱ ✱

SINCE SUPPOSED SIGHTINGS of Chessie began in the 1960s, they have only continued. Former CIA employee Donald Kyker and some neighbors saw not one, but four unidentified water creatures swimming near shore in 1978. Then in 1980, the creature was spotted just off Love Point, sparking a media frenzy. Two years later, Maryland resident Robert Frew was entertaining dinner guests with his wife, Karen, when the whole party noticed a giant water creature about 200 yards from shore swimming toward a group of people frolicking nearby in the surf. They watched the creature, which they estimated to be about 30 feet in length, as it dove underneath the unsuspecting humans, emerged on the other side, and swam away. Frew recorded several minutes of the creature's antics, and the Smithsonian Museum of Natural History reviewed his film. Although they could not identify the animal, they did concede that it was "animate," or living.

The Chessie Challenge

Some believe Chessie is a manatee, but they usually swim in much warmer waters and are only about ten feet long. Also, the fact that Chessie is often seen with several "humps" breaking the water behind its head leads other investigators to conclude that it could be either a giant sea snake or a large seal.

One Maryland resident has compiled a list of 78 different sightings over the years. And a tour boat operator offers sea-monster tours in hopes of repeating the events of 1980 when 25 passengers on several charter boats all spotted Chessie cavorting in the waves.

Giant Frogman Spotted in Ohio!

For the most part, frogs are rather unintimidating—unless they're more than four feet tall and standing along a dark road in the middle of the night.

✳ ✳ ✳ ✳

The First Encounter

ON MARCH 3, 1972, police officer Ray Shockey was driving his patrol car along Riverside Road toward the small town of Loveland, Ohio. At approximately 1:00 AM, Shockey saw what he thought was a dog lying alongside the road, but as he got closer, the creature suddenly stood up on two feet. Amazed, Shockey stopped his car and watched the creature climb over a guardrail and scamper down the ditch toward the Little Miami River. Shockey drove back to the police station and described what he'd seen to fellow officer Mark Matthews. Shockey said the creature was approximately four feet tall and weighed between 50 to 75 pounds. It stood on two legs and had webbed feet, clawed hands, and the head of a frog.

After hearing his story, Matthews accompanied Shockey back to the site of the encounter. The pair could not locate the frogman, but they did find strange scratch marks along the section of guardrail the creature had climbed over.

Frogman Returns

On the night of March 17, Matthews was on the outskirts of town when he saw an animal lying in the middle of the road. Thinking that the animal had been hit by a car, Matthews stopped his squad car. But when the animal suddenly stood up on two legs, Matthews realized that it was the same creature that Shockey had encountered. Just as before, the creature walked to the side of the road and climbed over a guardrail. Matthews simply watched, although some reports say he shot at the animal. Either way, the creature moved down the embankment toward the river and vanished.

The Aftermath

When news spread of a second Frogman sighting, the town of Loveland was inundated with calls from reporters across the country. Obviously, reports of four-foot-tall froglike creatures are rarely considered newsworthy, but two witnesses had seen the creature on different nights, and both were police officers.

In the beginning, Shockey and Matthews stuck to their stories and even had sketches made of the creature they'd encountered. But over time, the public turned on the officers, accusing them of fabricating the whole thing. In recent years, the officers now claim that what they encountered was merely an iguana. Most seem happy with that explanation. But it doesn't explain how an iguana stood up on two legs and walked across the road. Or why their sketches looked nothing like an iguana.

So Where Is the Frog Today?

A local farmer also claimed he saw the Frogman lumbering through his field one evening, but there have been no other sightings since the 1970s. Those who believe in the Loveland Frogman claim that after Matthews allegedly shot at it, it became frightened and moved to a more isolated area. Others think that Matthews's shot killed the creature. Of course, there are some who believe that the Loveland Frogman is still out there and has merely become more elusive. Just something to consider should you ever find yourself driving alongside the Little Miami River near Loveland on a dark, moonless night.

Ghosts of the *Queen Mary*

Once considered a grand jewel of the ocean, the decks of the Queen Mary *played host to such rich and famous guests as Clark Gable, Charlie Chaplin, Laurel and Hardy, and Elizabeth Taylor. Today, the* Queen Mary *is permanently docked, but she still hosts some mysterious, ghostly passengers!*

✳   ✳   ✳   ✳

The *Queen Mary* Goes to War

THE QUEEN MARY took her maiden voyage in May 1936, but a change came in 1940 when the British government pressed the ocean liner into military service. She was given a coat of gray paint and was turned into a troop transport vessel. The majestic dining salons became mess halls and the cocktail bars, cabins, and staterooms were filled with bunks. Even the swimming pools were boarded over and crowded with cots for the men. The ship was so useful to the Allies that Hitler offered a reward to the U-Boat commander who could sink her.

Although the *Queen Mary* avoided enemy torpedoes during the war, she was unable to avoid tragedy. On October 2, 1942, escorted by the cruiser HMS *Curacoa* and several destroyers, the *Queen Mary* was sailing on the choppy North Atlantic near Ireland. She was carrying about 15,000 American soldiers.

Danger from German vessels was always present, but things were quiet until suddenly, before anyone could act, the *Queen Mary's* massive bow smashed into the *Curacoa*. There was no way to slow down, no time for warning, and no distress calls to the men onboard. They had only seconds to react before their ship was sliced in two. Within minutes, both sections of the ship plunged below the surface of the icy water, carrying the crew with them. Of the *Curacoa's* 439-man crew, 338 of them perished on that fateful day. The *Queen Mary* suffered only minor damage and there were no injuries to her crew.

After that, the *Queen Mary* served unscathed for the remainder of the war. Following the surrender of Germany, she was used to carry American troops and GI war brides to the United States and Canada, before returning to England for conversion back to a luxury liner.

Last Days of an Ocean Liner

After the war, the *Queen Mary* and her sister ship, the *Queen Elizabeth*, were the preferred method of transatlantic travel for the rich and famous. But by the 1960s, airplane travel was faster and cheaper, and so, in late 1967, the *Queen Mary* steamed away from England for the last time. Her decks and staterooms were filled with curiosity seekers and wealthy patrons who wanted to be part of the ship's final voyage.

She ended her 39-day journey in Long Beach, California, where she was permanently docked as a floating hotel, convention center, museum, and restaurant. She is now listed on the National Register of Historic Places and is open to visitors year-round.

The Haunted Queen Mary

The *Queen Mary* has seen much tragedy and death, so it's no surprise that the ship plays host to a number of ghosts. Because of the sheer number of passengers who have walked her decks, accidents were bound to happen. One such mishap occurred on July 10, 1966, when John Pedder, an engine room worker, was crushed to death when an automatic door closed on him. There have been other reported deaths onboard, as well. For instance, during the war, when the ship was used for troop transport, a brawl broke out in one of the galleys and a cook was allegedly shoved into a hot oven, where he burned to death.

There are also reports of a woman drowning in the ship's swimming pool and stories of passengers falling overboard. Another strange death onboard was that of Senior Second Officer William Stark, whose ghost has often been spotted on deck and in his former quarters. Stark died after drinking lime juice mixed with cleaning solution, which he mistook for gin. He realized his error, and while he joked about it, he called the ship's doctor. Unfortunately, though, Stark soon felt the effects of the poison. As the young officer's condition worsened, he lapsed into a coma and died on September 22, 1949. Witnesses have also encountered a spectral man in gray overalls who has been seen below deck. He has dark hair and a long beard and is believed to be a mechanic or maintenance worker from the 1930s.

Another friendly spirit, dubbed "Miss Turner," is believed to have been a switchboard operator on the ship. A ghostly woman known as "Mrs. Kilburn" wears a gray uniform with starched white cuffs. She was once in charge of the stewardesses and bellboys, and she's still watching over the comings and goings on the ship. And although it is unknown who the ship's "Lady in White" might be, she haunts the *Queen*'s Salon and is normally seen wearing a white, backless evening gown. Witnesses say she dances alone near the grand piano as if listening to music only she can hear, then vanishes.

Security guards, staff members, and visitors have also reported doors unlocking, opening, and closing on their own, often triggering security alarms. Other unexplained occurrences include phantom voices and footsteps, banging and hammerings sounds, cold spots, inexplicable winds that blow through closed-off areas, and lights that turn on and off.

During a tour of the ship, one guest felt someone tugging on her purse and sweater and stroking her hair. Cold chills crept down her spine when she realized there was no one near her at the time!

In 1967, some 25 years after the tragic accident with the *Curacoa*, a marine engineer working inside the ship heard the terrible sound of two ships colliding. He even heard screams and shredding steel. Did the terrible events of 1942 somehow leave an impression on the atmosphere of this grand old ship? Or worse, is the crew of the *Curacoa* still doomed to relive that fateful October afternoon for eternity?

Echoing the Present

The stories of mysterious encounters and strange events go on and on. From ghostly music provided by happier times to ghostly screams provoked by sadder ones, it seems almost certain that the events of the past have left an indelible impression on the decks, corridors, and cabins of the *Queen Mary*, creating a haunting that is rivaled by few others in the annals of the supernatural.

Famous UFO Sightings

Unidentified flying objects, foo fighters, ghost rockets—whatever you call them, strange and unclassified objects in the sky remain one of the world's truly mysterious phenomena. Here are some of the most famous UFO sightings.

✳ ✳ ✳ ✳

The Battle of Los Angeles

O N FEBRUARY 25, 1942, just weeks after Japan's attack on Pearl Harbor and America's entry into World War II, late-night air-raid sirens sounded a blackout order throughout Los Angeles County in California. A silvery object (or objects) was spotted in the sky, prompting an all-out assault from ground troops. For a solid hour, antiaircraft fire bombarded the unidentified craft with some 1,400 shells, as numerous high-powered searchlights followed its slow movement across the sky. Several witnesses reported direct hits on the invader, though it was never downed. After the "all clear" was sounded, the object vanished, and it has never been identified.

The Marfa Lights

The town of Marfa, located far out in western Texas, is home to what many believe is the best concentration of "ghost lights" in the nation. Almost nightly, witnesses along Highway 67 can peer across the flatland north of the Chinati Mountains and spot glowing orbs of varying color and size, bobbing and floating among the brush. It's an event that's reportedly been witnessed since the 1880s. Though several scientists have conducted studies, no one has been able to determine their origin. Nevertheless, local officials have capitalized on the phenomenon and constructed an official roadside viewing area.

The Washington Flap

In two separate incidents just days apart in 1952, numerous objects were detected high above Washington, D.C., moving erratically at speeds as fast as 7,000 miles per hour. At one point, separate military radar stations detected the same objects simultaneously. Several eyewitnesses viewed the objects from the ground and from air control towers, and three pilots spotted them at close range, saying they looked like the lit end of a cigarette or like falling stars without tails. The official Air Force explanation was "temperature inversion," and the sightings were labeled "unexplained."

The Hill Abduction, aka the Zeta Reticuli Incident

By the 1960s, a number of people had reportedly seen UFOs but hadn't actually encountered aliens personally. But on September 19, 1961, Barney and Betty Hill found themselves being chased by a spacecraft along Route 3 in New Hampshire. The object eventually descended upon their vehicle, whereupon Barney witnessed several humanoid creatures through the craft's windows. The couple tried to escape, but their car began shaking violently, and they were forced off the road. Suffering lapses in memory from that moment on, the Hills later recalled being taken aboard the ship, examined, and questioned by figures with very large eyes. The incident was known only to locals and the UFO community until the 1966 publication of *The Interrupted Journey* by John Fuller.

The Apollo 11 Transmission

When American astronauts made that great leap onto the surface of the moon on July 20, 1969, they apparently weren't alone. Although the incident has been repeatedly denied, believers point to a transmission from the lunar surface that had been censored by NASA but was reportedly picked up by private ham-radio operators: "These babies are huge, sir! Enormous!... You wouldn't believe it. I'm telling you there are other spacecraft out there, lined up on the far side of the crater edge. They're on the moon watching us!"

Fire in the Sky

After completing a job along Arizona's Mogollon Rim on November 5, 1979, Travis Walton and six fellow loggers spotted a large spacecraft hovering near the dark forest road leading home. Walton approached the craft on foot and was knocked to the ground by a beam of light. Then he and the craft disappeared. Five days later, Walton mysteriously reappeared just outside of town. He said that during his time aboard the spacecraft, he had struggled to escape from the short, large-headed creatures that performed experiments on his body. Neither Walton nor any of his coworkers has strayed from the facts of their stories in the decades that followed.

The Rendlesham Forest Incident

In late December 1980, several soldiers at the Royal Air Force base in Woodbridge, Suffolk, England, saw a number of strange lights among the trees just outside their east gate. Upon investigation, they spotted a conical or disk-shape object hovering above a clearing. The object seemed aware of their presence and moved away from them, but the men eventually gave chase. No hard evidence has been provided by the military, but the event is often considered the most significant UFO event in Britain. The Forestry Commission has since created a "UFO Trail" for hikers near the RAF base.

JAL 1628

On November 17, 1986, as Japan Airlines flight 1628 passed over Alaska, military radar detected an object on its tail. When the blip caught up with the cargo jet, the pilot reported seeing three large craft shaped like shelled walnuts, one of which was twice the size of an aircraft carrier. The objects matched the airplane's speed and tracked it for nearly an hour. At one point, the two smaller craft came so close that the pilot said he could feel their heat. The incident prompted an official FAA investigation and made worldwide headlines.

The Phoenix Lights

In March 1997, hundreds, if not thousands, of witnesses throughout Phoenix, Arizona, and the surrounding area caught sight of what was to become the most controversial UFO sighting in decades. For at least two hours, Arizona residents watched an array of lights move across the sky, and many reportedly saw a dark, triangular object between them. The lights, which varied in color, were even caught on videotape. Nearby military personnel tried to reproduce the event by dropping flares from the sky, but most witnesses weren't satisfied with what was deemed a diversion from the truth.

Roswell

Undoubtedly the most famous UFO-related location, Roswell immediately brings to mind flying-saucer debris, men in black, secret military programs, alien autopsies, weather balloons, and government cover-ups. The incident that started it all occurred during the first week of July 1947, just before Roswell Army Air Field spokespersons claimed they had recovered parts of a wrecked "flying disc" from a nearby ranch. The report was quickly corrected to involve a weather balloon instead, which many insist was part of a cover-up. In later years, people claiming to have been involved in the recovery effort began to reveal insider information, insisting that not only was the wreckage of extraterrestrial origin, but that autopsies had been performed on alien bodies recovered from the site. Ever since, the name of this small New Mexico town has been synonymous with ufology, making Roswell a popular stop for anyone interested in all things alien.

Bigfoot: The King of All Monsters

Let's face it—if you had to pick one monster that stands head (and feet) above all others, it would be Bigfoot. Not only is it the stuff of legends, but its likeness has also been used to promote everything from pizza to beef jerky. Bigfoot has had amusement park rides and monster trucks named after it and was even one of the mascots for the 2010 Winter Olympics in Vancouver, British Columbia.

✳ ✳ ✳ ✳

Early Sightings

FOLKTALES FROM NATIVE American tribes throughout the Northwest, the area that Bigfoot traditionally calls home, are filled with references to giant, apelike creatures roaming the woods. They described the beast as between seven and ten feet tall and covered in brown or dark hair. (Sasquatch, a common term used for the big-footed beast, is actually an anglicization of a Native American term for a giant supernatural creature.)

Walking on two legs, Sasquatch had an almost human-like appearance, although its facial features more closely resembled that of an ape, and it had almost no neck. With looks like that, it's not surprising that Native American folklore often described the creature as cannibalistic, supernatural, and dangerous. Other tales, however, said Sasquatch appeared to be frightened of humans and mostly kept to itself.

It wasn't until the 1900s, when more and more woodlands were being devoured in the name of progress, that Sasquatch sightings started to increase. It was believed that, though generally docile, the beast did have a mean streak when feeling threatened. In July 1924, Fred Beck and several others were mining in a mountainous area of Washington State. One evening, the group spotted and shot at what appeared to be an apelike creature. After fleeing to their cabin, the group was startled when several more hairy giants began banging on the walls, windows, and doors. For several hours, the creatures pummeled the cabin and threw large rocks at it before disappearing shortly before dawn. After several such encounters in the same general vicinity, the area was renamed Ape Canyon.

My, What Big Feet You Have!

In August 1958, Jerry Crew, a bulldozer operator, showed up for work at a wooded site in Bluff Creek, California. Walking up to his bulldozer, which had been left there overnight, Crew found giant footprints in the dirt. At first, they appeared to be the naked footprints of a man, but with one major difference—these feet were huge! After the tracks appeared on several occasions, Crew took a cast of one of them and brought it to *The Humboldt Times* in Eureka, California. The following day, the newspaper ran a front-page story, complete with photos of the footprint and a name for the creature: Bigfoot. The story and photographs hit the Associated Press, and the name stuck.

Even so, the event is still rife with controversy. Skeptics claim that it was Ray Wallace, not Bigfoot, who made the tracks as a practical joke on his brother Wilbur, who was Crew's supervisor. Apparently the joke backfired when Crew arrived at the site first and saw the prints before Wilbur. However, Ray Wallace never admitted to faking the tracks or having anything to do with perpetrating a hoax.

Video Evidence?

In 1967, in response to numerous Bigfoot sightings in northern California, Roger Patterson rented a 16mm video camera in hopes of filming the elusive creature. Patterson and his friend, Robert Gimlin, spent several days on horseback traveling though the Six Rivers National Forest without coming across as much as a footprint.

Then, on October 20, the pair rounded a bend and noticed something dark and hairy crouched near the water. When the creature stood up on two legs and presented itself in all its hairy, seven-foot glory, that's when Patterson said he knew for sure he was looking at Bigfoot. Unfortunately, Patterson's horse saw the creature, too, and suddenly reared up. Because of this, it took Patterson several precious seconds to get off the horse and remove the video camera from his saddlebag. Once he did that, he ran toward the creature, filming as he went.

As the creature walked away, Patterson continued filming until his tape ran out. He quickly changed his film, and then both men retrieved their frightened horses and attempted to follow Bigfoot further before eventually losing sight of it.

When they arrived back in town, Patterson reviewed the film. Even though it was less than a minute long and extremely shaky in spots, the film appeared to show Bigfoot running away while occasionally looking toward the camera. For most Bigfoot enthusiasts, the Patterson–Gimlin film stands as the Holy Grail of Bigfoot sightings—physical proof captured on video. Skeptics, however, alleged that Patterson and Gimlin faked the entire incident and filmed a man in an expensive monkey suit. Nevertheless, more than 50 years after the event occurred, the Patterson–Gimlin film is still one of the most talked about pieces of Bigfoot evidence, mainly because neither man ever admitted to a hoax and the fact that no one has been able to figure out how they faked it.

Gone Sasquatching

The fact that some people doubt the existence of Bigfoot hasn't stopped thousands of people from heading into the woods to try to find one. Even today, the hairy creature makes brief appearances here and there. Of course, sites like YouTube have given rise to dozens of "authentic" videos of Bigfoot, some of which are quite comical.

Still, every once in a while, a video that deserves a second look pops up. For example, in 2005, ferry operator Bobby Clarke filmed almost three minutes of video of a Bigfoot-like creature on the banks of the Nelson River in Manitoba. And in late 2007, photos taken by a hunter in Pennsylvania's Allegheny National Forest were being analyzed.

Spotting Sasquatch

Throughout the world, it's called Alma, Yeti, Sasquatch, the Abominable Snowman, Wildman, and Bigfoot. Whatever the name, people agree that it's tall, hairy, doesn't smell good, and has a habit of showing up in locations around the globe— especially in North America.

✳ ✳ ✳ ✳

Jasper, Alberta, Canada (1811)

THIS WAS THE first known Bigfoot evidence found in North America. An explorer named David Thompson found 14-inch footprints in the snow, each toe topped by a short claw. He and his party didn't follow the tracks, fearing their guns would be useless against such a large animal. In his journal he wrote that he couldn't bring himself to believe such a creature existed.

British Columbia, Canada (1924)

In 1957, prospector Albert Ostman was finally able to come forward about a chilling event that happened to him more than 30 years prior. While camping at the head of Toba Inlet near Vancouver Island, Ostman was snatched up, still in his sleeping bag, and taken to a small valley where several Bigfoot were living. Held captive for several days, Ostman was only able to escape when one of the larger creatures tried to eat his snuff and chaos ensued.

Wanoga Butte, Oregon (1957)

After a long, uneventful morning hunting, Gary Joanis and Jim Newall were ecstatic when Joanis felled a deer with a single shot. But when a hairy creature "not less than nine feet tall" emerged from the woods, threw the deer over its shoulder, and lumbered off, the two men were left speechless.

Monroe, Michigan (1965)

On August 13, Christine Van Acker and her mother were driving when a large, hairy creature came out of the nearby woods. Frightened by the creature, the mother lost control of the car and grazed the beast. The car stalled and while the mother struggled to start it, the creature put its arm through the window, struck Christine in the face and slammed her mother's head against the car door, leaving both women with black eyes, photos of which were widely circulated in the press.

Spearfish, South Dakota (1977)

Betty Johnson and her three daughters saw two Bigfoot in a cornfield. The larger of the two was eight-feet tall; the other, slightly smaller. They both appeared to be eating corn and making a whistling sound.

Paris Township, Ohio (1978)

Herbert and Evelyn Cayton reported that a seven-foot-tall, 300-pound, fur-covered creature appeared at their house so frequently that their daughter thought it was a pet.

Jackson, Wyoming (1980)

On June 17, Glenn Towner and Robert Goodrich went into the woods on Snow King Mountain to check out a lean-to built by a friend of theirs. After hearing moaning and growling, the pair was chased out of the woods by a 12-foot-tall creature covered in hair. The creature followed them back to civilization, where it was last spotted standing briefly beneath a streetlight before vanishing back into the woods.

Crescent City, California (1995)

A TV crew was driving in their RV, filming the scenery in Jedediah Smith Redwoods State Park, when an eight-foot-tall hairy giant crossed their path and was caught on tape.

Cotton Island, Louisiana (2000)

Bigfoot surprised lumberjacks Earl Whitstine and Carl Dubois while they were clearing timber. The hairy figure returned a few days later, leaving behind footprints and hair samples.

Selma, Oregon (2000)

While hiking with his family near the Oregon Caves National Monument on July 1, psychologist Matthew Johnson smelled a strange musky odor. Hearing odd grunting noises coming from behind some trees, Johnson went to investigate and saw something very tall and hairy walking away. When asked to describe it, Johnson said that it could be "nothing else but a Sasquatch."

Granton, Wisconsin (2000)

As James Hughes was delivering newspapers early one morning, he saw a shaggy figure, about eight feet tall, carrying a goat. However, sheriffs called to the scene couldn't find any footprints or missing goats.

Mt. St. Helens, Washington (2002)

Jerry Kelso made his wife and two-year-old child wait in the car, while he chased what he thought was a man in a gorilla suit. When he was about 100 feet away, he realized that it wasn't a gorilla suit.

Cranbrook, British Columbia, Canada (2007)

Snowplow driver Gord Johnson drove by a large, hairy figure with a "conical head" walking along a snowy road.

Ghost Lights

The legends are similar, no matter the locale. It's whispered that mysterious lights that blink and wink in the night are the spirits of long-dead railroad workers, jealous and jilted lovers, or lost children. They go by many names: marsh lights, ghost lights, will-o'-the-wisp, feu follet, earth lights, and even, to the skeptical, swamp gas. They occur in remote areas, often near old railway tracks or power transmitters. Some are thought to issue from the geomagnetic fields of certain kinds of rock. But tales of lights that change color, follow people, foil electrical systems, or perform acrobatic stunts are harder to explain.

✳ ✳ ✳ ✳

The Peculiar Paulding Light

ACCORDING TO LEGEND, an old railway brakeman was killed near the Choate Branch Railroad tracks that used to run near Paulding, Michigan, along the northern Wisconsin–Michigan border. People have observed strange lights near the tracks for decades, and it is said that they're from the railman's ghostly lantern swinging as he walks his old beat. Others, armed with telescopes and binoculars, believe that the famed Paulding Light is actually caused by headlights shining from a highway a few miles away.

Still, many claim that the lights behave like anything but distant reflections. The lights are said to change from red to green, zoom up close as if peering into people's cars, chase people, flash through automobiles either cutting off all electric power or turning radios off and on, and zigzag through the nearby woods. Crowds flock to the Robins Wood Road site off Highway 45 to see the phenomenon for themselves, and a wooden sign has been erected.

The Fiery *Feu Follet*

During the mid-18th century, when Detroit was being settled by the French, aristocrats and working folks feared the *feu follet*—spirit lights of the marshy river area. One local legend tells of a rich landowner who nearly drowned one stormy night when the brilliant lights lured him into a swamp. Luckily, two guests staying at his house heard his terrified cries and managed to rescue him. At the time, the prevailing theory of the marsh lights was that windows had to be closed when the *feu follet* were near or they would enter the house, snake their way into the windpipes of those present, and choke them to death.

Baffling Brown Mountain Lights

Although scoffed at as nothing more than reflected train lights, the multicolored light show in the foothills of North Carolina's Blue Ridge Mountains has fascinated humans since an early explorer reported it in 1771, and even earlier according to Native American legend. Several centuries ago, many people were killed during a battle between the Cherokee and the Catawba tribes. Legend has it that the Brown Mountain Lights are the spirits of those lost warriors.

Another tale states that a plantation owner got lost hunting on Brown Mountain and that one of his slaves came looking for him, swinging a lantern to light his way. The slave never found his owner but still walks the mountainside with his eternal lantern. Still another legend claims the lights come from the spirit of a woman murdered on the mountain by her husband in 1850.

Whatever the source of the colorful lights, they come in many shapes, from glowing orbs to trailing bursts to still, white areas. Crowds flock to at least three locations to view the lights, but one of the most popular is the Brown Mountain overlook on Highway 181, 20 miles north of Morganton.

Glowing in Great Britain

For a week before Cornwall, England, suffered an earthquake in November 1996, people of the region began seeing unexplained lights in the sky that ranged from circular to rectangular in shape. Some saw the lights as precursors to the quake, but that didn't explain why several witnesses observed large golden spheres dropping from the clouds two years earlier or why others saw purple pixie lights hovering around the area's old tin mines.

The Lincolnshire region was notorious in the mid-1960s as the site of unexplained balls of colored light. On August 10, 1965, a woman named Rachel Atwill woke up just before 4:00 AM to see a reddish light over some nearby hills. The light persisted for almost a half hour, and Atwill reported that the experience gave her a headache.

The same light was seen about an hour later by a truck driver, but he had a more harrowing experience as the light hovered only 50 yards from his truck. The situation grew worse when the light zoomed right up to his windshield and sat there, lighting up the inside of the truck and waking his sleeping wife and daughter. Luckily, it soon lifted back into the atmosphere and disappeared. Others in the area also reported seeing lights of the same description, and one was even able to capture a photo that was published in a London newspaper.

Red Eyes Over Point Pleasant: The Mysterious Mothman

In 1942, the U.S. government took control of several thousand acres of land just north of Point Pleasant, West Virginia. The purpose was to build a secret facility capable of creating and storing TNT that could be used during World War II. For the next three years, the facility cranked out massive amounts of TNT, shipping it out or storing it in one of the numerous concrete "igloo" structures that dotted the area. In 1945, the facility was shut down and eventually abandoned, but it was here that an enigmatic flying creature with glowing red eyes made its home years later.

* * * *

"Red Eyes on the Right"

O N THE EVENING of November 15, 1966, Linda and Roger Scarberry were out driving with another couple, Mary and Steve Mallette. As they drove, they decided to take a detour that took them past the abandoned TNT factory.

As they neared the gate of the old factory, they noticed two red lights up ahead. When Roger stopped the car, the couples were horrified to find that the red lights appeared to be two glowing red eyes. What's more, those eyes belonged to a creature standing more than seven feet tall with giant wings folded behind it. That was all Roger needed to see before he hit the gas pedal and sped off. In response, the creature calmly unfolded its wings and flew toward the car. Incredibly, even though Roger raced along at speeds close to 100 miles per hour, the red-eyed creature was able to keep up with them without much effort.

Upon reaching Point Pleasant, the two couples ran from their car to the Mason County Courthouse and alerted Deputy Millard Halstead of their terrifying encounter. Halstead couldn't be sure exactly what the two couples had seen, but whatever it was, it had clearly frightened them. In an attempt to calm them down, Halstead agreed to accompany them to the TNT factory. As his patrol car neared the entrance, the police radio suddenly emitted a strange, whining noise. Other than that, despite a thorough search of the area, nothing out of the ordinary was found.

More Encounters

Needless to say, once word got around Point Pleasant that a giant winged creature with glowing red eyes was roaming around the area, everyone had to see it for themselves. The creature didn't disappoint. Dubbed Mothman by the local press, the creature was spotted flying overhead, hiding, and even lurking on front porches. In fact, in the last few weeks of November, dozens of witnesses encountered the winged beast. But Mothman wasn't the only game in town. It seems that around the same time that he showed up, local residents started noticing strange lights in the evening sky, some of which hovered silently over the abandoned TNT factory. Of course, this led some to believe that Mothman and the UFOs were somehow connected. One such person was Mary Hyre of *The Athens Messenger*, who had been reporting on the strange activities in Point Pleasant since they started. Perhaps that's why she became the first target.

Beware the Men in Black

One day, while Mary Hyre was at work, several strange men visited her office and began asking questions about the lights in the sky. Normally, she didn't mind talking to people about the UFO sightings and Mothman. But there was something peculiar about these guys. For instance, they all dressed exactly the same: black suits, black ties, black hats, and dark sunglasses. They also spoke in a strange monotone and seemed confused by ordinary objects such as ballpoint pens. As the men left, Hyre wondered whether they had been from another planet. Either way, she had an up-close-and-personal encounter with the legendary Men in Black.

Mary Hyre was not the only person to have a run-in with the Men in Black. As the summer of 1967 rolled around, dozens of people were interrogated by them. In most cases, the men showed up unannounced at the homes of people who had recently witnessed a Mothman or UFO sighting. For the most part, the men simply wanted to know what the witnesses had seen. But sometimes, the men went to great lengths to convince the witnesses that they were mistaken and had not seen anything out of the ordinary. Other times, the men threatened witnesses. Each time the Men in Black left a witness's house, they drove away in a black, unmarked sedan. Despite numerous attempts to determine who these men were and where they came from, their identity remained a secret. And all the while, the Mothman sightings continued throughout Point Pleasant and the surrounding area.

The Silver Bridge Tragedy

Erected in 1928, the Silver Bridge was a gorgeous chain suspension bridge that spanned the Ohio River, connecting Point Pleasant with Ohio. On December 15, 1967, the bridge was busy with holiday shoppers bustling back and forth between West Virginia and Ohio. As the day wore on, more and more cars started filling the bridge until shortly before 5:00 PM, when traffic on the bridge came to a standstill. For several minutes, none of the cars budged. Suddenly, there was a loud popping noise and then the unthinkable happened: The Silver Bridge collapsed, sending dozens of cars and their passengers into the freezing water below.

Over the next few days, local authorities and residents searched the river hoping to find survivors, but in the end, 46 people lost their lives in the bridge collapse. A thorough investigation determined that a manufacturing flaw in one of the bridge's supporting bars caused the collapse. But there are others who claim that in the days and weeks leading up to the collapse, they saw Mothman and even the Men in Black around, on, and even under the bridge. Further witnesses state that while most of Point Pleasant was watching the Silver Bridge collapse, bright lights and strange objects were flying out of the area and disappearing into the winter sky. Perhaps that had nothing to do with the collapse of the Silver Bridge, but the Mothman has not been seen since…or has he?

Mothman Lives!

There are reports that the Mothman is still alive and well and has moved on to other areas of the United States. There are even those who claim that he was spotted flying near the Twin Towers on September 11, 2001, leading to speculation that Mothman is a portent of doom and only appears when disasters are imminent. Some believe Mothman was a visitor from another planet who returned home shortly after the Silver Bridge fell. Still others think the creature was the result of the toxic chemicals eventually discovered in the area near the TNT factory. And then there are skeptics who say that the initial sighting was nothing more than a giant sand crane and that mass hysteria took care of the rest. Whichever theory you choose to believe, the Mothman Lives website compiles all sightings of the creature from the 1960s to the present.

Haunting the Sea: Oregon's Ghost Forests

The gnarled, twisted shapes rising up from Oregon's coastline are macabre memorials to the magnificent forests that stood here ages ago. Like a ghost town eerily preserved in time, these "ghost forests" are shrouded in mystery: What caused the mighty trees to fall? Why are they still here? And where are they going?

✳   ✳   ✳   ✳

An Eerie Appearance

THESE GROVES OF ancient tree stumps—called "ghost forests" because of their age (approximately 1,000 to 4,000 years old) and bleak appearance—emerge along the

46-mile stretch between Lincoln City and Tillamook. For years, tourists and scientists alike have been perplexed by the forests' strange beauty. Some trees extend out of the sand like angular sculptures; others are just visible as tiny tips poking through the water. All are remnants of the giant Sitka spruce forests, which towered 200 feet above Oregon's coastline for years. That is, until something knocked them down.

A Cataclysmic Collapse

No one knows for sure just what that "something" was, but experts agree that for such forests to be preserved, the trees must have been very suddenly submerged in sand, clay, or mud. This submersion would not only kill the trees but also keep them frozen in time by shutting off their oxygen.

The original (and still widely held) belief is that a giant earthquake, which suddenly dropped the ground 25 feet below sea level and immersed the trees in sand and water, toppled the forests. Another theory is that it wasn't an earthquake but a tsunami that struck, drowning the trees under a massive tidal wave. A third theory suggests that it was a combination of the two—an earthquake buried the trees and then caused a tsunami that lopped off the tree tops, leaving only stumps behind.

A newer theory is that the trees died as a result of sudden landscape changes, with sand levels rising over the course of a few decades (that's "sudden" when you're speaking in geologic terms) to eventually overwhelm the forest.

Seasonal Specters

For decades, ghost forests were seen only occasionally during the harsh winter months, when violent waves strip away layers of sand, exposing the tree stumps just briefly before the calmer waves of spring and summer carry sand back to the shores and bury them once again.

But lately, the ghost forests have become less of a rarity. Since 1998, more and more spooky spruces have been popping up—the result of a decade of rough winters, washing away as much as 17 feet of sand in some areas, combined with less sand recovery in the spring and summer. In 2007, Arch Cape saw stumps for the first time in 40 years, along with the mud-cliff remains of a forest floor, and in the winter of 2008, an unprecedented ten-foot drop in sand level revealed a new forest at Cape Kiwanda. Just a few miles away at Hug Point, the waves uncovered stumps that could date back 80,000 years to the Pleistocene era, when woolly mammoths and saber-toothed tigers roamed the earth. And the remains of roots marred by saws at Moolack Beach show that early European settlers harvested the trees for fire and shelter. Oregon's most impressive and most famous ghost forest is found at Neskowin, where 100 twisted shapes can be seen poking through the water year-round.

Grim Tide-ings

But the erosion that has newly exposed these phantom forests may also be destroying them. The stumps at Neskowin and Cape Lookout are reportedly showing so much that waves are ripping them out by the roots. Some experts believe this increased erosion means the coastline is gradually disappearing—and taking the ghost forests with it. Perhaps soon, the ghost forests of Oregon will haunt only our memories.

Giving Up the Ghost

When tropical storm Winston struck the Ra area of Fiji, many small coastal villages were devastated by the rising water and strong winds. The village of Nayavutoka saw the death of two of its village residents in the wake of the storm, both of whom the village respectfully buried as they returned to their storm-torn homes.

✳ ✳ ✳ ✳

ONE OF THE unfortunate people to lose their lives that day was thirty-two-year-old Pauliasi Naiova, who suffered from a disability that hindered him from walking at a fast pace. He was known throughout the town for his love of food—never turning down an occasion to eat—and his limp left leg, which dragged along as he walked. He was much slower than the rest of the village, which—unfortunately—thwarted him from making it to safety before the tidal surges hit the coast. The returning village found his body on the beach and buried him later that day.

Disasters like this were to be expected when living on the shore of an island in the ocean, and everyday life went back to normal as people repaired their homes and belongings. But—ostensibly—not everything was back to normal. Nayavutoka native Osea Balesavu, who knew and cared for Naiova, began to notice something strange around the village. That night after the storm, the village dogs barked without stopping. Usually, the dogs reserved their barking fits for predators stalking the village, but that night was different. The night after, the barking continued but everyone—being as relaxed as they are living the island life—took no mind of the noise.

Balesavu went to bed that night like any other night, but something woke him from his midnight slumber. The dogs still barking, Balesavu opened his tired eyes to an apparition of his old friend, Naiova. The sight was surreal in its clarity. Balesavu felt a heavy weight on his chest and saw the image of his late friend standing in front of him, whispering for food. Balesavu was not afraid but knew that the apparition of Naiova could not stay. He told the apparition that he must go, that he does not belong here in this world anymore, that he must leave the village alone and go where he must now go. Despite his wishes, the visitations continued.

Throughout the rest of that week, Balesavu continued to see his deceased friend roaming the village and asking for food. Balesavu reacted the same way every time, telling Naiova that he could not stay there. Although the encounters ceased, Balesavu still felt his friend lingering in the evenings as months worth of dinnertimes came and went.

Balesavu felt great pain for how his friend died, wishing that he could have done more to help him when the storm hit, but it all happened so quickly. Balesavu continues to hope that his friend can find where he must go and be in peace when he reaches his destination. Who knows what happens when you die, but you must seek peace in your place and be able to move away from the material sustenance of our transient world and into the unknown. Let us hope that we are not doomed to wander this planet alone and unperceived when we finally give up the ghost.

House on the Hill, Man in the Window

Michelle Widwinter recently bought a quaint home for herself and her daughter in England. After it had passed all of its inspections, the officials decided the home was acceptable to be moved into, but Widwinter soon realized they forgot one last test: a séance to determine whether a man who lived in the house during the 1870s was still living there.

✳   ✳   ✳   ✳

MICHELLE WIDWINTER DIDN'T look into the history of the house before she bought it, but she quickly realized something was afoot one day as she took a photo of the house's front-yard. Just like all of your worst nightmares, Widwinter looked at the photo and saw the face of a man staring back at her from inside the house. Startled, she ran back inside to make sure no one was there—which there wasn't—and then tried to determine what this apparition was.

Like anyone seeking a public opinion, she posted the photo onto Facebook to see if her friends had any logical explanations for the photo. Some claimed it was a reflection of the flowers in front of the window, others claimed she doctored the photo. Widwinter was a logical person, but logic couldn't explain how a man's face appeared in her window. She soon found herself slipping away from the rational self she had known herself to be when other occurrences began to happen around the house.

The face in the window made her question her own beliefs, and then waking up to a wall clock smashing onto the floor made her a believer. She denied any claim that she was making all of it up, but continued to have trouble proving what she was experiencing. Unable to come up with an explanation, Widwinter tried to block out the thoughts of her house being haunted, which was incredibly hard to do because of the persistent and strange noises heard behind the walls and flickering lights seen throughout the house.

It turns out that a local historian, Andrew Jones, had a little insight into the house's history and the man that might have been inhabiting it. Jones studied the life of a man by the name of Samuel Kent, who had lived in that house in the 19th century. Turns out that Kent was the original suspect of the Rode Hill House murder of 1860 before his daughter was convicted and imprisoned for the crime. Because of the dark history behind the house, Jones suspects that the spirit of Kent still lurks in the house, trying to come to terms with the murder of his three-year-old son.

The Grey Lady Keeps Her Eye on Hampton Court for the Royal Family

Cameras seem to be the best way to see something that—ostensibly—isn't there. You can take a photo of your friends in front of a bunch of ruins, but when you look at the photo you find that there is one more person in the photo that wasn't really there.

✳   ✳   ✳   ✳

FOR DECADES THE famous Grey Lady of Hampton Court in England has photo-bombed numerous photos, appearing in her greyish-blue gown. The recent photo captured by twelve-year-old Holly Hampsheir is truly terrifying.

Hampsheir took an ordinary photo—or so she thought—of her cousin as they were touring the Hampton Court, a palatial, English estate from the 16th century. She took a few more photos in the same room and continued on the tour. Little did Hampsheir know, she had caught a frighteningly vivid image of the Grey Lady standing right behind her cousin.

As she reviewed her photos the next day, she noticed the anomaly in this disturbing photo. She compared it to the other photos she shot in the room but couldn't make sense of what she was seeing. The Grey Lady appeared in one photo and was gone in the next. And this is not your standard out-of-focus photo of a ghost. The Grey Lady looks as real as Hampsheir's cousin but is dressed in an elegant greyish-blue dress with long brown hair. Hampsheir's aunt, Miss McGee, was with the girls when the photos were taken and was absolutely terrified when she saw them. Since the encounter, McGee and her daughter haven't slept properly at night, worrying about what the omen might have meant.

A Long History

Grey Lady sightings in Hampton Court have occurred since 1829, apparently after the palace's church was torn down, disturbing the Grey Lady's tomb. The Grey Lady's name was Dame Sybil, who died in 1562 after contracting smallpox while she took care of the sick infant and soon to be monarch, Elizabeth I. Dame Sybil was a servant at Hampton Court under four Tudor monarchs and had also nursed Prince Edward as a child. After her tomb was moved, many strange noises began to occur throughout the palatial estate. A person had once heard the sound of someone working a spinning wheel through the walls, which led to the discovery of an unknown chamber that contained a single spinning wheel in the center of the room.

Hampton Court is filled with history. It has been home to the British monarchy for more than five hundred years and welcomed history's most powerful people. From all of the servants—like Dame Sybil—who had their entire lives wrapped up in the routine of the palace, to Henry VIII who accused Catherine Howard of adultery and dragged her down the halls of the palace: the Hampton Court has many secrets within its walls. The Grey Lady will continue to walk the hall of Hampton Court to make sure everything remains in order.

Alleged Celebrity UFO Sightings

It's not just moonshine-swilling farmers in rural areas who claim to have seen UFOs hovering in the night sky. Plenty of celebrities have also reportedly witnessed unidentified flying objects and have been happy to talk about their experiences afterward.

✳ ✳ ✳ ✳

Jimmy Carter

NOT EVEN PRESIDENTS are immune from UFO sightings. During Jimmy Carter's presidential campaign of 1976, he told reporters that in 1969, before he was governor of Georgia, he saw what could have been a UFO. "It was the darndest thing I've ever seen," he said of the incident. He claimed that the object that he and a group of others had watched for ten minutes was as bright as the moon. Carter was often referred to as "the UFO president" after being elected because he filed a report on the matter.

David Duchovny

In 1982, long before he starred as a believer in the supernatural on the hit sci-fi series *The X-Files*, David Duchovny thought he saw a UFO. Although, by his own admission, he's reluctant to say with any certainty that it wasn't something he simply imagined as a result of stress and overwork. "There was something in the air and it was gone," he later told reporters. "I thought: 'You've got to get some rest, David.'"

Jackie Gleason

Jackie Gleason was a comedian and actor best known for his work on the sitcom *The Honeymooners* and his role as Minnesota Fats in *The Hustler* (1961). He was also supposedly a paranormal enthusiast who claimed to have witnessed several unidentified objects flying in the sky. Gleason's second wife, Beverly McKittrick, claimed that in 1974 President Nixon took Gleason to the Homestead Air Force Base in Florida, where he saw the wreckage of a crashed extraterrestrial spaceship and the bodies of dead aliens. The incident had such a profound affect on him that it curtailed his famous appetite for alcohol, at least for a while. Gleason was so inspired by the visit that he later built a house in upstate New York that was designed to look like a spaceship and was called "The Mother Ship."

John Lennon

In 1974, former Beatle John Lennon claimed that he witnessed a flying saucer from the balcony of his apartment in New York City. Lennon was with his girlfriend May Pang, who later described the craft as circular with white lights around its rim and said that it hovered in the sky above their window. Lennon talked about the event frequently and even referenced it in two of his songs, "Out of the Blue" and "Nobody Told Me," which contains the lyric, "There's UFOs over New York and I ain't too surprised . . ."

Ronald Reagan

Former actor and U.S. president Ronald Reagan witnessed UFOs on two occasions. Once during his term as California governor (1967–1975), Reagan and his wife Nancy arrived late to a party hosted by actor William Holden. Guests including Steve Allen and Lucille Ball reported that the couple excitedly described how they had just witnessed a UFO while driving along the Pacific Coast Highway. They had stopped to watch the event, which made them late to the party.

Reagan also confessed to a *Wall Street Journal* reporter that in 1974, when the gubernatorial jet was preparing to land in Bakersfield, California, he noticed a strange bright light in the sky. The pilot followed the light for a short time before it suddenly shot up vertically at a high rate of speed and disappeared from sight. Reagan stopped short of labeling the light a UFO, of course. As actress Lucille Ball said in reference to Reagan's first alleged UFO sighting, "After he was elected president, I kept thinking about that event and wondered if he still would have won if he told everyone that he saw a flying saucer."

William Shatner

For decades, the man who played Captain Kirk in the original *Star Trek* series claimed that an alien saved his life. When the actor and a group of friends were riding their motorbikes through the desert in the late 1960s, Shatner was inadvertently left behind when his bike wouldn't restart after driving into a giant pothole. Shatner said that he spotted an alien in a silver suit standing on a ridge and that it led him to a gas station and safety. Shatner later stated in his autobiography, *Up Till Now*, that he made up the part about the alien during a television interview.

Gordon Cooper

This former astronaut participated in a United Nations panel discussion on UFOs in New York in 1985. In the discussion, Cooper said, "I believe that these extraterrestrial vehicles and their crews are visiting this planet from other planets, which obviously are a little more technically advanced than we are here on Earth. I feel that we need to have a top-level, coordinated program to scientifically collect and analyze data from all over the Earth concerning any type of encounter, and to determine how best to interface with these visitors in a friendly fashion."

Muhammad Ali

This famous athlete has also claimed to have seen UFOs hovering over New York City. The occurrence was said to have taken place early in his career while he was working with his trainer, Angelo Dundee, in Central Park. Just before dawn, the two men observed a large, round UFO as it came out from behind the city skyline and moved slowly across the sky, a sighting that lasted about 15 minutes. Ali claimed at least 16 sightings. In one, he was a passenger in a car motoring along the New Jersey Turnpike when a cigar-shape craft hovered briefly over his vehicle.

Jimi Hendrix

Hendrix often claimed to have been followed around by UFOs and frequently referred to them in his lyrics. In addition, Hendrix allegedly was saved from freezing to death in 1965 by an eight-foot-tall angel-like alien who thawed the snowdrift in which the musician's van was stuck. He also once told a *New York Times* reporter that he was actually from Mars.

The Mysterious Orb

If Texas were a dartboard, the city of Brownwood would be at the center of the bull's-eye. Maybe that's how aliens saw it, too.

✳   ✳   ✳   ✳

BROWNWOOD IS A peaceful little city with about 20,000 residents and a popular train museum. A frontier town at one time, it became the trade center of Texas when the railroad arrived in 1885. Since then, the city has maintained a peaceful lifestyle. Even the massive tornado that struck Brownwood in 1976 left no fatalities. It's just a typical small town.

An Invader From the Sky

In July 2002, however, the city's peace was broken. Brownwood made international headlines when a strange metal orb fell from space, landed in the Colorado River, and washed up just south of town. The orb looked like a battered metal soccer ball—it was about a foot across, and it weighed just under ten pounds. Experts described it as a titanium sphere. When it was x-rayed, it revealed a second, inner sphere with tubes and wires wrapped inside.

That's all that anybody knows. No one is sure what the object is, and no one has claimed responsibility for it. The leading theory is that it's a cryogenic tank from some kind of spacecraft from Earth, used to store a small amount of liquid hydrogen or helium for cooling purposes. Others have speculated that it's a bomb, a spying device, or even a weapon used to combat UFOs.

It's Not Alone

The Brownwood sphere isn't unique. A similar object landed in Kingsbury, Texas, in 1997, and was quickly confiscated by the Air Force for "tests and analysis." So far, no further announcements have been made.

Of course, the Air Force probably has a lot to keep it busy. About 200 UFOs are reported each month, and Texas is among the top three states where UFOs are seen. But until anything is known for sure, those in Texas at night should keep an eye on the skies.

The Great Texas Airship Mystery

Roswell, New Mexico, may be the most famous potential UFO crash site, but did Texas experience a similar event in the 19th century?

* * * *

ONE SUNNY APRIL morning in 1897, a UFO crashed in Aurora, Texas. Six years before the Wright Brothers' first flight and 50 years before Roswell, a huge, cigar-shape UFO was seen in the skies. It was first noted on November 17, 1896, about a thousand feet above rooftops in Sacramento,

California. From there, the spaceship traveled to San Francisco, where it was seen by hundreds of people.

A National Tour

Next, the craft crossed the United States, where it was observed by thousands. Near Omaha, Nebraska, a farmer reported the ship on the ground, making repairs. When it returned to the skies, it headed toward Chicago, where it was photographed on April 11, 1897, the first UFO photo on record. On April 15, near Kalamazoo, Michigan, residents reported loud noises "like that of heavy ordnance" coming from the spaceship.

Two days later, the UFO attempted a landing in Aurora, Texas, which should have been a good place. The town was almost deserted, and its broad, empty fields could have been an ideal landing strip.

No Smooth Sailing

However, at about 6 AM on April 17, the huge, cigar-shape airship "sailed over the public square and, when it reached the north part of town, collided with the tower of Judge Proctor's windmill and went to pieces with a terrific explosion, scattering debris over several acres of ground, wrecking the windmill and water tank and destroying the judge's flower garden." That's how Aurora resident and cotton buyer S. E. Haydon described the events for *The Dallas Morning News*.

The remains of the ship seemed to be strips and shards of a silver-colored metal. Just one body was recovered. The newspaper reported, "while his remains are badly disfigured, enough of the original has been picked up to show that he was not an inhabitant of this world."

On April 18, reportedly, that body was given a good, Christian burial in the Aurora cemetery, where it may remain to this day. A 1973 effort to exhume the body and examine it was successfully blocked by the Aurora Cemetery Association.

A Firsthand Account

Although many people have claimed the Aurora incident was a hoax, an elderly woman was interviewed in 1973 and clearly recalled the crash from her childhood. She said that her parents wouldn't let her near the debris from the spacecraft, in case it contained something dangerous. However, she described the alien as "a small man."

Aurora continues to attract people interested in UFOs. They wonder why modern Aurora appears to be laid out like a military base. Nearby, Fort Worth seems to be home to the U.S. government's experts in alien technology. Immediately after the Roswell UFO crash in 1947, debris from that spaceship was sent to Fort Worth for analysis.

Is There Any Trace Left?

The Aurora Encounter, a 1986 movie, documents the events that began when people saw the spacecraft attempt a landing at Judge Proctor's farm. Today, the Oates gas station marks the area where the UFO crashed. Metal debris was collected from the site in the 1970s and studied by North Texas State University. That study called one fragment "most intriguing": It appeared to be iron but wasn't magnetic; it was shiny and malleable rather than brittle, as iron should be.

As recently as 2008, UFOs have appeared in the north central Texas skies. In Stephenville, a freight company owner and pilot described a low-flying object in the sky, "a mile long and half a mile wide." Others who saw the ship several times during January 2008 said that its lights changed configuration, so it wasn't an airplane. The government declined to comment.

Today, a plaque at the Aurora cemetery mentions the spaceship, but the alien's tombstone—which, if it actually existed, is said to have featured a carved image of a spaceship—was stolen many years ago.

Popping His Top: The Seaford Poltergeist

Poltergeists are the publicity hounds of the spirit world. While other ghosts are content to appear in the shadows and then vanish so that nobody's ever exactly sure what they saw, poltergeist activities are always very flashy and conspicuous. Need furniture rearranged or doors opened or slammed shut? How about knickknacks moved around or plates smashed? If so, just call your neighborhood poltergeist; they love to perform such mischief in plain sight. Poltergeists don't care—they aren't part of the ghostly union. They just enjoy annoying the living.

❋　❋　❋　❋

Pop! Pop! Pop!

THE SCIENCE OF investigating poltergeist activity has come a long way since the days when people blamed it all on witchcraft. One of the cases that got folks thinking that there might be more to it was the story of the Seaford Poltergeist.

This entity first made itself known to the Herrmann family of Seaford, Long Island, in early February 1958. Mrs. Herrmann had just welcomed her children Lucille and Jimmy home from school when several bottles in various rooms of the house all popped their tops and spewed their contents all over. The family considered various explanations, such as excess humidity or pressure building up in the bottles, but the tops were all of the twist-off variety. Short of a miniature tornado yanking the tops off, there seemed to be no rational explanation.

After the same thing happened several more times, Mr. Herrmann began to suspect that his son Jimmy—who had an interest in science—was somehow pulling a fast one on the family. However, after carefully watching the child while the incident happened, Herrmann knew that unless his son was a future Einstein, there was no way that the boy could be responsible. With no "ghost busters" to consult, Mr. Herrmann did the next best thing he could in 1958: He called the police.

Dubious at first, the police launched an investigation after witnessing some of the episodes firsthand. But answers were not forthcoming, and the incidents kept occurring. Even having a priest bless the house and sprinkle holy water in each of its rooms didn't help. An exorcism was considered but rejected because the incidents didn't resemble the work of a demon. Rather, they seemed to be the antics of a poltergeist (a noisy spirit).

Explanation Unknown

Word of the events attracted the attention of the media as well as curiosity seekers. All explanations—from the scientifically sound (sonic booms, strong drafts, freakish magnetic waves) to the weird and wacky (Soviet satellite *Sputnik*)—were considered and dismissed. Although this was the Cold War era, it was unclear how tormenting a single American family fit into the Soviets' dastardly scheme of world domination.

What was far more worrisome was that the incidents seemed to be escalating in violence. Instead of just bottles popping open, objects such as a sugar bowl, a record player, and a heavy bookcase were tossed around. Fortunately, help soon arrived in the form of experts from Duke University's Parapsychology Laboratory. Their theory was that someone in the house was unwittingly moving objects via Recurrent Spontaneous Psychokinesis (RSPK). Children seemed to attract such activity, and the Duke team discovered that Jimmy had been at or near the scene of the incidents most of the time.

When one of the researchers spent time with the boy—playing cards, helping him with his homework, or just talking—the unusual activity declined. Two more incidents occurred in early March before the Seaford Poltergeist apparently packed its bags and moved on. After 67 recorded incidents in five weeks, the lives of the Herrmann family returned to normal. To this day, it is still unknown exactly what caused the strange events in the Herrmann household in early 1958.

The Watseka Wonder: A Tale of Possession

Spiritual possession—in which a person's body is taken over by the spirit of another—is easy to fake, and legitimate cases are incredibly rare. One of the most widely publicized possessions occurred in Watseka, Illinois, in the late 1870s, when the spirit of Mary Roff, a girl who had died 12 years earlier, inhabited the body of 13-year-old Lurancy Vennum. This astounding case became known as the "Watseka Wonder."

✳ ✳ ✳ ✳

A Troubled Life

IN 1865, MARY Roff was just 18 years old when she died in an insane asylum following a lifelong illness that tormented her with frequent fits, seizures, and strange voices in her head. She'd also developed an obsession with bloodletting and would apply leeches to her body, poke herself with pins, and cut herself with razors. Doctors thought that Mary was mentally ill, but others—including her own family—came to believe that her problems were supernatural in origin.

At the time of Mary Roff's death, Lurancy Vennum was barely a year old. Born on April 16, 1864, Lurancy moved with her family to Watseka a few years after Mary Roff's death and knew nothing of the girl or her family.

In July 1877, about 12 years after Mary passed away, Lurancy started to exhibit symptoms similar to Mary's, including uncontrollable seizures. Her speech became garbled, and she often spoke in a strange language. She sometimes fell into trances, assumed different personalities, and claimed to see spirits, many of which terrified her.

The townspeople of Watseka didn't know what to make of Lurancy. Many thought that she was insane and should be committed, as Mary had been. But the Roffs, who had become ardent Spiritualists as a result of their daughter's troubles, believed that unseen forces were tormenting Lurancy. They felt that she was not insane but rather was possessed by the spirits of the dead. With the permission of Lurancy's parents, Asa Roff—Mary's father—met with the young girl in the company of Dr. E. Winchester Stevens, who was also a Spiritualist. During their visit, a friendly spirit spoke to Lurancy and asked to take control of her body to protect her from sinister forces. That spirit was Mary Roff.

Sent to Heaven

After Mary took possession of Lurancy's body, she explained that Lurancy was ill and needed to return to heaven to be cured. Mary said that she would remain in Lurancy's body until sometime in May. Over the next few months, it seemed apparent that Mary's spirit was indeed in control of Lurancy's body. She looked the same, but she knew nothing about the Vennum family or her life as Lurancy. Instead, she had intimate knowledge of the Roffs, and she acted as though they were her family. Although she treated the Vennums politely, they were essentially strangers to her.

In February 1878, Lurancy/Mary asked to go live with her parents—the Roffs. The Vennums reluctantly consented. On the way to the Roff home, as they traveled past the house where they'd lived when Mary was alive, Lurancy wanted to know why they weren't stopping. The Roffs explained that they'd moved to a new home a few years back, which was something that Lurancy/Mary would not have known. Lurancy/Mary spent several months living in the Roff home, where she identified objects and people that Lurancy could not have known.

On one occasion, Lurancy sat down at the Roff's family piano and began to play, singing the same songs Mary had sung in her youth. One member of the Roff family commented, "As we stood listening, the familiar [songs] were hers, though emanating from another's lips."

Once word spread of Lurancy's spiritual possession, interested people started to visit. Lurancy/Mary typically met them in the Roffs' front parlor, where she frequently demonstrated knowledge of events that had transpired long before Lurancy was even born.

During one encounter with a Mrs. Sherman, Mary was asked about the people she had met in the afterlife. Immediately, Mary started listing the names of some of Mrs. Sherman's deceased family members, as well as several of Mrs. Sherman's neighbors who had died. Again, this was information that Lurancy could not possibly have known.

Scene at a Séance

In April 1878, during a séance that was held in the Roff home and attended by several people (including Dr. Stevens), one member of the group became possessed by the spirit of another member's dead brother, who addressed the gathering. After the spirit had left the man's body, Mary removed herself from Lurancy's body (which immediately lolled over against the person next to her, as if dead) and possessed the body of a participant named Dr. Steel. Through him, Mary proved to everyone present that it was indeed her. She then abandoned Dr. Steel's body and reentered Lurancy's.

Going Home

Mary permanently left Lurancy's body on May 21, 1878. When Lurancy awoke from her trance, she was no longer afflicted by the numerous problems that had previously plagued her, nor did she have any recollection of being spiritually possessed by Mary. By all accounts, she came away from the experience a healthy young lady. Indeed, Lurancy grew to be a happy woman and exhibited no ill effects from the possession. She went on to marry and have 13 children.

But Mary didn't abandon Lurancy completely. According to some sources, Lurancy kept in touch with the Roff family, with whom she felt a strange closeness, although she had no idea why. She would visit with them once a year and allow Mary's spirit to possess her briefly, just like it did in the late 1870s.

The story of the Watseka Wonder still stands as one of the most authentic cases of spirit possession in history. It has been investigated, dissected, and ridiculed, but to this day, no clear scientific explanation has ever been offered.

Are You Going to Eat That Jesus?

Images of religious icons, particularly Jesus and the Virgin Mary, sometimes show up in the oddest places. Some people believe they are divine. What's the story?

✳ ✳ ✳ ✳

SIGHTINGS OF RELIGIOUS symbols or images, called religious simulacra, in unexpected places are common enough that they've become incorporated into pop culture. Many of the people who discover or are involved in these sightings consider them to be miraculous events. Some also claim that the objects in which the images appear have special properties, such as bringing good luck or being immune to the ravages of time.

Jesus and Mary

For Christians, Jesus and the Virgin Mary are among the most significant religious figures, and not coincidentally, they also seem to make the most common appearances—often in food. Perhaps the quintessential sighting of a Christian religious symbol in food occurred in 1978, when a New Mexico woman named Maria Rubio was making a burrito. She noticed that a burn on the tortilla appeared to be in the shape of Jesus' head. After receiving the blessing of a priest, she built a shrine to house the tortilla and even quit her job to tend to the shrine full-time.

Islamic Words

Not surprisingly, religious sightings do not always involve Christian figures or symbols. In the Islamic world, the perception of the Arabic word for Allah roughly parallels the sighting of Jesus, the Virgin Mary, or other religious figures by Christians. Similarly, the objects involved sometimes have mystical properties ascribed to them. In 2006, a Kazakh farmer discovered an egg that villagers claimed had the name of Allah on its shell. After the sighting was verified by the local mosque, Bites Amantayeva, the farmer who discovered the egg, decided to keep it, saying, "We don't think it'll go bad." The name of Allah has also been sighted on fish scales, on beans, and in tomato slices.

Selling Simulacra

Sightings of religious images can have commercial as well as spiritual implications. In 1996, someone at a coffee shop in Nashville, Tennessee, discovered a cinnamon bun that bore a striking resemblance to Mother Teresa. The coffee shop parlayed the discovery into a line of merchandise, including coffee mugs and T-shirts. The merchandise was marketed with a NunBun trademark after Mother Teresa asked the shop to stop using the phrase "Immaculate Confection."

The proliferation of internet auction sites such as eBay has created a market for these "miraculous" objects. One of the widest-known auctions occurred in 2004, when a Florida woman named Diane Duyser auctioned part of a grilled cheese sandwich she claimed bore the image of the Virgin Mary on eBay. Duyser asserted that the sandwich, which she had been storing since it was made in 1994, had never grown moldy and had brought her good luck, allowing her to win $70,000 at a casino. The sandwich was purchased by another casino for $28,000.

Religious sightings—especially if they have been contrived somehow—are not always viewed in a positive light. In 1997, Nike produced several models of basketball shoes that unintentionally featured a logo that, when viewed from right to left, resembled the Arabic word for Allah. The Council on American-Islamic Relations (CAIR) quickly demanded an apology, and Nike had little choice but to recall the shoes. The settlement between Nike and CAIR also included Arabic training for Nike graphic designers and Nike-built playgrounds in Muslim communities.

A Scientific Explanation?

While the parties involved in sightings of religious symbols often consider them to be miraculous in nature, the prevailing scientific view is that, rather than miraculous, they are occurrences of pareidolia, a psychological phenomenon in which random stimuli are interpreted as being meaningful in some way. As part of its intellectual process, the mind tries to make sense of what may be unrelated images. This is the same phenomenon that psychologists credit with forming the likeness of a man in the moon or shapes in clouds. It's also what's involved when the brain creates pictures from the famous Rorschach inkblots.

The Ghosts of the St. Valentine's Day Massacre

After Chicago gangsters lured their rivals into an ambush, they thought that they had enjoyed the last laugh. What they failed to consider was the existence of another syndicate—one that could reach out from beyond the grave.

✳   ✳   ✳   ✳

Requiem for Racketeers

DURING THE ROARING '20s, Al "Scarface" Capone ruled Chicago. Be it gambling, prostitution, bootleg whiskey, or anything else illegal or immoral, Capone and his gangsters controlled it. Almost no one—including the police—dared to stand up to Capone and his men because resistance certainly meant winding up on the wrong end of a gun. Still, one man was determined to dethrone Capone: George "Bugs" Moran.

Moran and his North Side Gang had been slowly muscling their way into Chicago in an attempt to force Capone and his men out. As 1929 began, rumors indicated that Capone was planning to "take care of" Moran. As the days turned into weeks and nothing happened, Moran and his men began to relax and let their guard down. That would prove to be a fatal mistake.

Gathering for the Slaughter

On February 14, 1929, six members of the North Side Gang gathered inside the SMC Cartage Company at 2122 North Clark Street. With them was mechanic John May, who was not a member of the gang but had been hired to work on a member's car. May had brought along his dog, Highball, and had tied him to the bumper of the car while he worked. At approximately 10:30 AM, two cars parked in front of the Clark Street entrance of the building. Four men—two dressed as police officers and two in street clothes—got out and walked into the warehouse.

Murderers in Disguise

Based on physical evidence, once the men were inside, it is believed they announced that the warehouse was being raided and ordered everyone to line up facing the back wall. Believing that the uniformed men were indeed police officers, all of Moran's men, along with John May, did as they were told. Suddenly, the supposed raiders began shooting, and in a hail of shotgun fire and more than 70 submachine-gun rounds, the seven men were brutally murdered.

After the slaughter was over, the two men in street clothes calmly walked out of the building with their hands up, followed by the two men dressed as police officers. To everyone nearby, it appeared as though a shootout had occurred and that the police had arrived and arrested two men.

"Nobody Shot Me"

Minutes later, neighbors called police after hearing strange howls coming from inside the building. When the real police arrived, they found all seven men mortally wounded. One of the men, Frank Gusenberg, lingered long enough to respond to one question. When authorities asked who shot him, Gusenberg responded, "Nobody shot me." The only survivor of the melee was Highball the dog.

When word of the massacre hit the newswire, everyone suspected that Al Capone had something to do with it. Although Capone swore that he wasn't involved, most people felt that he had orchestrated the whole thing as a way to get rid of Moran and several of his key men. There was only one problem: Bugs Moran wasn't in the warehouse at the time of the shooting. Why he wasn't there is not clear, but one thing is certain: February 14, 1929, was Bugs Moran's lucky day.

Police were unable to pin anything related to the crime on Capone, although they did charge two of his gunmen—John Scalise and Jack "Machine Gun" McGurn—with the murders. Scalise never saw the inside of the courthouse: He was murdered before his trial began. Charges against McGurn were eventually dropped; however, he was murdered seven years later—on Valentine's Day—in what appeared to be retaliation for the 1929 massacre.

Haunted by the Truth

Publicly, Al Capone may have denied any wrongdoing, but it appears that the truth literally haunted him until his dying day. In May 1929, Capone was incarcerated at Philadelphia's Eastern State Penitentiary, serving a one-year stint for weapons possession. Such a span was considered "easy time" by gangster standards, but Capone's time inside would be anything but. Haunted by the ghost of James Clark—who was killed in the St. Valentine's Day Massacre—Capone was often heard begging "Jimmy" to leave him alone.

The torment continued even after Capone was released. One day, Capone's valet, Hymie Cornish, saw an unfamiliar man in Capone's apartment. When he ordered the man to identify himself, the mysterious figure slipped behind a curtain and vanished. Capone insisted that Cornish, like himself, had seen the ghost of Clark. Some say that Clark didn't rest until Capone passed away on January 25, 1947.

Ghosts Still Linger

Over the years, the warehouse in which the St. Valentine's Day Massacre took place transformed into a morbid tourist attraction, as curiosity seekers felt compelled to see the site for themselves. It became a piece of Chicago history.

When the building was demolished in 1967, the wall against which the seven doomed men stood was dismantled brick by brick and sold at auction. An enterprising businessman purchased the bricks and eventually sold each one, but many of them were returned soon after. According to unhappy customers, their luck took a nosedive after they purchased the ghoulish souvenirs. Illness, financial ruin, divorce, and even death resulted, causing the frightened owners to believe that the bricks were cursed.

As for the infamous massacre site, nothing much is left there today. A nursing home owns the land and has left the area vacant, save for a parking lot and a few trees. Some people have reported hearing gunfire and screams as they pass by the site; and people walking their dogs near the lot claim that their furry friends pull on their leashes and try to get away from the area as soon as possible.

Perhaps they sense the ghostly remnants of the bloody slaughter that took place there so many years ago.

Ghosts of the Gold Rush

The California Gold Rush of 1848—its frenzy of ambition and greed is what made the Wild West truly wild. So it's little wonder that some folks would find it difficult to leave, even after they've supposedly passed on to the great gold mine in the sky. Check out these haunted locales next time you wander through California's Gold Rush territory.

✳ ✳ ✳ ✳

Jamestown Hotel

OVER THE YEARS since opening in 1858, the Jamestown Hotel in Jamestown has served as a boarding house, bordello, bus depot, and hospital. The resident ghost story is every bit as dramatic as the building's history. In 1938, Mary Rose, the granddaughter of a wealthy and influential prospector, fell in love with a handsome British soldier. Her grandfather was not pleased. The soldier was promptly shipped off to India, where he met a violent death. Mary Rose, desolate, pregnant, and unmarried, checked into what was then the Mother Lode Hospital to await the birth of her child. Unfortunately, neither mother nor child survived childbirth, but guests at the hotel say they've seen misty apparitions of the spirits of Mary Rose and her soldier.

1859 Historic National Hotel

Located in Jamestown, the 1859 Historic National Hotel's resident ghost, affectionately named Flo, usually remains upstairs, favoring the rooms toward the front of the building. She has occasionally been spotted floating through the downstairs dining room, but only in the early morning. Current hotel owner Stephen Willey says that, although he's never personally encountered Flo, he has come across many a hotel guest who arrived a skeptic and left a believer.

Willow Steakhouse & Saloon

A mine once ran underneath what is now the Willow Steakhouse (located in, you guessed it, Jamestown), and it plays a part in the restaurant's violent history. There, a mine collapse killed 23 miners; there were violent deaths at the Willow's bar; and a man was lynched in his own room. From the time the building was first built in 1862, a series of mysterious fires have plagued the property, the most recent in 1985. Some blame restless spirits, saying that the place is crowded with ghosts, including a short man who roams the upstairs halls, a dapper gambler who favors the bar, and a redheaded woman who was shot by her husband in the bar during the Gold Rush years.

City Hotel

Located within the Columbia State Historic Park, this Gold Rush-era hotel still welcomes guests, although visitors may share their lodgings with an unexpected roommate. When the hotel was restored for its current use, authentic period antiques reflecting Columbia's heyday (1850-1870) were brought in from nearby San Francisco. Among them was an especially ornate and finely carved wooden bed, originally imported from Europe more than a century before it found its way to the City Hotel. With the bed came the hotel's resident ghost, Elizabeth, a woman who reportedly died in it during childbirth. Since the arrival of the bed (and Elizabeth), doors now open and close at random in Room 1; a sweet perfume often wafts through the air; and guests, especially children, have reported seeing a woman in a white dress standing at the foot of the bed.

The Groveland Hotel

This historic hotel in Groveland is actually two buildings: One was built in 1849 and served as lodging for miners and prospectors working at the now defunct gold mine behind the building. The other was built in 1919 for workers doing construction on the Hetch Hetchy Dam. According to lore, a prospector named Lyle remains. A recluse, Lyle was dead for several days before anyone thought to check his room to see if he was all right. As a ghost, Lyle is quirky. He can't stand to see women's cosmetics on the dresser, and he's not shy about moving them. When people talk about him, Lyle tends to respond by flickering the lights or rushing by as a cold breeze. Once Lyle even helped current owner Peggy Mosley with her baking by flinging open the oven door at the precise moment the bread was finished. Sometimes Lyle disappears for weeks—perhaps to go prospecting—but he always returns to The Groveland Hotel.

Vineyard House

Modern visitors to this beautiful bed-and-breakfast in Coloma would never guess its troubled and violent past. Construction on the house finished in 1878, and a year later, its first owner reportedly went insane and had to be chained in the home's cellar "for his own protection." He went on a hunger strike, starving himself to death and leaving his wife in dire financial straights. The family's grapevines dried up and its wine business went under. The widow was forced to take in boarders to make ends meet and for a time even resorted to renting the house as a jail, a period when two hangings took place in the front yard. Misty apparitions roam the hotel, accompanied by the sound of rattling chains.

Bodie, California

Sure, it's not a hotel, but in its heyday, Bodie personified the Wild West. A Gold Rush town that seemingly sprang up over-night, more than 10,000 people called Bodie home in the late 1870s. No fewer than 70 saloons served up suds to the men who worked the area's 30 mines. Numerous bordellos, gam-bling halls, and opium dens provided further "amusement," and gunfights were common. During this period, at least one man was killed every day in Bodie. When the gold veins depleted, the town withered; by the time the last mine closed during World War II, only six people remained. Today about 160 buildings still stand, left just as they were when their inhabit-ants departed. However, some Bodie residents remain eternally.

The sound of a nonexistent piano often floats through the streets, and a spectral white mule haunts the Standard Mine on the outskirts of town.

The Ghosts of Gettysburg

The Battle of Gettysburg holds a unique and tragic place in the annals of American history: It was the turning point of the Civil War and its bloodiest battle. From July 1 through July 3, 1863, the Union and Confederate armies suffered a total of more than 50,000 casualties (dead, wounded, and missing) on the battlefields of Gettysburg, Pennsylvania. All that bloodshed and suffering is said to have permanently stained the town and left it brimming with ghosts.

✳   ✳   ✳   ✳

First Ghost Sighting

FEW PEOPLE REALIZE that the first sighting of a ghost at Gettysburg allegedly took place *before* the battle was even over. As the story goes, Union reinforcements from the 20th Maine Infantry were nearing Gettysburg but got lost as they traveled in the dark. As the troops reached a fork in the road, they were greeted by a man wearing a tricornered hat, who was sitting atop a horse; both the man and his horse appeared to be glowing. The man, who bore a striking resemblance to George Washington, motioned for the regiment to follow; believing the man to be a Union general, Colonel Joshua Chamberlain ordered his regiment to do so. Just as Chamberlain began to think that something was odd about the helpful fellow, the man simply vanished.

As the soldiers searched for the spectral stranger, they realized that they'd been led to Little Round Top—the very spot where, the following day, they would repel a Confederate advance in one of the turning points of the battle. To his dying day, Chamberlain, as well as the roughly 100 men who saw the ghostly figure that night, believed that they had been led to

Little Round Top by the ghost of George Washington himself, looking to save the country he had once led.

Pickett's Charge

On the final day of the conflict, Confederate General Robert E. Lee felt the battle slipping away from him, so in what many saw as an act of desperation, he ordered 12,000 Confederate soldiers to attack the Union forces that were firmly entrenched on Cemetery Ridge. During the attack that is now known as Pickett's Charge, the Confederates slowly and methodically marched across open fields toward the heavily fortified Union lines. The attack failed miserably: More than 6,000 Rebel soldiers were killed or wounded before they retreated. The defeat essentially signaled the beginning of the end of the Civil War.

To this day, it is said that if you stand atop Cemetery Ridge and look out across the field, you might catch a glimpse of row after ghostly row of Confederate soldiers slowly marching toward their doom at the hands of Union troops.

Jennie Wade

While the battle raged near Cemetery Ridge, 20-year-old Mary Virginia "Ginnie" Wade (aka Jennie Wade) was at her sister's house baking bread for the Union troops stationed nearby. Without warning, a stray bullet flew through the house, struck the young woman, and killed her instantly, making her the only civilian known to have died during the Battle of Gettysburg. Visitors to the historic Jennie Wade House often report catching whiffs of freshly baked bread. Jennie's spirit is also felt in the basement, where her body was placed until relatives could bury her. When *Ghost Lab* visited the Jennie Wade House in 2010, phantom footsteps were heard and other audio evidence was captured.

Farnsworth House

Though it is next to impossible to determine who fired the shot that killed Jennie Wade, it is believed that it came from the attic of the nearby Farnsworth House. Now a bed-and-breakfast, the building was taken over by Confederate sharpshooters during the Battle of Gettysburg. One in particular—the one who may have fired the shot that killed Jennie Wade—is said to have holed up in the building's attic. He didn't survive the battle, but judging by the dozens of bullet holes and scars along the sides of the Farnsworth House, he didn't go down without a fight. Perhaps that's why his ghost still lingers—to let us know what really happened in the Farnsworth attic. Passersby often report looking up at the attic window that faces the Jennie Wade House and seeing a ghostly figure looking down at them.

But the sharpshooter is just one of many spirits that haunt the Farnsworth House. Paranormal experts claim that the home features no less than 14 ghosts—some are friendly, and some are not. Representing the former, "Mary" sits beside the sick and lingers wherever there's cheering up to be done. Many believe that this compassionate phantom—which is dressed in 19th-century apparel—was a nurse or midwife during her mortal years.

Then there's "Walter"—the antithesis of Mary. Believed to be a Confederate soldier who was jilted by his lover before being killed, Walter's ghost seems determined to exact its revenge by hurting women. Reports state that a female guest was once attacked by an invisible presence. Another time, an unseen force hurled a chair at a female visitor; many blame Walter for both incidents.

Pennsylvania Hall at Gettysburg College

Built in 1832, Gettysburg College stands adjacent to the famous battlefield. During the conflict, some of its buildings served as operating rooms and makeshift morgues. Late one night in the early 1980s, two college administrators, who were working on an upper floor, got on an elevator and pushed the button for the first floor. But the elevator descended past the first floor and continued to the basement. Upon reaching the basement, the elevator doors opened. It didn't take long for the workers to realize that they'd somehow traveled back in time: The familiar surroundings of the basement had been replaced by bloody, screaming Confederate soldiers on stretchers. Doctors stood over the men, desperately trying to save their lives. Blood and gore were everywhere.

As the administrators frantically pushed the elevator buttons, one of the spectral doctors began walking toward them. Without a second to spare, the elevator doors closed just as the ghostly figure reached them. This time, the elevator rose to the first floor and opened its doors, revealing modern furnishings. Despite repeated return visits to the basement, nothing out of the ordinary has ever been reported again.

Unsettled Spirits at the Sanatorium

It was designed to save lives at a time when an epidemic was sweeping the nation. Little did its developers know that they were erecting a building in which scores of people would take their last gasping breaths. Is it any wonder that the halls of the Waverly Hills Sanatorium in Louisville, Kentucky, still echo with the footsteps of those who died there?

✳ ✳ ✳ ✳

Origins

AROUND 1883, THE first building was erected on the site of what is now the Waverly Hills Sanatorium. Major Thomas Hays, the owner of the property, decided that the local schools were too far away for his daughters to attend, so he constructed a small schoolhouse on the land and hired teacher Lizzie Harris to instruct the girls. Because of her love of Walter Scott's *Waverley* novels, Harris named the place Waverly School. Taken by the name, Hays decided to call his property Waverly Hill.

In the early 1900s, an outbreak of tuberculosis spread across the United States. In an effort to confine the highly contagious disease, the construction of TB sanatoriums and hospitals was planned. In 1908, the Board of Tuberculosis Hospitals purchased the Hays property, and in July 1910, a small two-story building was opened; it had the capacity to house nearly 50 patients.

They Just Keep Coming...

Without a cure in existence or any way to slow the disease, little could be done for TB patients at the time. Treatment often consisted of nothing more than fresh air and exposure to heat lamps. More and more patients arrived at the sanatorium; therefore, in the 1920s, expansion of the facility began, and in 1926, the building that stands today opened. This massive five-story structure could house nearly 400 patients. But once again, the rooms quickly filled up. The sad truth was that the sanatorium was only kept from overcrowding due to the fact that, without a cure, many of the patients died. Just how many people passed away there is the stuff of urban legends—some estimates go as high as 65,000. In truth, the number is probably closer to 8,000, but that's still a staggering number when one realizes that tuberculosis causes patients to slowly and painfully waste away over the course of weeks or even months.

In the 1940s, treatments for TB were introduced, and as a result, the number of patients at Waverly Hills consistently declined until the building was officially shut down in 1961.

The Final Years

A short time later, Waverly Hills was reopened as the Woodhaven Geriatric Center. This chapter of the building's history came to an end around 1980 amid whispers of patient cruelty and abuse. Before long, those whispers became full-blown urban legends involving depravities such as electroshock therapy. Not surprisingly, it wasn't long before people started saying that the abandoned, foreboding structure was haunted.

Meet the Ghosts

So who are the ghosts that are said to haunt Waverly Hills? Sadly, the identities of most of them are unknown, but many of them have been encountered. Almost every floor of the building has experienced paranormal activity, such as disembodied voices and ghostly footsteps. Doors have been known to open and close by themselves, and bits of debris have been thrown at unsuspecting visitors. It is said that all one has to do is wait quietly to spot one of the many shadow people that walk down the hallways. Of course, if you're looking for a more interactive ghost encounter, you can always head up to the third floor. There, you might find the spirit of a young girl in the solarium. If she's not there, check the nearby staircases—apparently she likes to run up and down them.

Waverly Hills is also home to the ghost of a young boy who likes to play with a small ball that sometimes appears on the floor. Not wanting to wait to find the ball, some visitors have resorted to bringing their own, which they leave in a certain spot, only to see it roll away or even vanish before it appears on a different floor altogether.

Welcome to Room 502

Of all the allegedly haunted areas at Waverly Hills, none holds a candle to Room 502. Most of the legends associated with the room center on two nurses, both of whom supposedly committed suicide on the premises. One nurse is said to have killed herself in the room in 1928. Apparently, she was a single woman who discovered that she was pregnant. Feeling that she had nowhere to turn, the young woman chose to slip a rope around her neck and hang herself. The other nurse who worked in Room 502 is said to have killed herself in 1932 by jumping from the roof, although the reason why is unclear. Although no documentation substantiating either of these suicides has been unearthed, that has not stopped visitors to Room 502 from experiencing paranormal activity. Upon entering the room, people often report feeling "heavy" or the sensation of being watched. It is quite common for guests to witness shadow figures darting around the room, and occasionally, a lucky visitor catches a glimpse of a spectral nurse standing by the window.

The Body Chute

When expansion of the building began in the 1920s, a rather morbid (though some would say essential) part of the sanatorium was constructed: the Body Chute—a 500-foot-long underground tunnel leading from the main building to a nearby road and set of railroad tracks. Some believe that the tunnel was created simply for convenience, while others think it was designed to prevent patients from seeing the truth—that many of them were dying. Although it was called a chute, bodies were never dumped into it; rather, they were walked through it on gurneys. The tunnel was even equipped with a motorized cable system to help with transportation.

People walking through the Body Chute have reported hearing disembodied voices, whispering, and even painful groans. Sometimes, shadowy figures are seen wandering through the tunnel. But because the only light down there comes from random air vents, the figures vanish almost as quickly as they appear.

Lights, Camera, Ghosts!

After the TV show *Scariest Places on Earth* featured Waverly Hills in a 2001 episode, numerous programs began filming at the sanatorium. *Ghost Hunters* visited there twice—once in 2006 and again in 2007 as part of its annual live Halloween investigation. *Most Haunted* came all the way from the UK in 2008, and *Ghost Adventures* spent a night locked inside the sanatorium in 2010. But of all the episodes filmed at Waverly Hills, none was more bizarre than that of the short-lived VH1 show *Celebrity Paranormal Project*.

The series' debut episode, which aired in October 2006, was shot at Waverly Hills and featured actor Gary Busey, comedian Hal Sparks, *Survivor* winner Jenna Morasca, model/actress

Donna D'Errico, and model Toccara Jones conducting an investigation. The supernatural activity began early in the evening, shortly after Busey and Morasca were sent to Room 418 to investigate. They weren't there long before their thermal-imaging camera picked up shapes moving around the room and even sitting on a bed near them. When Morasca was left in the room alone, she heard all sorts of strange noises and even encountered a small red ball, which wasn't there when the team first entered the room.

When Sparks was in the solarium, he rolled balls across the floor in an attempt to convince the spirits to play with him. The footage shows what appears to be one of the balls rolling back to him. At around the same time, Sparks reported seeing a small dark shape—like that of a child—run past the doorway. Later on in the evening, D'Errico reported feeling that someone was following her, an incident that was accompanied by the sound of footsteps. She also heard what sounded like people screaming. She was so frightened that she ran away from the building screaming. Once back in the company of the other investigators, D'Errico said that she actually saw the figure of a man standing in a hallway.

The evening ended with the entire group attempting to contact the spirits in Room 502. As they asked questions, banging noises and footsteps were heard coming from all around them. When they left the building, they were still hearing noises and encountered a child's ball that seemed to appear from out of nowhere.

"Come Join Us"

Waverly Hills Sanatorium is open for tours, both during the day and for overnight ghost hunts. Just be assured that no matter how many ghosts inhabit Waverly Hills, they always have room for more.

Meet the Ghosts of Owl's Head Light

Owl's Head Light, which watches over Rockland Harbor on Maine's West Penobscot Bay, has ghostly credentials to hoot about—so much so that in 2006, Coastal Living *magazine named it America's most haunted lighthouse.*

✳   ✳   ✳   ✳

THE ORIGINAL OWL'S Head Light was commissioned and built in 1825 after a boom in the lime-mining industry in nearby Rockland increased shipping traffic around the bay's rocky shores. A sturdier structure replaced this poorly built lighthouse in 1852, but it wasn't until recent times that ghosts began to visit the promontory where the original 30-foot tower and then its replacement have guarded the bay for nearly two centuries.

No one is sure exactly when the hauntings began, but at some point, caretakers began finding human footprints in the snow on the stairway that leads from the caretaker's house to the tower. The footprints started about halfway up the stairs, as if someone had materialized on the spot. Whoever made the prints had a purpose: The tracks often led to an open lighthouse door, and caretakers would find a fresh shine on the equipment inside.

Over the years, a strange white figure has also appeared in a window of the lighthouse. One caretaker's child reported seeing a mysterious woman sitting on a bedroom chair, and several caretakers claimed that they glimpsed a small spectral woman working in the kitchen. To make her presence known, the ghostly cook likes to jangle tableware and slam cupboard doors.

Bedroom Invader

One strange incident happened around 1985, when lighthouse keeper Andy Germann got up late one night to tend to some chores that he'd forgotten to do outside the house. As he left the bedroom, Andy saw a misty form float over the floor and pass into the room. He shrugged it off—figuring that it was just the bay's formidable fog—and continued with his task. Andy's wife Denise was trying to get back to sleep when she felt her husband lie down on his side of the bed. But when she turned to ask why he had returned so quickly, all she could see was a body-sized dent on the mattress. The impression could conceivably have been leftover from when Andy exited the bed ... except that it kept changing in depth, as if someone was fidgeting to get comfortable. This continued for several minutes before Denise surmised that it was the work of a ghostly intruder, and she kindly asked it to leave. It did, but other strange phenomena—such as doors opening and closing on their own and the sound of footsteps—continued to occur, especially in a particular upstairs room.

Only a few years later, new residents received a clue about who might have been making tracks in the snow, cleaning the great lighthouse lens, and trying to sleep in the main bedroom. After caretaker Gerard Graham, his wife Debbie, and their young daughter Claire moved into the structure, Claire would often describe a playmate that only she could see. He looked like an old-fashioned sea captain, she said. Claire began to spout technical nautical terms that her parents said she did not know, and she even warned her father when the foghorn needed to be turned on. Incidentally, Claire slept in the bedroom that the Germanns believed was haunted.

The Frozen Couple

Owl's Head Light is also famous as the site of the true story of the "frozen couple." This tale involves no ghosts, but it does include two people who were brought back from the dead. In 1850, a great storm lashed the bay a few days before Christmas. A small schooner anchored at a neighboring port was having a hard time in the crashing waves, and its captain left the vessel, perhaps to seek help.

Before the captain returned, the schooner's cables snapped and the storm propelled it toward Rockland Harbor. Aboard the schooner were three hapless souls: the first mate, Richard Ingraham; Ingraham's fiancée, Lydia Dyer; and a sailor, Roger Elliott. It did not take long before the vessel crashed aground near Owl's Head Light. It remained partially intact, but freezing water quickly drenched the three passengers, who were huddled together under blankets that began to collect ice.

Thawed Out

The engaged couple eventually lost consciousness, but Elliott managed to get off the ship and clamber over the rocks to the lighthouse. Fortunately, the caretaker passed by on a horse-drawn sleigh and saw the half-frozen man, who told him of his capsized friends.

The caretaker immediately gathered a rescue party, which found Ingraham and Dyer encased in ice. Both appeared to be dead, but their seemingly lifeless bodies were chipped out and brought back to the caretaker's home, although it took great effort to release the couple from their icy tomb.

The rescuers then managed to thaw the pair out by pouring water on them and rubbing their arms and legs to restore circulation. Much to the surprise and joy of all present, Ingraham and Dyer regained consciousness. They eventually married as planned and raised four children.

Death Takes No Holiday

Elliott was not so lucky; he died, possibly of hypothermia. No one knows for sure what happened to the schooner's captain. Perhaps he never made it ashore to seek help but ultimately found comfort in the caretaker's house, where he visited young Claire Graham more than a hundred years later.

Perhaps the most famous resident of the Owl's Head Light was a springer spaniel named Spot, who belonged to a keeper in the 1930s. Spot learned to use his teeth to sound the foghorn whenever a vessel came into sight. Once, when the foghorn was broken, Spot performed his duty by barking and was credited with preventing a mail boat from crashing into the rocks.

The Ghosts of Wisconsin's Black Point Mansion

Like many spectral beings, some ghost stories evaporate like misty ectoplasm when studied closely. In other words, they don't hold up to scrutiny when examined thoroughly. But the ghosts of the Black Point Mansion on Wisconsin's Geneva Lake boast a solid history to back up the spooky legend of their origin.

✳   ✳   ✳   ✳

IN 1888, WEALTHY Chicagoan Conrad Seipp built a 20-room summer home on the southern shore of Geneva Lake. Known as Black Point Mansion, Seipp's vacation house looks much the same today as it did back then, with an imposing four-story tower that rises above the black oak trees for which it was named. But according to local legend, on stormy nights, the cupola at the tower's peak holds the restless spirits of a priest and nuns who drowned in the lake many years ago.

Unlike many urban legends, this tale has elements of truth to it: On July 7, 1895, Father James Hogan, a beloved Catholic priest from Harvard, Illinois, did indeed drown in Geneva Lake within sight of Black Point Mansion. But the others who died were not Catholic sisters but rather Father Hogan's *actual* sister Mary; his brother Dr. John Hogan; the doctor's wife, Kittie; their two-year-old child; and a steamboat captain.

On that fateful day, the Hogan family had taken a train from Illinois to Williams Bay on the northwestern shore of Geneva Lake. From there, they boarded a small steamboat to visit friends who lived nearby. As the day wore on, storm clouds began to gather, so the family decided to make a fast retreat before the weather worsened. Eyeing the darkening sky, the captain of the steamer *Dispatch* advised the group to postpone their trip until after the storm had passed. But the Hogans persuaded him to make the trip anyway, and the *Dispatch* began what would be its final crossing of Geneva Lake.

The anxious passengers were more than halfway through their journey when a squall kicked up. The storm quickly turned so violent that the small vessel could not make it to the nearest landing—a park near Black Point Mansion. The captain blew his distress whistle over and over, but no one could get to the steamer before it capsized, tossing all five passengers and the captain into the deep spring-fed lake. The mansion's tower may well have been the last thing any of them saw before succumbing to the cold, dark water. Anguished witnesses on shore saw the baby's white dress fluttering in the harsh wind . . . and then the family was gone.

It took some time to recover the bodies, but newspapers said that the doctor was found on the lake bottom with his hands in an attitude of prayer; Mary still wore her ladylike gloves and held her purse; and Father Hogan was lying as if merely at rest. Seventy-five priests and a large crowd of parishioners attended his funeral.

A Lake Monster's Ball

Black Point Mansion's haunted tower is not the area's only supernatural claim to fame. Before European settlers came to Geneva Lake, the Potawatomi people who lived there believed that fierce water spirits fought with thunderbirds in the lake to cause the kind of sudden storm that sank the *Dispatch*. They also thought that the lake was home to an eel-like monster that would pull down canoes during bad weather. And in the mid-to-late 1800s, numerous residents and tourists claimed to have seen a giant creature—which they dubbed "Jenny"—swimming along the lakeshore.

One of the people who spotted Jenny was a minister from Delavan. And in July 1892—three years before the drowning of the Hogan family—the *Chicago Tribune* reported that three fishermen saw a 100-foot-long monster in the lake. The sighting occurred in front of the very park that the captain of the *Dispatch* was trying to reach when the steamer went down.

Take an Excursion on the Lake . . . If You Dare

Today, Black Point Mansion is owned by the state of Wisconsin; it serves as a museum, and despite the fact that it retains nearly all of its original furniture, the building itself is not believed to harbor any ghosts—just the open cupola. From May through October, tourists can still venture out on the lake by steamboat to get exactly the same view of the mansion and its tower that the ill-fated Hogan family had on that tragic day in 1895.

A Host of Ghosts Haunt the White Eagle Saloon

The building housing the White Eagle Saloon in Portland, Oregon, has been many things since it was constructed in the early 1900s: a hotel, a brothel, a rooming house, and, most recently, a tavern that features live music. For much of its history, it has also been haunted.

✳ ✳ ✳ ✳

OVER THE YEARS, a great deal of paranormal activity has been reported at the White Eagle Saloon. Most of it has been harmless—but not all of it. For example, many years ago, a waitress was walking to the basement after closing to tabulate the day's receipts when something unseen shoved her down the stairs. The woman's hysterical screams got the attention of the bartender and doorman, who had a bucket hurled at them by an invisible force. Not surprisingly, the waitress quit.

To date, this is the most violent outburst from the spirits at the White Eagle Saloon; however, many other, more innocuous events that simply defy explanation have occurred there.

Weirdness in the Bathroom

One of the White Eagle's ghosts seems to enjoy flushing the toilet in the men's room. Many people have observed this unusual activity, usually after closing. A faulty toilet? No way, says owner Chuck Hughes—the flushing has occurred with two different commodes, and it is sometimes accompanied by the sound of footsteps in the hallway outside the restroom.

Hughes has experienced quite a bit of unexplained phenomena over the years. For example, one day he was removing a lock from a door on the second floor when he heard what sounded like a woman crying at the other end of the hallway. But as he walked toward the source of the noise, the crying ceased. Hughes checked all of the rooms on the second floor but found nothing. When he returned to his work on the door, the crying began again. Hughes again tried to find the source of the sound, and this time, he felt an overwhelming chill.

Frightened, Hughes rushed downstairs and exited the tavern. Looking back at the building, he saw what he later described as a ghostly shape in one of the second-floor windows. After moving to the back of the building, Hughes saw the same specter at another window. Shaken, he refused to go upstairs again for nearly a year.

A Ghost Named Sam

It is believed that one of the ghosts haunting the White Eagle Saloon is a former employee named Sam, who some say was adopted at a young age by one of the building's early owners. A burly guy, Sam lived and worked at the White Eagle until his death in the 1930s.

After Sam died in his room at the White Eagle, his boss had his body removed and then locked the room and left it pretty much the way it was for a long time. Is Sam still hanging around the tavern? Many believe so. Hughes recalled that after he bought the White Eagle, the door to Sam's room would not stay open. Time after time, the door was left open, only to be found shut—and locked—a couple of days later. Apparently, Sam likes his privacy.

Hughes says that he's experienced enough unexplained phenomena at the White Eagle to fill a book. For example, he used to keep a bed in the basement to use when he worked late; one night, he awoke to find himself being nudged by invisible hands. Understandably disconcerted, he got dressed and went home. While working in the basement after hours, Hughes often heard voices and footsteps above him; sometimes the voices even called his name. But every time he went to investigate, no one was there.

Suspected Spooks

The White Eagle Saloon has hosted its share of wild times and even wilder characters over the years, so it's no surprise that it's haunted. Sam is believed to be the spook that flushes the men's room toilet, and the crying woman may be the spirit of one of the many prostitutes who worked there when the building housed a brothel.

But who pushed the waitress down the cellar stairs? Some suspect that it was the ghost of a Chinese bouncer known for harshly treating the African American prostitutes who worked in the basement. One day, the guy simply disappeared. Was he murdered? If so, it might explain why his angry spirit is still attached to the White Eagle.

"Lotz" of Ghosts Gather at Carter House

Franklin, Tennessee, which is located about 20 miles south of Nashville, has a population of 64,000—unless you count its ghosts. The site of what some historians consider the bloodiest one-day battle of the Civil War, Franklin is rich with history—and restless spirits. It seems that many of the soldiers who lost their lives in that famous battle are still hanging around the city.

✳   ✳   ✳   ✳

Before the Blood

IN 1830, FOUNTAIN Branch Carter built a beautiful home in the heart of Franklin. In 1858, Johann Lotz constructed his own house across the street on land that he'd purchased from Carter. Both were blissfully unaware of what would occur there just a few years later.

After the fall of Nashville in 1862, Franklin became a Union military post. In 1864, in an attempt to "take the bull by the horns," the Confederate army decided to attack the enemy head-on in Franklin, hoping to drive General Sherman's army north. It didn't quite work out that way; instead, during the Battle of Franklin on November 30, 1864, more than 4,000 lives were lost, and because the battlefield was small, the concentration of bloodshed was very high. And most of it took place right in front of the Lotz and Carter homes.

The Battle Begins

When the Confederate troops arrived in town, Union General Jacob Cox commandeered the Carter House as his base of operations. Fearing for their lives, the Carter family took refuge in the basement during the five long hours of the battle. In all, 23 people—including the Lotz family—crowded into the cellar. They all survived, and when the fighting was over, both houses were converted into field hospitals. Surgeries, amputations, and death filled the days and weeks that followed. Between the violence and the chaos, it's no wonder that some of the dead never found peace.

One of the men who was killed during the battle was Tod Carter, Fountain's son and a Confederate soldier who was thrilled to be heading home. He was wounded just 300 feet from his front door and was taken to his sister's bedroom, where he later died. Some say that his spirit remains there today.

History Comes to Life

In 1953, the Carter House was opened to the public. Today, it's a museum and a National Historic Landmark; its eight acres stand as a tribute to the battle that took place there so long ago. If you look closely, more than a thousand bullet holes can be found on the property. The Lotz House—which was added to the National Historic Register in 1976 and opened to the public in 2008—bears its share of scars as well: Bloodstains are evident throughout, and a round indentation in the wood floor is a reminder of a cannonball that crashed through the roof and flew through a second-floor bedroom before landing in the parlor on the first floor, leaving a charred path in its wake.

In the Spirit of Things

Visitors to the Carter House have reported seeing the specter of Tod Carter sitting on a bed or standing in the hallway. His sister Annie has also been spotted in the hallways and on the stairs. She's blamed for playful pranks such as rolling a ball along the floor and causing objects to appear and disappear. But then again, the mischief-maker might be the spirit of one of the children who took refuge in the cellar during the battle. After all, staff members and visitors have reported feeling the sensation of a child tugging at their sleeves, and one worker even saw a spectral child walking down the staircase.

The ghosts of soldiers and other family members may be responsible for some of the other unusual phenomena experienced in the house, such as furniture moving on its own, doors slamming, and apparitions peering through the windows.

Not to be outdone, the ghosts at the Lotz House manifest as phantom voices and household items that move on their own or come up missing. While they haven't been identified, they seem to be civilian spirits rather than military ones.

It's tough sharing space with so many ghosts, but the staff members are used to it, and they're happy to share the history—and the spirits—with visitors who stop by on the Franklin on Foot Ghost Tour. And don't worry: These lively spirits have never followed anyone home—at least not yet!

Don't Mess with the Lady in Black

In the opening days of the Civil War—the days of unrealistic expectations, when many thought that the war would be over in a matter of weeks or months—Andrew Lanier was preparing to leave his home in Georgia to serve in the Confederate Army. But before he left, he asked his beloved girlfriend Melanie to marry him. She did, and the two spent just one night together as husband and wife. The next day, Andrew headed off to war, undoubtedly assuming that he would return home soon. Little did either of them know that they would never again see each other as a free man and woman.

✳ ✳ ✳ ✳

A FEW MONTHS LATER, Andrew was captured by Union forces and was sent to Fort Warren, a military prison on Georges Island, which is located about seven miles off the coast of Boston. As military prisons go, Fort Warren was not as bad as some others, but to Lanier it was intolerable. He deeply missed Georgia and his wife, and he shared these sentiments with her in a letter.

After Melanie read the letter, she knew that she could not stand by idly while her husband rotted away in prison. So she cut her hair short, disguised herself as a man, and made her way across Union lines to Massachusetts. Finally, during a violent storm, she managed to slip inside the prison, which was not terribly secure. Soon, Melanie was reunited with her husband.

Foiled and Spoiled

The fort's other prisoners were likely pleased to see a Southern woman in their midst. They were certainly happy that she had brought along an old pistol and a short-handled pick. The prisoners hatched a scheme to tunnel underneath the fort's arsenal; once there, they planned to grab guns and seize the fort. Then they would turn the fort's artillery on Boston.

The prisoners worked on the tunnel for the next few weeks. However, they had miscalculated the distance to the arsenal, so when they tried to break through the ground, they were caught. One by one, they came out of the tunnel—except for Melanie. She had planned to wait until all of the others had been accounted for and then pop out of the hole with her pistol and take the guards by surprise.

It was a long shot, but it might have worked. Unfortunately for the Confederate prisoners, after Melanie emerged from the hole and ordered the guards to surrender, they quickly formed a circle around her and closed in. Just as Melanie pulled the trigger on her gun, it was knocked from her hand; the wayward bullet struck her husband and killed him instantly. Melanie was captured and was sentenced to hang as a Rebel spy.

On the day of her execution, Melanie made a final request: She wanted to wear a woman's dress for the hanging instead of the men's clothing that she had been wearing for weeks. She was given an old black dress that had been used for a theatrical performance at the fort. That should have been the end ... but it was only the beginning.

Un-"fort"-unate Occurrences

A short time later, a soldier named Cassidy was patrolling the area near where Melanie had been executed. He felt two hands grab him around the neck from behind. The hands began to squeeze, trying to strangle him. Struggling for breath, Cassidy managed to twist around so that he could see his attacker: He was staring into the ghostly face of Melanie Lanier.

Clad in the black dress in which she had died, Melanie was staring sinisterly at the soldier, her face pale but her eyes ablaze with hatred and revenge. Cassidy screamed, and managed to twist out of her grip. He then ran back to the other guards, crying out in terror. But not only did his story provoke fits of laughter, it also got him locked away in the guardhouse for 30 days for deserting his post. That was just fine with Cassidy, who vowed never to patrol that area after dark again.

The "Lady in Black" has been haunting Fort Warren ever since then. In 1891, female footprints were found in the snow, even though no woman had been on the island. Then, during World War II, an army sentry encountered the ghost of Melanie Lanier near the site where she had died. He was so frightened by the incident that he went insane and spent the next two decades in a mental institution.

A few years after World War II, Captain Charles Norris was stationed alone on the island. He was reading one night when he felt someone tap him on the shoulder. He turned around, but no one was there.

Later, when the telephone began to ring, Norris answered it only to hear the male operator ask, "What number please?"

Norris explained that he was answering a call, not making one. The operator said that Norris's wife had answered the phone previously and had taken a message. All alone on the island, Norris knew that only one female could have answered the phone: The Lady in Black.

The vengeful wraith still roams Fort Warren. Sentries on duty there have been known to shoot at ill-defined forms, and once, a stone rolled all the way across a floor under its own power. It seems that Melanie Lanier is still trying to devise ways to distract the guards stationed there. After all, it was her love for her husband that brought her to the island, and even though they're both long dead, her love—like her spirit—lives on.

Remember the Alamo!

While no one knows for certain why ghosts choose particular places to haunt, one explanation suggests that many earthbound spirits are victims of tragedy. One of the greatest tragedies in American history occurred when General Santa Anna's Mexican army slaughtered nearly 200 Texans during the Battle of the Alamo. The tales of those gallant men who refused to give up the mission-turned-fortress still resonate with us today. In fact, it seems as though many of those brave souls haven't left.

✳   ✳   ✳   ✳

Standing Their Ground

B Y EARLY FEBRUARY 1836, the fledgling government of Texas was in disarray, and its army couldn't muster much in the way of reinforcements. As a result, when Colonel James Bowie, Colonel William Travis, and Davy Crockett arrived in San Antonio, they knew that little help was on the way, so their scant garrison of around 180 soldiers prepared to face a Mexican army of more than 1,800.

General Santa Anna shelled the mission for 12 days before ordering his men to charge. The brave soldiers inside the fort were hopelessly outnumbered, but they fought valiantly, killing or wounding hundreds of Mexican soldiers. The battle was over in less than 90 minutes, and only a handful of the fighting Texans survived (they were later executed), along with the women and children who Santa Anna spared from the slaughter.

Protective Phantoms

Several weeks after the fateful battle took place, Santa Anna ordered his men to raze the Alamo, thus erasing any evidence of the Texans' brave stand. The task fell to Colonel Sanchez, who rode with his men to dismantle the old church. As they set about their task, however, six phantom monks appeared from the walls of the Alamo. The monks, armed with flaming swords, made their demands clear. "Do not touch the walls of the Alamo!" the spirits shrieked. Colonel Sanchez and his men—frightened for their lives and their very souls—retreated to camp to report to General Andrade. The general was not impressed by the story, so he brought a contingent of soldiers and a cannon back to the mission to finish the job himself. No sooner had he ordered the cannon aimed at the chapel door than the monks appeared again. Armed with their flaming swords and screaming their singular demand, they startled the troops and spooked their horses. General Andrade was thrown from his mount, and when he regained control of his horse, he turned his attention back to the Alamo. It was then that a wall of fire appeared to erupt from the ground, preventing him from getting any closer to the mission. To his further horror, the thick black smoke produced by the fire quickly took the form of a large man with a ball of fire in each of his spectral hands. The general ran and never returned, but this was only the beginning of the Alamo's supernatural history.

Guarding Ghosts

In the years after the Battle of the Alamo, the fort was used as a jail. During this time, newspapers reported sightings of a sentry patrolling the roof. The guard was spotted walking east to west and back again each night; however, the authorities claimed that they'd never stationed a man there. In fact, anyone who bothered to watch the guard for more than a moment noticed that he quickly vanished. Most guards and officers refused to patrol the building at night because they kept hearing horrible moans in the darkness. It sounded as if a soldier's final moments—perhaps being stabbed to death by bayonet-wielding Mexican soldiers—were being reenacted over and over again each night. The men also reported feeling as though eyes were following them throughout the building. This ominous presence seems to stalk visitors to the Alamo to this day.

Wandering Wraiths

The spirits guarding the Alamo aren't the only specters that make themselves known at the site. Visitors often report seeing a young blond-haired boy in a window over what is now a gift shop. Every year in early March, near the anniversary of the massacre, neighbors say that a horse can be heard galloping on the pavement at dawn; perhaps it's a spectral courier who is still trying to reach Colonel Travis. Artilleryman Anthony Wolfe's young sons, who died at the hands of the Mexican army like their father, are said to go along on the daily tours of the Alamo: Many tour groups have reported seeing the two young boys following them and have noted that the boys vanish when the groups reach the chapel. Park rangers have also seen a man dressed in period clothing; when they followed him across the grounds, he faded from view when he reached the chapel.

Celebrity Specters

Not all the ghosts at the Alamo are unknown figures. One spirit that is often spotted on the grounds wears a buckskin shirt, moccasins, and a coonskin cap. Sometimes he stands at attention, a flintlock rifle at his side; other times he's leaning on a wall near the chapel, dying from his wounds. One ranger even claimed that he got close enough to determine that it was definitely Davy Crockett and that he watched as phantom soldiers in Mexican uniforms attacked the famed frontiersman. Multiple people have even reported seeing Crockett from different vantage points at the same time.

Finally, there's the case of John Wayne, who became obsessed with the old mission while he was directing his epic western *The Alamo* (1960) on location. Since his death in 1979, "The

Duke" has been spotted at the Alamo on more than one occasion. He usually just wanders the grounds, but occasionally he is seen conversing with the other restless spirits. If John Wayne did indeed choose to haunt the Alamo, he certainly has plenty of company.

When the Gray Man Speaks, You Better Listen

One of the oldest summer resorts on the East Coast, Pawleys Island is a small barrier island located along the coast of South Carolina. Only a handful of people live there year-round, and one of the perennial residents is the Gray Man. Many say that this restless spirit has no face. However, that seems to be a minor inconvenience; after all, when it comes to warning the living of impending doom, a pretty face—or any face at all—is hardly necessary.

✳ ✳ ✳ ✳

Apparition Identity Crisis

ACCORDING TO LEGEND, before every major hurricane that has hit Pawleys Island since the early 1820s—including Hurricane Hugo in 1989—the Gray Man has appeared to certain folks on the island to warn them to leave before the approaching storm strikes. When they return after the storm, the people who encountered the Gray Man find their homes undamaged, while other buildings nearby have been destroyed.

The identity of the Gray Man is unknown, but there are several candidates. One theory suggests that it's Percival Pawley, the island's first owner and its namesake; others believe that the helpful spirit is Plowden Charles Jennett Weston, a man whose former home is now the island's Pelican Inn.

But the more romantic legends say that the Gray Man is the ghost of a young man who died for love. Stories about how he perished vary: One tale says that on his way to see his beloved, he fell into a bed of quicksand and died. Soon after, while the object of this deceased man's affection was walking along the beach, a figure in gray approached her and told her to leave the island. She did, and that night a hurricane slammed into the area, destroying just about every home—except hers. She believed she had been saved by the spirit of her beloved.

Another story concerns a woman who married a man after she thought that her beloved had died at sea. Later, when she met a man who had survived a shipwreck off Pawleys Island, she realized that he was her lost love, waterlogged but still very much alive. However, he didn't take the news of her marriage too well; he slinked away and died shortly thereafter. But according to legend, ever since then, he's been warning folks to flee when they're in danger from an upcoming storm.

The Ghostly Lifesaver

No matter who this ghost was in life, he has supposedly appeared before hurricanes in 1822, 1893, 1916, 1954, 1955, and 1989. And for decades, local fishermen have told stories of the Gray Man appearing to them hours before a sudden storm roiled up that would have put their lives in jeopardy.

The Gray Man is credited with saving many lives before the advent of contemporary forecasting techniques. In 1954, a couple was spending their honeymoon on the island when they heard a knock on their door at around 5 AM. When the husband opened the door, he saw a figure in gray whose clothes reeked of salty brine and whose features were obscured by a gray hat. The man in gray said that the Red Cross had sent him to warn people to evacuate because a huge storm was heading for the island. Before the honeymooning husband could question him further, the man in gray vanished. Realizing that this was no ordinary Red Cross worker, the man and his new bride left the island immediately.

Later that evening, ferocious Hurricane Hazel struck the island with the deadly force of a Category 4 storm, with winds gusting as high as 150 miles per hour. In her wake, Hazel left thousands of homes destroyed and 95 people dead. The newlywed couple, however, had been spared by the Gray Man's grace.

A Ghost Who Keeps on Giving

The Gray Man apparently doesn't care much for modern technology—he was still on the job as recently as 1989. That year, just before Hurricane Hugo hit, a couple walking along the beach spotted the Gray Man. Although the phantom vanished before the couple could speak to him, his reputation preceded him, and the couple fled the island. When they returned, their home was the only one in the area that had not been devastated by the storm. This incident got the Gray Man a moment in the national spotlight: He was featured on an episode of *Unsolved Mysteries* in 1990.

The Grey Lady of Evansville, Indiana

The Willard Library in Evansville, Indiana, has a long history of supernatural activity. But while multiple ghosts typically inhabit many haunted buildings, only one spirit seems to peruse the stacks at this old Victorian library—an entity known as "the Lady in Grey."

✳ ✳ ✳ ✳

Not Shy at All

ACCORDING TO LOCAL reports, the Lady in Grey has been haunting the Willard Library since at least the 1930s. The first known encounter with her occurred in 1937, when a janitor ran into the lonely ghost in the library's cellar. There, he saw a mysterious woman dressed all in gray. A veil was draped from her face to her shoes, and she glowed ethereally in the darkness.

That may have been the first confirmed encounter with the Grey Lady, but it certainly wasn't the last. In fact, according to library employees and patrons, this spirit seems to go out of its way to make its presence known.

On one occasion, the members of a local genealogy group noticed the distinct scent of perfume in the library's research room. None of the group members was wearing perfume at the time, and no one else had entered the room while they were there.

Margaret Maier, who worked at the library for more than four decades, also smelled the Grey Lady's musky perfume at her own home. Maier speculated that the spirit briefly followed her home while the children's room of the library was undergoing renovations. In addition to the scent of perfume, Maier and her sister reported feeling an unseen presence in their midst, as well as an inexplicable chill at Maier's home.

Spooky Shenanigans

She clearly means no harm, but the Lady in Grey isn't above playing pranks on library staffers. One night, Bettye Elaine Miller, who was head librarian from 1972 to 1975, was working late when she heard water running on the second floor. She rushed upstairs to find that a bathroom faucet had been mysteriously turned on. Later, another librarian using the same bathroom watched in horror as a faucet turned on by itself.

Over the years, reports of paranormal activity at the Willard Library have become so commonplace that, with the library's permission, the *Evansville Courier & Press* installed three internet-connected "ghost cams" in the building so that curious ghost hunters can try to catch a glimpse of the Grey Lady. The cameras have proven quite popular with fans of the paranormal, logging hundreds of thousands of hits since they first went online.

A Ghost Revealed

Of course, everyone wants to know the identity of the mysterious Grey Lady. Local historians believe that she is the ghost of Louise Carpenter, the daughter of Willard Carpenter, who funded the construction of the library and for whom it was named. According to reports, Louise was greatly displeased with the fact that when her father died, he left a great deal of his money for the construction of a public library. She even tried to sue the library's board of trustees, claiming that her father was "of unsound mind and...unduly influenced in establishing the library."

Louise's lawsuit was unsuccessful, and she was unable to stop the library's construction. A theory among many ghost hunters suggests that, upon her death in 1908, Louise's spirit came to reside within the library and will stay there until the property is returned to the Carpenter family, which is quite unlikely.

Libraries are popular haunts for ghosts, but few have logged as many reputable sightings and paranormal occurrences as the Willard Library. It very well may be the most haunted library in the United States, thanks to a gray-clad spirit that still holds a grudge, even from beyond the grave.

Werewolves in Wisconsin?

Do you believe in werewolves? If you head out to southeastern Wisconsin, you might just meet one face-to-fang.

✳ ✳ ✳ ✳

Meeting the Beast

THE FIRST RECORDED sighting of the Beast came in 1936, long before it even had a name. Security guard Mark Schackelman was walking the grounds of a convent near Jefferson shortly before midnight when he saw a strange creature digging on top of a Native American burial mound. As Schackelman got closer, the creature ran off into the darkness.

The scene repeated itself the following night, but this time, the creature stood up on its hind legs, growled at the shocked security guard, and simply walked away.

Encounters like this have continued through the years. Most people describe the creature as six to eight feet tall. It gets around on all fours but can also walk on two feet. Its entire body is covered with fur (similar to Bigfoot), but this Beast also has clawed hands, the head of a wolf, and bright yellow eyes. With a description like that, it's easy to see why some people believe that the creature is a werewolf. But several people have seen the Beast in broad daylight.

The Beast Gets a Name

In the early 1990s, an outbreak of Beast sightings in southeastern Wisconsin—specifically, along an isolated stretch of Bray Road, just outside the town of Elkhorn—led a local reporter to dub the creature "The Beast of Bray Road."

Today, the Beast continues to linger around southeastern Wisconsin, but it's seldom seen on Bray Road anymore. It was, however, spotted in Madison in 2004. So if you're ever driving through the area, keep an eye out for what might be lurking around the bend.

The Sisters at Kemper Hall

Kemper Hall—which is situated on the shore of Lake Michigan in Kenosha, Wisconsin—is one of the Dairy State's oldest buildings. The structure originally served as the home of Wisconsin's first congressman, Charles Durkee. When he became governor of the Utah Territory in 1865, Durkee donated the estate to the Kenosha Female Seminary. In 1878, the Sisters of Saint Mary took over the property, renamed it Kemper Hall, and turned it into a preparatory school for girls—and that's when many of its ghostly stories began.

✳ ✳ ✳ ✳

The Spectral Sister Superior

PERHAPS THE MOST famous of the ghost stories involving Kemper Hall revolves around Sister Margaret Clare, the school's first Sister Superior and the embodiment of the stereotypical stern parochial-school nun. Sister Margaret Clare was well liked in her order, but students knew her for her demanding nature and unrelenting temper. One legend says that the nun met her end when an angry student pushed her down the spiral staircase that led to the school's observatory; other rumors suggest that she fell down the stairs after tripping on her own habit. Not surprisingly, the observatory and staircase still attract visitors. Many who have peered down the stairwell at night claim that they have glimpsed her shattered body staring back at them from the bottom. The problem with these tales is that Sister Margaret Clare actually died of natural causes in 1921. Still, the reports of the fallen nun persist; perhaps it's a different nun.

A Mysterious Disappearance

Sister Margaret Clare may have gone to her grave harboring a sinister secret about the mysterious disappearance of another nun: Sister Augusta. In 1899, Sister Augusta arrived at Kemper Hall for an annual retreat; but shortly thereafter—on January 2, 1900—she vanished without a trace. Some said that she'd been driven to the edge of madness by the amount of work she'd been given and was granted a time-off request. But her disappearance seemed suspect to authorities, who undertook a search that stretched all the way back to Sister Augusta's hometown of St. Louis, Missouri. Then, on January 5, Kemper Hall sent word to the nun's family and the authorities that Sister Augusta had been found, safe and sound, in Springfield, Missouri. However, the school failed to offer an explanation for why she had left behind her handbag, her crucifix, and her insignia of the holy Sisterhood. Just three days later, Sister Augusta's body washed up on the shore of Lake Michigan. Her death was ruled a suicide, and to this day, locals still report seeing a spectral nun in tears walking along the beach. Many maintenance workers have also reported hearing a woman sobbing in Kemper Hall late at night, but when they investigate, they find no one. Sister Augusta may well be the crying nun that so many hear, but she does not cry alone.

Picture of the Paranormal

Kemper Center, Inc., has not allowed paranormal investigators to access Kemper Hall since it took control of the building shortly after the school closed in 1975. But much of the property is now a public park, and on several occasions, nighttime visitors have seen a nun—perhaps Sister Augusta or Sister Margaret Clare—peering at them from the windows of the former school. People visiting Kemper Hall for wedding receptions have also reported hearing crying and footsteps in hallways that are clearly unoccupied by the living.

In 1997, a television crew from WTMJ in Milwaukee filmed a story at the original Durkee Mansion. The shoot went off without issue, but when the crew was editing the footage, they found that the picture turned to static every time a portrait of Charles Durkee entered the frame. It seems that the Sisters of Kemper Hall have maintained an ethereal presence in the building.

The Most Haunted House in Dixie?

Located near Vicksburg, Mississippi, the McRaven House was haunted even before it became a Civil War hospital.

✳ ✳ ✳ ✳

THE OLDEST PARTS of the estate known as McRaven House were built in 1797. Over the next 40 years, its owners gradually added to the property until it became a classic southern mansion, standing proudly among the magnolia blossoms and dogwood trees of the Old South.

And like nearly all such mansions, it has its share of resident ghosts. Today, McRaven House is often referred to as "the most haunted house in Mississippi." Some researchers believe that environmental conditions on the property make it particularly susceptible to hauntings: Ghosts that may not be noticeable in drier, less humid climates seem to be more perceptible in the dews of the delta. Of course, it helps that the McRaven House has seen more than its share of tragedy and death during its 200-year history.

The Ghost of Poor Mary

In the early 1860s, the house's supernatural activity seemed to center on an upstairs bedroom in which Mary Elizabeth Howard had died during childbirth in 1836 at age 15. Mary's brown-haired apparition is still seen descending the mansion's grand staircase. Her ghost is blamed for the poltergeist activity—such as pictures falling from the wall—that is often reported in the bedroom where she died. And her wedding shawl, which is occasionally put on display for tourists, is said to emit heat.

Ghosts of the Civil War

Mary Elizabeth's ghost alone would qualify McRaven House as a notably haunted reminder of Mississippi's antebellum past, but she is far from the only spirit residing there, thanks in part to the bloody atrocities of the Civil War.

The Siege of Vicksburg, which took place in 1863, was one of the longest, bloodiest battles of the entire conflict. When General Ulysses S. Grant and his Union forces crossed the Tennessee River into Mississippi, Confederate forces retreated into Vicksburg, which was so well guarded that it was known as a "fortress city." But as more and more Union forces gathered in the forests and swamps around Vicksburg, Confederate General John C. Pemberton was advised to evacuate. Fearing the wrath of the local population if he abandoned them, Pemberton refused.

By the time the siege began in earnest, the Confederate troops were greatly outnumbered. Rebel forces surrendered the city of Vicksburg on July 4, 1863, after more than a month of fighting. Nearly all of the Confederate soldiers involved in the battle—around 33,000 in all—were captured, wounded, or killed. The Union victory put the entire Mississippi River in northern hands, and combined with the victory at Gettysburg that same week, it marked the beginning of the end for the Confederacy.

Captain McPherson's Last Report

In the middle of the action stood McRaven House. In the early days of the siege, it served as a Confederate hospital, and, at that time, it was full of the screams of anguished and dying men. Cannons from both armies shot at the mansion, destroying large portions of it.

Later, after Union forces captured the house, it served as the headquarters for General Grant and the Union army. One of the officers put in charge of the house was Captain McPherson, a Vicksburg native who had fled to the North to fight for the Union. Sometime during the siege, he disappeared. Soon after, according to legend, McPherson's commanding officer awoke to find the captain in his room. He was furious at the intrusion until he noticed McPherson's mangled, bloody face and torn uniform. The commanding officer then realized that this was not McPherson himself—it was his ghost, which had returned to deliver the message that Rebels, who couldn't forgive him for abandoning the South, had murdered him. McPherson's ghost reputedly still wanders the grounds dressed in Union blue with blood oozing from a bullet wound in his forehead.

Other Civil War Ghosts

Nearly a year after the siege ended, John Bobb—the owner of McRaven House at the time—spotted six Union soldiers picking flowers in his garden. Outraged by the trespassers, Bobb threw a brick at them and hit one of the Yankees in the head. After going to the local field commander to report the intruders, Bobb returned home to find 25 Union soldiers waiting for him; they marched him into the nearby bayou and shot him to death.His ghost has been seen roaming the property ever since.

The War Ended, But the Ghosts Kept Coming

Mary Elizabeth and the Civil War-era ghosts aren't the only spirits that haunt McRaven House. In 1882, William Murray purchased the home, and over the next 78 years, five members of his family died on the premises. The most recent death there was that of his daughter Ella, who spent her last years as a recluse in the house, where she reportedly burned furniture to stay warm. After her death in 1960, the mansion was restored, refurbished, and opened for tours and battle reenactments. In the early morning hours, tour groups and staffers have often spotted the ghosts of Ella and the other Murrays who died in the house.

Ghost hunters have been conducting investigations at the house since at least the 1980s, and they've frequently photographed mysterious forms outside the building, often around the portion of the property that served as a burial ground for soldiers; some are simply odd blobs of light, but others appear to be human-shaped forms.Few argue with the claim that McRaven House is "the most haunted house in Mississippi." In fact, some even call it "the most haunted house in Dixie."

The Worried Husband

"You never pay any attention to me!" is a common lament heard in marriages when a person feels neglected by his or her partner. But what about the opposite situation—when a person's concern for his or her spouse extends beyond the grave?

❋   ❋   ❋   ❋

IN THE LATE 1940s, Elaine and her husband lived in an apartment in Oskaloosa, Iowa. They shared the floor with a single woman named Patricia, whose husband had died in an industrial accident. The devastated young woman had moved there to try to regroup.

One evening while her husband was working, Elaine decided to take a bath. Just as she was about to turn on the bathroom light, she smelled pipe smoke and then saw a young man with black hair and a horseshoe-shaped scar on his cheek; he was holding a pipe. After a moment, Elaine realized that the man was not really looking at her, he was sort of looking through her. She then deduced that the man was a ghost. Elaine watched as he began to move through her apartment. She followed him as he glided down the hall toward Patricia's apartment. When he got to Patricia's door, he vanished.

Uncertain of what she was doing, Elaine turned the doorknob to Patricia's apartment; it was unlocked, so Elaine went inside. There, she found Patricia lying on her bed, barely alive: She had slashed her wrists, and her lifeblood was quickly draining away. Elaine bandaged Patricia as best she could and called her husband. He raced home with a doctor, who treated Patricia's injuries.

The next day, Patricia thanked Elaine for saving her life. She said that she had been deeply saddened by her husband's death and had turned to the bottle as a result. Overcome by grief, the idea of joining her husband seemed appealing to her, so she had slit her wrists. If it had not been for Elaine, her plan would have succeeded.

Elaine said nothing about why she had entered Patricia's apartment in the first place. But when Patricia showed Elaine a picture of her late husband, everything suddenly made sense: The man in the photo was the same man who Elaine had seen in her apartment.

Chapter 3

How Did This Happen?

Strange Catastrophes

Life is full of surprises, some less pleasant than others. From beer floods to raining frogs to exploding whales, headlines continually prove that truth is sometimes stranger than fiction.

✳ ✳ ✳ ✳

The London Beer Flood

IN 1814, A vat of beer erupted in a London brewery. Within minutes, the explosion had split open several other vats, and more than 320,000 gallons of beer flooded the streets of a nearby slum. People rushed to save as much of the beer as they could, collecting it in pots, cans, and cups. Others scooped the beer up in their hands and drank it as quickly as they could. Nine people died in the flood—eight from drowning and one from alcohol poisoning.

The Great Siberian Explosion

Around 7:00 AM on June 30, 1908, 60 million trees in remote Siberia were flattened by a mysterious 15-megaton explosion. The huge blast, which occurred about five miles above the surface of the earth, traveled around the world twice and triggered a strong, four-hour magnetic storm. Magnetic storms occur about once every hundred years, and can create radiation similar to a nuclear explosion. These storms start in space and are typically accompanied by solar flares.

The 1908 explosion may have started with a comet of ice, which melted and exploded as it entered Earth's atmosphere. Or, it may have been an unusual airburst from an asteroid. Others believe that the source was a nuclear-powered spacecraft from another planet. However, no physical evidence of the cause has ever been found.

The Boston Molasses Disaster

On an unusually warm January day in 1919, a molasses tank burst near downtown Boston, sending more than two million gallons of the sticky sweetener flowing through the city's North End at an estimated 35 miles per hour. The force of the molasses wave was so intense that it lifted a train off its tracks and crushed several buildings in its path. When the flood finally came to a halt, molasses was two to three feet deep in the streets, 21 people and several horses had died, and more than 150 people were injured. Nearly 90 years later, people in Boston can still smell molasses during sultry summer days.

It's Raining...Frogs

On September 7, 1953, clouds formed over Leicester, Massachusetts—a peaceful little town near the middle of the state. Within a few hours, a downpour began, but it wasn't rain falling from the sky—thousands of frogs and toads dropped out of the air. Children collected them in buckets as if it was a game. Town officials insisted that the creatures had simply escaped from a nearby pond, but many of them landed on roofs and in gutters, which seemed to dispute this theory. It is still unclear why the frogs appeared in Leicester or why the same thing happened almost 20 years later in Brignoles, France.

Oregon's Exploding Whale

When an eight-ton sperm whale beaches itself in your town, what do you do? That's a question residents of Florence, Oregon, faced in November 1970. After consulting with the U.S. Navy, town officials decided to blow up the carcass with a half ton of dynamite. Spectators and news crews gathered to watch but were horrified when they were engulfed in a sandy, reddish mist and slapped by flying pieces of whale blubber. A quarter mile away, a car was crushed when a gigantic chunk of whale flesh landed on it. No one was seriously hurt in the incident, but when the air cleared, most of the whale was still on the beach. The highway department hauled the rest of it away.

Back From the Dead

Nothing is certain but death and taxes…yet sometimes that's not so true. History is riddled with strange tales of people who just weren't content staying dead.

✳ ✳ ✳ ✳

✳ After a major automobile accident in 2007, Venezuelan Carlos Camejo was declared dead. The coroner had just begun the autopsy by cutting into Camejo's face when the man began to bleed. Immediately realizing that the crash victim was still alive, the doctor became even more stunned when Camejo regained consciousness as he was stitching up the incision. "I woke up because the pain was unbearable," Camejo told reporters after his ordeal.

✳ Ann Greene, a young servant in Oxford, England, was convicted of killing her illegitimate newborn child after the baby was stillborn in 1650. After she was hanged, Greene's body was cut down and transported to Oxford University where it was to be used for anatomy classes. As the lesson progressed, Greene began to moan and regained consciousness. The students helped revive her and treated her injuries. Eventually she was given a pardon, gained a level of celebrity, married, and had several children.

✳ In 1674, Marjorie Erskine died in Chirnside, Scotland, and was buried in a shallow grave by a sexton with less than honorable intentions. Erskine was sent to her eternal rest with some valuable jewelry the sexton was intent on adding to his own collection. After digging up her body, the sexton was trying to cut off her finger to steal her ring when, much to his surprise, she awoke.

* After being found unconscious and sprawled on the floor of her Albany, New York, apartment by paramedics in 1996, Mildred Clarke, 86, was pronounced dead by a coroner. About 90 minutes later an attendant noticed that the body bag containing Clarke was, in fact, moving. Clarke recovered but unfortunately only lived for another week, giving into the stress of age and heart failure.

* When 19th-century Cardinal Somaglia took ill and passed out, he was thought to be dead. Because he was a high-ranking church official, embalming was begun immediately so he could lie in state, as was customary. As a surgeon began the process by cutting into the cardinal's chest, he noticed that the man's heart was still beating. Somaglia awoke and pushed the knife away. However, the damage was done, and he died from the embalming process.

* Oran was a devout sixth-century monk on Iona, a small island off the coast of Scotland. According to legend, he was buried alive by his own urging to sanctify the island but was dug up three days later and found alive. He told his fellow monks that he had seen heaven and hell and a host of other sights. "There is no such great wonder in death, nor is hell what it has been described," he claimed as he was pulled from the ground. The head monk, Columba, ordered that he be reburied immediately as a heretic. To this day, when someone in the region broaches an uncomfortable subject, people will tell the person to "throw mud in the mouth of St. Oran."

* In 1740, 16-year-old William Duell was convicted of rape and murder and sentenced to death by hanging. After his lifeless body was removed from the gallows it was taken to the local college for dissection. His body was stripped and

laid out in preparation for the process when a servant who was washing the corpse noticed it was still breathing. After a full recovery, he was returned to prison, but it was decided that instead of being hanged again he would be exiled to the then-prison state of Australia.

* A victim of the horrors of war, three-year-old Lebanese Hussein Belhas had his leg blown off in an Israeli attack in 1996. Declared dead, the boy's body was placed in a morgue freezer, but when attendants returned he was found alive. After he recovered from his injuries, Belhas took a stoic stance on his fate. "I am the boy who died, and then came back to life. This was my destiny," he said.

* In late 1995, Daphne Banks of Cambridgeshire, England, was declared dead. On New Year's Day, 1996, as she lay in the mortuary, an undertaker noticed a vein twitching in her leg. Examining closer, the attendant could hear snoring coming from the body. The 61-year-old Banks was quickly transferred to a local hospital where she made a full recovery.

* As mourners sadly paid their last respects to the Greek Orthodox bishop Nicephorus Glycas on the island of Lesbos in 1896, they were met with quite a shock. Glycas had been lying in state for two days as preparations for his burial were being made. Suddenly, he sat up and looked around at the stunned congregation. "What are you staring at?" he reportedly asked.

* During the 16th century, a young man named Matthew Wall died in the village of Braughing, England. As pallbearers were carrying him to his final resting place, they dropped his coffin after one of them stumbled on a stone. When the coffin crashed to the ground, Wall was revived and went on to live a full life. When he actually did pass away years later, the terms of his will stipulated that Old Man's Day be celebrated in the village every October 2, the anniversary of his return from the dead.

The Devil Is Alive and Well…
And Living in New Jersey

The Pine Barrens consist of more than a million acres of forested land in central and southern New Jersey. So named because the area's sandy, acidic soil is bad for growing crops, it has proven a fertile home for an amazing collection of trees and plants. Of course, if the stories are true, the area is also home to a bizarre winged creature known as the Jersey Devil.

✳ ✳ ✳ ✳

Birth of the Devil

THERE ARE MANY legends concerning the origin of the Jersey Devil. The most popular involves the Leeds family, who came to America from Europe in the 1730s and settled in the southern area of the Pine Barrens. The Leeds family quickly grew by leaps and bounds, and before long, their house was filled with a dozen children. Needless to say, when Mother Leeds found out she was pregnant with child number 13, she was less than enthusiastic. In fact, she supposedly yelled out that she was done having children and that this child "could be the devil" for all she cared. Apparently someone was listening, for when the 13th child was born, it allegedly resembled a devil, complete with wings, a tail, and cloven hooves. Once born, the child devoured its 12 siblings and its parents, then promptly disappeared into the Pine Barrens, where it still lives to this day.

The First Sightings

One of the first, and most intriguing, sightings of the Jersey Devil took place in the early 1800s when Commodore Stephen Decatur saw a bizarre creature flying overhead as he was test-firing cannons at the Hanover Iron Works. Perhaps wishing to test the accuracy of the cannons, Decatur took aim and fired upon the creature overhead, striking one of its wings. To the amazement of Decatur and the other onlookers, the creature didn't seem to care that it had just been shot by a cannonball and casually flew away.

From the mid-1800s until the early 1900s, there were numerous sightings of the Jersey Devil throughout the Pine Barrens and beyond. Those who actually witnessed it described it as being everything from short and hairy to tall and cranelike. But there was one thing everyone agreed upon—whatever the creature was, it was not of this earth.

1909: The Year of the Devil

At the beginning of 1909, thousands of people encountered the beast in the span of a week. On Saturday, January 16, a winged creature believed to be the Jersey Devil was spotted flying over the town of Woodbury, New Jersey. The following day, residents of Bristol, Pennsylvania, also reported seeing something strange flying in the sky. Later the same day, bizarre tracks were discovered in the snow. Then on Monday, January 18, residents of Burlington, New Jersey, and neighboring towns were perplexed by the strange tracks in the snow on their rooftops. They had no clue as to who or what left them. All the while, reports kept coming in of something strange flying overhead with a head resembling a horse and hooves for feet.

In the early morning hours of January 19, Nelson Evans and his wife got up close and personal with the Jersey Devil outside their Gloucester, New Jersey, home. At approximately 2:30 AM, a creature standing more than eight feet tall with a "head like a collie dog and a face like a horse" peered into the Evanses' window. Although they were petrified, Nelson mustered up the courage to open the window and yell at the creature. Startled, the creature turned, made a barking sound, and then flew off. Later that day, two Gloucester hunters claimed they had tracked strange footprints in the snow for nearly 20 miles. They noticed that whatever this creature was, it not only had the ability to fly or leap over large areas, but it could also squeeze underneath fences and through small spaces.

By Wednesday, January 20, local towns were forming posses intent on tracking down the Jersey Devil. They were all unsuccessful, although they did have several sightings of the winged creature flying toward neighboring towns. Then on Thursday, things really got out of hand. The day began with the Devil reportedly attacking a trolley car in Haddon Heights. It was also during this time that local farmers reported finding some of their livestock missing or dead. And in Camden, New Jersey, a dog was attacked by the Jersey Devil and only managed to survive when its owner chased the beast away.

By Friday, the Devil had been spotted all over New Jersey and in parts of Pennsylvania. During that time, the creature had been shot at (and was supposedly struck by several bullets) and was even hosed down by a local fire department, but this didn't seem to phase the beast at all.

Sightings Continue

As news of the Jersey Devil spread, it seemed that the entire nation descended upon New Jersey in an attempt to catch a glimpse of or, better yet, capture, the creature. But despite all the searching and even a $10,000 reward for the beast's capture, it was never caught.

It appears that after its very busy week in 1909, the Jersey Devil decided to lay low. In fact, though sightings did continue through the years, they were few and far between. Because of this, people started to believe that the Jersey Devil was a harbinger of doom and would only be sighted when something bad was going to happen. Of course, this did not stop hundreds of people from wandering through the Pine Barrens in search of the beast. But no matter how hard people looked, not a single photograph or piece of video exists of the creature. Part of the reason certainly has to be that the Pine Barrens has remained virtually the same vast and undeveloped area, making it the perfect place for a devil to hide. So for now, the Pine Barrens is keeping its secret.

The Kuano River Boy

Around the world, feral (or wild) children have reportedly been raised by wolves, monkeys, and even ostriches, but a boy seen splashing about the banks of a river in northern India in the 1970s was rumored to have been raised by fish or lizards.

✳ ✳ ✳ ✳

From the Black Lagoon

THE BOY, ABOUT 15 years old when first discovered in 1973 by residents of the small town of Baragdava, had blackish-green skin and no hair. His head appeared malformed in a strange bullet shape, and he was entirely naked. "Lizard people" complete with green scales have been reported from time to time around the world, but this boy lacked scales, gills, or even webbed toes. He lived amid the crocodiles in the Kuano River without fear of attack and was able to hold his breath and stay underwater longer than thought humanly possible. But strangest of all, hundreds of people, including police and reporters, saw him run across the surface of the water. This may have been explained by the slightly submerged dam surface. A person dashing across it might have appeared to be running on water to observers at a distance. Either way, there was no question that the boy was strangely at home in the river habitat.

Son of a Water Spirit

Although his initial appearance was a shock, a village woman named Somni, who found the boy lying in a field one day, noticed a birthmark on his back that was identical to that of the infant son she had lost in the swirling river several years earlier. Somni even had an explanation for why her son, whom she'd named Ramchandra, ended up as a "merman." Somni claimed that she had been raped and impregnated by a giant water spirit during a rainstorm. Villagers accepted Somni's story; however, her husband displayed the same bullet-shape skull as the River Boy.

The Amphibious Life

Although Ramchandra, if that was indeed his true identity, preferred to remain in the river most of the time, he did seem curious about the human villagers living nearby and would sometimes approach them. Several times he was captured and brought to the village by force. He enjoyed eating vegetables left for him along the riverbank, although his main sustenance came from raw fish and frogs that he gulped from the river without using his hands.

Not Easy Being Green

For nine years, the River Boy interacted with the villagers of Baragdava, but eventually he came to a terrible end. In 1982, after two policemen tried to catch him, he made an escape from what had been his home village and swam to another river town about 12 miles away. There he approached a woman tending a small tea shop. The woman was so frightened by his naked, greenish appearance that she doused him with a pan of boiling water. Ramchandra ran back to the river where he died from severe burns. His body was eventually retrieved floating on the water. The Kuano River Boy's age at the time of his tragic death was estimated at 24.

The River Boy's green-tinted skin was never definitively explained, although it was presumed to have been from long-time contact with the river water and perhaps algae. But strangely, there are records of other green children of unknown origin. In 1887, some field workers observed a boy and a girl as they timidly emerged from a cave in Banjos, Spain. The skin of both children was bright green, and they wore clothing made from an unrecognizable fabric. They spoke a language no one understood, but when the girl learned some Spanish, she told the villagers that a whirlwind had brought them to the cave from another land where the sun was never seen. Both children perished young—the boy after some days and the girl after about five years—but their skin turned a paler and paler green the longer they were out of the cave.

The Black Dahlia Murder Mystery

One of the most baffling murder mysteries in U.S. history began innocently enough on the morning of January 15, 1947. Betty Bersinger was walking with her young daughter in the Leimert Park area of Los Angeles, when she spotted something lying in a vacant lot that caused her blood to run cold. She ran to a nearby house and called the police. Officers Wayne Fitzgerald and Frank Perkins arrived on the scene shortly after 11:00 AM.

✳   ✳   ✳   ✳

A Grisly Discovery

LYING ONLY SEVERAL feet from the road, in plain sight, was the naked body of a young woman. Her body had numerous cuts and abrasions, including a knife wound from ear to ear that resembled a ghoulish grin. Even more horrific was that her body had been completely severed at the midsection, and the two halves had been placed as if they were part of some morbid display. That's what disturbed officers the most: The killer appeared to have carefully posed the victim close to the street because he wanted people to find his grotesque handiwork.

Something else that troubled the officers was that even though the body had been brutally violated and desecrated, there was very little blood found at the scene. The only blood evidence recovered was a possible bloody footprint and an empty cement package with a spot of blood on it. In fact, the body was so clean that it appeared to have just been washed. Shortly before removing the body, officers scoured the area for a possible murder weapon, but none was recovered. A coroner later determined that the cause of death was from hemorrhage and shock due to a concussion of the brain and lacerations of the face, probably from a very large knife.

Positive Identification

After a brief investigation, police were able to identify the deceased as Elizabeth Short, who was born in Hyde Park,

Massachusetts, on July 29, 1924. At age 19, Short had moved to California to live with her father, but she moved out and spent the next few years moving back and forth between California, Florida, and Massachusetts. In July 1946, Short returned to California to see Lt. Gordon Fickling, a former boyfriend, who was stationed in Long Beach. For the last six months of her life, Short lived in an assortment of hotels, rooming houses, and private homes. She was last seen a week before her body was found, which made police very interested in finding out where and with whom she spent her final days.

The Black Dahlia Is Born

As police continued their investigation, reporters jumped all over the story and began referring to the unknown killer by names such as "sex-crazed maniac" and even "werewolf." Short herself was also given a nickname: the Black Dahlia. Reporters said it was a name friends had called her as a play on the movie *The Blue Dahlia*, which had recently been released. However, others contend Short was never called the Black Dahlia while she was alive; it was just something reporters made up for a better story. Either way, it wasn't long before newspapers around the globe were splashing front-page headlines about the horrific murder of the Black Dahlia.

The Killer Is Still Out There

As time wore on, hundreds of police officers were assigned to the Black Dahlia investigation. They combed the streets, interviewing people and following leads. Although police interviewed thousands of potential suspects—and dozens even confessed to the murder—to this day, no one has ever officially been charged with the crime. More than 70 years and several books and movies after the crime, the Elizabeth Short murder case is still listed as "open." We are no closer to knowing who killed Short or why than when her body was first discovered.

There is one bright note to this story. In February 1947, perhaps as a result of the Black Dahlia case, the state of

California became the first state to pass a law requiring all convicted sex offenders to register themselves.

Lingering Spirits of the *Eastland* Disaster

The city of Chicago has a dark history of disaster and death, with devastating fires, horrific accidents, and catastrophic events. One of the most tragic took place on July 24, 1915. On that overcast, summer afternoon, hundreds of people died in the Chicago River when the Eastland capsized just a few feet from the dock. This calamity left a ghostly impression on the Windy City that is still felt today.

✳ ✳ ✳ ✳

Company Picnic Turns Tragic

JULY 24 WAS GOING to be a special day for thousands of Chicagoans. It was reserved for the annual summer picnic for employees of the Western Electric Company, which was to be held across Lake Michigan in Michigan City, Indiana. And although officials at the utility company had encouraged workers to bring along friends and relatives, they were surprised when more than 7,000 people arrived to be ferried across the lake on the five excursion boats chartered for the day. Three of the steamers—the *Theodore Roosevelt*, the *Petoskey*, and the *Eastland*—were docked on the Chicago River near Clark Street.

On this fateful morning, the *Eastland*, a steamer owned by the St. Joseph–Chicago Steamship Company, was filled to its limit. The boat had a reputation for top-heaviness and instability, and the new federal Seaman's Act, which was passed in 1915 as a result of the *Titanic* tragedy, required more lifeboats than previous regulations did. All of this resulted in the ship being even more unstable than it already was. It was a recipe for disaster.

Death and the *Eastland*

As passengers boarded the *Eastland*, she began listing back and forth. This had happened on the ship before, so the crew emptied the ballast compartments to provide more stability. As the boat was preparing to depart, some passengers went below deck, hoping to warm up on the cool, cloudy morning, but many on the overcrowded steamer jammed their way onto the deck to wave to onlookers on shore. The *Eastland* tilted once again, but this time more severely, and passengers began to panic. Moments later, the *Eastland* rolled to her side, coming to rest at the bottom of the river, only 18 feet below the surface. One side of the boat's hull was actually above the water's surface in some spots.

Passengers on deck were tossed into the river, splashing about in a mass of bodies. The overturned ship created a current that pulled some of the floundering swimmers to their doom, while many of the women's long dresses were snagged on the ship, tugging them down to the bottom.

Those inside were thrown to one side of the ship when it capsized. Heavy furniture onboard crushed some passengers and those who were not killed instantly drowned a few moments later when water rushed inside. A few managed to escape, but most of them didn't. Their bodies were later found trapped in a tangled heap on the lowest side of the *Eastland*.

Firefighters, rescue workers, and volunteers soon arrived and tried to help people escape through portholes. They also cut holes in the portion of the ship's hull that was above the water line. Approximately 1,660 passengers survived the disaster, but they still ended up in the river, and many courageous people from the wharf jumped in or threw life preservers as well as lines, boxes, and anything that floated into the water to the panicked and drowning passengers. In the end, 844 people died, many of them young women and children. Officially, no clear explanation was given for why the vessel capsized, and the St. Joseph–Chicago Steamship Company was not held accountable for the disaster.

The bodies of those who perished in the tragedy were wrapped in sheets and placed on the *Theodore Roosevelt* or lined up along the docks. Marshall Field's and other large stores sent wagons to carry the dead to hospitals, funeral homes, and makeshift morgues, such as the Second Regiment Armory, where more than 200 bodies were sent.

After the ship was removed from the river, it was sold and later became a U.S. warship as the gunboat U.S.S. *Wilmette*. The ship never saw any action but was used as a training ship during World War II. After the war, it was decommissioned and eventually scrapped in 1947. The *Eastland* may be gone, but its story and ghosts continue to linger nearly a century later.

Hauntings at Harpo Studios

At the time of the *Eastland* disaster, the only public building large enough to be used as a temporary morgue was the Second Regiment Armory, located on Chicago's near west side. The dead were laid out on the floor of the armory and assigned identification numbers. Chicagoans whose loved ones had perished in the disaster filed through the rows of bodies, searching for familiar faces, but in 22 cases, there was no one left to identify them. Those families were completely wiped out. The names of these victims were learned from neighbors who came searching for their friends. The weeping, crying, and moaning of the bereaved echoed off the walls of the armory for days. The last body to be identified was Willie Novotny, a seven-year-old boy whose parents and older sister had also perished on the *Eastland*. When extended family members identified the boy nearly a week after the disaster took place, a chapter was closed on one of Chicago's most horrific events.

As years passed, the armory building went through several incarnations, including a stable, a bowling alley, and Harpo Studios, which was home to the production company of Oprah

Winfrey. A number of *The Oprah Show's* staff members, security guards, and maintenance workers claimed that the studio was haunted by the spirits of those who tragically lost their lives on the *Eastland*. Many employees experienced unexplained phenomena, including the sighting of a woman in a long gray dress who walked the corridors and then mysteriously vanished into the wall. Some believe she is the spirit of a mourner who came to the armory looking for her family and left a bit of herself behind at a place where she felt her greatest sense of loss.

The woman in gray may not be alone in her spectral travels through the old armory. Staff members also witnessed doors opening and closing on their own and heard people sobbing, whispering, and moaning, as well as phantom footsteps on the lobby's staircase. Those who have experienced these strange events believe that the tragedy of yesterday is still manifesting itself in the old armory building's present state.

Chicago River Ghosts

In the same way that the former armory seems to have been impressed with a ghostly recording of past events, the Chicago River seems haunted, too. For years, people walking on the Clark Street bridge have heard crying, moaning, and pleas for help coming from the river. Some have even witnessed the apparitions of victims helplessly splashing in the water. On several occasions, some witnesses have called the police for help. One man even jumped into the river to save what he thought was an actual person drowning. When he returned to the surface, he discovered that he was in the water alone. He had no explanation for what he'd seen, other than to admit that it might have been a ghost.

So it seems that the horror of the *Eastland* disaster has left an imprint on this spot and continues to replay itself over and over again, ensuring that the unfortunate victims from the *Eastland* will never truly be forgotten.

Murder in the Heartland

If you ever find yourself in northwestern Kansas looking for the village of Holcomb, don't blink or you'll miss it. It's the kind of place where nothing ever seems to happen. And yet, back in 1959, Holcomb became one of the most notorious locations in the history of American crime.

✳ ✳ ✳ ✳

"Everyone Loved the Clutters..."

IN THE 1940S, successful businessman Herb Clutter built a house on the outskirts of town and started raising a family with his wife, Bonnie. The Clutters quickly became one of the most popular families in the small village, due largely to their friendly nature. People would be hard-pressed to find someone who had a bad word to say about them.

On the morning of Sunday, November 15, 1959, Clarence Ewalt drove his daughter Nancy to the Clutter house so she could go to church with the family as she did every week. She was a good friend of the Clutters' teenage daughter, who was also named Nancy. Nancy Ewalt knocked on the door several times but got no response. She went around to a side door, looked around and called out, but no one answered. At that point, Mr. Ewalt drove his daughter to the Kidwell house nearby and picked up Susan Kidwell, another friend. Susan tried phoning the Clutters, but no one answered. So the three drove back to the Clutter house. The two girls entered the house through the kitchen door and went to Nancy Clutter's room, where they discovered her dead body.

Unspeakable Acts

Sheriff Robinson was the first officer to respond. He entered the house with another officer and a neighbor, Larry Hendricks. According to Nancy Ewalt, the three men went first to Nancy Clutter's room, where they found the teenager dead of an apparent gunshot wound to the back of the head. She was lying on her bed facing the wall with her hands and ankles bound. Down the hallway in the master bedroom, the body of Bonnie Clutter was discovered. Like her daughter, Bonnie's hands and feet were also bound, and she appeared to have been shot point-blank in the head.

In the basement of the Clutter home, police found the bodies of Herb Clutter and his 15-year-old son, Kenyon. Like his mother and sister, Kenyon had been shot in the head; his body was tied to a sofa.

As atrocious as the other three murders were, Herb Clutter appeared to have suffered the most. Like the others, he had been shot in the head, but there were slash marks on his throat, and his mouth had been taped shut. And although his body was lying on the floor of the basement, there was a rope hanging from the ceiling suggesting that, at some point, he may have been hung from the rope.

Dewey's Task Force

Alvin A. Dewey of the Kansas City Bureau of Investigation (KBI) was put in charge of the investigation. Even though Dewey was a police veteran and had seen his fair share of violent murders, the Clutter murders hit him hard. Herb Clutter was a friend, and their families had attended church together.

At his first press conference after the bodies were discovered, Dewey announced that he was heading up a 19-man task force that would not rest until they found the person or persons responsible for the horrific murders. But he knew it was going to be a tough case. For one, the amount of blood and gore at the scene suggested that revenge might have been the motive. But the Clutters were upstanding members of the community and loved by all, as evidenced by the nearly 600 mourners who showed up for the family's funeral service. The idea that the murders were the result of a robbery gone bad was also being pursued, but Dewey had his doubts about that, as well. For him, it just didn't fit that the entire Clutter family would have walked in on a robbery and then been killed the way they had. For that reason, Dewey began to believe that there had been more than one killer.

A Secret Clue

There was not a lot of evidence left behind at the crime scene. Not only was the murder weapon missing, but whoever pulled the trigger had taken the time to pick up the spent shells. However, Dewey did have an ace up his sleeve, and it was something not even the press was made aware of. Herb Clutter's body had been found lying on a piece of cardboard. On that cardboard were impressions from a man's boot. Both of the victims found in the basement, Herb and Kenyon Clutter, were barefoot, which meant the boots may have belonged to the killer. It wasn't much to go on, but for Dewey, it was a start. Still, as Christmas 1959 crept closer, the case was starting to come to a standstill. Then, finally, a big break came from an unlikely place: Lansing Prison.

A Break in the Case

The man who would break the case wide open was Lansing Prison inmate Floyd Wells. Earlier in the year, Wells had been sentenced to Lansing for breaking and entering. His cellmate was a man named Richard Hickock. One night, the two men were talking, and Hickock mentioned that even though he was going to be released from prison soon, he had nowhere to go. Wells told him that back in the late 1940s, he had been out looking for work and stumbled across a kind, rich man named Clutter who would often hire people to work around his farm. Once he mentioned Herb Clutter, Hickock seemed obsessed with the man. He wouldn't stop asking Wells to tell him everything he knew about Clutter. How old was he? Was he strong? How many others lived in the house with him?

One night, Hickock calmly stated that when he was released, he and his friend Perry Smith were going to rob the Clutters and murder anyone in the house. Wells said that Hickock even went so far as to explain exactly how he would tie everyone up and shoot them one at a time. Wells further stated that he never believed Hickock was serious until he heard the news that the Clutters had been murdered in exactly the way Hickock had described.

Captures and Confessions

On December 30, after attempting to cash a series of bad checks, Hickock and Smith were arrested in Las Vegas. Among the items seized from the stolen car they were driving was a pair of boots belonging to Hickock. When confronted with the fact that his boots matched the imprint at the crime scene, Hickock broke down and admitted he had been there during the murders. However, he swore that Perry Smith had killed the whole family and that he had tried to stop him.

When Smith was informed that his partner was putting all the blame on him, he decided it was in his best interest to explain his side. Smith gave a very detailed version of how Hickock had devised a plan to steal the contents of a safe in Herb Clutter's home office. The pair had arrived under cover of darkness at approximately 12:30 AM. Finding no safe in the office, the pair went up into the master bedroom, where they surprised Herb Clutter, who was sleeping alone in bed. When told they had come for the contents of the safe, Herb told them to take whatever they wanted, but he said there was no safe in the house.

Not convinced, Smith and Hickock rounded up the family and tied them up, hoping to get one of them to reveal the location of the safe. When that failed, Smith and Hickock prepared to leave. But when Hickock started bragging about how he had been ready to kill the entire family, Smith called his bluff, and an argument ensued. At that point, Smith said he snapped and stabbed Herb Clutter in the throat. Seeing the man in such pain, Smith said he then shot him to end his suffering. Smith then turned the gun on Kenyon. Smith ended his statement by saying that he'd made Hickock shoot and kill the two women.

The Verdict

The murder trial of Richard Hickock and Perry Smith began on March 23, 1960, at Finney County Courthouse. Five days later, the case was handed over to the jury, who needed only 40 minutes to reach their verdict: Both men were guilty of all charges. They recommended that Hickock and Smith be hanged for their crimes.

Sitting in the front row when the verdicts were read was Truman Capote, who had been writing a series of articles about the murders for *The New Yorker*. Those articles would later inspire his best-selling novel *In Cold Blood*.

After several appeals, both men were executed at Lansing Prison, one right after the other, on April 14, 1965. Richard Hickock was the first to be hanged, with Perry Smith going to the same gallows roughly 30 minutes later. Agent Alvin Dewey was present for both executions.

Several years after the murders, in an attempt to heal the community, a stained-glass window at the First Methodist Church in Garden City, Kansas, was posthumously dedicated to the memory of the Clutter family. Despite an initial impulse to bulldoze the Clutter house, it was left standing and today is a private residence.

Gone Without a Trace

While we all watch in amazement as magicians make everything from small coins to giant buildings disappear, in our hearts, we all know it's a trick. Things don't just disappear, especially not people. Or do they?

❋   ❋   ❋   ❋

Louis Le Prince

THE NAME LOUIS Aimé Augustin Le Prince doesn't mean much to most people, but some believe he was the first person to record moving images on film, a good seven years before

Thomas Edison. Whether or not he did so is open to debate, as is what happened to him on September 16, 1890. On that day, Le Prince's brother accompanied him to the train station in Dijon, France, where he was scheduled to take the express train to Paris. When the train reached Paris, however, Le Prince and his luggage were nowhere to be found. Theories about his disappearance range from his being murdered for trying to fight Edison over the patent of the first motion picture to his family forcing him to go into hiding to keep him safe from people who wanted his patents for themselves. Others believe that Le Prince took his own life because he was nearly bankrupt.

Jimmy Hoffa

On the afternoon of July 30, 1975, Jimmy Hoffa, former president of the International Brotherhood of Teamsters, stepped onto the parking lot of the Manchus Red Fox Restaurant near Detroit and into history. Scheduled to meet with known mobsters from New Jersey and New York, Hoffa vanished and was never seen or heard from again. Since that day, wild theories involving mob hits and political assassinations have run rampant. But despite hundreds of anonymous tips, confessions from mob hitmen, and even the wife of a former mobster accusing her husband of the hit, it is still unknown what happened to Hoffa or where he's buried, and the case officially remains open. As recently as May 2006, FBI agents were still following leads and digging up yards in Michigan trying to find out what happened to Hoffa.

Dorothy Arnold

After spending most of December 12, 1910, shopping in Manhattan, American socialite Dorothy Arnold told a friend she was planning to walk home through Central Park. She never made it. Fearing their daughter had eloped with her one-time boyfriend George Griscom, Jr., the Arnolds immediately hired the Pinkerton Detective Agency, although they did not report her missing to police until almost a month later. Once the press heard the news, theories spread like wildfire, most of them pointing the finger at Griscom. Some believed he had murdered Arnold, but others thought she had died as the result of a botched abortion. Still others felt her family had banished her to Switzerland and then used her disappearance as a cover-up. No evidence was ever found to formally charge Griscom, and Arnold's disappearance remains unsolved.

Frederick Valentich

To vanish without a trace is rather unusual. But to vanish in an airplane while chasing a UFO—now that's unique. Yet that's exactly what happened to 20-year-old pilot Frederick Valentich on the night of October 21, 1978. Shortly after 7:00 PM, while flying a Cessna 182L to King Island, Australia, Valentich radioed that an "unidentified craft" was hovering over his plane. For the next several minutes, he attempted to describe the object, which had blinking lights and was "not an aircraft." At approximately 7:12 PM, Valentich stated that he was having engine trouble. Immediately after that, the flight tower picked up 17 seconds of "metallic, scraping sounds." Then all was silent. A search began immediately, but no trace of Valentich or his plane was ever found. Strangely enough, the evening Valentich disappeared, there were numerous reports of UFOs seen all over the skies of Australia.

Frank Morris, John Anglin, and Clarence Anglin

Officially, records show that there was never a successful escape from Alcatraz Prison while it was in operation. Of course, those records leave out the part that three men *might* have made it, but they disappeared in the process.

After spending two years planning their escape, inmates Frank Morris and brothers Clarence and John Anglin placed home-made dummies in their bunks, crawled through hand-dug tunnels, and made their way to the prison roof. Then they apparently climbed down, hopped aboard homemade rafts, and made their way out into San Francisco Bay.

The next day, one of the largest manhunts in history began. Pieces of a raft and a life preserver were found floating in the bay, as well as a bag containing personal items from the escapees, but that was all. The official report stated that in all likelihood, the men drowned. However, a 2003 episode of *Mythbusters* determined that the men may have survived.

Mike the Headless Chicken

Chickens are known not for their intelligence but for their pecking, their much-emulated dance, and, in one special case, a chicken named Mike was known for losing his head.

✳ ✳ ✳ ✳

A Slip of the Knife

O N A FALL day in 1945, on a farm in Fruita, Colorado, chickens were meeting their maker. It was nothing out of the ordinary; Lloyd and Clara Olsen slaughtered chickens on their farm all the time. But this particular day was fortuitous for Lloyd and one of his chickens. As Lloyd brought down his knife on the neck of a future meal, the head came off, clean as a whistle. The decapitated chicken flapped and danced around, which is what normally happens when a chicken loses its head.

But this chicken didn't stop flapping and dancing around. Most headless chickens only live a few minutes before going to that big chicken coop in the sky, but this particular bird was alive and well several hours (and then several months) after it had lost its, er, mind.

Open Mike

Lloyd was fascinated by this chicken that had somehow cheated death. The chicken continued to behave exactly like the other chickens on the farm—he just didn't have a head. Mike, as he was named, even attempted to cluck, although it sounded more like a gurgle since it came out of a hole in his neck.

Lloyd was starting to see the entrepreneurial possibilities that Mike had created—a living, breathing headless chicken was sure to be a goldmine. But Lloyd knew he had to devise a way for Mike to get nutrients or he would die. Using an eyedropper, a mixture of ground-up grain and water was sent down Mike's open esophagus, and little bits of gravel were dropped down his throat to help his gizzard grind up food.

That'll Be a Quarter

Mike the Headless Chicken was not some magical beast with the ability to cheat death; he was just an ordinary chicken that got lucky. Scientists who examined Mike determined that Lloyd had done a shoddy job of butchering him. Most of his head was actually gone, but the slice had missed Mike's jugular vein, and a blood clot prevented him from bleeding to death. Most of a chicken's reflex actions originate in the brain stem, and Mike's was pretty much untouched.

None of this mattered to the general public. When Mike went on a national sideshow tour in 1945, people lined up to see this wonder chicken and paid a quarter for the privilege. At his most popular, Mike was drawing in about $4,500 per month, which is equivalent to about $50,000 today. He was insured for $10,000 and featured in *Life* magazine. What became of Mike's head is a mystery. Most photos show a chicken head alongside Mike, either at his feet or pickled in a jar.

A Moment of Silence, Please

It's wasn't the lack of a head that was toughest on Mike—he had a problem with choking on his own mucus. The Olsens employed a syringe to suck the mucus out of Mike's neck, but one fateful night, Mike was traveling back home to Fruita, roosting with the Olsens in their motel room. Lloyd and Clara heard Mike choking in the middle of the night and reached for the syringe. Alas, they discovered they had left it in the last town where Mike had appeared. Mike finally succumbed to death that night in Phoenix in 1947.

These days, Fruita holds an annual Mike the Headless Chicken Day every third weekend in May in honor of their most famous resident.

The Death of John Dillinger...or Someone Who Looked Like Him

On July 22, 1934, outside the Biograph Theater on Chicago's north side, John Dillinger, America's first Public Enemy Number One, passed from this world into the next in a hail of bullets. Or did he? Conspiracy theorists believe that FBI agents shot and killed the wrong man and covered it all up when they realized their mistake. So what really happened that night? Let's first take a look at the main players in this gangland soap opera.

❋   ❋   ❋   ❋

Hoover Wants His Man

BORN JUNE 22, 1903, John Dillinger was in his early thirties when he first caught the FBI's eye. They thought they were through with him in January 1934, when he was arrested after shooting a police officer during a bank robbery in East Chicago, Indiana. However, Dillinger managed to stage a daring escape from his Indiana jail cell using a wooden gun painted with black shoe polish.

Once Dillinger left Indiana in a stolen vehicle and crossed into Illinois, he was officially a federal fugitive. J. Edgar Hoover, then director of the FBI, promised a quick apprehension, but Dillinger had other plans. He seemed to enjoy the fact that the FBI was tracking him—rather than go into hiding, he continued robbing banks. Annoyed, Hoover assigned FBI Agent Melvin Purvis to ambush Dillinger. Purvis's plan backfired, though, and Dillinger escaped, shooting and killing two innocent men in the process. After the botched trap, the public was in an uproar and the FBI was under close scrutiny. To everyone at the FBI, the message was clear: Hoover wanted Dillinger.

The Woman in Red

The FBI's big break came in July 1934 with a phone call from a woman named Anna Sage. Sage was a Romanian immigrant who ran a Chicago-area brothel. Fearing that she might be deported, Sage wanted to strike a bargain with the feds. Her proposal was simple: In exchange for not being deported, Sage was willing to give the FBI John Dillinger. According to Sage, Dillinger was dating Polly Hamilton, one of her former employees. Melvin Purvis personally met with Sage and told her he couldn't make any promises but he would do what he could about her pending deportation.

Several days later, on July 22, Sage called the FBI office in Chicago and said that she was going to the movies that night with Dillinger and Hamilton. Sage quickly hung up but not before saying she would wear something bright so that agents could pick out the threesome in a crowd. Not knowing which movie theater they were planning to go to, Purvis dispatched several agents to the Marbro Theater, while he and another group of agents went to the Biograph.

At approximately 8:30 PM, Purvis believed he saw Dillinger, Sage, and Hamilton enter the Biograph. As she had promised, Sage indeed wore something bright—an orange blouse. However, under the mar-quee lights, the blouse's color appeared to be red, which is why Sage was forever dubbed "The Woman in Red."

Purvis tried to apprehend Dillinger right after he purchased tickets, but he slipped past Purvis and into the darkened theater. Purvis went into the theater but was unable to locate Dillinger in the dark. At that point, Purvis left the theater, gathered his men, and made the decision to apprehend Dillinger as he was exiting the theater. Purvis positioned himself in the theater's vestibule, instructed his men to hide outside, and told them that he would signal them by lighting a cigar when he spotted Dillinger.

"Stick 'em up, Johnny!"

At approximately 10:30 PM, the doors to the Biograph opened and people started to exit. All of the agents' eyes were on Purvis. When a man wearing a straw hat, accompanied by two women, walked past Purvis, the agent quickly placed a cigar in his mouth and lit a match. Perhaps sensing something was wrong, the man turned and looked at Purvis, at which point Purvis drew his pistol and said, "Stick 'em up, Johnny!" In response, the man turned as if he was going to run away, while at the same time reaching for what appeared to be a gun. Seeing the movement, the other agents opened fire. As the man ran away, attempting to flee down the alleyway alongside the theater, he was shot four times on his left side and once in the back of the neck before crumpling on the pavement. When Purvis reached him and checked for vitals, there were none. Minutes later, after being driven to a local hospital, John Dillinger was pronounced DOA. But as soon as it was announced that Dillinger was dead, the controversy began.

Dillinger Disputed

Much of the basis for the conspiracy stems from the fact that Hoover, both publicly and privately, made it clear that no matter what, he wanted Dillinger caught. On top of that, Agent Purvis was under a lot of pressure to capture Dillinger, especially since he'd failed with a previous attempt. Keeping that in mind, it would be easy to conclude that Purvis, in his haste to capture Dillinger, might have overlooked a few things. First, it was Purvis alone who pointed out the man he thought to be Dillinger to the waiting agents. Conspiracy theorists contend that Purvis fingered the wrong man that night, and an innocent man ended up getting killed as a result. As evidence, they point to Purvis's own statement: While they were standing at close range, the man tried to pull a gun, which is why the agents had to open fire. But even though agents stated they recovered a .38-caliber Colt automatic from the victim's body (and even had it on display for many years), author Jay Robert Nash discovered that that particular model was not even available until a good five months after Dillinger's alleged death! Theorists believe that when agents realized they had not only shot the wrong man, but an unarmed one at that, they planted the gun as part of a cover-up.

Another interesting fact that could have resulted in Purvis's misidentification was that Dillinger had recently undergone plastic surgery in an attempt to disguise himself. In addition to work on his face, Dillinger had attempted to obliterate his fingerprints by dipping his fingers into an acid solution. On top of that, the man who Purvis said was Dillinger was wearing a straw hat the entire time Purvis saw him. It is certainly possible that Purvis did not actually recognize Dillinger but instead picked out someone who merely looked like him. If you remember, the only tip Purvis had was Sage telling him that she was going to the movies with Dillinger and his girlfriend. Did Purvis see Sage leaving the theater in her orange blouse and finger the wrong man simply because he was standing next to Sage and resembled Dillinger? Or was the whole thing a setup orchestrated by Sage and Dillinger to trick the FBI into executing an innocent man?

So Who Was It?

If the man shot and killed outside the theater wasn't John Dillinger, who was it? There are conflicting accounts, but one speculation is that it was a man named Jimmy Lawrence, who was dating Polly Hamilton. If you believe in the conspiracy, Lawrence was simply in the wrong place at the wrong time. Or possibly, Dillinger purposely sent Lawrence to the theater hoping FBI agents would shoot him, allowing Dillinger to fade into obscurity. Of course, those who don't believe in the conspiracy say the reason Lawrence looked so much like Dillinger is because he was Dillinger using an alias. Further, Dillinger's sister, Audrey Hancock, identified his body. Finally, they say it all boils down to the FBI losing the gun Dillinger had the night he was killed and inadvertently replacing it with the wrong one.

Not really, though. It seems that whenever someone comes up with a piece of evidence to fuel the conspiracy theory, some-one else has something to refute it. Some have asked that Dillinger's body be exhumed and DNA tests be performed, but nothing has come of it yet. Until that happens, we'll probably never know for sure what really happened on that hot July night back in 1934. But that's okay, because real or imagined, everyone loves a good mystery.

Rebel with a Curse: James Dean and "Little Bastard"

From the moment James Dean first walked onto a Hollywood set, countless people have emulated his cool style and attitude. When Dean died in a car crash in 1955 at age 24, his iconic status was immortalized. Perhaps this is partly due to the strange details that surrounded his death. Did a cursed car take the rising star away before his time?

✳   ✳   ✳   ✳

How Much Is that Porsche in the Window?

IN 1955, HEARTTHROB James Dean purchased a silver Porsche 550 Spyder, which he nicknamed "Little Bastard." Dean painted the number "130" on the hood and the car's saucy name on the back.

On the morning of September 30, Dean drove the Porsche to his mechanic for a quick tune-up before heading to a race he was planning to enter. The car checked out, and Dean left, making plans to meet up with a few friends and a *Life* magazine photographer later that day.

Everyone who knew Dean knew he liked to drive fast. The movie star set out on the highway, driving at top speeds in his beloved Porsche. He actually got stopped for speeding at one point but got back on the road after getting a ticket.

But when the sun got in his eyes and another car made a quick left turn, Dean couldn't stop in time. Screeching brakes, twisted metal, and an ambulance that couldn't make it to the hospital in time signaled the end of James Dean's short life.

You Need Brake Pads, a New Alternator, and a Priest

Within a year or so of Dean's fatal car crash, his Porsche was involved in a number of unusual—and sometimes deadly—incidents. Were they all coincidental, or was the car actually cursed? Consider the following:

Two doctors claimed several of Little Bastard's parts. One of the docs was killed and the other seriously injured in separate accidents. Someone else purchased the tires, which blew simultaneously, sending their new owner to the hospital.

The Fresno garage where the car was kept for a while after Dean's death was the site of a major fire. The California State Highway Patrol removed the car from Fresno, figuring they could show the charred remains of Dean's car to warn teenagers about the dangers of careless driving. When the vehicle transporting the remains of the car crashed en route to the site, the driver was thrown from his vehicle and died.

The display the Highway Patrol produced was incredibly popular, of course, but it also turned out to be dangerous. The legs of a young boy looking at the car were crushed when three of the cables holding the vehicle upright suddenly broke, bringing the heavy metal down onto the boy's body. When the car left the exhibit, it broke in half on the truck used to haul it away and killed a worker involved in the loading process.

In 1959, there was another attempt to display the car. Though it was welded together, legend has it that the car suddenly broke into 11 pieces. The following year, the owner had finally had enough and decided to have the Porsche shipped from Miami back to California. Little Bastard was loaded onto a sealed boxcar, but when the train arrived in L.A., the car was gone. Thieves may have taken the car, sure, but there were reports that the boxcar hadn't been disturbed. Whether or not the car was cursed, with all the trouble it caused, perhaps it was for the best that it finally disappeared.

Mysterious Disappearances in the Bermuda Triangle

Few geographical locations on Earth have been discussed and debated more than the three-sided chunk of ocean between the Atlantic coast of Florida and the regions of San Juan, Puerto Rico, and Bermuda known as the Bermuda Triangle.

✳   ✳   ✳   ✳

OVER THE CENTURIES, hundreds of ships and dozens of airplanes have mysteriously disappeared while floating in or flying through the region commonly called the Bermuda Triangle. Myth mongers propose that alien forces are responsible for these dissipations. Because little or no wreckage from the vanished vessels has ever been recovered, paranormal pirating has also been cited as the culprit. Other theorists suggest that leftover technology from the lost continent of Atlantis— mainly an underwater rock formation known as the Bimini Road (situated just off the island of Bimini in the Bahamas)— exerts a supernatural power that grabs unsuspecting intruders and drags them to the depths.

A Deadly Adjective

Although the theory of the Triangle had been mentioned in publications as early as 1950, it wasn't until the '60s that the region was anointed with its three-sided appellation. Columnist Vincent Gaddis wrote an article in the February 1964 edition of *Argosy* magazine that discussed the various mysterious disappearances that had occurred over the years and designated the area where myth and mystery mixed as the "Deadly Bermuda Triangle." The use of the adjective deadly perpetrated the possibility that UFOs, alien anarchists, supernatural beings, and metaphysical monsters reigned over the region.

In 1975, historian, pilot, and researcher Lawrence David Kusche published one of the first definitive studies that dismissed many of the Triangle theories. In his book *The Bermuda Triangle Mystery—Solved*, he concluded that the Triangle was a "manufactured mystery," the result of bad research and reporting and, occasionally, deliberately falsified facts.

Before weighing anchor on Kusche's conclusions, however, consider that one of his next major publications was a tome about exotic popcorn recipes.

Explaining Odd Occurrences

Other pragmatists have insisted that a combination of natural forces—a double whammy of waves and rain that create the perfect storm—is most likely the cause for these maritime misfortunes. Other possible "answers" to the mysteries include rogue waves (such as the one that capsized the Ocean Ranger oil rig off the coast of Newfoundland in 1982), hurricanes, underwater earthquakes, and human error. Whatever the causes, the Coast Guard receives almost 20 distress calls every day from amateur sailors attempting to navigate the slippery sides of the Triangle.

Modern-day piracy—usually among those involved in drug smuggling—has been mentioned as a probable cause for odd occurrences, as have unusual magnetic anomalies that screw up compass readings. Other possible explanations include the Gulf Stream's uncertain current, the high volume of sea and air traffic in the region, and even methane hydrates (gas bubbles) that produce "mud volcanoes" capable of sucking a ship into the depths. But let's take a closer look at some of the stranger occurences.

Flight 19

On the afternoon of December 5, 1945, five Avenger torpedo bombers left the Naval Air Station at Fort Lauderdale, Florida, with Lt. Charles Taylor in command of a crew of 13 student pilots. About 90 minutes into the flight, Taylor radioed the base to say that his compasses weren't working, but he figured he was somewhere over the Florida Keys. The lieutenant who received the signal told Taylor to fly north toward Miami, as long as he was sure he was actually over the Keys. Although he was an experienced pilot, Taylor got horribly turned around, and the more he tried to get out of the Keys, the further out to sea he and his crew traveled. As night fell, radio signals worsened, until, finally, there was nothing at all from Flight 19. A U.S. Navy investigation reported that Taylor's confusion caused the disaster, but his mother convinced them to change the official report to read that the planes went down for "causes unknown." The planes have never been recovered.

The *Spray*

Joshua Slocum, the first man to sail solo around the world, never should have been lost at sea, but it appears that's exactly what happened. In 1909, the *Spray* left the East Coast of the United States for Venezuela via the Caribbean Sea. Slocum was never heard from or seen again and was declared dead in 1924. The ship was solid, and Slocum was a pro, so nobody knows what happened. Perhaps he was felled by a larger ship or maybe he was taken down by pirates. No one knows for sure that Slocum disappeared within the Triangle's waters, but Bermuda buffs claim Slocum's story as part of the area's mysterious and supernatural legacy.

USS *Cyclops*

As World War I heated up, America went to battle. In 1918, the *Cyclops*, commanded by Lt. G. W. Worley, was sent to Brazil to refuel Allied ships. With 309 people onboard, the ship left Rio de Janeiro in February and reached Barbados in March. After that, the *Cyclops* was never seen or heard from again. The Navy says in its official statement, "The disappearance of this ship has been one of the most baffling mysteries in the annals of the Navy, all attempts to locate her having proved unsuccessful. There were no enemy submarines in the western Atlantic at that time, and in December 1918, every effort was made to obtain from German sources information regarding the disappearance of the vessel."

Star Tiger

The *Star Tiger*, commanded by Capt. B. W. McMillan, was flying from England to Bermuda in early 1948. On January 30, McMillan said he expected to arrive in Bermuda at 5:00 AM, but neither he nor any of the 31 people onboard the *Star Tiger* were ever heard from again. When the Civil Air Ministry launched an investigation, they learned that the S.S. *Troubadour* had reported seeing a low-flying aircraft halfway between Bermuda and the entrance to Delaware Bay. If that aircraft was the *Star Tiger*, it was drastically off course. According to the Civil Air Ministry, the fate of the *Star Tiger* remains unknown.

Star Ariel

On January 17, 1949, a Tudor IV aircraft like the *Star Tiger* left Bermuda with seven crew members and 13 passengers en route to Jamaica. That morning, Capt. J. C. McPhee reported that the flight was going smoothly. Shortly afterward, another more cryptic message came from the captain, when he reported that he was changing his frequency, and then nothing more was heard—ever. More than 60 aircraft and 13,000 people were deployed to look for the *Star Ariel*, but no hint of debris or wreckage was ever found. After the *Star Ariel* disappeared, production of Tudor IVs ceased.

Flight 201

This Cessna left for Fort Lauderdale on March 31, 1984, en route for Bimini Island in the Bahamas, but it never made it. Not quite midway to its destination, the plane slowed its airspeed significantly, but no distress signals came from the plane. Suddenly, the plane dropped from the air into the water, completely vanishing from the radar. A woman on Bimini Island swore she saw a plane plunge into the sea about a mile offshore, but no wreckage has ever been found.

Teignmouth Electron

Who said that the Bermuda Triangle only swallows up ships and planes? Who's to say it can't also make a man go mad? Perhaps that's what happened on the *Teignmouth Electron* in 1969. The *Sunday Times* Golden Globe race of 1968 left England on October 31 and required each contestant to sail his ship solo. Donald Crowhurst was one of the entrants, but he never made it to the finish line. The *Electron* was found abandoned in the middle of the Bermuda Triangle in July 1969. Logbooks recovered from the ship reveal that Crowhurst was deceiving organizers about his position in the race and going a little bit nutty out there in the big blue ocean. The last entry of his log was dated June 29—it is believed that Crowhurst jumped overboard and drowned himself in the Triangle.

Creepy Coincidences

From a prophetic book written decades before a tragic event took place to a man struck repeatedly by lightning, life's great coincidences are often truly mind-boggling.

✳ ✳ ✳ ✳

The Numbers Don't Lie

THE TERROR ATTACKS of September 11, 2001, brought with them much speculation. Was this heinous act perpetrated by a group of rogue extremists or part of a larger conspiracy? Did everything happen precisely as reported, or was the public being misled? While these questions and others were being pondered, a curious and underreported event took place.

On September 11, 2002, the one-year anniversary of the attacks, the New York State Lottery conducted one of two standard daily drawings. In the three-number contest, the balls drawn were 9–1–1. Statisticians point out that this isn't particularly astounding, given the less than astronomical odds in a three-ball draw. Even so, that's one creepy coincidence.

Womb for One More

As if one womb were no longer good enough to get the job done, Hannah Kersey of Great Britain was born with two. Then, in 2006, to confound the medical world even more, the 23-year-old woman gave birth to triplets—identical twins Ruby and Tilly were delivered from one of Kersey's wombs, while baby Gracie was extracted from the other. All three girls came into the world seven weeks premature via cesarean section and were quite healthy upon arrival. For the record, there have been about 70 known pregnancies in separate wombs in the past 100 years, but the case of triplets is the first of its kind and doctors estimate the likelihood is about one in 25 million.

He's "Awl" That

Most people recognize the name Louis Braille, the world-renowned inventor of the Braille system of reading and writing for the blind. But what many people don't know is how Braille himself became blind and how it led to his invention.

When he was only three years old, Braille accidentally poked himself in the eye with a stitching awl owned by his father, a saddle maker. At first his injury didn't seem serious, but when an autoimmune disease known as sympathetic ophthalmia set in, he went blind in both eyes.

Over the years, Braille adapted well to his disability. Then, in 1824, at age 15, he invented a system of raised dots that enabled the blind to read and write through use of their fingertips. To form each dot on a page, Braille employed a common hand tool found at most saddle maker's shops—a stitching awl, the same tool that had injured him as a child.

Lotsa Luck

Evelyn Adams had a couple of bucks and a dream. In 1985, she purchased a New Jersey lottery ticket and crossed her fingers. When the winning numbers were called, she realized she had hit the jackpot. The following year, Adams amazingly hit the jackpot once more. Her combined take for both wins totaled a cool $5.4 million. It was enough money to easily live out her days in comfort. But it wasn't to be.

Due to Adams's innate generosity and love of gambling, she eventually went broke. Today, she lives in a trailer and laments the past: "I wish I had the chance to do it all over again. I'd be much smarter about it now."

Think of Laura

On a whim, ten-year-old Laura Buxton of Burton, Staffordshire, England, jotted her name and address on a luggage label in 2001. She then attached it to a helium balloon and released it into the sky. Supported by air currents for 140 miles, the balloon eventually touched down in a garden in Pewsey, Wiltshire, England. Bizarrely, another ten-year-old girl named Laura Buxton read the note, got in touch with its sender, and the girls became fast friends. In addition to their identical names and ages, each child had fair hair and owned a black Labrador retriever, a guinea pig, and a rabbit.

Attractive Gent

Do some people attract lightning the way a movie star attracts fans? In the case of Major Walter Summerford, an officer in the British Army, the evidence nods toward the affirmative. In 1918, Summerford received his first jolt when he was knocked from his horse by a flash of lightning. Injuries to his lower body forced him to retire from the military, so he moved to Vancouver, British Columbia.

In 1924, Summerford spent a day fishing beside a river. Suddenly, a bolt of lightning struck the tree he was sitting beneath, and he was zapped again. But by 1926, Summerford had recovered from his injuries to the degree that he was able to take walks. He continued with this therapy until one tragic summer's day in 1930 when, unbelievably, lightning found him yet again. This time it paralyzed him for good. He died two years after the incident.

The story should end there, but it doesn't. In 1936, a lightning bolt took aim at a cemetery and unleashed its 100,000-volt charge. Luckily, no living soul was nearby at the time, and the bolt passed its energy harmlessly into the ground, as do the vast majority of lightning strikes. Still, before hitting the ground, the lightning bolt injected its fearsome energy into Major Summerford's headstone.

Four's a Crowd

In 1838, Edgar Allan Poe, famous author of the macabre, penned a novel entitled *The Narrative of Arthur Gordon Pym of Nantucket*. His fictitious account centers around four survivors of a shipwreck who find themselves adrift in an open lifeboat. After many days of hunger and torment, they decide the only way for any of them to survive is if one is sacrificed for food. They draw straws, and cabin boy Richard Parker comes up short. He is subsequently killed, and the three remaining seamen partake of his flesh.

In 1884, some 46 years after the tale was first told, the yacht *Mignonette* broke apart during a hurricane in the South Atlantic. Its four survivors drifted in a lifeboat for 19 days before turning desperate from hunger and thirst. One sailor, a cabin boy, became delirious after guzzling copious quantities of seawater. Upon seeing this, the other three determined that the man was at death's door and decided to kill him. They then devoured his remains. His name: Richard Parker.

Downed Damsels

Mary Ashford was born in 1797, and Barbara Forrest in 1954, yet circumstances surrounding their eventual murders are eerily similar. On May 27, 1817, Ashford was raped and killed in

Erdington, England. On May 27, 1974, Forrest was also raped and murdered in Erdington, just 400 yards away from the site of Ashford's murder. The day preceding both of the murders was Whit Monday, a floating religious holiday on the Christian calendar celebrated mostly in Europe. The murders occurred at approximately the same time of day, and attempts had been made to conceal both bodies.

That's not all. Each woman had visited a friend on the night before Whit Monday, changed into a new dress during the evening, and attended a dance. Curiously, suspects in both cases shared the surname "Thornton." Both were tried and acquitted.

Naughty but Nice

Whenever Brownsville, Texas, waitress Melina Salazar saw cantankerous customer Walter "Buck" Swords walking into her café, she felt an urge to walk out. Nevertheless, Salazar persevered through a fusillade of demands and curses heaped upon her by her most demanding, albeit loyal, customer. When 89-year-old Swords passed away, no one was more shocked than Salazar to learn that he'd bequeathed her $50,000 and his car. Describing Swords as, "kind of mean," the waitress told a television news crew, "I still can't believe it."

Hitler's Death, a Hoax?

Rumors of Hitler's survival persisted for years. The charred corpse was a double; he had offspring; he was living in South America, keeping that old Nazi spirit alive. Some of the wilder tales were fueled by Soviet propaganda. They were false. In 1993 the Russian government opened the old Soviet files. We now know beyond any reasonable doubt what happened.

✳   ✳   ✳   ✳

THE NKVD (RUSSIAN intelligence) investigation began the moment Soviet troops overran the Führerbunker. They exhumed the Hitler and Goebbels bodies, bringing in close acquaintances for positive I.D.; for example, Eva and Adolf's former dentist and his assistant both recognized their own professional handiwork. The original announcement had been correct: Adolf Hitler had died April 30, 1945. After sending Hitler's jaw back to Moscow for safekeeping, the NKVD secretly reburied the other remains at a military base near Magdeburg, German Democratic Republic (East Germany).

In 1970, the Soviet military prepared to transfer the Magdeburg base to East German control. The KGB (successor to the NKVD) dared not leave the Nazi remains. On April 4, 1970, the KGB exhumed the fragmentary remains of Adolf and Eva Hitler and the Goebbels family. Hitler's skull was identified, and the bullet-holed portion was sent to Moscow. The next day, the KGB incinerated the rest of the remains, crushed them to dust and dumped it in a nearby river. Therefore, of Eva Braun and the Goebbels family nothing at all remains. Of Hitler, today only his jaw and a skull fragment exist in Russian custody.

Rumors of War

Plenty of myths have come out of World War II, but few are as unfounded as the claim that President Franklin Delano Roosevelt allowed the Japanese to attack Pearl Harbor so the United States could enter the conflict.

✳   ✳   ✳   ✳

UNFORTUNATELY, THIS RUMOR has followed FDR's legacy almost from the moment the attack occurred, and many people continue to believe it today. But countless investigations and studies have failed to uncover a "smoking gun" that proves the president could have engineered such a monumental act of treason. Let's look at some of the arguments and their counter-arguments to spot the facts.

Coded Knowledge

Conspiracy theorists frequently note that the U.S. military had successfully broken Japanese codes and thus knew in advance of the attack. This is partially true—Japanese codes had been broken, but they were diplomatic codes, not military ones. The military *had* received notice from other sources, including the British, that an attack was pending. What wasn't known was where the attack would take place. Almost everyone assumed it would be against the Philippines or some other Pacific territory, and no one had reason to believe that the target would be the military base at Pearl Harbor.

Another common assumption is that Roosevelt had the Pacific Fleet moved from San Diego to Pearl Harbor to lure the Japanese into attacking. However, it wasn't Roosevelt who made that decision. Rather, it was the State Department, which hoped to deter Japanese aggression with a show of naval force.

Ships at Sea

Many conspiracy theorists also like to claim that the American aircraft carriers based at Pearl Harbor had been sent on maneuvers prior to the attack as a precaution, so the attack wouldn't be as damaging as it could have been. In fact, the Japanese devastated the Pacific Fleet, sinking four U.S. battleships and severely damaging four others. In addition, three light cruisers, three destroyers, and four smaller vessels were demolished or heavily damaged, and 75 percent of the island's military air fleet was annihilated before the planes could take to the sky. The value of the aircraft carriers that survived because they were on maneuvers wouldn't be realized until months later, at the Battle of Midway.

An Excuse to Fight

Perhaps most important is that Roosevelt didn't need a Japanese attack to bring the United States into the war. Though officially neutral at the time, the country was actively engaged in fighting the Axis by providing war materials to Great Britain and other Allied nations via the Lend-Lease Act. Furthermore, antiwar sentiment was waning dramatically as Americans grew increasingly angered by Japanese and German aggression. It was just a matter of time before the United States took off the gloves and waded into the war that was engulfing the world.

The Men on the Moon

On July 20, 1969, millions of people worldwide watched in awe as U.S. astronauts became the first humans to step on the moon. However, a considerable number of conspiracy theorists contend that the men were just actors performing on a soundstage.

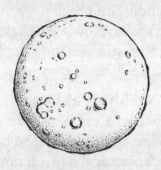

* * * *

THE NATIONAL AERONAUTICS and Space Administration (NASA) has been dealing with this myth for nearly 40 years. In fact, it has a page on its official website that scientifically explains the pieces of "proof" that supposedly expose the fraud. These are the most common questions raised.

If the astronauts really did take photographs on the moon, why aren't the stars visible in them? The stars are there but are too faint to be seen in the photos. The reason for this has to do with the fact that the lunar surface is so brightly lit by the sun. The astronauts had to adjust their camera settings to accommodate the brightness, which then rendered the stars in the background difficult to see.

Why was there no blast crater under the lunar module?
The astronauts had slowed their descent, bringing the rocket on the lander from a maximum of 10,000 pounds of thrust to just 3,000 pounds. In addition, the lack of atmosphere on the moon spread the exhaust fairly wide, lowering the pressure and diminishing the scope of a blast crater.

If there is no air on the moon, why does the flag planted by the astronauts appear to be waving? The flag appears to wave because the astronauts were rotating the pole on which it was mounted as they tried to get it to stand upright.

When the lunar module took off from the moon back into orbit, why was there no visible flame from the rocket? The composition of the fuel used for the takeoff from the surface of the moon was different in that it produced no flame.

Conspiracy theorists present dozens of "examples" that supposedly prove that the moon landing never happened, and all of them are easily explained. But that hasn't kept naysayers from perpetuating the myth.

Twenty-three years after the moon landing, on February 15, 2001, Fox TV stirred the pot yet again with a program titled *Conspiracy Theory: Did We Land on the Moon?* The show trotted out the usual array of conspiracy theorists, who in turn dusted off the usual spurious "proof." And once again, NASA found itself having to answer to a skeptical but persistent few.

Many people theorize that the landing was faked because the United States didn't have the technology to safely send a crew to the moon. Instead, it pretended it did as a way to win the final leg of the space race against the Soviet Union. But consider the situation: Thousands of men and women worked for almost a decade (and three astronauts died) to make the success of *Apollo 11* a reality. With so many people involved, a hoax of that magnitude would be virtually impossible to contain, especially after almost four decades.

For additional proof that the moon landing really happened, consider the hundreds of pounds of moon rocks brought back by the six *Apollo* missions that were able to retrieve them. Moon rocks are unique and aren't easily manufactured, so if they didn't come from the moon, what is their source?

Finally, there's no denying the fact that the *Apollo* astronauts left behind a two-foot reflecting panel equipped with dozens of tiny mirrors. Scientists are able to bounce laser pulses off the mirrors to pinpoint the moon's distance from Earth.

The myth of the faked moon landing will probably never go away. But the proof of its reality is irrefutable. In the words of astronaut Charles Duke, who walked on the moon in 1972 as part of the *Apollo 16* mission: "We've been to the moon nine times. Why would we fake it nine times, if we faked it?"

Ohio's Greatest Unsolved Mystery

From 1935 until 1938, a brutal madman roamed the Flats of Cleveland. The killer—known as the Mad Butcher of Kingsbury Run—is believed to have murdered 12 men and women. Despite a massive manhunt, the murderer was never apprehended.

✳   ✳   ✳   ✳

IN 1935, THE Depression had hit Cleveland hard, leaving large numbers of people homeless. Shantytowns sprang up on the eastern side of the city in Kingsbury Run—a popular place for transients—near the Erie and Nickel Plate railroads. It is unclear who the Butcher's first victim was. Recent research suggests it may have been an unidentified woman found floating in Lake Erie—in pieces—on September 5, 1934; she would be known as Jane Doe I but dubbed by some as the "Lady of the Lake." The first official victim was found in the Jackass Hill area of Kingsbury Run on September 23, 1935. The unidentified body, labeled John Doe, had been dead for almost a month. A mere 30 feet away from the body was another victim, Edward

Andrassy. Unlike John Doe, Andrassy had only been dead for days, indicating that the spot was a dumping ground.

After a few months passed without another body, police thought the worst was over. Then on January 26, 1936, the partial remains of a new victim, a woman, were found in downtown Cleveland. On February 7, more remains were found at a separate location, and the deceased was identified as Florence Genevieve Polillo. Despite similarities among the three murders, authorities had yet to connect them—serial killers were highly uncommon at the time.

Tattoo Man, Eliot Ness, and More Victims

On June 5, two young boys passing through Kingsbury Run discovered a severed head. The rest of the body was found near the Nickel Plate railroad police station. Despite six distinctive tattoos on the man's body (thus the nickname "Tattoo Man"), he was never identified and became John Doe II.

At this point, Cleveland's newly appointed director of public safety, Eliot Ness, was officially briefed on the case. While Ness and his men hunted down leads, the headless body of another unidentified male was found west of Cleveland on July 22, 1936. It appeared that the man, John Doe III, had been murdered several months earlier. On September 10, the headless body of a sixth victim, John Doe IV, was found in Kingsbury Run. Ness officially started spearheading the investigation. Determined to bring the killer to justice, Ness's staff fanned out across the city, even going undercover in the Kingsbury Run area. As 1936 drew to a close, no suspects had been named nor new victims discovered. City residents believed that Ness's team had run the killer off.

The Body Count Climbs

A woman's mutilated torso washed up on the beach at 156th Street on February 23, 1937. The rest would wash ashore two months later. (Strangely, the body washed up in the same location as the "Lady of the Lake" had three years earlier.)

On June 6, 1937, teenager Russell Lauyer found the decomposed body of a woman inside of a burlap sack under the Lorain-Carnegie Bridge in Cleveland. With the body was a newspaper from June of the previous year, suggesting a timeline for the murder. An investigation indicated the body might belong to one Rose Wallace; this was never confirmed, and the victim is sometimes referred to as Jane Doe II. Pieces of another man's body (the ninth victim) began washing ashore on July 6, just below Kingsbury Run. Cleveland newspapers were having a field day with the case that the "great" Eliot Ness couldn't solve. This fueled Ness, and he promised justice.

Burning of Kingsbury Run

The next nine months were quiet, and the public began to relax. When a woman's severed leg was found in the Cuyahoga River on April 8, 1938, however, people debated its connection to the Butcher. But the rest of Jane Doe III was soon found inside two burlap sacks floating in the river (*sans* head, of course).

On August 16, 1938, the last two confirmed victims of the Butcher were found together at the East 9th Street Lakeshore Dump. Jane Doe IV had apparently been dead for four to six months prior to discovery, while John Doe VI may have been dead for almost nine months.

Something snapped inside Eliot Ness. On the night of August 18, Ness and dozens of police officials raided the shantytowns in the Flats, ending up in Kingsbury Run. Along the way, they interrogated or arrested anyone they came across, and Ness ordered the shanties burned to the ground. There would be no more confirmed victims of the Mad Butcher of Kingsbury Run.

Who Was the Mad Butcher?

There were two prime suspects in the case, though no one was ever charged. The first was Dr. Francis Sweeney, a surgeon with the knowledge many believed necessary to mutilate the victims the way the killer did. (He was also a cousin of Congressman Martin L. Sweeney, a known political opponent of Ness.)

In August 1938, Dr. Sweeney was interrogated by Ness, two other men, and the inventor of the polygraph machine, Dr. Royal Grossman. By all accounts, Sweeney failed the polygraph test (several times), and Ness believed he had his man, but he was released due to lack of evidence. Two days after the interrogation, on August 25, 1938, Sweeney checked himself into the Sandusky Veterans Hospital. He remained institutionalized at various facilities until his death in 1965. Because Sweeney voluntarily checked himself in, he could have left whenever he desired.

The other suspect was Frank Dolezal, who was arrested by private investigators on July 5, 1939, as a suspect in the murder of Florence Polillo, with whom he had lived for a time. While in custody, Dolezal confessed to killing Polillo, although some believe the confession was forced. Either way, Dolezal died under mysterious circumstances while incarcerated at the Cuyahoga County Jail before he could be charged.

As for Eliot Ness, some believe his inability to bring the Butcher to trial weighed on him for the rest of his life. Ness went to his grave without getting a conviction. To this day, the case remains open.

A Fiery Debate: Spontaneous Human Combustion

Proponents contend that the phenomenon—in which a person suddenly bursts into flames—is very real. Skeptics, however, are quick to explain it away.

✳ ✳ ✳ ✳

The Curious Case of Helen Conway

A PHOTO DOCUMENTS THE gruesome death of Helen Conway. Visible in the black-and-white image—taken in 1964 in Delaware County, Pennsylvania—is an oily smear that was her torso and, behind, an ashen specter of the upholstered bedroom chair she occupied. The picture's most haunting feature might be her legs, thin and ghostly pale, clearly intact and seemingly unscathed by whatever it was that consumed the rest of her.

What consumed her, say proponents of a theory that people can catch fire without an external source of ignition, was spontaneous human combustion. It's a classic case, believers assert: Conway was immolated by an intense, precisely localized source of heat that damaged little else in the room. Adding to the mystery, the investigating fire marshal said that it took just twenty-one minutes for her to burn away and that he could not identify an outside accelerant.

If Conway's body ignited from within and burned so quickly she had no time to rise and seek help, hers wouldn't be the first or last death to fit the pattern of spontaneous human combustion.

The phenomenon was documented as early as 1763 by Frenchman Jonas Dupont in his collection of accounts, published as *De Incendis Corporis Humani Spontaneis*. Charles Dickens's 1852 novel *Bleak House* sensationalized the issue with the spontaneous-combustion death of a character named Krook. That humans have been reduced to ashes with little damage to their surroundings is not the stuff of fiction, however. Many documented cases exist. The question is, did these people combust spontaneously?

How It Happens

Theories advancing the concept abound. Early hypotheses held that victims, such as Dickens's Krook, were likely alcoholics so besotted that their very flesh became flammable. Later conjecture blamed the influence of geomagnetism.

A 1996 book by John Heymer, *The Entrancing Flame*, maintained emotional distress could lead to explosions of defective mitochondria. These outbursts cause cellular releases of hydrogen and oxygen and trigger crematory reactions in the body. That same year, Larry E. Arnold—publicity material calls him a parascientist—published *Ablaze! The Mysterious Fires of Spontaneous Human Combustion*. Arnold claimed sufferers were struck by a subatomic particle he had discovered and named the "pyrotron."

Perhaps somewhat more credible reasoning came out of Brooklyn, New York, where the eponymous founder of Robin Beach Engineers Associated (described as a scientific detective agency) linked the theory of spontaneous human combustion with proven instances of individuals whose biology caused them to retain intense concentrations of static electricity.

A Controversy Is Sparked

Skeptics are legion. They suspect that accounts are often embellished or important facts are ignored. That the unfortunate Helen Conway was overweight and a heavy smoker, for instance, likely played a key role in her demise.

Indeed, Conway's case is considered by some to be evidence of the wick effect, which might be today's most forensically respected explanation for spontaneous human combustion. It holds that an external source, such as a dropped cigarette, ignites bedding, clothing, or furnishings. This material acts like an absorbing wick, while the body's fat takes on the fueling role of candle wax. The burning fat liquefies, saturating the bedding, clothing, or furnishings, and keeps the heat localized.

The result is a long, slow immolation that burns away fatty tissues, organs, and associated bone, leaving leaner areas, such as legs, untouched. Experiments on pig carcasses show it can take five or more hours, with the body's water boiling off ahead of the spreading fire.

Under the wick theory, victims are likely to already be unconscious when the fire starts. They're in closed spaces with little moving air, so the flames are allowed to smolder, doing their work without disrupting the surroundings or alerting passersby.

Nevertheless, even the wick effect theory, like all other explanations of spontaneous human combustion, has scientific weaknesses. The fact remains, according to the mainstream science community, that evidence of spontaneous human combustion is entirely circumstantial, and that not a single proven eyewitness account exists to substantiate anyone's claims of "Poof—the body just went up in flames!"

Anything but Splendor: Natalie Wood

The official account of Natalie Wood's tragic death is riddled with holes. For this reason, cover-up theorists continue to run hog-wild with conjecture. Here's a sampling of the questions, facts, and assertions surrounding the case.

✳   ✳   ✳   ✳

A Life in Pictures

THERE ARE THOSE who will forever recall Natalie Wood as the adorable child actress from *Miracle on 34th Street* (1947) and those who remember her as the sexy but wholesome grown-up star of movies such as *West Side Story* (1961), *Splendor in the Grass* (1961), and *Bob & Carol & Ted & Alice* (1969). Both groups generally agree that Wood had uncommon beauty and talent.

Wood appeared in her first film, *Happy Land* (1943), in a bit part alongside other people from her hometown of Santa Rosa, California, where the film was shot. She stood out to the director, who remembered her later when he needed to cast a child in another film. Wood was uncommonly mature and professional for a child actress, which helped her make a relatively smooth transition to ingenue roles.

Although Wood befriended James Dean and Sal Mineo—her troubled young costars from *Rebel Without a Cause* (1955)—and she briefly dated Elvis Presley, she preferred to move in established Hollywood circles. By the time she was 20, she was married to Robert Wagner and was costarring with Frank Sinatra in *Kings Go Forth* (1958), which firmly ensconced her in the Hollywood establishment. The early 1960s represent the high point of Wood's career, and she specialized in playing high-spirited characters with determination and spunk. She added two more Oscar nominations to the one she received for *Rebel* and racked up five Golden Globe nominations for Best Actress. This period also proved to be personally turbulent for Wood, as she suffered through a failed marriage to Wagner and another to Richard Gregson. After taking time off to raise her children, she remarried Wagner and returned to her acting career.

Shocking News

And so, on November 29, 1981, the headline hit the news-wires much like an out-of-control car hits a brick wall. Natalie Wood, the beautiful, vivacious 43-year-old star of stage and screen, had drowned after falling from her yacht the *Splendour*, which was anchored off California's Santa Catalina Island. Wood had been on the boat during a break from her latest film, *Brainstorm*, and was accompanied by Wagner and *Brainstorm* costar Christopher Walken. Skipper Dennis Davern was at the helm. Foul play was not suspected.

In My Esteemed Opinion

After a short investigation, Chief Medical Examiner Dr. Thomas Noguchi listed Wood's death as an accidental drowning. Tests revealed that she had consumed "seven or eight" glasses of wine, and the coroner contended that in her intoxicated state Wood had probably stumbled and fallen overboard while attempting to untie the yacht's rubber dinghy. He also stated that cuts and bruises on her body could have occurred when she fell from the boat.

Doubting Thomases

To this day, many question Wood's mysterious demise and believe that the accidental drowning theory sounds a bit too convenient. Pointed questions have led to many rumors: Does someone know more about Wood's final moments than they're letting on? Was her drowning really an accident, or did someone intentionally or accidentally *help* her overboard? Could this be why she sustained substantial bruising on her face and the back of her legs? Why was Wagner so reluctant to publicly discuss the incident? Were Christopher Walken and Wood an item as had been rumored? With this possibility in mind, could a booze-fueled fight have erupted between the two men? Could Wood have then tried to intervene, only to be knocked overboard for her efforts? And why did authorities declare Wood's death accidental so quickly? Would such a hasty ruling have been issued had the principals not been famous, wealthy, and influential?

Ripples

At the time of Wood's death, she and Wagner were seven years into their second marriage to each other. Whether Wood was carrying on an affair with Walken, as was alleged, may be immaterial, even if it made for interesting tabloid fodder. But Wagner's perception of their relationship could certainly be a factor. If nothing else, it might better explain the argument that ensued between Wagner and Walken that fateful night.

Case Closed?

Further information about Wood's death is sparse because no eyewitnesses have come forward. However, a businesswoman whose boat was anchored nearby testified that she heard a woman shouting for help, and then a voice responding, "We'll be over to get you," so the woman went back to bed. Just after dawn, Wood's body was found floating a mile away from the *Splendour*, approximately 200 yards offshore. The dinghy was found nearby; its only cargo was a stack of lifejackets.

In 2008, after 27 years of silence, Robert Wagner recalled in his autobiography, *Pieces of My Heart: A Life*, that he and Walken had engaged in a heated argument during supper after Walken had suggested that Wood star in more films, effectively keeping her away from their children. Wagner and Walken then headed topside to cool down. Sometime around midnight, Wagner said he returned to his cabin and discovered that his wife was missing. He soon realized that the yacht's dinghy was gone as well. In his book, he surmised that Wood may have gone to secure the dinghy that had been noisily slapping against the boat. Then, tipsy from the wine, she probably fell into the ocean and drowned. Walken notified the authorities.

Was Natalie Wood's demise the result of a deadly mix of wine and saltwater as the coroner's report suggests? This certainly could be the case. But why would she leave her warm cabin to tend to a loose rubber dinghy in the dark of night?

Perhaps we'll never know what happened that fateful night, but an interview conducted shortly before Wood's death proved prophetic: "I'm frightened to death of the water," said Wood about a long-held fear. "I can swim a little bit, but I'm afraid of water that is dark."

5 of History's Coldest Cases

They were gruesome crimes that shocked us with their brutality. But as time passed, we heard less and less about them until we forgot about the crime, not even realizing that the perpetrator remained among us. Yet the files remain open, and the families of the victims live on in a state of semi-paralysis. Here are some of the world's most famous cold cases.

✳ ✳ ✳ ✳

1. **The Zodiac Killer:** The Zodiac Killer was responsible for several murders in the San Francisco area in the 1960s and 1970s. His victims were shot, stabbed, and bludgeoned to

death. After the first few kills, he began sending letters to the local press in which he taunted police and made public threats, such as planning to blow up a school bus. In a letter sent to the *San Francisco Chronicle* two days after the murder of cabbie Paul Stine in October 1969, the killer, who called himself "The Zodiac," included in the package pieces of Stine's blood-soaked shirt. In the letters, which continued until 1978, he claimed a cumulative tally of 37 murders.

2. **Swedish Prime Minister Olof Palme:** On February 28, 1986, Swedish Prime Minister Olof Palme was gunned down on a Stockholm street as he and his wife strolled home from the movies unprotected around midnight. The prime minister was fatally shot in the back. His wife was seriously wounded but survived.

   In 1988, a petty thief and drug addict named Christer Petterson was convicted of the murder because he was picked out of a lineup by Palme's widow. The conviction was later overturned on appeal when doubts were raised as to the reliability of Mrs. Palme's evidence. In 2020, Swedish police declared the case closed. They said they beileved the killer was a man named Stig Engström, known as an eyewitness to the crime, who had later committed suicide.

3. **Bob Crane:** In 1978, Bob Crane, star of TV's *Hogan's Heroes*, was clubbed to death in his apartment. Crane shared a close friendship with John Carpenter, a pioneer in the development of video technology. The two shared an affinity for debauchery and sexual excesses, which were recorded on videotape. But by late 1978, Crane was tiring of Carpenter's dependence on him and had let him know that the friendship was over.

   The following day, June 29, 1978, Crane was bludgeoned to death with a camera tripod in his Scottsdale, Arizona, apartment. Suspicion immediately fell on Carpenter, and a small spattering of blood was found in Carpenter's rental car, but police were unable to connect it to the crime. Examiners also found a tiny piece of human tissue in the car. Sixteen years after the killing, Carpenter finally went to trial, but he was acquitted due to lack of evidence.

4. **Tupac Shakur:** On September 7, 1996, successful rap artist Tupac Shakur was shot four times in a drive-by shooting in Las Vegas. He died six days later. Two years prior to that, Shakur had been shot five times in the lobby of a Manhattan recording studio the day before he was found guilty of sexual assault. He survived that attack, only to spend the next 11 months in jail. The 1994 shooting was a major catalyst for an East Coast-West Coast feud that would envelop the hip-hop industry and culminate in the deaths of both Shakur and Notorious B.I.G. (Christopher Wallace).

On the night of the fatal shooting, Shakur attended the Mike Tyson-Bruce Seldon fight at the MGM Grand in Las Vegas. After the fight, Shakur and his entourage got into a scuffle with a gang member. Shakur then headed for a nightclub, but he never made it. No one was ever arrested for the killing.

5. **JonBenét Ramsey:** In the early hours of December 26, 1996, Patsy Ramsey reported that her six-year-old daughter, JonBenét, had been abducted from her Boulder, Colorado, home. Police rushed to the Ramsey home where, hours later, John Ramsey found his little girl dead in the basement. She had been battered, sexually assaulted, and strangled.

Police found several tantalizing bits of evidence—a number of footprints, a rope that did not belong on the premises, marks on the body that suggested the use of a stun gun, and DNA samples on the girl's body. The ransom note was also suspicious. Police found that it was written with a pen and pad of paper belonging to the Ramseys. The amount demanded, $118,000, was a surprisingly small amount, considering that John Ramsey was worth more than $6 million. It is also interesting to note that Mr. Ramsey had just received a year-end bonus of $118,117.50.

A number of suspects were considered, but one by one they were cleared. Finally, the police zeroed in on the parents. For years, the Ramseys were put under intense pressure by authorities and the public alike to confess to the murder. However, a grand jury investigation ended with no indictments. In 2003, a judge ruled that an intruder had killed JonBenét. Then, in August 2006, John Mark Karr confessed, claiming that he was with the girl when she died. However, Karr's DNA did not match that found on JonBenét. He was not charged, and the case remains unsolved.

Famous Curses

No one really knows for sure if there's any truth to these curses, but if you want to take James Dean's car for a spin, or dig up an ancient mummy, don't expect us to help!

✳ ✳ ✳ ✳

1. **"The Club":** If you're a rock star and you're about to turn 27, you might want to consider taking a year off to avoid membership in "The Club." Robert Johnson, an African-American musician, who Eric Clapton called "the most important blues musician who ever lived," played the guitar so well that some said he must have made a deal with the devil. So when he died at 27, folks said it must have been time to pay up. Since Johnson, a host of musical geniuses have gone to an early grave at age 27. Brian Jones, founding member of the Rolling Stones, died at age 27 in 1969. Then it was both Jimi Hendrix and Janis Joplin in 1970 and Jim Morrison the following year. Kurt Cobain joined

"The Club" in 1994. Fast-forward to 2011, when British chanteuse Amy Winehouse succumbed to alcohol poisoning at the age of—you guessed it—27. Coincidence? Or were these musical geniuses paying debts, too?

2. **"Da Billy Goat" Curse:** In 1945, William "Billy Goat" Sianis brought his pet goat, Murphy, to Wrigley Field to see the fourth game of the 1945 World Series between the Chicago Cubs and the Detroit Tigers. Sianis and his goat were later ejected from the game, and Sianis reportedly put a curse on the team that day. And for 71 years, the Cubs have had legendarily bad luck. Over the years, Cubs fans have experienced agony in repeated late-season collapses when victory seemed imminent. In 1969, 1984, 1989, and 2003, the Cubs were painfully close to advancing to the World Series but couldn't hold the lead. Even those who don't consider themselves Cubs fans blame the hex for the weird and almost comical losses year after year. But the curse was broken in 2016 when the Cubs won the World Series against Cleveland. The Cubs hadn't won a World Series since 1908—no other team in the history of the game has gone that long without a championship.

3. **Rasputin and the Romanovs:** Rasputin, the self-proclaimed magician and cult leader, wormed his way into the palace of the Romanovs, Russia's ruling family, around the turn of the last century. After getting a little too big for his britches, a few of the Romanovs allegedly decided to have him killed. But he was exceptionally resilient. Reportedly it took poison, falling down a staircase, and repeated gunshots before Rasputin was finally dead. It's said that Rasputin mumbled a curse from his deathbed, assuring Russia's ruling monarchs that they would all be dead within a year. That did come to pass, as the Romanov family was brutally murdered in a mass execution less than a year later.

4. Tecumseh and the American Presidents: The curse of Tippecanoe, or "Tecumseh's Curse," is a widely held explanation of the fact that from 1840 to 1960, every U.S. president elected (or reelected) every twentieth year has died in office. Popular belief is that Tecumseh administered the curse when William Henry Harrison's troops defeated the Native American leader and his forces at the Battle of Tippecanoe. Check it out:

* William Henry Harrison was elected president in 1840. He caught a cold during his inauguration, which quickly turned into pneumonia. He died April 4, 1841, after only one month in office.

* Abraham Lincoln was elected president in 1860 and reelected four years later. Lincoln was assassinated and died April 15, 1865.

* James Garfield was elected president in 1880. Charles Guiteau shot him in July 1881. Garfield died several months later, from complications following the gunshot wound.

* William McKinley was elected president in 1896 and reelected in 1900. On September 6, 1901, McKinley was shot by Leon F. Czolgosz, who considered the president an "enemy of the people." McKinley died eight days later.

* Three years after Warren G. Harding was elected president in 1920, he died suddenly of either a heart attack or stroke while traveling in San Francisco.

* Franklin D. Roosevelt was elected president in 1932 and reelected in 1936, 1940, and 1944. His health wasn't great, but he died rather suddenly in 1945, of a cerebral hemorrhage or stroke.

* John F. Kennedy was elected president in 1960 and assassinated in Dallas three years later.

* Ronald Reagan was elected president in 1980, and though he was shot by an assassin in 1981, he did survive. Some say this broke the curse.

5. The Curse of the Kennedy Family: Okay, so maybe if this family had stayed out of politics and off airplanes, their fate might be different. Regardless, the number of Kennedy family tragedies have led some to believe there must be a curse on the whole bunch. You decide:

* JFK's brother Joseph, Jr., and sister Kathleen both died in separate plane crashes in 1944 and 1948, respectively.

* JFK's other sister, Rosemary, was institutionalized in a mental hospital for years.

* John F. Kennedy himself, America's 35th president, was assassinated in 1963 at age 46.

* Robert Kennedy, JFK's younger brother, was assassinated in 1968.

* Senator Ted Kennedy, JFK's youngest brother, survived a plane crash in 1964. In 1969, he was driving a car that went off a bridge, causing the death of his companion, Mary Jo Kopechne. His presidential goals were pretty much squashed after that.

* In 1984, Robert Kennedy's son David died of a drug overdose. Another son, Michael, died in a skiing accident in 1997.

* In 1999, JFK, Jr., his wife, and his sister-in-law died when the small plane he was piloting crashed into the Atlantic Ocean.

Thelma Todd: Suicide or Murder?

During her nine-year film career, Thelma Todd costarred in dozens of comedies with the likes of Harry Langdon, Laurel and Hardy, and the Marx Brothers. Today, however, the "Ice Cream Blonde," as she was known, is best remembered for her bizarre death, which remains one of Hollywood's most enduring mysteries. Let's explore what could have happened.

✳   ✳   ✳   ✳

Sins Indulged

TODD WAS BORN in Lawrence, Massachusetts, in 1906 and arrived in Hollywood at age 20 via the beauty pageant circuit. Pretty and vivacious, she quickly became a hot commodity and fell headlong into Tinseltown's anything-goes party scene. In 1932, she married Pasquale "Pat" DiCicco, an agent of sorts who was also associated with gangster Charles "Lucky" Luciano. Their marriage was plagued by drunken fights, and they divorced two years later.

For solace, Todd turned to director Roland West, who didn't approve of her drinking and drug use, but he could not stop her. With his help, Todd opened a roadhouse called Thelma Todd's Sidewalk Café, located on the Pacific Coast Highway, and the actress moved into a spacious apartment above the restaurant. Shortly after, Todd began a relationship with gangster "Lucky" Luciano, who tried to get her to let him use a room at the Sidewalk Café for illegal gambling. Todd repeatedly refused.

On the morning of December 16, 1935, Todd was found dead in the front seat of her 1934 Lincoln Phaeton convertible, which was parked in the two-car garage she shared with West. The apparent cause of death was carbon monoxide poisoning, though whether Todd was the victim of an accident, suicide, or murder remains a mystery.

Little evidence supports the suicide theory, outside the mode of death and the fact that Todd led a fast-paced lifestyle that sometimes got the better of her. Indeed, her career was going remarkably well, and she had purchased Christmas presents and was looking forward to a New Year's Eve party. So suicide does not seem a viable cause, though it is still mentioned as a probable one in many accounts.

The Accident Theory

However, an accidental death is also a possibility. The key to her car was in the "on" position, and the motor was dead when Todd was discovered by her maid. West suggested to investigators that the actress turned on the car to get warm, passed out because she was drunk, and then succumbed to carbon monoxide poisoning. Todd also had a heart condition, according to West, and this may have contributed to her death.

Nonetheless, the notion of foul play is suggested by several incongruities found at the scene. Spots of blood were discovered on and in Todd's car and on her mouth, and her nose was broken, leading some to believe she was knocked out then placed in the car to make it look like a suicide. (Police attributed the injuries to Todd falling unconscious and striking her head on the steering wheel.) In addition, Todd's blood-alcohol level was extremely high—high enough to stupefy her so that someone could carry her without her fighting back—and her high-heeled shoes were clean and unscuffed, even though she would have had to ascend a flight of outdoor, concrete stairs to reach the garage, which was a 271-step climb behind the restaurant. Investigators also found an unidentified smudged handprint on the left side of the vehicle.

Two With Motive

If Todd was murdered, as some have suggested, who had motive? Because of her wild lifestyle, there are several potential suspects, most notably Pasquale DiCicco, who was known to have a violent temper, and "Lucky" Luciano, who was angry at Todd for refusing to let him use her restaurant for illegal activities.

Despite the many questions raised by the evidence found at the scene, a grand jury ruled Todd's death accidental. The investigation had been hampered by altered and destroyed evidence, threats to witnesses, and cover-ups, making it impossible to ever learn what really happened. An open-casket service was held at Forest Lawn Memorial Park, where the public viewed the actress bedecked in yellow roses. After the service, Todd was cremated, eliminating the possibility of a second autopsy. Later, when her mother, Alice Todd, died, the actress's ashes were placed in her mother's casket so they could be buried together in Massachusetts.

The King Is Dead . . . Wait, Not Yet

On January 20, 1936, England's beloved King George V—grandfather of the reigning Queen Elizabeth II—died in his sleep. Or was it actually murder? You be the judge.

✳ ✳ ✳ ✳

Case Files

ON JANUARY 17, 1936, Queen Mary called the royal physician, Lord Bertrand Dawson, to attend to her 71-year-old husband, King George V, who couldn't seem to shake his bronchitis. Over the next three days, the king slipped in and out of consciousness. On the morning of January 20, the king held a ten-minute meeting with his counselors and, at some point, summoned his private secretary, Wigram, to discuss the nation's business. "How is the Empire?" he asked, in what would allegedly be his final words. Exhaustion overcame him before the conversation could continue.

That night after dinner, Dawson gave the king a shot of morphine to help him sleep. At 9:25 PM, Dawson issued a brief medical bulletin to prepare the nation for the inevitable: "The King's life is moving peacefully towards its close," it said. An hour and a half later—five minutes before midnight—the king was dead.

For half a century, this is the story that the public (and biographers) believed. But some startling details later came to light, revealing what may in fact be a case of murder in the first degree.

Stop the Presses!

November 28, 1986, was a day that literally rewrote history. It was on this day, nearly 50 years after the king's death and 41 after Dawson's, that the physician's personal diary was published in the Windsor archives. The sordid truth about the king's demise was exposed.

According to the doctor's notes, the king simply wasn't dying quickly enough. Around 11:00 PM on January 20—an hour and a half after Dawson released the bulletin announcing the king's imminent passing—he realized it was not going to be a speedy process. "The last stage might endure for many hours," he wrote, "unknown to the patient but little comporting with the dignity and serenity which he so richly merited." What's worse, the king's delay would mean that his obituary wouldn't run in the morning edition of the London *Times*, the paper considered most appropriate for national news, but rather in some "less appropriate" evening publication. How bourgeois!

Taking matters into his own hands, Dawson called his wife and asked her to contact the *Times* to have them hold publication;

there was going to be some big news coming yet that night. Then, at 11:25 PM, Dawson prepared a lethal cocktail of three-quarters of a gram of morphine and one gram of cocaine, and he injected it into the king's jugular vein. Thirty minutes later, King George was dead—just in time to make the morning news. "A Peaceful Ending at Midnight," read the *Times* headline.

In his notes, Dawson describes his actions as "a facet of euthanasia or so-called mercy killing," done to protect the reputation of the king. He also claims that both the queen and Prince Edward were in agreement that the king's life should not be prolonged if his illness was fatal. That said, his notes say nothing about his efforts to consult them of his decision. Most likely, he made it on his own.

Murder or Mercy?

Euthanasia is defined as "the intentional killing of a dependent human being for his or her alleged benefit." Euthanasia by action means "intentionally causing death by performing an action such as giving a lethal injection," while nonvoluntary euthanasia means doing it without the patient's consent. Murder, on the other hand, is to "kill unlawfully and with premeditated malice." If the question is intent, then it's hard to argue that Dawson's actions make him a murderer, even though many in England, including the medical community, believe that's just what the prominent physician was. From a legal perspective, euthanasia is and always has been "unlawful" in England, as it is in most places throughout the world.

In fact, Dawson himself opposed euthanasia as a legal practice. Just ten months after the king's passing, Dawson spoke against a bill that would have legalized it, arguing that it should be a choice left to the individual doctor, not the federal government. In what can now perhaps be seen as an attempt to excuse his own actions, Dawson went on to say that a doctor "should make the act of dying more gentle and more peaceful, even if it does involve the curtailment of the length of life."

Although Dawson died in 1945 with a glowing reputation for his years of service to the royal family, today his name is a source of anger and disgrace. As recently as 1994, the *British Medical Journal* published an article deriding him for his selfishness and "arrogance," claiming that he committed a "convenience killing" of the king in order to return to his own busy private practice in London.

Now, it's true that King George asked Wigram, "How is the Empire?" and then drifted into sleep. But those words actually weren't the last ones spoken by the dying king. According to Dawson's notes, the king's last worst words were uttered just as the doctor injected him with the first dose of morphine: "God damn you."

Other Instances of Euthanasia

While the story of King George is shocking, others have sought the right to end their own life on their own terms.

In Switzerland, assisted suicide has been legal since the 1940s. According to a 1997 Reuters UK article, many terminally ill people from other countries travel to Switzerland to end their lives.

In 1994, Oregon passed the Death with Dignity Act, becoming the first state to legalize physician-assisted suicide, in which a patient voluntarily enlists the help of a doctor to end his or her life. (Think Dr. Jack Kevorkian.) The law didn't go into effect until 1997.

Speaking of Dr. Kevorkian (aka "Dr. Death"), the physician was released from prison in June 2007 following an eight-year sentence for second-degree murder, of which he was convicted after administering a fatal injection to Michigan patient Thomas Youk, who suffered from Lou Gehrig's disease. Prosecutors had previously failed on four different occasions to convict Kevorkian for assisting in the suicides of terminal patients.

Testimony From the Other Side

When Zona Heaster Shue of Greenbrier County, West Virginia, died suddenly at age 23, her doctor attributed her passing to natural causes. But when Zona's mother encountered her ghost, a shocking tale of murder was revealed. Would testimony from the Other Side help to nab Zona's killer?

✳   ✳   ✳   ✳

Gone Too Soon

ON JANUARY 23, 1897, a boy who was doing chores at the Shue home discovered Zona's limp body lying at the bottom of the stairs. He ran to tell her husband—Edward Stribbling "Trout" Shue—and then he summoned a doctor. When Dr. George W. Knapp arrived, Shue escorted him to the bedroom where he'd moved Zona's lifeless body. Although Shue had already dressed Zona for burial, Knapp examined her body. As the doctor went about his duties, Shue became noticeably distressed, so Knapp cut the examination short. Suspecting natural causes as the reason for Zona's passing and not wishing to upset her husband any further, Knapp reported her cause of death as "everlasting faint" but later changed the finding to "childbirth." Although Zona hadn't told anyone that she was pregnant, the doctor surmised that complications from a pregnancy must have been the culprit because he'd recently treated her for "female trouble." During his hasty examination, Knapp noticed a few bruises on Zona's neck but quickly passed them off as unrelated.

Whirlwind Courtship

Little is known about her life, but it is believed that Zona Heaster was born in Greenbrier County, West Virginia, around 1873. In October 1896, she met Shue, a drifter who had recently moved to the area to work as a blacksmith.

Only months after they met, Zona Heaster and Edward Shue married. But for reasons that she couldn't quite explain, Zona's mother—Mary Jane Heaster—had taken an instant disliking to her son-in-law. Despite her concerns, the newlyweds seemed to get along until that tragic day when Zona was found dead. In an instant, Mary Jane's world was turned upside down. She grieved, as would any mother who must bury a child, but she sharply disagreed with Dr. Knapp's determination of her daughter's cause of death. In her mind, there was only one way that her daughter could have died at such a young age: Shue had killed her and had covered it up.

It All Comes Out in the Wash

At Zona's wake, those who came to pay their respects noticed Shue's erratic behavior: He continued to openly mourn his wife's passing, but something seemed odd about the way he grieved. His mood alternated between extreme sadness and sudden manic energy. He tended to his wife's body like a man possessed, allowing no one to get close to it. He also tied a large scarf around his wife's neck for no apparent reason, and even stranger, he placed a pillow on one side of Zona's head and a rolled-up cloth on the other; he told puzzled onlookers that they would help her "rest easier." And when Zona's body was moved to the cemetery for burial, several people noticed a strange looseness to her neck as they transported her. Not surprisingly, people began to talk.

Mary Jane Heaster did not have to be convinced that Shue was acting suspiciously about Zona's death. She had always hated him and wished that her daughter had never married him. She had a sneaking suspicion that something wasn't right, but she didn't know how to prove it.

After the funeral, Mary Jane Heaster washed the sheet that had lined her daughter's coffin. To her horror, the water inside the basin turned red. Then, even more shockingly, the sheet turned pink and the water again turned clear. Mary Jane was convinced that this was a sign, so she began praying that her daughter would come to her to reveal the truth.

Ghostly Visions

According to Mary Jane, Zona's apparition came to her over the course of four nights. It described how abusive Shue had been throughout their marriage and stated that he was responsible for her death. The tragedy occurred because Shue thought that Zona hadn't cooked meat for supper; he went into a rage, strangled her, and broke her neck. To demonstrate the brutality of Shue's attack, Zona's ghost rotated her head completely around. This horrified Mary Jane, but it also brought her some relief: Her beloved daughter had returned from the grave to seek the justice that she deserved. Armed with the unbridled power of a mother's love, Mary Jane was determined to avenge her daughter's death.

Please Believe Me!

Mary Jane immediately told local prosecutor John Alfred Preston of her ghostly visit, and begged him to investigate. Whether or not he took Mary Jane at her word is open to debate, but Preston did agree to interview Knapp and others associated with the case.

After learning that Dr. Knapp's examination had been cursory at best, Preston and Knapp agreed that an autopsy would help to clear things up, so Zona's body was exhumed. A local newspaper reported that Edward Shue "vigorously complained" about the exhumation but was forced to witness the proceedings. When Dr. Knapp proclaimed that Zona's neck was indeed broken, Shue was arrested and charged with his wife's murder.

While Shue awaited trial, tales of his unsavory past started coming to light. It was revealed that he'd been married twice before. His first marriage (to Allie Estelline Cutlip) had ended in divorce in 1889, while Shue was incarcerated for horse theft. In their divorce decree, Cutlip claimed that Shue had frequently beaten her. In 1894, Shue married Lucy Ann Tritt; however, the union was short-lived—Tritt died just eight months into their marriage under "mysterious" circumstances.

In the autumn of 1896, Shue moved to Greenbrier County, where he met Zona Heaster. Was there a pattern of violence with this lethal lothario?

Trial

Shue's trial began on June 22, 1897. Both the prosecution and the defense did their best to discredit each other: For every witness who spoke of Shue's ill temper, another likened him to an altar boy. After Shue took the stand, many agreed that he handled himself skillfully. Then it was Mary Jane Heaster's turn. When questioned by the prosecution, her ghostly encounter with her daughter was not mentioned. But when she was cross-examined by Shue's attorney, Mary Jane recalled in great detail how Zona's spirit had fingered Shue as her abuser and killer. The defense characterized Mary Jane's "visions" as little more than a grieving mother's ravings, assuming that the jury would agree. They were wrong. When the trial concluded, the jury quickly rendered a guilty verdict. Not only had they believed Mary Jane's supernatural tale, they fell just short of delivering the necessary votes to hang Shue for his evil deeds; instead, he was sentenced to life in prison. And as it turned out, that wouldn't be very long.

Epilogue

In July 1897, Shue was transferred to the West Virginia Penitentiary in Moundsville, where he lived out the rest of his days. The convicted murderer died on March 13, 1900, of an epidemic that was sweeping the prison. But his name lives on, as does the ghostly legend of Zona Heaster Shue. A historical marker located beside Route 60 in Greenbrier County reads:

Greenbrier Ghost

"Interred in nearby cemetery is Zona Heaster Shue. Her death in 1897 was presumed natural until her spirit appeared to her mother to describe how she was killed by her husband Edward. Autopsy on the exhumed body verified the apparition's account. Edward, found guilty of murder, was sentenced to the state prison. Only known case in which testimony from ghost helped convict a murderer."

The Philip Phenomenon: Creating a Ghost out of Thin Air

Which came first: the ghost or the séance? That's the million-dollar question regarding the Philip Phenomenon—an astonishing experiment that successfully conjured up a spirit. The only problem is that this ghost never really lived... Or did it?

* * * *

I T ALL BEGAN in 1972, when members of the Toronto Society for Psychical Research (TSPR) conducted an experiment to determine if they could "create" a ghost and study how the power of suggestion affected the results. They wanted to know if they could work with a totally fictitious character—a man they invented from scratch—and somehow make contact with its spirit. And they did.

Dr. A.R.G. Owen, the organization's chief parapsychology researcher, gathered a group of eight people who were interested in the paranormal but had no psychic abilities of their own. The Owen Group, as it was called, was made up of people from all walks of life, including Owen's wife, an accountant, an industrial designer, a former MENSA chairwoman, a housewife, a student, and a bookkeeper. Dr. Joel Whitton, a psychologist, was also present at many of the meetings as an observer.

The Making of a Ghost

The first order of business was to create the ghost, giving it physical characteristics and a complete background story. According to Dr. Owen, it was important to the study that the spirit be totally made-up, with no strong ties to any historical figure.

The group named the ghost Philip and proceeded to bring him to life—on paper, that is. A sketch artist even drew a picture of Philip as the group imagined him. Here is his story:

Philip Aylesford was an aristocratic Englishman who was born in 1624. As a supporter of the King, he was knighted at age 16 and went on to make a name for himself in the military. He married Dorothea, the beautiful daughter of a nobleman who lived nearby. Unfortunately, Dorothea's appearance was deceiving, as her personality was cold and unyielding. As a Catholic, Philip wouldn't divorce his wife, so he found escape by riding around the grounds of his estate. One day, he came across a Travelers' camp. There, he found true love in the arms of the raven-haired Margo, whose dark eyes seemed to look into his soul. He brought her to Diddington Manor, his family home, and hid her in the gatehouse near the stable. But it wasn't meant to be: Dorothea soon discovered her husband's secret affair and retaliated by accusing Margo of stealing and practicing witchcraft. Afraid of damaging his own reputation, Philip did not step forward in Margo's defense, and she was burned at the stake. After the death of his beloved, Philip was tormented with guilt and loneliness; he killed himself in 1654 at age 30.

Focus, Focus, Focus

In September 1972, after the tale was written, the group began meeting regularly. Reports of these meetings vary. Some accounts describe them as mere gatherings in which group members would discuss Philip and meditate on the details of his life. With no results after about a year, the group moved on to a more traditional method of communing with ghosts: holding séances in a darkened room, sitting around a table with appropriate music and objects that might have been used by Philip or his family. Another version has the group beginning with séances and switching to the more casual setting later.

The setting itself is ultimately secondary to the results: Through the focus and concentration of the group, Philip soon began to make his presence known. He answered questions by tapping on the table for "yes" or "no." Just to be sure, a "yes" tap confirmed that he was, indeed, Philip.

A Physical Presence

After communication was established, the Philip Phenomenon took on a life of its own. Through the tapping, Philip was able to answer questions about the details of his life. He was also able to correctly answer questions about people and places of that historical time period, although these were all facts that were familiar to at least one member of the group. Philip even seemed to develop a personality, exuding emotions that changed the atmosphere of the entire room. But most amazingly, he was able to exhibit some remarkable physical manifestations, such as making objects move, turning lights on and off at the group's request, and performing incredible feats with the table: It shifted, it danced on one leg, and it even moved across the room.

In order to demonstrate the results of this experiment, the group held a séance in front of an audience of 50 people; the session was also videotaped. Philip rose to the occasion—and so did the table. In addition to tapping on the table and manipulating the lights, Philip made the entire table levitate half an inch off the ground!

The experiment was deemed a success, as there was little doubt that something paranormal was occurring during the sessions. However, the Owen Group never actually realized its original goal of getting the ghost of Philip to materialize. But the TSPR did go on to re-create the experiment successfully on several other occasions with a new group and a new fictional "ghost."

Real, Random, or Re-creation?

So what can be concluded from all this? No one knows for sure, but several schools of thought have developed regarding the matter. Some believe that Philip was a real ghost and that he had once been a living, breathing person. Perhaps he had a few of the characteristics of the fictional Philip and simply responded to the group's summons. Some who believe in the ghost theory say that it may have been a playful spirit (or a demonic one) that just pretended to be Philip as a prank.

A less-popular theory suggests that someone close to the group was aware of the background information as well as the times and places of the meetings. He or she might have planned an elaborate hoax to make it appear as though the ghost was real. But it is also possible that after creating Philip, the Owen Group put forth enough energy, focus, and concentration to bring him to life, in a manner of speaking. Ghosts may well be products of our imaginations, existing only in our minds, but this study does prove one thing: When people put those minds together, anything is possible—even a visit from the "Other Side."

1924 Murder Mystery

Who's at the heart of the cloaked-in-secrets demise of Thomas Ince? Who, of the loads of lovelies and gallons of gents on the infamous Oneida *yacht that night, was the killer? Curious minds demand to know.*

✳ ✳ ✳ ✳

THE NIGHT IS November 15, 1924. The setting is the *Oneida* yacht. The principal players are: Thomas H. Ince, Marion Davies, Charlie Chaplin, and William Randolph Hearst.

The Facts

By 1924, William Randolph Hearst had built a huge newspaper empire; he dabbled in filmmaking and politics; he owned the *Oneida*. Thomas Ince was a prolific movie producer. Charlie Chaplin was a star comedian. Marion Davies was an actor. The web of connections went like this: Hearst and Davies were lovers; Davies and Chaplin were rumored to be lovers.

For Ince's birthday, Hearst planned a party on his yacht. It was a lavish one—champagne all around. In the era of Prohibition, this was not just extravagant, it was also illegal. But Hearst had ulterior motives: He'd heard rumors that his mistress, Davies, was secretly seeing Chaplin, and so he invited Chaplin to the party. The *Oneida* set sail from San Pedro, California, headed to San Diego on Saturday, November 15.

An unfortunate but persistent fog settled over the events once the cast of characters were onboard the yacht. What is known definitively is that Ince arrived at the party late, due to business, and that he did not depart the yacht under his own power. Whether he was sick or dead depends on which version you believe, but it's a fact that Ince left the yacht on a stretcher on Sunday, November 16. What happened? Various scenarios have been put forward over the years.

* Possibility 1: Hearst shoots Ince. Hearst invites Chaplin to the party to observe his behavior around Davies and to verify their affair. After catching the two in a compromising position, he flies off the handle, runs to his stateroom, grabs his gun, and comes back shooting. In this scenario, Ince tries to break up the trouble but gets shot by mistake.

* Possibility 2: Hearst shoots Ince. It's the same end result as possibility 1, but in this scenario, Davies and Ince are alone in the galley after Ince comes in to look for something to settle the queasiness caused by his notorious ulcers. Entering and seeing the two people together, Hearst assumes Chaplin—not Ince—is with Davies. He pulls his gun and shoots.

* Possibility 3: Chaplin shoots Ince. Chaplin, a week away from marrying a pregnant 16-year-old to avoid scandal and the law, is forlorn to the point where he considers suicide. While contemplating his gun, it accidentally goes off, and the bullet goes through the thin walls of the ship to hit Ince in the neighboring room.

* Possibility 4: An assassin shoots Ince. In this scenario, a hired assassin shoots Ince so Hearst can escape an unwanted business deal with the producer.

* Possibility 5: Ince dies of natural causes. Known for his shaky health, Ince succumbs to rabid indigestion and chronic heart problems. A development such as this would not surprise his friends and family.

Aftermath

Regardless of which of the various scenarios might actually be true, Ince was wheeled off Hearst's yacht. But what happened next? That's not so clear, either. The facts of the aftermath of Ince's death are as hazy as the facts of the death itself. All reports agree that Ince did, in fact, die. There was no autopsy, and his body was cremated. After the cremation, Ince's wife, Nell, moved to Europe. But beyond those matters of record, there are simply conflicting stories.

The individuals involved had various reasons for wanting to protect themselves from whatever might have happened on the yacht. If an unlawful death did indeed take place, the motivation speaks for itself. But even if nothing untoward happened, Hearst was breaking the Prohibition laws. The damage an investigation could have caused was enough reason to make Hearst cover up any attention that could have come his way from Ince's death. As a result, he tried to hide all mention of any foul play. Although Hearst didn't own the *Los Angeles Times*, he was plenty powerful. Rumor has it that an early edition of the paper after Ince's death carried the screaming headline, "Movie Producer Shot on Hearst Yacht." By later in the day, the headline had disappeared.

For his part, Chaplin denied being on the *Oneida* in the first place. In his version of the story, he didn't attend the party for Ince at all. He did, however, claim to visit Ince—along with Hearst and Davies—later in the week. He also stated that Ince died two weeks after that visit. Most reports show that Ince was definitely dead within 48 hours of the yacht party. Davies agreed that Chaplin was never aboard the *Oneida* that fateful night. In her version, Ince's wife called her the day after Ince left the yacht to inform her of Ince's death. Ince's doctor claimed that the producer didn't die until Tuesday, two days later.

So, what really happened? Who knows? Most of the people on the yacht never commented on their experience. Louella Parsons certainly didn't. The famed gossip columnist was reportedly aboard the *Oneida* that night (although she denied it as well). She had experienced some success writing for a Hearst newspaper, but shortly after this event, Hearst gave her a lifetime contract and wide syndication, allowing her to become a Hollywood power broker. Coincidence? No one can say for certain.

Olympic Disasters

After years of training, even Olympic-caliber athletes are vulnerable to last-minute injuries that dash their hopes. Athletes are sidelined by everything from the common pulled muscle or cold to more unexpected ailments. For instance, in 1912 Sweden's cyclist Carl Landsberg was hit by a motor wagon during a road race and was dragged down the road. The performance of runners Pekka Vasala (Finland) and Silvio Leonard (Cuba) suffered in 1968 and 1976 when Vasala got Montezuma's Revenge and Leonard cut his foot on a cologne bottle. Perhaps the most memorable Olympic disaster was when Janos Baranyai of Hungary dislocated his elbow while lifting 148 kg during the 2008 Beijing Olympics. Here are some other instances.

✳ ✳ ✳ ✳

* The U.S. track-and-field team for the 1900 Paris games was weakened because the French unexpectedly held events on the Sabbath. Several universities forbade their collegiate athletes to compete.

* Runner Harvey Cohn was almost swept overboard, and six athletes required medical treatment, when the SS *Barbarossa* was hit by a large wave enroute to Athens in 1906. Several favored U.S. athletes did poorly or dropped out because of their "ocean adventure."

* Francisco Lazaro of Portugal collapsed during the 1912 marathon and died the next day from sunstroke.

* After losing his opening round at the Berlin 1936 Olympics, Thomas Hamilton-Brown, a lightweight boxer from South Africa, drowned his sorrows with food. But the competitors' scores had accidentally been switched. Sadly, the damage was done—a five-pound weight gain kept Hamilton-Brown from the final round.

* Shortly after arriving in London for the 1948 Olympics, Czech gymnast Eliska Misakova was hospitalized. She died of infantile paralysis the day her team competed and won the gold. At the award ceremony, the Czech flag was bordered in black.

* During the 1960 cycling road race in Rome, Dane Knut Jensen suffered sunstroke, fractured his skull in a fall, and died.

* In 1960, Wym Essajas, Suriname's sole athlete, misunderstood the schedule and missed his 800-meter race. Suriname couldn't send another athlete to the Olympics until 1972.

* Australian skier Ross Milne died during a practice run for the men's downhill at Innsbruck in 1964 after smashing into a tree.

* Mexico City's altitude of 7,347 feet slowed the times of endurance events in the 1968 games. Three men running the 10,000-meter were unable to finish while others fell unconscious at the finish line.

* The Munich Massacre of 1972 resulted in the deaths of eleven Israeli athletes, five Palestinian terrorists, and one German policeman after the kidnapping of the athletes.

* In 1972, U.S. runners Eddie Hart, Rey Robinson, and Robert Taylor, supplied with an outdated schedule, rushed to the 100-meter semifinals at the last minute. Hart and Robinson, both winners in the quarterfinals, missed their heats. Taylor ran and won the silver medal.

* Sixteen-year-old swimmer Rick DeMont took two Marex pills for an asthma attack the day before his 400-meter freestyle race. His gold medal was revoked when he failed the drug test. The 1972 team physicians never checked to see whether his prescription contained banned substances.

* The same thing happened to Romanian gymnast Andreea Raducan in 2000. She was stripped of her gold medal for the all-around competition when she tested positive for the banned substance pseudoephedrine—an ingredient in the cold medicine provided by team doctors.

* In 1996, two people were killed and 111 were injured when American Eric Robert Rudolph detonated a bomb at the Atlanta Olympics.

* During the 2010 Winter Olympics in Vancouver, Georgian luger Nodar Kumaritashvili died during a training run on the luge track, losing control of his sled in a tight turn and crashing headlong into a steel support pole. Kumaritashvili's death prompted officials to alter the luge course in an attempt to make it less dangerous. Sadly, the modifications came too late for Nodar.

Three-Ring Disasters

For more than 200 years, various circuses have brought smiles to the faces of American children of all ages. They're popular attractions, but they've also been the scene of horrendous disasters. Here are some of the most memorable.

✳   ✳   ✳   ✳

The Wallace Brothers Circus Train Disaster

ON AUGUST 6, 1903, two trains owned by the Wallace Brothers Shows were involved in a calamitous rear-end collision at the Grand Trunk Railroad Yard in Durand, Michigan. Twenty-three people were killed instantly, and several others died shortly after; nearly 100 individuals were injured. Numerous animals also perished in the crash, including three camels, an Arabian horse, a Great Dane, and an elephant named Maud.

The *Owosso Argus Press* described the aftermath this way: "The scene that followed is indescribable, the cries and groans from the injured persons and frightened passengers, the roars from the terrified animals and the escaping steam aroused the whole city, and hundreds rushed to the scene to assist in every way in the sad task of caring for the dead and wounded."

The Hagenbeck-Wallace Circus Train Disaster

In the early morning hours of June 22, 1918, the Hagenbeck-Wallace Circus train was struck by an empty troop train just outside Hammond, Indiana. Of the 300 passengers asleep in the circus train, 86 were killed and more than 127 were injured. As a result of the ensuing fire, fed by the wood-constructed Pullman cars, many of the dead were burned beyond recognition. Thanks to assistance from its competitors, including Ringling Brothers and Barnum & Bailey, which loaned equipment and performers, the Hagenbeck-Wallace Circus had to cancel only two performances.

Political Scandals

Political scandals in the United States have been around since the birth of the nation and don't show any signs of going away, much to the satisfaction of late-night comedians and talk show hosts. Who needs soap operas when real life in Washington is so scandalous? Check out these infamous political scandals.

Teapot Dome Scandal

THE TEAPOT DOME Scandal was the largest of numerous scandals during the presidency of Warren Harding. Teapot Dome is an oil field reserved for emergency use by the U.S. Navy located on public land in Wyoming. Oil companies and politicians claimed the reserves were not necessary and that the oil companies could supply the Navy in the event of shortages. In 1922, Interior Secretary Albert B. Fall accepted $404,000 in illegal gifts from oil company executives in return for leasing the rights to the oil at Teapot Dome to Mammoth Oil without asking for competitive bids. The leases were legal but the gifts were not. Fall's attempts to keep the gifts secret failed, and, on April 14, 1922, *The Wall Street Journal* exposed the bribes. Fall denied the charges, but an investigation revealed a $100,000 no-interest loan in return for leases that Fall had forgotten to cover up. In 1927, the Supreme Court ruled that the oil leases had been illegally obtained, and the U.S. Navy regained control of Teapot Dome and other reserves. Fall was found guilty of bribery in 1929, fined $100,000, and sentenced to one year in prison. He was the first cabinet member imprisoned for his actions while in office. President Harding was not aware of the scandal at the time of his death in 1923, but it contributed to his administration being considered one of the most corrupt in history.

Chappaquiddick

After being elected to the Senate in 1962, Edward M. "Ted" Kennedy became known as a liberal who championed causes such as education and health care, but he had less success in his personal life. On July 18, 1969, Kennedy attended a party on Chappaquiddick Island in Massachusetts. He left the party with 29-year-old Mary Jo Kopechne, who had campaigned for Ted's late brother Robert. Soon after the two left the party, Kennedy's car veered off a bridge and Kopechne drowned. An experienced swimmer, Kennedy said he tried to rescue her but the tide was too strong. He swam to shore, went back to the party, and returned with two other men. Their rescue efforts also failed, but Kennedy waited until the next day to report the accident, calling his lawyer and Kopechne's parents first, claiming the crash had dazed him. There was speculation that he tried to cover up that he was driving under the influence, but nothing was ever proven. Kennedy pleaded guilty to leaving the scene of an accident, received a two-month suspended jail sentence, and lost his driver's license for a year. The scandal may have contributed to his failed presidential bid in 1980, but it didn't hurt his reputation in the Senate. In April 2006, *Time* magazine named him one of "America's 10 Best Senators," and he was remembered with fondness when he died.

Chapter 4

What Goes on There?

A Favorite Celebrity Haunt

San Diego's grand Hotel del Coronado sparkles in the California sun. It's a popular seaside resort, a National Historic Landmark, and a very haunted hotel. Affectionately called "the Del," the hotel is proud of Kate Morgan, its resident ghost. Her story is just one of the hotel's many spine-tingling tales.

✳   ✳   ✳   ✳

The Mysterious Mrs. Morgan

O N NOVEMBER 24, 1892, Kate Morgan checked into the Hotel del Coronado under the name Lottie A. Bernard from Detroit. She looked pale and said she wasn't feeling well. She mentioned that she was planning to meet her brother, a doctor.

After a few days, the staff began to worry. The mysterious woman had checked in with no luggage. Her brother hadn't arrived, and she had barely left her room.

On Monday, November 28, the woman went into town and purchased a gun. Her body was found early the next morning on stairs that led from the hotel to the beach. From the gunshot wound to her head, it appeared she had committed suicide. When police investigated, they found few personal belongings in her hotel room.

Murder or Suicide?

After Kate's death, police determined that "Lottie A. Bernard" was an alias. They sent a sketch of her to newspapers, which described her as "the beautiful stranger." Further investigation uncovered that "Lottie" had been born Kate Farmer in Iowa, and married Tom Morgan in 1885.

Morgan was reputed to be a conman and a gambler. He allegedly worked the rails and enlisted Kate's help in stealing money from train passengers. According to a witness, somewhere between Los Angeles and San Diego, Kate and Morgan had an intense argument on a train. Morgan departed before reaching San Diego; Kate continued on the train and then checked into the Del.

Some people claim that the clues at the scene add up to murder rather than suicide. Attorney Alan May's 1990 book, *The Legend of Kate Morgan*, claims the bullet that killed Kate was a different caliber than the gun she'd purchased.

Haunting in Room 302

Whatever happened, Kate's ghost has lingered at the Del. She often manifests as eerie eyes and lips appearing in the mirror or reflected in the window of her room. Kate's spirit may be responsible for strange noises and unexplained breezes around her room as well. The curtains on closed windows billow for no reason, and lights and televisions turn themselves on and off. Kate also appears as a pale young woman in a black lace dress. A sweet fragrance lingers after her apparition disappears.

Kate stayed in Room 302. Later, during remodeling the hotel changed the room number to 3327. The haunted room is so popular that people ask for it as "the Kate Morgan room." The hotel welcomes questions about the ghost, and everyone treats Kate as an honored guest.

The Mysterious Maid

Room 3519 at the Del is also haunted, perhaps even more intensely than Kate's room. In 1983, a Secret Service agent stayed in Room 3519 while guarding then-Vice President George H.W. Bush. The special agent bolted from the room in the middle of the night claiming that he'd heard unearthly gurgling noises and that the entire room seemed to glow.

The Secret Service agent may have encountered a ghost related to the Kate Morgan mystery. According to one legend, while Kate was at the hotel, a maid stayed in what would later be Room 3519. In some versions of the story, the maid was traveling with Kate; in others, the maid had simply befriended her. Whatever the connection between the two, the maid allegedly vanished the same morning Kate was found dead.

That's not the only ghost story connected with Room 3519. Another story goes that in 1888, the year the hotel was built, a wealthy man kept his mistress in that room. When the woman found out she was pregnant, she killed herself. Her body was removed from the Del, and nothing else is known about her, not even her name. Ghost hunters believe she is the one who causes the lights in the room to flicker and is responsible for the unexplained cold spot in front of the room's door.

The Blonde on the Beach

In recent years, some hotel guests have reported sightings of the ghost of Marilyn Monroe. She loved the Hotel del Coronado when she stayed there to film the movie *Some Like It Hot*. Monroe's ghost has appeared at several of her favorite places, including Hollywood's Roosevelt Hotel, where people see her in the lobby's mirror. At the Del, Monroe is supposedly seen outdoors as a fleeting, translucent apparition near the door to the hotel or on the beach nearby. Those who see Monroe's ghost comment on her windswept blonde hair and her fringed shawl that flutters in the breeze. Others have allegedly heard her light giggle in the second and third floor hallways.

Whether they're from a rural farm or the silver screen, guests and ghosts love the Hotel del Coronado. If you choose to stay in one of its most haunted rooms, just remember that you're never alone.

The Body Farm

When will an employee not be reprimanded for laying down on the job? When that worker is a Body Farm recruit. Hundreds of rotting corpses get away with such shenanigans every day at the University of Tennessee's "Body Farm," and they have yet to be written up for it. In fact, they are praised for their profound contributions to science.

✳ ✳ ✳ ✳

A Eureka Moment

FORENSIC ANTHROPOLOGIST WILLIAM M. Bass had a dream. As an expert in the field of human decomposition, he couldn't fathom why a facility devoted to this under-studied process didn't exist. So, in 1972, working in conjunction with the University of Tennessee, he founded the Body Farm or, more specifically, the University of Tennessee Forensic Anthropology Facility.

Body Snatchers

If you're going to start a body farm, it doesn't take a forensic anthropologist to realize that there might be a problem in obtaining bodies. One way is to use bodies that have been donated for medical studies. Another focuses on cadavers that rot away each year at medical examiners offices, with nary a soul to claim them. Enter Bass and his associates. Like "pods" from *Invasion of the Body Snatchers*, these scientists grab every body they can lay their hands on.

A Creepy Joint

Just outside of Knoxville, the eerie three-acre wooded plot that Bass claimed for his scientific studies is where an unspecified number of cadavers in various states of decomposition are kept. While some hang out completely in the open, others spend their time in shallow graves or entombed in vaults. Others dip their toes and other body parts in ponds. And a few spend eternity inside sealed car trunks.

Dying for the Cause

So why is this done? What can be learned from observing human flesh and bone decay in the hot Tennessee sun? Plenty, according to scientists and members of the media who have studied the Body Farm. "Nearly everything known about the science of human decomposition comes from one place— forensic anthropologist William Bass' Body Farm," declared CNN in high praise of the facility. The bodies are strewn in different positions and under varying circumstances for reasons far from happenstance. Each cadaver will display differing reactions to decomposition, insect and wildlife interference, and the elements. These invaluable indicators can help investigators zero-in on the cause and time of death in current and future criminal cases.

Stiff Legacy

Bass himself claims that knowledge gleaned from Body Farm studies has proven especially helpful to murder investigations. "People will have alibis for certain time periods, and if you can determine death happened at another time, it makes a difference in the court case," said Bass. Even the prestigious FBI uses the Body Farm as a real-world simulator to help train its agents. Every February, representatives visit the site to dig for bodies that farm hands have prepared as simulated crime scenes.

Further Afield

At another facility at the University of New Mexico, scientists have collected over 500 human skeletons and store them as "skeletal archives" to create biological profiles based on what happens to bones over time. And in Germany, the Max Planck

Institute for Computer Science has been working on a 3-D graphics program based on forensic data to produce more accurate likenesses of the victims.

Although many other proposed farms never got off the ground due to community protest, since the inception of Bass's original Body Farm, another farm has been established at Western Carolina University. Ideally, Bass would like to see body farms all over the nation. Since decaying bodies react differently depending on their climate and surroundings, says Bass, "It's important to gather information from other research facilities across the United States."

The Restless Spirits of the LaLaurie Mansion

There is no city in the American South as haunted as New Orleans, which is not surprising given its dark history of death, murder, war, slavery, and on occasion, downright depravity. New Orleans is a city that stands as a prime example of the deeds of the past creating the hauntings of today.

✳ ✳ ✳ ✳

THERE ARE SCORES of ghost stories in the city, but there is no story as famous as that of the LaLaurie Mansion. It has long been considered the French Quarter's most haunted house, and in many early writings of the city, its infamy was so great that it was simply referred to as "the haunted house."

The origins of the ghostly tales centering on 1140 Royal Street began around 1832, when Dr. Louis LaLaurie and his wife, Delphine, moved into the mansion. It was regarded as one of the finest houses in the city and one that befit their social status—the family was noted for its grand affairs and respected for its wealth and prominence.

Madame LaLaurie was considered one of the most intelligent, beautiful, and influential women in the city. She was known for her grand dinner parties that showed off her fine china and imported rugs and fabrics. One of the things that nearly all of her guests recalled about her was her extraordinary kindness.

A Darker Side

This was the side of Madame LaLaurie that her friends and admirers saw. But beneath the delicate and refined exterior was a cruel, cold-blooded, and possibly insane woman—a side that some were forced to see on a regular basis.

The finery of the LaLaurie house was attended to by dozens of slaves. Many guests to the mansion remembered the finely dressed servants, who made sure that guests wanted for nothing. Other slaves, sometimes glimpsed in passing, were not so elegant. In fact, they were surprisingly thin and hollow-chested. Rumors began to swirl that Madame LaLaurie abused these slaves. It was said that she kept her cook chained to the kitchen's fireplace and that many other slaves were subjected to treatment that went far beyond mere cruelty.

Mr. Montreuil, a neighbor on Royal Street, was one of the first to become suspicious that something was not quite right with the slaves in the LaLaurie house. Parlor maids were replaced with no explanation, and stable hands suddenly disappeared, never to be seen again. Montreuil made a report to the authorities, but little, if anything, was done.

One day, another neighbor heard a scream and saw Madame LaLaurie chasing a young servant girl across the courtyard with a whip. The neighbor watched as the girl was pursued from floor to floor until she and Madame LaLaurie at last appeared on the rooftop. The child ran down the steeply pitched roof and vanished. Moments later, the neighbor heard a horrible thud as the child's small body struck the flagstones below. Stunned, the neighbor watched the house and told authorities that she witnessed the girl being buried in a shallow grave.

When the authorities investigated the neighbor's claims, the LaLaurie slaves were impounded and sold at auction. Unfortunately, Madame LaLaurie coaxed some relatives into secretly buying them back for her. The entire incident had been a terrible accident, she said. Some believed her, but many others didn't, and the LaLaurie social standing began to slowly decline. Soon, everyone would know the truth.

Unspeakable Horrors

In April 1834, a huge fire broke out in the kitchen of the LaLaurie Mansion. The story goes that the fire was set by the cook, who couldn't handle any more torture at the hands of Madame LaLaurie. As the fire swept through the house and smoke filled the rooms, the streets outside began filling with people. Soon the volunteer fire department was on hand carrying buckets of water, and bystanders began crowding into the house, trying to offer assistance.

Throughout the chaos, Madame LaLaurie remained calm. She directed the volunteers to carry out expensive paintings and smaller pieces of furniture. She was intent on saving the house but would not allow panic to overcome her. Montreuil, the neighbor who had been suspicious of Madame LaLaurie, came to assist during the fire. He asked if the slaves were in danger from the blaze and was told by Madame LaLaurie not to interfere in her family business. Montreuil appealed to a local official who was also present. They began searching for the rest of the servants and were joined by several firefighters. They tried to enter the attic but the door was locked, so firefighters broke it down.

What they saw in the attic was unlike anything they could have imagined. They found slaves chained to the walls. Cruel experiments had been carried out with mouths sewn shut, eyes poked out, limbs removed, and skulls opened while the slaves were still alive. The men were overwhelmed by the terrifying sight, as well as the stench of death permeating the confined chamber.

Although the chamber contained a number of dead bodies, many of the slaves were still alive. Some were unconscious and some cried in pain, begging to be killed and put out of their misery. The men fled the scene in disgust, and once the fire was extinguished, bystanders helped the surviving slaves out of the attic and provided them with food and water. It is uncertain just how many slaves were found in Madame LaLaurie's torture chamber. Only a few were strong enough to leave the chamber of horrors under their own power.

As the mutilated slaves were carried out of the house, a crowd gathered outside. Nothing happened for hours, but word of the atrocities began to spread. Madame LaLaurie alone, it was said, was responsible for the atrocities in the house, and the people wanted vengeance. Threats were shouted as the crowd grew restless. Suddenly, the gates to the mansion opened and a carriage clattered onto the street. The coach sped past, carrying its passengers out of sight. Madame LaLaurie had escaped, fleeing to a ship that took her far away from New Orleans.

The seething mob on Royal Street was enraged. They decided to take their anger out on the mansion the LaLauries had left behind. They broke furniture, shattered windows, and looted the fine china, expensive glassware, and imported foods before the authorities arrived and restored order. The house was eventually closed and sealed, and it sat on Royal Street, completely empty for years. Or so it seemed at the time.

The Haunted House on Royal Street

Recently discovered letters signed by Madame LaLaurie show that she escaped to France where her dark past was unknown. No legal action was ever taken against her, and she was never seen in New Orleans, or her mansion, again. The same cannot be said for her victims.

Tales of ghosts at 1140 Royal Street began soon after the LaLauries fled. As the mansion began to fall into disrepair, neighbors and passersby claimed to hear cries of terror from the deserted property. They saw apparitions of slaves peering out from the windows and walking in the overgrown gardens.

The house was eventually sold, but the first owner kept it for only three months. He heard groaning sounds and cries in the darkness and soon abandoned the place. He attempted to operate it as a boarding house, but renters usually only stayed for a few days and then moved out. Finally, he gave up, and the house was abandoned again.

The LaLaurie house switched owners several times until the late 1890s, when it was converted into a boarding house for recent immigrants.

A number of strange events occurred during that time. One story told of a tenant being attacked by a naked man in chains, who quickly vanished. There were stories of children being chased by a spectral woman with a whip; screams and weeping sounds from the attic; and on one occasion, a mother was frightened to see a woman in a formal gown gazing into the crib where her infant slept. Even cheap rent was not enough to convince tenants to stay for longer than a week or two, and soon the house was empty once again.

The Haunted Saloon

Over the years, the house served as a saloon, a furniture store, and a refuge for poor and homeless men. In 1969, the mansion was converted into 20 apartments before a new owner, a retired New Orleans doctor, purchased it. The house was restored to its original condition and turned into condominiums. Apparently, tenants are a little easier to keep today than they were a century ago.

That owner did not observe any supernatural occurrences in the house, but past tenants have told of doors that opened and closed by themselves, water faucets that inexplicably turned on, toilets that flushed under their own power, and other small irritations. Others told of a lingering scream that was sometimes heard in the courtyard at night. The LaLaurie Mansion was later purchased by actor Nicholas Cage, who previously bought another property in the Garden District from famous horror writer Anne Rice. The house has been quiet as of late, but perhaps Cage will draw out the spirits of this terrible tragedy.

Madame LaLaurie's Secret Graveyard

During a remodeling of the house that took place some years ago, workers discovered an unmarked graveyard under the floorboards of the house. The skeletal remains had been placed there haphazardly and with no sense of organization or ceremony. When officials investigated, they found the remains to be from the early to mid-1800s.

Some believe that Madame LaLaurie may have buried these bodies in secret, solving the mystery of why some of the slaves simply disappeared. But how many of her slaves did she kill? And how many of them have never found peace?

Dinner With a Ghost

Next time you enjoy a meal at your favorite restaurant, know that you may be dining with some unseen guests. Here are a few eateries where a ghostly good time is always on the menu.

✳ ✳ ✳ ✳

Stone's Public House, Ashland, Massachusetts

SINCE 1834, STONE'S Public House has been serving up food and drink to area residents and visitors alike. Should you choose to stop in for a bite, first take a good look at the photo of John Stone hanging over the bar's fireplace, so you'll be sure to recognize his ghost when it appears. Stone's spirit is said to be one of a handful that haunts the inn. Other spirits include a man that Stone accidentally murdered in an argument during a card game. According to the legend, Stone and several friends buried the man in the basement. The spirits make their presence known by breaking glasses, causing cold breezes, and appearing as shadowy figures.

Arnaud's, New Orleans, Louisiana

The ghost of a man dressed in an old-fashioned tuxedo is often spotted near the windows of the main dining room. But this ghost, believed to be that of Arnaud Cazenave, the first owner of the establishment, is not alone. A ghostly woman has been seen walking out of the restroom and moving silently across the restaurant before disappearing into a wall.

Country House Restaurant, Clarendon Hills, Illinois

As the story goes, many years ago, a woman who was dating one of the restaurant's bartenders stopped in and asked him to watch her baby for a while. When he refused, the woman put the baby back in her car, sped off down the road, and promptly crashed into a tree, killing herself and her child. Apparently the ghost of both the young woman and her baby found their way back to the restaurant. The young woman's ghost has been blamed for banging on walls and doors and the jukebox playing on its own. She has also been seen walking through the restaurant and sometimes people outside see the ghostly woman in an upstairs window. Patrons and employees have also reported hearing a baby cry, even when there were no babies present.

Poogan's Porch, Charleston, South Carolina

Originally built as a house in 1888, the building underwent major renovations and reopened as a restaurant in 1976. Perhaps it was those renovations that brought the ghost of Zoe St. Amand, former owner of the house, back to see what all the fuss was about. Zoe's ghost is described as an older woman in a long black dress who silently wanders through the establishment at all hours of the day and night.

Big Nose Kate's Saloon, Tombstone, Arizona

Named after Mary Katherine Haroney, thought to be the first prostitute in Tombstone, the building was originally known as the Grand Hotel. At this establishment, there are several ghosts who seem to enjoy passing the time touching patrons and employees, moving objects, and appearing in the occasional photograph. The most famous ghost, however, is that of a man known as the Swamper. Legend has it that the man lived in the basement of the saloon and had dug a secret tunnel under the street and into a nearby silver mine. He would sneak into the mines late at night and make off with untold amounts of silver. The strange sounds and muffled voices still coming from this long-abandoned tunnel seem to prove that even in death, the Swamper continues his underhanded and illegal mining practices.

A Haunting on Chicago's Magnificent Mile

Chicago's Water Tower stands more than 150 feet tall along the world-famous Magnificent Mile—one of the city's most popular tourist attractions. However, many visitors don't realize that the site is haunted by a hero who died there during the Great Chicago Fire of 1871.

✳ ✳ ✳ ✳

Mrs. O'Leary Lit a Lantern in the Shed

ON THE EVENING of October 8, 1871, the Great Chicago Fire began behind the O'Leary home. Contrary to popular belief, the fire was not started by a cow kicking over a lantern. Nevertheless, the flames spread quickly from the O'Leary barn. When the smoke cleared a couple of days later, charred buildings and ashes littered the city. The fire had blazed a path nearly a mile wide and four miles long, leaving more than 100,000 people homeless. Approximately 300 people died in the fire, but the heat was so intense that only 125 bodies were recovered. One of those bodies was a suicide victim found inside the Chicago Water Tower.

A Hero's Last Resort?

According to legend, a lone fireman remained steadfast at the water-pumping station in Chicago's Streeterville neighborhood trying to save as many homes as possible. But as the flames closed in around him, he realized it was a losing battle. With his back to the Chicago Water Tower, there was simply no place to run.

As the fire edged closer, the brave fireman considered his options. Apparently, a slow death by fire seemed more frightening than a quicker end by his own hand. So the story goes that the fireman climbed the stairs inside the water tower, strung a rope from a beam near the top of the structure, and, in a moment of desperation, looped the rope around his neck and jumped to his death.

The Solitary Ghost

The heat of the fire did not destroy the Chicago Water Tower, but it did scorch everything inside. The heroic fireman's identity was never known, but his spirit lingers. Hundreds of people have seen the sad figure of the hanging man and smelled a suggestion of smoke inside the tower, especially on October nights around the anniversary of the tragedy.

From outside the historic structure, some people see a pale man staring down at them from a window near the top of the tower. His expression is sad and resigned, and he seems to look right through those on the ground.

Other visitors have reported an eerie, sorrowful whistling that seems to come from inside the structure. It echoes through the tower, and then it stops abruptly.

However, most people who've seen the Water Tower ghost describe him with a rope around his neck, swinging and turning slowly. His face is twisted, grotesque, and highlighted as if flames are just beneath him. The ghost appears so real that many witnesses have called police to report a suicide. But responding officers, who have often seen the apparition themselves, know that he's a ghost…and a reminder of valor during a tragic fire more than a century ago.

Share a Toast With a Ghost

Visitors to the Golden Fleece, a 16th-century pub and inn in York, England, can spend a few minutes or a full night with numerous ghosts at the city's most haunted site. Located at the end of one of Europe's best-preserved medieval streets known as "the Shambles," the Golden Fleece is a well kept but ancient building surrounded by a mysterious atmosphere.

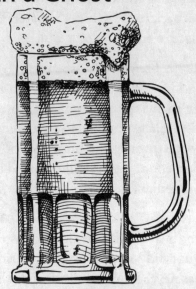

* * * *

Enjoy Some Spirits with Some Spirits

UPON ENTERING THE Golden Fleece, visitors sense spirits from the pub's past. Even when the front room is nearly empty, many visitors glance around nervously, expecting to see other guests standing in a dark corner. Unexplained shadows move and then vanish, and the sound of phantom glasses clinking can be heard. It's truly an eerie place.

Many guests will witness the Golden Fleece's ghosts if they go looking for them. For the best ghostly encounters, explore the pub's quirky corridors and cozy public rooms. Ghosts have been reported in every part of the pub and also in the haunted yard immediately behind it. Most people see the spirits as flickering figures, off to one side. Others see full apparitions, such as the colorful ghost of Lady Alice Peckett.

Lady Peckett Kept Her Head,
But Thomas Percy Didn't

Lady Alice Peckett haunts both the Golden Fleece and Lady Peckett's Yard directly behind it. Her husband, John, who owned the building, was the Lord Mayor of the city of York in 1701. He left the pub when he died, but his wife decided to stay. No one is certain why she lingers, but some claim that she was too spirited and fun-loving for her more serious politician husband. Perhaps she doesn't want to miss out on anything at the Golden Fleece.

Lady Alice generally manifests as an older woman wearing sweet perfume, but don't let her serene demeanor fool you. She's a mischievous ghost who likes to surprise people by walking through solid walls around the Function Room.

Another ghost to keep an eye out for is Thomas Percy, the Seventh Earl of Northumberland. Also know as the Headless Earl, Percy, a relatively harmless ghost, floats around the Shambles, near the entrance to the Golden Fleece, in search of his missing head.

During the reign of Queen Elizabeth I, when Catholics were burned at the stake, Percy held steadfast in his Catholic beliefs. Despite this, Percy was a favorite of the queen for many years. Unfortunately, Thomas didn't realize his vulnerability. In 1569, he led a rebellion against Elizabeth and planned to replace her with her Catholic cousin, Mary, Queen of Scots. When the rebellion failed, Percy was beheaded in a public execution not far from the Golden Fleece. Though his body was buried, his head was left on public display as a warning to others. After some time, the head was simply thrown away.

A Fine "Cold Spot" in the Pub

If the weather is sultry or the pub is crowded, find a seat at the booth in the back corner of the pub. The spirits will oblige by keeping that corner cool and breezy. During a June 2007 visit, a group of American tourists complimented the staff on how well the booth was cooled. They were startled to learn that there is no air conditioning in the pub.

The chilling effect may be thanks to "One Eyed Jack," a 17th-century ghost dressed in a red coat, wig, and crisply pressed breeches. He's sometimes seen carrying a flintlock pistol and creates a refreshing breeze as he paces up and down the room, waiting to be served.

A Full Night of Good Spirits

Above the pub is an inn, and guests can spend the night encountering various spirits. Look for the gruesome, blue-tinted face of an inebriated World War II airman who fell to his death from a window.

Or listen for the confused whimpering of a little boy who appears in Victorian clothing. In the late 1800s, he was crushed to death as a cart backed up to the pub door to deliver ale. He's often seen around the front room of the pub and has even been known to pick pockets.

If you encounter a ghost wearing a noose, that spirit has escaped from the pub's basement. After being executed, corpses were sometimes stored in the cellar of the Golden Fleece, but in many cases, the bodies were never claimed, and they may be buried in the basement. Perhaps they're wandering the Golden Fleece hoping that someone will recognize them and give them a proper burial. Most often, overnight guests at the Golden Fleece hear music and loud laughter from downstairs. When they investigate the noise, they discover that the pub is closed, the lights are off, and the downstairs rooms are empty…unless you count the ghosts, of course.

Just remember that if you see a Roman soldier who seems to be walking on his knees, nothing terrible happened to his legs. He's haunting from a time when the streets of York were several feet lower than they are now. That's the level where his ghostly feet are.

A Condemned Man Leaves His Mark

In 1877, Carbon County Prison inmate Alexander Campbell spent long, agonizing days awaiting sentencing. Campbell, a coal miner from northeastern Pennsylvania, had been charged with the murder of mine superintendent John P. Jones. Authorities believed that Campbell was part of the Molly Maguires labor group, a secret organization looking to even the score with mine owners. Although evidence shows that he was indeed part of the Mollies, and he admitted that he'd been present at the murder scene, Campbell professed his innocence and swore repeatedly that he was not the shooter.

❋   ❋   ❋   ❋

The Sentence

CONVICTED LARGELY ON evidence collected by James McParlan, a Pinkerton detective hired by mine owners to infiltrate the underground labor union, Campbell was sentenced to hang. The decree would be carried out at specially prepared gallows at the Carbon County Prison. When the prisoner's day of reckoning arrived, he rubbed his hand on his sooty cell floor then slapped it on the wall proclaiming, "I am innocent, and let this be my testimony!" With that, Alexander Campbell was unceremoniously dragged from cell number 17 and committed, whether rightly or wrongly, to eternity.

The Hand of Fate

The Carbon County Prison of present-day is not too different from the torture chamber that it was back in Campbell's day. Although it is now a museum, the jail still imparts the horrors of man's inhumanity to man. Visitors move through its claustrophobically small cells and dank dungeon rooms with mouths agape. When they reach cell number 17, many visitors feel a cold chill rise up their spine, as they notice that Alexander Campbell's handprint is still there!

"There's no logical explanation for it," says James Starrs, a forensic scientist from George Washington University who investigated the mark. Starrs is not the first to scratch his head in disbelief. In 1930, a local sheriff aimed to rid the jail of its ominous mark. He had the wall torn down and replaced with a new one. But when he awoke the following morning and stepped into the cell, the handprint had reappeared on the newly constructed wall! Many years later Sheriff Charles Neast took his best shot at the wall, this time with green latex paint. The mark inexplicably returned. Was Campbell truly innocent as his ghostly handprint seems to suggest? No one can say with certainty. Is the handprint inside cell number 17 the sort of thing that legends are made of? You can bet your life on it.

Bachelor's Grove: America's Most Haunted Cemetery?

Hidden away inside the Rubio Woods Forest Preserve near Midlothian, Illinois, lies Bachelor's Grove Cemetery, widely reported to be one of the most haunted cemeteries in the United States. Haunted or not, the cemetery certainly has an intriguing history that raises many questions but provides few answers.

Like almost everything associated with the cemetery, the very origins of Bachelor's Grove are surrounded in mystery. Some claim that the cemetery got its name in the early 1800s when several unmarried men built homes nearby, causing locals to nickname the area Bachelor's Grove. Others, however, believe the name was actually Batchelder's Grove, named after a family that lived in the area.

❋ ❋ ❋ ❋

Abandoned and Vandalized

DESPITE ITS SMALL size (about an acre), the cemetery became a popular site over the years because of its convenient location right off the Midlothian Turnpike. The quaint pond at the rear of the cemetery added to the allure, and as a result, about 200 individuals made Bachelor's Grove their final resting place.

All that changed during the 1960s when the branch of the Midlothian Turnpike that ran past the cemetery was closed, cutting it off from traffic. With the road essentially abandoned, people stopped coming to the cemetery altogether. The last burial at Bachelor's Grove took place in 1965, although there was an interment of ashes in 1989.

Without a proper road to get to the cemetery, Bachelor's Grove fell into a state of disrepair. Along with the cover of the Rubio Woods, this made the cemetery an attractive location for late-night parties and senseless vandalism. Today, of the nearly 200 graves, only 20 or so still have tombstones. The rest have been broken or gone missing. This, combined with rumors that some graves were dug up, is why many believe that the spirits of Bachelor's Grove do not rest in peace.

Glow in the Dark

Who haunts Bachelor's Grove? For starters, the ghost of a woman dressed in white has been spotted late at night walking among the tombstones or sitting on top of them. So many people have seen her throughout the years that she is commonly known as the Madonna of Bachelor's Grove.

There are also reports of strange, flashing lights moving around the cemetery, especially near the algae-covered pond in the back. Some believe that the pond was used as an impromptu "burial ground" for Chicago-area gangsters and that the lights are the spirits of their victims. Others believe the strange orbs are related to the legend that, many years ago, a man plowing the nearby fields died when his horse became spooked and ran into the pond, drowning both man and horse.

Probably the most fascinating paranormal activity reported at Bachelor's Grove is that of the ghost house. On certain nights, a spectral house is said to appear in the distance along the abandoned road leading to the cemetery. Those who have witnessed this strange apparition say that the house slowly fades away until it disappears without a trace. Similarly, others have spotted a ghostly car barreling down the road, complete with glowing headlights.

Should you wish to visit Bachelor's Grove in the hopes of encountering some of these spirits, it is open every day but only during daylight hours. The abandoned road now serves as a well-worn path through the woods up to the cemetery. Just remember that you are visiting hallowed ground and the final resting places of men, women, and children. Be sure to treat it as such.

Spending Eternity on "The Rock"

Alcatraz, nicknamed "The Rock," was the ultimate American prison—a place that hardened criminals and assorted public enemies such as Al Capone called home. Surrounded by the heavy mist and rolling fog of San Francisco Bay, the damp prison on Alcatraz Island kept more than a thousand dangerous men cloistered from the rest of the world. The cold winds and chilly waters of the bay made Alcatraz one of the loneliest prisons in the world.

From 1934 to 1963, during its reign as a federal prison, Alcatraz was not a facility for rehabilitating hardened criminals; it was a place of harsh punishment and limited privilege. Those who endured their stay were fortunate to leave with their sanity or—as many believe—their souls.

✳ ✳ ✳ ✳

The Island of Pelicans

WHEN THE SPANISH first explored the area in 1775, they dubbed the island *La Isla de los Alcatraces,* or "the Island of the Pelicans." What they found was a rocky piece of land that was completely uninhabited, sparsely vegetated, and surrounded by churning water and swift currents.

The U.S. military took over Alcatraz Island in 1850. For several decades, it was the army's first long-term prison, and it quickly gained a reputation for being a tough facility. The military used the island until 1934, when high operating costs coupled with the financial constraints of the Great Depression forced their exit.

America's Devil's Island

The rise of criminal activity in the 1920s and early 1930s put a new focus on Alcatraz. Federal authorities decided to construct an imposing, escape-proof prison that would strike fear into even the hardest criminals, and Alcatraz was the chosen site. In 1934, the Federal Bureau of Prisons took control of the facility and implemented a strict set of rules and regulations. The top guards and officers of the federal penal system were transferred to the island, and soon Alcatraz was transformed into an impregnable fortress.

Across the country, prison wardens were asked to send their worst inmates to Alcatraz. This included inmates with behavioral issues, those who had previously attempted to escape, and the most notorious criminals of the day, including Al Capone, George "Machine Gun" Kelly, Doc Barker (of the Ma Barker Gang), and Alvin "Creepy" Karpis.

Life on "The Rock" was anything but luxurious. Each cell measured five feet by nine feet and featured a fold-up bunk, desk, chair, toilet, and sink. Each day was exactly the same, from chow times to work assignments. The routine never varied and was completely methodical. Compliance was expected, and the tough guards sometimes meted out severe punishment if rules were not followed.

If prisoners broke the rules, they could be sent to a punishment cell known as "the hole." There were several of these cells, which were dreaded by the convicts. Here, men were stripped of all but their basic right to food. During the daytime, mattresses were taken away and steel doors blocked out any natural light. Prisoners might spend as long as 19 days in "the hole" in complete isolation from other inmates. Time spent there usually meant psychological and physical abuse from the guards as well. Screams from hardened criminals could be heard echoing throughout the entire building in a stark warning to the other prisoners.

After time spent in "the hole," men often came out with pneumonia or arthritis after spending days or weeks on the cold cement floor with no clothing. Others came out devoid of their sanity. Some men never came out of "the hole" alive.

Alcatraz and "Scarface" Al Capone

Al Capone arrived at Alcatraz in August 1934. He was fairly well behaved, but life on "The Rock" was not easy for the ex-crime boss. He was involved in a number of fights during his incarceration, was once stabbed with a pair of scissors, and spent some time in isolation while at Alcatraz.

Attempts on his life, beatings, and the prison routine itself took their toll on Capone. Seeking a diversion, he played the banjo in a prison band. Some legends say that Scarface spent most of his time strumming his banjo alone, hoping to avoid other prisoners. In reality, after more than three years in Alcatraz, Capone was on the edge of total insanity. He spent the last year of his federal sentence in the hospital ward, undergoing treatment for an advanced case of syphilis.

When Capone left Alcatraz, he definitely seemed worse for the wear. It appeared that "The Rock" (and his nasty case of syphilis) had completely broken him. In January 1939, he was transferred to another prison to serve out a separate sentence. Capone was released to his family and doctors in November 1939 and became a recluse at his Florida estate. He died, broken and insane, in 1947.

Al Capone was not the only inmate to lose his grip on reality at Alcatraz. While working in the prison garage, convicted bank robber Rufe Persful picked up an ax and chopped the fingers off his left hand. Laughing maniacally, he asked another prisoner to cut off his right hand as well. An inmate named Joe Bowers sustained a superficial wound when he tried to slash his own throat with a pair of broken eyeglasses. Ed Wutke, who was at Alcatraz for murder, managed to use a pencil sharpener blade to fatally cut through his jugular vein. These were not the only suicide attempts, and many other men suffered mental breakdowns at Alcatraz.

Escapes From Alcatraz

During Alcatraz's 29 years as a federal prison, 34 different men tried to escape the island in 14 separate attempts. In almost every case, the escapees were killed or recaptured. Two escape attempts are particularly infamous.

In May 1946, six inmates captured a gun cage, obtained prison keys, and took over a cell house in less than an hour. Unfortunately for them, the only key they did not get was the one that would let them out of the cell building, which effectively grounded the escape plot. The prison break turned into a heated gunfight that led to the deaths of three of the escapees, as well as several guards. When it was over, two of the surviving escapees were sentenced to death and the third received a life sentence.

Though the 1946 incident may have been the most violent escape attempt at Alcatraz, it is not the most famous. That distinction belongs to a 1962 attempt by Frank Morris and brothers Clarence and John Anglin. Over several months, the men chipped away at the vent shafts in their cells using tools they had stolen from work sites. They also created makeshift rafts and inflatable life vests using raincoats. They even collected hair from the barbershop and made lifelike dummies to fool the guards on duty during the escape. Then, on the night of June 11, 1962, after making their way out of the prison, the trio boarded their rafts and set out into the cold waters of the bay, never to be seen again.

More than four decades later, it is still unclear whether or not the escapees survived. According to the Bureau of Prisons, the men are either missing or presumed drowned. The story of the escape was brought to the silver screen in the 1979 film *Escape from Alcatraz*, starring Clint Eastwood.

The Haunted Prison

On March 23, 1963, less than a year after this last escape attempt, Alcatraz ended its run as a federal prison, and the island remained largely abandoned until the early 1970s. Congress placed the island under the purview of the National Park Service in 1972, and Alcatraz opened to the public in 1973. It is now one of the most popular historic sites in America.

In the daytime, the former prison bustles with the activity of tour guides and visitors, but at night, the buildings play host to some unexplainable phenomena. Many believe that some of those who served time on "The Rock" linger for all eternity.

Accounts of hauntings have been widely reported since Alcatraz first shut its doors. Park service employees and visitors to Alcatraz report weird, ghostly encounters in the crumbling, old buildings. Unexplained clanging sounds, footsteps, and disembodied voices and screams are commonly heard coming from the empty corridors and long-abandoned cells. Some guides have reportedly witnessed strange events in certain areas of the prison, such as the infamous "holes," where prisoners suffered greatly.

But perhaps the most eerie sound is the faint banjo music sometimes heard in the shower room. Legend has it that Al Capone would often sit and strum his banjo in that spot rather than risk going out into the yard. Is it the broken spirit of Al

Capone that creates this mournful melody on his phantom instrument? Or is it another ghostly inmate, unable to escape, even after death?

America's Most Haunted Lighthouse

Built in 1830, the historic Point Lookout Lighthouse is located in St. Mary's County, Maryland, where the Potomac River meets Chesapeake Bay. It is a beautiful setting for hiking, boating, fishing, camping, and ghost-hunting.

✲ ✲ ✲ ✲

The Most Ghosts

POINT LOOKOUT LIGHTHOUSE has been called America's most haunted lighthouse, perhaps because it was built on what later became the largest camp for Confederate prisoners of war. Marshy surroundings, tent housing, and close quarters were a dangerous combination, and smallpox, scurvy, and dysentery ran rampant. The camp held more than 50,000 soldiers, and between 3,000 and 8,000 died there.

Park rangers and visitors to the lighthouse report hearing snoring and footsteps, having a sense of being watched, and feeling the floors shake and the air move as crowds of invisible beings pass by. A photograph of a former caretaker shows the misty figure of a young soldier leaning against the wall behind her, although no one noticed him when the photo was taken during a séance at the lighthouse.

The Lost Ghost

In December 1977, Ranger Gerald Sword was sitting in the lighthouse's kitchen on a stormy night when a man's face appeared at the back door. The man was young, with a floppy cap and a long coat, and peered into the bright room. Given the awful weather, Sword opened the door to let him in, but the young man floated backward until he vanished entirely. Later, after a bit of research, Sword realized he had been face-to-face with Joseph Haney, a young officer whose body had washed ashore after the steamboat he was on sank during a similar storm in 1878.

The Host Ghost

One of Point Lookout's most frequent visitors is the apparition of a woman dressed in a long blue skirt and a white blouse who appears at the top of the stairs. She is believed to be Ann Davis, the wife of the first lighthouse keeper. Although her husband died shortly after he took the post, Ann remained as the keeper for the next 30 years, and, according to inspection reports, was known for clean and well-kept grounds. Caretakers claim to hear her sighing heavily.

Who Said That?

Point Lookout's reputation drew Hans Holzer, Ph.D., a renowned parapsychologist, who tried to capture evidence of ghostly activity. Holzer and his team claimed to have recorded 24 different voices in all, both male and female, talking, laughing, and singing. Among their recordings, the group heard male voices saying "fire if they get too close," "going home," and more than a few obscenities.

Take Care, Caretaker

One former caretaker reported waking in the middle of the night to see a ring of lights dancing above her head. She smelled smoke and raced downstairs to find a space heater on fire. She believes that the lights were trying to protect her and the lighthouse from being consumed by flames.

A Full House

The lighthouse was decommissioned in 1966, after 135 years of service. In 2002, the state of Maryland purchased it, and it is now open for tours and paranormal investigations. The Point Lookout Lighthouse continues to have a steady stream of visitors—even those who are no longer among the living.

No Humans Allowed

Every dog has its day. But when your dog's day has passed, or your cat has used up all of its nine lives, if you live near L.A., you might take your departed friend to the Pet Memorial Park.

✳ ✳ ✳ ✳

ORIGINALLY NAMED THE Los Angeles Pet Cemetery, these ten acres of land in Calabasas, California, have served as the final resting place for cats, dogs, horses, and virtually every other kind of pet imaginable since 1928, making it one of the oldest pet cemeteries on the West Coast. It's now the final resting place of several famous animals, including Petey from *The Little Rascals* and Rudolph Valentino's dog, Kabar.

Saving the Cemetery

In 1973, the entire property was donated to the Los Angeles Society for the Prevention of Cruelty to Animals (LASPCA). In the early 1980s, when word spread that the LASPCA was considering selling the cemetery to developers, pet lovers throughout Los Angeles decided something had to be done to save it. Several individuals banded together to create S.O.P.H.I.E. (Save Our Pets' History In Eternity), a nonprofit organization to save the Los Angeles Pet Cemetery.

Through a series of fundraisers, S.O.P.H.I.E. was able to purchase the entire property, and, in September 1986, the cemetery was reopened as the Los Angeles Pet Memorial Park. The facility is now a fully operational animal funeral home, complete with a crematory and an area with couches and chairs where owners can spend a few minutes saying their final good-byes to their faithful, furry friends.

Teacher's Pet

Visitors to the Los Angeles Pet Cemetery often find it hard to locate specific monuments because upright markers are not allowed. Of course, rules were made to be broken. In this case, they were broken for a special cat named Room Eight.

Shortly after the 1952 school year kicked off, one of the students in Room 8 at Elysian Heights Elementary School in Los Angeles noticed a black-and-white cat sneaking into the classroom through an open window. For the rest of the school year, the cat, which the students named Room Eight, visited the classroom. At the end of the school year, as the students were filing out for summer vacation, Room Eight jumped out the window and scampered off as if he had summer plans, too. Everyone thought that was the last they would see of Room Eight, until the start of school the following year, when a familiar black-and-white tomcat popped through the window. Once again, Room Eight stayed the entire school year and then took off for parts unknown for summer break, only to return again in September.

Year after year, students, faculty, and even reporters, waited eagerly to see if and when Room Eight would show up again. For the next 16 years, Room Eight returned to the school. Sadly, he passed away in 1968. Following his death, an upright monument was placed over his grave in the Los Angeles Pet Memorial Park. Hundreds of students and faculty members from Elysian Heights Elementary School attended the beloved cat's funeral and burial.

The Legend and Lore of Ohio's Most Haunted House

Cleveland's Franklin Castle, a foreboding stone building, has earned the dubious distinction of being Ohio's most haunted house. Frightening tales have been told of doors flying off their hinges, light fixtures spinning on their own, ghostly babies crying, and a woman dressed in black peering from a window. But what could have caused this house to become so haunted?

✳   ✳   ✳   ✳

Myths, Mysteries, and Murder at Franklin Castle

TRUTH AND LEGEND are easily confused at Franklin Castle. However, it is known that in 1866, a German immigrant named Hannes Tiedemann, his wife Luise, and their children moved to the spot where the mansion would later be built.

In January 1881, the Tiedemann's daughter Emma died, and shortly after, Hannes's elderly mother also passed away. Legend has it that within the next few years, the Tiedemanns lost three more children. In the face of such events, real or imagined, rumors began to spread that the family was cursed.

Possibly to distract his wife from the tragic family events, Tiedemann hired a renowned architectural firm to design a grand mansion for the family. He spared no expense and incorporated turrets, gargoyles, and steep gables into the design, adding to the four-story castle's gothic appearance. The 26-room mansion also included moving panels, concealed doors, hidden passageways, secret rooms, and five fireplaces.

When Luise died in 1895, rumors once again began to spread about the numerous unfortunate deaths in the Tiedemann family. A few years later, Hannes sold the castle to the Mullhauser family, who were in the brewing business. By the time Tiedemann died in 1908, his entire family was gone, and he was left without an heir.

Even with Tiedemann gone, stories and speculation about the man and strange events in his former home continued. Rumors circulated that he had been an unfaithful husband and had illicit encounters within the vast mansion. Eventually, this speculation led to stories of murder. One grisly tale alleged that Hannes killed his niece by hanging her in a secret hallway connected to the castles ballroom. Apparently, Tiedemann murdered the girl because he believed she was insane and he wanted to end her suffering.

According to legend, Hannes also killed a servant girl named Rachel after she rejected his advances. In another incarnation of the story, Rachel was actually Tiedemann's mistress, and she suffocated when he bound and gagged her after discovering her plan to marry someone else. Could it be that Rachel's spirit is the castle's woman in black who appears in the mansion's windows? Some past residents believe they've heard a woman choking in that part of the house. Others have even claimed to feel that they themselves were being choked while visiting the room.

New Owners, New Stories

The stories of murder and foul play in the house do not end with Tiedemann. In 1913, the Mullhauser family sold the house to the German Socialist Party, who used the house only for meetings and gatherings or so they claimed. Legend has it that the new residents were actually German spies and that an underground group of Nazis executed a large group of people in one of the secret passageways. Whatever might have happened, the group sold the house in the late 1960s.

Perhaps the most gruesome secret uncovered in the house was in one of the hidden rooms, where, in the 1970s, the skeletons of a dozen babies were found. It was suggested that perhaps they were the victims of a doctor's botched experiments or even medical specimens, but no one knows for sure. A medical examiner was only able to determine that they were old bones.

The Haunted Castle

James Romano, along with his wife and children, moved into Franklin Castle in January 1968. On the day they moved in, the children came down from playing upstairs to ask if they could take a cookie to their new friend, a little girl who was crying. When Mrs. Romano accompanied the children upstairs, the sad little girl was gone. After this happened several times, the Romanos began to wonder if they were getting ghostly visits from the Tiedemann children.

While living in the house, Mrs. Romano also believed she heard footsteps moving through the hallways and organ music playing, despite the fact that there was no organ in the house. On the third floor, she heard voices and glasses clinking, even though she was alone in the house. Eventually, the Romanos consulted a priest about the strange events in their home. But the priest refused to perform an exorcism, stating that he felt an evil presence and that the family should move.

By 1974, fed up with their strange home, the Romanos sold the castle to Sam Muscatello who, after finding out about the mansion's ghoulish history, began providing guided tours. Some of his visitors reported hearing odd sounds and encountering the mysterious woman in black.

Interest in the house's checkered past caused Muscatello to begin looking for the hidden doors and passageways. During his search, he made a ghastly find when he discovered a skeleton hidden behind a panel in the tower room, where, according to legend, a bloody ax murder once took place. The Cleveland coroner's office examined the bones and judged that they belonged to someone who had been dead for a very long time. Muscatello was never able to convert the place into a successful tourist attraction, and he eventually sold it.

The End of the Haunting?

Franklin Castle was sold and resold several times, but proposed renovations or plans to develop the house never seemed to pan out. To make matters worse, a fire set by a vagrant caused damage to the interiors. Has the alleged bloody past of the house left a ghostly mark on the building? Are the tragic events of days gone by being repeated in the present? Do the ghosts of yesterday still wander the corridors of this gothic house? We may never know for certain, but some claim that strange experiences still occur in the daunting mansion.

Celebrity Haunts

It's not surprising that so many celebrity ghosts hang out near Hollywood. What other town could inspire such dreams and passions, highs and lows?

✳ ✳ ✳ ✳

Marilyn Monroe

HOLLYWOOD'S ROOSEVELT HOTEL, home of the first ever Academy Awards in 1929, eternally hosts at least two celebrity spooks (along with a handful of other less famous specters). The ghostly reflection of silver-screen goddess Marilyn Monroe has often been seen in a wood-framed mirror that used to hang in the room where she frequently stayed. Today, visitors can simply visit the lower level, just outside the elevators, to get a glimpse of the mirror. Being a restless sort, Monroe's ghost has also been reported hovering near her tomb in the Westwood Memorial Cemetery and at San Diego's Hotel del Coronado.

Montgomery Clift

Marilyn Monroe isn't lonely at the Roosevelt. Her good friend, four-time Oscar nominee Montgomery Clift, has also never left the hotel that served as his home for more than three months in 1952 while filming *From Here to Eternity*. To commune with Clift, reserve Room 928, where he is said to leave the phone off the hook, pace the floor, and cause inexplicable loud noises. One guest even reported feeling an unseen hand tap her on the shoulder.

Rudolph Valentino

The ghost of romantic hero Rudolph Valentino has been spotted all over Hollywood, including near his tomb at the Hollywood Forever Memorial Park, floating over the costume department at Paramount Studios, and at his former Beverly Hills mansion. Throughout the years, owners of his former home have reported seeing "The Sheik" roaming the hallways, hanging out in his former bedroom, and visiting the stables (now turned into private residences). Others report seeing his specter enjoying the view of Los Angeles from the second-floor windows of the main house.

Ozzie Nelson

Bandleader and television star Ozzie Nelson can't seem to leave the Hollywood Hills home he shared with Harriet, David, and Ricky for more than 25 years. Reports of Nelson's ghost started circulating in Tinseltown soon after Harriet sold the house in 1980. Subsequent residents of the house have reported seeing doors open and close by unseen hands and lights and faucets turning on and off by themselves. One female homeowner even reported that the ghost pulled down the bed covers and got amorous with her.

Orson Welles

One of Hollywood's most respected writers, actors, and directors, Orson Welles still reportedly spends time at his favorite Hollywood bakery. As he was known as a man with gourmet tastes, it's no wonder Welles's spirit lingers at Melrose Avenue's Sweet Lady Jane, legendary for their extraordinary desserts. Tales of Welles's apparition have circulated among staff and guests of the restaurant for years. Visions of him seated at his favorite table are often accompanied by the scent of his favorite cigar and brandy.

John Wayne

Drive down the coast about an hour or so from Los Angeles, and you'll come to Newport Beach, home of the *Wild Goose*.

The vessel served as a minesweeper for the Canadian Navy during World War II before actor John Wayne purchased her in 1965 and converted her into a luxury yacht. The ship was said to be "Duke's" favorite possession, and he put her to good use during countless family vacations, star-studded parties, and poker sessions with buddies such as Dean Martin, Bob Hope, and Sammy Davis, Jr. Shortly after Wayne's death in 1979, new owners claimed to see a tall smiling man in various places on the yacht. Sightings of John Wayne's ghost on the *Wild Goose* have continued ever since. Those who want to try to see Duke's ghost for themselves can charter the *Wild Goose* for private events. But be prepared to bring your wallet—prices to charter the haunted boat start at $1,450 per hour.

Benjamin "Bugsy" Siegel

One ghost who can't seem to decide where to haunt is gangster Bugsy Siegel. Some stories claim that Siegel's ghost haunts the Beverly Hills home that once belonged to his girlfriend Virginia Hill, where he was gunned down in 1947. But the most prevalent Siegel sightings occur at the Flamingo Hotel in Las Vegas. Though the hotel has changed completely since Siegel opened it in the early 1940s, his ghost is said to still linger around the pool, as well as the statue and memorial to him in the hotel's gardens. Guests in the hotel's presidential suite have been sharing their lodgings with Siegel's spirit for years. He seems to favor spending time near the pool table when he's not in the bathroom.

Elvis Presley

Apparently, Elvis has NOT left the building, or so claim stage-hands at the Las Vegas Hilton, formerly the International Hotel. Presley made his big comeback there and continued to draw sellout crowds in the hotel's showroom until his death in 1977. The most common place to spot the King's sequined jumpsuit-clad ghost is backstage near the elevators. Elvis is also known to haunt his Memphis home, Graceland.

Keeping the Flame: The Loyal Keeper of the White River Light

Are you dedicated enough to your job to perform your duties until the day you die? What about the day after?

✳ ✳ ✳ ✳

Let There Be Light

IN THE LATE 1850s, local mill owners and merchants became concerned about frequent shipwrecks occurring where the White River emptied into Lake Michigan near Whitehall, Michigan. The narrow river connected the lumber mills of White Lake (an area called "The Lumber Queen of the World") and the Great Lakes shipping channels. The state legislature responded by approving the construction of and funding for a lighthouse; however, the White River Light would not be built for another 12 years.

In 1872, a beacon light was set up at the area's South Pier, and shipping captain William Robinson was granted the position of light keeper. In 1875, the White River Light Station was built, and Robinson and his beloved wife, Sarah, moved into the keeper's residence, where they happily raised their 11 children. Robinson often said he was so happy there that he would stay until his dying day. That happiness was marred by Sarah's unexpected death in 1891. Robinson, who had expected to live with her at the lighthouse until his retirement, was inconsolable. Grief-stricken, he poured all of his attention into tending the lighthouse.

Like (Grand)father, Like (Grand)son

As Robinson grew older, the Lighthouse Board began to consider his replacement, finally awarding the post to his grandson (and assistant keeper), Captain William Bush, in 1915. Although the board expected Bush to immediately take over Robinson's duties, he kindly allowed his grandfather to continue as keeper and remain in the keeper's residence for several years.

In 1919, after 47 years of loyal service, the board demanded that Robinson vacate the premises, but he refused. The board allegedly met and agreed to take legal action against Robinson if he didn't leave, but they never got the chance. Two weeks later, on the day before the deadline, Robinson died in his sleep. Bush moved into the residence, and the board was satisfied with their new man. But Captain Robinson stayed on, apparently still refusing to budge.

Thump, Thump, Tap

The lighthouse was decommissioned in 1960 and was turned into a museum in 1970. Today, museum staff and visitors believe that Robinson still occupies the building and continues his duties as lighthouse keeper. Curator Karen McDonnell lives in the lighthouse and reports hearing footsteps on the circular staircase in the middle of the night. She attributes this to Robinson, rather than natural causes, because of the unmistakable sound of his walking cane on the stairs.

McDonnell believes Robinson may have also gotten his wish— to stay in the lighthouse with his wife—because Sarah seems to have returned to the lighthouse as well. She helps with dusting and light housework, leaving display cases cleaner than they were before. Museum visitors often talk about feeling warm and safe inside the building and feeling a sense of love and peace. One tourist felt the presence of a smitten young couple, sitting in one of the window nooks.

We'll Leave the Light on for You

Visitors are welcome to explore the museum, which is open from June through October, and learn more about the shipping history of the Great Lakes. Perhaps you could even get a guided tour from the light's first and most loyal keeper.

America's Haunted Hotels

Looking for ghosts can be a tiring experience, and sometimes, while on the road, even the most intrepid ghost hunter needs a good night's sleep. But if a peaceful night is what you're looking for, you may want to go elsewhere. In these places, no one rests in peace!

✳ ✳ ✳ ✳

Admiral Fell Inn (Baltimore, Maryland)

THE ADMIRAL FELL Inn, located just steps away from the harbor on historic Fell's Point in Baltimore, was named for a shipping family who immigrated from England in the 18th century. With parts of the inn dating back to the 1700s, it's a charming place with stately rooms, an intimate pub, and wonderful service. It is also reportedly home to a number of spirits.

The ghosts at the Admiral Fell Inn include a young boy who died from cholera, a woman in white who haunts Room 218, and a man who died in Room 413. Staff members claim this room is always chilly and has strange, moving cold spots.

In 2003, during Hurricane Isabel, the hotel's guests were evacuated to safety, but several of the hotel managers stayed behind. At one point in the night, they reported the sounds of music, laughter, and dancing from the floor above the lobby. When they checked to see what was going on, they discovered no one else in the building.

Blennerhassett Hotel (Parkersburg, West Virginia)

The Blennerhassett Hotel was designed and built in 1889 by William Chancellor, a prominent businessman. The hotel was a grand showplace and has been restored to its original condition in recent years. These renovations have reportedly stirred the ghosts who reside there into action.

There are several ghosts associated with the hotel, including a man in gray who has been seen walking around on the second floor and the infamous "Four O'Clock Knocker," who likes to pound on guest room doors at 4:00 AM. There is also a ghost who likes to ride the elevators, often stopping on floors where the button has not been pushed. But the most famous resident spirit is that of hotel builder William Chancellor. Guests and employees have reported seeing clouds of cigar smoke in the hallways, wafting through doorways, and circling a portrait of Chancellor that hangs in the library.

Stanley Hotel (Estes Park, Colorado)

The Stanley Hotel has gained quite a reputation over the years, not only as a magnificent hotel with a breathtaking view but also as the haunted hotel that provided the inspiration for Stephen King's book *The Shining*.

In 1909, when Freelan Stanley opened his grand hotel, it immediately began to attract famous visitors from all over the country. Today, it attracts a number of ghostly guests as well.

The hotel's most notable ghost is Stanley himself; his apparition is often seen in the lobby and the billiard room. Legend has it that Stanley's wife, Flora, still entertains guests by playing her piano in the ballroom. Many people have reportedly seen the keys moving on the piano as music plays, but if they try to get close to it, the music stops. Another resident ghost seems especially fond of Room 407, where he turns lights on and off and rattles the occupants with inexplicable noises.

The Lodge (Cloudcroft, New Mexico)

Opened in the early 1900s, The Lodge has attracted famous visitors such as Pancho Villa, Judy Garland, and Clark Gable. And since 1901, every New Mexico governor has stayed in the spacious Governor's Suite.

The Lodge is reportedly haunted by the ghost of a beautiful young chambermaid named Rebecca, who was murdered by her lumberjack boyfriend when he caught her cheating on him. Her apparition has frequently been spotted in the hallways, and her playful, mischievous spirit has bedeviled guests in the rooms. She is now accepted as part of the hotel's history, and there is even a stained-glass window with her likeness prominently displayed at The Lodge.

The hotel's Red Dog Saloon is reputedly one of Rebecca's favorite spots. There she makes her presence known by turning lights on and off, causing alcohol to disappear, moving objects around, and playing music long after the tavern has closed. Several bartenders claim to have seen the reflection of a pretty, red-haired woman in the bar's mirror, but when they turn around to talk to her, she disappears.

Beer, Wine, and Spirits: The Haunted Lemp Mansion

There is no other place in St. Louis, Missouri, with a ghostly history quite like the Lemp Mansion. It has served as many things over the years—stately home, boarding house, restaurant, bed-and-breakfast—but it has never lost the notoriety of being the most haunted place in the city. In fact, in 1980, Life magazine called the Lemp Mansion "one of the ten most haunted places in America."

* * * *

THE LEMP BREWERY, and the Lemp family itself, gained recognition during the mid-1800s. Although they were credited with making one of the first lager beers in the United States and once rivaled the annual sales of Anheuser–Busch, few people remember much about the Lemps today—most people in St. Louis can barely even recall that the Lemps once made beer. They are now more familiar with the family's mansion on the city's south side than with the decaying brewery that stands two blocks away. The Lemps have been gone for years, but their old house stands as a reminder of their wealth and the tragedies that plagued them. Perhaps that's why there's still an aura of sadness looming over the place.

During the day, the house is a bustling restaurant, filled with people and activity, but at night, many people believe the old mansion is haunted. Are its ghosts the restless spirits of the Lemps wandering the corridors of their former home? It seems possible, given the enormous number of tragedies that struck the prominent family.

The Lemp Empire Begins

Adam Lemp left Germany in 1836, and by 1838 had settled in St. Louis. He had learned the brewer's trade as a young man, and he soon introduced the city to one of the first American lagers, a crisp, clean beer that required months of storage in a cool, dark place to obtain its unique flavor. This new beer quickly became a regional favorite.

Business prospered, and by the 1850s, thanks to the demand for lager, Lemp's Western Brewing Company was one of the largest in the city. When Adam Lemp died in 1862, his son William took the reins, and the company entered its period of greatest prominence.

After the death of his father, William began a major expansion of the brewery. He purchased more land and constructed a new brewery—the largest in St. Louis. In 1899, the Lemps introduced their famous Falstaff beer, which became a favorite across the country. Lemp was the first brewery to establish coast-to-coast distribution of its beer, and the company grew so large that as many as 100 horses were needed to pull the delivery wagons in St. Louis alone.

In 1876, during the time of his company's greatest success, William purchased a home for his family a short distance away from the brewery. He immediately began renovating and expanding the house, which had been built in the early 1860s, decorating it with original artwork, hand-carved wood decor, and ornately painted ceilings. The mansion featured a tunnel that traveled from the basement of the house along a quarried shaft and exited at the brewery. Ironically, it was in the midst of all this success that the Lemp family's troubles began.

Death Comes Calling

The first death in the family was that of Frederick Lemp, William's favorite son and heir to the Lemp empire. As the most ambitious and hardworking of the Lemp children, he'd been groomed to take over the family business. He was well liked and happily married but spent countless hours at the brewery working to improve the company's future. In 1901, his health began to fail, and, in December of that year, he died at age 28. Many believe that he worked himself to death.

Frederick's death devastated his parents, especially his father. William's friends and coworkers said he was never the same afterward. He was rarely seen in public and walked to the brewery using the tunnel beneath the house.

On January 1, 1904, William suffered another crushing blow with the death of his closest friend, fellow brewer Frederick Pabst. This tragedy left William nervous and unsettled, and his physical and mental health began to deteriorate. On February 13, 1904, his suffering became unbearable. After breakfast, he went upstairs to his bedroom and shot himself with a revolver. No suicide note was ever found.

In November 1904, William, Jr., became president of the William J. Lemp Brewing Company. With his inheritance, he filled the house with servants, built country houses, and spent huge sums on carriages, clothing, and art.

Will's wife, Lillian, nicknamed the "Lavender Lady" because of her fondness for that color, was soon spending the Lemp fortune as quickly as her husband. They eventually divorced in 1906, causing a scandal throughout St. Louis. When it was all over, the Lavender Lady went into seclusion.

Less Drinking, More Death

In 1919, the 18th Amendment was passed, prohibiting the manufacture, transportation, and sale of alcohol in the United States. This signaled the end for many brewers, including the Lemps. Many hoped that Congress would repeal the amendment, but Will decided not to wait. He closed down the plant without notice, thus closing the door on the Lemp empire.

Will sold the famous Lemp "Falstaff" logo to brewer Joseph Griesedieck for $25,000. In 1922, he sold the brewery to the International Shoe Co. for a fraction of its estimated worth ($7 million before Prohibition).

With Prohibition destroying the brewery, the 1920s looked to be a dismal decade for the Lemp family. And it began on a tragic note, with the suicide of Elsa Lemp Wright in 1920. The second member of the family to commit suicide, Elsa was the wealthiest woman in St. Louis after inheriting her share of her father's estate. After a stormy marriage to wealthy industrialist Thomas Wright between 1910 and 1918, the couple divorced but then remarried in March 1920. Shortly after, Elsa inexplicably shot herself. No letter was ever found.

Will and his brother Edwin rushed to Elsa's house when they heard of their sister's suicide. Will had only one comment: "That's the Lemp family for you."

Will's own death came a short time later. While sitting in his office in the mansion, Will shot himself in the chest. His secretary found him lying in a pool of blood, and he died before a doctor could be summoned. As with his father and sister before him, Will had left no indication as to why he had ended his life.

Oddly, Will seemed to have had no intention of killing himself. After the sale of the brewery, he had discussed selling off the rest of his assets and said he wanted to rest and travel. He and his second wife were even planning a trip to Europe. Friends were baffled by his sudden death.

With William, Jr., gone and his brothers, Charles and Edwin, involved with their own endeavors, it seemed that the days of the Lemp empire had come to an end. But the days of Lemp tragedy were not yet over.

Charles was never very involved with the Lemp Brewery. His work had mostly been in the banking and financial industries, and he sometimes dabbled in politics as well. In the 1920s, Charles moved back into the Lemp Mansion.

Charles was a mysterious figure who became odd and reclusive with age. A lifelong bachelor, he lived alone in the rambling old house, and by age 77, he was arthritic and ill. He had grown quite eccentric and developed a morbid attachment to the Lemp family home. Because of the history of the place, his brother Edwin often encouraged Charles to move out, but he refused. Finally, when he could stand it no more, he became the fourth member of the Lemp family to take his own life.

On May 10, 1949, one of the staff members found Charles dead in his second-floor bedroom. He had shot himself at some point during the night. He was the only member of the family to leave a suicide note behind. He wrote: "In case I am found dead, blame it on no one but me."

The Lemp family, once so large and prosperous, had been nearly destroyed in less than a century. Only Edwin Lemp remained, and he had long avoided the life that had turned so tragic for the rest of his family. He was known as a quiet, reclusive man who lived a peaceful life on his secluded estate. In 1970, Edwin, the last of the Lemps, passed away quietly of natural causes at age 90.

Lemp Mansion Hauntings

After the death of Charles Lemp, the grand family mansion was sold and turned into a boarding house. It soon fell on hard times and began to deteriorate along with the neighborhood. In later years, stories emerged that residents of the boarding house often complained of ghostly knocks and phantom footsteps inside. As these tales spread, it became increasingly hard to find tenants to occupy the rooms, so the old Lemp Mansion was rarely filled.

The decline of the house continued until 1975, when Dick Pointer and his family purchased it. The Pointers began remodeling and renovating the place, working for years to turn it into a restaurant and inn. But the Pointers soon realized they were not alone in the house. Workers told of ghostly events occurring, such as strange sounds, tools that vanished and appeared again in other places, and an overwhelming feeling that they were being watched by people unseen.

After the restaurant opened, staff members began to report their own odd experiences. Glasses were seen lifting off the bar and flying through the air, inexplicable sounds were heard, and some people even glimpsed actual apparitions. Visitors to the house reported that doors locked and unlocked on their own, voices and sounds came from nowhere, and even the Lavender Lady was spotted on occasion.

These strange events continue today, so it is no surprise that the inn attracts ghost hunters from around the country. Many spend the night in the house and report their own bizarre happenings, from eerie sounds to strange photographs. One woman awoke to see the specter of a lady standing next to her bed. The ghost raised a finger to her lips, as if asking the woman not to scream, and then vanished.

Paul Pointer manages the business today, along with his sisters, Mary and Patty. They all accept the ghosts as part of the ambience of the historic old home. As Paul once said, "People come here expecting to experience weird things, and fortunately for us, they are rarely disappointed."

Winchester Mystery House

By the time she was 22, Sarah Pardee was seriously popular—she spoke four languages, played the piano, and was exceedingly pretty. Nicknamed the "Belle of New Haven," she had her pick of suitors. She chose a young man named William W. Winchester, the only son of Oliver Winchester, a stockholder with the successful New Haven Arms Company. When Sarah and William married in 1862, William had plans to expand the business by buying out some of his competition and introducing the repeating rifle. The gun became known as "The Gun that Won the West," and the now fabulously wealthy Winchester name was woven into the fabric of American history.

✳   ✳   ✳   ✳

Can't Buy Me Love

IN THE SUMMER of 1866, Sarah gave birth to a daughter, but the joy of a new baby was brief. The child was born sickly, diagnosed with marasmus, a protein deficiency that typically afflicts infants in third-world countries. The baby was unable to gain weight and succumbed to the disease in just a few weeks.

Sarah and William were both bereft, but Sarah took it the hardest. She sank into a serious depression from which she would never totally recover.

Fifteen years later, when Oliver Winchester passed away, William stepped into his dad's shoes at the family business. However, he had only held the job for a few months when he lost a battle with tuberculosis and died in 1881.

Sarah was now 41 years old and without the family she had built her life around. She was also extremely wealthy. In the late 1880s, the average family income hovered around $500 per year. Sarah was pulling in about $1,000 per day! Because her husband left her everything, she had more than 700 shares of stock in addition to income from current sales. Sarah was up to her eyeballs in money. When William's mother died in 1898, Sarah inherited 2,000 more shares, which meant that she owned about 50 percent of the business. Sarah Winchester was all dressed up and had absolutely nowhere to go—even if she did have someplace, there was no one with whom she could share it.

"I See Dead People"

Today, most people regard psychics with more than a little suspicion and skepticism, but in the late 19th century, psychics had grabbed much of the public's attention and trust. The period after the Civil War and the onslaught of new industry had left so much destruction and created so much change for people that many were looking for answers in a confusing world. With claims that they could commune with the "Great Beyond," psychics were consulted by thousands hoping for some insight.

Sarah was not doing well after the death of her husband. Losing her child had been a debilitating blow, but after her husband's passing, she was barely able to function. Fearing for her life, one of Sarah's close friends suggested she visit a psychic to see if she could contact her husband or daughter or both.

Sarah agreed to visit a Boston medium named Adam Coons, who wasted no time in telling her that William was trying to communicate with her, and the message wasn't good.

Apparently, William was desperate to tell Sarah that the family was cursed as a result of the invention of the repeating rifle. Native Americans, settlers, and soldiers all over the world were dead, largely due to the Winchester family. The spirits of these people were out for Sarah next, said William through the medium. The only way for her to prolong her life was to "head toward the setting sun," which meant, "move to California." The medium told her that once she got there, she would have to build a house where all those spirits could live happily together—but the house had to be built big and built often. Sarah was told that construction on the house could never cease, or the spirits would claim her and she would die. So Sarah packed up and left New Haven for California in 1884.

Now That's a House!

Sarah bought an eight-room farmhouse on the outskirts of the burgeoning town of San Jose, on the southern end of San Francisco Bay. Legend has it that she hired more than

20 workmen and a foreman and kept them working 24 hours a day, 365 days a year. To ensure that they would keep quiet about what they were doing—and not leave because the house was more than a little weird—she paid them a whopping $3 per day—more than twice the going rate of the time.

The workmen took the money and built as their client wished, though it made no sense whatsoever. Sarah was not an architect, but she gave the orders for the house's design. Sarah's odd requests, the constant construction, and an endless stream of money resulted in a rather unusual abode—stairs lead to ceilings, windows open into brick walls, and some rooms have no doors. There are also Tiffany windows all over the place, many containing the number 13, with which Sarah was obsessed. There are spiderweb-paned windows, which, although lovely, didn't do much to dispel rumors that Sarah was preoccupied with death and the occult.

The house kept on growing, all because the spirits were supposedly "advising" Sarah. Chimneys were built and never used. There were so many rooms that counting them was pointless. Reportedly, one stairway in the house went up seven steps and down eleven, and one of the linen closets is bigger than most three-bedroom apartments.

Very few people ever saw the lady of the house. When she shopped in town, merchants came to her car, as she rarely stepped out. Questions and rumors were rampant in San Jose: Who was this crazy lady? Was the house haunted by spirits or just the energy of the aggrieved widow who lived there? Would the hammers ever stop banging? The workers knew how weird the house was, but no one knew for sure what was going on inside Sarah's head.

Still, Sarah was generous in the community. She donated to the poor, occasionally socialized, and, in the early days, even threw a party every once in a while. She had a maid she was quite fond of and was exceedingly kind to any children she encountered. But as the house grew and the years passed, the rumors became more prevalent and the increasingly private Winchester retreated further into her bizarre hermitage.

The End

In 1922, Sarah Winchester died in her sleep, and the construction finally ceased after 38 years. In her will, Sarah left huge chunks of her estate to nieces, nephews, and loyal employees. The will was divided into exactly 13 parts and was signed 13 times. Her belongings, everything from ornate furniture to chandeliers to silver dinner services, were auctioned off. It took six weeks to remove everything.

And as for the house itself, it wasn't going to find a buyer any time soon: The structure at the time of Sarah's passing covered several acres and had more than 10,000 window panes, 160 rooms, 467 doorways, 47 fireplaces, 40 stairways, and 6 kitchens. A group of investors bought the house in hopes of turning it into a tourist attraction, which they did. What they didn't do was employ guides or security, however, so for a small fee, thousands of curious people came from all over the country to traipse through the house, scribbling graffiti on the walls and stealing bits of wallpaper. It wasn't until the house was purchased in the 1970s and renamed the Winchester Mystery House that it was restored to its original state. Millions of people have visited the house, which continues to be one of the top tourist attractions in California.

The Footnote

With so many people going in and out of the house over the years, it's not surprising that there are tales of "strange happenings" in the Winchester mansion. People have claimed that they've heard and seen banging doors, mysterious voices, cold spots, moving lights, doorknobs that turn by themselves, and more than a few say that Sarah herself still roams the many rooms. Psychics who have visited the house solemnly swear that it is indeed haunted.

This can't be proven, of course, but it doesn't stop the claims, and it didn't stop the lady of the house from undertaking one of the world's most incredible construction projects.

A Realtor's Worst Nightmare

It seems every town in the world has a local haunted house—the one house that animals and locals avoid like the plague. But when it comes to haunted houses that can chill your bones with just one glance and give you nightmares for weeks, nothing can hold a ghostly candle to a foreboding Dutch Colonial in Amityville, New York, which once glared down at passersby with windows that seemed to resemble demonic eyes.

✳   ✳   ✳   ✳

Brutal Beginnings

MOST HAUNTINGS BEGIN with tragic circumstances, and the house at 112 Ocean Avenue is no exception. In the early morning hours of November 13, 1974, someone fatally shot six of the seven members of the DeFeo family—father Ronald, Sr., his wife, Louise, and four of their children: Mark, John, Allison, and Dawn. The only one to escape the massacre was 23-year-old Ronnie "Butch" DeFeo, who was subsequently arrested and charged with all six murders. He eventually confessed and was sentenced to 25 years to life in prison. During the trial, there were rumors that demonic voices had directed DeFeo to commit the murders, although prosecutors claimed he was only trying to collect the family's $200,000 insurance policy.

The DeFeo house stood alone and abandoned until December 1975, when new owners came calling.

The Horror Begins

George and Kathy Lutz knew they had a bargain on their hands when their realtor showed them 112 Ocean Avenue. The house had six bedrooms, a pool, and even a boathouse, all for the unbelievable price of $80,000. Of course, an entire family had been murdered in the house, and some of their belongings were still inside, but after a family meeting, the Lutzes decided it was too good a deal to pass up. So George and Kathy moved in with their three young children: Daniel, Christopher, and Missy.

Shortly thereafter, the nightmare began. To the Lutzes, it quickly became obvious that there were demonic forces at work inside the house. Some of the paranormal experiences that allegedly took place in the home include:

* George had trouble sleeping and would continually wake up at exactly 3:15 AM, believed to be the time the DeFeo murders took place.

* Daughter Missy began talking to an imaginary friend: a girl named Jodie who sometimes appeared as a pig. Standing outside the house one night, George looked up and saw a giant pig with glowing red eyes staring back at him from Missy's room. Later, cloven hoofprints were found in the snow outside the house.

* Even though it was the middle of winter, certain rooms in the house, especially the sewing room, were constantly infested with flies.

* A small room painted blood red was found hidden behind shelving in the basement. Dubbed the Red Room, the entire family felt there was something evil in the room. Even the family dog, Harry, refused to go near it.

* During an attempt to bless the house, a priest suddenly became violently ill and heard an inhuman voice yell at him to "Get out!"

* When George and Kathy attempted to bless the house on their own, they heard voices screaming, "Will you stop?"

* Green slime oozed out of the toilets and dripped from the walls.

✳ George began (unintentionally) taking on the mannerisms of Ronald DeFeo, Jr., and even grew out his beard, causing him to resemble DeFeo. Apparently the likeness was so uncanny that when Lutz walked into a bar DeFeo used to frequent, patrons thought he was DeFeo.

On January 14, 1976, unable to cope with the unseen forces at work in the house, George and Kathy Lutz gathered up their children and their dog and fled the house in the middle of the night. The following day, George sent movers out to gather up all their belongings. The Lutzes themselves never again set foot inside 112 Ocean Avenue.

Searching for Evil

In an attempt to understand exactly what happened to his family inside the house, George brought in demonologists Ed and Lorraine Warren, who arrived at the house with a local news crew on March 6, 1976. Lorraine said that she sensed a very strong evil presence in the house. Several years later, a series of time-lapse infrared photographs were released that appeared to show a ghostly boy with glowing eyes standing near one of the staircases.

Jay Anson's book *The Amityville Horror—A True Story* was released in September 1977. The book, which chronicled the Lutz family's harrowing ordeal, was compiled from more than 40 hours of tape-recorded interviews with George and Kathy and became a best seller almost immediately. With that, everyone started taking a closer look into what really happened at 112 Ocean Avenue.

Controversy Begins

Once people started looking at the specifics in Anson's book, things didn't seem to add up. For one, a check of weather conditions showed there was no snow on the ground when George claimed to have found the strange cloven footprints outside the house. Likewise, windows and doors that ghostly forces had supposedly broken or demolished in the book were found to still be intact. Reporters interviewing neighbors along Ocean Avenue found that not a single person could remember ever seeing or hearing anything strange going on at the house. And despite the book mentioning numerous visits by local police to investigate strange noises at the Lutz house, the Amityville Police Department publicly stated that during the whole time the Lutzes lived at 112 Ocean Avenue, they never visited the home or received a single phone call from the family.

The Lawsuits

In May 1977, George and Kathy Lutz filed a series of lawsuits against numerous magazines and individuals who had either investigated 112 Ocean Avenue or had written about the reported hauntings. They alleged that these people had invaded their privacy and caused their family mental distress. There was one other name in the lawsuit that raised more than a few eyebrows: William Weber, Ronald DeFeo, Jr.'s defense lawyer. Even more surprising was that Weber filed a countersuit for $2 million for breach of contract.

Weber contended that he had met with the Lutzes and that "over many bottles of wine" the three made up the story of the house being haunted. When Weber found out that the Lutzes had taken their story to Jay Anson and essentially cut him out of the deal, he sued. In September 1979, U.S. District Court judge Jack B. Weinstein dismissed all of the Lutzes' claims and also made some telling remarks in his ruling, including that he felt the book was basically a work of fiction that relied heavily upon Weber's suggestions. Weber's countersuit was later settled out of court for an undisclosed amount.

What Really Happened?

Even though it's been more than 30 years since the Lutzes occupied the house at 112 Ocean Avenue, many questions still remain. A series of books and movies all bearing the name *The Amityville Horror* were released, which continued to blur the lines between what really happened in the home and what was a fabrication. In 2005, a remake of *The Amityville Horror* movie was released that added many new elements to the story that have yet to be substantiated, including a link between the house in Amityville and a mythical figure, John Ketcham, who was reportedly involved with witchcraft in Salem, Massachusetts.

Kathy Lutz died of emphysema in August 2004. George Lutz passed away from complications of heart disease in May 2006. Both went to their graves still proclaiming that what happened to them inside 112 Ocean Avenue did indeed occur and was not a hoax.

The house itself is still standing. You would think that with a building as famous (or infamous) and well known as the Amityville Horror house is, it would be easy to find. Not so. In order to stop the onslaught of trespassing thrill seekers, the address has been changed, so 112 Ocean Avenue technically no longer exists. The famous quarter-moon windows have also been removed and replaced with ordinary square ones.

Since the Lutz family moved out, the property has changed hands several times, but none of the owners have ever reported anything paranormal taking place there. They did acknowledge being frightened from time to time but that was usually from being startled by the occasional trespasser peering into their windows trying to get a glimpse of the inside of this allegedly haunted house.

The Mysterious Area 51

Conspiracy theorists believe many things. But they all agree on one thing—these conspiracies pale in comparison to the mother of all conspiracies: Area 51.

✳   ✳   ✳   ✳

ALIEN AUTOPSIES. COVERT military operations. Tests on bizarre aircraft. These are all things rumored to be going on inside Area 51—a top secret location inside the Nevada

Test and Training Range (NTTR) about an hour northwest of Las Vegas. Though shrouded in secrecy, some of the history of Area 51 is known. For instance, this desert area was used as a bombing test site during World War II, but no facility existed on the site until 1955. At that time, the area was chosen as the perfect location to develop and test the U-2 spy plane. Originally known as Watertown, it came to be called Area 51 in 1958 when 38,000 acres were designated for military use. The entire area was simply marked "Area 51 on military maps. Today, the facility is rumored to contain approximately 575 square miles. But you won't find it on a map because, officially, it doesn't exist.

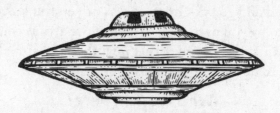

An Impenetrable Fortress

Getting a clear idea of the size of Area 51, or even a glimpse of the place, is next to impossible. Years ago, curiosity seekers could get a good view of the facility by hiking to the top of two nearby mountain peaks known as White Sides and Freedom Ridge. But government officials soon grew weary of people climbing up there and snapping pictures, so in 1995, they seized control of both. Currently, the only way to legally catch a glimpse of the base is to scale 7,913-foot-tall Tikaboo Peak. Even if you make it that far, you're still not guaranteed to see anything because the facility is more than 25 miles away and is only visible on clear days with no haze.

The main entrance to Area 51 is along Groom Lake Road. Those brave (or foolhardy) souls who have ventured down the road to investigate quickly realize they are being watched. Video cameras and motion sensors are hidden along the road, and signs alert the curious that if they continue any further, they will be entering a military installation, which is illegal "without the written permission of the installation commander." If that's not enough to get unwanted guests to turn around, one sign clearly states: "Use of deadly force authorized." Simply put, take one step over that imaginary line in the dirt, and they will get you.

Camo Dudes

And just exactly who are "they"? They are the "Camo Dudes," mysterious figures watching trespassers from nearby hillsides and jeeps. If they spot something suspicious, they might call for backup—Blackhawk helicopters that will come in for a closer look. All things considered, it would probably be best to just turn around and go back home. And lest you think about hiring someone to fly you over Area 51, the entire area is considered restricted air space, meaning that unauthorized aircraft are not permitted to fly over, or even near, the facility.

Who Works There?

Most employees are general contractors who work for companies in the area. But rather than allow these workers to commute individually, the facility has them ushered in secretly and en masse in one of two ways. The first is a mysterious white bus with tinted windows that picks up employees at several unmarked stops before whisking them through the front gates of the facility. Every evening, the bus leaves the facility and drops the employees off.

The second mode of commuter transport, an even more secretive way, is JANET, the code name given to the secret planes that carry workers back and forth from Area 51 and Las Vegas McCarran Airport. JANET has its own terminal, which is located at the far end of the airport behind fences with special security gates. It even has its own private parking lot. Several times a day, planes from the JANET fleet take off and land at the airport.

Bob Lazar

The most famous Area 51 employee is someone who may or may not have actually worked there. In the late 1980s, Bob Lazar claimed that he'd worked at the secret facility he referred to as S-4. In addition, Lazar said that he was assigned the task of reverse engineering a recovered spaceship in order to determine how it worked. Lazar had only been at the facility for a short time, but he and his team had progressed to the point where they were test flying the alien spaceship. That's when Lazar made a big mistake. He decided to bring some friends out to Groom Lake Road when he knew the alien craft was being flown. He was caught and subsequently fired.

During his initial interviews with a local TV station, Lazar seemed credible and quite knowledgeable as to the inner workings of Area 51. But when people started trying to verify the information Lazar was giving, not only was it next to impossible to confirm most of his story, his education and employment history could not be verified either. Skeptics immediately proclaimed that Lazar was a fraud. To this day, Lazar contends that everything he said was factual and that the government deleted all his records in order to set him up and make him look like a fake. Whether or not he's telling the truth, Lazar will be remembered as the man who first brought up the idea that alien spaceships were being experimented on at Area 51.

What's Really Going On?

So what really goes on inside Area 51? One thing we do know is that they work on and test aircraft. Whether they are alien spacecraft or not is still open to debate. Some of the planes worked on and tested at Area 51 include the SR-71 Blackbird and the F-117 Nighthawk stealth fighter. Currently, there are rumors that a craft known only by the codename Aurora is being worked on at the facility.

If you want to try and catch a glimpse of some of these strange craft being tested, you'll need to hang out at the

"Black Mailbox" along Highway 375, also known as the Extraterrestrial Highway. It's really nothing more than a mailbox along the side of the road. But as with most things associated with Area 51, nothing is as it sounds, so it should come as no surprise that the "Black Mailbox" is actually white. It belongs to a rancher, who owns the property nearby. Still, this is the spot where people have been known to camp out all night just for a chance to see something strange floating in the night sky.

The Lawsuit

In 1994, a landmark lawsuit was filed against the U.S. Air Force by five unnamed contractors and the widows of two others. The suit claimed that the contractors had been present at Area 51 when large quantities of "unknown chemicals" were burned in trenches and pits. As a result of coming into contact with the fumes of the chemicals, the suit alleged that two of the contractors died, and the five survivors suffered respiratory problems and skin sores. Reporters worldwide jumped on the story, not only because it proved that Area 51 existed but also because the suit was asking for many classified documents to be entered as evidence.

Would some of those documents refer to alien beings or space-craft? The world would never know because in September 1995, while petitions for the case were still going on, President Bill Clinton signed Presidential Determination No. 95–45, which basically stated that Area 51 was exempt from federal, state, local, and interstate hazardous and solid waste laws. Shortly thereafter, the lawsuit was dismissed due to a lack of evidence, and all attempts at appeals were rejected. In 2002, President George W. Bush renewed Area 51's exemptions, ensuring once and for all that what goes on inside Area 51 stays inside Area 51.

So at the end of the day, we're still left scratching our heads about Area 51. We know it exists and we have some idea of what goes on there, but there is still so much more we don't know. More than likely, we never will know everything, but then again, what fun is a mystery if you know all the answers?

Spirits in Chains

Peering out over miles of farmland is one of southern Illinois's most haunted locations. When it was completed in 1838, the large home known as Hickory Hill was a horrific place to the men and women who were brought there in chains. Thanks to this part of its history, Hickory Hill has been nicknamed the "Old Slave House."

Since the early 1900s, people have come from all over the country to see this strange and ominous place. The atrocities that occurred there were revealed years ago, but many stories claim that the dead of Hickory Hill do not rest in peace.

✳   ✳   ✳   ✳

Working in the Salt Mines

HICKORY HILL WAS built by John Hart Crenshaw, a descendant of an old American family with ties to the founding of the country. He was born in November 1797, on the border of North and South Carolina, but his family moved west and settled in New Madrid, Missouri, only to have their home destroyed by the earthquake of 1811. A short time later, they moved to southern Illinois and started a farm.

By the time he was in his mid-thirties, Crenshaw had amassed such a fortune in the salt industry that, at one point, he paid one-seventh of all the taxes collected in the state. But Crenshaw is best remembered for Hickory Hill and his ties to the kidnapping of slaves. Although Illinois was a free state, it allowed slaves to be leased for work in the salt mines of southern Illinois. Work in the salt mines was backbreaking attracted only the most desperate workers. Because of this, slavery became essential to the success of the salt-mining operations.

Slaves had no protection under the law and free Blacks had very little. And few officials interfered with the men who seized Black people and carried them south for sale at auction. Perhaps those most guilty of this practice were the "night riders" of the 1830s and 1840s—bands of men who posted riders along the Ohio River at night to capture escaped slaves and return them for a reward. They also kidnapped free Black men and their children and sold them in the South. The night riders were the opposite of the Underground Railroad, sending escaped slaves back to the southern plantations rather than to the northern cities and freedom.

Allegedly, Crenshaw, who leased slaves to work the salt mines, kept a number of night riders in his employ. He used this as a profitable sideline to his legitimate businesses. Rather than collecting any rewards, Crenshaw realized that he could make much more money by working the captured slaves or by selling them back into the southern market.

Most people viewed Crenshaw as an upstanding businessman and community leader who was active in his church. No one knew that he was holding illegal slaves or that he was suspected of kidnapping Black families and selling them into slavery. They would have been even more surprised to learn that the slaves were being held captive in the barred chambers of the attic of Hickory Hill. The men were often subjected to cruelty and the women to the "breeding chamber," which made even more money for Crenshaw. A pregnant slave on the southern market was worth much more than a female with no child. The practice turned a handsome profit and kept Crenshaw supplied with workers.

The Old Slave House

Crenshaw built Hickory Hill, his classic Greek plantation house, on a hill overlooking the Saline River. The house was certainly grand, but it had some unusual and less visible additions. Legend says there was once a tunnel connecting the basement to the banks of the Saline River to load and unload slaves at night. Another large passageway at the rear of the house allowed wagons to enter the house so that slaves could be unloaded where they would not be seen from the outside.

Located on the third floor of Hickory Hill were the infamous confines of the attic and proof that Crenshaw had something sinister in mind when he had the house built. The attic can still be reached today by a flight of narrow, well-worn stairs that end at a wide hallway containing about a dozen cell-like rooms with flat, wooden bunks facing the narrow corridor that runs between them. The slaves spent their time in these cells chained to the walls. Barred windows at either end provided the only light and the only ventilation. During the summer, the heat in the attic was unbearable.

Downfall

In 1842, Crenshaw was indicted on criminal charges. It was reported that he had engineered the kidnapping of a free Black woman and her children. He allegedly had them taken from their home and carried by wagon out of state. Unfortunately, the prosecutor couldn't prove this, and Crenshaw was set free.

But soon, rumors began to spread about Crenshaw's business activities. These rumblings, combined with the earlier indictment, started to upset a lot of people in the area. In March 1842, a steam mill that Crenshaw owned was burned to the ground. It is believed that the fire was started by a group of free Black men, angry over Crenshaw's actions.

In 1846, Crenshaw's business holdings began to decline. In addition to several civil court actions against him, demand fell for Illinois salt. Even worse, Crenshaw was attacked by one of his workers, resulting in the loss of a leg. After that, he sold off his slaves and closed down most of his salt operations. During the Civil War, he sold Hickory Hill, but when he died in December 1871, he was buried in Hickory Hill Cemetery.

Ghosts in the Attic

John Crenshaw has been in his grave for more than a century, but according to local legend, many of the slaves that he once kept chained in his attic do not rest in peace. These stories, which come from southern Illinois folklore and scholarly works alike, maintain that eerie voices are sometimes heard in the attic of the house as they moan, cry, and whisper of the horrific things that were done to them in centuries past.

George Sisk, a former owner of the Old Slave House, insisted that the place was haunted, and many visitors to the house agree. The old slave quarters are often hot and cramped and at other times are inexplicably cold.

In the 1920s, Sisk opened the house to tourists. Soon after, visitors began complaining of weird happenings in the house, such as inexplicable sounds in the attic, especially crying, moaning, whimpering, and even the rattling of chains. A number of people told of uncomfortable feelings in the slave quarters, such as sensations of intense fear, sadness, and of being watched. Others felt as if they'd been touched by invisible hands or had unseen figures brush by them.

Other legends soon became attached to Hickory Hill, such as a story that arose in the 1920s, which claimed that no one could spend the night in the attic of the house and survive. Many would-be thrill seekers tried, but no one managed to make it to daybreak in the attic of Hickory Hill until 1978, when a reporter from Harrisburg, Illinois, managed to make it through the night, beating out more than 150 previous challengers. The reporter felt pretty good afterward but confessed that he didn't want to make it an annual event.

Still Haunted?

People still claim to feel cold chills and hear voices in the house, but for most visitors, a visit to Hickory Hill is not so bizarre. Many experience nothing, while others say they feel unsettled, frightened, or overwrought with emotion in the attic. Perhaps this is not a sign of the supernatural, but the attic is certainly an eerie place with a great deal of odd energy.

The Old Slave House closed down in 1996 but was purchased by the state of Illinois a few years later. Eventually, the house will reopen as a historic site. Whether or not the ghosts will be a part of the new attraction is uncertain. At the very least, visitors should take a moment to remember those unfortunate souls who once suffered in the house and pray that they have finally found peace on the other side.

The Haunting of Hull House

In the late 1880s, Hull House represented a bastion in social equality and was intended to help raise the poorest residents of Chicago above their poverty and poor education. Unfortunately, it became known for its ghost stories and one infamous supernatural creature forever known as the "Devil Baby."

In 1856, wealthy businessman Charles J. Hull constructed a mansion at Halsted and Polk streets on Chicago's near west side, at the time one of the most fashionable sections of the city. But the Great Fire of 1871 sent wealthy Chicagoans to other parts of the city, and the near west side began to attract a large population of Italian, Greek, and Jewish immigrants. It became one of the most dangerous slums in the city, and by the 1880s, Hull House was surrounded by factories, bordellos, taverns, and rundown tenement houses. In 1889, it was exactly the sort of neighborhood that Jane Addams was seeking.

Jane Addams's Hull House

BORN INTO AN affluent family in 1860, Jane Addams knew nothing of poverty as a child. But when her father died, she sank into a deep depression, so she traveled to Europe to escape from her grief. It was there, in the slums of London, that she realized her life's calling.

Jane and Ellen Gates Starr, her friend and traveling companion, volunteered with the poor at Toynbee Hall, a settlement house in the poverty-stricken Whitechapel neighborhood. There, affluent students like Jane and Ellen worked alongside the most undesirable members of British society, offering food, education, and medical care while lobbying for social reform and improved standards of living for the poor. Jane was invigorated by her work at Toynbee Hall and soon made plans to start a similar project in Chicago.

By the time Addams came to the west side with the intention of starting a settlement house, the crowded neighborhood was teeming with poverty, crime, and prostitution. Numerous brothels, saloons, and dope dealers victimized the refugees and immigrants who came to America with little money and were often unable to speak English. It was to these people that Jane Addams became the "voice of humanity."

Impressed by Jane's plans for a settlement house, Helen Culver, Charles Hull's niece, offered the mansion to Addams with a rent-free lease. Addams and Starr converted the mansion into a safe and comfortable place that offered food, shelter, and education for the impoverished. As the operation increased in popularity, 12 more buildings were added, until eventually Hull House spread out over an entire city block.

When Jane Addams died in 1935, the Hull House Association took over the property and continued her efforts until the 1960s, when the University of Illinois at Chicago bought the property. Hull House was named a historic site, but the additional buildings around the mansion were torn down. And though much has changed, some things remain the same—such as the resident ghosts of Hull House, including a spirit that Jane Addams herself witnessed on numerous occasions!

The Ghost of Mrs. Hull

Charles Hull's wife had died of natural causes in a second-floor bedroom of the mansion several years before Jane Addams took up residence in the home. Addams occupied Mrs. Hull's former bedroom and was awakened by the sound of footsteps pacing back and forth. When Ellen confessed that she'd heard the same noises, too, Addams moved to another bedroom.

Jane, Ellen, and other staff members were not the only ones to witness the strange occurrences in the house. Visitors and overnight guests experienced Mrs. Hull's presence, too. Author Helen Campbell claimed to see a ghostly woman standing next to her bed when she spent the night in the haunted room. When she turned on a light, the apparition disappeared.

In Jane Addams's autobiography, *Twenty Years at Hull House*, she stated that earlier tenants of the mansion believed that the attic was haunted, so they always left a bucket of water on the steps because they thought a ghost would not be able to pass it and descend to the lower floors.

The ghostly tale of Mrs. Hull is still recounted today, but unfortunately for Jane Addams, this would not be the only supernatural tale surrounding Hull House.

The "Devil Baby"

By 1913, rumors were circulating that Hull House was the refuge of a "Devil Baby," and the organization's reputation as a great example of social reform was tarnished. According to the widely spread story, this horribly deformed child was the son of a Catholic woman whose husband was an atheist. When the young woman hung a picture of the Virgin Mary in her home, her husband angrily tore it down, screaming that he would rather have the devil himself in his home than a picture of the Virgin Mary. He soon got his wish!

When his wife became pregnant a short time later, she was carrying the "Devil Baby" in her womb. Allegedly, the baby was born with pointed ears, horns, and a tail. Unable to endure the insults and tormenting by his neighbors, the husband abandoned the child at Hull House.

The baby, who was born with the ability to speak both English and Latin, continued to be a nuisance while at Hull House. While being baptized, he purportedly leapt from the priest's arms and began dancing, laughing, and singing. Unable to make the child behave, Jane reportedly had him locked away in the attic of Hull House, safe from prying eyes.

Stories about the "Devil Baby" quickly spread around town and, believing them to be true, people flocked to Hull House in droves, hoping to get a peek at the freakish child. Jane turned away dozens of curiosity seekers every day and tried to assure them that there was no truth to the rumors. The pandemonium eventually died down, but decades later, many people still believe that the story of the "Devil Baby" had some elements of truth to it. People have speculated that the child was actually a badly deformed infant brought to Hull House by a poor, young mother who could not care for it. But once the rumors got started, they took on a life of their own.

Those who believe that the "Devil Baby" tale is true insist that the disfigured boy was hidden away in the attic of Hull House for many years. They claim this explains why a deformed face was often seen looking out of the upstairs windows. Believers state that the boy grew up at Hull House, tucked safely out of sight, and when Jane Addams died, he was moved to another settlement house on the north side of the city, where he later died.

Hauntings Today

What remains of Hull House today is located on Halsted Street and is open as a historical site. The University of Illinois at Chicago built its campus around the mansion in the 1960s, leaving no trace of the old neighborhood that once existed. The crumbling tenements, brothels, and saloons have been replaced by loft apartments, parking lots, and ethnic restaurants.

Today, Hull House remains an attraction for tourists, history buffs, and ghost enthusiasts. It is not uncommon for motion sensors to be triggered, even when no one is at the house. Officers report that no other building on campus gets as many false alarm calls as Hull House. They have also answered calls about people looking out of the windows after the museum is closed, but they have never found anyone in the place after hours.

One incident that remains unexplained occurred when a front window of the house was shattered a few years ago. Officers rushed to the scene but found no one there. The strange thing was that the window appeared to be broken from inside the house, yet police found no evidence of a break-in and no sign that anyone had been in the house at all.

Visitors who have come to Hull House during the evening hours often report strange occurrences. There are many claims of lights turning on and off, shadowy figures seen moving inside, and shutters that open and close by themselves.

There are many possible suspects in the haunting of this house, including the ghost of Mrs. Hull, the lingering spirit of one of the poor people that Jane Addams tried to save, and, of course, the "Devil Baby," whose spirit may still be trapped in the mansion's attic. It might be any one of these restless spirits, or perhaps all of them. It's no surprise that many call Hull House the most haunted house in Chicago!

A Bump in the Light: America's Haunted Lighthouses

More than 60 lighthouses in the United States are believed to be haunted. Some are home to eerie ghosts, while others host more playful spirits. Whether they stick around because of tragedy, love, or some other reason, these spectral visitors add an otherworldly element to already-fascinating places.

✳ ✳ ✳ ✳

St. Simons Island Lighthouse, Georgia

THIS LIGHTHOUSE MAY have been cursed from the start. Originally constructed in 1811, the first building was destroyed by Confederate soldiers. While the lighthouse was being rebuilt, the architect fell ill and died of yellow fever. Then, on a stormy night in 1880, a dispute between the lighthouse keeper and his assistant resulted in gunshots. The keeper died after days of suffering from his wounds, but the assistant was never charged with the crime. The new keeper maintained he could hear strange footsteps on the spiral staircase to the tower. To this day, subsequent lighthouse keepers, their families, and visitors have also heard the same slow tread on the tower's 129 steps.

Minots Ledge Lighthouse, Massachusetts

Despite the sweet nickname, the ghosts of the "I Love You" lighthouse tell a tragic story. The first Minots Ledge Lighthouse began operating in 1850, and being its keeper was arguably the most frightening assignment around. Built directly in the rough waters around the Cohasset Reefs, the spidery metal skeleton swayed and buckled in the wind and waves. On April 17, 1851, a sudden nor'easter stranded the keeper on the mainland—he could only watch as the storm slowly destroyed the lighthouse, with his two assistants inside. Their bodies were found after the storm cleared.

A new storm-proof stone tower was built, and the spirits of those who perished in the first lighthouse seem to reside in the new building. Subsequent keepers have heard them working, and sailors see them waving from the external ladder. On stormy nights the light blinks "1–4–3," which locals say is code for "I love you." They believe this is the assistants' message to their loved ones, passing ships, and anyone caught in a storm.

Yaquina Bay Lighthouse, Oregon

In 1899, Lischen M. Miller wrote a story for *Pacific Monthly* about a girl who disappeared at the Yaquina Bay Lighthouse. The girl, a captain's daughter, was left with a caretaker while her father was at sea. One day she and her friends went to explore the abandoned lighthouse. When she got separated from her friends, they heard her shriek. They searched for her but only found some blood and her handkerchief. A door that had been open only moments before was locked. Although many maintain that this story is pure fiction, the spectral figure of a girl has been seen around the tower.

St. Augustine Lighthouse, Florida

St. Augustine is often called America's most haunted city, and the lighthouse there might claim its own "most haunted" title. So many different spirits are rumored to haunt this light that it's probably a bit crowded. Visitors report seeing a young girl with a bow in her hair. She is thought to be the ghost of a girl who died during the tower's construction. A tall man is often seen in the basement of the keeper's house, and doors unlock mysteriously, footsteps follow visitors, and cold spots move around the buildings. The spirits seem harmless, but construction workers have complained of foreboding feelings and freak accidents.

Fairport Harbor Light, Ohio

This lighthouse is rumored to have two rather playful ghosts. The first is of a keeper's young son who died. The second appears to be a charming gray kitten that routinely seeks out museum staff and visitors to play. Its spectral nature becomes apparent when visitors realize the kitten has no feet—it simply hovers above the ground. Although a former keeper's wife had a beloved kitten while she lived in the lighthouse, the "ghost cat" story was dismissed as silly until workers found the body of a cat in a crawl space there.

Old Presque Isle Lighthouse, Michigan

This lighthouse was decommissioned in 1870 and became a museum. In 1977, when George and Lorraine Parris were hired as caretakers, they ran the light regularly until the Coast Guard warned that running a decommissioned light was hazardous and illegal. To ensure it wouldn't happen again, the machinery that rotated the light was removed. But since George's death in 1992, the lighthouse has frequently glowed at night—not so brightly as to cause harm but bright enough to be seen by passing ships and across the bay. Although the Coast Guard has classified it as an "unidentified" light, Lorraine believes that it is George, still happily working in his lighthouse.

Gettysburg's Ghosts

You learned about some of Gettysburg's reported ghosts on page 170. But there are rumors of others as well.

✳   ✳   ✳   ✳

Devil's Den

A T THE BASE of Little Round Top and across a barren field lies an outcropping of rocks known as Devil's Den. It was from this location that Confederate sharpshooters took up positions and fired at the Union soldiers stationed along Little Round Top. Eventually, Union soldiers followed the telltale sign of gun smoke and picked off the sharpshooters one by one.

After Devil's Den was secured by Union forces, famous Civil War photographer Alexander Gardner was allowed to come in and take photos of the area. One of his most famous pictures, "A Sharpshooter's Last Sleep," was taken at Devil's Den and shows a Confederate sharpshooter lying dead near the rocks. There was only one problem: The photograph was staged. Gardner apparently dragged a dead Confederate soldier over from another location and positioned the body himself. Legend has it that the ghost of the Confederate soldier was unhappy with how his body was treated, so his ghost often causes cameras in Devil's Den to malfunction.

Incidents of the War.

Spangler's Spring

As soon as the Battle of Gettysburg was over, soldiers began relating their personal experiences to local newspapers. One story that spread quickly centered on the cooling waters of Spangler's Spring. It was said that at various times during the fierce fighting, both sides agreed to periodic ceasefires so that Union and Confederate soldiers could stand side-by-side and drink from the spring. It's a touching story, but in all likelihood, it never actually happened. Even if it did, it doesn't explain the ghostly woman in a white dress who is seen at the spring. Some claim that the "Woman in White" is the spirit of a woman who lost her lover during the Battle of Gettysburg. Another theory is that she was a young woman who took her own life after breaking up with her lover years after the war ended.

Phantom Ships and Ghostly Crews

Ghost ships come in a variety of shapes and sizes, but they all seem to have the ability to slip back and forth between the watery veil of this world and the next, often making appearances that foretell of impending doom. Come with us now as we set sail in search of some of the most famous ghost ships in maritime history and supernatural lore.

* * * *

The *Palatine*

ACCORDING TO LEGEND, shortly after Christmas 1738, the *Princess Augusta* ran aground and broke into pieces off the coast of Block Island, Rhode Island. Roughly 130 years later, poet John Greenleaf Whittier renamed the European vessel and told his version of the shipwreck in his poem *The Palatine*, which was published in *Atlantic Monthly*. Today, strange lights are still reported in the waters surrounding Block Island, especially on the Saturday between Christmas and New Year's Day.

Mary Celeste

The *Amazon* was cursed from the beginning. During her maiden voyage, the *Amazon*'s captain died. After being salvaged by an American company that renamed her the *Mary Celeste*, the ship left New York on November 7, 1872, bound for Genoa, Italy. Onboard were Captain Benjamin Briggs, his family, and a crew of seven.

Nearly a month later, on December 4, the crew of the *Dei Gratia* found the abandoned ship. There was plenty of food and water onboard the *Mary Celeste*, but the only living soul on the ship was a cat. The crew and the captain's family were missing, and no clues remained as to where they went. The last entry in the captain's logbook was dated almost two weeks prior to the ship's discovery, meaning it had somehow piloted itself all that time.

To this day, the fate of the members of the *Mary Celeste* remains unknown, as does how the ship piloted its way across the ocean non-crewed for weeks. Many believe she was piloted by a ghostly crew that kept her safe until she was found.

Iron Mountain

A ship disappearing on the high seas is one thing, but on a river? That's exactly what happened to the *Iron Mountain*. In June 1872, the 180-foot-long ship left New Orleans heading for Pittsburgh via the Mississippi River with a crew of more than 50 men. A day after picking up additional cargo, which was towed behind the ship in barges, the *Iron Mountain* steamed its way north and promptly vanished.

Later that day, the barges were recovered floating in the river, but the *Iron Mountain* and its entire crew were never seen nor heard from again. For years after it disappeared, ship captains would whisper to each other about how the *Iron Mountain* was simply sucked up into another dimension through a ghostly portal.

Edmund Fitzgerald

When it comes to ghost ships, the *Edmund Fitzgerald* is the biggest—literally. At more than 720 feet long, the freighter shuttled iron ore across the Great Lakes beginning in the late 1950s. On November 9, 1975, Captain Ernest M. McSorley and his crew pulled the *Edmund Fitzgerald* out of dock at Superior, Wisconsin, with a load of iron ore to be delivered to a steel mill near Detroit. The following day, "The Fitz" sank during a violent storm without ever issuing a distress signal. All 29 members of the crew were presumed dead, but their bodies were never found.

Almost ten years to the day after it sank, a strange, dark ship was seen riding along the waves of Lake Superior. One look at the monstrous ship was all witnesses needed to recognize it as the *Edmund Fitzgerald*.

Flying Dutchman

Easily the world's most famous ghost ship, the story of the *Flying Dutchman* is legendary. Stories say that during the 1800s, a Dutch ship captained by Hendrick Vanderdecken was attempting to sail around the Cape of Good Hope when a violent storm came up. Rather than pull into port, the *Dutchman's* stubborn captain claimed he would navigate around the Cape even if it took him all of eternity to do so. The ship and all of the crew were lost in the storm, and as foreshadowed by Vanderdecken, they were, indeed, condemned to sail the high seas for all of eternity.

Almost immediately, people from all over the world began spotting the Dutch ship silently moving through the ocean, often cast in an eerie glow. Because of the legend associated with Captain Vanderdecken, sightings of the *Flying Dutchman* are now thought to be signs of bad things to come. Case in point: The most recent sighting of the vessel occurred off the coast of North Carolina's Outer Banks prior to Hurricane Isabel in 2003.

Centralia, Pennsylvania: It's Hot, Hot, Hot

There's a lot going on underfoot in any given place: sewage systems, tree roots, animal dens, subway tunnels, maybe even some caves, depending on where you live. But if you're one of the few people who still happen to live in Centralia, Pennsylvania, you've got a lot more going on beneath the ground. Read on to discover the stranger-than-fiction truth about this now-defunct mining community.

✳   ✳   ✳   ✳

Whoops!

FOR MOST OF the first half of the 20th century, the northeastern Pennsylvania mining town of Centralia was a perfectly functional Smalltown, U.S.A. The population hovered around 3,000, and there were shops and cafés, businesses and schools. Miners worked hard in the coal-rich region, and all was well, with small problems but not major catastrophes.

Then in 1962, the fate of Centralia changed forever. Though the logic seems dubious now, it was common practice in those days to turn open mine pits into garbage dumps. After all, the mining holes were wide dips in the earth, which made for perfect fire pits—there was little risk of starting forest fires because the garbage would burn below ground level. No one thought about the possibility of the fire going underground. But that's exactly what happened.

The garbage dumpers picked a very, very bad place to set their trash alight. As it turns out, the pit, an abandoned mine in the southeastern part of town, was smack in the middle of a robust coal vein. And what does coal do best? Burn. The trash ignited the trail of coal, and the coal began to slowly burn underground, spidering out to other coal veins beneath the surface of Centralia. This was not good.

Everybody Out

The underground fire sizzled its way into coal veins under the businesses, schools, and homes of Centralia. Over time, the fire started causing health problems for residents. Carbon monoxide gases caused lightheadedness and hacking coughs as the smoke continued to curl up from the ground. Wildlife was making a mass exodus, and the air smelled bad. Pavement started to crack, building foundations were at risk, and it began to dawn on the people of Centralia that this underground fire wasn't going to fizzle out on its own.

The next two decades were spent trying to extinguish the fire but to no avail. Firefighters, engineers, and concerned individuals came up with plan after failed plan. Some thought the best solution was to flush the mines with water; others tried to excavate the burning material. Some figured that drilling holes into the ground might help locate the boundaries of the fire, but that only fed the fire with more oxygen.

By the early 1980s, the fire was burning under a few hundred acres. After a young boy fell into a burning sinkhole in the sidewalk, the government stepped in to help Centralians relocate. Eventually, the few remaining buildings in town were condemned, and the government took ownership of the land.

Pennsylvania's government seriously looked into putting the fires out for good, but ultimately, it seemed more reasonable to just move people out rather than shell out the $660 million price tag for trenching the entire area, which was not guaranteed to work. Several million dollars had already been spent on the fire, and apparently, that was enough.

Visit Scenic Centralia...or Not

An engineering study in 1983 concluded that the mine fires could burn for another couple of centuries or more, perhaps spreading over more than 3,500 acres before burning out. That means that if you want to visit a slow-roasted town, you've got plenty of time. You'll have to look hard for Centralia, though— the town doesn't even exist on a lot of maps these days. Visitors will occasionally see smoke rising from cracks in the road or catch a whiff of sulfur here and there. Though tourism is obviously not encouraged—and we certainly don't advise it—it's not against the law to explore the town. Just keep an eye out for burning sinkholes, of course.

Europe's Most Haunted Hotels

Many of Europe's haunted hotels are located in Britain and Ireland, where ghosts are often considered as friends or even members of the family, and are given the same respect as any living person—or even more. Other European cultures aren't as comfortable with ghosts—opting to tear down haunted hotels instead of coexisting with spirits—but there are still a few places in Europe where ghost hunters can explore.

❋ ❋ ❋ ❋

Comlongon Castle, Dumfries, Scotland

LADY MARION CARRUTHERS haunts Scotland's beautiful Comlongon Castle. On September 25, 1570, Lady Marion leaped to her death from the castle's lookout tower rather than submit to an arranged marriage. Visitors can easily find the exact spot where she landed; for more than 400 years, it's been difficult to grow grass there. Because Lady Marion's death was a suicide, she was denied a Christian burial, and it seems her spirit is unable to rest in peace. Dressed in green, her ghost wanders around the castle and its grounds. In 2007, Comlongon Castle was voted the "Best Haunted Hotel or B&B" in the UK and Ireland.

Ettington Park Hotel, Alderminister, England

You may feel chills when you see the Ettington Park Hotel, where the classic 1963 horror movie *The Haunting* was filmed. It was an apt choice for the movie locale because the hotel features several ghosts.

The Shirley family rebuilt this Victorian Gothic structure in the mid-1800s, and the ghost of the "Lady in Gray" has appeared on the staircase regularly since that time. Her identity is unknown, unlike the phantom "Lady in White," who was supposedly a former governess named Lady Emma. The voices of crying children are probably the two Shirley children who drowned nearby in the River Stour; they're buried by the church tower.

Watch out for poltergeists in the Library Bar, where books fly across the room. And don't be alarmed if you hear a late-night snooker game when no one is in the room—it's just the ghosts having fun.

Ye Olde Black Bear, Tewkesbury, England

If you're looking for headless ghosts dragging clanking chains, Ye Olde Black Bear is just the place. Built in the early 1300s, the structure is the oldest inn in Gloucestershire. The hotel's headless ghost may be one individual or several—without a head, it's difficult to tell. However, the ghost's uniform suggests that he was a soldier killed in a battle around the 1470s. Those who've seen the figure at the hotel suspect he doesn't realize he's dead—Ye Olde Black Bear was supposedly a favorite hangout for soldiers during his era.

Renvyle House Hotel, Galway, Ireland

Renvyle House Hotel is not old by haunted hotel standards. The site has been built on, destroyed, built again, destroyed again—once by a fire set by the IRA—and so on, until the current hotel was erected in the 1930s. But its ghosts have an impressive pedigree, dating back to a 16th-century Irish pirate queen, Gráinne O'Malley. A redheaded boy is a more recent spirit, possibly a son of the Blake family who owned the site in the 19th century. The hotel is haunted by so many spirits that it was regularly visited by celebrities, such as poet W. B. Yeats, who conducted séances there. Today, Renvyle House Hotel is still a favorite destination for ghost hunters, and it is included in many "haunted hotel" tours.

Royal Lion Hotel, Lyme Regis, England

The Royal Lion Hotel was built in 1601 as a coaching inn, but some of its ghosts may visit from across the street, where executions allegedly took place. Other misty, ghostly figures around the hotel may be the spirits of pirates who sailed into the port, or they could be some of the rebels who were hung and quartered on the nearby beach after trying to overthrow King James

II in 1685. Waterfront hotels are often haunted due to their association with pirates and wrecked ships. However, with several dozen different spirits, this site reports more ghosts than most.

Dragsholm Slot Hotel, Nekselø Bay, Denmark

In Danish, the word slot means "castle," and the Dragsholm is one of the world's great haunted castle hotels. According to legend, Dragsholm's "Gray Lady"—a 12th-century maid who loved working at the hotel—visits on most nights. She silently checks on guests to be sure they are comfortable. The "White Lady" haunts the corridors nightly. She may be the young woman who was allegedly walled up inside the castle; her ancient corpse was found during 19th-century renovations.

James Hepburn, the Fourth Earl of Bothwell, is the castle's most famous ghost. Hepburn became the third husband of Mary, Queen of Scots, after he helped murder her previous spouse. For his role in that crime, Bothwell spent the last ten years of his life chained to a pillar in Dragsholm. If you think you've seen his ghostly apparition, you can compare it to his mummified body in a nearby church in Faarevejle.

Hotel Scandinavia, Venice, Italy

The Hotel Scandinavia is in a building dating back to the year 1000, and it's surrounded by stories of ghosts and apparitions. In the 15th century, the apparition of a wealthy (and rather buxom) Madonna first appeared close to the hotel's palazzo. Witnesses report hearing sounds from the sorrowful ghosts of condemned prisoners who long ago crossed the nearby Bridge of Sighs. This famous bridge was where convicts caught a final glimpse of Venice before being imprisoned. These spirits apparently visit the hotel, and their voices are most often heard in the lobby. Because of the location's unique ghosts and how often they're heard, the Hotel Scandinavia is consistently ranked as one of the world's top five haunted hotels.

Canada's Most Haunted Resort

The Fairmont Banff Springs Hotel looks like an elegant castle fit for a fairy tale. Truly one of the most luxurious resorts in the world, it is also one of the most haunted.

* * * *

Wandering Spirits

THE STORY BEGINS in 1883, when three off-duty Canadian Pacific Railway workers were hiking around Banff and discovered the now famous hot springs. Construction of a hotel was started about four years later, and in 1888, the Banff Springs Hotel opened. It was a large, partly wooden structure nestled in spectacular mountains about two hours from Calgary. For years, the only way to visit the hotel was by rail, making it an ideal, scenic getaway for tourists...and for ghosts.

From the hotel's earliest days, security staff noticed dark, shadowy figures floating in the hallways. The apparitions seemed to linger in one area before vanishing into a nearby wall where no hotel room existed. Banff's staff and owners were baffled, and guests were a little frightened.

Then in 1926, a fire destroyed part of the hotel. During the cleanup, workers uncovered a builder's mistake. At the exact location where ghosts had been sighted, the cleanup crew found an interior room with no windows or doors. People speculated that the secluded room had been the ghosts' home, or a portal to "the other side." The hotel was rebuilt without the odd, hidden room, so when it reopened in 1928, most people thought the phantom figures were gone for good, but they were wrong....

The Ghostly Bride

According to legend, during the 1920s, a woman left the hotel's bridal suite wearing her wedding gown. As she walked down the candlelit staircase, a gust of wind lifted the train of her gown and caught it on fire. Struggling to put out the flames, the bride lost her balance and fell, which caused her to break her neck and killed her instantly. Scorch marks on the marble stairs still indicate where she fell.

Since then, staff and guests have seen the ghostly bride on the stairs. Witnesses say she appears as a translucent figure before bursting into flames and vanishing. People have also noticed unexplained gusts of wind around the haunted staircase. Others have seen the ghostly bride dancing alone in the ballroom or seemingly waiting for someone at the hotel's Rob Roy Lounge. She fades away slowly if you continue to watch her. She may also haunt the bridal suite, where guests have reported recurring "cold spots." But the bridal suite isn't nearly as haunted as another room at the hotel.

Ghosts on the Eighth Floor

If you're looking for a murder mystery, visit the eighth floor of the Banff Springs Hotel. Staff members won't talk about it, but Room 873 has been sealed and its number removed. Nearby doors are numbered 871 and 872, followed by 874 and 875.

According to rumors, a family was murdered in Room 873. Afterward, the hotel cleaned the room and prepared it for new guests. However, each time the staff cleaned the large mirror in Room 873, a child's fingerprints reappeared. Eventually, the hotel closed the room and sealed it. Some guests say the outline of the door is still visible. Others have taken photos outside the sealed room, and vivid, unexplained orbs have reportedly appeared in the pictures.

Those orbs are dramatic, but there's an even more intense, ghostly manifestation at Banff. The ghost of a former hotel bellman, Sam McCauley, appears so real that guests often think he's a regular hotel employee.

Some Scots Never Leave

McCauley arrived from Scotland in the 1930s and worked as a porter at the Banff Springs Hotel for nearly 40 years. Before he died, he promised to return to the hotel as a ghost. It seems he kept his word: McCauley has been seen in the hallways and sometimes helps guests with their luggage. When they turn to tip the elderly man, he vanishes. McCauley is popular with staff and guests alike and is spotted regularly in the lobby and on the ninth floor, where he used to store his tips.

Another Scotsman haunts the Banff Springs Hotel, too. Very late at night, a Scottish piper appears around the Rob Roy Lounge. Some people apparently see him in full Scottish garb, but because this ghost is headless, his real identity is unknown.

In addition, a portrait hanging in the MacKenzie Room appears to be haunted. According to legend, a ghost comes out of the portrait's eyes. First, the eyes seem to light up slightly, then something with jagged edges appears to swirl out of the eyes. The apparition is so scary that no one has remained in the room long enough to see what happens next. Some say this ghost was partly responsible for a fire in the hotel in 1946.

The Helpful Housekeeper and the Singing Men

One of the hotel's newest ghosts is a former housekeeper. She allegedly visits rooms and straightens the covers on the beds—sometimes while guests are still sleeping! She's harmless, but it can be unsettling to wake up in the morning and find the bed more tidy than when you went to sleep.

For your listening pleasure, it has been reported that around 3:00 AM, a male voice sings loudly in the downstairs ladies' washroom. He's never seen, nor is the male chorus that sings in the men's washroom near the ballrooms.

Other Figures and Phantom Lights

Though most people believe the hotel's earliest shadowy ghosts left when the resort was rebuilt in the 1920s, some have reported seeing those fleeting forms again. They're dark and move silently through the halls, like something out of a movie, then they vanish, passing through walls and locked doors. Other guests describe eerie, unexplained lights hovering outside their hotel room windows. These guests say that the lights aren't frightening, merely odd.

One thing is certain: Banff Springs Hotel is popular with everyone who visits it…including ghosts.

A Museum's Shrouded Mystery

Texas' Fort Worth Museum of Science and Industry began to notice strange occurrences happening throughout the building after they received the traveling Titanic exhibit. What was caught on camera still can't be explained.

✳   ✳   ✳   ✳

ONCE THE EXHIBIT came to the musuem, security guards began seeing things move across the floor seemingly all by themselves. They heard strange whispers down dark hallways, and they watched security monitors and light fixtures flash on and off. They knew something creepy was about but nothing confirmed their fears more than a recent photo posted online.

The photo—taken in the children's section of the museum—is a shot of a young boy playing with a hands-on activity, but in the background is a figure so distorted and absolutely evil looking that the fun the child is having would be nonexistent if he had seen what was behind him. This figure is shrouded and about the same color as what you'd imagine a mummy to be. Standing in the basket of a child-size grocery cart, the figure's lower half seems to taper off thinner and thinner, while its top half is covered in a tattered fabric with its dead-gray hands holding an undefined object.

Many comments on the page doubt the authenticity of the photograph, saying the figure casts a shadow, or that it must be standing behind the cart, or that because the photo is lacking a time signature that it could have easily been altered. But the fact alone is that something this creepy, standing in the middle of a children's exhibit, would have never been ignored by children. It's horrifying and the children would have been terrified if they actually saw someone dressed like that. Doubts and rumors continue to fly around the photo, but we think its paranormal assessment is dead on.

Ohio's Mysterious Hangar 18

An otherwordly legend makes its way from New Mexico to Ohio when the wreckage from Roswell ends up in the Midwest. Even those who aren't UFO buffs have probably heard about the infamous Roswell Incident, where an alien spaceship supposedly crash-landed in the New Mexico desert, and the U.S. government covered the whole thing up. But what most people don't know is that according to legend, the mysterious aircraft was recovered (along with some alien bodies), secreted out of Roswell, and came to rest just outside of Dayton, Ohio.

✳   ✳   ✳   ✳

Something Crashed in the Desert

WHILE THE EXACT date is unclear, sometime during the first week of July 1947, a local Roswell rancher by the name of Mac Brazel decided to go out and check his property for fallen trees and other damage after a night of heavy storms and lightning. Brazel allegedly came across an area of his property littered with strange debris unlike anything he had ever seen before. Some of the debris even had strange writing on it.

Brazel showed some of the debris to a few neighbors and then took it to the office of Roswell sheriff George Wilcox, who called authorities at Roswell Army Air Field. After speaking with Wilcox, intelligence officer Major Jesse Marcel drove out to the Brazel ranch and collected as much debris as he could. He then returned to the airfield and showed the debris to his commanding officer, Colonel William Blanchard, commander of the 509th Bomb Group that was stationed at the Roswell Air Field. Upon seeing the debris, Blanchard dispatched military vehicles and personnel back out to the Brazel ranch to see if they could recover anything else.

"Flying Saucer Captured!"

On July 8, 1947, Colonel Blanchard issued a press release stating that the wreckage of a "crashed disk" had been recovered. The bold headline of the July 8 edition of the *Roswell Daily Record* read: "RAAF Captures Flying Saucer on Ranch in Roswell Region." Newspapers around the world ran similar headlines. But then, within hours of the Blanchard release, General Roger M. Ramey, commander of the Eighth Air Force in Fort Worth, Texas, retracted Blanchard's release for him and issued another statement saying there was no UFO. Blanchard's men had simply recovered a fallen weather balloon.

Before long, the headlines that had earlier touted the capture of a UFO read: "It's a Weather Balloon" and "'Flying Disc' Turns Up as Just Hot Air." Later editions even ran a staged photograph of Major Jesse Marcel, who was first sent to investigate the incident, kneeling in front of weather balloon debris. Most of the general public seemed content with the explanation, but there were skeptics.

Whisked Away to Hangar 18?

Those who believe that aliens crash-landed near Roswell claim that, under cover of darkness, large portions of the alien spacecraft were brought out to the Roswell Air Field and loaded onto B-29 and C-54 aircrafts. Those planes were then supposedly flown to Wright-Patterson Air Force Base, just outside of Dayton. Once the planes landed, they were taxied over to Hangar 18 and unloaded. And according to legend, it's all still there.

There are some problems with the story, though. For one, none of the hangars on Wright-Patterson Air Force Base are officially known as "Hangar 18," and there are no buildings designated with the number 18. Rather, the hangars are labeled 1A, 1B, 1C, and so on. There's also the fact that none of the hangars seem large enough to house and conceal an alien spacecraft. But just because there's nothing listed as Hangar 18 on a Wright-Patterson map doesn't mean it's not there. Conspiracy theorists believe that hangars 4A, 4B, and 4C might be the infamous Hangar 18.

As for the overall size of the hangars, it's believed that most of the wreckage has been stored in giant underground tunnels and chambers deep under the hangar, both to protect the debris and to keep it safe from prying eyes. It is said that Wright-Patterson is currently conducting experiments on the wreckage to see if scientists can reverse-engineer the technology.

So What's the Deal?

The story of Hangar 18 only got stranger as the years went on, starting with the government's Project Blue Book, a program designed to investigate reported UFO sightings across the United States. Between 1947 and 1969, Project Blue Book investigated more than 12,000 UFO sightings before being disbanded. And where was Project Blue Book headquartered? Wright-Patterson Air Force Base.

Adding to the furor, in the early 1960s, Arizona senator Barry Goldwater, himself a retired major general in the U.S. Army Air Corps (and a friend of Colonel Blanchard), became interested in what, if anything, had crashed in Roswell. When Goldwater discovered Hangar 18, he first wrote directly to Wright-Patterson and asked for permission to tour the facility but was quickly denied. He then approached another friend, General Curtis LeMay, and asked if he could see the "Green Room" where the UFO secret was being held. Goldwater claimed that LeMay gave him "holy hell" and screamed at Goldwater, "Not only can't you get into it, but don't you ever mention it to me again."

Most recently, in 1982, retired pilot Oliver "Pappy" Henderson attended a reunion and announced that he was one of the men who had flown alien bodies out of Roswell in a C-54 cargo plane. His destination? Hangar 18 at Wright-Patterson. Although no one is closer to a definitive answer, it seems that the legend of Hangar 18 will never die.

Hollywood's Urban Legends

If ever there was a breeding ground for urban legends, it would be in the Hollywood Hills. Simply put, people love to hear all sorts of gossip about stars and movies... the weirder the better. Here are some of the strangest urban legends to come out of Hollywood.

✳ ✳ ✳ ✳

Humphrey Bogart Was the Gerber Baby

EVERYONE KNOWS THE famous black-and-white drawing of the baby that graces Gerber baby food products. Well, there's an urban legend that the baby is none other than actor Humphrey Bogart. This legend probably took off due to the fact that Bogart's mother, Maud, was a commercial illustrator who actually did sell drawings to advertising agencies. In fact, she did allow one of her drawings of her sonHumphrey to be used in a baby food advertisement—for Mellin's Baby Food. However, Gerber did not start producing baby food until 1928, and by that time, Bogart was 29 years old, making it unlikely—but not impossible—that Bogart could be the Gerber baby. We now know that Ann Turner Cook was the lucky model in 1928. She was drawn by artist Dorothy Hope Smith, who submitted the drawing to Gerber.

Disney on Ice

In life, Walt Disney warmed the hearts of millions. In death, Disney is rumored to have had himself frozen until such a time that scientists could warm him up and bring him back to life. What sounds like something out of a sci-fi movie may have been rooted in the fact that Walt Disney liked to keep his personal life private, so when he died, specifics about his burial were kept under wraps, leading to all sorts of speculation. Rumors were further fueled when Disney was buried in Forest Lawn Cemetery in Glendale, California, which does not publicly list who is interred there. But Walt Disney's unfrozen remains are indeed there, in the Freedom Mausoleum.

Three Men and a Baby... and a Ghost!

There's a scene in the movie *Three Men and a Baby* (1987) in which Ted Danson's character, Jack, and his mother are walking through Jack's house while the mother is holding the baby. As they walk in front of a window, the ghostly image of a boy is seen standing in the background. When the characters walk by the window a second time, the boy has been replaced by what appears to be a shotgun. Legend has it that the ghost belongs to a boy who accidentally shot himself to death with a shotgun in the house where the movie was filmed.

Of course, the truth is a little less spooky. What many people mistake for the boy's apparition is nothing more than a cardboard cutout of Danson, which was supposed to be part of a subplot involving Jack's appearance in a dog food commercial. And those scenes weren't filmed in a house, either. They all took place on a studio set in Toronto.

Munchkin Suicide in *The Wizard of Oz*

In *The Wizard of Oz* (1939), shortly after Dorothy and the Scarecrow convince the Tin Man to join their posse, they begin singing and skipping down the Yellow Brick Road. As they round the bend in the road and dance off the screen, a strange, dark shape can be seen moving in a bizarre fashion to the left of the road. It is said that one of the Munchkins, heartbroken over a failed love affair, chose to take his own life as the cameras rolled. It makes for a creepy story, but there's no truth to it. What people are actually seeing is nothing more than an exotic bird flapping its wings. Prior to filming, the director decided that adding strange, exotic birds to the scene would add a bit more color, so he rented several such birds from the Los Angeles Zoo and allowed them to roam freely about the set.

The Texas Chain Saw Massacre Is a True Story

When Tobe Hooper's *The Texas Chain Saw Massacre* first hit theaters in 1974, it was touted as being based on a true story, even using the line "It happened!" on movie posters. But the truth isn't so black and white. Hooper did base the character Leatherface on a real person—murderer and grave robber Ed Gein. But although Gein was a convicted killer who also fashioned human body parts into jewelry and furniture, there is no evidence that he offed anyone with a chain saw. And he lived in Wisconsin, not Texas. Apparently *The Wisconsin Rifle-Shootin' Massacre* wasn't as scintillating.

O. J. Simpson Was Considered for the Lead Role in *The Terminator*

Most people are familiar with the iconic image of Arnold Schwarzenegger as the murderous Terminator cyborg. What many people don't know, though, is that one of the actors considered for the lead role was none other than O. J. Simpson. Producers passed on Simpson because they felt he was too "nice" and wouldn't be believable playing the role of a killer. Although ironic, this tale appears to be true.

Disney's Snuff Film

In the 1958 Disney documentary *White Wilderness*, dozens of lemmings are shown jumping to their deaths off a cliff into the ocean as part of a bizarre suicide ritual. There was only one glitch: Lemmings don't commit suicide en masse. When principal photographer James R. Simon arrived in Alberta, Canada to film, he was informed of this. But rather than scrap the project, Simon had the lemmings herded up and forced off the cliff while the cameras rolled. As the creatures struggled to keep from drowning, the narrator delivered the disturbing and all-too-telling line: "It's not given to man to understand all of nature's mysteries."

Despite the film winning an Oscar for Best Documentary in 1959, once the truth about what happened on those cliffs was revealed, it quickly and quietly was locked away, becoming one of Disney's deep, dark secrets.

The Death of Actor Vic Morrow Can Be Seen in *Twilight Zone: The Movie*

In the early morning of July 23, 1982, actor Vic Morrow and two children were re-creating a Vietnam War battle scene—complete with helicopters and explosions—for *Twilight Zone: The Movie.*

The scene began fine, but then one of the helicopter pilots lost control and crashed, killing Morrow and the two child actors. Multiple cameras were rolling at the time and caught the carnage on film, but the footage was locked away. However, while the deaths don't appear in the *Twilight Zone* film, some of the tragic scenes appeared in the 1992 direct-to-video flick *Death Scenes 2.*

The Poltergeist Movies Are Cursed

A series of strange, unexpected deaths surrounding actors who worked on the popular *Poltergeist* films have led many to believe that the supernatural theme of the movies has conjured up curses over those associated with them. There have been several untimely deaths, including 22-year-old Dominique Dunne, who played older daughter Dana Freeling in the original *Poltergeist*. She died in November 1982 as a result of injuries sustained when she was attacked by her abusive boyfriend. Little blonde Heather O'Rourke, who starred in all three movies as the perpetually haunted Carol Anne, died of septic shock on February 1, 1988, at age 12. Today, her grave site is a stop on the popular "Haunted Hollywood" tour.

Other cast member deaths were more expected. When Julian Beck, who played Kane in *Poltergeist II: The Other Side*, passed away in September 1985, he was 60 years old and had been battling stomach cancer for nearly two years. Similarly, Will

Sampson, the lovable Native American guide from *Poltergeist II*, died from complications after receiving a heart and lung transplant. It's not apparent there's a *Poltergeist* curse, but there sure has been a lot of real-life tragedy.

Top-Secret Locations You Can Visit

There are plenty of stories of secret government facilities hidden in plain sight. Places where all sorts of strange tests take place, far away from the general public. Many of the North American top-secret government places have been (at least partially) declassified, allowing average Joes to visit. We've listed some locations where you can play Men in Black.

✳ ✳ ✳ ✳

Titan Missile Silo

JUST A LITTLE south of Tucson, Arizona, lies the Sonoran Desert, a barren, desolate area where nothing seems to be happening. That's exactly why, during the Cold War, the U.S. government hid an underground Titan Missile silo there.

Inside the missile silo, one of dozens that once littered the area, a Titan 2 Missile could be armed and launched in just under 90 seconds. Until it was finally abandoned in the 1990s, the government manned the silo 24 hours a day, with every member being trained to "turn the key" and launch the missile at a moment's notice. Today, the silo is open to the public as the Titan Missile Museum. Visitors can take a look at one of the few remaining Titan 2 missiles in existence, still sitting on the launch pad (relax, it's been disarmed). Folks with extra dough can also spend the night inside the silo and play the role of one of the crew members assigned to prepare to launch the missile at a moment's notice.

Peanut Island

You wouldn't think a sunny place called Peanut Island, located near Palm Beach, Florida, could hold many secrets. Yet in

December 1961, the U.S. Navy came to the island on a secret mission to create a fallout shelter for then-President John F. Kennedy and his family. The shelter was completed, but it was never used and was all but forgotten when the Cold War ended. Today, the shelter is maintained by the Palm Beach Maritime Museum, which conducts weekend tours of the space.

Los Alamos National Laboratory

Until recently, the U.S. government refused to acknowledge the Los Alamos National Laboratory's existence. But in the early 1940s, the lab was created near Los Alamos, New Mexico, to develop the first nuclear weapons in what would become known as the Manhattan Project. Back then, the facility was so top secret it didn't even have a name. It was simply referred to as Site Y. No matter what it was called, the lab produced two nuclear bombs, nicknamed Little Boy and Fat Man—bombs that would be dropped on Hiroshima and Nagasaki, effectively ending World War II. Today, tours of portions of the facility can be arranged through the Lab's Public Affairs Department.

Fort Knox

It is the stuff that legends are made of: A mythical building filled with over 4,700 tons of gold, stacked up and piled high to the ceiling. But this is no fairytale—the gold really does exist, and it resides inside Fort Knox.

Since 1937, the U.S. Department of the Treasury's Bullion Depository has been storing the gold inside Fort Knox on a massive military campus that stretches across three counties in north-central Kentucky. Parts of the campus are open for tours, including the General George Patton Museum. But don't think you're going to catch a glimpse of that shiny stuff—visitors are not permitted to go through the gate or enter the building.

Nevada Test Site

If you've ever seen one of those old black-and-white educational films of nuclear bombs being tested, chances are it was filmed at the Nevada Test Site, often referred to as the Most Bombed Place in the World.

Located about an hour north of Las Vegas, the Nevada Test Site was created in 1951 as a secret place for the government to conduct nuclear experiments and tests in an outdoor laboratory that is actually larger than Rhode Island. Out there, scientists blew everything up from mannequins to entire buildings. Those curious to take a peek inside the facility can sign up for a daylong tour.

Of course, before they let you set foot on the base, visitors must submit to a background check and sign paperwork promising not to attempt to photograph, videotape, or take soil samples from the site. Visit as your own risk!

The Magnetic Hill Phenomenon

It has taken researchers hundreds of years to finally solve the mystery of magnetic hills, or spook hills, as they're often called. This phenomenon, found all over the world, describes places where objects—including cars in neutral gear—move uphill on a slightly sloping road, seemingly defying gravity.

✳   ✳   ✳   ✳

MONCTON, IN NEW Brunswick, Canada, lays claim to one of the more famous magnetic hills, called, appropriately, Magnetic Hill. Over the years, it has also been called Fool's Hill and Magic Hill. Since the location made headlines in 1931, hundreds of thousands of tourists have flocked there to witness this phenomenon for themselves.

Go Figure

Much to the dismay of paranormal believers, people in science once assumed that a magnetic anomaly caused this event. But advanced physics has concluded this phenomenon is due "to the visual anchoring of the sloping surface to a gravity-relative eye level whose perceived direction is biased by sloping surroundings." In nonscientific jargon, all that says is that it's an optical illusion.

Papers published in the journal of the Association of Psychological Science supported this conclusion based on a series of experiments done with models. They found that if the horizon cannot be seen or is not level then people may be fooled by objects that they expect to be vertical but aren't. False perspective is also a culprit; think, for example, of a line of poles on the horizon that seem to get larger or smaller depending on distance.

Engineers with plumb lines, one made of iron and one made of stone, demonstrated that a slope appearing to go uphill might in reality be going downhill. A good topographical map may also be sufficient to show which way the land is really sloping.

I Know a Place

Other notable magnetic hills can be found in Wisconsin, Pennsylvania, California, Florida, Barbados, Scotland, Australia, Italy, Greece, and South Korea.

Mansfield Reformatory

North of the Lincoln Highway, outside of Mansfield, is an imposing medieval-type castle that seems very much out of place in Ohio's heartland. This site has been home to more than 150,000 inmates, a set for four major motion pictures, and a midnight location for numerous paranormal television shows, including Scariest Places on Earth. *It even holds a place in Guinness World Records.*

MANSFIELD REFORMATORY (AKA Ohio State Reformatory) was built to hold juvenile first offenders. Given the population, it did not have an electric chair or a gallows, but, over the years, prisoners, guards, and the family of staff died within its walls—and not always by disease or natural causes.

Two guards were killed during escape attempts, one in 1926 and the other in 1932. In both cases, the killers were convicted and executed in the electric chair at the Ohio Penitentiary in Columbus. The wife of Warden Arthur Glattke accidently shot herself in 1950 when she knocked a loaded revolver off a closet shelf. She died three days later of pneumonia. Arthur followed in 1959, dying of a heart attack in his office. There are also other, less documented stories that circulate of unnatural deaths within the walls of the prison.

Mansfield in the Movies

In an early scene of the 1994 movie *The Shawshank Redemption*, the character Andy Dufresne, convicted of killing his wife and her lover, is on a bus headed to prison. The bus turns down a tree-lined street, heading toward a large stone building. The camera slowly glides toward and over the building, panning down on a massive prison yard filled with inmates. This and a number of other scenes from the movie were filmed in Mansfield.

Closed only four years earlier, the almost 100-year-old prison boasted the world's largest freestanding cell block, six stories high, noted in *Guinness World Records*. Prior to the prison's closing in 1990, portions of two other movies were filmed within its walls. James Caan and Elliott Gould visited the prison during the making of *Harry and Walter Go to New York* in 1976, and Sylvester Stallone and Kurt Russell were in the prison filming *Tango & Cash* the year before it closed. By the time *The Shawshank Redemption* was filmed, all inmates had been transferred out. The prison yard, captured by the aerial view at the start of *Shawshank Redemption,* had been torn down when small parts of *Air Force One* were filmed on the site in 1997.

Ghostly Activities

While no major pictures have been shot there in recent years, several minor movies, music videos, and television programs have continued to bring attention to the Gothic castle. Paranormal studies of the location have discovered several "hot spots" where researchers have experienced strange visions, noises, and even the scent of perfume from the living quarters where Helen Glattke was shot. Ghost tours have become a popular means of visiting the remaining structure. Some explorers even stay overnight to better their chances of communicating with the spirits of those who once inhabited the prison. Visitors to the Ohio State Reformatory may not run into Sylvester Stallone or Tim Robbins, but there is a chance Arthur or Helen Glattke or one of the many deceased inmates or guards may make their presence known. Not a bad addition to an afternoon tour.

The Ghosts of Seattle's Pike Place Market

Each year, millions of people visit Seattle's Pike Place Market, which is known for the store where employees toss fish at each other at a dizzying pace. As it turns out, however, human visitors aren't the only ones attracted to the market.

✳ ✳ ✳ ✳

Where Shopping Can Be a Spiritual Experience

PIKE PLACE MARKET, which opened in August 1907, is one of the oldest farmers' markets in the United States. On its first day in business, more than 10,000 shoppers besieged the eight farmers who had brought their wares to Seattle's waterfront. By year's end, the market's first building was open, and it hasn't looked back since. Perhaps that's a good thing, because looking back might well reveal something else besides shoppers: ghosts.

One of the market's most frequent phantom visitors is Princess Angeline, the daughter of Chief Seattle, who was a leader of the tribes that lived in the area before the arrival of white settlers. By the late 1850s, many Native Americans had left the area due to the terms of a treaty between the tribes and the U.S. government. But Angeline stayed in Seattle and was a familiar figure along the waterfront. She became a local celebrity and was frequently photographed later in life.

Angeline died in 1896 at age 85. So when Pike Place Market was built on the site of her former home, it was like sending out an open invitation for her to hang around for a while, and Angeline has apparently accepted the offer. Her apparition has been spotted at many different locations in the market, but she seems particularly fond of a wooden column on the lower level. Abnormally cold air is said to surround this column, and photographs of it reputedly show things that aren't apparent to the naked eye.

With her braided gray hair, slow way of moving, and habit of browsing, Angeline's ghost easily passes for an elderly shopper. She has often fooled people, who react to her as if she's a fellow consumer until she startles them by vanishing right before their eyes. Sometimes, Angeline even treats folks to a light show, changing from a glowing white figure to blue, lavender, or pink.

You're Never Alone at Pike Place Market

While Angeline does her best to make as many ghostly appearances at the market as possible, she's not the only spectral spectacle at Pike Place. Workers have heard disembodied lullabies drifting through the air late at night after the market is closed; allegedly, they come from the ghost of a heavyset female barber who used to softly sing her customers to sleep and then pick their pockets while they snoozed. Unfortunately, she was not as good at walking as singing, and one day she fell through a weak floor to her death. Another spirit that calls Pike Place home is Arthur Goodwin, the market's director from 1918 to 1941. Ever the workaholic, Arthur's silhouette can often be seen looking down at the market from his former office on the upper floor. What's more, a small spectral boy is seen in a craft shop that sells beads. He's been known to open and shut the cash register and tug at sleeves to get attention. At one point during renovations to the store, a small cache of beads was discovered in a wall; it's believed that the ghostly boy was stashing beads there to play with later, as kids often do.

A Specter With a Sweet Tooth

Some more temperamental ghosts have been heard arguing inside the walk-in freezer of a Pike Place deli. A few deli employees simply refuse to go into the freezer because they're afraid of being drawn into whatever disagreement these spirits have with each other.

Other ghostly goings-on occur in a bookshop, where employees—who swear that they're the only ones in the store—sometimes hear footsteps echoing through the aisles. And proving that even a ghost can have a sweet tooth, a candy store at the market has its own resident ghost. On several occasions, employees have put the candy scoops away at night, only to find them back out the next morning. The next time you're in Seattle, be sure to visit Pike Place Market, and remember that the person standing next to you might just be a visitor from the Other Side.

West Point's Spirited Residents

The United States Military Academy at West Point has an illustrious history. Since 1802, it has educated young men (and women, beginning in 1976) preparing to serve their country as officers in the U.S. Army; prior to that time, West Point was a military fort. With that much history, it's no surprise that these hallowed halls are home to a ghost or two.

✳   ✳   ✳   ✳

KEEPING IN LINE with the pomp and circumstance of the academy, cadets and visitors have reported seeing soldiers from different eras in full-dress uniforms. And back in the 1920s, a spirit inhabiting a house on Professor's Row had to be exorcised. It is unknown whether this was a malevolent ghost or a demonic force, but whatever it was and whatever it did, it frightened two servant girls so terribly that they ran out of the house screaming in the middle of the night.

A cranky Irish cook named Molly is thought to haunt the superintendent's mansion, where she once worked. "Miss Molly"—as she was called when she lived there in the early 19th century—was the maid of Brigadier General Sylvanus Thayer. A hard worker even in death, Molly is often seen kneading bread in the mansion's kitchen.

The Pickpocket Poltergeist

In October 1972, demonologists Ed and Lorraine Warren were invited to give a lecture at West Point. While they were there, they were asked to investigate some paranormal activity that had been occurring at the superintendent's house. It seems that, among other things, personal items and wallets of guests had come up missing . . . only to be discovered later, neatly arranged on the dresser in the master bedroom. Lorraine was able to communicate with the "Pickpocket Poltergeist," who identified himself as a man named Greer. In the early 1800s, he had been wrongly accused of murder, and although he was ultimately exonerated, he was anguishing in sorrow and was unable to move on. Lorraine urged him to go into the light.

Room 4714

But it is Room 4714 in the 47th Division Barracks that has caused the most supernatural speculation. Paranormal activity was first reported there shortly after the Warrens' visit, when students Art Victor and James O'Connor shared the room. One day, when O'Connor went to take a shower, he noticed that his bathrobe was swinging back and forth—but nothing was blowing it. Then suddenly, the temperature in the room dropped several degrees.

A couple of days later, O'Connor saw an apparition of a soldier wearing a uniform and carrying a musket. The following evening, both boys felt an extreme drop in temperature and then saw a man's upper body float through the room; it hovered between the floor and ceiling for a few minutes before disappearing.

One night shortly thereafter, two fellow cadets—Keith Bakken and Terry Meehan—volunteered to spend the night in Room 4714. During the night, Meehan awoke and caught a glimpse of a ghostly figure near the ceiling. By the time Bakken woke up, the apparition was gone, but both boys experienced an extreme drop in temperature. After the campus newspaper published an article about the strange activity, several other cadets offered to sleep in the room. A thermocouple was used to scientifically measure any temperature changes. The coldest temperature was always found right next to O'Connor. Oddly, one night when other cadets were in his room waiting for the ghost, O'Connor saw the specter in *another* room while the boys in Room 4714 saw nothing.

Although a significant number of cadets saw the apparition and felt the drastic temperature change in Room 4714, the identity of this spirit remains unknown. The 47th Division barracks are located near the site of a disastrous house fire that killed an officer. The building is also close to a graveyard in which some Revolutionary War-era soldiers are buried. Could the ghost be one of these military men attempting to bond with the new breed of cadet? If so, the spirit eventually gave up—it hasn't been seen or felt since the 1970s.

Sleepless at the Empire State Building

As an international icon, the 102-story Empire State Building welcomes visitors from all over the world every day. In fact, it is estimated that 110 million people have made trips to the top of the revered skyscraper. But some guests never leave: These are the ghosts of the Empire State Building.

❋   ❋   ❋   ❋

LOCATED IN THE center of Manhattan, the Empire State Building represents financial success as well as architectural beauty, but it wasn't always that way. The Art Deco building opened in 1931, during the Great Depression when times were tough. You'd never know that now, however, as the building bustles with activity. Workers, sweethearts, families, and tourists are all attracted to the structure, and with all the activity that has taken place within its walls—especially on the observation deck—it's no wonder that a few spirits have lingered.

What Makes a Ghost a Ghost?

Throughout the history of the Empire State Building, numerous people have died there of natural causes. Others may have passed away elsewhere but returned to haunt the building because it held a special place in their hearts in life: Perhaps they worked there or met their spouse there and wanted to spend a little more time there—maybe eternity. The process of building a skyscraper of this size can also produce a few ghosts. Official records document only five deaths related to the construction of the Empire State Building, but you can be sure that some of those workers have remained to see the finished project.

In addition, on July 28, 1945, a 10-ton B-25 bomber headed for Newark encountered fog, and the plane crashed into the 79th floor of the Empire State Building, killing 11 office workers.

Choosing the Afterlife

Over the years, many people who have fallen on hard times have gone to the Empire State Building to end their lives: The structure has been the site of at least 30 suicides. Due to the violent nature of such deaths, suicide victims probably account for most of the unsettled spirits found there. Although several suicide attempts were made from the observation deck in the building's early years, the problem wasn't addressed until a jumper injured a pedestrian upon landing in January 1947. This near miss, coupled with a rash of suicide attempts that year, forced the building's owners to erect a high fence strong enough to deter future jumpers. But that hasn't stopped the spirits of those who succeeded from lingering on the observation deck, usually late at night.

Most of the spirits seen by workers and tourists are of the generic variety—white, filmy, and silent. Who they were and why they stayed behind is unknown, but apparitions do seem to roam the building: In fact, many people have reportedly caught glimpses of a ghostly figure that runs straight through the fence and plunges over the edge.

The Ghost of World War II

More than one person has reported seeing a distraught female spirit on the observation deck. She has been described as a pale, distracted woman wearing red lipstick. She sticks out to all those who tell the story because her clothing appears to be from the 1940s. And unlike many specters, this ghost speaks directly to the living. "My man died in the war," she says, adding that they were childhood sweethearts and were planning to marry when he got home from Germany... but he never returned. She tells of how much she loved her beau and says that she can't live without him. And that is apparently what drove the woman over the edge—literally. One visitor, who encountered the ghostly woman in 1985, actually saw her plunge over the wall, only to return a short time later to tell the same story in the exact same words to another unsuspecting tourist.

Every day, visitors go to the Empire State Building to admire the wonderful Art Deco architecture and take in the spectacular view of New York City and the surrounding area. But if you ever visit the building, keep an eye out for the poor souls that remain there. And if you use your camera, be sure to check your pictures carefully: That white blob may not be a photographic error after all.

Unsettling Happenings Aboard *UB-65*

You've probably heard of ghost ships or ghosts that inhabit ships, but how about a submarine that takes such spooky folklore beneath the waves? German sub UB-65 was one such vessel. From ghostly sightings to freakish tragedies that led many to fear for life and limb, the tale of the "Iron Coffin" is an ominous part of military history.

✳ ✳ ✳ ✳

Das Boot

DURING WORLD WAR I, the German U-boat was feared above all other war machines. It could sink other vessels from great distances without being detected. But the U-boat had its drawbacks. For example, unlike conventional vessels that floated on the water's surface, U-boats were virtually doomed if underwater explosives were detonated near them while they were submerged. But submariners—who are a uniquely brave lot—generally accept such perils as part of their job. This makes the fantastic tale of German submarine *UB-65* all the more interesting.

Commissioned in 1917, *UB-65* seemed cursed from the start. From mysterious mishaps and tragic accidents to ethereal events associated with the "Iron Coffin" suggest that it was one wicked vessel.

Devil's Playground

Most warships manage to celebrate their launches before any casualties occur onboard. Not so with *UB-65*. While still under construction at a shipyard in Hamburg, Germany, a structural girder broke free of its chain and fell directly on top of a workman. Pinned by its crushing weight for a full hour, the man shrieked in pain. When the girder was finally lifted off of him, the man died.

Later, just prior to the submarine's launch, another tragedy occurred. This time, a chloride gas leak claimed three lives in the vessel's engine room when dry-cell battery tests went awry. Were such tragedies simply unfortunate coincidences, or was *UB-65* showing distinct signs of being cursed? No one could say with certainty, but many sailors leaned toward the latter.

Chilling Sea Trials

After launching on June 26, 1917, *UB-65* moved into her sea-trial phase. Designed to debug the vessel before it commenced active duty, *UB-65's* "shakedown" tests would prove deadly. Macabre events began when *UB-65* surfaced to perform a hatch inspection. Clearly underestimating the ferocity of a storm that was raging outside in the turbulent North Atlantic, the seaman performing the inspection was swept overboard to his death. This event took a heavy toll on the crew's morale, but sadly, even more misfortune was yet to come.

During a test dive, a ballast tank ruptured and seawater began to fill the engine room; noxious vapors that greatly sickened all on board were produced as a result. It took 12 long hours before events were finally brought under control. This time, the seamen had survived and had seemingly beaten the curse, but just barely. The next event would turn the tables once again and grant the Grim Reaper his much-pursued bounty.

Kaboom!

If there were any doubts about *UB-65* being cursed, they were quickly erased by an incident that took place when the vessel was being fitted with armaments for its first patrol. As crew members loaded torpedoes into firing tubes, one of the warheads inexplicably detonated. The blast claimed the life of the second officer, injured many others, and sent shudders through the submarine.

Afterward, crew members were given several days off to bury their fallen comrade. It was a somber period and a much-needed time for healing. Unfortunately, ethereal forces were about to wreak further havoc on the submarine and rattle the men's nerves like never before.

Second Life for the Second Officer

After the crew reboarded for *UB-65*'s first mission, a scream was heard coming from the gangplank. It came from an officer who had witnessed something that his mind couldn't quite grasp. Later, when pressed about the incident, the officer swore to the captain that his recently buried comrade had boarded the sub directly in front of him. Soon after, another crewman reported seeing the dead sailor as well. Believing that his crew was suffering from hysteria, the captain pushed on with the mission. But the situation only got worse when the engine room staff reported seeing the deceased officer's apparition standing where he had perished. Hoping to stave off panic, the captain ordered all talk of ghosts to cease.

Everything went well until January 1918—the pivotal month when the captain himself became a believer. The turnabout took place while *UB-65* was cruising on the surface. A frightened lookout bolted below deck claiming that he'd seen the second officer's ghost topside. Hoping to put an end to spirit-related nonsense, the captain grabbed the lookout and led him back up the ladder. When they reached the deck, the captain's smugness morphed into terror. There, just inches before him, stood the ghost of the dead second officer.

Exorcism

With numerous documented sightings on their hands, the German Navy knew that it had a problem. The sub was temporarily decommissioned, and a Lutheran minister was brought on board to perform an exorcism. Afterward, a new crew was assembled and the vessel was put back into service, but it didn't take long for the fright-fest to start all over again. In May 1918, at least three ghost sightings were reported. One sailor was so frightened to see the second officer's spirit that he jumped overboard and drowned.

That was the last death aboard *UB-65* until mid-July 1918, when the sub mysteriously disappeared while patrolling in the North Atlantic. Conjecture abounds over what exactly happened aboard *UB-65*: Accidental causes or explosive depth charges head up the list of probable culprits for the vessel's demise. In 2004, an underwater expedition located *UB-65* in the vicinity of Padstow, England, but researchers still couldn't produce a conclusive reason for why the sub was lost. What is known for sure is that this cursed "Iron Coffin" took 37 souls down with her. The Grim Reaper, determined as always, had received his ill-gotten spoils.

Here Lie the Ghosts of Prisoners Past

There's something about a prison that's a little scary ... to most of us, anyway. But add the elements of murder, brutal assault, suicide, and riots, and you have an atmosphere ripe for paranormal activity. Society wanted these hardened criminals to remain behind bars for life, but some are bound there for eternity.

* * * *

Burlington Prison (Mount Holly, New Jersey)

ARCHITECT ROBERT MILLS designed the Burlington Prison to accommodate just 40 convicts when it was built in 1811. Like most other prisons, however, it eventually became overcrowded: By 1965, when it closed, nearly 100 inmates were confined there.

The prison is now a museum, and when remodeling began in 1999, ghosts started making their presence known. Not surprisingly, workers weren't too thrilled to be sharing the building with the spirits of the dead, so paranormal investigators were called in to quell their fears. Unfortunately, that strategy backfired when the ghost hunters declared the place to be haunted. Some of the unexplained activity included missing tools showing up in different locations, unusual noises, and two visible ghosts—one in the shower area and another that is thought to be a prisoner who hung himself in a maximum-security cell. Before it closed, Burlington Prison was the oldest operating prison in the United States. Many of the former inmates are still there to welcome visitors—at least in spirit.

Idaho State Penitentiary (Boise, Idaho)

The early inmates at the Idaho State Penitentiary (which opened around 1870) were model prisoners, but by the 1930s, the convicts admitted there were much more violent and cunning. The prison closed in the 1970s due to riots brought on by the prison's pitiful living conditions. Where there is violence, there's also a good chance that spirits will linger behind. It's no surprise that a tremendous feeling of sadness is experienced in the execution chamber, but visitors' reactions to it are unusually strong: Some have become agitated and overcome with a feeling of dread, while others have dissolved into tears and reported feeling physically ill. And then there are the noises—crying, moaning, and the sounds of guards walking the halls emanate from this facility's walls. The prison, which is now an official historic site, is used as a museum and is open for public tours.

Old City Jail (Charleston, South Carolina)

Before Charleston's city jail was built in 1802, the land on which it stands was designated for public use. Runaway slaves were held at a workhouse there, and the homeless came by for free meals and medical care. The area became less gentrified after the jail was built and hardened criminals and the criminally insane moved in. Over the years, the facility held pirates of the high seas and a great number of slaves who were involved in a revolt in 1822. With its long history and unusual combination of residents, it's no surprise that the Old City Jail has more than a few ghosts hanging around.

One of the specters frequently observed at the jail is an African American male, who probably worked on the premises as a slave. His clothing is ragged and he appears to be carrying a heavy load on his shoulders; he seems oblivious to his living counterparts. But a more violent presence also resides at the jail. Visitors have experienced the sensation that they were being pushed, tugged, or tapped by an unseen force, and many have actually felt physically ill. Today, the Old City Jail building houses the American College of the Building Arts and is an official "Save America's Treasures" project.

Southern Ohio Correctional Facility (Lucasville, Ohio)

One of the worst prison riots in history took place in April 1993 at the Southern Ohio Correctional Facility. For ten days, some 450 prisoners staged an uprising in Cellblock L of this maximum-security prison. In the end, five prisoners were sentenced to death for their roles in the fracas that left nine prisoners and one guard dead. Since then, guards patrolling Cellblock L have reported seeing apparitions in the area. They've also heard doors slam and seen shadows when no one else was around. One guard followed a prisoner who was walking the halls after lockdown, only to watch the man vanish before his very eyes.

Haunted Restaurants

Choosing a place to dine is never simple. What type of cuisine? Formal or informal? What type of spirits? And speaking of spirits: Do you want fully apparitional ghosts or invisible entities? In many restaurants across America, the question isn't whether to dine with a ghost or be haunt-free, but rather how many ghosts might join the meal.

❋   ❋   ❋   ❋

Country Tavern (Nashua, New Hampshire)

IN 1741, A merchant-ship owner known to history only as Captain Ford built a farmhouse for himself and his young wife Elizabeth. His business often took him away from home for long periods of time; however, after one trip that lasted for about a year, Ford returned home to discover that Elizabeth had recently given birth to a baby girl. Furious, he locked Elizabeth in a closet and killed the infant. After he released Elizabeth from captivity, he stabbed her. Ford buried the baby in the yard and dumped his wife's body in a well.

In the early 1980s, when the Country Tavern opened in the old farmhouse, the ghost of Elizabeth—who had been seen on the grounds of her former abode many times since her death—made herself at home: A blonde woman in a white Colonial-style dress with blue ribbons has been spotted in the quaint establishment's dining rooms, kitchen, and women's restroom. Elizabeth isn't shy, either. Sometimes she moves plates—occasionally while diners are still eating off of them. She also likes to play with female patrons' hair and tinker with small items. Visitors have also noticed Elizabeth peering through a window in an adjacent barn. Elizabeth is the primary ghost at the Country Tavern, but people have also heard a baby's faint cry.

Arnaud's (New Orleans, Louisiana)

In 1918, Arnaud Casenave—a French wine salesman—opened a restaurant in the heart of New Orleans; it's been a family-owned center of fine dining in the Crescent City ever since, but it's not without its ghosts. The specter of a man dressed in an old-fashioned tuxedo is often spotted near the windows of the main dining room; this ghost is believed to be none other than Arnaud himself, still watching over his beloved restaurant. A spectral woman has also been seen walking out of the restroom and moving silently down the hall before disappearing into a wall.

Old Bermuda Inn (Staten Island, New York)

When Martha Mesereau's husband was away fighting in the Civil War, she lit a candle and sat by her bedroom window every night, waiting for his safe return. When she learned that her husband had died in battle, Martha locked herself in her room and died of a broken heart. But she still makes her presence known at her former home, which is now the Old Bermuda Inn—a banquet hall and bed-and-breakfast. Moving cold spots permeate the building, and locked doors open on their own. Staff members have also heard Martha crying. In recent years, when the building was undergoing renovations, a portrait of Martha spontaneously burst into flames in the hallway; perhaps she was showing her disapproval of the changes being made to her house. Diners have seen a woman resembling Martha walking through the dining room, and others have seen her sitting in the window, just like she did in life while waiting for her husband's return.

Poogan's Porch (Charleston, South Carolina)

In 2003, the Travel Channel voted Poogan's Porch the "Third Most Haunted Place in America." Staff members and guests have seen a woman in a long black dress disappear in front of their eyes. The same woman has been sighted waving from a second story window; she is believed to be the ghost of Zoe St. Amand, a former schoolteacher who lived in the building until the 1950s. Then there's the ghost of the restaurant's namesake: Poogan was a stray dog that wandered the neighborhood begging for scraps. While the restaurant was being renovated in the 1970s, he liked to hang out on the porch to watch. The lovable mutt died in 1979, but people relaxing on the porch have felt an animal rub against their legs even though no creature was there. Not many restaurants can claim a resident ghost dog.

The Happiest Haunted Place on Earth?

According to the proprietors of Disneyland, the Haunted Mansion is home to 999 ghosts . . . and there's room for one more. But some people believe that the 1,000th ghost is already there—and that it is no special effect! In fact, many spirits are said to linger at the Magic Kingdom long after the last guest has left for the day.

✳ ✳ ✳ ✳

The Haunted Mansion

THE MOST FAMOUS "real" ghost at the Haunted Mansion is that of "Timmy," a young boy who loved the attraction so much that, after he met an unfortunate and untimely death, his mother asked for the park's permission to scatter his ashes on the ride. When the park refused, she was appalled. How could Disneyland deny the simple request of a grieving mother?

As the story goes, the poor woman took matters into her own hands. She boarded the ride with her son's ashes in hand and waited until she came to the "Séance Room," where a harp, tambourine, and other instruments float in mid-air while Madame Leota—the face in the crystal ball—calls the spirits to come forth and join the party. Timmy's mother allegedly scattered her son's ashes as her "Doom Buggy" moved through the room. Ever since then, guests have claimed to see the ghost of young Timmy crying in the area where people exit the ride.

Could the story be true? No one has ever been able to verify Timmy's actual identity, but someone could easily scatter ashes while on the ride. In fact, the park is known to intentionally keep the Mansion dusty, so it's certainly conceivable that human ashes could have been hidden somewhere along the dark ride's journey.

During slow periods when they had the ride pretty much to themselves, some guests have reported hearing loud knocks on the backs of their Doom Buggies, even though no one was in the car behind them and no cast members were nearby. Some claim that Buggy No. 55 is the haunted buggy. No one is certain who is haunting it (perhaps it's Timmy), but having a chance to ride in it is considered the "Holy Grail" among Haunted Mansion enthusiasts.

Uncle Walt's Keeping Watch

While the Haunted Mansion may be the most logical location for ghosts to hang out at Disneyland, it's certainly not the only place they've been sighted. In fact, rumors have long swirled that Walt Disney himself haunts a room that was originally intended to be his apartment. He never actually lived in the space, which is tucked away near the Pirates of the Caribbean ride, but some say that he loved the idea of having his own apartment inside the park so much that he sometimes comes back from beyond the grave to visit it.

The Sad Tale of Disco Debbie

Another ghost that is seen at the park is "Disco Debbie," a former employee that is said to haunt Space Mountain—an indoor roller coaster. According to legend, during the summer of 1979, Debbie's job was to liven up the crowd and encourage guests to dance on the "Space Stage" outside the attraction. After work one day, she was found dead of a brain aneurysm backstage at Space Mountain. She has since been seen on several occasions—often as a pale green apparition that's visible through the ride's windows.

REAL Skeletons!

Other dead bodies have been in the park known as "The Happiest Place on Earth," and people lined up to see them. Believe it or not, when the Pirates of the Caribbean ride first opened in the late 1960s, its designers had not yet created realistic-looking skeletons. Their solution? Use actual cadavers! Scoff if you will, but the tale is reportedly true—every skeleton on the ride was real when it first opened, and the skull and crossbones above the captain's bed still is! The story is hard to believe and the company doesn't like to talk about it, but the "Disney Underground" community insists that it's true.

And as for the rumor that Walt Disney's cryogenically frozen body lies in a secret chamber under the Pirates of the Caribbean attraction? Well, that's a whole other story!

New Jersey's Haunted Union Hotel

A New Jersey hotel that witnessed a major event continues to make history of its own—haunted history, that is.

✳   ✳   ✳   ✳

A Shocking Event

IN EARLY 1932, in an event that was as sad as it was sensational, Charles Lindbergh—the first man to fly solo across the Atlantic Ocean—again made headlines; however, this time it was for something that would have anything but a happy ending. On the night of March 1, 1932, the famous flyer's 20-month-old son was kidnapped from the family home in Hopewell, New Jersey. Although Lindbergh paid the requested ransom, the boy's body was eventually found half-buried in a roadside thicket not far from his home. Suspect Bruno Richard Hauptmann, a carpenter and small-time crook, was taken into custody on September 19, 1934. A transfixed American public anxiously awaited Hauptmann's trial, which was scheduled to begin on January 3, 1935, at the Hunterdon County courthouse in Flemington, New Jersey.

The Trial of the Century

Due to Lindbergh's fame and the revolting nature of the crime, the five-week proceeding was dubbed the "trial of the century." As such, it drew members of the press like moths to a flame. To keep reporters close to the action, the Union Hotel, which was located just across the street from the Hunterdon County courthouse, was tapped as the press headquarters. The Victorian building was an apt choice: Built in 1877, the four-story hotel was near the site of the trial, and it had a bar on its premises—just the thing to soothe battle-weary correspondents looking to unwind.

On February 13, 1935, the jury handed down a guilty verdict, which carried with it the death penalty. Happy that the villain had received his due, Americans rejoiced. Hauptmann went to the electric chair on April 3, 1936. Since that day, however, speculation regarding his culpability in the crime has stirred relentlessly. But that's not the only thing that's been stirring.

Harrowing Happenings

After the press departed the Union Hotel, little more was heard about the inn—little more of an *earthly* nature, that is. Staff reports of paranormal occurrences began trickling in, with each story sounding just a tad more terrifying than the one that preceded it. Over the years, several businesses have opened in the building—most recently a restaurant, which closed in 2008. According to witnesses, the ghosts of the Union Hotel have a penchant for vigorously spinning barstools. After this gets the attention of the intended eyewitness, which it unfailingly does, their next trick is to slam doors . . . loudly.

One night after closing, a bouncer locked the doors to the hotel's foyer and then joined staff members for a drink. Suddenly, the doors flew open—completely unaided—and a cold breeze blew past the group. Dumbfounded by what he had witnessed, the bouncer again closed the doors. As he did, he saw a phantom pair of children's shoes scrambling up the main stairway. Horrified, he turned and fled. In another incident, a waitress was carrying her cash drawer upstairs after closing. As she reached the top step, she heard a disembodied voice humming a lullaby. Like the bouncer, she fled the scene, never to return again.

Spirits and Other Spirits

At least one ghost at the Union Hotel has its disembodied heart in the right place. While going over her books late one night, a night manager sensed a sudden presence. Startled, she moved back from her desk, and an invisible intruder moved up against her and pressed against her chest. She asked it to move away and the ghost respectfully complied. While some might categorize this turn of events as fortunate, the woman isn't so sure: She regrets telling the entity to back away for fear that she may never have such an encounter again.

Had the manager met the ghost of the condemned man? It's doubtful, since Hauptmann never stayed at the hotel. It's more likely that she brushed up against the spirit of a reporter left over from the days of the Hauptmann trial that was feeling a little frisky after unwinding in the bar.

Confessions From a Counterfeit House

On a hill overlooking the Ohio River in Monroe Township, Adams County, sits a house that isn't what it seems. Its modest size and quiet exterior hide countless architectural and historical secrets—secrets that have earned it the nickname "The Counterfeit House."

✳ ✳ ✳ ✳

IN 1850, OLIVER Ezra Tompkins and his sister, Ann E. Lovejoy, purchased 118 acres and built a rather peculiar house to suit the needs of their successful home-based business. Tompkins and Lovejoy were counterfeiters who specialized in making fake 50-cent coins and $500 bills. They needed a house that could keep their secrets. Although passersby could see smoke escaping from the house's seven chimneys, only two of those chimneys were connected to working fireplaces; the others were fed by ductwork and filled with secret compartments. The front door featured a trick lock and a hidden slot for the exchange of money and products, and the gabled attic window housed a signal light.

The counterfeiting room was a windowless, doorless room in the rear of the house, accessible only through a series of trapdoors. A trapdoor in the floor led to a sizeable tunnel that provided an escape route through the bedrock of the surrounding hills to a cliff. Although no records exist to support the imagined use of these features, local historians believe the reports to be true.

Visitors Not Welcome

While Lovejoy was in Cincinnati spending some of her counterfeit money, she was noticed by the police. A Pinkerton agent followed her home and watched as she opened the trick lock. He waited until she was inside, then followed her in, hoping to capture the criminals.

Immediately past the door, in a 10-foot by 45-foot hallway, Tompkins was waiting—he beat the agent to death. To this day, bloodstains are still visible on the walls and floor. Tompkins and Lovejoy buried the agent's body in one of the nearby hills, and Tompkins used the hidden tunnel to escape to a friendly riverboat, collapsing the tunnel with explosives as he went. Lovejoy held a mock funeral for Tompkins and inherited his estate, although shortly after she went into debt and moved away.

Keeping Up the Counterfeit House

Although Tompkins never returned to the house, both his ghost and that of the agent are said to haunt it. Tourists have reported seeing a man's shape in the front doorway and have complained of unexplained cold spots and an unfamiliar "presence."

In 1896, a great-great uncle of Jo Lynn Spires, the current owner, purchased the property. It passed to Spires's grandparents in the 1930s, and Spires and her parents lived in the house with her grandfather. Although privately owned, the house was a tourist attraction, and Spires regularly kept the house clean, repaired, and ready for the stream of visitors that would trickle in each weekend. Unable to keep up with the repairs on the house, however, Spires moved into a trailer on the property in 1986. She continues to welcome approximately 1,000 tourists each summer.

In February 2008, windstorms caused severe damage to the house. One of the false chimneys blew apart, and the roof ripped off. Although Spires was able to prevent damage to the antiques and furnishings within the house, she was unsure how she would find the money to restore the roof and prevent future leaks. Perhaps she should consider printing some.

Haunted Hospitals Have Tales to Tell

If they could speak, hospitals would have incredible stories to tell. Within their walls, lives are saved and lives are lost. People undergo surgeries, heal from injuries, and some simply never leave. Doctors and nurses have personal dramas and patients have near-death experiences, so it's not surprising that hospitals are among the most haunted places you'll find.

✳ ✳ ✳ ✳

Carrie Tingley Children's Hospital (Albuquerque, New Mexico)

ORIGINALLY ESTABLISHED IN the city of Truth or Consequences, New Mexico, Carrie Tingley Children's

Hospital was founded in 1937 to help kids suffering from polio. It was later moved to Albuquerque, where it became affiliated with the University of New Mexico Medical Center. Some unused areas of the hospital are said to have invisible force fields that sometimes prevent people from moving through certain hallways or doors. Employees know to listen for a telltale hissing sound that is heard just before a barrier is encountered. Glowing rooms, disembodied voices, and phantom heartbeats and sobbing are all elements of the haunting there.

Doctors Hospital (Perry Heights, Ohio)

You'd expect former patients to be the spirits haunting a hospital, but the ghost of a former nurse's aide also wanders Doctors Hospital, humming just the way she used to in life. An elderly woman who died there also reportedly haunts the room in which she died. After she passed in the late 20th century, patients felt cold spots in the room and even had their blankets pulled off of them. The room was eventually sealed off and was no longer in use when the hospital closed its doors in 2008.

The Ohio Exploration Society, which investigates the paranormal, visited the hospital in March 2010. They tried to record electronic voice phenomena (EVPs) in the patient's room without success, but that doesn't mean all was quiet—the investigators did capture an unexplained voice in the hospital lab.

Linda Vista Community Hospital (Los Angeles, California)

A hospital with too many unexplained deaths sounds like the perfect place to find a ghost or two. Linda Vista, which was built in 1904, is now closed and is said to be haunted by both patients and staff. Elevators start and stop by themselves; a green light glows faintly throughout the night and other lights flicker on and off; moans and screams have been heard; the image of a doctor has been observed in an upper window; and on the third floor, unexplained foul odors can often be smelled.

Visitors also report seeing a spectral girl playing outside and hearing her laugh. Apparently Hollywood types don't scare too easily: The building has been used in movies, music videos, and commercials, as well as the pilot episode of NBC's long-running hospital drama *ER* (1994).

Madison Civil War Hospital (Madison, Georgia)

When the Madison Civil War Hospital served as a military medical facility, it certainly saw its share of sick and injured soldiers...and death. Although it's no longer in use, the building still has some life in it—afterlife, that is. Paranormal investigators have heard phantom footsteps in an empty stairwell and rustling sounds in a seemingly unoccupied basement; they've also seen a ball bouncing down a hallway by itself.

Plymouth County Hospital (Hanson, Massachusetts)

In the early part of the 20th century, the Hanson Tuberculosis Hospital opened to treat terminally ill TB patients from the Boston area. When the tuberculosis epidemic died down, it became Plymouth County Hospital, and in 1992, its doors were closed for good. Since then, people have reported feeling like they are being watched, and odd noises—mostly screams and laughter—have been reported coming from within.

San Diego's Whaley House

Even if you don't believe in ghosts, you've got to be intrigued by all the chatter surrounding the Whaley House in San Diego. According to late ghost hunter Hans Holzer, this old family homestead might be the most haunted house in America. The U.S. Department of Commerce lists the building as an authentic Haunted House (it is one of only two structures in the country to hold this distinction), and the television show America's Most Haunted *called it the Most Haunted House in the United States.*

✳ ✳ ✳ ✳

How It All Began

THE FIRST TWO-STORY building in San Diego and now the oldest on the West Coast, the Whaley House needs all of its space to house the many spirits that reside inside it. Built by prominent Californian Thomas Whaley in 1856, it began as a one-story granary with an adjacent two-story residence. By the next year, Whaley had opened a general store on the premises. Over the years, the building also served as a county courthouse, a ballroom, a billiards hall, and a theater, among other things. Now it's a California State Historic Landmark and a museum.

Squatter's Rights

Hindsight is always 20/20, but perhaps Thomas Whaley should have thought twice about buying the property on which "Yankee Jim" Robinson was publicly hanged in 1852. Accused of attempted grand larceny, Robinson was executed in a particularly unpleasant display. The gallows were situated on the back of a wagon that was set up at the site; however, being a tall man, Yankee Jim was able to reach the wagon with his feet, thus delaying his death for several minutes. According to newspaper reports, when his legs were finally pulled out from under him, he "swung back and forth like a pendulum" until he died.

Although Whaley was actually present at Robinson's execution, he apparently didn't associate the property with the gruesome event that had taken place there. Nevertheless, soon after the house was completed, he and his family began to hear heavy disembodied footsteps, as if a large man was walking through the house. Remembering what had taken place there a few years earlier, the Whaleys believed that the spirit of Yankee Jim himself was sharing their new home. Apparently, Robinson was not a malevolent ghost because the Whaleys' youngest daughter, Lillian, remained in the house with the spirit until 1953. But to this day, visitors to the site still report hearing the heavy-footed phantom.

Family Spirits

After the house became a historic landmark and was opened to the public in 1960, staff, tourists, and ghost hunters alike began to experience paranormal phenomena such as apparitions, noises, and isolated cold spots. Some have even caught glimpses of a small spotted dog running by with its ears flapping, which just might be the spirit of the Whaleys' terrier, Dolly Varden. Although Thomas and Anna Whaley lived in several different houses, the couple must have dearly loved their original San Diego home because they don't seem quite ready to leave it, even a century after their deaths. They have been seen—and heard—going about their daily business and doing chores in the house. Don't they know there's a cleaning service for that?

The couple has also been captured on film acting as though it was still the 19th century. Thomas was seen wandering through the house and smoking a pipe near an upstairs window, while Anna seems to have kept up her duties as the matron of the house: People have seen her rocking a baby, tucking a child into bed, and folding clothes. Sometimes, the family's rocking chair is seen teetering back and forth all by itself.

Children are especially likely to see the building's former occupants. Employees frequently notice youngsters smiling or waving at people who the adults are unable to see. And the sound of piano music that sometimes drifts through the air? Most say that it's Anna, still playing the tunes that she loved most in life.

Long before he became one of America's most beloved TV personalities, Regis Philbin worked at a television station in San Diego. In 1964, when he and a companion paid a visit to the Whaley House to investigate the ghostly tales, Philbin was startled to see the wispy figure of Anna Whaley moving along one of the walls. When he turned on a flashlight to get a better look, she disappeared, leaving only her portrait to smile back at him.

Wilted Violet

Thomas and Anna's daughter Violet had a particularly sad life and is thought to haunt the old house where she once lived. In 1882, in a double wedding with her sister Anna Amelia, the beautiful Violet was married at the Whaley House to a man that her parents did not trust.

Unfortunately, the marriage lasted only two weeks, after which Violet was granted a divorce. Divorce was highly uncommon in those days, and the scandal was humiliating for both Violet and her family. Violet became extremely depressed, and in 1885, she took her own life by shooting herself in the heart.

It is believed that Violet makes her presence known by turning on lights in the upstairs rooms and setting off the burglar alarm. Her spirit is also thought to be responsible for the phantom footsteps that emanate from the second floor and the sudden icy chills often felt by visitors—as though a spirit had just walked right through them.

Ghosts Galore

Most of the spirits at the Whaley House seem to be related to the family or the site. A young girl has been seen in several locations in and around the house. Dressed in 19th-century clothing, she plays with toys in the playroom, sniffs flowers in the garden, and darts in and out of the dining room very quickly. Some say that she was a playmate of the Whaley children and that she died on the property when she got tangled in a clothesline and either broke her neck or was strangled; however, there is no record of such a death occurring at the Whaley House.

Another female ghost seems to be attached to the part of the house that once served as a courtroom. One visitor said that as she walked into the room, she saw a woman dressed in a calico skirt typical of the 1800s. The spirit didn't seem evil, but it didn't seem to be particularly welcoming either. The visitor captured the spectral woman's shadowy figure in a photo. It seems likely that the ghost is somehow connected to an event that took place in the courtroom. The ghost of a man dressed in a businesslike frock coat has also appeared in the former courtroom. However, his spirit may not be strongly attached to the building because it fades away more quickly than others that are seen there.

Haunted Happenings

In addition to these apparitions, visitors, volunteers, and employees have reported other odd phenomena inside the house. Unexplained singing, organ music, and whistling have been heard, as has a toddler crying in an upstairs nursery. Some have witnessed levitating furniture, and others have noticed mysterious scents, such as perfume, cigar smoke, and the scent of holiday baking coming from an empty kitchen.

When visitors first enter the house, they can examine photos taken by previous visitors. These images all have one thing in common: They contain mysterious objects such as shadows, orbs, and misty figures. One visitor reported trying to take photos with an otherwise reliable camera; as soon as she tried to focus, the camera beeped, indicating that she was too close to her subject despite the fact that she was nowhere near the closest (visible) object. Once developed, the photos featured an orb or filmy shadow in nearly every shot.

At least the Whaley House spirits take some responsibility for the place. Once, after an especially long day at the museum, a staff member was getting ready to close up when all the doors and windows on both floors suddenly locked on their own, all at the same time.

Sometimes spirits just need a little alone time.

Ghosts That Like Country Music

Just over the Ohio River from downtown Cincinnati is the town of Wilder, Kentucky, home of Bobby Mackey's—a country-music nightclub and allegedly one of the most haunted locations in the United States. Over the years, the property is said to have seen such atrocities as a beheading, a poisoning, a suicide, numerous unsolved murders, and even a case of possession.

❋ ❋ ❋ ❋

Hell's Gate

T HE FIRST BUILDING that is believed to have stood on the property now occupied by Bobby Mackey's was a slaughterhouse, which operated from the 1850s until the late 1880s. During that time, it was said to have been so busy that the ground floor was often literally coated with blood. To alleviate that, a well was dug in the basement, which allowed the blood to be washed off the floor and carried out to the nearby river. Needless to say, gallons upon gallons of blood and other assorted matter were dumped into that well. Perhaps that's why legend has it that after the slaughterhouse closed, a satanic cult used the well as part of its rituals. Some even claim that these rituals opened a portal to the Other Side, a portal that—to this day—has yet to be closed.

An Unspeakable Crime

On February 1, 1896, the headless body of Pearl Bryan was found less than two miles from the site of the former slaughterhouse. It was later discovered that Bryan's boyfriend, Scott Jackson, and his friend, Alonzo Walling, had murdered her after a botched abortion attempt. The two men were arrested, but they refused to reveal the location of Bryan's head. Both men were hanged for the crime in March 1897, without ever disclosing the location of Bryan's head. The consensus was that the head was probably thrown into the old slaughterhouse well. Perhaps that's why Pearl Bryan's ghost is seen wandering around inside Bobby Mackey's, both with and without her head. And although Jackson and Walling did not take their last breaths on the property, it is believed that their ghosts are stuck there too; they have both been seen throughout the building, but Jackson's ghost seems to be more active...and angry. Those who have encountered his ghost—usually around the well in the basement—say that it is a dark and unhappy spirit.

Gangsters and Unsolved Murders

Shortly after the executions of Jackson and Walling, the former slaughterhouse was torn down, leaving only the well. In the 1920s, the building now known as Bobby Mackey's was built on the property directly over the well. During Prohibition, it functioned as a ruthless speakeasy and gambling den where several people lost their lives. Eventually, the building was shut down and cleared out—presumably of everything except the restless spirits.

In 1933, after Prohibition was lifted, E. A. "Buck" Brady purchased the building and renamed it The Primrose. Brady was competing with powerful gangsters who began showing up at The Primrose trying to scare him into giving them a cut of the profits. But Brady refused to be intimidated and continually turned them down. All this came to a head on August 5, 1946, when Brady and gangster Albert "Red" Masterson were involved in a shootout. After that, Brady decided that he was done. After many years of having to continually (and often forcibly) reject advances by Cincinnati-area gangsters, Brady sold the building. But if the stories are to be believed, as he handed over the keys, he cursed the building, saying that because he couldn't run a successful business there, no one should.

Today, the ghosts of both Buck Brady and Red Masterson are seen inside Bobby Mackey's. Brady's ghost has been identified from photographs taken of him when he was alive. And even though he cursed the building, his ghost seems harmless enough. Masterson's ghost, on the other hand, has been described as "not friendly" and has been blamed for some of the alleged attacks on bar patrons.

Johanna

After Brady sold the building, it reopened as The Latin Quarter. According to legend, Johanna, the daughter of The Latin Quarter's owner, fell in love with (and became pregnant by) Robert Randall, one of the singers at the nightclub. After Johanna's father found out about the pregnancy, he ordered Randall killed. When Johanna learned of her father's involvement in her boyfriend's death, she first unsuccessfully tried to poison him and then committed suicide in the basement of the building.

Johanna's ghost is seen throughout the building, but it is most often reported on the top floor and in the stairwells, where she will either push or hug people. She is also said to hang out in the Spotlight Room, a secret place in the attic where she allegedly wrote a poem on the wall before committing suicide. Even those who cannot see her apparition can always tell that Johanna is around by the scent of roses.

One of the strangest phenomena attributed to Johanna's ghost is that the turned-off (and unplugged) jukebox sometimes springs to life by playing "The Anniversary Waltz"—despite the fact that the song is not even a selection on the device's menu.

Bobby Mackey's Music World

In the spring of 1978, musician Bobby Mackey purchased the building, and it has been in operation ever since. Besides operating as a bar, Bobby Mackey's has a stage and a dance floor and has featured performances by many country music acts.

Shortly after her husband purchased the building, Janet Mackey was working in the upstairs apartment when she was shoved out of the room toward the stairs while being told to "Get out" by a spirit that she later identified as Alonzo Walling. After that, Janet refused to set foot in the room. So Bobby hired Carl Lawson as a caretaker and allowed him to stay in the apartment. Upon moving in, Lawson reportedly heard strange noises and saw shadowy figures moving around the bar late at night. Believing that the spirits were coming in through the well in the basement, Lawson threw holy water down the hole. As a result, Lawson claimed that he became possessed and was only able to break free from the demon's grasp after an exorcism was performed on him.

In 1993, a man sued Bobby Mackey's alleging that while he was in the bar's men's room, he was punched and kicked by a "dark-haired apparition" wearing a cowboy hat. The victim stated that he might have angered the ghost because he dared it to appear shortly before being attacked. While the suit was thrown out, it did result in the now-famous sign that hangs above the front doors of Bobby Mackey's, which alerts guests to the possibility that the building may be haunted and that they are entering at their own risk.

Prime-Time Ghosts

Bobby Mackey repeatedly turned down requests to have his bar investigated; however, in 2008, he allowed the TV show *Ghost Adventures* to film an episode at his nightclub, which yielded some interesting and controversial footage. Among other things, investigators encountered odd cold spots and claimed to have heard the voice of a woman. While using the men's room, investigator Nick Groff also heard banging noises, which startled him so much that he ran out of the restroom without zipping up his pants. The team also captured some odd video of what appeared to be a man in a cowboy hat moving around in the basement.

But the episode will forever be remembered as the one in which overly dramatic ghost hunter Zak Bagans claimed to have been attacked by a demonic entity after challenging the evil forces in the basement. As proof, Bagans proudly displayed three scratch marks on his back. Bagans was so shaken by the event that he proclaimed it to be one of the scariest things he had ever encountered. But that didn't stop *Ghost Adventures* from returning to Bobby Mackey's in 2010.

Investigators spending time at Bobby Mackey's might be a bit disappointed if they don't experience as much paranormal activity as the *Ghost Adventures* team, but that doesn't mean that the place isn't active. For example, when the organization Ghosts of Ohio visited Bobby Mackey's, the investigation seemed uneventful. But when the team members reviewed their audio afterward, they found that a recorder set up near the infamous well picked up a voice clearly saying, "It hurts."

They're Waiting for You

While Bobby Mackey states that he does not believe in ghosts and doesn't think that his bar is haunted, reports of paranormal activity still continue to pour in. So should you ever find yourself sitting at the bar at Bobby Mackey's late at night, make sure you take a look around and keep in mind that just because the barstool next to you appears to be empty, you may not be drinking alone.

Griggs Mansion

A notoriously haunted house in St. Paul, Minnesota, changes hands, and then all paranormal activity ceases. Was the house ever haunted? If so, what made the once-frisky ghosts decide to pack up and leave? It's a question that is difficult to answer. A house that's haunted to some seems completely benign to others. Who is right? Let's examine the evidence.

✳ ✳ ✳ ✳

First Frights

BUILT IN 1883 BY wholesale grocery tycoon Chauncey W. Griggs, the imposing 24-room Griggs Mansion features high ceilings, a dark interior, and a stone facade that looks decidedly menacing. Although the home bears his name, Griggs lived there for only a scant four years before moving to sunnier climes on the West Coast. After that, the house changed hands quite frequently, which some say is a sure sign that the place was haunted.

The first ghost sightings at the house date back to 1915, when a young maid—who was despondent over a breakup—hanged herself on the mansion's fourth floor. Soon after the woman's burial, her spirit was allegedly seen roaming the building's hallways. According to witnesses, the ghost of Charles Wade arrived next. In life, he was the mansion's gardener and caretaker; in death, he liked to cruise the building's library.

Unexplained Activity

Strange occurrences are the norm at the Griggs Mansion. Over the years, residents have reported hearing disembodied footsteps traveling up and down the staircases, seeing doors open and close by themselves, hearing voices coming from unoccupied rooms, and experiencing all manner of unexplainable incidents, which suggest that the Griggs Mansion is indeed haunted.

In 1939, the mansion was donated to the St. Paul Gallery and School of Art. During the 1950s, staffer Dr. Delmar Rolb claimed that he saw the apparition of a "tall thin man" in his apartment in the basement of the building. In 1964, Carl L. Weschcke—a publisher of books relating to the occult—acquired the house. He said that as soon as he would close a particular window, it would mysteriously reopen. Determined to stop this game, Weschcke nailed the window shut; however, when he returned home the next day, it was open once again.

Ghostbusters

In 1969, reporters from a local newspaper spent a night at the Griggs Mansion. The journalists—who were all initially skeptics—became believers after spending a harrowing night on the premises; unexplained footsteps and an unnerving feeling that a presence accompanied them were enough to do the trick. The frightened reporters fled the mansion in the wee hours of the morning and never returned.

More Skeptics

In 1982, Tibor and Olga Zoltai purchased the mansion. "When we first moved in, there were people who would cross to the other side of the street to pass the house," Olga recalled in an interview with a local newspaper. "One even threw a piece of Christ's cross into the yard."

However, in nearly three decades of living inside the reputedly haunted house, the couple has never experienced anything out of the ordinary. To show just how silly they found the ghost stories, the playful couple assembled an "emergency kit" that contained a clove of garlic, a bottle of holy water, a crucifix, and a stake. They figured that these items would provide ample protection against any restless spirits in the house.

The Historic (and Haunted) Roosevelt Hotel

Situated at 7000 Hollywood Boulevard, the 12-story Roosevelt Hotel is an integral part of Hollywood's history. For more than 80 years, this hotel has served as a temporary home away from home for some of the world's biggest celebrities, who love to soak in the atmosphere. In fact, many of the stars who visit the Roosevelt enjoy themselves so much that they frequently return... even in death.

✳   ✳   ✳   ✳

Now Open for Business

THE ROOSEVELT, NAMED after President Theodore Roosevelt, was the brainchild of a group that included actor Douglas Fairbanks and was designed to function as a haven for actors who lived on the East Coast but found themselves in Hollywood making movies. When the doors swung open for business on May 15, 1927, nearly $3 million had been spent building the 400-room hotel. The design captured the flavor of southern California with its Spanish colonial style.

It didn't take long for the who's who of Hollywood to start visiting the Roosevelt, using it for industry functions and doing business in its sunken lobby or elegant Library Bar. The era's biggest stars, including Mary Pickford, Gloria Swanson, Greta Garbo, Charlie Chaplin, and Will Rogers, were present at the hotel's inaugural ball. The Roosevelt was even the site of the very first Academy Awards ceremony, which was held in the hotel's Blossom Room on May 16, 1929. The ceremony included several activities, but the actual awards presentation was the shortest in Academy Awards history, lasting approximately five minutes with only 15 awards handed out.

Over the years, more and more stars made the Roosevelt their hotel of choice, including Clark Gable, Errol Flynn, Hugh Hefner, Frank Sinatra, Elizabeth Taylor, Judy Garland, and Al Jolson. In addition, a variety of lesser-known but important personnel, from musicians to voice instructors to writers, stayed for extended periods of time on the studios' tabs while working on various movies.

But the years began to take their toll on the Roosevelt, and by the 1980s, the building had fallen into such disrepair that it came close to being demolished. A major hotel chain saved it from the wrecking ball and began making extensive renovations. They worked hard to reflect the Roosevelt's original charm and color schemes, focusing a lot of attention on the sunken Spanish-style lobby adorned with rounded Moorish windows and a bubbling fountain. The renovators discovered the lobby's huge, original, wrought-iron chandelier in pieces in the basement and spent six months putting it back together. It has been said that all of the banging during the renovation was enough to wake the dead—literally.

You're Never Alone at the Roosevelt

The first documented encounter with a ghost at the Roosevelt came in December 1985. The hotel was scheduled to reopen a month later, so employees were frantically working to complete the renovation. Employee Alan Russell was working in the Blossom Room when he felt a cold spot. Alarmed, he called some of his coworkers over and they felt it too, although they couldn't find a rational explanation.

Since then, guests and employees alike have reported seeing a man in dark clothing standing in precisely the same spot where Russell felt the cold spot. Who this man is remains a mystery. Shortly after the newly renovated Roosevelt opened for business, the front desk started getting calls from confused guests who reported hearing disembodied voices coming from empty hallways. At other times, guests would call to complain about a loud conversation coming from the room next door, only to be told that the room was empty and locked up tight.

Ghosts and More Ghosts

The ghosts of the Roosevelt might have started out being heard rather than seen, but that was to change, too. Guests and employees have also reported seeing dark figures roaming the hallways late at night. In one instance, the ghost of a man dressed all in white was seen walking through the walls of the hotel. Over time, the ninth floor of the hotel became a haven for much of the paranormal activity. Things were said to have gotten to the point that some Roosevelt employees refused to go up to the floor alone at night.

In 1992, in an attempt to find some answers, psychic Peter James was invited to the Roosevelt. As he wandered the halls of the hotel, James claimed to have encountered several famous ghosts. He felt Humphrey Bogart's spirit near the elevators and bumped into Carmen Miranda's specter while walking down the hallway on the third floor. James stated that when he ventured down to the Blossom Room, the ghosts of Edward Arnold and Betty Grable were present.

Are there really ghosts there? What ghosts might you see? You'd have to book a room and see...

The Top 5 Most Haunted Places in Texas

The Big Star State sure has some big hauntings under its belt.

* * * *

* The Alamo, San Antonio: It's probably no surprise that Texas's most famous fort and battle site also reports Texas's most hauntings, from General Santa Anna to John Wayne. Since 1836, visitors and passersby have noticed eerie lights and ghostly figures here, day and night.

* Texas Governor's Mansion, Austin: Across the street from Texas's state capitol, the governor's mansion has been the site of drama, victory, tragedy, and hauntings. According to legend, former governor Sam Houston haunts the mansion, where he's hiding from his third wife. She tried to reform Sam into a sober, churchgoing man. He'd rather spend his afterlife without her.

* Market Square, Houston: Downtown Houston may be haunted by 19th-century madam Pamelia Mann. According to staff and patrons at establishments such as La Carafe, the late Ms. Mann is a nightly visitor. Dressed in a white Victorian gown, she has reportedly been seen outside on Congress Avenue and inside some of the buildings. She checks the ladies' rooms on the Market Square block where her brothel once stood.

* The Jail at La Grange: Many people know La Grange for "the best little whorehouse in Texas." Nearby, Fayette County Jail is known for tales of the ghost of Marie Dach, who starved herself while on death row. Today, the jail is the La Grange Chamber of Commerce, and the gaunt figure of Mrs. Dach haunts her former cell. Ironically, it's part of the chamber of commerce's kitchen.

* Driskill Hotel, Austin: For celebrity ghosts in an elegant setting, look no further than Austin's downtown Driskill Hotel. Some say that former U.S. President Lyndon Baines Johnson is among the hotel's famous ghosts. The spirit of LBJ appears around the hotel mezzanine, where he used to celebrate on election nights.

The Hockey Hall of Fame— Where Legends Live On

The Hockey Hall of Fame in Toronto was created to showcase all things hockey: the best players, games, and coaches. It's no surprise that legends come alive there--it's a place where stars of the sport live on forever. So you probably wouldn't be surprised to find a ghost hanging around its hallowed halls, but you might be surprised to learn that she has absolutely nothing to do with hockey.

* * * *

Dorothy Who?

SITUATED ON THE corner of Yonge and Front Streets in downtown Toronto, the Hockey Hall of Fame resides in a beautiful old building that has the look of a cathedral, complete with a stained-glass dome. Built in 1885, the structure was home to the Bank of Montreal before it closed in 1982; the Hall moved into the building a decade later.

Over the years, there have been many theories regarding the building's resident ghost, Dorothy. As you can imagine, a lot of speculation has surrounded how the young woman died...and why she stayed. Some thought that she was the victim of a robbery gone wrong. Others thought she was involved in an embezzling scheme and that she took her own life when the crime was uncovered. But most believed she was  caught up in a tragic love affair. One version of the tale suggested that her boyfriend left to take "a job on the boats."

In 2009, the *Toronto Star* conducted a thorough investigation of Dorothy and her mysterious demise. With that, the pieces started coming together.

In 1953, 19-year-old Dorothea Mae Elliott was working at the Bank of Montreal as a teller. She was a vivacious brunette, popular with coworkers and customers alike. Orphaned at nine years old, Dorothy didn't let her sad childhood get her down; in fact, friends and coworkers described her as "the most popular girl in the bank" and "the life of the party."

But on March 11, 1953, when Dorothy arrived at the bank, she appeared to be distressed and her clothing was disheveled. It would later be discovered that she had been involved in a romantic liaison with her bank manager--a married man--and when he chose to end the relationship, she was heartbroken. At some point, she discreetly removed the bank's .38-caliber revolver from a drawer and headed to the women's restroom on the second floor. At around 9 A.M., another female employee entered the room and began to scream: Dorothy had shot herself in the head and no one had even heard the gunshot. She died the next morning at a local hospital.

Cold Spots

Over the years, many employees, customers, and other visitors to the building have experienced odd phenomena, all of which have been attributed to Dorothy. Lights turn on and off on their own, and locked doors open by themselves when no one is around. People working in the building late at night have heard mysterious footsteps, and many have reported hearing moans and screams.

One worker who was setting up for an event witnessed a chair spinning around and around until it moved right into his hand. And while performing at an event in the building, harpist Joanna Jordan actually saw Dorothy's ghost along the second-floor ceiling. When she was invited to play there again, Jordan refused to venture onto that floor alone.

So attached was Dorothy to the old bank building that she remained there even after it was taken over by hockey fans and memorabilia. One young boy visiting the Hall also saw Dorothy's apparition; he screamed after glimpsing a woman with long dark hair gliding back and forth through the walls. Isn't there a penalty for that?

Chapter 5

What Is This?

Unidentified Submerged Objects

Much like their flying brethren, unidentified submerged objects captivate and mystify. But instead of vanishing into the skies, USOs, such as the following, plunge underwater.

✳　✳　✳　✳

Sighting at Puerto Rico Trench

In 1963, while conducting exercises off the coast of Puerto Rico, U.S. Navy submarines encountered something extraordinary. The incident began when a sonar operator aboard an accompanying destroyer reported a strange occurrence. According to the seaman, one of the subs traveling with the armada broke free from the pack to chase a USO. This quarry would be unlike anything the submariners had ever pursued.

Underwater technology in the early 1960s was advancing rapidly. Still, vessels had their limitations. The U.S.S. *Nautilus*, though faster than any submarine that preceded it, was still limited to about 20 knots (23 miles per hour). The bathyscaphe *Trieste*, a deep-sea submersible, could exceed 30,000 feet in depth, but the descent took as long as five hours. Once there, the vessel could not be maneuvered side to side. Knowing this, the submariners were stunned by what they witnessed. The USO was moving at 150 knots (170 miles per hour) and hitting depths greater than 20,000 feet! No underwater vehicles on Earth were capable of such fantastic numbers. Even today, modern nuclear subs have top speeds of about 25 knots (29 miles per hour) and can operate at around 800-plus feet below the surface.

Thirteen separate crafts witnessed the USO as it criss-crossed the Atlantic Ocean over a four-day period. At its deepest, the mystery vehicle reached 27,000 feet. To this day, there's been no earthly explanation offered for the occurrence.

USO With a Bus Pass

In 1964, London bus driver Bob Fall witnessed one of the strangest USO sightings. While transporting a full contingent of passengers, the driver and his fares reported seeing a silver, cigar-shape object dive into the nearby waters of the River Lea. The police attributed the phenomenon to a flight of ducks, despite the obvious incongruence. Severed telephone lines and a large gouge on the river's embankment suggested something far different.

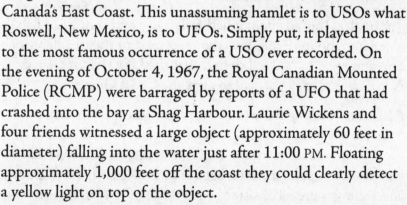

Shag Harbour Incident

The fishing village of Shag Harbour lies on Canada's East Coast. This unassuming hamlet is to USOs what Roswell, New Mexico, is to UFOs. Simply put, it played host to the most famous occurrence of a USO ever recorded. On the evening of October 4, 1967, the Royal Canadian Mounted Police (RCMP) were barraged by reports of a UFO that had crashed into the bay at Shag Harbour. Laurie Wickens and four friends witnessed a large object (approximately 60 feet in diameter) falling into the water just after 11:00 PM. Floating approximately 1,000 feet off the coast they could clearly detect a yellow light on top of the object.

The RCMP promptly contacted the Rescue Coordination Center in Halifax to ask if any aircraft were missing. None were. The object sank into the depths of the water and disappeared from view. When local fishing boats went to the USO crash site, they encountered yellow foam on the water's surface and detected an odd sulfuric smell. No survivors or bodies were ever found. The Royal Canadian Air Force officially labeled the occurrence a UFO, but because the object was last seen under water, such events are now described as USOs.

Pascagoula Incident

On November 6, 1973, at approximately 8:00 PM, a USO was sighted by at least nine fishermen anchored off the coast of Pascagoula, Mississippi. They witnessed an underwater object an estimated five feet in diameter that emitted a strange amber light.

First to spot the USO was Rayme Ryan. He repeatedly poked at the light-emitting object with an oar. Each time he made contact with the strange object, its light would dim and it would move a few feet away, then brighten once again.

Fascinated by the ethereal quality of this submerged question mark, Ryan summoned the others. For the next half hour, the cat-and-mouse game played out in front of the fishermen until Ryan struck the object with a particularly forceful blow. With this action, the USO disappeared from view.

The anglers moved about a half mile away and continued fishing. After about 30 minutes, they returned to their earlier location and were astounded to find that the USO had returned. At this point, they decided to alert the Coast Guard.

After interviewing the witnesses, investigators from the Naval Ship Research and Development Laboratory in Panama City, Florida, submitted their findings: At least nine persons had witnessed an undetermined light source whose characteristics and actions were inconsistent with those of known marine organisms or with an uncontrolled human-made object. Their final report was inconclusive, stating that the object could not be positively identified.

Pleasant Valley: Louis Bromfield's Malabar Farm

Malabar Farm State Park features camping, fishing, hiking, a youth hostel, a scenic overlook, a historic mansion, and a working farm dedicated to promoting sustainable agriculture. But more important than what it offers today is all that was witnessed there in its not-so-distant past.

✳ ✳ ✳ ✳

LOUIS BROMFIELD WAS a Mansfield-born farm boy who studied at Cornell Agricultural College before attending Columbia University for journalism. Although he didn't complete his studies at either school, both disciplines shaped his interests for the rest of his life.

Bromfield wrote his first novel in 1924 and won a Pulitzer Prize for fiction for the novel *Early Autumn* in 1927. He dedicated himself to writing, publishing 33 novels and several screenplays over the next 33 years. He moved his family to France, where they lived for 13 years, socializing with other expatriate writers and artists such as Edith Wharton, Pablo Picasso, Sinclair Lewis, and Gertrude Stein. He helped then-unknown Ernest Hemingway find publication.

Farming and agriculture remained an interest, and he was constantly researching ways to improve topsoil and groundwater while producing greater crop yields without using pesticides. Many of his practices are still used in organic farming today, earning him the reputation as the father of "New Agriculture."

The Big House

Bromfield brought his family back from Europe in 1939 and purchased four adjacent farms in the Pleasant Valley region, collectively calling them Malabar Farm. He selected a farmhouse, demolished all but four rooms, and with the help of architect Louis Lamoreux he added 28 more rooms to the structure, including nine bedrooms, six baths, and four half-baths—all designed to look as if the "Big House" had been constructed over decades, rather than months.

Through his screenplays and time in France, Bromfield had made friends with many of the day's glitterati, and his rural Ohio farm was a surprising mecca for the glamorous. On May 21, 1945, his friends Humphrey Bogart and Lauren Bacall were married in the entrance hall of the Big House. They honeymooned on the grounds.

In 1976, Malabar Farm was opened to the public as a state park. The Big House is open for tours and features many of Bromfield's original furnishings, including his 28-drawer desk (which he never used, preferring a nearby card table instead) and two Grandma Moses paintings. Wedding ceremonies are frequently held on the site of Bogart and Bacall's, although only 25 guests (including the wedding party) are permitted, and all are required to stand due to space constraints.

The Ceely Rose Murders

Not all the farm's ghosts are glamorous or content. Within view of the Big House is the site of a series of sensational murders, retold in Bromfield's novel, *Pleasant Valley*.

Celia "Ceely" Rose, a 23-year-old described as unattractive and slow-witted by newspapers of the day, loved a neighborhood boy who was pleasant and kind to her but didn't return her feelings. Not wishing to hurt her, he told her they could never marry because of her parents' disapproval. Heartbroken, Ceely mixed arsenic into her family's breakfast cottage cheese one day in 1896, killing her father within the day and her brother within the week. Her mother recovered and even helped hide her daughter's crime, but when she spoke of moving, Ceely poisoned her again—this time fatally.

Ceely was tricked into confessing to a family friend and then confined to a mental institution for the rest of her life.

Although her family is limited to haunting the Pleasant Valley cemetery where they are interred, local legend says Ceely's ghost peers sadly out of the upstairs windows of her former house on Malabar Farm.

The Pulitzer Prize wasn't Louis Bromfield's only award: He was posthumously inducted into the Ohio Agricultural Hall of Fame in 1989. (Yes, Ohio has its own Agricultural Hall of Fame.)

Was *The Exorcist* Really Based on a True Story?

Almost everyone is familiar with the movie The Exorcist. The 1973 film stars Ellen Burstyn, Jason Miller, and—most memorably—Linda Blair as a young girl who is possessed by a demon. Naturally, everyone wants to know if the story—which was based on a best-selling novel by William Peter Blatty—is true. The answer to that question is...maybe. hhhh

IN JANUARY 1949, a 13-year-old boy named Roland (some sources say that his name was Robbie) and his family—who lived in Mount Rainier, Maryland—began hearing scratching sounds from behind the walls and inside the ceiling of their house. Believing that their home was infested with mice, Roland's parents called an exterminator. However, the exterminator found no evidence of rodents in the house. After that, the family's problem got worse: They began to hear unexplained footsteps in the home, and objects such as dishes and furniture seemed to relocate on their own.

But these incidents would seem minor compared to what came next: Roland claimed that an invisible entity attacked him and that his bed shook so violently that he couldn't sleep. The sheets and blankets were repeatedly ripped from his bed and tossed onto the floor. One time, Roland tried to grab them, but he was yanked onto the floor with the bedcovers still clenched in his fists.

Roland liked board games, and his aunt "Tillie"—a woman who had a strong interest in the supernatural—had taught him how to use a Ouija board before she died. Some blamed the Ouija board for causing the trouble, claiming that it had allowed a demonic being to come into the home and target Roland for terror.

Not Such Good Vibrations

By this time, the family was convinced that an evil entity was afoot, so they appealed to a Lutheran minister named Schulze for help. Reverend Schulze prayed for Roland and had his congregation do so as well. He even took Roland to his own home so the boy could get some sleep. However, both the bed and an armchair that Roland tried to sleep in there vibrated and moved, allowing the boy no rest. Schulze noted that Roland seemed to be in a trance while these incidents occurred.

If Schulze had any doubt that it was time to call in the cavalry, he was certainly convinced when scratches mysteriously materialized on Roland's body. These marks were then replaced by words that appeared to be made by claws. The word *Louis* was clearly visible, which was interpreted as St. Louis—Roland's mother's hometown. With all signs pointing to the need for an exorcism, Father Edward Albert Hughes of St. James Catholic Church was summoned.

Truth or Fiction?

At this point, accounts of the story begin to splinter, as no two versions are alike. According to the version that has been more or less accepted as fact, Father Hughes went to see Roland and was disturbed when the boy addressed him in Latin—a language that was unknown to the youth. Hughes decided to perform an exorcism, during which a loose bedspring slashed him. The priest was supposedly so shaken by the ordeal that he was never the same again. (However, according to some sources, this part of the story never happened; they say that Hughes only saw Roland once at St. James, Roland never spoke in Latin, and Hughes never performed an exorcism on the boy, nor was he physically or emotionally affected by it. It is unclear why someone felt that dramatic license needed to be taken here, because the actual events are strange enough.)

During Roland's visit to Hughes, the priest suggested using blessed candles and special prayers to help the boy. But when Roland's mother did this, a comb flew across the room, hitting the candles and snuffing them out. Other objects also flew around the room, and at one point, a Bible was thrown at the boy's feet. Supposedly, Roland had to stop attending school because his desk shook so badly.

It seems that an attempt was made to baptize Roland into the Catholic faith as a way of helping him. However, this didn't work out so well: As his uncle drove him to the ceremony, the boy grabbed him by the throat and screamed that the baptism wouldn't work.

The Battle of St. Louis

Finally, at their wits' end, the family decided to stay with relatives in the St. Louis area. Unfortunately, the distance between Maryland and Missouri proved to be no deterrent to the invisible entity, and the assaults on Roland continued. In St. Louis, a relative introduced the boy and his family to Jesuit priest Father William Bowdern, who, in turn, employed Father Raymond J. Bishop, a pastor at St. Francis Xavier Church in St. Louis, in his efforts to help the family.

Father Bishop made several attempts to stop the attacks on the boy but to no avail. After Bishop sprinkled the boy's mattress with holy water in the shape of a cross, the attacks ceased. However, after Bishop left the room, the boy suddenly cried out in pain; when his pajama top was pulled up, Roland had numerous scratches across his abdomen. He could not have done it to himself, as he was in the presence of several witnesses at all times.

After more nights of violence against Roland, Father Bishop returned—this time with Father Bowdern. They prayed in the boy's room and then left. But as soon as they departed, loud noises began emanating from the room. When family members investigated, they found that an extremely heavy bookcase had swiveled around, a bench had overturned, and the boy's mattress was once again shaking and bouncing. It was at this point that another exorcism was deemed the only sensible course of action left.

The exorcism was a desperate battle that was waged over the course of several months. Some of it took place in the rectory at St. Francis Xavier Church, some of it at a hospital, and some of it at Roland's home; one source says that the boy was exorcised no less than 20 times. During this time, practically everything and anything typically associated with an exorcism occurred: Roland's body jerked in uncontrollable spasms, he experienced projectile vomiting, and he spit and cursed at the priests; he also conveyed information that he couldn't possibly have known. However, his head didn't spin completely around like Linda Blair's did in *The Exorcist*.

Gone, but Certainly Not Forgotten

Eventually, Bowdern's persistence paid off. He repeatedly practiced the ritual and ignored the torrent of physical and verbal abuse hurled at him by the entity that was residing inside the boy. Finally, in mid-April 1949, Roland spoke with a voice that identified itself as St. Michael. He ordered Satan and all demons to leave the boy alone. For the next few minutes, Roland went into a titanic rage, as if all the furies of the world were battling inside of him. Suddenly, he became quiet, turned to the priests, and simply said, "He's gone."

The entity was gone, and fortunately, Roland remembered little about the ordeal. Some months later, a 20-year-old Georgetown University student named William Peter Blatty spotted an article in *The Washington Post* about Roland's experience. He let the idea of demonic possession percolate in his brain for years before finally writing his book, which became a best seller. Out of privacy concerns, Blatty changed so many details from the actual case that the source was virtually unrecognizable—until the intense publicity surrounding the movie forced the "real" story out.

Over the years, numerous theories regarding the incident have been suggested: Some say that it was an elaborate hoax gone too far, while others claim that it was the result of poltergeist activity or an actual possession. Regardless, this case continues to resonate in American culture.

The Real Hound of the Baskervilles

In March 1901, Sir Arthur Conan Doyle believed that he was going on a relaxing golf holiday. At the time, he also thought that he was finished writing Sherlock Holmes stories. But he was wrong on both counts. His experiences at England's Royal Links Hotel in the town of Cromer led to the most famous Holmes adventure ever, and it all began with the story of a shaggy dog.

Soon after he arrived at the Royal Links Hotel, the famous author heard an amazing tale. A huge, sinister, ghostly dog was said to haunt the nearby coast, and the animal could be seen from the hotel on stormy nights. Supposedly, the black dog was the size of a calf and had glowing red eyes and an odor like brimstone. In Conan Doyle's words, it was "a spectral hound, black, silent, and monstrous." The author immediately began searching for this extraordinary beast.

✳   ✳   ✳   ✳

England's Black Shuck

Throughout most of England, this type of terrifying hound is called a "black shuck." Some people describe it as an unusually large black wolfhound; others say it is a hound from hell. Shucks have been reported for hundreds of years, including some late 20th-century encounters with the police.

Most shuck sightings occur along England's picturesque southeastern coast. The town of Cromer, where Conan Doyle vacationed, is at the heart of this area. During the daytime, Cromer is a deceptively quaint and peaceful town, but on stormy nights, the town has a much darker reputation. In his 1901 book, *Highways and Byways of East Anglia*, author William Dutt described Cromer's black shuck. "He takes the form of a huge black dog, and prowls along dark lanes and lonesome field footpaths, where, although his howling makes the hearer's blood run cold, his footfalls make no sound."

Neither an Officer nor a Gentleman

Squire Richard Cabell—the basis of Arthur Conan Doyle's villain, Hugo Baskerville—may have been the first person killed by a black shuck. Cabell was born around 1620 and grew up in Brook Manor near what is now England's eerie Dartmoor National Park. Like his father, Cabell supported the Royalists, who taxed peasants rather than landowners. This made the Cabell family unpopular with their neighbors, and some people claimed that Richard Cabell had sold his soul to the devil.

The Black Shuck's Revenge

When the Royalists were defeated in the English Civil War, Cabell hastily married Elizabeth Fowell, the daughter of the local tax collector. According to local lore, Cabell resented his wife and was also insanely jealous and abusive toward her. One night, Elizabeth and her dog attempted to flee across the moor as Squire Cabell chased after them.

When Cabell caught up with his wife and began to beat her, the dog increased in size and its skin stretched over its expanding frame, giving the hound a skeletal appearance. Then, his eyes began to glow with rage, or perhaps the fires of hell. The dog ripped Cabell's throat out and then disappeared across the moor, leaving the corpse at Elizabeth's feet. From that moment on, similar hounds have been sighted around Dartmoor as well as along Norfolk's coastline.

The Devil Claims His Own

Soon after Richard Cabell was interred in the Holy Trinity Church graveyard, people began reporting strange occurrences at the cemetery. Some claimed they'd seen Cabell on stormy nights, rising from his grave and leading a pack of phantom hounds on a hunt across the moor, possibly searching for Elizabeth. According to legend, the squire's eyes glowed red with rage, and he would attack anyone who crossed his path.

Allegedly for protection, the town placed a heavy stone slab over Cabell's grave. Still, the reports of his ghost continued, along with sightings of the black shuck. Later, a huge stone building—referred to as "the sepulchre"—was constructed around the grave. A heavy wooden door was added, along with metal bars on the windows, to keep Cabell's spirit inside.

To this day, people report an ominous red glow emanating from inside the building. According to local lore, if you run around the crypt seven times and reach through the window, either Cabell or the devil will lick or bite your fingertips.

Cabell's Revenge

Whether these stories of Cabell's afterlife prison are true or not, the graveyard and the church next to it have been the victims of extraordinarily bad luck since the 1800s.

First, the cemetery became a target for body snatchers in the 1820s. Then the church caught fire several times, including a blaze in 1849 that was attributed to arson. Later, around 1885, the church was struck by lightning. Some years after that, the stained-glass windows shattered and had to be replaced. The church was plagued by problems like these until 1992, when a fire started under the altar. The flames were so intense that the church's ancient Norman font exploded from the heat. Area residents, weary of such calamities, decided not to repair the church. Today, Holy Trinity Church is an empty shell and perhaps a monument to the Cabell curse.

The Real Baskerville

Sir Arthur Conan Doyle's novel *The Hound of the Baskervilles* matches many of the chilling details of the Richard Cabell legend. He describes the fictional Hugo Baskerville as "a most wild, profane, and godless man" with "a certain wanton and cruel humour." In the novel, Baskerville kidnaps the lovely daughter of a nearby landowner and holds her captive until she marries him. After mistreating his wife, Baskerville is attacked and killed by a vicious, phantom hound.

Conan Doyle intended *The Hound of the Baskervilles* to be fiction, so he did not choose to call his villain Richard Cabell. Instead, the author whimsically used the surname of William Henry "Harry" Baskerville, the coachman who drove him around Devon during his research. Interestingly, Harry was a distant relative of Elizabeth Fowell, whose storied flight from Richard Cabell was the inspiration for the legend of Dartmoor's black shucks.

The Shucks Still Roam

On stormy days and damp nights, many believe that black shucks can still be seen throughout England. Some also think that a black shuck left scratches and burn marks on the door at Blythburgh's Holy Trinity Church, also called the Cathedral of the Marshes. Throughout the 20th century, shuck sightings continued to be reported. Shuck Lane in the coastal Norfolk town of Overstrand was given that name because the beast is said to frequently appear there.

According to paranormal researchers, the best place to find a black shuck is at Coltishall Bridge just north of Norwich. If you walk that bridge at night, you may sense or hear the beast. If you are especially unlucky, you may actually see it. But close your eyes if you think a black shuck is nearby, for—as William Dutt reported in his book—"to meet him is to be warned that your death will occur by the end of the year."

Unexplained Phenomena

If a phenomenon can't be readily explained, does that make it any less true to those who witnessed it?

✳ ✳ ✳ ✳

The Philadelphia Experiment

THE PHILADELPHIA EXPERIMENT (aka Project Rainbow) is one for the "too strange not to be true" file. Allegedly, on October 28, 1943, a supersecret experiment was being conducted at the Philadelphia Naval Shipyard. Its objective? To make the *USS Eldridge* and all of its inhabitants disappear! That day, some reported that the *Eldridge* became almost entirely invisible amidst a flash of blue light. Inexplicably, it had not only vanished but also tele-transported—at the same instant, it was witnessed some 375 miles away at the U.S.

Naval Base in Norfolk, Virginia. Legend has it that most sailors involved in the experiment became violently ill afterward. They were the lucky ones. Others were supposedly fused to the ship's deck or completely vaporized and were never seen again. Justifiably horrified by these results, the navy is said to have pulled the plug on future experiments and employed brainwashing techniques to help the affected seamen forget what happened.

Moodus Noises

The Moodus Noises are thunderlike sounds that emanate from caves near East Haddam, Connecticut, where the Salmon and Moodus Rivers meet. The name itself is derived from the Native American word *machemoodus*, which means "place of noises." When European settlers filtered into the area in the late 1600s, the Wangunk tribe warned them about the odd, supernatural sounds. Whether or not anything otherworldly exists there is open to debate. In 1979, seismologists showed that the noises were always accompanied by small earthquakes (some measuring as low as magnitude 2 on the Richter scale) spread over a small area some 5,000 feet deep by 800 feet wide. But this doesn't explain the fact that no known faultline exists at Moodus. Nor does it describe how small tremors—producing 100 times less ground motion than is detectable by human beings—can generate big, bellowing booms. The mystery and the booms continue.

Rock Concert

Visitors looking to entertain themselves at Pennsylvania's Ringing Rocks Park often show up toting hammers. Seems odd, but they're necessary for the proper tone. Ringing Rocks is a seven-acre boulder field that runs about ten feet deep. For reasons that are still unexplained, some of these rocks ring like bells when struck lightly by a hammer or other object. Because igneous diabase rocks don't usually do this, the boulder field has caused quite a stir through the years. In 1890, Dr. J. J. Ott held what may have been the world's first "rock concert" at the park. He assembled rocks of different pitches, enlisted the aid of a brass band for accompaniment, and went to town.

Cry Me a Red River

Tales of "crying" statues have become almost commonplace. Sometimes they're revealed as hoaxes, but other times they can truly confound the senses. The Mother Mary statue that cries "tears of blood" at the Vietnamese Catholic Martyrs Church in Sacramento apparently began crying in November 2005 when parishioners discovered a dark reddish substance flowing from her left eye. A priest wiped it away only to see it miraculously reappear a moment later. News of the incident spread like... well, like news of a crying Mother Mary statue. Soon, hordes of the faithful made a pilgrimage to witness the miracle. Skeptics say that black paint used as eyeliner on the statue is the true culprit and that her "tears" are closer to this color than red. The faithful think the nonbelievers are blinded by anything but the light because the tears continually reappear even after the excess substance is wiped away.

The Year Without a Summer

"The Year Without a Summer" may sound like Armegeddon, but these words describe an actual year in human history—the year 1816, which Americans nicknamed "eighteen-hundred-and-froze-to-death." It was a year of floods, droughts, and unparalleled summertime frosts that destroyed crops, spread diseases, incited riots, and otherwise wrought havoc upon the world. The culprit of this global meteorological mayhem was the eruption of Tambora, a volcano on the Indonesian island of Sumbawa—the largest explosive eruption in recorded history.

✳ ✳ ✳ ✳

Monster Eruption

TAMBORA WAS CONSIDERED inactive until 1812, when a dense cloud of smoke was seen rising above its summit. But neither the smoke, which grew denser and denser over the next three years, nor the occasional rumbles heard from the mountain, could prepare the islanders for what was to come.

When Tambora exploded in April 1815, the blast was heard 1,700 miles away and so much ash was ejected into the atmosphere that islands 250 miles away experienced complete darkness. Only a couple thousand of the island's 12,000 inhabitants survived the fiery three-day cataclysm. Altogether, the eruption and its after-effects killed more than 90,000 people throughout Indonesia, mostly through disease, pollution of drinking water, and famine. Ash rains destroyed crops on every island within hundreds of miles.

Global Cooling

Along with about 140 gigatons of magma, Tambora expelled hundreds of millions of tons of fine ash, which was spread worldwide through winds and weather systems. It is this ash that scientists now blame for the subsequent "Year Without a Summer." The sulfate aerosol particles contained in it remained in the atmosphere for years and reflected back solar radiation, cooling the globe. The effect was aggravated by the activity of other volcanoes: Soufrière St. Vincent in the West Indies (1812), Mount Mayon in the Philippines (1814), and Suwanose–Jima in Japan, which erupted continuously from 1813 to 1814. To make matters worse, all this took place during an extended period of low solar energy output called the Dalton Minimum, which lasted from about 1795 to the 1820s.

Spring of 1816 in the New World

Although the last three months of 1815 and February 1816 were all warmer than usual, the mild winter hesitated to turn into spring. Under the influence of the hot ash winds from the equator, the low-pressure system usually sitting over Iceland at this time of year shifted south toward the British Isles, and America was penetrated by polar air masses. By March, weather was becoming erratic.

On Sunday, March 17, Richmond, Virginia, was treated to summerlike temperatures; however, the next day, there was hail and sleet, and on Tuesday morning, the flowers of apricot and peach trees were covered with icicles. At the end of May, there were still frosts and snowfall from Ohio to Connecticut.

June 1816

The first days of June were deceptively warm, with 70s, 80s, and even low 90s in the northeastern United States. But on June 6, temperatures suddenly dropped into the 40s and it began to rain. Within hours, rain turned into snow, birds dropped dead in the streets, and some trees began shedding their still unexpanded leaves. This distemper of nature continued through June 11, when the wind shifted and the cold spell was over...or so people thought.

But strange weather continued to vex the population. Gales and violent hailstorms pummeled crops. On June 27, West Chester, Pennsylvania, reportedly experienced a torrential storm where hailstones the size of walnuts fell from the sky.

July 1816

Just as the farmers were beginning to think that the damage to their crops might be minimal, another cold spell checked their hopes. On July 6, a strong northwestern wind set in, and for the next four days, winter descended upon New England and the Mid-Atlantic states once more as temperatures again dropped to the 30s and 40s. The outlook for a successful harvest was looking bleaker day by freezing day; what vegetation remained intact in New England was flavorless and languid.

August 1816

The folk wisdom that bad things come in threes proved itself before the end of the summer. On August 20, another wave of frost and snow finished off the fruit, vegetables, vines, and meager remains of the corn and bean crops. The fields were said to be "as empty and white as October." For many farmers, that spelled ruin. Even though wheat and rye yielded enough to carry the country through to the next season without mass starvation, panic and speculation drove the price of flour from $3 to nearly $20 per barrel. Animal feed became so expensive that cattle had to be slaughtered en masse. Many New England farmers, unable to cope with the disastrous season, loaded up their belongings and headed west.

Summer Overseas

Meanwhile, Europe was faring no better. Snow fell in several countries in June. Alpine glaciers advanced, threatening to engulf villages and dam rivers. In France, grapes were not ripe enough to be harvested until November, and the wine made from them was undrinkable. Wheat yields in Europe reportedly fell by 20 to 40 percent, both because of cold and water damage and because rains delayed and hampered harvesting.

Famine hit Switzerland especially hard. People began eating moss, sorrel, and cats, and official assistance had to be given to the populace to help them distinguish poisonous and nonpoisonous plants. In Rhineland, people reportedly dug through the fields for rotten remains of the previous year's potato harvest. Wheat, oats, and potatoes failed in Britain and Ireland, and a typhus epidemic swept the British Isles, killing tens of thousands. Grain prices doubled on average; in west-central Europe, they rose between three and seven times their normal price. This was a disaster for the masses of poor people, whose average expenditures for bread totaled between one-quarter and one-half of their total income.

Dearth led to hunger, and high prices led to increased poverty, which led to mass vagrancy and begging. People looted grain storages and pillaged large farms. There was a wave of emigrations to America. The European economy was still unsteady from the aftermath of the Napoleonic wars, and the crisis of 1816 led to a massive retreat from liberal ideas. By 1820, Europe was in the grip of political and economic conservatism—thanks to a volcanic eruption in Indonesia.

Who's to Blame?

Theories for why summer failed to come in 1816 abound. Many lay the blame directly on the sun. Due to volcanic particles in the air, the solar disk had been dimmed all year, which made large sunspots visible to the naked eye. Others believed that the ice persisting in the Atlantic and the Great Lakes was absorbing great quantities of heat from the atmosphere.

Silver Lining

In 1816, Geneva, Switzerland, had experienced the coldest summer it would face between 1753 and 1960. It was this bad weather that kept Mary Wollstonecraft Godwin, Percy Shelley, and Lord Byron indoors at the Villa Diodati on the shores of Lake Geneva in June 1816. As they listened to the wind howl and watched the awesome thunderstorms rage over the lake, they recited poetry and told each other ghost stories, which they vowed to record on paper.

His mood very much under the weather, Byron penned his lengthy poem *Darkness*, a vivid imagination of the Apocalypse, which the weather made seem altogether at hand. ("Morn came and went, and came, and brought no day....") And Mary Wollstonecraft Godwin, who would later become Mary Shelley, Percy's wife, began work on a masterpiece that would eventually bear the title *Frankenstein or the Modern Prometheus*.

Strange Structures

Humans have the capacity to achieve great things, conquer the seemingly impossible, and invent wonders that make our world a better place. However, sometimes they just like to build things that are big, tall, or strange.

✳   ✳   ✳   ✳

Personal Vanity Gets Etched in Stone

SOUTH DAKOTA HAS Mount Rushmore, but nestled in the Catskill Mountains is the town of Prattsville, New York, which features Pratt Rocks—a set of relief carvings begun 84 years before its famous western counterpart. Zadock Pratt, who founded the world's largest tannery in the 1830s, commissioned a local sculptor to immortalize his visage high up on a mountainside. The numerous stone carvings include a coat of arms, Pratt's own bust, his business milestones, and even his personal accomplishments, such as his two terms in the U.S. House of Representatives. Carvings also include a shrine to Pratt's son George, who was killed during the Civil War. But the strangest bit found at this site is a recessed tomb that was intended to house Pratt's decaying corpse for eternity. It leaked, Pratt balked, and the chamber remains empty.

Mega-Megaliths

The offbeat dream of Bill Cohea, Jr., and Frederick Lindkvist, two highly spiritual fellows, Columcille was designed to resemble an ancient Scottish religious retreat located on the Isle of Iona. More than 80 oblong stones are "planted" in a Bangor, Pennsylvania, field to approximate the ancient site, a place where some say "the veil is thin between worlds." In addition to the megaliths, Columcille has enchanting chapels, altars, bell towers, cairns, and gates—enough features to lure Harry Potter fans into an entire day of exploration. Cohea and Lindkvist began their ever-evolving project as a spiritual retreat in 1978. They encourage everyone to visit their nondenominational mystical park. Their request? Simply "be."

Stacked Really High

It's quite surprising to encounter a 1,216-foot-tall smokestack, especially when that chimney is located in a rural town deep in western Pennsylvania. Homer City Generating Station produces electricity by burning coal. But the process has one troubling side effect: Its effluence can be toxic in certain quantities. The super-tall smokestack's purpose is to harmlessly disperse this undesirable by-product, thereby rendering it safe. It does this by releasing the agents high up in the atmosphere where they (theoretically) have ample time to dilute before falling back to Earth. At present, this soaring chunk of steel-reinforced concrete ranks as the third tallest in the world, just behind a 1,250-foot-tall smokestack located in Canada and a 1,377-foot-tall monster over in Kazakhstan.

Fee! Fie! Foe! Fum!

A drive through Staunton, Virginia, may leave some wondering if they've mistakenly entered the land of the giants. After all, an 18-foot-tall watering can and a six-foot-tall flowerpot are displayed on the main boulevard. But fear not. It's no giant who dwells in this hamlet but rather an average-size gent named Willie Ferguson. A large concentration of this metal fabricator's giant works can be seen on the grounds of his sculpture studio. At this metal "imaginarium," visitors will find a six-foot-long dagger, a ten-foot-long set of crutches, a six-foot-tall work boot—everything, it seems, but the proverbial beanstalk.

Cross With Caution

If you've crossed Vermont's Brookfield Floating Bridge by car, you're aware of its treachery. If you tried it on a motorcycle, you probably took an unplanned swim. That's because the lake that the bridge is supposed to cross occasionally crosses it. The 320-foot-long all-wooden Brookfield Bridge rests on 380 tarred, oaken barrels that were designed to adjust to the level of Sunset Lake and keep the bridge deck high and dry. But more often than not, they allow the bridge to sink several inches below the surface. Why does this bridge float in the first place? Sunset Lake is too deep to support a traditional, pillared span, so since 1820, impromptu "water ballet" maneuvers have been taking place as vehicles amble across.

Tower City

As drivers creep along I-76 just west of Philadelphia, they witness a stand of super-tall broadcasting masts towering over a suburban neighborhood. The Roxborough Antenna Farm is to broadcasting towers what New York City is to skyscrapers. In the land of broadcasting, height equals might, so the higher the tower, the better the signal strength. With eight TV/FM masts jutting above the 1,000-foot mark (the tallest stretches to 1,276 feet), the array easily outclasses most skyscrapers in height.

The reason these big sticks exist in such a concentrated area? Location, location, location. The Roxborough site is a unique setting that features geographical height, proper zoning clearances, and favorable proximity to the city—a trifecta by industry standards.

Circle Marks the Spot: The Mystery of Crop Circles

The result of cyclonic winds? Attempted alien communication? Evidence of hungry cows with serious OCD? There are many theories as to how crop circles, or grain stalks flattened in recognizable patterns, have come to exist. Most people dismiss them as pranks, but there are more than a few who believe there's something otherworldly going on.

✳   ✳   ✳   ✳

Ye Ole Crop Circle

SOME EXPERTS BELIEVE the first crop circles date back to the late 1600s, but there isn't much evidence to support them. Other experts cite evidence of more than 400 simple circles 6 to 20 feet in diameter that appeared worldwide hundreds of years ago. The kinds of circles they refer to are still being found today, usually after huge, cyclonic thunderstorms pass over a large expanse of agricultural land. These circles are much smaller and not nearly as precise as the geometric, mathematically complex circles that started cropping up in the second half of the 20th century. Still, drawings and writings about these smaller circles lend weight to the claims of believers that the crop circle phenomenon isn't a new thing.

The International Crop Circle Database reports stories of "UFO nests" in British papers during the 1960s. About a decade or so later, crop circles fully captured the attention (and the imagination) of the masses.

No, Virginia, There Aren't Any Aliens

In 1991, two men from Southampton, England, came forward with a confession. Doug Bower and Dave Chorley admitted that they were responsible for the majority of the crop circles found in England during the preceding two decades.

Inspired by stories of "UFO nests" in the 1960s, the two decided to add a little excitement to their sleepy town. With boards, string, and a few simple navigational tools, the men worked through the night to create complex patterns in fields that could be seen from the road. It worked, and before long, much of the Western world was caught up in crop circle fever. Some claimed it was irrefutable proof that UFOs were landing on Earth. Others said God was trying to communicate with humans "through the language of mathematics." For believers, there was no doubt that supernatural or extraterrestrial forces were at work. But skeptics were thrilled to hear the confession from Bower and Chorley, since they never believed the circles to be anything but a prank in the first place.

Before the men came forward, more crop circles appeared throughout the 1980s and '90s, many of them not made by Bower and Chorley. Circles "mysteriously" occurred in Australia, Canada, the United States, Argentina, India, and even Afghanistan. In 1995, more than 200 cases of crop circles were reported worldwide. In 2001, a formation that appeared in Wiltshire, England, contained 409 circles and covered more than 12 acres.

Many were baffled that anyone could believe these large and admittedly rather intricate motifs were anything but human-made. Plus, the more media coverage crop circles garnered, the more new crop circles appeared. Other people came forward, admitting that they were the "strange and unexplained power" behind the circles. Even then, die-hard believers dismissed the hoaxers, vehemently suggesting that they were either players in a government cover-up, captives of aliens forced to throw everyone off track, or just average Joes looking for 15 minutes of fame by claiming to have made something that was clearly the work of nonhumans.

Scientists were deployed to ascertain the facts. In 1999, a well-funded team of experts was assembled to examine numerous crop circles in the UK. The verdict? At least 80 percent of the circles were, beyond a shadow of a doubt, created by humans. Footprints, abandoned tools, and video of a group of hoaxers caught in the act all debunked the theory that crop circles were created by aliens.

But Still...

So if crop circles are nothing more than hoaxers having fun or artists playing with a unique medium, why are we still so interested? Movies such as *Signs* in 2002 capitalized on the public's fascination with the phenomenon, and crop circles still capture headlines. Skeptics will scoff, but from time to time, there is a circle that doesn't quite fit the profile of a human-made prank.

There have been claims that fully functional cell phones cease to work once the caller steps inside certain crop circles. Could it be caused by some funky ion-scramble emitted by an extra-terrestrial force? Some researchers have tried to re-create the circles and succeeded, but only with the use of high-tech tools and equipment that wouldn't be available to the average prankster. If all of these circles were made by humans, why are so few people busted for trespassing in the middle of the night? And where are all the footprints?

Eyewitness accounts of UFOs rising from fields can hardly be considered irrefutable evidence, but there are several reports from folks who swear they saw ships, lights, and movement in the sky just before crop circles were discovered.

Deadly Bling?: The Curse of the Hope Diamond

Diamonds are a girl's best friend, a jeweler's meal ticket, and serious status symbols for those who can afford them. But there's one famous diamond whose brilliant color comes with a cloudy history. The Hope Diamond is one of the world's most beautiful gemstones—and one that some say causes death and suffering to those who possess it. So is the Hope Diamond really cursed? There's a lot of evidence that says "no," but there have been some really strange coincidences.

✳ ✳ ✳ ✳

The Origin of Hope

IT'S BELIEVED THAT this shockingly large, blue-hued diamond came from India several centuries ago. At the time, the exceptional diamond was slightly more than 112 carats, which is enormous. (On average, a diamond in an engagement ring ranges from a quarter to a full carat.) According to legend, a thief stole the diamond from the eye of a Hindu statue, but scholars don't think the shape would have been right to sit in the face of a statue. Nevertheless, the story states that the young thief was torn apart by wild dogs soon after he sold the diamond, making this the first life claimed by the jewel.

Courts, Carats, and Carnage

In the mid-1600s, a French jeweler named Tavernier purchased the diamond in India and kept it for several years without incident before selling it to King Louis XIV in 1668, along with several other jewels. The king recut the diamond in 1673, taking it down to 67 carats. This new cut emphasized the jewel's clarity, and Louis liked to wear the "Blue Diamond of the Crown" around his neck on special occasions. He, too, owned the gemstone without much trouble.

More than a hundred years later, France's King Louis XVI possessed the stone. In 1791, when the royal family tried to flee the country, the crown jewels were hidden for safekeeping, but they were stolen the following year. Some were eventually returned, but the blue diamond was not.

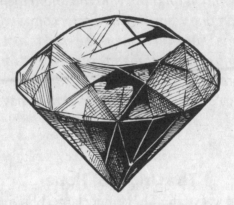

King Louis XVI and his wife Marie Antoinette died by guillotine in 1793. Those who believe in the curse are eager to include these two romantic figures in the list of cursed owners, but their deaths probably had more to do with the angry mobs of the French Revolution than a piece of jewelry.

Right This Way, Mr. Hope

It is unknown what happened to the big blue diamond from the time it was stolen in France until it appeared in England nearly 50 years later. When the diamond reappeared, it wasn't the same size as before—it was now only about 45 carats. Had it been cut again to disguise its identity? Or was this a new diamond altogether? Because the blue diamond was so unique in color and size, it was believed to be the diamond in question.

In the 1830s, wealthy banker Henry Philip Hope purchased the diamond, henceforth known as the Hope Diamond. When he died (of natural causes) in 1839, he bequeathed the gem to his oldest nephew, and it eventually ended up with the nephew's grandson, Francis Hope.

Francis Hope is the next person supposedly cursed by the diamond. Francis was a notorious gambler and was generally bad with money. Though he owned the diamond, he was not allowed to sell it without his family's permission, which he finally got in 1901 when he announced he was bankrupt. It's doubtful that the diamond had anything to do with Francis's bad luck, though that's what some believers suggest.

Coming to America

Joseph Frankel and Sons of New York purchased the diamond from Francis, and by 1909, after a few trades between the world's most notable jewelers, the Hope Diamond found itself in the hands of famous French jeweler Pierre Cartier. That's where rumors of a curse may have actually originated.

Allegedly, Cartier came up with the curse concept in order to sell the diamond to Evalyn Walsh McLean, a rich socialite who claimed that bad luck charms always turned into good luck charms in her hands. Cartier may have embellished the terrible things that had befallen previous owners of his special diamond so that McLean would purchase it—which she did. Cartier even inserted a clause in the sales contract, which stated that if any fatality occurred in the family within six months, the Hope Diamond could be exchanged for jewelry valued at the $180,000 McLean paid for the stone. Nevertheless, McLean wore the diamond on a chain around her neck constantly, and the spookiness surrounding the gem started picking up steam.

Whether or not anything can be blamed on the jewel, it certainly can't be denied that McLean had a pretty miserable life starting around the time she purchased the diamond. Her eldest son died at age nine in a fiery car crash. Years later, her 25-year-old daughter killed herself. Not long after that, her husband was declared insane and was committed to a mental institution for the rest of his life. With rumors swirling about the Hope Diamond's curse, everyone pointed to the necklace when these terrible events took place.

In 1947, when McLean died (while wearing the diamond) at age 60, the Hope Diamond and most of her other treasures were sold to pay off debts. American jeweler Harry Winston forked over the $1 million asking price for McLean's entire jewelry collection.

Hope on Display

If Harry Winston was scared of the alleged curse, he didn't show it. Winston had long wanted to start a collection of gemstones to display for the general public, so in 1958, when the Smithsonian Institute started one in Washington, D.C., he sent the Hope Diamond to them as a centerpiece. These days, it's kept under glass as a central figure for the National Gem Collection at the National Museum of Natural History. So far, no one's dropped dead from checking it out.

Getting a Charge Out of Life

It may seem odd to compare the human body to an electric power generator, but rare cases around the world have shown that some people are born with shocking abilities...literally. Jacqueline Priestman, a British woman, consistently produces ten times the static electricity of a normal human being.

✳   ✳   ✳   ✳

How to "Conduct" Oneself

PRIESTMAN, WHO IRONICALLY married an electrician before she knew about her strange ability, grew up with no more than the usual mild electromagnetic field that surrounds every human. But when she turned 22, sparks began to fly. Priestman noticed that her mere touch would cause ordinary household appliances to short out and fizzle, while others could use the same appliances with no problem. She could also change the channels on her TV by going near it.

Priestman has had to buy at least 30 new vacuum cleaners in her married life, plus five irons and several washing machines.

Michael Shallis, a lecturer at Oxford University and a former astrophysicist, studied Priestman and told a British newspaper in 1985 that she was actually able to transmit tiny bolts of "lightning" that could affect any electrical system nearby. He had no explanation for the phenomenon but did say that most similar cases he had investigated involved women. For example, Pauline Shaw flooded her house every time she tried to do laundry because the washing machine fuses would blow when she touched the dials. The washer's door would then pop open and turn the machine into a fountain.

For more than four years, Shallis studied 600 people with Priestman's condition and, eventually, wrote a book about them called *The Electric Connection*.

SLI-ding Through Life

There is a name for those like Priestman and Shaw. Because people with abnormal amounts of static electricity often cause streetlights to flicker when they pass by, scientists call the strange disorder Street Light Interference, or SLI. People with the condition are called SLI-ders, or Sliders.

An older name for the phenomenon is High Voltage Syndrome, or HVS. Around 1930, one HVS patient, Count John Berenyi of Hungary, was reportedly able to make neon light tubes glow merely by holding them. And according to author Vincent Gaddis, the National Safety Council investigates what he calls "human spark plugs"—people who can start fires with the electrical abundance of their mere presence. One woman made a rather poor vocational choice in the early 1940s when she got a job gluing shoes together with rubber cement, a highly flammable substance. She allegedly started at least five fires in the factory and could ignite a pail of rubber cement merely by standing near it. She had to quit after suffering severe burns in one of the fires.

Even babies can act as superconductors. In 1869, a child born in France was so highly charged that anyone who approached him received a sharp electric shock. He even exhibited a faint glow around his hands. The infant died from undetermined causes when he was only nine months old, and, according to witnesses, his entire body radiated light at the time of his passing.

Radiant Blood

The strange baby was not the only human known to glow. Luminous people have been reported in many circumstances, and their abilities are often tied to medical conditions. Anna Monaro, an Italian woman, gained attention in 1934, when her breasts began to spontaneously emit blue phosphorescent light while she was sleeping. The weird condition lasted for weeks and drew many eminent doctors and scientists to study her firsthand. They were even able to capture the glow on film. Many theories were offered, from "electrical and magnetic organisms in the woman's body" to "radiant blood." Eventually, the bizarre condition went away and did not return.

Through No Fault of Her Own

A Welsh woman named Mary Jones set off a religious fervor in 1905, when amazing forms of light appeared to emit from her body. Jones had already gained some notoriety as a local preacher when people began to observe glowing, exploding balls of lightning and electric-blue rectangles hovering near her as she spoke. The light show lasted for several months and attracted hundreds of believers, along with a cadre of scientific observers. Various explanations were offered for the lights, from a misidentification of the planet Venus to fault lines under the chapel where Jones preached. Scientists speculated that movements of the earth had stressed the bedrock, issuing gases that resulted in geomagnetic anomalies in the air above.

Lightning Reactions

Not everyone with an electric attraction finds the sensation enjoyable. Grace Charlesworth, a woman from the UK, had lived in a house for almost 40 years when, in 1968, she began receiving unexplainable shocks both indoors and out. The weird voltage was strong enough to spin Charlesworth's body in a complete circle, and at times, it would even make her head shake uncontrollably. The voltage was sometimes visible as sparks, and she could escape only by leaving her house or yard, as she was never bothered elsewhere.

Charlesworth blamed her problem on the noise from a compressor in a nearby factory, but fixing the compressor did not stop the mysterious electricity. One possible contributing factor was that the house had been hit by lightning five times.

Some people become so sensitive to electrical currents that they cannot even live in homes with any sort of wiring or appliances. An Irish woman named Margaret Cousins had to move to a cabin with no utilities in 1996 because her condition had become so painful. But two years later she had to move again after two cell phone towers were installed nearby and caused her pain to return.

An Underground Mystery: The Hollow Earth Theory

For centuries, people have believed that Earth is hollow. They claim that civilizations may live inside Earth's core or that it might be a landing base for alien spaceships. This sounds like fantasy, but believers point to startling evidence, including explorers' reports and modern photos taken from space.

✳   ✳   ✳   ✳

A Prize Inside?

HOLLOW EARTH BELIEVERS agree that our planet is a shell between 500 and 800 miles thick, and inside that shell is another world. It may be a gaseous realm, an alien outpost, or home to a utopian society.

Some believers add a spiritual spin. Calling the interior world Agartha or Shambhala, they use concepts from Eastern religions and point to ancient legends supporting these ideas.

Many Hollow Earth enthusiasts are certain that people from the outer and inner worlds can visit each other by traveling through openings in the outer shell. One such entrance is a hole in the ocean near the North Pole. A November 1968 photo by the ESSA-7 satellite showed a dark, circular area at the North Pole that was surrounded by ice fields. Another hole supposedly exists in Antarctica. Some Hollow Earth enthusiasts say Hitler believed that Antarctica held the true opening to Earth's core. Leading Hollow Earth researchers such as Dennis Crenshaw suggest that President Roosevelt ordered the 1939 South Pole expedition to find the entrance before the Germans did.

The poles may not hold the only entrances to a world hidden deep beneath our feet. Jules Verne's famous novel *Journey to the Center of the Earth* supported yet another theory about passage between the worlds. In his story, there were many access points, including waterfalls and inactive volcanoes. Edgar Allan Poe and Edgar Rice Burroughs also wrote about worlds inside Earth. Their ideas were based on science as well as fantasy.

Scientists Take Note

Many scientists have taken the Hollow Earth theory seriously. One of the most noted was English astronomer Edmund Halley, of Halley's Comet fame. In 1692, he declared that our planet is hollow, and as evidence, he pointed to global shifts in Earth's magnetic fields, which frequently cause compass anomalies. According to Halley, those shifts could be explained by the movement of rotating worlds inside Earth. In addition, he claimed that the source of gravity—still debated in the 21st century—could be an interior world.

In Halley's opinion, Earth is made of three separate layers or shells, each rotating independently around a solid core. We live on the outer shell, but the inner worlds might be inhabited, too. Halley also suggested that Earth's interior atmospheres are luminous. We supposedly see them as gas leaking out of Earth's fissures. At the poles, that gas creates the *aurora borealis*.

Scientists Look Deeper

Hollow Earth researchers claim that the groundwork for their theories was laid by some of the most notable scientific minds of the 17th and 18th centuries. Although their beliefs remain controversial and largely unsubstantiated, they are still widely discussed and have a network of enthusiasts.

Some researchers claim that Leonhard Euler (1707–1783), one of the greatest mathematicians of all time, believed that Earth's interior includes a glowing core that illuminates life for a well-developed civilization, much like the sun lights our world. Another mathematician, Sir John Leslie (1766–1832), suggested that Earth has a thin crust and also believed the interior cavity was filled with light.

In 1818, a popular lecturer named John Cleves Symmes, Jr., proposed an expedition to prove the Hollow Earth theory. He believed that he could sail to the North Pole, and upon reaching the opening to Earth's core, he could steer his ship over the lip of the entrance, which he believed resembled a waterfall. Then he would continue sailing on waters inside the planet. In 1822 and 1823, Symmes petitioned Congress to fund the expedition, but he was turned down. He died in 1829, and his gravestone in Hamilton, Ohio, is decorated with his model of the Hollow Earth.

Proof Gets Woolly and Weird

In 1846, a remarkably well-preserved—and long extinct—woolly mammoth was found frozen in Siberia. Most woolly mammoths died out about 12,000 years ago, so researchers were baffled by its pristine condition.

Hollow Earth enthusiasts say there is only one explanation: The mammoth lived inside Earth, where those beasts are not extinct. The beast had probably become lost, emerged into our world, and froze to death shortly before the 1846 discovery.

Eyewitnesses at the North Pole

Several respected scientists and explorers have visited the poles and returned with stories that suggest a hollow Earth.

At the start of the 20th century, Arctic explorers Dr. Frederick A. Cook and Rear Admiral Robert E. Peary sighted land—not just an icy wasteland—at the North Pole. Peary first described it as "the white summits of a distant land." A 1913 Arctic expedition also reported seeing "hills, valleys, and snow-capped peaks." All of these claims were dismissed as mirages but would later be echoed by the research of Admiral Richard E. Byrd, the first man to fly over the North Pole. Hollow Earth believers suggest that Byrd actually flew into the interior world and then out again, without realizing it. They cite Byrd's notes as evidence, as he describes his navigational instruments and compasses spinning out of control.

Unidentified Submerged Objects

Support for the Hollow Earth theory has also come from UFO enthusiasts. People who study UFOs have also been documenting USOs, or unidentified submerged objects. These mysterious vehicles have been spotted—mostly at sea—since the 19th century.

USOs look like "flying saucers," but instead of vanishing into the skies, they plunge beneath the surface of the ocean. Some are luminous and fly upward from the sea at a fantastic speed… and without making a sound. UFO enthusiasts believe that these spaceships are visiting worlds beneath the sea. Some are certain that these are actually underwater alien bases. Other UFO researchers think that the ocean conceals entries to a hollow Earth, where the aliens maintain outposts.

The Search Continues

Scientists have determined that the most likely location for a northern opening to Earth's interior is at 84.4 N Latitude, 141 E Longitude. It's a spot near Siberia, about 600 miles from the North Pole. Photos taken by *Apollo 8* in 1968 and *Apollo 16* in 1972 show dark, circular areas confirming the location.

Some scientists are studying seismic tomography, which uses natural and human-made explosions as well as earthquakes and other seismic waves to chart Earth's interior masses. So far, scientists confirm that Earth is comprised of three separate layers. And late 20th-century images may suggest a mountain range at Earth's core.

What may seem like fantasy from a Jules Verne novel could turn out to be an astonishing reality. Hollow Earth societies around the world continue to look for proof of this centuries-old legend…and who knows what they might find?

Eerie Haunted Objects

Many ghost hunters believe that solid objects, such as buildings, furnishings, and decorative items, retain psychic energy. People who come into contact with these objects may sense stored emotions, as though they're revisiting the original events surrounding the items. Usually these "flashbacks" are associated with past tragedies and death. Others objects appear to channel actual spirits. Either way, they're just plain creepy.

✳   ✳   ✳   ✳

What Is a Haunted Object?

A HAUNTED OBJECT IS an item that seems to give off a certain energy or vibe. Paranormal occurrences accompany the object itself and begin after the object is acquired. Sometimes, human characteristics—such as breathing or tapping sounds—are associated with the item. In other cases, a person can place a haunted object in one place only to find that it mysteriously moves while he or she is absent from the room, is sleeping, or is away from home.

Becoming Haunted

No one knows for sure what causes an object to become haunted. Some people think that the items are possessed. Renowned psychic Sylvia Browne says that oftentimes a spirit has a "lingering fondness" for an object and may just stop by to visit it. She stresses that all items are capable of holding imprints, which are not always pleasant.

Another explanation is that certain objects are cursed, but that doesn't seem as likely. Most experts feel that a "haunting" comes from residual energy associated with the people or places connected to the item. For example, a beloved doll or stuffed animal may retain some energy from its human owner. This is especially likely to be the case with an item that was near—or even involved in—a violent event such as a murder, the death of a child, or even a heated argument. The "haunting" occurs when the residual energy plays back or reenacts the traumatic event. Like other residual phenomena, haunted objects can't communicate or interact with humans.

When people experience a paranormal event, they often assume that the building in which the incident occurs is haunted, but sometimes it's just one item. Here's a look at some objects that are reportedly haunted.

Robert, the Haunted Doll

Few dolls are as haunted as "Robert," a straw doll once owned by Florida artist Robert "Gene" Otto. During Otto's lifetime (he died in 1974), the doll was often heard walking, humming, and singing in the attic. Some witnesses even claim they saw the doll staring out the window at them. Today, the doll resides in the Fort East Martello Museum in Key West, where he continues to frighten visitors. As ghost hunter David Sloan quipped after investigating Robert, "Be careful of the objects you possess, or one day they may end up possessing you."

A Haunted Painting

A disturbing—and apparently haunted—painting entitled *Hands Resist Him* became famous on eBay in February 2000. The painting portrayed a little boy standing in front of a window and next to a girl with jointed, doll-like arms.

Artist Bill Stoneham painted the picture in 1972. Within a year of the art's first showing, both the gallery owner and the Los Angeles critic who reviewed it were dead. No one is certain what happened after the painting's original owner, actor John Marley, died on May 22, 1984, but years later, the art was found behind a brewery.

People continue to report strange events after merely viewing photos of the painting online. (An internet search for "haunted painting" will lead you to such photos.) One person heard an eerie, disembodied voice when viewing the artwork. Others talk about fainting as soon as they look at it. Some say that they have been visited by spirits from the painting.

Comte LeFleur's Ghostly Portrait

If you dine at Brennan's Restaurant in New Orleans, be sure to visit the Red Room upstairs and watch the portrait of Comte LeFleur for several minutes. Many guests watch his smile change to an expression far more sinister.

Wealthy Comte LeFleur was well liked in colonial New Orleans. One day, he cheerfully went around town making funeral and burial arrangements for three people. Then he returned home and killed his wife and his college-age son. The count then hanged himself from the sturdy gas chandelier overlooking the corpses of his family.

Today, the LeFleur residence is home to Brennan's Restaurant. Like the ghosts of the count and his family, the chandelier is still there. But it is the painting of Comte LeFleur that catches the eye of most visitors. Those who spend a few minutes watching the killer's image understand why it is one of America's most frightening portraits. LeFleur's head tilts slightly, and his expression changes from a mild smile to an evil grin until you blink or glance away.

An Especially Spooky Ouija Board

Many people avoid Ouija boards because they may connect us with "the other side" or with evil entities. This certainly seemed to be the case with the board Abner Williams loaned to a group of El Paso "Goths." In mid-2000, after the board was returned to him, Williams complained of scratching noises coming from the board, along with a man's voice addressing him, followed by the sound of children chanting nursery rhymes at his window. When Williams tried to throw the board in the trash, it reappeared in his house. A paranormal investigator borrowed the board, and a hooded figure appeared from nowhere and growled at his son.

When a paranormal research team investigated the Ouija board, they found spots of blood on the front of it and a coating of blood on the back. They measured several cold spots over areas of the board, and photos revealed a strange ectoplasm rising from it. The board was eventually sent to a new owner, who did not want it cleared of negative energy. That person has remained silent about more recent activity surrounding the board.

Although this is an unusually well-documented haunted Ouija board, this is not an uncommon tale. Many psychics warn that, if you ask a spirit to communicate with you through a Ouija board, it's like opening a door between the worlds. You never know what kind of spirits—good or evil—will use that Ouija board to visit you. In general, it's wise to be cautious with "spirit boards" of any kind.

Nathaniel Hawthorne and the Haunted Chair

You may have seen a creepy old chair or two, but when author Nathaniel Hawthorne encountered one that was actually haunted, he wrote a short story about it. Hawthorne's "true family legend," which he titled "The Ghost of Dr. Harris," wasn't published until 30 years after the author's death.

According to Hawthorne, Dr. Harris used to sit and read the newspaper in the same chair at the Boston Athenaeum each morning. When the old man died, his ghost continued to visit, and Hawthorne, who was researching at the library, saw it daily until he had the courage to look him in the eye. There, the author reported a "melancholy look of helplessness" that lingered for several seconds. Then the ghost vanished. So if you visit the Boston Athenaeum, be careful where you sit. Dr. Harris may be in that "empty" chair.

Annabelle and the Haunted Doll

Raggedy Ann and Andy dolls have been popular for decades. But after a young woman named Donna received a Raggedy Ann doll in the 1970s, she didn't have such a warm and fuzzy experience. The doll would often change positions on its own: Once, it was found kneeling—a position that was impossible for Donna and her roommate Angie to create due to the soft and floppy nature of the doll's body. The girls also found mysterious notes that were written in a childish scrawl. Worried, Donna and Angie called in a medium, who told them that their apartment building was once the home of a young girl named Annabelle. But after the doll attacked Angie's boyfriend, the girls called in demonologists Ed and Lorraine Warren, who determined that "Annabelle" was not the friendly, playful spirit of a young girl, but instead was a demonic entity. The doll went to live with the Warrens, who knew how to handle its antics, and it now resides in a glass case at the Warren Occult Museum in Connecticut.

The Haunted Wedding Dress at the Baker Mansion

In the 19th century, the Baker Mansion in Altoona, Pennsylvania, was home to the Baker family. As the story goes, daughter Anna fell in love with and became secretly engaged to one of her father's employees. But when her father discovered the romance, he sent the suitor away. Poor Anna never got over her lost love, and she never married.

When the Blair County Historical Society took over the building in the 1920s, a beautiful wedding dress that belonged to Anna's rival, Elizabeth Bell, was put on display. Although the dress was showcased under glass in Anna's bedroom, it often moved and swayed of its own accord. Caretakers attributed the movement to a loose floorboard that jarred the case when visitors walked past. But security cameras recorded the dress moving when no one else was around. Eventually, like Anna's suitor, the wedding dress was removed.

Although the haunted dress is no longer displayed at the mansion, some Baker family spirits have apparently remained there. Apparitions have been seen in a mirror and on a staircase, and photos have also shown orbs and misty shadows.

Watt an Accomplishment: Obsessive Art in Los Angeles

What is nearly 100 feet tall, is comprised of 17 pieces, was decorated mostly from recycled materials, can withstand a force equivalent to nearly 80 mile-per-hour winds, and lives in Los Angeles? No, it's not some computer-generated monster starring in the latest summer blockbuster: It's Watts Towers, the strange but oddly attractive creation of an Italian immigrant who became a bit obsessed with an extracurricular art project.

✳ ✳ ✳ ✳

Buon Giorno, Signor Rodia

BORN IN SOUTHERN Italy in 1879, Simon Rodia immigrated to the United States with his older brother in the mid-1890s. The boys settled on the East Coast, where they worked various jobs in coalfields, rock quarries, and railroad camps. When his brother was killed in a jobsite accident, Rodia relocated to Seattle, where he met his wife and started a family before moving to Watts, a section of Los Angeles. Soon after, Rodia began an art project in his backyard to pay tribute to his adopted country. It would take him 33 years to complete.

The Towers

Rodia had been trained as a tile-layer, not as a carpenter or an engineer, so when he decided to build super tall towers on his modest one-tenth of an acre plot, he had to get creative. By tying beams together with chicken wire and scaling the sides of the towers (which were glued together with cement) as he built them, he got the job done. The steel pipes and rods, wire mesh, and crude mortar used for support might have been primitive and rather unorthodox, but they worked for Rodia. As he built the structure, he decorated it. Way before "going green" was cool, Rodia chose to recycle old materials to adorn his edifice. By pressing broken dishes, glass, ceramic bits, and other shiny stuff into the concrete, he created a mosaic over every inch of Watts Towers—he even inlaid the floor. The multicolored chips form hearts, Rodia's initials, the dates 1921 and 1923 (the years his children were born), and flowers, but most of the tiles create swirls of random, free-form designs.

When he stepped off the final tower and declared he was finished, Rodia was 75 years old. Unfortunately, a general lack of understanding had plagued the structures for some time. During the 1930s and 1940s, rumors had spread that the towers were transmitting signals to the Communists and the Japanese. Annoyed by government officials and disheartened by a steady stream of vandals, Rodia signed the property over to his neighbor and friend, Louis H. Saucedo, and left town in the mid-1950s.

Trouble in Cement Paradise

Though the Watts Towers had survived numerous earthquakes throughout the years, in 1959, the city of Los Angeles threatened to raze the structures on account of them being an "unauthorized public hazard." Public outcry demanded that the towers be tested before being demolished, and the city agreed. More than a thousand people watched as 10,000 pounds of force were applied to the tallest tower. Ironically, the testing apparatus itself bent from the force, but the tower withstood the pressure just fine. The towers were reopened a year later and soon the Los Angeles community felt a sense of pride toward their unique landmark.

In 1978, the land on which the Watts Towers stood was deeded to the state of California, and the structures underwent extensive repair for seven years. After that, the towers were named a national historic landmark and were later named an official California State Park. Today, the towers are visited by thousands of people every year who enjoy the bizarre but fascinating work of the Italian-American folk artist.

The Legend of Gore Orphanage

Though it's not much to look at today—in fact, there's nothing left to see—an old sign and an abandoned mansion add up to a long legend in Vermilion, Ohio. Travelers who find themselves on the outskirts of the town of Vermilion should keep their eyes peeled for a road sign that has given rise to one of Ohio's longest-standing legends. The faded green sign simply reads, "Gore Orphanage Road."

✻　✻　✻　✻

The Legend

NOT SURPRISINGLY, THERE was at one point an orphanage located along what is now Gore Orphanage Road. The story goes that "Old Man" Gore, the man who ran the orphanage, was rather wicked and often mistreated the children. It is claimed that one night, in a fit of rage, he even burned down the orphanage, with all of the children still inside. (In an alternate version of the story, a mysterious "old man" living in the woods is blamed for the fire.)

Few visitors make their way to the ruins of the orphanage, but it is said that those who do will hear all sorts of strange noises coming from within—perhaps the screams of the children as they are being burned alive. If curiosity seekers are really lucky, they'll catch a glimpse of ghostly children running through the woods, burning. But even if the ephemeral children aren't seen, they might still make their presence known by leaving tiny handprints all over the cars of those who park there.

The Facts

An orphanage was indeed located along Gore Orphanage Road. The Reverend John Sprunger started the Light of Hope Orphanage around 1902. Sprunger and his wife ran the orphanage for roughly a dozen years until Sprunger passed away. Mrs. Sprunger was eventually forced to sell off everything and move away; orphans who remained were sent to live with relatives or found homes in the community. There is nothing in the records about any children dying in a fire. Some of the outbuildings may have ultimately burned down, but that was many years after they had been abandoned. So if there was no Gore Orphanage, where did the name of the road come from? Simple: A *gore* is a surveyor's term used to describe a triangular piece of land. In other words, the road ran through the gore that was near the orphanage.

Swift Mansion

There even seems to be some confusion as to where the actual orphanage was located. In reality, the Light of Hope Orphanage was made up of several buildings. There are ruins of a burned building on Gore Orphanage Road, but they are the ruins of the Swift Mansion. In the early 1840s, wealthy farmer Joseph Swift created a farm at the bottom of the ravine, causing all of the townsfolk to nickname the mansion he erected "Swift's Folly." Swift operated the farm for several years until some bad investments forced him to sell the mansion and land to Nicholas Wilber. And with that transaction, the final piece of the Gore Orphanage legend fell into place.

The Wilbers were apparently very interested in spiritualism. So when several Wilber grandchildren sadly fell victim to the diphtheria epidemic that swept through the area in early 1893, as legend has it, the Wilbers would hold seances in the Swift Mansion to contact them. When Nicholas died in 1901, the mansion was left empty and soon acquired the reputation of being haunted, possibly by the ghosts of the Wilber children. Years later, the mansion fell victim to arson, which may be what brought about the legend of ghosts of burning children.

The House of David

The only thing more startling than seeing men with waist-length hair and long beards playing baseball in the early 1900s might have been knowing every player on this early barnstorming team was a member of a highly controversial religious sect known as the House of David.

✳ ✳ ✳ ✳

From Kentucky to the Second Coming

BASED IN BENTON Harbor, Michigan, this religious sect centered around its charismatic leader, Benjamin Franklin Purnell, and his wife, Mary. The couple believed that they were God's appointed messengers for the Second Coming of Christ, and that the human body could have eternal life on Earth. They also believed that both men and women should imitate Jesus by never cutting their hair. Purnell based his teachings on those of an 18th-century English group called the Philadelphians, which were developed from the prophecies of a woman named Joanna Southcott who claimed she was the first of seven messengers to proclaim the Second Coming. Purnell somehow deduced that he was also one of those seven.

Growing Hair, Religion, and Crowds

Born in Kentucky in March 1861, Purnell and Mary traveled around the country for several years while polishing their doctrine. After being booted out of a small town in Ohio, possibly because Benjamin was accused of adultery with a local farmer's wife, they landed in Benton Harbor in March 1903. Members of a sect related to the Philadelphians called the Jezreelites lived in nearby Grand Rapids, and Purnell had been in touch with the Bauschke brothers of Benton Harbor, who were sympathetic to his cause.

With the backing of the Bauschkes and other prominent local citizens, Purnell soon attracted a crowd of believers and called his group the Israelite House of David. The 700 or so members lived chaste, commune-style lives on a cluster of farms and land, served vegetarian meals, and started successful cottage industries, such as a toy factory, greenhouse, and canning facility.

As word spread of the long-haired, oddly dressed members and their colony, the curious began making Sunday trips to observe them. Purnell turned this into a cash opportunity by opening an aviary, a small zoo, a vegetarian restaurant, an ice-cream parlor, and, ironically, a barber shop. The crowds grew, and, in 1908, he started work on his own amusement park, which included an expanded zoo and a miniature, steam-powered railway whose trains ran throughout the grounds.

Entertainment Evangelism

In the meantime, some members of the group had formed a baseball team that also drew crowds, so Purnell added a large stadium next to the amusement park. The team traveled as well, and added to their popularity with comical routines, such as hiding the ball under their beards. Building on the sports theme, the colony also featured exhibition basketball, and later, miniature car racing.

The colony also boasted a popular brass band, whose members capitalized on their showy long tresses by starting each concert facing away from the audience, hair covering half of their snazzy uniforms. They often played jazzy, crowd-pleasing numbers rather than the expected somber religious tunes.

Religious activities continued, too. Adopting the title "The Prince of Peace," Purnell often held teaching sessions, including one in which he was photographed allegedly changing water into wine.

Problems in Paradise

As happens with any large social enterprise, some members became disgruntled and left. Purnell referred to them as "scorpions." Rumors flew concerning improper relations between Purnell and young females in the group, especially when the colony purchased an island in northern Michigan where they ran a prosperous lumber business. Newspaper reports alleged that rebellious group members were killed and buried there and that Purnell kept a group of young girls as sex slaves. The public was also suspicious of mass weddings he conducted. Lawsuits had begun against Purnell in Ohio and continued to mount even as the Michigan colony progressed.

In 1926, Purnell was finally arrested on charges that included religious fraud and statutory rape. He endured a lengthy trial, but he was ill for most of it, and much of his testimony was deemed incoherent. Most charges were eventually dismissed.

Purnell died in Benton Harbor on December 16, 1927, at age 66. But shortly before passing, he told his followers that, like Jesus, he would be back in three days. As far as anyone knows, he wasn't. His preserved remains were kept in a glass-covered coffin on the colony grounds for decades, although at one time Mary's brother reportedly insisted that the body was not Purnell's but that of another colony member.

Remains of the Day

After his death, some of the believers switched their allegiance to Purnell's widow, Mary, who lived until 1953 and started a new colony called Mary's City of David, which still plays baseball and runs a museum in Benton Harbor. The grounds and businesses were split between the two groups, and only a handful of members remain in either. The zoo closed in 1945, with the animals given to Chicago's Lincoln Park Zoo, and the amusement park, remembered fondly by many local residents, closed in the early 1970s. The original area east of Benton Harbor's city limits still serves as the headquarters for the two groups. And many credit Benjamin Purnell as the forerunner of later, high-style evangelical leaders such as Jim Bakker and Oral Roberts. The House of David team played in the first professional night baseball game, in Independence, Kansas, in 1930.

Strange Collections

Judging from the number of online museums and collectors' guides, it seems that many people are trying to make a name for themselves with one-of-a-kind collections. American Idol contestant Brandon Green even proudly displayed his toenail and fingernail collection for a national television audience.

✳ ✳ ✳ ✳

Navel Fluff

IN 1984, GRAHAM Barker of Perth, Australia, started collecting his navel lint. Since then, he has seldom missed a day's "harvest" and collects an average of 3.03 milligrams each day; he currently has about $2^1/_2$ jars of lint. He was rewarded for his efforts in 2000 when *Guinness World Records* declared his navel lint collection the world's largest. Barker also collects his own beard clippings, bakery bags, and ski-lift tickets.

Adhesive Bandages

Marz Waggener of Long Beach, California, has been collecting (unused) adhesive bandages since February 1994, after convincing her mother that she needed a box of Incredible Crash Dummies bandages for a Girl Scout badge. Her collection reached 3,300 different bandages, including a 1979 Superman bandage and some rare samples from the 1950s.

Traffic Signs and Signals

Stephen Salcedo asks visitors to his website to refrain from calling the cops on him—all 500-plus traffic signs and signals in his collection were obtained legally. Salcedo started his collection in 1986 at age five. The Fort Wayne, Indiana, collector has always been attracted to the graphic design aspect of road signs and has a special fondness for older ones (pre-1960). The "treasure" of his collection is the street sign that stood on the corner near his childhood home in Merrillville, Indiana.

Police and Prison Restraints

If the handcuff-collecting world has a celebrity, it is Stan Willis of Cincinnati. Since 1969, Willis has been collecting police and prison restraints and has built his reputation selling rare cuffs to other collectors. In 2003, *Guinness World Records* recognized his collection as the largest—it now contains nearly 1,400 items. He also collects police and fire department-related items, such as badges, lanterns, and helmets.

Mustard

Barry Levenson began his mustard collection in October 1986, with 12 jars he bought to soothe his grief when the Boston Red Sox lost to the New York Mets in the World Series. He vowed to assemble the largest collection of prepared mustard in the world. In April 1992, he opened the Mount Horeb Mustard Museum in Mount Horeb, Wisconsin.

He now displays nearly 5,000 mustards from all 50 states and more than 60 countries, as well as historic mustard memorabilia. He is currently working on getting widespread recognition of the first Saturday in August as World Mustard Day, which is already celebrated at the museum.

Toothpaste

Dentist Val Kolpakov began collecting toothpaste and dental artifacts in March 2002 as a way to advertise his new dental practice. His hobby became a mission, however, and he now displays more than 1,400 tubes in his Saginaw, Michigan, dental office.

Although the star of his collection is a rare silver Georgian tooth powder box from 1801, he is especially interested in vintage toothpastes, tubes from around the world, toothpastes from TV and movie sets, and flavors other than the traditional mint. Dr. Kolpakov boasts a variety of liquor-flavored pastes (including bourbon, Scotch, wine varietals, and champagne) as well as curry, lavender, and pumpkin pudding. Kolpakov believes his to be the largest collection in the world and is in the process of applying for a Guinness Record Certificate.

Barf Bags

Although Steve Silberberg of Massachusetts has never been out of the United States, his 2,000-plus barf bags come from around the world. Silberberg began collecting "happy sacks"— as they're known in piloting circles—in 1981 and now has a wide range of bus, car, train, and helicopter bags as well. Although not the largest collection in the world (he guesses it might be the tenth largest), he does have the largest collection of non-transportation bags, including novelty bags not intended for use, as well as political and movie sickness bags. The treasures of his collection include those given away on the Disneyland Star Tours ride and one from the Space Shuttle.

Mechanical Memorabilia

Marvin Yagoda has been a pharmacist for 50 years, but he is best known for his hobby of collecting mechanical novelties, vintage oddities, strange curiosities, and wonders, as he calls them. He started his collection of vintage coin-operated games and toys in the early 1960s and displayed some pieces in a local food court. After the food court closed in 1988, he opened Marvin's Marvelous Mechanical Museum in 1990—a 5,500-square-foot building in a strip mall in Farmington Hills, Michigan. Yagoda has packed the 40-foot ceilings with such things as fortune-tellers-in-a-box, nickelodeons, a carousel, more than 50 model airplanes, antique electric fans, animatronic dummies, vintage arcade games (from the early 1900s through present day), prize machines, one of the infamous P. T. Barnum Cardiff Giant statues, the electric chair from Sing Sing Prison, and much, much more.

More than a thousand electrical outlets power the machines, which are all in working condition. Even the walls are not overlooked, sporting his collection of magic posters and 20-foot-long carnival canvases. Admission to his museum is free, but be sure to come with a few rolls of quarters.

The Multimillion-Dollar Manhattan Mystery

When a family hired an architect to design their new 4,200-square-foot apartment, they had no idea what they'd gotten themselves into.

✳   ✳   ✳   ✳

IN 2003, THE Klinsky family decided they wanted their recently purchased Manhattan home to be unique. It was an understandable request; after all, they paid $8.5 million for the place. So when the family found architect Eric Clough and heard his impressive vision, they immediately hired him for the job. Of course, what they didn't know then was that they'd heard only half of Clough's plan for their home—and that the other half wouldn't be discovered until months after they'd moved in.

The Conception

Clough says it all started when Mr. Klinsky handed him a poem he'd written and asked to have it put into a bottle and hidden behind a wall as a sort of time capsule for his family. The concept gave Clough the idea that would eventually make national news: He would create a complex mystery built into the apartment, complete with clues that would take the family on a fictional journey through time. He researched ciphers and codes, secret compartments, and contraptions and spent years creating the most majestic design he'd ever imagined.

The Discovery

Fast forward to May 2006. The Klinsky family (including mom, dad, four children, and a dog) moved into their apartment. They were pleased with the results; everything looked great and seemed normal. Well, it did for about four months.

The first mystery was discovered when one of the sons and a friend were playing in his bedroom. The boy was looking intently at the room's radiator when he noticed letters carved into the grille. Somehow, the child realized they were in a code (later identified as the Caesar Shift cipher, in which each letter is replaced by a letter three positions lower in the alphabet). Decoded, the words spelled the son's name.

Several more unusual events unfolded, all with Clough refusing to give any explanation. Finally, the family received a cryptic letter with a poem directing them to a hidden panel. That's when the true scavenger hunt began.

The First Clue

Inside the panel, the family found a book that Clough had custom-written and bound. Clue by clue, the story took them through trap doors and hidden compartments within their own home, producing a complex web that took weeks to unravel.

Eighteen difficult clues later, the mystery led them to a set of hallway panels. The Klinskys had to take off two decorative doorknockers and form them together to make a crank. In turn, that crank opened hidden panels in a dining room cabinet that contained another series of keys and keyholes. Once the family figured out what keys matched with what holes, they discovered a set of drawers with a crossword puzzle. The puzzle led to more hidden panels in another room, which led to a hidden magnet, which opened more hidden panels, which contained—at long last—the original poem the father had asked Clough to hide.

The Process

This intense mystery spared no expense. Clough's fee for the renovation was more than $1.2 million—a number he says didn't even begin to cover the project's cost. (Granted, he was only hired for the renovation, and not the mystery.) While the renovation itself took about a year and a half, the creation of the unusual scavenger hunt took a full four years. Clough says he ate most of the overhead, and he had a few dozen friends who volunteered their time. In 2008, it was reported that Paramount Pictures bought the rights to the story of the Klinsky mystery apartment. Now *that's* what we call a housewarming.

Ghost in the Machine

Sometimes the last thing you want to see is another email in your inbox that you have to respond to, and other times you receive an email that you cannot help but open. Pennsylvania residents Tim Hart and Jimmy McGraw received an email after their cousin's death that they couldn't help themselves from opening.

✳   ✳   ✳   ✳

JACK FROESE DIED at the young age of thirty-two from heart arrhythmia, but somehow his email account stayed active after his passing. Both Hart and McGraw were totally confounded and a little freaked out when they received awfully specific emails from their deceased cousin. About six months after Froese's death, the two cousins received emails that were incredibly pertinent and related to the last conversations they had each had with him.

Hart received an ominous and downright creepy email from his deceased cousin with the subject heading of "I'm watching!" That alone might have been enough to make most of us freak out and run out of the house screaming, but Hart didn't freak out—at least not yet. He opened the email and it read, "Did you hear me? I'm at your house. Clean your attic!!!"

At that point, Hart felt himself pale of all color. Hart's messy attic was the last thing Froese and Hart had talked about, and now—in true ghost fashion—Froese was probably in Hart's attic looking for a cool, clean, and dry place to hang out for a while. Hart responded to the email, but never received a response.

Froese wasn't done with the internet yet. He purportedly sent another email to McGraw about an ankle injury McGraw had received after Froese's death. McGraw did believe that it was his cousin, contacting him in an attempt to stay connected with his family, but couldn't explain how or why.

Froese's mother, Patty, told the two that what they encountered was a gift and that they should appreciate the mystery. Although some people were upset by the possibility of an online prank, both McGraw and Hart remained confident that their cousin continued in this world as an online presence.

It's a Bird! It's a Plane! It's ... Avrocar?!?

Not all UFOs are alien spaceships. One top-secret program was contracted out by the U.S. military to an aircraft company in Canada.

✳ ✳ ✳ ✳

OH, THE 1950S—A time of sock hops, drive-in movies, and the Cold War between America and the Soviet Union. It was also a time when discussion of life on other planets was rampant, fueled by the alleged crash of an alien spaceship near Roswell, New Mexico, in 1947.

Watch the Skies

Speculation abounded about the unidentified flying objects (UFOs) spotted nearly every week by everyone from farmers to airplane pilots. As time passed, government authorities began to wonder if the flying saucers were, in fact, part of a secret Russian program to create a new type of air force. Fearful that such a craft would upset the existing balance of power, the U.S. Air Force decided to produce its own saucer-shape ship.

In 1953, the military contacted Avro Aircraft Limited of Canada, an aircraft manufacturing company that operated in Malton, Ontario, between 1945 and 1962. Project Silverbug was initially proposed simply because the government wanted to find out if UFOs could be manufactured by humans. But before long, both the military and the scientific community were speculating about its potential. Intrigued by the idea, designers at Avro—led by British aeronautical engineer John Frost—began working on the VZ-9-AV Avrocar. The round craft would have been right at home in a scene from the classic science fiction film *The Day the Earth Stood Still*. Security for the project was so tight that it probably generated rumors that America was actually testing a captured alien spacecraft.

Of This Earth

By 1958, the company had produced two prototypes, which were 18 feet in diameter and 3.5 feet tall. Constructed around a large triangle, the Avrocar was shaped like a disk, with a curved upper surface. It included an enclosed 124-blade turbo-rotor at the center of the triangle, which provided lifting power through an opening in the bottom of the craft. The turbo also powered the craft's controls. Although conceived as being able to carry two passengers, in reality a single pilot could barely fit inside the cramped space. The Avrocar was operated with a single control stick, which activated different panels around the ship. Airflow issued from a large center ring, which was controlled by the pilot to guide the craft either vertically or horizontally.

The military envisioned using the craft as "flying Jeeps" that would hover close to the ground and move at a maximum speed of 40 mph. But that, apparently, was only going to be the beginning. Avro had its own plans, which included not just commercial Avrocars, but also a family-size Avrowagon, an Avrotruck for larger loads, Avroangel to rush people to the hospital, and a military Avropelican, which, like a pelican hunting for fish, would conduct surveillance for submarines.

But Does It Fly?

The prototypes impressed the U.S. Army enough to award Avro a $2 million contract. Unfortunately, the Avrocar project was canceled when an economic downturn forced the company to temporarily close and restructure. When Avro Aircraft reopened, the original team of designers had dispersed. Further efforts to revive the project were unsuccessful, and repeated testing proved that the craft was inherently unstable. It soon became apparent that whatever UFOs were spotted overhead, it was unlikely that they came from this planet. Project Silverbug was abandoned when funding ran out in March 1961, but one of the two Avrocar prototypes is housed at the U.S. Army Transportation Museum in Fort Eustis, Virginia.

Unbelievable Beliefs

Faith is a very personal experience, and by definition, it is not based on fact. Over the centuries, people have expressed their faith in a variety of unique philosophies.

✳ ✳ ✳ ✳

The Millerites

WILLIAM MILLER, A farmer in northern New York, founded a doomsday cult in the 1800s. Studying the Bible convinced Miller that humanity was due for damnation. He began preaching this message in the early 1830s. His first prediction was that Jesus Christ would "come again to the earth, cleanse, purify and take possession of the same" between March 1843 and March 1844. When a comet appeared early in 1843, a number of his followers killed themselves, believing the end was near.

However, when his prophecy didn't come to pass and the world survived, Miller stood by his message but became reluctant to set actual dates. Some of his followers took it upon themselves to announce October 22, 1844, as the big day, and Miller reluctantly agreed. This date came to be known as The Great Disappointment.

Regardless, Miller and his followers established a basis on which the Seventh-Day Adventist Church was later founded.

The Raelian Movement

A belief in unidentified flying objects has haunted humanity for generations, with thousands claiming to have had direct contact with alien beings from other worlds. Claude Vorilhon, a French race car driver and onetime musician, asserted that he was visited by an extraterrestrial in 1973. It was a life-altering experience for him that caused him to change his name to Rael and found the Raelian Church. Rael's religion proclaims that the Elohim ("those who came from the sky") created everything on Earth. Although many turn a skeptical eye toward Vorilhon, whose faith also preaches free love, the Raelian Movement is said to include as many as 65,000 members worldwide.

The Vampire Church

With offices located throughout the United States, Canada, and Australia, the Vampire Church provides the initiated and the curious with an opportunity to learn more about vampirism. However, don't expect to find much about the "undead," as vampires have been portrayed in stories since Bram Stoker wrote *Dracula* in 1897. Instead, the church offers insight into vampirism as a physical condition that sometimes requires unusual energy resources, such as blood. In addition, it explains the difference between psychic vampires and elemental vampires.

The Church of Euthanasia

"Save the Planet—Kill Yourself." These words are the battle cry of the Church of Euthanasia, which was established by Boston resident Chris Korda in 1992. Korda, a musician, had a dream one night about an alien who warned her that Earth was in serious danger. The extraterrestrial, which Korda dubbed "The Being," stressed the importance of protecting the planet's environment through population control.

As a result of the encounter, Korda established the Church of Euthanasia, which supports suicide, abortion, and sodomy (defined as any sex act that is not intended for procreation). According to the church's website, members are vegetarian, but they "support cannibalism for those who insist on eating flesh."

Although it reportedly has only about 100 members in the Boston area, the church claims that thousands worldwide have visited its website and been exposed to its message.

Satanic Marketing

What's behind the vicious rumor that put mega-corporation Procter & Gamble on many churches' hit lists?

∗ ∗ ∗ ∗

PROCTER & GAMBLE, one of the largest corporations in the world, manufactures a plethora of products that range from pet food to potato chips. The company takes pride in its reputation as a business that can be trusted, so it came as a huge shock when, starting in the 1960s, Christian churches and individuals around the country spread the rumor that P&G was dedicated to the service of Satan.

The Devil Is in the Details

How the rumor got started remains a mystery. According to one of the most popular versions of the story, the president of P&G appeared on *The Phil Donahue Show* in March 1994 and announced that, because of society's new openness, he finally felt comfortable revealing that he was a member of the Church of Satan and that much of his company's profits went toward the advancement of that organization. When Donahue supposedly asked him whether such an announcement would have a negative impact on P&G, the CEO replied, "There aren't enough Christians in the United States to make a difference."

There's one problem with this story—and with the variations that place the company president on *The Sally Jessy Raphael Show*, *The Merv Griffin Show*, and *60 Minutes*: It didn't happen.

Lose the Logo

Adding fuel to the fable was the company's logo, which featured the image of a "man in the moon" and 13 stars. Many interpreted this rather innocuous design to be Satanic, and some even claimed that the curlicues in the man's beard looked like the number 666—the biblical "mark of the Beast" referred to in the Book of Revelation. By 1985, the company had become so frustrated by the allegations that it had no choice but to retire the logo, which had graced P&G products for more than 100 years.

Speaking Out

Procter & Gamble did all it could to quell the rumors, which resulted in more than 200,000 phone calls and letters from concerned consumers. Company spokespeople vehemently denied the story, explaining in a press release: "The president of P&G has never discussed Satanism on any national televised talk show, nor has any other P&G executive. The moon-and-stars trademark dates back to the mid-1800s, when the "man in the moon" was simply a popular design. The 13 stars in the design honor the original 13 colonies."

In addition, the company turned to several prominent religious leaders, including evangelist Billy Graham, to help clear its name, and when that didn't work, it even sued a handful of clergy members who continued to spread the offending story.

Talk show host Sally Jessy Raphael also denied the allegations, noting, "The rumors going around that the president of Procter & Gamble appeared on [my] show and announced he was a member of the Church of Satan are not true. The president of Procter & Gamble has never appeared on *The Sally Jessy Raphael Show*."

Senseless Allegations

Of course, like most urban legends, this story falls apart under the slightest scrutiny. Foremost, one must ask why the CEO of an international conglomerate (especially one that must answer to stockholders) would risk decades of consumer goodwill— not to mention billions of dollars in sales—to announce to the world that his company was run by and catered to Satanists. And even if that were the case, he needn't bother announcing it, since any deals made with the devil would be a matter of public record.

In 2007, a jury awarded Procter & Gamble $19.25 million in a civil lawsuit filed against four former Amway distributors accused of spreading false rumors about the company's ties to the Church of Satan. The distributors were found guilty of using a voicemail system to inform customers that P&G's profits were used to support Satanic cults.

One Reptile to Rule Them All

Some people are ruled by their pets; others are ruled by their work. Conspiracy theorist David Icke believes that we're all being ruled by reptilian humanoids.

✳   ✳   ✳   ✳

Worldwide Domination

DAVID ICKE HAS worn many hats: journalist, news anchor for the BBC, spokesman for the British Green Party, and professional soccer player. But after a spiritual experience in Peru in 1991, he took on another role: famed conspiracy theorist.Like many other conspiracy theorists, Icke believes that a group called the Illuminati, or "global elite," controls the world. According to these theorists, the group manipulates the economy and uses mind control to usher humanity into a submissive state. Icke also believes that the group is responsible for organizing such tragedies as the Holocaust and the Oklahoma City bombings.

Some of the most powerful people in the world are members, claims Icke, including ex-British Prime Minister Tony Blair and former U.S. President George H. W. Bush, as well as leaders of financial institutions and major media outlets. However, not all members are human. According to Icke, those at the top of the Illuminati bloodlines are vehicles for a reptilian entity from the constellation Draco. These shape-shifters can change from human to reptile and back again, and they are essentially controlling humanity.

Is Icke Onto Something?

In the documentary *David Icke: Was He Right?*, Icke claims that many of his earlier predictions, including a hurricane in New Orleans and a "major attack on a large city" between the years 2000 and 2002, have come true. But are we really being ruled by reptilian humanoids or is Icke's theory a bunch of snake oil? Icke was nearly laughed off the stage in a 1991 appearance on a BBC talk show. But with 20 published books, thousands attending his speaking engagements, and nearly 200,000 weekly hits to his website, perhaps it's Icke who's having the last laugh. Icke continues to espouse insensitive views on Judaism that many have seen as anti-semitic, and his reposnse to the COVID-19 epidemic has disregarded health concerns held by many officials.

Legendary Lake Mills

Along the interstate between Madison and Milwaukee is the small town that dubbed itself "Legendary Lake Mills." It's legendary, indeed, and controversial too.

✳   ✳   ✳   ✳

An Underwater Mystery

SINCE THE 1840s, locals have buzzed about "stone tepees" standing at the bottom of Rock Lake. The idea seems plausible. Less than three miles due east is Aztalan State Park, an archeological site where the ancient remains of a Middle-Mississippian village, temple mounds, and ceremonial complex have been restored.

But Native American legend and local folklore, combined with years of third-party research, have not been enough to persuade top scientists that there are pyramids beneath Rock Lake's waters. In fact, the phenomena has been dubbed "North America's most controversial underwater archeological discovery of the 20th century."

One theory holds that Ancient Aztecs believed that their ancestors hailed from a land far north of Mexico, called Aztalan. The legend goes that in 1066, the Aztalans of Lake Mills appealed to the gods for relief from a long drought by building sacrificial pyramids. Rain came down, creating a beautiful lake and submerging the pyramids. They named the lake *Tyranena*, meaning "sparkling waters."

Fast-forward 800 years. When the first white settlers set up camp along Tyranena's banks in the 1830s, the resident Winnebago people shared the story of Tyranena with them. But even the Winnebago didn't quite understand the story, as it came from a "foreign tribe." The lore remained as elusive as the small islands that settlers reported as floating above the water. Soon after the settlers arrived, a sawmill and a gristmill were built on the lake's edge, subsequently raising the water level. What little was left to see of the supposed pyramids was submerged.

Doubt and Circumstance

Over the next 200 years, the lake would be caught up in a continuous cycle of sensationalism and doubt, false starts, and circumstance. In the early 1900s, two brothers, Claude and Lee Wilson, went out duck hunting one hot, clear day during a drought and were able to reach down and touch the so-called pyramid's apex with an oar. Local residents would find the pyramid again the next day, but by the time a reporter got onto the lake a week later rain had fallen, ending the drought and raising the water level. Through the decades, anglers would declare their belief in the structures when they snagged their lines and nets, but interest waned.

The lore was rekindled in the 1930s when a local school-teacher, Victor Taylor, took it upon himself to canvass residents and dive over the pyramids, without diving equipment. He described four conical underwater structures. With this "evidence," state and national agencies threw money into the effort, even hiring professional divers to explore the underwater structures. But these divers were literally mired by the lake's deteriorating, muddy bottom, mucking up belief in the pyramids once again.

Eventually the controversy would reach an MIT engineer, Max Nohl, the man who invented the first scuba-type device. A master excavator, Nohl made it his personal mission to uncover the truth beneath the lake. He rekindled the town's pyramid fever with his extensive dives and written accounts with detailed measurements.

Debunked?

While Nohl successfully made his case, the curious fact remained that no professional archeologist wanted to be associated with Rock Lake. The establishment theory contends that the lake bottom anomalies are merely glacial castoffs from the last Ice Age. In an article in the September 1962 issue of *The Wisconsin Archeologist*, the pyramids were wholly debunked by the state's academes, who alleged that Native Americans didn't work in stone and that mound-building only began 2,000 years prior, whereas Rock Lake was at least 10,000 years old. Case closed. Or not.

In July 1967, Jack Kennedy, a professional diver from Illinois, was sport diving with friends on Rock Lake. Near the end of the day, after all of his comrades had run out of air, Kennedy took one last dive . . . over a pyramid. Shocked at his discovery, he removed three rocks from its wall. Further analysis revealed the rocks were made of quartzite from a riverbed. The first concrete evidence was now in hand.

Kennedy continued to dive at Rock Lake, eventually making a sketch of a structure 70 feet long, 30 feet wide, and 15 feet tall, which appeared in *Skin Diver* magazine. His discovery led to a resurgence in the exploration of Rock Lake, a summer haven for leisure boaters and beachgoers. Explorers have documented stone rings, tombs, curiously long rock bars, and pyramidal structures in dives, sonic sonar, and aerial photography. In 1998, two Rock Lake enthusiasts, Archie Eschborn and Jack LeTourneau, formed Rock Lake Research Society to "document and help preserve these archeological treasures that could rewrite North American history... and persuade state officials to declare Rock Lake a historical site."

History Still Unwritten

Does the Aztalan connection hold water? How does glacial activity fit in the picture?

To date, Rock Lake remains just that, a lake, which is still unprotected as a historical site. But locals continue to believe, if not for the archeological and anthropological truth, then for the opportunities the lore and legend provide. In Lake Mills, you can stay at the Pyramid Motel or throw back a Stone Tepee Pale Ale, made by the city's resident Tyranena Brewing Company. Or perhaps you can head to one of the city's three beaches and try your hand at uncovering the mysteries of the "sparkling waters" yourself.

Mermaids: Real or Fish-ction?

The idea that mermaids actually exist is, well, a bit fishy. But anyone who has ever watched The Little Mermaid *or* Splash, *knows that there's a magic surrounding mermaids that is irresistible. In 2012 a Discovery Channel documentary stunned viewers with their suggestion that the answer is "maybe."*

✳   ✳   ✳   ✳

T**HE EARLIEST IMAGE** of a mermaid comes from 1000 BC in Syria, where the goddess Atargatis tried to take on the form of a fish by diving into the sea. She was not allowed to give up her great beauty, however, and the result was half fish and half human—a goddess of the sea with a beautiful face, long flowing hair and the sleek glimmering tail of a fish.

Homer's *The Odyssey* expanded on that idea by creating half human sea creatures called "sirens." Beautiful? Yes. But a little evil as well. These mermaids sang harmonious tunes, luring sailors to their death in the sea. Stories of their existence have been told and retold for a couple thousand years. And artists have depicted the mythical creatures in their artwork for just as long. Almost every country and culture has tales of mermaids and many people claim to have seen one. It begs the question: before mass communication as we know it today, how did all these separate cultures come up with the same imaginary creature with so many of the same characteristics?

So Could They Be Real?

The answer is maybe. The Discovery Channel program follows the scientific investigation of two former National Oceanic Atmospheric Administration (NOAA) scientists who started out to learn more about the beaching of whales in 2007. What they discovered were some mysterious underwater sounds—like nothing they had ever heard before.

Underwater singing? There must be mermaids! Well, it wasn't quite that simple, but the team did feel that the noises merited additional investigation—especially since they were convinced that this mysterious creature was attempting to communicate with them.

When another whale-beaching occurred along the coast of South Africa, the scientists traveled there and found that African scientists had recorded similar underwater communications. Further investigation revealed the remains of this sea creature in the belly of a great white shark—and it was definitely a marine animal. And a human. In short, it appeared to be a mermaid.

This creature was not a Disney princess by any means. But it did appear to possess the tail of a fish along with the clearly defined hands associated with the human body. If nothing else, this unusual creature supported an old "aquatic ape" theory about ancient mammals that lived on both land and sea. But alas, the government took possession of these remains, leaving the scientists with nothing but their recording of an unusual sea-sound.

As is often the case with government actions, their decision to confiscate the remains only convinced the scientists—and everyone hearing the story—that they were on to something. They tracked down a local teenager who claimed to have seen the body of a mermaid on the beach along with the whales. And surprise—he had taken a video with his cell phone.

Unfortunately the video wasn't clear and the government denies any discovery or cover-up of mermaids. The NOAA has also issued a statement saying there's no evidence that "aquatic humanoids" have ever been found.

One Heck of a Hoax? The Mysterious Voynich Manuscript

Dubbed the "World's Most Mysterious Book," the Voynich manuscript contains more than 200 vellum pages of vivid, colorful illustrations and handwritten prose. There's only one small problem: No one knows what any of it means. Or whether it means anything at all.

✻   ✻   ✻   ✻

IT WAS "DISCOVERED" in 1912 after being hidden from the world for almost 250 years. An American antique book dealer named Wilfried Voynich came across the medieval manuscript at an Italian Jesuit College. Approximately nine inches by six inches in size, the manuscript bore a soft, light-brown vellum cover, which was unmarked, untitled, and gave no indication as to when it had been written or by whom.

Bound inside were approximately 230 yellow parchment pages, most of which contained richly colored drawings of strange plants, celestial bodies, and other scientific matter. Many of the pages were adorned by naked nymphs bathing in odd-looking plumbing and personal-size washtubs. Handwritten text written in flowing script accompanied the illustrations.

Although Voynich was an expert antiquarian, he was baffled by the book's contents. And today—nearly a century later—the manuscript that came to bear his name remains a mystery.

Weird Science

The mystery surrounding the Voynich manuscript begins with its content, which reads (so to speak) like a work of weird science presented in six identifiable "sections":

* a botanical section, containing drawings of plants that no botanist has ever been able to identify

* an astronomical section, with illustrations of the sun, moon, stars, and zodiac symbols surrounded by naked nymphs bathing in individual washtubs

* a "biological" section, showing perplexing anatomical drawings of chambers or organs connected by tubes—and which also features more nymphs swimming in their inner liquids

* a cosmological section, consisting mostly of unexplained circular drawings

* a pharmaceutical section, depicting drawings of plant parts (leaves, roots) placed next to containers

* a recipe section, featuring short paragraphs "bulleted" by stars in the margin

Weirder still are the ubiquitous nymphs—a nice touch perhaps, but how they relate to the subject matter is really anyone's guess.

Many Mysteries, Still No Answers

And then there's the manuscript's enigmatic text. The world's greatest cryptologists have failed to unravel its meaning. Even the American and British code breakers who cracked the Japanese and German codes in World War II were stumped. To this day, not a single word of the Voynich manuscript has been deciphered.

This, of course, has led to key unsolved questions, namely:

* Who wrote it? A letter found with the manuscript, dated 1666, credits Roger Bacon, a Franciscan friar who lived from 1214 to 1294. This has since been discredited because the manuscript's date of origin is generally considered to be between 1450 and 1500. There are as many theories about who wrote it as there are nymphs among its pages. In fact, some believe Voynich forged the whole thing.

* What is it? It was first thought to be a coded description of Bacon's early scientific discoveries. Since then, other theories ranging from an ancient prayer book written in a pidgin Germanic language to one big, elaborate hoax (aside from that supposedly perpetrated by Voynich) have been posited.

* Is it real writing? Is the script composed in a variation of a known language, a lost language, an encrypted language, an artificial language? Or is it just plain gibberish?

What Do We Know?

Despite the aura of mystery surrounding the manuscript, it has been possible to trace its travels over the past 400 years. The earliest known owner was Holy Roman Emperor Rudolph II, who purchased it in 1586. By 1666, the manuscript had passed through a series of owners to Athanasius Kircher, a Jesuit scholar who hid it in the college where Voynich found it 250 years later. After being passed down to various members of Voynich's estate, the manuscript was sold in 1961 to a rare-book collector who sought to resell it for a fortune. After failing to find a buyer, he donated it to Yale University, where it currently resides—still shrouded in mystery—in the Beinecke Rare Book and Manuscript Library.

The Search for Meaning Continues...

To this day, efforts to translate the Voynich manuscript continue. And still, the manuscript refuses to yield its secrets, leading experts to conclude that it's either an ingenious hoax or the ultimate unbreakable code. The hoax theory gained some ground in 2004 when Dr. Gordon Rugg, a computer-science lecturer at Keele University, announced that he had replicated the Voynich manuscript using a low-tech device called a Cardan grille. According to Rugg, this proved that the manuscript was likely a fraud—a volume of jibberish created, perhaps, in an attempt to con money out of Emperor Rudolph II. Mystery solved? Well, it's not quite as simple as that. Many researchers remain unconvinced. Sure, Rugg may have proven that the manuscript might be a hoax. But the possibility that it is not a hoax remains. And thus, the search for meaning continues...

The Vanishing Treasure Room

In the Age of Enlightenment, kings and emperors built immense palaces to outdo one another—each one bigger and more gilded and bejeweled than the last. But one of Russia's greatest 18th century treasures became one of the 20th century's greatest unsolved mysteries.

✳ ✳ ✳ ✳

THE STORIED HISTORY of the Amber Room begins in 1701, when it was commissioned by Frederick I of Prussia. Considered by admirers and artists alike to be the "Eighth Wonder of the World," the sparkling, honey-gold room consisted of wall panels inlaid with prehistoric amber, finely carved and illuminated by candles and mirrors. In 1716, Prussian King Freidrich Wilhelm I gifted the panels to then-ally Russian Tsar Peter the Great to ornament the imperial palace at his new capital, St. Petersburg.

After sitting at the Winter Palace for four decades, the Amber Room was moved to Tsarskoye Selo, the Romanov palace just south of St. Petersburg. During the mid-18th century, Prussia's King Frederick the Great sent Russia's Empress Elizabeth more of the amber material from his Baltic holdings, and Elizabeth ordered her court's great Italian architect, Bartolomeo Rastrelli, to expand the Amber Room into a masterpiece.

The golden room was not finished until 1770, under the reign of Catherine the Great. Incorporating more than six tons of amber and accented with semiprecious stones, the fabled room became not only a prized jewel of the Russian empire, but a symbol of the alliance between Prussia and Russia.

From Peace to War

Two centuries after the Amber Room was removed to the Catherine Palace, the world was a much darker place. Prussia and Russia, formerly faithful allies, were locked in a deadly struggle that would bring down both imperial houses. By 1941, the former dominions of Frederick and Peter were ruled by Adolf Hitler and Joseph Stalin.

In a surprise attack, Hitler's armies drove across the Soviet border in June 1941 to launch the most destructive war in history. German panzers drove from the Polish frontier to the gates of Moscow in an epic six-month campaign, devouring some of the most fertile, productive territory in Eastern Europe.

One of the unfortunate cities in the path of the Nazi onslaught was St. Petersburg, renamed Leningrad by its communist masters. Frantic palace curators desperately tried to remove the Amber Room's antique panels, but the brittle prehistoric resin began to crumble as the panels were detached. Faced with probable destruction of one of Russia's greatest treasures or its abandonment to the Nazis, the curators attempted to hide the room's precious panels by covering them with gauze and wallpaper.

Although Leningrad withstood a long, bloody siege, German troops swept through the city's suburbs, capturing Tsarskoye Selo intact in October 1941. Soldiers discovered the treasure hidden behind the wallpaper, and German troops disassembled the room's panels over a 36-hour period, packed them in 27 crates, and shipped them back to Königsberg, in East Prussia.

The fabled Amber Room panels were put on display in Königsberg's castle museum. They remained there for two years—until the Third Reich began to crumble before the weight of Soviet and Anglo-American military forces. Sometime in 1944, the room's valuable panels were allegedly dismantled and packed into crates, to prevent damage by British and Soviet bombers. In January 1945, Hitler permitted the westward movement of cultural treasures, including the Italo-Russo-German masterpiece.

And from there, the Amber Room was lost to history.

The Great Treasure Hunt

The world was left to speculate about the fate of the famous imperial room, and dozens of theories have been spawned about the room's whereabouts. Some claim the Amber Room was lost—sunk aboard a submarine, bombed to pieces, or perhaps burned in Königsberg. This last conclusion was eventually accepted by Alexander Brusov, a Soviet investigator sent to find the Amber Room shortly after the war's end. Referring to the destruction of Königsberg Castle by Red Army forces on April 9, 1945, he came to the conclusion: "Summarizing all the facts, we can say that the Amber Room was destroyed between 9 and 11 April 1945."

An in-depth hunt by two British investigative journalists pieced together the last days of the Amber Room and concluded that its fate was sealed when Soviet troops accidentally set fire to the castle compound during the last month of combat, destroying the brittle jewels and obscuring their location.

Other treasure hunters, however, claim the room still sits in an abandoned mine shaft or some long-forgotten Nazi bunker beneath the outskirts of Königsberg. One German investigator claimed former SS officers told him the room's panels were packed up and hidden in an abandoned silver mine near Berlin; a Lithuanian official claimed witnesses saw SS troops hiding the panels in a local swamp. Neither has been able to prove his claims.

The Trail Goes Cold

The hunt for the Amber Room has been made more difficult because its last witnesses are gone—several under mysterious circumstances. The Nazi curator in charge of the room died of typhus the day before he was scheduled to be interviewed by the KGB, and a Soviet intelligence officer who spoke to a journalist about the room's whereabouts died the following day in a car crash. In 1987, Georg Stein, a former German soldier who had devoted his life to searching for the Amber Room, was found murdered in a forest, his stomach slit open by a scalpel.

In 1997, the world got a tantalizing glimpse of the long-lost treasure when German police raided the office of a Bremen lawyer who was attempting to sell an amber mosaic worth $2.5 million on behalf of one of his clients, the son of a former German lieutenant. The small mosaic—inlaid with jade and onyx as well as amber—had been stolen from the Amber Room by a German officer and was separated from the main panels. After its seizure, this last true remnant of the legendary tsarist treasure made its way back to Russia in April 2000.

Decades of searches by German and Soviet investigators have come up empty. The fate of the fabled room—worth an esti-

mated $142 million to $250 million in today's currency—has
remained elusive for investigators looking for the Holy Grail of
Russian baroque artwork.

Picking Up the Pieces

In 1979, the Soviet government, with help from a dona-
tion made by a German gas firm in 1999, began amassing
old photographs of the Amber Room and pieces of the rare
amber to create a reconstructed room worthy of its prede-
cessor. Carefully rebuilt at a cost exceeding $7 million, the
reconstructed room was dedicated by the Russian president
and German chancellor at a ceremony in 2003, marking
the tricentennial of St. Petersburg's founding. The dazzling
Amber Room is now on display for the thousands of tourists
who come to Tsarskoye Selo to view the playground of one of
Europe's great dynasties.

The Nazca Lines—Pictures Aimed at an Eye in the Sky?

*Ancient works of art etched into a desert floor in South America
have inspired wild theories about who created them and why. Did
space aliens leave them on long-ago visits? Decades of scientific
research reject the popular notion, showing that the lines were
the work of mere Earthlings.*

✳   ✳   ✳   ✳

FLYING ABOVE THE rocky plains northwest of Nazca, Peru,
in 1927, aviator Toribio Mejía Xesspe was surprised to see
gigantic eyes looking up at him. Then the pilot noticed that
the orbs stared out of a bulbous head upon a cartoonish line
drawing of a man, etched over hundreds of square feet of the
landscape below. The huge drawing—later called "owl man" for
its staring eyes—turned out to be just one of scores of huge,
2,000-year-old images scratched into the earth over almost
200 square miles of the parched Peruvian landscape.

There is a 360-foot-long monkey with a whimsically spiraled tail, along with a 150-foot-long spider, and a 935-foot pelican. Other figures range from hummingbird to killer whale. Unless the viewer knows what to look for, they're almost invisible from ground level. There are also geometric shapes and straight lines that stretch for miles across the stony ground.

The Theory of Ancient Astronauts

The drawings have been dated to a period between 200 BC and AD 600. Obviously, there were no airplanes from which to view them back then. So why were they made? And for whose benefit? In his 1968 book *Chariots of the Gods?*, Swiss author Erich Von Däniken popularized the idea that the drawings and lines were landing signals and runways for starships that visited southern Peru long before the modern era. In his interpretation, the owl man is instead an astronaut in a helmet. Von Däniken's theory caught on among UFO enthusiasts. Many science-fiction novels and films make reference to this desert in Peru's Pampa Colorado region as a site with special significance to space travelers.

Coming Down to Earth

Examined up close, the drawings consist of cleared paths— areas where someone removed reddish surface rocks to expose the soft soil beneath. In the stable desert climate—averaging less than an inch of rain per year—the paths have survived through many centuries largely intact.

Scientists believe the Nazca culture—a civilization that came before the Incas—drew the lines. The style of the artwork is similar to that featured on Nazca pottery. German-born researcher Maria Reiche (1903–1998) showed how the Nazca could have laid out the figures using simple surveying tools such as ropes and posts. In the 1980s, American researcher Joe Nickell duplicated one of the drawings, a condor, showing that the Nazca could have rendered parts of the figures "freehand"—that is, without special tools or even scale models.

Nickell also demonstrated that despite their great size, the figures can be identified as drawings even from ground level. No alien technology would have been required to make them.

Still Mysterious

As for why the Nazca drew giant doodles across the desert, no one is sure. Reiche noted that some of the lines have astronomical relevance. For example, one points to where the sun sets at the winter solstice. Some lines may also have pointed toward underground water sources—crucially important to desert people.

Most scholars think that the marks were part of the Nazca religion. They may have been footpaths followed during ritual processions. And although it's extremely unlikely that they were intended for extraterrestrials, many experts think it likely that the lines were oriented toward Nazca gods—perhaps a monkey god, a spider god, and so on, who could be imagined gazing down from the heavens upon likenesses of themselves.

Shroud of Turin: Real or Fake?

Measuring roughly 14 feet long by 3 feet wide, the Shroud of Turin features the front and back image of a man who was 5 feet, 9 inches tall. The man was bearded and had shoulder-length hair parted down the middle. Dark stains on the Shroud are consistent with blood from a crucifixion.

✳ ✳ ✳ ✳

FIRST PUBLICLY DISPLAYED in 1357, the Shroud of Turin has apparent ties to the Knights of Templar. At the time of its first showing, the Shroud was in the hands of of the family of Geoffrey de Charney, a Templar who had been burned at the stake in 1314 along with Jacques de Molay. Some accounts say it was the Knights who removed the cloth from Constantinople, where it was kept in the 13th century.

Some believe the Shroud of Turin is the cloth that Jesus was wrapped in after his death. All four gospels mention that the body of Jesus was covered in a linen cloth prior to the resurrection. Others assert that the cloth shrouded Jacques de Molay after he was tortured by being nailed to a door. Still others contend that the Shroud was the early photographic experiments of Leonardo da Vinci. He mentioned working with "optics" in some of his diaries and wrote his notes in a sort of mirrored handwriting style, some say, to keep his experiments secret from the church.

Is the Shroud of Turin authentic? In 1988, scientists using carbon-dating concluded that the material in the Shroud was from around AD 1260 to 1390, which seems to exclude the possibility that the Shroud bears the image of Jesus.

The Hitler Diaries Hoax

In 1983, Germany's popular magazine Stern *dropped a bomb: It now had access to Adolf Hitler's secret diaries. Experts soon revealed them as phonies authored by a modern crook, leaving prominent historians and major media looking ridiculous.*

✳   ✳   ✳   ✳

Counterfeit Collectibles

THE CROOK WAS Konrad Kujau, a man of numerous aliases and lies. He was born in 1938, and after World War II he lived in East Germany. He moved to West Germany in 1957 and began a life of petty crime, quickly specializing in forgery.

A lifetime Hitler fan, Kujau became a noted Nazi memorabilia "collector." Naturally, he manufactured most of his collection, including authentication documents. He built a favorable reputation as a dealer specializing in ostensibly authentic Hitler stuff: signatures, writing, poetry, and art. The public display of Nazi anything is illegal in Germany, as is Holocaust denial. Even WWII games sold in modern Germany cannot use the swastika. Nazi memorabilia collections remain strictly on the down low. Modern Germans overwhelmingly repudiate Nazism, and those born post-war also dislike association with a horror they didn't perpetrate. It's a painful subject.

Still, every country has closet Hitler admirers, and Germany is no exception. *Stern* journalist Gerd Heidemann was one—he even bought Hermann Goering's old yacht. In 1979, a collector (Kujau under an alias) invited Heidemann to check out his Nazi collection, including a bound copy of a diary supposedly authored by Hitler. The diary, which covered a period from January to June 1935, had been salvaged from a late-war plane crash in East Germany. The collector also claimed that there were 26 other volumes, each covering a six-month period.

Faulty Fact-Checking

Using his journalistic training, Heidemann went to East Germany and found a backstory that verified a plane crash. Although he didn't dig much deeper, he had a good excuse. At the time, the world thought in terms of East and West Germany. In East Germany, a socialist police state, no one nosed around except where the state approved (which it rarely did). Heidemann and *Stern's* West German homeland was the mainstay of NATO, and the border between East and West Germany bristled with a surprising percentage of the world's military power. *Stern* lacked an easy way to verify anything in East Germany.

So Heidemann basically pitched what he had to *Stern*, and the magazine swung from its heels. Salivating at the "find of a generation," *Stern* authorized Heidemann to offer an advance of $1 million (approximate U.S. equivalent) for the diaries. Kujau played coy, explaining that the other 26 volumes hadn't yet been smuggled out of East Germany. In reality, he needed time to forge them. He finally finished in 1981 and handed over the first volume to Heidemann. At this point, everyone was too excited to bother with that tedious step called "authentication." *Stern* hadn't even learned Kujau's identity; it was too busy counting its future profit from serialization rights. Anyone who voiced worries about fraud was hushed. Some surprisingly big names entered bids, including *Newsweek*, *Paris Match*, and the *London Times*.

Stretching the Truth

The diaries themselves purported to reveal a kinder, gentler Hitler, a generally okay guy who wasn't even fully aware of the Holocaust. This Hitler is what modern Nazi sympathizers like to imagine existed, not the weird megalomaniac of actual history. But its improbability also spurred skeptics into gear.

In an attempt to deal with the naysayers, *Stern* got a bit hysterical, even insisting that noted British historian Hugh Trevor-Roper had pronounced the diaries authentic. But skeptics faulted the diaries' paper, handwriting, and style. After some controversy, West German authorities ran forensics. The testing proved that the paper, ink, and even glue were of post-WWII manufacture. *Stern* had been bamboozled.

Because *Stern* is to Germany what *Time* and *Newsweek* are to the United States, it had a significant amount of credibility to lose. Several *Stern* editors were soon looking for new jobs. To say that the West German government was "annoyed" is an understatement. After *Stern* fired Heidemann, the police charged him with fraud. Heidemann, in his smartest move in a long time, implicated Kujau. When this news was made public in the media, Kujau went into hiding. In May 1983, he decided to turn himself into the police, who were anxiously waiting to arrest him. After several days of intense questioning, the authorities learned that Kujau was a reflexive, perpetual liar who invented falsehoods to cover his fictions.

The High Price of Greed

Kujau and Heidemann were each sentenced to several years in jail. The judge said *Stern* had "acted with such naiveté and negligence that it was virtually an accomplice in the fraud." The roughly $5 million the magazine ultimately gave Heidemann to pay Kujau was never recovered. Heidemann's increasingly lavish lifestyle during the forgeries and subsequent investigations suggests that he spent the majority of the money offshore.

After his release, Kujau tried his hand at politics, replica painting, and (again) forgery. He died of complications from cancer in 2000, but his crime is considered one of the most bold and successful hoaxes of the century. Declassified East German files later showed that Heidemann had been an East German spy, though it's uncertain whether that had anything to do with the hoax. He claims he was actually a double agent working for West German authorities. With his career prospects impaired, he now keeps a low profile.

The Black Angel of Death

The "Black Angel of Death" is unlike other angel statues at Oakland Cemetery in Iowa City, Iowa. For starters, at eight and a half feet tall (not including its pedestal), it towers high above the others. The eyes of the other angel statues gaze up toward heaven, and their wings are folded on their backs, which signals hope. But with its wings spread wide and pointing toward the ground, the Black Angel stares down upon the grave of Eddie Dolezal, who died in 1891 at age 18. The other angels are made of white marble; the Black Angel was sculpted out of bronze, which turned black over the years due to oxidation (or, as some speculate, the sins of Eddie's mother, who commissioned the statue in 1912). The Black Angel is different from the other angels in another important way: According to legend, it likes to take new victims.

T**HE BLACK ANGEL** doesn't like to be touched inappropriately or witness public displays of affection. Locals know that girls should not be kissed near the statue: The consequence is death within six months. Anyone who touches the statue on Halloween night has only seven more years to live. Worse, giving the Angel a kiss can stop a person's heart.

The Black Angel is said to take its ultimate revenge on those who desecrate it. Legend says that four boys died in a car crash not long after urinating on the Black Angel. Another story tells of a young man who removed the thumb of the Angel; soon after, his body was found hundreds of miles away in the Chicago River, dead from strangulation. A single thumbprint was imprinted on his neck. Not long after, a bronze thumb, blackened with age, was reportedly found at the base of the Black Angel.

Whether or not the Black Angel has actually killed anyone is debatable, but photos do often reveal strange lights around it. One couple found that every one of their pictures featured a red light where the angel's heart would be. Other snapshots have included orbs, which signify the presence of spirits. For whatever reason, the Black Angel does not rest well. Anyone in its presence should beware of its powers.

Losing Philip K. Dick's Head

Consider the sorts of things an air traveler might accidentally leave in an overhead bin: a novel, a jacket, a laptop computer... or perhaps the $750,000 android head of author Philip K. Dick.

✳ ✳ ✳ ✳

Meet David Hanson

I**N THE WORLD** of robotics, David Hanson is known as the genius inventor of "frubber"—an uncannily authentic-looking synthetic skin. With this breakthrough, Hanson has created robots modeled after popular figures, anyone ranging from Albert Einstein to rocker David Byrne. In 2004, his firm, Hanson Robotics, led a team of artists, scientists, and literary scholars to create an android modeled after science fiction writer Philip K. Dick, who died in 1982. To build the android's body of synthetic knowledge, a team led by artificial intelligence (AI) expert Andrew Olney scanned 20 of Dick's novels as well as interviews, speeches, and biographical information into its computer brain.

After six months of work, the completed android was an impressive achievement. Using a camera for its eyes, the android could follow movement, make eye contact, and recognize familiar faces in a crowd. The android's cutting-edge AI applications allowed it to respond to queries using its inputted source material (though its replies were often off-topic and bordered on the surreal—not unlike the real-life Dick, according to friends). The team called him "Phil."

David Hanson Loses His Head

In June 2005, Phil made his debut appearance at Chicago's NextFest technology exhibition. He was a sensation. The technically minded marveled at the feat of engineering, the sci-fi fans thrilled at the wonderful irony of interacting with an android replication of their long-dead hero, and the merely curious were rewarded by the eerie sense of humanity that Phil inspired.

At the San Diego Comic-Con, Phil took part in a panel discussing the upcoming release of *A Scanner Darkly*. Phil was a sensation: Hanson and Phil made appearances in Memphis, New Orleans, and Dallas. There was talk of a tour to promote the movie, an appearance on the *Late Show with David Letterman*, and a stint in the Smithsonian Institute's traveling collection.

In early 2006, Phil was on his way to Mountain View, California. He was stored face down in Styrofoam, bundled in a gym bag, and stowed in the overhead bin on the plane. Hanson, bleary from sleep, changed flights in Las Vegas. Soon afterward, he realized that Phil was still on the plane. The airline confirmed that Phil had traveled with the plane to Orange County. The android was supposed to be put on a flight to San Francisco but never arrived. Phil has not been seen since.

All Is Not Lost

Though the unique Philip K. Dick head has vanished, Hanson's laptop, containing Phil's brain, is safe. Despite the heartbreaking loss, Hanson eventually built another head for Phil. A failed lawsuit against the airline, however, means that, ironically, like the real-life Philip K. Dick, Phil must wait for the two things most precious to a struggling writer: time and money.

Welcome to Ohio: Don't Lose Your Head!

Sure, New York has its Headless Horseman, but Ohio can do that one better: a headless motorcycle ghost. And not just one, either. It's been said that the state of Ohio has more headless motorcycle ghosts per capita than any other state.

✳　✳　✳　✳

CONSIDERED THE FATHER of all Ohio headless motorcycle ghosts, the legend of the Elmore Rider became popular in the 1950s and may have existed even further back. As the story goes, a young motorcycle enthusiast from Elmore was forced to leave his true love behind when he went to serve his country in World War I. Upon his return on the evening of March 21, the first thing the soldier did was hop on his motorcycle and race off to reunite with her. Imagine the man's shock and horror when, arriving at her home, he found her in the arms of another man. Full of rage, the young man jumped on his motorcycle and sped off into the night. As he crossed a bridge, he lost control of his bike and crashed, decapitating himself in the process.

Today, it is said that if the curious go out to the bridge on March 21, the anniversary of the young man's death, and flash their lights three times, the ghostly light from a phantom motorcycle will begin coming toward them. As soon as the light crosses the bridge, it vanishes.

Calling Out the Rider

Having heard about the Elmore Rider for years, a man named Richard Gill decided to try a series of experiments to test the tale's validity. In 1968, Gill and a friend visited that bridge on March 21 to catch a glimpse of the headless ghost. Armed with video and still cameras, the pair sat in Gill's car and flashed the headlights three times. Almost immediately, they saw a single white light come down the hill toward the bridge. As the pair looked on in amazement, the light crossed the bridge and vanished into thin air. Believing they were on to something, Gill and his friend strung a piece of string across the road and flashed their lights again. Almost on cue, the light appeared, came down the hill, and promptly disappeared when it reached the other side of the bridge. Amazingly, when Gill checked the string, it was still intact—even though the light had appeared to go right through it.

As a final experiment, Gill managed to convince his friend to stand in the middle of the road, directly in the path of the phantom headlight. Gill went to the car and flashed the lights three times, summoning the ghost. The light appeared and, from Gill's viewpoint, looked like it went right through his friend before disappearing. Running onto the bridge, Gill found that his friend was no longer there. He was lying in a ditch alongside the road, unconscious. When he came to, the friend remembered nothing. Weirdly, the video and audio tapes revealed nothing except a strange whining noise, without so much as a flicker of light visible.

So ended Gill's experiments. But even the threat of bodily harm hasn't stopped people from showing up in droves every March 21, hoping to see a real-life ghost...or at least its headlight.

The Oxford Motorcycle Ghost

Having only been around since the 1980s, the headless motorcycle ghost of Oxford could be considered the newcomer. But the legend is unique in that it contains an explanation as to why people have to flash their lights three times to get the ghost to appear.

The Oxford story begins with a young couple, both of whom were living on Oxford-Milford Road while falling madly in love with each other. There was only one problem: The girl's parents didn't approve of the fact that the boy rode a motorcycle, and they forbade her from seeing him. The lovestruck girl secretly disobeyed her parents, and the couple devised a plan. As soon as the girl's parents were fast asleep, she would flash her front porch light three times. Upon seeing the light, the boy would push his motorcycle over to the girl's house, located around a sharp bend. Once he got there, the girl would creep out, and they would push the motorcycle back down the road before racing off.

The plan worked fine until one fateful night when the boy fell asleep waiting for his girlfriend to flash the porch light. Some say he grew tired because he had been in town drinking earlier that night. Regardless, when he woke up, he saw that his girlfriend had been frantically flashing the porch light over and over. Not wanting to keep her waiting a minute longer, he cranked up his motorcycle and sped toward her house. In too much of a hurry, he was unable to navigate the sharp bend, and he crashed through a barbed wire fence, coming out the other side minus his head.

It is said that even today, the headless ghost still rides his motorcycle down Oxford-Milford Road. The girlfriend's house is long gone, but if ghost chasers go to the spot near the sharp curve where it once stood and flash their lights three times, the ghost will come speeding down the road. The light will then go barreling off the road when it reaches the bend.

Blue Light Cemeteries

Under the full moon, some cemeteries in Texas are known for eerie, flashing blue lights and ghostly figures hovering over certain graves.

✳ ✳ ✳ ✳

TEXAS'S MANY INTRIGUING mysteries include "blue light" cemeteries. Many people believe that these blue lights and figures are ghosts, angels, or even demons. Others blame the phenomena on swamp gas or foxfire, a luminescent fungus that glows in the dark. The more likely explanation is more simple... and perhaps more mystical.

Geologists explain that normal flashes occur when the mineral labradorite is exposed to bright, natural light. Although they can happen at any time, these flashes become especially obvious at night. The effect is so unique, it's called *labradorescence*.

No Need to Be Alarmed

Labradorite is a blue-green stone that's found in Finland, Nova Scotia, Newfoundland, and Labrador. The mineral has been used for gravestones, especially in Louisiana and Texas. Unfortunately, natural cracks and refractions within the mineral cause it to crumble, especially after years in the hot sun.

Thus, in cemeteries throughout Texas, pieces of crumbled labradorite glisten beneath the moon. Hidden in the grass, those shards reflect moonlight and spark ghost stories.

Or Is There?

According to folklore, labradorite can connect the living to the spirit world. Some psychics use labradorite to communicate with "the other side."

One of Texas's most famous blue light cemeteries is just west of Houston near Patterson Road. For more than 20 years, curiosity seekers have ignored poison ivy, spiders, snakes, and barbed wire to explore Hillendahl-Eggling Cemetery. It's been called "Blue Light Cemetery" since the 1940s when the surrounding German community moved to make room for a Houston reservoir. Other Texas "blue light" cemetery locations include Andice, Cason, and Spring.

The Easter Island Tablets

Considered to be one of the most remote islands in the world, Easter Island is more than 1,200 miles away from its nearest inhabited neighbor. Yet, amazingly, Polynesian explorers braved the open Pacific Ocean and somehow found their way to the island around the year 1200. Archaeologists believe that these people created a thriving community, evidenced most notably by the nearly 1,000 enormous stone moai on the island. These monolithic human figures, which all feature unusually large heads, are said to represent the ancestors of the Rapa Nui people.

Studying these stone monoliths, and Easter Island itself, has provided researchers with valuable information about the Rapa Nui people and their culture. There are other artifacts found on the island, however, that have proven to be much more mysterious than the famous moai figures.

✳ ✳ ✳ ✳

Mysterious Symbols

IN THE 19TH century, a Roman Catholic missionary named Eugene Eyraud visited Easter Island and kept a journal of his thoughts and impressions. He wrote of discovering dozens of "wooden tablets or sticks covered in several sorts of hieroglyphic characters." Ultimately, 26 objects were recovered from Easter Island that contained this peculiar script. The writing seems to mostly depict animals, plants, humans, and geometric forms.

The script was dubbed "rongorongo," which, in the Rapa Nui language, means "to recite, to declaim, to chant out." The writing on the tablets is neat and tidy, with many of the wooden objects "fluted" with grooves to provide a straight-lined guide. According to oral tradition, expert scribes of rongorongo used small stones or shark teeth to carve the figures. It is also said that students of the language often wrote on banana leaves, however, no examples of this writing survive.

Lost in Translation

To this day, the rongorongo writing on these tablets has proved indecipherable. Making translation of the tablets especially difficult are several factors. First is the fact that very few inhabitants of Easter Island were literate. The handful that were—the expert scribes, priests, and tribal leaders who inscribed the tablets—were wiped out, either due to epidemics of illness or during slave raids. Another problem is the very limited number of texts that have been found, giving researchers limited context to decipher the script. And finally, the Rapa Nui language spoken today is vastly different from what was spoken centuries ago, as influence from Tahiti and other Polynesian islands affected the language. In fact, today, as a territory of Chile, Spanish is most commonly spoken on Easter Island. Although we don't know what the Rapa Nui people wanted to convey on these tablets, they believed it was important enough to painstakingly carve it into these artifacts. Perhaps one day, this linguistic mystery will be solved.

Chapter 6

Do You Know What Happened?

The Curse of King Tut's Tomb

If you discovered a mummy's tomb, would you go in? The curse of King Tut's tomb is a classic tale, even if there's a lot of evidence that says there was never anything to worry about.

✳ ✳ ✳ ✳

Curse, Schmurse!

IN THE EARLY 1920s, English explorer and archeologist Howard Carter led an expedition funded by the Fifth Earl of Carnarvon to unearth the tomb of Egyptian King Tutankhamun. Most of the tombs of Egyptian kings had been ransacked long ago, but Carter had reason to believe that King Tut's 3,000-year-old tomb was probably still full of artifacts from the ancient world. He was right.

Within the king's burial chamber were vases, precious metals, statues, even whole chariots, all buried with the king to aid him in the afterlife. Due to the hard work of Carter and his team, we now know a great deal more about the life of ancient Egyptian people during King Tut's time. Carter had been warned about the dangers of disrupting an ancient tomb, but he didn't buy into the rumors of curses and hexes. After opening the tomb, however, it was hard to deny that some strange, unpleasant events began to take place.

Curse or Coincidence?

During the 1920s, several men involved in the excavation died shortly after entering King Tut's tomb. The first one to go—the Fifth Earl of Carnarvon—died only a few months after completing the excavation. Legend has it that at the exact moment the earl died, all the lights in the city of Cairo mysteriously went out. That morning, his dog allegedly dropped dead, too.

Egyptologists claim that the spores and mold released from opening an ancient grave are often enough to make a person sick or worse. The earl had been suffering from a chronic illness before he left for Egypt, which could have made him more susceptible to the mold, and, therefore, led to his death.

Other stories say that the earl was bitten by a mosquito. Considering the sanitary conditions in Egypt at the time, a mosquito bite in Cairo could have some serious consequences, including malaria and other deadly diseases. Some reports indicate that the bite became infected and he died as a result—not because an ancient pharaoh was annoyed with him.

There were other odd happenings, and the public, already interested in the discovery of the tomb itself, was hungry for details of "the curse of the pharaohs." Newspapers reported all kinds of "proof": the earl's younger brother died suddenly five months after the excavation, and on the morning of the opening of the tomb, Carter's pet bird was swallowed by a cobra—the same kind of vicious cobra depicted on the mask of King Tut. Two of the workers hired for the dig died after opening the tomb, though their passing was likely due to malaria, not any curse.

Six of the 26 explorers involved died within a decade. But many of those involved in the exploration lived long, happy lives, including Carter. He never paid much attention to the curse, and, apparently, it never paid much attention to him. In 1939, Carter died of natural causes at age 64, after working with King Tut and his treasures for more than 17 years.

King Tutankhamun's sarcophagus and treasures have toured
the world on a nearly continual basis since their discovery
and restoration. When the exhibit went to America in the
1970s, some people tried to revive the old curse. When a San
Francisco police officer suffered a mild stroke while guarding a
gold funeral mask, he unsuccessfully tried to collect compensation, claiming his stroke was due to the pharaoh's curse.

A Superior Haunting: The *Edmund Fitzgerald*

*Many ships have been lost to the dangers of the Great Lakes,
but few incidents have fascinated the world like the sinking of
the* Edmund Fitzgerald *off the shores of northern Michigan on
November 10, 1975. The mysterious circumstances of the tragedy,
which took 29 lives, and lingering tales of a haunting—all
memorialized in a 1976 song by Gordon Lightfoot—have kept
the horrific story fresh for more than three decades.*

✳ ✳ ✳ ✳

Least Likely to Sink

LAKE SUPERIOR IS well known among sailors for its treachery, especially when the unusually strong autumn winds
sailors call the "Witch of November" roil the waves. But the
729-foot-long *Edmund Fitzgerald* was considered as unsinkable
as any steamer ever launched, and its cost of $8.4 million made
it the most expensive freighter in history at the time.

At its christening in June 1958, the ship was the Great Lakes'
largest freighter, built with state-of-the-art technology, comfortable crew quarters, and elegant staterooms for guests. Its
name honored Edmund Fitzgerald, the son of a sea captain and
the president of Northwestern Mutual Insurance Company,
who had commissioned the boat.

During the christening, a few incidents occurred that some saw as bad omens from the get-go. As a crowd of more than 10,000 watched, it took Mrs. Fitzgerald three tries to shatter the bottle of champagne. Then, when the ship was released into the water, it hit the surface at the wrong angle and kicked up a wave that splattered the entire ceremonial area with lake water, and knocked the ship into a nearby dock. If that weren't enough, one spectator died on the spot of a heart attack.

The Last Launch

The weather was unseasonably pleasant the morning of November 9, 1975, so much so that the crew of 29 men who set sail from Superior, Wisconsin, that day were unlikely to have been concerned about their routine trip to Zug Island on the Detroit River. But the captain, Ernest McSorley, knew a storm was in the forecast.

McSorley was a 44-year veteran of the lakes, had captained the *Fitzgerald* since 1972, and was thought to have been planning his retirement for the following year. He paid close attention to the gale warnings issued that afternoon, but no one suspected they would turn into what weather-watchers called a "once in a lifetime storm." However, when the weather report was upgraded to a full storm warning, McSorley changed course to follow a route safer than the normal shipping lanes, instead chugging closer to the Canadian shore.

Following the *Fitzgerald* in a sort of "buddy" system was another freighter, the *Arthur Anderson*. The two captains stayed in contact as they traveled together through winds measuring up to 50 knots (about 58 miles per hour) with waves splashing 12 feet or higher. Around 1:00 PM, McSorley advised Captain Cooper of the *Anderson* that the *Fitzgerald* was "rolling." By about 2:45 PM, as the *Anderson* moved to avoid a dangerous shoal near Caribou Island, a crewman sighted the *Fitzgerald* about 16 miles ahead, closer to the shoal than Cooper thought safe.

About 3:30 PM, McSorley reported to Cooper that the *Fitzgerald* had sustained some minor damage and was beginning to list, or roll to one side. The ships were still 16–17 miles apart. At 4:10 PM, with waves now lashing 18 feet high, McSorley radioed that his ship had lost radar capability. The two ships stayed in radio contact until about 7:00 PM when the *Fitzgerald* crew told the *Anderson* they were "holding [their] own." After that, radio contact was lost and the *Fitzgerald* dropped off the radar. Around 8:30 PM, Cooper told the Coast Guard at Sault Ste. Marie that the *Fitzgerald* appeared to be missing. The search was on.

Evidently, the *Fitzgerald* sank sometime after 7:10 PM on November 10, just 17 miles from the shore of Whitefish Point, Michigan. Despite a massive search effort, it wasn't until November 14 that a navy flyer detected a magnetic anomaly that turned out to be the wreck of the *Fitzgerald*. The only other evidence of the disaster to surface was a handful of lifeboats, life jackets, and some oars, tools, and propane tanks. A robotic vehicle was used to thoroughly photograph the wreck in May 1976.

One Mysterious Body

One troubling aspect of the *Fitzgerald* tragedy was that no bodies were found. In most lakes or temperate waters, corpses rise to the surface as decomposition causes gases to form, which makes bodies float. But the Great Lakes are so cold that decomposition and the formation of these gases is inhibited, causing bodies to remain on the lake bottom. One explanation was that the crew had been contained in the ship's enclosed areas. The wildest speculation surmised that the ship was destroyed by a UFO and the men were abducted by aliens.

In 1994, a Michigan businessman named Frederick Shannon took a tugboat and a 16-foot submarine equipped with a full array of modern surveillance equipment to the site, hoping to produce a documentary about the ship. But his crew was surprised when they discovered a body near the bow of the wreck, which had settled into the lake bottom. The remains were covered by cork sections of a deteriorated canvas life vest and were photographed but not retrieved. However, there was nothing to conclusively prove that this body was associated with the *Fitzgerald*. Two French vessels were lost in the same region in 1918, and none of those bodies had been recovered either. A sailor lost from one of them could have been preserved by the lake's frigid water and heavy pressure.

Many have pondered whether the men of the *Edmund Fitzgerald* might have been saved had they had better disaster equipment, but survival time in such cold water is only minutes. Most of the life jackets later floated to the surface, indicating that the crewmen never put them on. The seas were much too rough to launch wooden lifeboats, and there was probably no time to find and inflate rubber life rafts.

What Sank the Mighty *Fitz*?

She went down fast, that much was evident. Three different organizations filed official reports on the ship's sinking without coming to any common conclusions. It was thought impossible for such a large, well-built, and relatively "young" ship, only in its 18th year, to break up and sink so quickly, particularly in this age of modern navigation and communication equipment.

One popular theory is that the *Fitzgerald* ventured too close to the dangerous Six-Fathom Shoal near Caribou Island and scraped over it, damaging the hull. Another is that the ship's hatch covers were either faulty or improperly clamped, which allowed water infiltration. Wave height may also have played its part, with the storm producing a series of gargantuan swells known as the "Three Sisters"—a trio of lightning-fast waves that pound a vessel with a 1–2–3 punch—the first washes over the deck, the second hits the deck again so fast that the first has not had time to clear itself, and the third quickly adds another heavy wash, piling thousands of gallons of water on the ship at once. Few ships have the ability to remain afloat under such an onslaught.

In addition, the ship was about 200 feet longer than the 530-feet-deep water where it floundered. If the waves pushed the ship bowfirst down into the water, it would have hit bottom and stuck (which is what appears to have happened), snapping the long midsection in two as a result of continuing wave action and exploding steam boilers. The ship's 26,000-pound cargo of iron ore pellets shifted as the ship twisted and sank, adding to the devastation.

Some fingers pointed to the ship's prior damages. The *Fitzgerald* had been knocked around a bit during its career on the lakes: In 1969, it crunched ground near the locks at Sault Ste. Marie, Michigan, and less than a year later, in April 1970, it sustained a minor collision with the S.S. *Hochelaga*. In September of that year, the *Fitzgerald* slammed a lock wall for a total of three damaging hits within the span of 12 months. It's possible that these impacts inflicted more structural problems than were realized or that they were not repaired properly.

Spirits of the Lake

Author Hugh E. Bishop says that since the mighty *Fitz* went down, sailors have claimed to see a ghostly ship in the vicinity of the sinking. The captain of a Coast Guard cutter, the *Woodrush*, was on duty near the *Fitzgerald* site in 1976 and spent a night stuck in shifting ice masses directly over the wreckage. All throughout the night, the captain's normally carefree black Labrador whined and cowered, avoiding certain spots on the ship as if some invisible presence existed.

Bishop also noted that on October 21, 1975, a San Antonio psychic named J. Nickie Jackson recorded in her diary a dream she'd had that foretold the *Fitzgerald*'s doom. In her dream, she saw the freighter struggling to stay afloat in giant waves before it finally plunged straight down into the depths. The real-life event occurred just three weeks later. Jackson was familiar with the *Edmund Fitzgerald* because she had previously lived in Superior but was surprised to dream about it in her new life in Texas.

For Whom the Bell Tolls...

On July 4, 1995, a year after the lone body was documented, the bell of the *Edmund Fitzgerald* was retrieved from the wreckage and laid to rest in the Great Lakes Shipwreck Historical Museum in Whitefish Bay, Michigan. With the wreckage, the diving crew left a replica of the bell, which symbolizes the ship's "spirit." Every year on November 10, during a memorial service, the original, 200-pound, bronze bell is now rung 29 times—once for each crew member who perished on the *Edmund Fitzgerald*.

Who Wants to Be a Billionaire?

According to legend, more than $2 billion in gold may be hidden on Oak Island in Mahone Bay, about 45 minutes from Halifax, Nova Scotia. For more than 200 years, treasure hunters have scoured the island, looking for the bounty, but the pirates who buried the treasure hid it well...and left booby traps, too.

✳ ✳ ✳ ✳

Folklore Leads to Fact

SINCE 1720, PEOPLE have claimed that pirate treasure was buried on Oak Island. Then, in the fall of 1795, young Daniel McGinnis went hunting on the island and found evidence that those stories might be true. But he found something rather odd: An oak tree had been used with a hoist to lift something very heavy. When McGinnis dug at that spot, he found loose sand indicating a pit about 12 feet in diameter.

He returned the next day with two friends and some digging tools. When the boys had dug ten feet down, they encountered a wooden platform—beneath it was more dirt. Ten feet further down, they reached another wooden platform with more dirt beneath it. At that point, the boys had to give up. They needed better tools and engineering expertise to continue their search.

They didn't get the help they needed, but one thing was certain: Something important had been buried on Oak Island. Soon, more people visited the island hoping to strike it rich.

An Encouraging Message

In the early 1800s, a Nova Scotia company began excavating the pit. The slow process took many years, and every ten feet, they found another wooden platform and sometimes layers of charcoal, putty, or coconut fiber.

About 90 feet down, the treasure hunters found an oily stone about three feet wide. It bore a coded inscription that read, "Forty feet below, two million pounds lie buried." (Gold worth two million pounds in 1795 would be worth approximately $2 billion today.)

However, as they dug past that 90-foot level, water began rushing into the hole. A few days later, the pit was almost full of seawater. No matter how much the team bailed, the water maintained its new level, so the company dug a second shaft, parallel to the first and 110 feet deep. But when they dug across to the original tunnel, water quickly filled the new shaft as well. The team abandoned the project, but others were eager to try their luck.

More Digging, More Encouragement, More Water

Since then, several companies have excavated deeper in the original shaft. Most treasure hunters—including a team organized by Franklin D. Roosevelt—have found additional proof that something valuable is buried there. For example, at 126 feet—nearly "forty feet below" the 90-foot marker—engineers found oak and iron.

Farther down, they also reached a large cement chamber, from which they brought up a tiny piece of parchment, which encouraged them to dig deeper.

A narrow shaft dug in 1971 allowed researchers to use special cameras to study the pit. The team thought they saw several chests, some tools, and a disembodied hand floating in the water, but the shaft collapsed before they could explore further.

Since then, flooding has continued to hamper research efforts, and at least six people have been killed in their quests to find buried treasure. Nevertheless, the digging continues. As of late 2007, the 1971 shaft had been redug to a depth of 181 feet. It offers the greatest promise for success. But just in case, investors and engineers plan to continue digging.

A Vacation Worth a Fortune?

The digging isn't limited to professionals. Oak Island has become a unique vacation spot for people who like adventure and the chance to go home with a fortune. Canadian law says any treasure hunter can keep 90 percent of his or her findings. Some vacationers dig at nearby islands, believing that the Oak Island site may be an elaborate, 18th-century "red herring." There are more than 100 other lovely islands in Mahone Bay. Perhaps the treasure is actually buried on one of them?

Underground Cities: What's Going on Down There?

Most of us give little thought to what is going on beneath our feet. Under many cities, however, there exists another city that contains other people—or did at one time.

✳   ✳   ✳   ✳

Edinburgh, Scotland

IN THE 1700S, space was at a premium in Edinburgh. Hemmed in by hills and surrounded by protective walls, Edinburgh had no more clear land to build upon within the city limits. Arched bridges, such as South Bridge, were built to connect hilltop to hilltop, and, in a marvel of architectural design, small honeycombed chambers and tunnels were built into the vaults. At first, fashionable shops used these rooms for storage and workspace areas. But their underground nature attracted the seedier members of society, and the area quickly became a breeding ground for disease and crime. Although the vaults were closed in the mid-1800s, they were rediscovered and excavated in 1995. Today, a few restaurants, nightclubs, and ghost tours operate in the vaults.

Seattle, Washington

In 1889, the Great Seattle Fire destroyed more than 25 city blocks near the waterfront. In rebuilding the Pioneer Square area, city leaders decided to raise the street level to avoid flooding. With street level now a full story higher, merchants moved most of their businesses to their second (now ground) floors. Sidewalks built at the new street level created underground tunnels connecting the taverns and businesses that remained open. In 1907, fear of crime and disease caused the underground to be condemned, but a few of these abandoned tunnels and rooms have been restored and are currently open to the public.

Cappadocia, Turkey

It is believed that hundreds of underground cities exist underneath the Cappadocia rock, although only 40 have been found and a mere six are open to visitors. These cities first appeared in literature around 400 BC, and were used for storage and protection. Carved out of soft volcanic rock, the largest of these cities has 600 doors leading to the surface, as well as connecting rooms that tunneled underground eight excavated stories—and possibly as many as 12 unexcavated levels below those—and could hold as many as 30,000 people.

Paris, France

Built upon a network of 12th-century quarries, Paris sits atop 170 miles of tunnels. From 1785 until the 1880s, these tunnels received the bones of nearly six million people from condemned or overcrowded cemeteries around the city. During World

War II, the tunnels were used to hide Resistance fighters. Today, a portion of the catacombs is open as a museum to visitors, but the rest is left to foolhardy explorers, illegal partiers, and the dead.

Montreal, Quebec, Canada

Montreal is sometimes called two cities in one due to its subterranean counterpart. The underground city was started in 1962 as a shopping center, and it eventually grew to connect important buildings and house more shopping space. Now, 60 percent of offices in Montreal are linked to the underground city and there are more than 200 entrances. The underground city's 22 miles of corridors are used by more than 500,000 people every day to go to work, school, or any of the bus terminals, metro stations, 1,700 shops, 1,615 apartments, 200 restaurants, 40 banks, 40 cinemas and entertainment venues, 8 hotels, or other places that are part of the network.

Hey, It's The Freemasons!

For many, talk of "Freemasonry" conjures up images of intricate handshakes, strange rituals, and harsh punishment for revealing secrets about either. In actuality, the roots of the order are brotherhood and generosity. Throughout the ages, Masons have been known to fiercely protect their members and the unique features of their society.

T HE FANTASTICALLY NAMED Most Ancient and Honorable Society of Free and Accepted Masons began like other guilds; it was a collection of artisans brought together by their common trade, in this case, stone cutting and crafting. (There are many speculations as to when the society first began. Some believe it dates back to when King Solomon's temple was built.

Others believe the guild first formed in Scotland in the 16th century.) The Freemasons made the welfare of their members a priority. Group elders devised strict work regulations for masons, whose skills were always in demand and were sometimes taken advantage of.

Organized Freemasonry emerged in Great Britain in the mid-17th century with the firm establishment of Grand Lodges and smaller, local Lodges. (No one overarching body governs Freemasonry as a whole, though lodges worldwide are usually linked either to England or France.) In 1730, transplanted Englishmen established the first American Lodge in Virginia, followed in 1733 by the continent's first chartered and opened Grand Lodge in Massachusetts.

Boasting early American members including George Washington, Benjamin Franklin, and John Hancock, Freemasonry played a part in the growth of the young nation in ways that gradually attracted curiosity, speculation, and concern.

The source of the organization's mysterious reputation lay partly in its secrecy: Masons were prohibited from revealing secrets (some believed Masons would be violently punished if they revealed secrets, though the Masons deny such rumors). The Masonic bond also emphasized a commitment to one another. Outsiders feared the exclusivity smacked of conspiracy and compromised the motives of Masons appointed to juries or elected to public office.

Nonmembers wondered about the meanings of the Freemasons' peculiar traditions (such as code words and other secretive forms of recognition between members) and symbolism (often geometric shapes or tools, such as the square and compass). Design elements of the one-dollar bill, including the Great Seal and the "all-seeing eye," have been credited to founding fathers such as Charles Thomson and other Masons.

Freemasonry in the United States suffered a serious blow in September 1826 when New York Masons abducted a former "brother" named William Morgan. Morgan was about to publish a book of Masonic secrets, but before he could, he was instead ushered north to the Canadian border and, in all likelihood, thrown into the Niagara River. His disappearance led to the arrest and conviction of three men on kidnapping charges (Morgan's body was never found)—scant penalties, locals said, for crimes that surely included murder. The affair increased widespread suspicion of the brotherhood, spawning an American Anti-Mason movement and even a new political party dedicated to keeping Freemasons out of national office.

In the decades following the Civil War, men were again drawn to brotherhood and fellowship as they searched for answers in a changing age, and Freemasonry slowly regained popularity.

Today, Freemasonry remains an order devoted to its own members, charitable causes, and the betterment of society. It has a worldwide membership of at least five million. Its members are traditionally male, though certain associations now permit women. Despite the name, most members are not stonemasons. They are, however, required to have faith in a supreme being, but not necessarily the Christian god.

The Philadelphia Experiment

In 1943, the Navy destroyer USS Eldridge *reportedly vanished, teleported from a dock in Pennsylvania to one in Virginia, and then rematerialized—all as part of a top-secret military experiment. Is there any fact to this fiction?*

✳ ✳ ✳ ✳

The Genesis of a Myth

THE STORY OF the Philadelphia Experiment began with the scribbled annotations of a crazed genius, Carlos Allende, who in 1956 read *The Case for the UFO*, by science enthusiast

Morris K. Jessup. Allende wrote chaotic annotations in his copy of the book, claiming, among other things, to know the answers to all the scientific and mathematical questions that Jessup's book touched upon. Jessup's interests included the possible military applications of electromagnetism, antigravity, and Einstein's Unified Field Theory.

Allende wrote two letters to Jessup, warning him that the government had already put Einstein's ideas to dangerous use. According to Allende, at some unspecified date in October 1943, he was serving aboard a merchant ship when he witnessed a disturbing naval experiment. The USS *Eldridge* disappeared, teleported from Philadelphia, Pennsylvania, to Norfolk, Virginia, and then reappeared in a matter of minutes. The men onboard the ship allegedly phased in and out of visibility or lost their minds and jumped overboard, and a few of them disappeared forever. This strange activity was part of an apparently successful military experiment to render ships invisible.

The Navy Gets Involved

Allende could not provide Jessup with any evidence for these claims, so Jessup stopped the correspondence. But in 1956, Jessup was summoned to Washington, D.C., by the Office of Naval Research, which had received Allende's annotated copy of Jessup's book and wanted to know about Allende's claims and his written comments. Shortly thereafter, Varo Corporation, a private group that does research for the military, published the annotated book, along with the letters Allende had sent to Jessup. The Navy has consistently denied Allende's claims about teleporting ships, and the impetus for publishing Allende's annotations is unclear. Morris Jessup committed suicide in 1959, leading some conspiracy theorists to claim that the government had him murdered for knowing too much about the experiments.

The Fact Within the Fiction

It is not certain when Allende's story was deemed the "Philadelphia Experiment," but over time, sensationalist books and movies have touted it as such. The date of the ship's disappearance is usually cited as October 28, though Allende himself cannot verify the date nor identify other witnesses. However, the inspiration behind Allende's claims is not a complete mystery.

In 1943, the Navy was in fact conducting experiments, some of which were surely top secret, and sometimes they involved research into the applications of some of Einstein's theories. The Navy had no idea how to make ships invisible, but it *did* want to make ships "invisible"—i.e., undetectable—to enemy magnetic torpedoes. Experiments such as these involved wrapping large cables around Navy vessels and pumping them with electricity in order to descramble their magnetic signatures.

The Intergalactic Journey of Scientology

There are few who don't know about the aura of mystery and scandal that surrounds the Church of Scientology, which boasts a small membership and a seismic pocketbook. Scientology frequently graces the headlines, with stories ranging from accounts of Tom Cruise tomfoolery to an endless stream of lawsuits and accusations of bribery and abuse.

✳ ✳ ✳ ✳

THE FANTASTICAL ELEMENTS to the saga of Scientology were perhaps written into the religion from its beginning, given that Scientology sprang from the fertile mind of its late creator, pulp fiction writer turned religious messiah, L. Ron Hubbard. Hubbard, born in 1911, began his writing career in the 1930s after flunking out of college. Hubbard had always preferred imagination to reality: Accounts of his past reveal hallucinogenic drug abuse and an obsession with black magic and Satanism. In between prolific bouts of writing, Hubbard served in the Navy during World War II, became involved in various start-up ventures, and, of course, dabbled in black magic ceremonies. Allegation has it that Hubbard and wealthy scientist friend John Parsons performed a ritual in which they attempted to impregnate a woman with the antichrist. The woman was Parsons's girlfriend, but she soon became Hubbard's second wife—though he was still married to his first wife.

Down to a Science

In 1949, Hubbard developed a self-help process that he called Dianetics. All of humanity's problems, according to Dianetics, stem from the traumas of past lives. These traumas are called *engrams,* and Hubbard's own e-meter (a machine using simple lie detector technology) can identify and help eliminate these engrams. Getting rid of engrams can have amazing results—from increasing intelligence to curing blindness. The first Dianetics article appeared in a sci-fi publication called *Astounding Science Fiction.* In 1950, Hubbard opened the Hubbard Dianetic Research Foundation in New Jersey, and in that same year *Dianetics: The Modern Science of Mental Health* was published and sold well.

Hubbard and his followers attempted to establish Dianetics as an official science. But the medical profession didn't appreciate Dianetics masquerading as science. The Dianetic Research Foundation came under investigation by the IRS and the American Medical Association. Hubbard closed his clinics and fled New Jersey.

Actually, It's a Religion...

Dianetics wasn't making the cut as a scientific theory, so Hubbard played another card. Years before, Hubbard is reputed to have told a friend "writing for a penny a word is ridiculous. If a man really wants to make a million dollars, the best way would be to start his own religion." After fleeing Jersey, Hubbard moved to Phoenix, Arizona, declared Dianetics an "applied religious philosophy," and, in 1954, Hubbard's organization was recognized as a religion by the IRS and granted tax-exempt status.

Thus the Church of Scientology was born. Hubbard added new stories to the original Dianetics creation, and by the 1960s, humans were spiritual descendants of the alien Thetans, who were banished to live on Earth by the intergalactic terrorist dictator Xenu 75 million years ago. Scientologist disciples must not only expel the traumas of past lives but of past lives on different planets. Discovering these traumas is an expensive process, so the Church actively recruits wealthy devotees. As for Hubbard, he died in 1986, soon after the IRS accused him of stealing $200 million from the Church. Today, Scientology and its various offshoot nonprofit groups and private business ventures continue to hold a vast fortune, and Scientology's ongoing litigation with the IRS, the press, and ex-devotees (hundreds of lawsuits are pending) are so bizarre, they seem almost out of this world.

The Mystery of the 700-Year-Old Piper

It's an intriguing story about a mysterious piper and more than 100 missing children. Made famous by the eponymous Brothers Grimm, this popular fairy tale has captivated generations of boys and girls. But is it actually more fact than fiction?

✳ ✳ ✳ ✳

THE LEGEND OF The Pied Piper of Hameln documents the story of a mysterious musician who rid a town of rats by enchanting the rodents with music from his flute. The musician led the mesmerized rats to a nearby river, where they drowned. When the townsfolk refused to settle their debt, the rat catcher returned several weeks later, charmed a group of 130 children with the same flute, and led them out of town. They disappeared—never to be seen again.

It's a story that dates back to approximately AD 1300 and has its roots in a small German town called Hameln. Several accounts written between the 14th and 17th centuries tell of a stained-glass window in the town's main church. The window pictured the Pied Piper with hands clasped, standing over a group of youngsters. Encircling the window was the following verse (this is a rough translation): "In the year 1284, on John's and Paul's day was the 26th of June. By a piper, dressed in all kinds of colors, 130 children born in Hameln were seduced and lost at the calvarie near the koppen."

The verse is quite specific: precise month and year, exact number of children involved in the incident, and detailed place names. Because of this, some scholars believe this window, which was removed in 1660 and either accidentally destroyed or lost, was created in memory of an actual event. Yet, the verse makes no mention of the circumstances regarding the departure of the children or their specific fate. What exactly happened in Hameln, Germany, in 1284? The truth is, no one actually knows—at least not for certain.

Theories Abound

Gernot Hüsam, the current chairman of the Coppenbrügge Castle Museum, believes the word "koppen" in the inscription may reference a rocky outcrop on a hill in nearby Coppenbrügge, a small town previously known as Koppanberg. Hüsam also believes the use of the word "calvarie" is in reference to either the medieval connotation of the gates of hell—or since the Crusades—a place of execution.

One theory put forward is that Coppenbrügge resident Nikolaus von Spiegelberg recruited Hameln youth to emigrate to areas in Pomerania near the Baltic Sea. This theory suggests the youngsters were either murdered, because they took part in summertime pagan rituals, or drowned in a tragic accident while in transit to the new colonies.

But this is not the only theory. In fact, theories concerning the fate of the children abound. Here are some ideas about what really happened:

* They suffered from the Black Plague or a similar disease and were led from the town to spare the rest of the population.

* They were part of a crusade to the Holy Land.

* They were lost in the 1260 Battle of Sedemünder.

* They died in a bridge collapse over the Weser River or a landslide on Ith Mountain.

* They emigrated to settle in other parts of Europe, including Maehren, Oelmutz, Transylvania, or Uckermark.

* They were actually young adults who were led away and murdered for performing pagan rituals on a local mountain.

Historians believe that emigration, bridge collapse/natural disaster, disease, or murder are the most plausible explanations.

Tracing the Piper's Path

Regardless of what actually happened in Hameln hundreds of years ago, the legend of the Pied Piper has endured. First accounts of the Piper had roots to the actual incident, but as time passed, the story took on a life of its own.

Earliest accounts of the legend date back to 1384, at which time a Hameln church leader, Deacon von Lude, was said to be in possession of a chorus book with a Latin verse related to the legend written on the front cover by his grandmother. The book was misplaced in the late 17th century and has never been found.

The oldest surviving account—according to amateur Pied Piper historian Jonas Kuhn—appears as an addition to a 14th-century manuscript from Luneburg. Written in Latin, the note is almost identical to the verse on the stained-glass window and translates roughly to:

"In the year of 1284, on the day of Saints John and Paul on the 26th of June 130 children born in Hamelin were seduced By a piper, dressed in all kinds of colors, and lost at the place of execution near the koppen."

Sixteenth-century physician and philosopher Jobus Fincelius believed the Pied Piper was the devil. In his 1556 book, *Concerning the Wonders of His Times*, Fincelius wrote: "It came about in Hameln in Saxony on the River Weser...the Devil visibly in human form walked the lanes of Hameln and by playing a pipe lured after him many children...to a mountain. Once there, he with the children...could no longer be found."

In 1557, Count Froben Christoph von Zimmern wrote a chronicle detailing his family's lineage. Sprinkled throughout the book were several folklore tales including one that referenced the Pied Piper. For some unknown reason, the count introduced rats into his version of the story: "He passed through the streets of the town with his small pipe...immediately all the rats...collected outside the houses and followed his footsteps." This first insertion of rodents into the legend led other writers to follow suit.

In 1802, Johan Wolfgang Goethe wrote "Der Rattenfanger," a poem based on the legend. The monologue was told in the first person through the eyes of the rat catcher. Goethe's poem made no direct reference to the town of Hameln, and in Goethe's version the Piper played a stringed instrument instead of a pipe. The Piper also made an appearance in Goethe's literary work *Faust*.

Jacob and Wilhelm Grimm began collecting European folktales in the early 1800s. Best known for a series of books that documented 211 fairy tales, the brothers also published two volumes between 1816 and 1818 detailing almost 600 German folklore legends. One of the volumes contained the story of *Der Rattenfanger von Hameln*.

The Grimm brothers' research for *The Pied Piper* drew on 11 different sources, from which they deduced two children were left behind (a blind child and a mute child); the piper led the children through a cave to Transylvania; and a street in Hameln was named after the event.

No End in Sight

While the details of the historical event surrounding the legend of *The Piped Piper* have been lost to time, the mystique of the story endures. Different versions of the legend have even appeared in literature outside of Germany: A rat catcher from Vienna helped rid the nearby town of Korneuburg of rats. When he wasn't paid, he stole off with the town's children and sold them as slaves in Constantinople. A vagabond rid the English town of Newton on the Isle of Wight of their rats, and when he wasn't paid, led the town's children into an ancient oak forest where they were never seen again. A Chinese version had a Hangchow district official use magic to convince the rats to leave his city.

The legend's plot has been adapted over time to fit whichever media is currently popular and has been used as a story line in children's books, ballet, theatre, and even a radio drama. The intriguing story of the mysterious piper will continue to interest people as long as there is mystery surrounding the original event.

In Mushrooms We Trust

John Allegro: linguist, showman, and certifiable eccentric. He made some...atypical, let's say...suggestions about Biblical history.

✳   ✳   ✳   ✳

IT'S NOT OFTEN that the world of academia produces a character like John Marco Allegro. Born in 1923, Allegro first studied for the Methodist ministry but later became a brilliant scholar of Hebrew dialects. This latter course of study made him a perfect fit for the international team assembled to decipher the Dead Sea Scrolls, the earliest surviving manuscripts of the Bible.

Because Allegro was part scholar and part showman, he became a star in the otherwise sober world of biblical scholarship. At the time, the historical importance of the scrolls was a cause for controversy, and Allegro gleefully submerged himself into the debate.

Suddenly, however, Allegro took the debate in an absurd direction with his infamous book: *The Sacred Mushroom and the Cross*. In it, he argued that Biblical figures like Moses and Christ were actually literary inventions. In fact, he contended that the Jewish and Christian scriptures were allegories, written to promote an ancient fertility cult. To Allegro, Jesus represented a hallucinogenic mushroom, which followers ingested to enhance their perception of God.

Allegro tried to prove that the Bible was actually a coded text written to preserve the secrets of this drug-worshipping cult. When the writers of these "folktales" died, he argued, their original meaning was forever lost. Subsequent followers—early Christians—began taking scripture literally and interpreted as factual what Allegro maintained had always been meant as fable.

This peculiar thesis was roundly panned by the academic community. Allegro's reputation was destroyed. Though he died in disrepute, Allegro did inspire a group of supporters who, even to this day, still try to defend the man and his zany thesis.

The Library of the Muses

By far the most famous library in history, the Library of Alexandria held an untold number of ancient works. Its fiery destruction meant the irrecoverable loss of a substantial part of the world's intellectual history.

✳ ✳ ✳ ✳

The Library's Beginnings

THE CITIES OF ancient Mesopotamia (e.g., Uruk, Nineveh, Babylon) and Egypt (e.g., Thebes, Memphis) had cultivated archives and libraries since the Bronze Age, but the idea for a library as grand as Alexandria did not occur in Greek culture until the Hellenistic Age, when Alexander the Great's conquests brought both Greece and these former civilizations under Macedonian rule. Previous Greek libraries were owned by individuals; the largest belonged to Aristotle (384–322 BC), whose work and school (the Lyceum) in Athens were supported by Alexander.

When Alexander died suddenly in 323 BC, his generals carved his empire into regional dynasties. The Hellenistic dynasties competed with each other for three centuries (until each was in turn conquered by either Rome or Parthia). Each dynasty desired cultural dominance, so they invited famous artists, authors, and intellectuals to live and work in their capital cities. Alexander's general Ptolemy, who controlled Egypt, decided to develop a collection of the world's learning (the Library) and a research center, the Mouseion (the Museum, or "Temple of the Muses"), where scholars on subsidy could study and add their research to the collection. This idea may well have come from Demetrius of Phaleron (350–280 BC), Ptolemy's advisor and the former governor of Athens, who had been a pupil at the Lyceum, but the grand project became one of the hallmarks of the Ptolemaic dynasty. Under the first three Ptolemies, the Museum, a royal library, and a smaller "daughter" library at the Temple of Serapis (the Serapeum) were built and grew as Alexandria became the intellectual, as well as commercial, capital of the Hellenistic world.

Egypt and Alexandria offered the Ptolemies distinct advantages for accomplishing their goals. Egypt was not only immensely rich, which gave it the wealth to purchase materials and to bring scholars to Alexandria, but it was the major producer of papyrus, a marsh reed that was beaten into a flat surface and made into scrolls for writing and copying. Alexandria was also the commercial hub of the Mediterranean, and goods and information from all over the world passed through its port.

Bibliomania: So Many Scrolls, So Little Time

Acquiring materials for the libraries and Museum became somewhat of an obsession for the Ptolemies. Although primarily focused on Greek and Egyptian works, their interests included translating other traditions into Greek. Among the most important of these efforts was the production of the Septuagint, a Greek version of the Jewish scriptures. Besides employing agents to scour major book markets and to search out copies of works not yet in the library, boats coming into Alexandria were required to declare any scrolls on board. If they were of interest, the scrolls were confiscated and copied, and the owners were given the copies and some compensation. Ptolemy III (285–222 BC) may have acquired Athens' official state collection of the plays of Aeschylus, Sophocles, and Euripides in a similar way—putting up 15 talents of silver as a guarantee while he had the plays copied, then foregoing the treasure in favor of keeping the originals. Whether or not this is true, it speaks to the value he placed on getting important works and the resources he had at his disposal to do so.

Alexandria's efforts were fueled by a fierce competition with the Hellenistic kingdom of Pergamum (modern Bergamo, Turkey), which created its own library. Each library sought to claim new finds and to produce new editions, leading at times to the acquisition of forgeries and occasional embarrassment. Alexandria finally tried to undercut its rival by cutting off papyrus exports, but Pergamum perfected a method for making writing material out of animal skins (now called "parchment" from the Latin *pergamina*) and continued to build its holdings. Eventually, however, Alexandria got the upper hand when the Roman general Marcus Antonius (Mark Antony) conquered Pergamum and made a present of its library to his lover, the Ptolemaic Queen Cleopatra.

Estimates as to the number of volumes in the Alexandrian library ranged wildly even in antiquity, generally between 200,000 and 700,000. Estimates are complicated by the fact that it isn't clear whether the numbers originate from works or scrolls: Some scrolls contained one work, some multiple works, and long works like the *Iliad* took multiple scrolls. Over time, a complex cataloguing system evolved, which culminated in a bibliographic survey of the library's holdings called the Pinakes. The survey was put together by the great Hellenistic scholar and poet Callimachus of Cyrene (305–240 BC). Unfortunately, this important work only exists in fragments today.

Burning Down the House

The Royal Library and its holdings were accidentally set aflame in 48 BC when Caesar (who had taken Cleopatra's side in her claim to the throne against her brother) tried to burn his way out of being trapped in the port by opposing forces. Further losses probably occurred in AD 271 when Emperor Aurelian destroyed part of the Museum while recapturing Alexandria from Queen Zenobia's forces. The "daughter" library of the Serapeum was finally destroyed by Christians under Emperor Theodosius near the end of the 4th century. But by then, much of the contents (like the contents of other great civic libraries of antiquity) had decayed or found their way into other hands, leaving the classical heritage scattered and fragmented for centuries. Much later, Christians dramatically blamed the burning of the library holdings on Muslim conquerors. Although this made for a good story, the legendary contents of the library were already long gone.

The Mound Builders: Mythmaking In Early America

The search for an improbable past, or, how to make a mountain out of a molehill.

✳ ✳ ✳ ✳

IN THE EARLY 1840s, the fledgling United States was gripped by a controversy that spilled from the parlors of the educated men in Boston and Philadelphia—the core of the nation's intellectual elite—onto the pages of the newspapers printed for mass edification. In the tiny farming village of Grave Creek, Virginia (now West Virginia), on the banks of the Ohio River stood one of the largest earthen mounds discovered during white man's progress westward. The existence of these mounds, spread liberally throughout the Mississippi Valley, Ohio River Valley, and much of the southeast, was commonly known and had caused a great deal of speculative excitement since Europeans had first arrived on the continent. Hernando de Soto, for one, had mentioned the mounds of the Southeast during his wandering in that region.

Money Well Spent

The colonists who settled the East Coast noticed that the mounds, which came in a variety of sizes and shapes, were typically placed near excellent sites for villages and farms. The Grave Creek mound was among the first of the major earthworks discovered by white men in their westward expansion. By 1838, the property was owned and farmed by the Tomlinson family. Abelard B. Tomlinson took an interest in the mound on his family's land and decided to open a vertical shaft from its summit, 70 feet high, to the center. He discovered skeletal remains at various levels and a timbered vault at the base containing the remains of two individuals. More importantly, he discovered a sandstone tablet inscribed with three lines of characters of unknown origin.

Who Were the Mound Builders?

Owing to the general belief that the indigenous people were lazy and incapable of such large, earth-moving operations and the fact that none of the tribes who dwelt near the mounds claimed any knowledge of who had built them, many 19th-century Americans believed that the mound builders could not have been the ancestors of the Native American tribes they encountered. Wild and fantastic stories arose, and by the early 19th century, the average American assumed that the mound builders had been a pre-Columbian expedition from the Old World—Vikings, Israelites, refugees from Atlantis—all these and more had their champions. Most agreed, however, that the New World had once hosted and given rise to a civilization as advanced as that of the Aztecs and Incas who had then fallen into disarray or been conquered by the people that now inhabited the land. Speculation on the history of the mound builders led many, including Thomas Jefferson, to visit mounds and conduct their own studies.

Mormons and the Mounds

Meanwhile, the Grave Creek tablet fanned the flames of a controversy that was roaring over the newly established, and widely despised, Church of Jesus Christ of Latter Day Saints, founded by Joseph Smith. The Mormon religion is based upon the belief that the American continent was once inhabited by lost tribes of Israel who divided into warring factions and fought each other to near extinction. The last surviving prophet of these people, Mormon, inscribed his people's history upon gold tablets, which were interred in a mound near present-day Palmyra, New York, until they were revealed to fifteen-year-old Joseph Smith in 1823. Though many Americans were ready to believe that the mounds represented the remains of a non-indigenous culture, they were less ready to believe in Smith's new religion. Smith and his adherents were persecuted horribly, and Smith was killed by an angry mob while leading his followers west. Critics of the Saints (as the Mormons prefer to be called) point to the early 19th-century publication of several popular books purporting that the earthen mounds of North America were the remains of lost tribes of Israel. These texts claimed that evidence would eventually be discovered to support their author's assertions. That the young Smith should have his revelation so soon after these fanciful studies were published struck many observers as entirely too coincidental. Thus, Abelard Tomlinson's excavation of the sandstone tablet with its strange figures ignited the passions of both Smith's followers and his detractors.

Enter the Scholar

Into this theological, and ultimately anthropological, maelstrom strode Henry Rowe Schoolcraft, a mineralogist whose keen interest in Native American history had led to his appointment as head of Indian affairs. While working in Sault Ste. Marie, Schoolcraft married a native woman and mastered the Ojibwa language. Schoolcraft traveled to Grave Creek to examine Tomlinson's tablet and concluded that the figures were indeed a language but deferred to more learned scholars to determine just which language they represented. The opinions were many and varied—from Celtic runes to early Greek; experts the world over weighed in with their opinions.

Nevertheless, Schoolcraft was more concerned with physical evidence and close study of the mounds themselves, and he remained convinced that the mounds and the artifacts they carried were the products of ancestors of the Native Americans. Schoolcraft's theory flew in the face of both those who sought to defend and those who sought to debunk the Mormon belief, and it would be more than three decades until serious scholarship and the emergence of true archeological techniques began to shift opinion on the subject.

Answers Proposed, but Questions Still Abound

History has vindicated Schoolcraft's careful and thoughtful study of the mounds. Today, we know that the mound builders were not descendants of Israel, nor were they the offspring of Vikings. They were simply the ancient and more numerous predecessors of the Native Americans, who constructed the mounds for protection from floods and as burial sites, temples, and defense strongholds. As for the Grave Creek tablet: Scholars today generally agree that the figures are not a written language but simply a fanciful design whose meaning, if ever there was one, has been lost to the ages. Though the Smithsonian Institute has several etchings of the tablet in its collection, the whereabouts of the actual tablet have been lost to the ages.

The Mystery of Easter Island

On Easter Sunday in 1722, a Dutch ship landed on a small island 2,300 miles from the coast of South America. Polynesian explorers had preceded them by a thousand years or more, and the Europeans found the descendants of those early visitors still living on the island. They also found a strange collection of almost 900 enormous stone heads, or moai, standing with their backs to the sea, gazing across the island with eyes hewn out of coral. The image of those faces haunts visitors to this day.

✳ ✳ ✳ ✳

Ancestors at the End of the Land

EASTER ISLAND LEGEND tells of the great Chief Hotu Matu'a, the Great Parent, striking out from Polynesia in a canoe, taking his family on a voyage across the trackless ocean in search of a new home. He made landfall on Te-Pito-te-Henua, the End of the Land, sometime between AD 400 and 700. Finding the island well-suited to habitation, his descendants spread out to cover much of the island, living off the natural bounty of the land and sea. With their survival assured, they built *ahu*—ceremonial sites featuring a large stone mound—and on them erected moai, which were representations of notable chieftains who led the island over the centuries. The moai weren't literal depictions of their ancestors, but rather embodied their spirit, or mana, and conferred blessings and protection on the islanders.

The construction of these moai was quite a project. A hereditary class of sculptors oversaw the main quarry, located near one of the volcanic mountains on the island. Groups of people would request a moai for their local ahu, and the sculptors would go to work, their efforts supported by gifts of food and other goods. Over time, they created 887 of the stone moai, averaging just over 13 feet tall and weighing around 14 tons, but ranging from one extreme of just under four feet tall to a behemoth that towered 71 feet. The moai were then transported across the island by a mechanism that still remains in doubt, but that may have involved rolling them on the trunks of palm trees felled for that purpose—a technique that was to have terrible repercussions for the islanders.

When Europeans first made landfall on Easter Island, they found an island full of standing moai. Fifty-two years later, James Cook reported that many of the statues had been toppled, and by the 1830s none were left standing. What's more, the statues hadn't just been knocked over; many of them had boulders placed at strategic locations, with the intention of decapitating the moai when they were pulled down. What had happened?

A Culture on the Brink

It turns out the original Dutch explorers had encountered a culture on the rebound. At the time of their arrival, they found two or three thousand living on the island, but some estimates put the population as high as fifteen thousand a century before. The story of the islanders' decline is one in which many authors find a cautionary tale: The people simply consumed natural resources to the point where their land could no longer support them. For a millennium, the islanders simply took what they needed: They fished, collected bird eggs, and chopped down trees to pursue their obsession with building moai. By the 1600s, life had changed: The last forests on the island disappeared, and the islanders' traditional foodstuffs disappeared from the archaeological record. Local tradition tells of a time of famine and even rumored cannibalism, and it is from this time that island history reveals the appearance of the spear. Tellingly, the Polynesian words for "wood" begin to take on a connotation of wealth, a meaning found nowhere else that shares the language. Perhaps worst of all, with their forests gone, the islanders had no material to make the canoes that would have allowed them to leave their island in search of resources. They were trapped, and they turned on one another.

The Europeans found a reduced society that had just emerged from this time of terror. The respite was short-lived, however. The arrival of the foreigners seems to have come at a critical moment in the history of Easter Island. Either coincidentally or spurred on by the strangers, a warrior class seized power across the island, and different groups vied for power. Villages were burned, their resources taken by the victors, and the defeated left to starve. The warfare also led to the toppling of an enemy's moai—whether to capture their mana or simply prevent it from being used against the opposing faction. In the end, none of the moai remained standing.

Downfall and Rebound

The troubles of Easter Island weren't limited to self-inflicted chaos. The arrival of the white man also introduced smallpox and syphilis; the islanders, with little natural immunity to the exotic diseases, fared no better than native populations elsewhere. As if that weren't enough, other ships arrived, collecting slaves for work in South America. The internal fighting and external pressure combined to reduce the number of native islanders to little more than a hundred by 1877—the last survivors of a people who once enjoyed a tropical paradise. Easter Island, or Rapa Nui, was annexed by Chile in 1888. As of 2009, there are 4,781 people living on the island. There are projects underway to raise the fallen moai. As of today, dozens have been returned to their former glory.

Shhh! It's A Secret Society

Though documentation proves this secret organization to preserve the Southern cause did indeed exist, many mysteries remain about the Knights of the Golden Circle.

✳   ✳   ✳   ✳

THE KNIGHTS OF the Golden Circle was a pro-South organization that operated out of the Deep South, the border states, the Midwest, and even parts of the North both before and during the Civil War. Much of its history is unknown due to its underground nature, but it is known that this secret society, bound by passwords, rituals, and handshakes, intended to preserve Southern culture and states' rights. Its precise origin, membership, and purpose are documented in a handful of primary sources, including the club's handbook, an exposé published in 1861, and a wartime government report that revealed the K.G.C. to be a serious threat to the federal government and its effort to quash the rebellion and maintain the Union.

Some historians trace the organization of the Knights of the Golden Circle back to the 1830s, though the name did not surface publicly until 1855. According to a report by the U.S. government in 1864, the organization included as many as 500,000 members in the North alone and had "castles," or local chapters, spread across the country. Members included everyone from notable politicians to the rank and file, all prepared to rise up against federal coercion as they saw their rights to slavery slipping away.

What's in a Name?

The group's name referred to a geographic "Golden Circle" that surrounded the Deep South. Its boundaries were the border states on the north, America's western territories, Mexico, Central America, and even Cuba. Southern leaders and organization members hoped to gain control of these lands to create a strong, agrarian economy dependent on slavery and plantations. This would either balance the numbers of slave states to free states in the federal government or provide a distinct nation that could separate from the Union. The proslavery leader John C. Calhoun of South Carolina was the group's intellectual mentor, although the K.G.C. didn't likely achieve great numbers before his death in 1850. The 1864 government report cited that members initially used nuohlac, Calhoun spelled backward, as a password.

Adding Fuel to the Fire

Once the Civil War began, the K.G.C. became a concern for both state and federal governments. The most obvious public figure associated with the K.G.C. was Dr. George Bickley, an eccentric pamphleteer of questionable character. He is credited with organizing the first castle of the Knights of the Golden Circle in his hometown of Cincinnati. He also sent an open letter to the Kentucky legislature declaring that his organization had 8,000 members in the state, with representatives in every county. The legislature called for a committee to investigate the organization, which had begun to menace that state's effort to remain neutral by importing arms and ammunition for the secession cause.

Federal officers arrested Bickley in New Albany, Indiana, in 1863 with a copy of the society's Rules, Regulations, and Principles of the K.G.C. and other regalia on his person. He was held in the Ohio state prison until late 1865. Bickley died two years later, never having been formally charged with a crime.

Methods and Tactics

The underground group used subversive tactics to thwart the Lincoln administration's effort once the war began. A telegram between a Union colonel and Secretary of War Edwin Stanton states how the "Holy Brotherhood" sought to encourage Union soldiers to desert and to paint the conflict as a war in favor of abolition. Some of the government's more questionable wartime tactics, such as the suspension of habeas corpus and the quelling of some aspects of a free press, were rallying points in the Midwest, and they were issues that surely connected northern dissidents such as Copperheads with the Knights in spirit if not in reality.

When antiwar sentiment and Peace Democrats influenced populations in Indiana, a U.S. court subpoenaed witnesses for a grand jury to learn more about the organization. The grand jury claimed the secret organization had recruited 15,000 members in Indiana alone and indicted 60 people in August 1862. The Union army attempted to infiltrate the organization and expose its subversive operations by sending new recruits back home to join the K.G.C.

Political Ties

Nationally known political leaders were also allegedly tied to the group. The 1861 exposé referred to a certain "Mr. V—of Ohio" as one of the few reliable members among prominent Northern politicians. It would likely have been assumed that this referred to leading Copperhead and Ohio Representative Clement Vallandigham, who decried abolition before the war and criticized Republicans in Congress and the administration. Union officers arrested Vallandigham, and a military court exiled him to the South.

Another possible member was John C. Breckenridge, vice president under James Buchanan and a presidential candidate in 1860. Even former President Franklin Pierce was accused of having an affiliation with the organization.

Assassination Conspiracy

Some also believe that the K.G.C. had a hand in the assassination of Abraham Lincoln. The contemporary exposé stated, "Some one of them is to distinguish himself for—if he can, that is—the assassination of the 'Abolition' President." According to a later anonymous account, Lincoln's assassin, John Wilkes Booth, took the oath of the society in a Baltimore castle in the fall of 1860.

The organization had several counterparts during the war, including the Knights of the Golden Square, the Union Relief Society, the Order of American Knights, and the Order of the Sons of Liberty, to name a few.

The Mystery of Montauk

Montauk, a beach community at the eastern tip of Long Island in New York State, has been deigned the Miami Beach of the mid-Atlantic. Conspiracy theorists, however, tell another tale. Has the U.S. government been hiding a secret at the former Camp Hero military base there?

✳   ✳   ✳   ✳

IN THE LATE 1950s, Montauk was not the paradise-style resort it is today. It was an isolated seaside community boasting a lighthouse commissioned by George Washington in 1792, an abandoned military base called Camp Hero, and a huge radar tower. This tower, still standing, is the last semiautomatic ground environment radar tower still in existence and features an antenna called AN/FPS-35. During its time of Air Force use, the AN/FPS-35 was capable of detecting airborne objects at a distance of more than 200 miles. One of its uses was detecting potential Soviet long-distance bombers, as the Cold War was in full swing. According to conspiracy theorists, however, the antenna and Camp Hero itself had a few other tricks lurking around the premises, namely human mind control and electro-magnetic field manipulation.

What's in the Basement?

Camp Hero was closed as an official U.S. Army base in November 1957, although the Air Force continued to use the radar facilities. After the Air Force left in 1980, the surrounding grounds were ultimately turned into a state park, which opened to the public in September 2002.

Yet the camp's vast underground facility remains under tight government jurisdiction, and the AN/FPS-35 radar tower still stands. Many say there is a government lab on-site that continues the alleged teleportation, magnetic field manipulation, and mind-control experiments that originated with Project Rainbow. One reason for this belief is that two of the sailors onboard the *Eldridge* on October 24, 1943—Al Bielek and Duncan Cameron—claimed to have jumped from the ship while it was in "hyperspace" between Philadelphia and Norfolk, and landed at Camp Hero, severely disoriented.

Though Project Rainbow was branded a hoax, an urban legend continues to surround its "legacy," which is commonly known as the Montauk Project. Theorists cite experiments in electromagnetic radiation designed to produce mass schizophrenia over time and reduce a populace's resistance to governmental control, which, they believe, would explain the continual presence of the antenna. According to these suspicions, a large number of orphans, loners, and homeless people are subjected to testing in Camp Hero's basement; most supposedly die as a result.

Interestingly, some conspiracy theorists believe that one outcropping of the experiments is the emergence and rapid popularity of the cell phone, which uses and produces electromagnetic and radio waves.

The Secret of the Stones

Part of the enduring charm of Stonehenge—that curious structure of rocks located in Wiltshire County, southern England—is that it continues to defy explanation, baffling experts throughout the centuries.

✳   ✳   ✳   ✳

THOUGH NO ONE can definitively say who erected this massive monument, when and why they built it, and how they did so without the aid of modern machinery, there are no shortage of theories. So let's hear from the experts:

Archaeologists: Speculate that the site first took shape about 5,000 years ago, with the first stones being laid in 3000 BC. The monument was finally completed in 1500 BC., perhaps serving as a memorial to fallen warriors, as the burial mounds that surround the site might indicate.

Geologists: Claim that 80 of the 4-ton rocks at Stonehenge, known as bluestones, were quarried from the Prescelly Mountains in Wales—240 miles away—and then transported by sled and barge to their current location.

Astronomers: Observe that builders placed the rocks in concentric circles, thus creating a massive solar observatory through which early man could predict the arrival of eclipses and follow the passage of the seasons. On the longest day of the year, the rising sun appears directly behind one of the main stones, the so-called "Heel Stone."

Historians: Think that the stones form the walls of an ancient temple—a place for people to worship the heavens. In later times, it was used by Druids to celebrate their pagan festivals.

Conspiracy theorists: Believe Stonehenge was placed there by a UFO.

The Anasazi

Across the deserts and mesas of the region known as the Four Corners, where Arizona, New Mexico, Colorado, and Utah meet, backcountry hikers and motoring tourists can easily spot reminders of an ancient people. From the towering stone structures at Chaco Culture National Historical Park to cliff dwellings at Mesa Verde National Park to the ubiquitous scatters of broken pottery and stone tools, these remains tell the story of a culture that spread out across the arid Southwest during ancient times.

✳ ✳ ✳ ✳

Who Were the Anasazi?

THE ANASAZI ARE believed to have lived in the region from about AD 1 through AD 1300 (though the exact beginning of the culture is difficult to determine because there is no particular defining event). In their everyday lives, they created black-on-white pottery styles that distinguish subregions within the culture, traded with neighboring cultures (including those to the south in Central America), and built ceremonial structures called kivas, which were used for religious or communal purposes.

The Exodus Explained

Spanish conquistadors exploring the Southwest noted the abandoned cliff dwellings and ruined plazas, and archaeologists today still try to understand what might have caused the Anasazi to move from their homes and villages throughout the region. Over time, researchers have posed a number of theories, including the idea that the Anasazi were driven from their villages by hostile nomads, such as those from the Apache or Ute tribes. Others believe that the Anasazi fought among themselves, causing a drastic reduction in their populations, and a few extraterrestrial-minded theorists have suggested that the Anasazi civilization was destroyed by aliens. Today, the prevalent hypothesis among scientists is that a long-term drought affected the area, destroying agricultural fields and forcing people to abandon their largest villages. Scientists and archaeologists have worked together to reconstruct the region's climate data and compare it with material that has been excavated. Based on their findings, many agree that some combination of environmental and cultural factors caused the dispersal of the Anasazi from the large-scale ruins seen throughout the landscape today.

Their Journey

Although many writers—of fiction and nonfiction alike—romanticize the Anasazi as a people who mysteriously disappeared from the region, they did not actually disappear. Those living in large ancient villages and cultural centers did indeed disperse, but the people themselves did not simply disappear. Today, descendents of the Anasazi can be found living throughout New Mexico and Arizona. The Hopi tribe in northern Arizona, as well as those living in approximately 20 pueblos in New Mexico, are the modern-day descendants of the Anasazi. The Pueblos in New Mexico whose modern inhabitants consider the Anasazi their ancestors include: Acoma, Cochiti, Isleta, Jemez, Laguna, Nambe, Picuris, Pojoaque, San Felipe, San Ildefonso, Ohkay Owingeh (formerly referred to as San Juan), Sandia, Santa Ana, Santa Clara, Santo Domingo, Taos, Tesuque, Zia, and Zuni.

Lily Dale, New York— U.S. Headquarters of the Spiritualism Movement

For centuries, the bereaved have sought ways to speak to their loved ones on the Other Side. In the 1840s, the Spiritualism movement swept across the United States. Spiritualists believe that an afterlife awaits us all, and that in it, ethereal beings retain many of the interests they had during their time on earth. They also believe that with the help of mediums—people who are able to see and communicate with the dead—the living can make contact with their deceased loved ones during formal sessions known as séances.

✳   ✳   ✳   ✳

The Awakening of the Spirits

IN THE MID-1870S, a group of committed Spiritualists began hosting summer meetings at Cassadaga Lake in southwestern New York. Believing that nothing is preordained or destined, the Spiritualists emphasized free will; they felt that it was up to the living to make choices based on guidance from the spirits.

To practice their religion, the Spiritualists purchased 20 acres of land near Cassadaga Lake and established the community of Lily Dale in 1879. In addition to offering the services of mediums, psychics, and other faith healers, the Lily Daleans also offered summer classes to followers of the Spiritualism movement. Lily Dale became so popular that a hotel was built in the town in 1880, and in 1883, a 1,200-seat auditorium was added.

Over the years, Lily Dale's freethinkers attracted many famous people: Susan B. Anthony spoke there frequently, Mae West visited the assembly, and, in 1916, the cottage of sisters Margaret and Kate Fox was moved to Lily Dale. (In 1848, the Fox sisters claimed that they had communicated with the spirit of a murdered peddler at their home in Hydesville, New York. This incident is often cited as the beginning of the Spiritualist movement.) Unfortunately, the Fox sisters' cottage burned down in a fire in 1955.

Haunting the Spiritualists

Given the presence of so many mediums, it is no surprise that ghosts are often seen in Lily Dale. The full spectrum of spirits—from full-bodied apparitions to shadows and orbs—regularly appear in photos taken around the town. The

Maplewood Hotel's lobby is decorated entirely with "spirit precipitated art"—art that was created with the assistance of spirits. Sometimes during a séance, a medium will set out a bowl of paints and a blank canvas; when the session is over, a painting—usually a portrait of the spirit that has just made its presence known—will be complete. One of the paintings in the hotel's lobby depicts a figure with a white beard wearing a white robe; it is unknown who this man was in life, but several guests have seen his apparition in the building's hallways. A blind, mute, quadriplegic woman created a spirit-assisted tapestry over a period of nine years. While the woman was in a trance, the spirits guided her and helped her to embroider the tapestry using only her mouth.

Modern Spiritualist Living

These days, groups often gather around Inspiration Stump (a grove in the Leolyn Woods) during the summertime. At these meetings, a medium gives short messages to the people in attendance from the various spirits present. People sit quietly, barely moving, so as not to disturb the medium's work. Even those who do not receive a message from a spirit feel rejuvenated, and many find themselves more aware of spiritual energies while at Inspiration Stump. Afterward, audience members often book individual sessions with the dozens of certified mediums who live year-round in the Lily Dale community.

People who wish to plan a trip to Lily Dale will find an extensive guide to workshops, lectures, and classes online. Keep in mind that although the Spiritualists practice their religion year-round, Lily Dale's two hotels are closed from late September until June. During the off-season, those wishing to visit a medium or attend a workshop can arrange to stay at a private home through the Lily Dale Spiritualist Church or the Church of the Living Spirit. In order to live amongst the spirits full time, one must become a member of the Lily Dale community and apply to the Lily Dale Assembly Board of Directors to earn the right to call this hauntingly beautiful town home.

Ghosts of Higher Education

Colleges and universities are some of the oldest institutions in America, so it's not surprising that they might harbor ghosts of those who passed through their hallowed halls in times past. College buildings and their surrounding grounds are often home to eternal residents that give new meaning to the term school spirit.

✳ ✳ ✳ ✳

Eastern Illinois University (Charleston, Illinois)

THE RESIDENT GHOST of Eastern Illinois University's Pemberton Hall was a young woman who was brutally raped and murdered there by a school custodian in 1917. Fortunately for current students, the fourth floor—where the crime took place—has been closed off for years, but maintenance workers still report seeing bloody footprints appear and then disappear on that floor. Residents elsewhere in the dormitory have heard piano music coming from the vacant floor above, where the murdered coed is said to play her spirited song.

Harvard University (Cambridge, Massachusetts)

Harvard's Thayer Hall—which was once used as a textile mill—is now inhabited by ghosts of years past. Spirits dressed in Victorian apparel have been seen entering and exiting through doors that no longer exist. Perhaps they're seeking the warmth of the building because they are often seen during the winter months.

Huntingdon College (Montgomery, Alabama)

If you visit Pratt Hall at Huntingdon College in Montgomery, Alabama, you might just encounter the ghost of a young lady named Martha. Better known today as the "Red Lady," Martha left her native New York and enrolled at Huntingdon in the early 1900s because it was her grandmother's alma mater. She was known on campus for her love of red: She decorated her room with red drapes and a red rug, and she often wore red dresses. Lonely and taunted by her peers, Martha killed herself in despair. She now haunts Pratt Hall (which once housed her dorm), where residents occasionally catch a glimpse of a young lady dressed in red. In recent years, she seems to have gotten bolder, as students have reported cold blasts of air surrounding those who are caught picking on their classmates.

Kenyon College (Gambier, Ohio)

Established in 1824, Kenyon is one of Ohio's most haunted colleges. At least three students who committed suicide in different dormitories now haunt them: One rearranges furniture in Manning Hall; one turns off lights, knocks on doors, and flushes toilets in Lewis Hall; and one roams around Norton Hall late at night. And back when Bolton Dance Studio was known as "The Greenhouse" (so named because of the building's glass roof) and housed the college pool, swimmers would occasionally hear a voice calling out to them. More recently, dancers have seen wet footprints in the studio, heard splashing sounds, and observed showers in the locker room turn on and off when no one is present. These strange occurrences are attributed to the "Greenhouse Ghost," which is thought to be the spirit of a male student who died at the pool in a diving accident during the 1940s.

Luther College (Decorah, Iowa)

The ghost of Gertrude—a Decorah high school student who desperately wanted to attend Luther College back in the days before women students were admitted there—is said to make her presence known at Larsen Hall. Students living there have blamed Gertrude for walking the halls at all hours of the night, sounding the fire alarm, and stealing items—especially modern lingerie—and sometimes leaving behind her own old-fashioned garments. She was killed in 1918 when she was hit by a car while riding her bicycle, ending her collegiate dreams before they even started.

St. Joseph's College (Emmitsburg, Maryland)

In 1810, Mother Elizabeth Seton, a Catholic nun, founded St. Joseph's Academy and Free School for Catholic girls. In 1902, the school became St. Joseph's College until it closed entirely in 1973. Mother Seton was buried on campus and was canonized in 1975. Today, her ghost is often seen gliding through the hallways of the school she knew so well. Observers have seen her walking with the ghost of an unidentified doctor who carries a medical bag, both apparently still searching for suffering souls to heal.

University of Notre Dame (South Bend, Indiana)

The hallowed halls of Notre Dame are home to several ghosts, including Father Edward Sorin, the university's founder, who is said to wander all over the campus, including in the Main Building and near the famous golden dome. Native Americans from the Potawatomi tribe are thought to haunt Columba Hall, which is located between the two campus lakes—on land where they once lived and buried their dead. In addition, Washington Hall is rumored to be the home of a few ghosts, among them a steeplejack who fell to his death in 1886 and Brother Canute Lardner, who died peacefully while watching a movie there in 1946. And then, of course, there's the ghost of George Gipp, Notre Dame's famous football star. Gipp died of pneumonia and strep throat, which he may have contracted after spending the night on Washington Hall's front steps because he stayed out after curfew and was locked out of the dorm. On his deathbed, he allegedly told coach Knute Rockne that when his players need a pep talk, he should tell them to "win one for the Gipper." Since Gipp's death in 1920, students have heard unexplained footsteps, doors slamming, and ghostly music in Washington Hall.

San Jose State University (San Jose, California)

San Jose was one of the U.S. cities where Japanese Americans were told to report for assignment to internment camps during World War II. It was in the old campus gymnasium at San

Jose State that these people gathered for processing before they were sent to their new "homes." So it's really no surprise that ghostly voices have been heard crying and speaking in a foreign language at the gym. Students there have also heard footsteps and doors closing when no one else is present.

The Ghosts of Chicago's Old Town Tatu

When ghost hunters from the Chicago branch of the American Ghost Society first investigated Old Town Tatu in 2006, their goal was to look for ghosts from the days when the building served as a funeral home. But in later investigations, they turned their attention to communicating with more recent spirits.

✳ ✳ ✳ ✳

Generations of Hauntings

FOR NEARLY 75 YEARS, the building that now houses Old Town Tatu on Chicago's north side was the home of the Klemundt Funeral Home. And for years, the Klemundt family had told stories about the building being haunted.

In 2002, the building was purchased for use as a tattoo parlor, and soon after, the new occupants began to experience strange poltergeist activity and other supernatural phenomena: Decorations fell off the walls as though pushed by an unseen force, and small objects—such as ashtrays—flew across the room. One tattoo artist even told of an ashtray that zipped through the air and landed upside down without spilling a single ash.

In the main entryway, several employees encountered the ghost of a young girl. Her presence was usually felt but not seen, so some researchers speculated that the phenomenon was not the ghost of a girl who died in the building but rather residual energy from a girl who was terrified after being left alone in the building years before.

Employees and customers also reported seeing the shadowy specters of a man in a brown suit, a man in a light blue suit, and a woman in a white dress. One employee even claimed to hear a disembodied voice in the basement that made a spooky noise like a ghost in a cartoon.

Ghosts Exposed

Prior to the American Ghost Society's first formal investigation of Old Town Tatu (then known as Odin Tatu) in 2006, no one was entirely sure how seriously to take these spooky stories. Veteran ghost hunters are used to people making up tales about women in white and ghosts making scary sounds. But they suspected that the tattoo artists weren't fabricating the stories; after all, the Klemundt family had been telling similar tales for years.

During their investigation, the researchers found a cold spot in the northeastern corner of the basement, and one team member felt something tap him on the shoulder. When one of the investigators called out "What's your name?," the team heard nothing; however, upon reviewing evidence from their audio recorder, they discovered that it had picked up a voice saying the name "Walter."

One theory suggests that this was the ghost of Walter Loeding, whose funeral was held in the building in the 1960s. Klemundt family members recalled that Walter didn't own a suit at the time of his death, so they had to buy one in which to bury him. The suit that they bought was brown, which leads some to believe that Walter is the ghost in a brown suit that some have seen.

"If I Die in This Place..."

None of this activity seemed to surprise Richard "Tapeworm" Herrera, the owner of the tattoo parlor. Not only did Tapeworm work in the building, he also lived there, and over the years, he had seen several ghosts, including the man in the brown suit, whom he saw while he worked.

"I stopped what I was doing and tried to motion for other people to look," Tapeworm said during the first investigation. "But I wouldn't take my eye[s] off him for one second, man, 'cause I knew that if I looked away for a second, he'd be gone. And he was! The second I looked away, he vanished."

Herrera also claimed that ghosts would mess with the appliances in his apartment above the tattoo parlor and would even open the window while he was in the bathroom. Most of the experiences seemed to amuse Tapeworm more than scare him, but the entity that he encountered on the staircase to his apartment did genuinely frighten him.

Having grown up in the neighborhood, Herrera had always been leery of the old tiled stairway—the only part of the funeral home that could be seen from the front windows. "I remember being a kid in this neighborhood, and you could see those stairs in the window. I was always all superstitious about it because of what the place was, you know. It was where the dead people were. And now...lo and behold, 30 years later, I'm living here. And twice, when I've been walking down those stairs, I felt like something was trying to push me! And that freaks me out because everyone knows you can't fight back with these cats! So the first time it happened, I just looked up and shouted, 'Listen! If I die in this place, it is on.

The investigators and Tapeworm all shared a hearty laugh. Later, when the researchers reviewed their audio, they found that the sound of ghostly laughter had been recorded on the staircase at the exact moment that a psychic, who was assisting with the investigation, claimed that a ghost thought it was very funny that Tapeworm was afraid of being pushed down the stairs. Tragically, barely three weeks after the first investigation, Tapeworm had a heart attack in his apartment. He died at age 37, just steps away from the staircase.

You Can't Keep a Good Ghost Down

After Tapeworm's death, his friends and coworkers came to believe that he was haunting the place, which was renamed Old Town Tatu. The equipment at Tapeworm's old station would frequently malfunction (or not work at all) when anyone who was not a friend of Tapeworm's tried to use it. In addition, motion-activated cameras that had been recently installed recorded unusual orblike blobs that floated up to the camera and briefly hovered in front of it before drifting away.

Then, on Halloween night, a few months after Tapeworm's untimely death, the tattoo parlor's employees were enjoying their annual Halloween party when one of them checked his cell phone and noticed a missed call—from Tapeworm's old number. He called the number the next day and found that it belonged to a confused young woman who had been asleep when the call was made.

One member of the American Ghost Society said that when he returned to the building (after Tapeworm's death), he felt as though someone was pulling his hair and flicking his ear—things that a prankster like Tapeworm would do in life.

Current employees also claim that Tapeworm's ghost seems especially active when they play techno music, which Tapeworm despised. To make his presence (and his dislike of the music) known, Tapeworm likes to make equipment malfunction and cause electrical disturbances. If employees play punk or heavy metal music, which were Tapeworm's favorites, the parlor is much calmer.

Tapeworm has also been known to announce his presence verbally: A psychic investigator who toured the building in 2007 was given no information about the place, yet he said that he sensed the presence of a particularly foul-mouthed ghost. And in 2009, Brad and Barry Klinge from *Ghost Lab* noted a 20-degree temperature drop after calling out, "Hey Richie!" They also picked up an EVP (electronic voice phenomenon) of a voice that Tapeworm's friends identified as his. The voice said a few things that cannot be repeated here (or on television, for that matter).

Whether Tapeworm's spirit is actually engaged in an otherworldly battle with the funeral parlor ghosts is, of course, unknown. But the presence of his ghost has been reported much more frequently than those of others in the years since his death, which leads some to wonder if he kicked their butts so far into oblivion that they're afraid to show up anymore. Those who knew Tapeworm have no doubt about it.

Chicago's Oriental Theatre Is Never Completely Empty

When Chicago's Iroquois Theatre opened for business, one patron is known to have described the place as "a death trap." However, according to records, the building was fully in compliance with the fire code, and advertisements billed it as "absolutely fireproof." Unfortunately, that first description proved to be true.

✳ ✳ ✳ ✳

False Advertising

WHEN THE IROQUOIS Theatre opened in November 1903, it was easy to feel safe while sitting underneath its ornate, 60-foot-high ceiling and among its white marbled walls and grand staircases. But, unbeknownst to patrons, when the theater was under construction, its owners had cut corners to open in time for the 1903 holiday season.

In retrospect, it's easy to wonder if the owners of the Iroquois were purposely inviting trouble. After all, they had declined to install sprinkler systems, and not all of the fire escapes were completed when the theater opened. In addition, exit signs were either missing or obscured by thick drapes, there were no backstage phones or fire buckets, and no fire alarm system was in place; in fact, the only fire-fighting equipment in the theater was a few canisters of a chemical product called Kilfyre. The owners had even skimped on the stage's safety curtain: Instead of using fireproof asbestos to make it, the owners saved about $50 by having the builders use a blend of asbestos, cotton, and wood pulp. But at the time, it was not uncommon for building inspectors and city officials to accept bribes to look the other way as builders ignored one safety law after another.

"A Death Trap"

On December 30, barely a month after the theater opened, vaudeville star Eddie Foy and his company were onstage performing the musical *Mr. Blue Beard* to a standing-room-only crowd that was estimated to be around 2,000 people—a few hundred more than the theater could safely hold.

At the beginning of the second act, a calcium light arced and sent a spark onto a muslin drape on a wall near the stage. The orchestra stopped playing, but Foy urged the audience to remain calm and stay in their seats. Even after the flames jumped to pieces of scenery that were hanging in the rafters— most of which were painted with highly flammable oil-based paint—Foy stayed onstage and begged the audience to remain calm and exit the theater in an orderly fashion. But Foy was no fool: He knew that when the scenery in the rafters caught fire, the situation was going to get a lot worse. Above and behind him, the fire spread quickly, and the cast and crew dashed for a backstage exit. Lighting gear jammed the fire curtain after it dropped only a few feet, which left the audience fully exposed to the flames on the stage.

Unbeknownst to the performers who scrambled to open the back door, the owners had ordered the ventilation system nailed shut. This kept the cold December air from getting inside, but it also effectively turned the building into a gigantic chimney. The minute the door was opened, a back draft turned the flames on stage into what eyewitnesses described as a "balloon of fire."

This massive fireball shot through the auditorium, incinerating some people right where they stood.

Naturally, the crowd panicked and ran for the fire exits, which the owners had locked to keep people from sneaking into the theater without paying. Those who weren't trampled trying to reach the fire exits ran for the front doors, hoping to rush out onto Randolph Street. But the doors opened in toward the lobby, not out toward the street, so rather than escaping through the doors, the people crashed *into* them, and then into each other. More people died from being crushed in the melee than from burns or smoke inhalation.

Meanwhile, the only hallway that led downstairs from the balcony was blocked by a metal accordion gate, which was placed there to keep people from sneaking into better seats, effectively trapping the unfortunate people in the upper reaches of the burning building. Some tried to jump from the balcony to escape; others opened the balcony's fire exit, which was miraculously kept unlocked. However, by the time those who opened the door realized that there *was* no fire escape behind the door, the crowd was pushing too hard for them to turn back: They were shoved out the door and dropped nearly 60 feet into the alley below. By the time the situation had calmed down, more than a hundred people had fallen to their demise in what newspapers called "Death Alley."

In the Wake of Tragedy

The exact number of lives lost in the Iroquois Theatre fire is uncertain. Around 600 people are known to have perished, but the actual number is probably much higher because some families picked up their dead before they could be counted. To this day, the fire at the Iroquois Theatre is the deadliest single-building fire in U.S. history. But on the positive side, steel fire curtains, clearly marked exits, and exit doors that swing out toward the street are all provisions that were mandated because of the Iroquois tragedy.

Following the incident, a number of city officials were brought to trial for gross negligence, but they all got off on technicalities. The only people ever successfully prosecuted for crimes surrounding the Iroquois fire were a few of the crooks who broke into the theater to shimmy rings off fingers, yank necklaces from necks, and dig money out of the pockets of the deceased (and the vast majority of these people were never prosecuted, either).

The Building May Be Gone, But the Ghosts Remain

Ghost sightings at the Iroquois Theatre began before the flames had even stopped smoldering: Photographs taken of the ruined auditorium shortly after the fire contain strange blobs of light and mist that some believe are the spirits of the unfortunate victims.

The theater was soon repaired and reopened, and it operated under various names for another 20 years before it was torn down. In its place, a new venue—the Oriental Theatre—was erected in 1926. For years, it was one of Chicago's premier movie theaters until it fell on hard times in the 1970s, when it mainly played kung fu movies. The Oriental Theatre finally shut its doors in 1981, and it seemed as though the Iroquois and its tragic tale had faded into Chicago's history.

But since 1998, when the Oriental Theatre reopened to host touring Broadway shows, employees have found that the ghosts have stuck around. During rehearsals, spectators are frequently seen in the balcony seats. When staff members are sent to ask them to leave, they find the balcony empty.

Many people who work in the building have reported seeing the specter of a woman in a tutu. This is thought to be the ghost of Nellie Reed, an aerialist who was in position high above the audience when the fire broke out. Although she was rescued from her perch, she suffered severe burns and died a few days later.

Other actors and crew members have encountered the ghost of a young girl who makes her presence known by giggling and flushing one of the toilets backstage. Her happy laugh has been picked up on audio recorders on more than one occasion and can often be heard in the hallways next to the main auditorium.

Staff members who work late at night, after all of the theater-goers have left the building, have reported seeing shadowy blobs that they call "soft shapes." These mysterious forms are seen zipping through the empty auditorium toward the places where the fire exits would have been in 1903.

And the ghosts in the theater may not only be spirits from the fire; female staff members have reportedly been harassed and threatened by a strange male voice in one of the sub-basements located far below the street. Historians suggest that this ghost may be from the 19th century, when the section of Randolph Street where the theater now stands was known as "Hairtrigger Block" and was home to the rowdiest gambling parlors in town.

Sometimes, when a building is torn down, its ghosts seem to go away. But other times, as seems to be the case with the Iroquois Theatre, they only get louder and more active.

The Haunted Destroyer

Shortly after the Japanese attack on Pearl Harbor, five brothers from Waterloo, Iowa—George, Francis, Joseph, Madison, and Albert Sullivan—enlisted in the U.S. Navy and served together aboard the light cruiser USS Juneau. Sadly, their inspiring story of family patriotism turned tragic when the Juneau was sunk by a Japanese submarine in November 1942, sending all five Sullivan brothers to a watery grave. Their story was immortalized in the movie The Fighting Sullivans (1944) and served as an inspiration for Steven Spielberg's Saving Private Ryan (1998).

In 1943, the Navy honored the Sullivan brothers by naming a destroyer after them: USS The Sullivans. It was a proud ship that served valiantly during the remainder of World War II, in the Korean War, and then in various hot spots around the world as part of the 6th Fleet. But after the vessel was decommissioned in 1965, the Navy had a difficult time finding people willing to clean and maintain it. The reason? The spirits of the Sullivan brothers were apparently haunting the ship.

✳   ✳   ✳   ✳

Haunted Happenings Begin

THE GHOSTS WERE quiet while the ship was on active duty, but they started making themselves known upon its retirement. Those who worked aboard *The Sullivans* after it was decommissioned reported seeing flying objects and hearing weird sounds and terrifying moans. Fleeting glimpses of young men dressed in World War II-era naval uniforms were also common sights.

One of the first acknowledgments that something bizarre was occurring aboard *The Sullivans* came when an electrician's mate refused an order to make a routine check of the ship. It was Friday the 13th he explained, and the last time he had been aboard the ship on that traditionally superstitious day, an unseen hand had reached out from a bulkhead, grabbed him by the ankle, and tripped him.

More Incidents Revealed

After the sailor's story was made public, others came forward with tales of their own frightening encounters aboard the destroyer. Another electrician's mate reported that something had reached out and snatched away the toolbox he had been carrying, and another sailor claimed that five glowing spheres passed him in a darkened hatchway while he stood paralyzed with fear.

In another account, a sailor assigned to work on the vessel said that he felt a chill and a sense of dread the moment he set foot aboard the ship. Within minutes, he was having trouble breathing, and he experienced an odd buzzing in his ears. "I felt like I had stepped into another world, and it wasn't a world where I wanted to be," said the sailor, who, until that day, had never believed in ghosts. "I knew there and then that I was never going back aboard that ship."

Most of the supernatural phenomena reported aboard *The Sullivans* occurred while the destroyer was docked in Philadelphia. For reasons unknown, removing the ship from active service apparently triggered a tremendous amount of activity from the spirits of the five Sullivan brothers. When the ship was relocated, however, ghost sightings and paranormal activity slowed dramatically.

Now a Museum

In 1977, *The Sullivans* was donated to the Buffalo and Erie County Naval & Military Park in Buffalo, New York, where it was turned into a memorial museum that is open for public tours. In 1986, the fabled vessel was declared a National Historic Landmark.

The story of the five Sullivan brothers and their untimely deaths captured the nation's attention and led to immediate policy changes within the U.S. Navy, which worked to ensure that no American family would ever again suffer such a grave loss. The story of the ship's haunting isn't well known outside of the small fraternity of people who worked aboard the vessel and experienced the brothers' spirited antics firsthand. Why the restless spirits of the brothers manifested when they did, did what they did, and then quieted down remains a mystery.

Myrtles Plantation: A Blast from the Past

Listed on the National Register of Historic Places and boasting more than 200 years of history, the Myrtles Plantation is a beautiful and sprawling old home in St. Francisville, Louisiana. Now used as a bed-and-breakfast, the mansion has seen its share of drama, including romance, death, and even murder. What better setting for a good old Southern-style haunting?

✳ ✳ ✳ ✳

Tales to Tell

IN 1796, DAVID Bradford built what would eventually become the Myrtles Plantation on 650 acres of land about 30 miles outside of Baton Rouge. At the time, the house—which was originally known as Laurel Grove—was much smaller than it is today. In 1834, Ruffin Stirling purchased and remodeled the plantation, doubling its size and renaming it after the many myrtle trees on the property.

Over the years, many people lived and died at the Myrtles Plantation, so it's not surprising that the place is home to a few restless spirits. Whether it's strange noises, disembodied voices, apparitions, or reflections in a haunted mirror, plenty of paranormal activity can be found at Myrtles Plantation.

In 2005, investigators from the television show *Ghost Hunters* paid a visit to the mansion and documented several strange phenomena. Thermal-imaging video cameras recorded the torso of something not really present, as well as a shadow that appeared to be moving up and down. The team also caught the unexplained movement of a lamp across a table: Over the course of a few minutes, it moved several inches with no help from anyone in the room.

If you visit the Myrtles Plantation, be sure to check out the Myrtles mirror: It is said to reflect the spirit of someone who died in front of it. People have repeatedly seen handprints on the mirror and orbs or apparitions in photos of it. Although many stories say that the images belong to one of the plantation's early owners and her children—all of whom were poisoned—the mirror was actually brought to the house in the 1970s. If it is indeed haunted, the ghosts may not be from the home originally.

A Spirited Place

Several ghosts are commonly seen inside the house. One is thought to be a French woman who wanders from room to room. Another is a regular at the piano; unfortunately, this spirit only seems to know one chord, which is heard over and over, stopping suddenly when anyone walks into the room. A third is the ghost of a young girl, who only appears right before thunderstorms.

The spirits of two young girls have also been seen playing outside on the veranda, and guests have also felt their presence at night while lying in bed. Sometimes, visitors feel pressure on the bed, as though someone is jumping on it. Soon after, people report seeing the spirit of a maid, who appears to smooth the covers. Another young girl with long curly hair has been seen floating outside the window of the toy room; she appears to be cupping her hands as if she's trying to see inside.

Some visitors report seeing a Confederate soldier on the porch; others have seen the spirit of a man that warns them not to go inside. Many people have glimpsed apparitions of slaves doing chores inside the mansion. And two other resident ghosts that are certainly entertaining but have little connection to the plantation's rich history are those of a ballet dancer clad in a tutu and a Native American woman who appears naked in the outdoor gazebo.

The ghost of William Winter is also said to haunt the mansion. Winter lived at the Myrtles Plantation from 1860 to 1868 and again from 1870 until his death in 1871, when an unknown assailant shot him as he answered the door. By some accounts, he staggered back inside and died on the 17th step of the staircase, where his slow dragging footsteps can be heard to this day.

Chloe

Perhaps the best-known ghost at the Myrtles Plantation is that of Chloe, a former slave. Her spirit is thought to walk between the main house and the old slave quarters. People describe her apparition as that of a slender woman wearing a green turban.

As the story goes, David Bradford's daughter Sara married Clark Woodruff, who—it is rumored—had an affair with a beautiful slave girl named Chloe. After enjoying her station in the main house, Chloe was upset when Woodruff ended the affair. When he later caught her eavesdropping, Woodruff became enraged and cut off her ear. Two versions of the next part of this story exist: One has Chloe seeking revenge on Woodruff by poisoning his family; the other says that she poisoned them to secure her position as a nursemaid and nanny, so that she would be needed inside to nurse the family back to health, and therefore, she wouldn't be sent to work in the fields.

In either case, Chloe allegedly crushed up oleander petals and added them to a cake she was baking for the oldest daughter's birthday. Clark Woodruff didn't eat any of it, but his wife and two daughters did, and they soon died from poisoning. The other slaves, fearing punishment, dragged Chloe to the yard, where she was hanged. Legend has it that her ghost can be seen in the yard and wandering through the house in her signature headwear.

It's a great story, but researchers who have dug through old court records have found no evidence that there ever was a Chloe: There is nothing to suggest that a slave by that name (or anything close to it) ever lived at Myrtles Plantation. And although death records show that Sara Woodruff and two of the children did die young, all the deaths were attributed to yellow fever, not poison.

So there you have it. Myrtles Plantation is rife with ghosts, but we may never know exactly who they were in life or why they're still attached to the mansion. Chloe may or may not have existed in the real world, but you never know what you may encounter at one of the most haunted houses in America.

The Sad Fate of British Airship R101

On October 5, 1930, the British airship R101 crashed during its maiden flight, killing nearly all aboard. Two days later, a woman with absolutely no knowledge of airships explained the incident in highly technical and freakishly accurate detail. Were the ghosts of the tragedy speaking through her?

✳   ✳   ✳   ✳

Foretellers or Frauds

PSYCHICS AFFECT PEOPLE in different ways. Those who believe in concepts such as mental telepathy and extrasensory perception can find validity in a medium's claims. Skeptics, on the other hand, aren't so sure. Psychic researcher Harry Price straddled the fence between the two camps: He deplored fakery but had witnessed enough of the supernatural to believe that there was indeed something to it. At his National Laboratory of Psychical Research, Price worked diligently to separate the wheat from the chaff—the real from the fake.

On October 7, 1930, Price arranged a séance with a promising medium named Eileen J. Garrett. Price's secretary Ethel Beenbarn and reporter Ian D. Coster were enlisted to record the proceedings. Price hoped to contact the recently deceased author Sir Arthur Conan Doyle (of *Sherlock Holmes* fame) and publish an account of the proceedings. Like Price, Doyle held a keen interest in the paranormal. Making contact with him could bring Price the evidence that he sought about the existence of an afterlife.

Strange Contact

Just two days before Price and Garrett met, a horrific tragedy occurred. The British airship *R101* crashed in France, killing 48 of the 55 people on board. A Court of Inquiry was assembled to answer queries about the crash, but not before Price and Garrett had their meeting.

At the séance, Garrett fell into a trance and then began to speak. In a deep, animated voice, she identified herself as Flight Lieutenant H. Carmichael Irwin, commander of the *R101* (not Sir Arthur Conan Doyle, whom Price had hoped to contact), and began to speak words that were as confusing as they were disjointed:

"I must do something about it. The whole bulk of the dirigible was entirely and absolutely too much for her engine's capacity. Engines too heavy... Oil pipe plugged. Flying too low altitude and never could rise... Severe tension on the fabric, which is chafing... Never reached cruising altitude—same in trial... Almost scraped the roofs of Achy!"

Coster recognized Irwin's name from the recent *R101* tragedy. After the séance, the reporter published highlights from the meeting. Shortly thereafter, a man named Will Charlton contacted Price. Charlton worked as a supply officer at the base where the *R101* was built and was familiar with the airship's construction. He asked the researcher for a transcript of the séance and studied it intently. What he saw amazed him: Garrett—who had no prior knowledge of or interest in airships—had spoken about one in highly technical terms. Moreover, she seemed to be explaining *why* the *R101* had crashed.

Passing Muster

As details of the crash emerged, Garrett's words proved even more insightful. It was revealed that the airship had passed over the village of Achy so low that it almost scraped a church tower, as Garrett had stated during the séance. Garrett also spoke of an "exorbitant scheme of carbon and hydrogen" as being "completely wrong" for the airship. When Charlton and other airship officials heard this, they were stunned. Only a handful of project team members had been privy to this top-secret information. Parlor tricks, no matter how clever, couldn't possibly account for Garrett's knowledge of this information.

The transcript yielded more than 40 highly technical details related to the airship's final flight. Charlton and his colleagues pronounced it an "amazing document." Before launching an official inquiry, they decided to stage another séance. Major Oliver Villiers of the Ministry of Civil Aviation sat down with Eileen Garrett and observed her as she drifted into a trance. This time, the medium channeled the spirits of others who had perished in the crash. Villiers asked pointed questions regarding the airframe of the *R101*, and the medium responded in startling detail:

Villiers: "What was the trouble? Irwin mentioned the nose."

Garrett: "Yes. Girder trouble and engine."

Villiers: "I must get this right. Can you describe exactly where? We have the long struts labeled from A to G."

Garrett: "The top one is O and then A, B, C, and so on downward. Look at your drawing. It was starboard of 5C. On our second flight, after we had finished, we found the girder had been strained, not cracked, and this caused trouble to the cover…"

Conclusion

When the Court of Inquiry's report was released, Garrett's words matched almost precisely with the findings. The phenomenon so impressed Charlton that he himself became a Spiritualist. After Garrett's death in 1970, Archie Jarman—a psychic researcher and columnist for the *Psychic News*—revealed that the medium had asked him to dig deeper into the *R101* case: She wished to learn just how close her description of the event was to reality. After six months of dogged research,

Jarman concluded that the technical terms expressed so vividly by the medium could only have come from the Other Side. In the end, the goal of contacting Sir Arthur Conan Doyle was not achieved; however, this fantastic development had advanced psychical studies immeasurably. Without question, Price had found his "wheat" and the answers to his questions.

"I feel that the period will sooner or later arrive when I must abandon life and reason together, in some struggle with the grim phantasm, FEAR."

—EDGAR ALLAN POE, "THE FALL OF THE HOUSE OF USHER"

The Curse of Griffith Park

Griffith Park in Los Angeles, California, is one of the largest urban parks in America. Many who visit it snap photos of the Hollywood sign, take in the view of the city, gaze at the heavens at the Griffith Observatory, and marvel at the animals at the Los Angeles Zoo. Others, however, come away from their visits to Griffith Park with bone-chilling tales of paranormal encounters.

✳ ✳ ✳ ✳

Where There's a Will...

THE DARK HISTORY of Griffith Park began in 1863, when it was called Rancho Los Feliz. That year, owner Don Antonio Feliz passed from this world, and many expected that his blind niece, Doña Petranilla, would inherit his fortune. Unbeknownst to Petranilla, however, local lawyer Don Antonio Coronel had visited Feliz to help him rewrite his will. When Feliz succumbed to smallpox, most of his wealth went to Coronel. Petranilla was outraged, and from the family adobe, she laid a curse upon the land that is still felt to this day.

A Curse Fit for a Colonel

Following Petranilla's curse, the Coronels and other subsequent owners were all plagued with misfortune and disease until Colonel Griffith J. Griffith, a wealthy industrialist, purchased the property. When Griffith acquired the land in 1882, opening a park was the last thing on his mind: His first order of business was to build housing developments on the land, but that venture soon failed. Griffith also allowed a small ostrich farm to open on the property, and surprisingly, it was quite successful. However, in 1884, storms plagued the area and the ostriches stampeded every night. Ranch hands claimed that the cause of the ruckus was a phantom rider that appeared in the rain. Some said that it was the ghost of Don Feliz, but others believed that it was Doña Petranilla, back from the dead to fulfill the curse that she imposed on the land. Regardless of who it was, Griffith refused to visit the property except at midday, and in 1896, to rid himself of the ghost once and for all, he donated 3,015 acres of his land to the city of Los Angeles.

However, that didn't stop the spirit from making appearances from time to time. In 1898, when the city's wealthy and influential residents gathered for a fiesta at Griffith Park, an ethereal horseback rider chased them out. Over the years, many visitors to the park have reported seeing this spirit sitting atop a horse and roaming the park's trails, or riding through the park at night.

Unfortunately, Griffith's mind deteriorated after that, and in 1903, he tried to kill his wife because he thought that she was conspiring against him with the Pope; he spent nearly two years in San Quentin for the crime. When he died in 1919, Colonel Griffith bequeathed his remaining fortune to the city of Los Angeles. If he relieved himself of the cursed property in an attempt to appease its restless spirits, the maneuver seems to have failed.

To Live and Die in Hollywood

In the 1930s, Griffith Park claimed another victim. Like so many others, Peg Entwistle had come to Hollywood to realize her dream of seeing her visage on the silver screen. However, after receiving poor reviews for her performance in her first motion picture, Entwistle concluded that her career was a failure. And so, on the night of September 16, 1932, she climbed to the top of the Hollywood sign's "H" and leaped to her death in the ravine below. A suicide note was found in her purse, and within days, she had achieved the fame she wanted in life.

Over the years, several hikers and park rangers have reported seeing a woman dressed in 1930s-era attire near the sign. And from time to time, a spectral blonde woman has been known to set off motion sensors located near the sign. When the rangers investigate, they notice the scent of gardenias.

The City of Angels' Lady in White

Park rangers spend more time in Griffith Park than anyone else, and they know that they're not alone. In their headquarters in the old Feliz adobe, the rangers have reportedly caught glimpses of a ghostly Hispanic woman who is dressed all in white. Most people seem to think that this is the tormented spirit of Doña Petranilla, the woman who originally cursed the land back in 1863. She died soon after placing the curse, and she is one of the property's oldest lost souls. In 1884, the worst of the storms that ripped through the area stripped most of the vegetation from the land. Around that time, Griffith's ranch hands witnessed the Lady in White cursing the land and all who lived on it, just as she had done in life. Some have reported hearing her wailing near the Los Angeles Zoo and the golf course, but her favorite haunt seems to be her former home. Although the park is closed overnight, Petranilla seems to prefer to make nocturnal appearances, and like her uncle and Colonel Griffith, she is sometimes seen on horseback going for a midnight ride.

Reversing the Curse

Those who might avoid one of the nation's most beautiful public parks for fear of its ghosts probably shouldn't: Most of the spirits that are said to haunt the grounds of Griffith Park seem to visit at night, often after the park is closed. Also, many movies and television shows have been filmed there over the years, all without a single apparition having been captured on film. In the years since the land passed from Colonel Griffith to the city of Los Angeles, no mysterious tragedies have befallen visitors to the park, but if you find yourself on the property at night— perhaps hiking in view of the Hollywood sign or the historic Feliz home—know that there's a good chance you're not alone.

Rogues' Hollow

Coal miners lived a hard life in the 19th century. Most of the digging was done by hand, and they had to live with everyday hazards such as poor ventilation, cave-ins, and machinery accidents. As a result, miners not only worked hard, but they played hard, as well. And when they wanted to play, they went to Rogues' Hollow.

✳ ✳ ✳ ✳

IN THE 1820s, Doylestown was a quiet place to live, with most of its citizens being farmers—that is, until coal was discovered in the area. Soon people from all over came to work in the coal mines that sprung up around town. By the time the coal industry left the area in the 1940s, more than 50 coal mines had operated in the area.

Originally, Rogues' Hollow consisted only of a store or two, a mill, and a single saloon just southeast of Doylestown. In order to meet the thirsty needs of the miners, more saloons opened up. And while most had tame names such as Smith's Saloon, several bore more foreboding monikers, including the infamous Devil's Den, run by Billy Gallagher. Some of the bloodiest fights to take place in the Hollow were said to have started in the Devil's Den.

For those who weren't in the mood for their own fight, customers could head across the street to Walsh's Saloon to watch (and bet on) illegal cockfights that took place every night.

Often the betting would get so fierce that drunken patrons would rip dollar bills in half and try to make 50-cent bets. But as rowdy as things got inside Walsh's, everyone knew to give the owner, Mike Walsh, a wide berth: He struck a hulking figure at more than 300 pounds and needed two "normal-size" chairs to sit comfortably.

Murder and Mayhem

Surprisingly, the number of deaths inside Rogues' Hollow proper was quite low, but the number of disappearances was quite high. In most cases, miners simply picked up and moved to another town. In other cases, drunken miners took a wrong turn while stumbling home drunk and met a swift death by falling into a mine shaft—in fact, quite a number of bodies were discovered at the bottom of mine shafts. Whispers throughout the town claimed that some of those accidental deaths were really murders.

Wanted criminals often hid out in the Hollow, and even the bravest officer of the law refused to enter the town. Moreover, the abandoned mines that riddled the countryside were fantastic places for men to hole up . . . literally. One famous criminal often associated with Rogues' Hollow is Richard Hulett of Akron, who was arrested and charged with counterfeiting large amounts of half-dollars and dollars in November 1893. While Hulett was convicted, he never gave up the location of his counterfeiting operation, leading many to believe Hulett had set up shop in one of the Hollow's abandoned mines. One long-standing legend even claims that Jesse James himself hid in the Hollow for a few days.

The Ghosts of Rogues' Hollow

With all the violence and death that took place in Rogues' Hollow, it would stand to reason that the place would be home to more than a few restless spirits. Perhaps the most famous is the ghost said to haunt Chidester's Mill. The wool mill owned and run by Samuel Chidester had been operating in Rogues'

Hollow for several years when, according to legend, a young boy working there was accidentally crushed to death. Today, his ghost is said to still wander the long-since silent remains of the mill.

Several other reports of spooky activity in Rogues' Hollow include ghostly figures in white as well as picks and axes that "dance" on their own. Of course, since there was so much drinking going on in Rogues' Hollow, one wonders if what the witnesses saw was the result of spirits from inside a bottle rather than spirits from the other side. Today, little remains from the rough-and-tumble era of Rogues' Hollow save for a few buildings. But curiosity seekers and history buffs can still visit the area, which is maintained by the Chippewa-Rogues' Hollow Historical Society, and, just maybe, the restless spirits of 19th-century miners.

The Smurl Incident

In the 1970s, the "Amityville Horror" story ignited a firestorm of controversy that's still debated today. The Smurl haunting is another incident that's not as well known but is equally divisive.

✳ ✳ ✳ ✳

Spirit Rumblings

IN 1973, JACK and Janet Smurl and their daughters Dawn and Heather moved into a duplex in West Pittston, Pennsylvania. Jack's parents occupied half of the home and Jack and Janet took the other. Nothing out of the ordinary occurred during the first 18 months that they lived there, but then odd things started to happen: Water pipes leaked repeatedly, even though they had been soldered and resoldered; claw marks were found on the bathtub, sink, and woodwork; an unexplained stain appeared on the carpet; a television burst into flames; and Dawn saw people floating in her bedroom.

In 1977, Jack and Janet welcomed twin daughters Shannon and Carin to the family. By then, the home had become Spook Central: Unplugged radios played, drawers opened and closed with no assistance, toilets flushed on their own, empty porch chairs rocked back and forth, and putrid smells circulated throughout the house.

Unfortunately, by 1985, events at the Smurl home had taken a dangerous turn. The house was always cold, and Jack's parents often heard angry voices coming from their son's side of the duplex, even though Jack and Janet were not arguing.

In February of that year, Janet was alone in the basement doing laundry when something called her name several times. A few days later, she was alone in the kitchen when the room became frigid; suddenly, a faceless, black, human-shaped form appeared. It then walked through the wall and was witnessed by Jack's mother.

At this point, the situation became even more bizarre. On the night Heather was confirmed into the Catholic faith, Shannon was nearly killed when a large light fixture fell from the ceiling and landed on her. On another night, Janet was violently pulled off the bed as Jack lay next to her, paralyzed and unable to help his wife as a foul odor nearly suffocated him. Periodically, heavy footsteps were heard in the attic, and rapping and scratching sounds came from the walls. Not even the family dog escaped: It was repeatedly picked up and thrown around.

"Who You Gonna Call?"

Unwilling to be terrorized out of their home, in January 1986, the Smurls contacted psychic researchers and demonologists Ed and Lorraine Warren, who confirmed that the home was haunted by four evil spirits, including a powerful demon. The Warrens theorized that the emotions generated as the older Smurl daughters entered puberty had somehow awoken a dormant demon.

The Warrens tried prayer and playing religious music, but this only angered the demon even more. It spelled out "You filthy bastard. Get out of this house" on a mirror, violently shook drawers, filled the TV set with an eerie white light, and slapped and bit Jack and Janet.

One day, Janet decided to try communicating with the demon on her own. She told it to rap once for "yes" if it was there to harm them; it rapped once. Next, the entity unleashed a new weapon: sexual assault. A red-eyed, green-gummed succubus with an old woman's face and a young woman's body raped Jack. An incubus sexually assaulted Janet, Dawn was nearly raped, and Carin fell seriously ill with a high fever. Pig noises—which supposedly signal a serious demonic infestation—emanated from the walls.

The Smurls could not escape even by leaving their home. The creature followed them on camping trips and even bothered Jack at his job, giving new meaning to the phrase "work is hell." The family appealed to the Catholic Church for help but to no avail. However, a renegade clergyman named Robert F. McKenna did try to help the Smurls by performing an exorcism in the spring of 1986, but even that didn't help.

Going Public

Finally, in August 1986, the family went to the media with their story. The incidents continued, but the publicity drew the attention of Paul Kurtz, chairman of the Buffalo-based Committee for the Scientific Investigation of Claims of the Paranormal (CSICOP). He offered to investigate, but the Smurls turned him down, stating that they wanted to stay with the Warrens and the Church.

The Smurls did, however, contact a medium, who came to the same conclusion as the Warrens—that there were four spirits in the home: One she couldn't identify, but she said that the others were an old woman named Abigail, a murderer named Patrick, and a very strong demon.

Another exorcism was performed in the summer of 1986, and that seemed to do the trick because the incidents stopped. But just before Christmas of that year, the black form appeared again, along with the banging noises, foul odors, and other phenomena.

Surrender

The Smurls finally moved out of the home in 1988; the next owner said that she never experienced any supernatural events while she lived there.

That same year, *The Haunted*, a book based on the Smurl family's experiences, was released. And in 1991, a TV movie with the same title aired.

But the controversy surrounding the alleged haunting was just beginning. In an article written for *The Skeptical Inquirer*, CSICOP's official magazine, Paul Kurtz cited financial gains from the book deal as a reason to doubt that the incidents were authentic. He also said that for years, residents in the area had complained about foul odors coming from a sewer pipe. He cited other natural explanations for some of the incidents and raised questions about Dawn Smurl's accounts of some of the events. He further claimed that the Warrens gave him a number of conflicting reasons for why he couldn't see the video and audio evidence that they said they'd compiled.

And that's where matters stand today, with the true believers in the Smurl family's account on one side and the doubters on the other. Like the Amityville incident, the Smurl haunting is likely to be debated for a long time to come.

St. Louis Cemetery Is Number One Among Spirits

In one of the most haunted cities in America, you're bound to find ghosts if you know where to look. And even if you don't, keep in mind that old buildings, new buildings, and cemeteries all attract restless spirits. Among the cemeteries in New Orleans, one is known as the most haunted of them all: St. Louis Cemetery No. 1.

✳ ✳ ✳ ✳

Looking Spooky

WHEN EUROPEAN IMMIGRANTS first settled in New Orleans, they needed a place to bury their dead. Unfortunately in New Orleans, that isn't as easy as it sounds. The city lies below sea level, so anything buried (i.e., a coffin) eventually pops back up to the surface due to the water level. That's why the city is full of aboveground cemeteries where the dead are encased in tombs or vaults. So instead of the tiny tombstones you see in graveyards in other parts of the country, the cemeteries in New Orleans are full of structures that are large enough to hold a coffin (or several). Those cemeteries are known as "cities of the dead."

Near the French Quarter, you'll find St. Louis Cemetery No. 1. Established in 1789, it's a beautiful place that's full of historical significance … and ghosts. In fact, many consider it the most haunted cemetery in the United States.

Just the look of St. Louis Cemetery No. 1 is enough to send a shiver down your spine. That's probably why it has been featured in several Hollywood movies, including *Easy Rider* (1969) and *Interview with the Vampire* (1994).

New Orleans is known for its eclectic mix of cultures, and the variety of burial traditions on display at St. Louis Cemetery No. 1 showcase this. French, Irish, and Spanish settlers are among the earliest people who were buried there, and today, their marble tombs mix with crumbling rocks. The grave-yard's narrow rows and winding paths lead to dead ends and confusion.

It's no wonder that visitors report hearing eerie sounds sur-rounding them in this otherworldly place. Is it the wind? Or is it the sound of spirits filling the air with their weeping and moaning?

Ghostly figures and phantom mists hover near the tombs. Some of the spirits are thought to be well-known people; oth-ers are anonymous but no less frightening.

Downcast Spirits

One oft-seen spirit is "Henry," who gave the deed to his tomb to a lady friend to have on hand when he died. Unbeknownst to him, she sold the plot while he was still alive, and upon his death some years later, he was buried in a potter's field. To this day, Henry is seen wandering through the cemetery, perhaps searching for a better place to spend his eternal rest. Some say that he has even asked mourners if there would be room for him in their loved one's tomb.

And if you like animals, St. Louis Cemetery No. 1 is a place to meet a few pets that are quite low maintenance. Ghosts of dogs and cats wander along the rows. All are friendly and are thought to be pets that belonged to a 19th-century grounds-keeper. They seem to be looking for their beloved master.

Voodoo Resides Here

The most famous spirit at St. Louis Cemetery No. 1, however, is that of Marie Laveau. Considered the Voodoo Priestess of New Orleans, Laveau died in 1881, but her spirit still haunts these grounds. Some say that she comes alive each year on June 23 (St. John's Eve) to lead her Voodoo followers. Between these periods of resurrection, her spirit is often seen wearing a distinctive red-and-white turban with seven knots. And if you don't happen to spot her ghost, you might just hear her mumbling Voodoo curses. She has also been known to appear in feline form as a huge black cat; you'll recognize this specter by its glowing red eyes.

Those brave enough to approach Laveau's tomb will want to heed this ritual: Make three Xs on the tombstone, turn around three times, and then knock three times on the stone, and your wish will be granted. And whatever you do, be sure to leave an offering—you definitely don't want to anger the Voodoo Priestess.

No Ghostly Groupie for This Celeb

Apparently, celebrities don't intimidate ghosts. Actor Charles S. Dutton has been in more than 80 films and TV shows— including *Rudy* (1993), *Roc*, and *The L Word*—but that didn't matter to one ghostly resident of St. Louis Cemetery No. 1. As Dutton recounted in an episode of *Celebrity Ghost Stories*, he was in New Orleans directing a movie in 2006, when he and his girlfriend decided to visit the old cemetery to look for the grave of Marie Laveau.

After much searching, they found the tomb and were admiring the many offerings in front of it when they noticed that a nearby grave—which was marked "Duplessy 1850"—had been broken open. The casket was pulled out and its lid was open about five inches. Pure curiosity made them look inside, where they saw a skeleton with a colorful scarf around its neck. Dutton decided to close the coffin and shove it back into the tomb so that it wasn't exposed to the elements. It was getting late by then and his girlfriend pleaded with him to leave, but he kept working.

Suddenly, the couple felt a presence behind them. They turned and saw a raggedly dressed man wearing the same scarf around his neck as the skeleton in the coffin. The two men made eye contact, and Dutton described the moment as feeling as though the man was looking straight through his soul. The man eventually turned around and walked away, but when Dutton tried to follow him, he simply turned a corner and vanished. Dutton was convinced that he and his girlfriend had just met Mr. Duplessy, the man into whose casket they had just peered.

Some Guests Stay Forever at the Chelsea

Since opening in 1884, New York City's famous Chelsea Hotel has been the home of great writers, musicians, artists, and directors, and until 1899, it was the tallest building in the Big Apple. With a rich history and a long list of famous former tenants, it's easy to imagine that the Chelsea may house some notable ghosts. Here are a few of the restless spirits that still call the Chelsea home.

✳   ✳   ✳   ✳

Thomas Wolfe (1900–1938)

THOMAS WOLFE WAS one of the greatest American writers of the early 20th century, and he penned *You Can't Go Home Again* while living in Room 829 at the Chelsea. Although Wolfe didn't die at the Chelsea, it's clear that the author considered the hotel his home, and apparently you *can* go home again . . . even after death: Wolfe's ghost is said to appear throughout the eighth floor. Many folks who snap photos of mysterious orbs there believe that they are the manifestation of Wolfe, still roaming the halls.

Dylan Thomas (1914–1953)

Welshman Dylan Thomas, who is best known for his poem "Do Not Go Gentle Into That Good Night," died of pneumonia in 1953 while visiting the United States. Before he fell ill, Thomas lived in Room 206 at the Chelsea. Several guests have awoken to see Thomas staring at them intently, deathly pale and with the sunken look of a drunk. One woman claimed that she awoke in the night when her room suddenly grew frigid, and then she heard footsteps. She looked up from her bed and saw a grimacing face staring at her in the mirror, and then the face suddenly vanished. She wasn't familiar with Thomas, but she later identified him from a photograph of famous people who had stayed at the Chelsea.

Eugene O'Neill (1888–1953)

One of America's most famous playwrights, Eugene O'Neill lived at the Chelsea on and off from the 1910s through the 1940s. O'Neill wrote plays such as *The Iceman Cometh*, and he often stayed at the Chelsea (which is only blocks from the theater district) when his works were in production on Broadway. Even so, his spirit has only been seen at the Chelsea sporadically. Despite the amount of time he spent there, O'Neill actually died at the Sheraton Hotel in Boston, which is now the Shelton Hall dormitory at Boston University; students in Room 401 often claim to see his specter there as well.

Herbert Huncke (1915–1996)

A notable poet from the Beat Generation, Herbert Huncke lived in Room 828 of the Chelsea until his death in 1996. He is credited with coining the term "Beat Generation," and his friends included William S. Burroughs and Jack Kerouac. But while his friends rose to prominence, Huncke had to settle for appearing as characters, such as Elmer Hassel in Kerouac's *On the Road*. In fact, Huncke didn't garner much fame of his own until he published his auto-biography (*Guilty of Everything*) in 1990, just six years before he passed. Current residents claim that Huncke likes to leave the communal bathroom door open on his old floor. They also say that if you listen to the drafts in the air vents, it's his voice that you'll hear wailing on cold nights.

Sid Vicious (1957–1979)

On the morning of October 12, 1978—in one of the most notorious moments in the history of the Chelsea—Sex Pistols' bassist Sid Vicious awoke in Room 100 after a drug binge to find his girlfriend, Nancy Spungen, stabbed to death in the bathroom. The bed was soaked with her blood, and Sid had been so high that he didn't know if he had murdered the love of his life or if they'd been attacked. After being charged with her murder, the punk-rock icon was so distraught that he overdosed on heroin before he went to trial. Since then, numerous people have witnessed Sid's ghost getting on the elevator at the Chelsea; sometimes he's covered in blood and other times he's accompanied by Nancy. Regardless of what happened that night, Sid seems doomed to spend eternity at the Chelsea Hotel.

Tombstone Shadows

In its heyday, Tombstone, Arizona, was known as "the town too tough to die." Apparently, its ghosts liked that moniker because there are so many spirits roaming its streets that Tombstone is a strong contender for the title of "Most Haunted Town in America." Here are a few of the most notable phantoms that still call this Wild West town home.

✳ ✳ ✳ ✳

Virgil Earp

A MAN IN A long black frock coat stands on a sidewalk in Tombstone; the people who see him assume that he's a reenactor in this former rough-and-tumble Wild West town. But as he starts across the street, a strange thing happens: He vanishes in mid-stride. Only then do people realize that they've just seen one of the many ghosts that haunt this legendary town.

It is usually assumed that the man in the black coat is the ghost of U.S. Deputy Marshal Virgil Earp, who may be reliving one of his life's darkest moments. On December 28, 1881, he was shot and wounded when outlaws who sought revenge for the infamous Gunfight at the O.K. Corral two months prior ambushed him. Virgil survived the attack, but his left arm was permanently maimed.

Morgan Earp

In March 1882, another group of outlaws—who were also seeking revenge for the Gunfight at the O.K. Corral—gunned down Morgan Earp, the brother of noted lawmen Virgil and Wyatt Earp. Morgan was shot in the back and killed while playing pool. Some say that you can still hear his dying words whispered at the location where he was murdered.

Big Nose Kate

Big Nose Kate was the girlfriend of gunslinger Doc Holliday, a friend of the Earps. Her ghost is reportedly responsible for the footsteps and snatches of whispered conversation that swirl through the Crystal Palace Saloon. Lights there turn on and off by themselves, and gambling wheels sometimes spin for no reason, causing speculation that, just as in life, Kate prefers the company of rowdy men.

Swamper

Big Nose Kate's Saloon was originally the Grand Hotel, and a man known as Swamper used to work there as a handyman. He lived in the basement, not far from some of the town's silver mines, so when he wasn't working, Swamper dug a tunnel to one of the mines and began supplementing his income with silver nuggets.

After all the effort that he'd put into obtaining the silver, Swamper was not about to let it go easily... not even after he died. He reportedly haunts Big Nose Kate's Saloon; perhaps he's still hanging around to protect his loot, which has never been found. Naturally, he's often spotted in the basement, but he also likes to show up in photos taken by visitors.

The Bird Cage Theatre

Anyplace where 26 people were violently killed is almost certain to be a spectral smorgasbord. Such is the case with Tombstone's infamously bawdy Bird Cage Theatre. One of the most frequently seen apparitions at the Bird Cage is that of a man who carries a clipboard and wears striped pants and a card-dealer's visor. He's been known to suddenly appear on stage, glide across it, and then walk through a wall. Visitors have raved to the management about how authentic-looking the Wild West costumes look, only to be told that nobody at the Bird Cage dresses in period clothing.

One night, an employee watched on a security monitor as a vaporous woman in white walked slowly through the cellar long after closing time. And although smoking and drinking are now prohibited at the Bird Cage, the scents of cigar smoke and whiskey still linger there. Visitors also hear unexplained sounds, such as a woman singing, a female sighing, glasses clinking, and cards shuffling, as if the ghosts are trying to finish a game that's gone on for far too long.

Nellie Cashman's Restaurant

Nellie Cashman's is another haunted hot spot in Tombstone. Patrons at the eatery report hearing strange noises and seeing dishes suddenly crash to the floor. And the ghosts at Nellie Cashman's have no patience for skeptics: A patron who once noisily derided all things supernatural found herself suddenly wearing the contents of a mustard container that inexplicably leaped off a table.

Fred White

Of the many deaths in Tombstone during the days of the Wild West, one of the most tragic was that of town marshal Fred White. In October 1880, White was trying to arrest "Curly Bill" Brocius when Brocius's gun accidentally went off, killing the lawman. White is rumored to haunt a street near where he was killed, apparently still angry with the way his life was so abruptly taken from him.

Boothill Graveyard

It would almost defy belief if Tombstone's legendary Boothill Graveyard wasn't haunted, but not to worry: The final resting place of so many who were violently taken from this life is said to harbor many restless spirits, including that of Billy Clanton, one of the victims of the Gunfight at the O.K. Corral. Clanton's apparition has been seen rising from his grave and walking toward town. Strange lights and sounds are also said to come from the cemetery.

George Buford

Violent death came in all forms in Tombstone. One of those occurred when a man named George Buford shot his lover and then himself. His aim was better the second time, though: She lived, but he died. He is said to haunt the building where he once lived, which is now a bed-and-breakfast. His spirit has been seen in and around the building; random lights appear there for no reason, and the doorbell sometimes rings on its own in the middle of the night. And ghostly George hasn't lost his fondness for the ladies: Women in the house have felt their hair being stroked and sensed light pressure on the backs of their necks. Of course, when they turn around, no one is there.

An Eternal Seaside Retreat: Cape May's Ghosts

Located at the very southern tip of New Jersey, Cape May was one of the first resort towns in the United States; it offered visitors exotic thrills long before Atlantic City and Las Vegas. In the second half of the 19th century, Cape May experienced a building boom that saw many opulent summer "cottages" (i.e., lavish mansions) spring up around town; many of these Victorian homes are now lovingly restored B & Bs. Some say that ghosts are attracted to water and old buildings; if that's true, it explains why the following ghosts are so fond of Cape May.

* * * *

The Haunted Bunker

IN CAPE MAY Point State Park, a hulking deserted concrete bunker that was built during World War II looks like a typical haunted structure. It is covered with moss and stains, seemingly just about to collapse into the water, and decay hangs heavy in the quiet air around it. Abandoned for decades, the bunker is now home only to seagulls—and ghosts. Visitors have heard a phantom crew still performing its duties: Commands are shouted and soldiers are heard laughing and yelling to each other. Some say that they've seen crew members running about on top of the bunker, only to find it deserted upon closer inspection.

The Inn at 22 Jackson

Jackson Street is one of the oldest and most haunted streets in Cape May. Rumor has it that up to eight buildings along the street harbor ghosts; perhaps the most notable is the Inn at 22 Jackson, one of the street's charming B & Bs. According to one story, while a man was talking to the inn's owner, he asked if she knew that the place was haunted and if she'd ever encountered Esmerelda. The owner said no and closed the front porch door, as it had suddenly gotten very cold. When she did this, she took her eye off the man for a brief moment, and he disappeared.

The owner later asked a longtime guest if she'd encountered any ghosts; the guest said that she'd seen a woman sitting at the edge of her bed. Subsequent research revealed that the original owners of the building had a nanny named Esmerelda.

Higbee Beach

Higbee Beach is located on the Delaware Bay side of Cape May Point. Legend has it that Mr. Higbee, who once owned the land, was buried facedown somewhere on the beach so that he could meet Satan face-to-face. Many think it's Higbee's spirit that roams the beach as a glowing, gray apparition that glides toward the water.

A phantom pirate also floats along the beach until he disappears. And the spirit of an elderly African American male—who is thought to have been Higbee's servant—is said to guard his master's grave.

Queen's Hotel

The Queen's Hotel was once home to a pharmacy that served as a brothel and a speakeasy on the side. Even though it's an upstanding establishment today, the building can't seem to put its past totally behind it. The ghost of a former prostitute haunts the third floor, where the faint scent of perfume sometimes lingers in the air and unexplained cold spots come and go. According to legend, this former working girl likes to feel appreciated, so leaving a dollar or two on the nightstand is a good way to stay in her good graces.

Other Haunted Inns

Many inns in town have paranormal tales but don't want them spread for fear that they might hurt business. Such is the case with an inn where a couple in a second-floor room continually heard the sound of a door slamming on the third floor and then children noisily clambering down the wooden stairs right outside their room. Frustrated, the man waited by the door to catch the young perpetrators in the act. The next time he heard the kids running down the stairs, he yanked open the door, ready to confront them, but the hallway was vacant. The man and his wife were so spooked that they left immediately; they wanted nothing more to do with the inn or its resident ghosts.

At another anonymous establishment, a male guest had gone to bed by himself one night. As he was lying on his side, he suddenly felt the other side of the bed depress, and he knew that he was not alone. The man lay there, wondering what to do. (How do you politely kick a ghost out of bed?) Eventually, he heard the bedsprings creak and felt the mattress rise up, and he knew that the spirit had solved his dilemma for him by leaving of its own accord.

Winterwood Gift & Christmas Gallery

The Winterwood Gift & Christmas Gallery, which was once the site of a dentist's office, is the home of a ghostly man in a white coat who carries something in his hand; he vanishes before anyone can see what he's holding.

While they were alive, the Knerr sisters owned the building, which they operated as a ladies' hat store. Apparently, they still like to keep watch over things, even from the Other Side. After the sisters died, the building became a bookstore. The sisters' spirits could often be heard giggling and knocking books off the shelves until the owner shouted at them to stop. His scolding may have convinced the mischievous sisters to cut it out, but they still like to knock Christmas decorations off the wall from time to time.

The Cape May Lighthouse

The Cape May Lighthouse is yet another haunted spot in town. There, a spectral woman has often been spotted on the first-floor landing. She wears a white dress and holds a child in one hand and a lantern in the other. Another ghost that supposedly resides at the lighthouse is that of a man who fell to his death there in 1995.

More Cape May Ghosts

This list is only a small sampling of the ghosts that reside in Cape May. Many local restaurants report strange occurrences, such as odd odors, chairs and plates that mysteriously move on their own, and misty shapes that manifest from out of nowhere and then suddenly vanish. And a phantom horse-and-carriage clops along like any of the other horse-drawn vehicles in town, only to disappear before unsuspecting visitors' eyes. It seems that the Victorian crown jewel of the Jersey Shore is also a hot spot for paranormal activity.

Fort Delaware Prison Hosts Ghosts Through the Ages

Pea Patch Island. Sounds quaint, doesn't it? Hardly the name of a place that you'd imagine would host a military prison... or the ghosts of former inmates who still can't seem to escape, even in death. But then, the hardships and horrors that were experienced there might just trump the loveliness that the name suggests.

✳   ✳   ✳   ✳

SHAPED LIKE A pentagon, Fort Delaware Prison was completed in 1859, just prior to the Civil War. With a moat surrounding its 32-foot-high walls, it was a very secure place to hold Confederate POWs.

With no extra blankets or clothing, Fort Delaware's inmates struggled to keep warm and suffered through the cold, harsh winters that are typical in the Mid-Atlantic region. Malaria, smallpox, and yellow fever were commonplace, and they traveled quickly through the facility; estimates suggest that between 2,500 and 3,000 people may have died there—and many tormented souls seem to remain.

Now Appearing...

One ghost that has been seen by many workers at the Fort Delaware Prison—which is now a living-history museum—is not the spirit of a prisoner at all: It's that of a former cook who now spends her time hiding ingredients from the current staff. Visitors have reported hearing a harmonica in the laundry area, where a ghost has been spotted threading buttons in a long string.

In the officer's quarters, a spectral child is known to tug on people's clothes and a ghostly woman taps visitors on the shoulder. Books fall from shelves, and chandelier crystals swing back and forth by themselves.

And then there are the darker, more sinister spirits—the ones that suffered in life and found no relief in death. Moans, muffled voices, and rattling chains fill the basement with spooky sounds of prisoners past. The halls echo with noises that resemble the sounds of someone trying to break free from chains. Apparitions of Confederate soldiers have been seen running through the prison, and sailors have witnessed lights on shore where there were none. Screams and desperate voices plead for help, but so far, no one has been able to calm these restless souls.

Ghost Hunter Endorsed

If you're searching for proof that these ghosts are the real deal, check out a 2008 episode of *Ghost Hunters* that was shot at Fort Delaware. Jason Hawes, Grant Wilson, and their team of investigators found quite a bit of paranormal activity when they visited the old prison. In the basement's tunnels, they heard unexplained footsteps and voices, as well as something crashing to the ground. A thermal-imaging camera picked up the apparition of a man who appeared to be running away from the group. And in the kitchen, the investigators heard a very loud banging sound that seemingly came from nowhere.

In the Spirit of Things

It's not *all* terror at the old prison. Today, Fort Delaware is part of a state park that's open to tourists and offers many special programs. One event that appeals to athletes and history buffs alike is the "Escape from Fort Delaware" triathlon: Each year when the starting musket blasts, participants reenact the escape route of 52 inmates who broke out of Fort Delaware Prison during the Civil War.

During the Civil War, so much misery was experienced at Camp Sumter—a prison for captured Union soldiers near Andersonville, Georgia—that the absence of a haunting there would be remarkable. It only served as a POW camp for a little more than a year, but during that time, 13,000 Union soldiers died there. Captain Henry Wirz, who was in charge of the prison, was hanged after the war for conspiracy and murder. His angry spirit still wanders the compound, and many visitors have smelled a vile odor that they attribute to his ghost.

Atchison, Kansas: A True Ghost Town

According to census records, approximately 10,000 people call Atchison, Kansas, home. While this is a good indication of how many people live in the town, it doesn't measure another important piece of data: how many ghosts reside there. Considering the ratio of ghosts to living residents, Atchison could quite possibly be the most haunted town in the United States.

✳ ✳ ✳ ✳

Madam of the Missouri River

ONE OF ATCHISON'S oldest ghost stories traces its origin back more than a hundred years, when what is currently Atchison Street was called Ferry Street. This road travels down the side of a steep hill and ends at the Missouri River. In years past, the riverside site was used to board ferries, and legend has it that a woman lost control of her buggy and crashed into the water, where she drowned. Her lonely spirit supposedly tries to lure men into her watery grave.

Mournful Molly of Jackson Park

Jackson Park is the site of a purported haunting by a female spirit named Molly. One story suggests that Molly was a Black woman who was lynched by a mob for having an affair with a white man. Another version indicates that Molly was a high school girl who fought with her date on prom night, leaving his car in disgust and entering the park; the next morning, her body was supposedly found hanging from a tree with her dress torn and tattered. Other stories contend that after Molly's boy-friend broke up with her, she jumped to her death from a high ledge in the park. Whoever the female spirit is, she often moans and unleashes shrill screams in the park around midnight, and some claim that they have seen her ghostly figure hanging from a tree.

The Abandoned Baby of Benedictine College

Two dorms at Benedictine College—a Catholic university founded in Atchison in 1858—are haunted: one by a baby and the other by one of the school's founding monks. The monks protect the school, and one has often been sighted at Ferrell Hall. The ghost-baby resides in Memorial Hall; legend has it that a female student once gave birth in the closet of her dorm room, but the newborn died. Several residents of Memorial Hall have reported feeling a phantom baby in their beds at night. Even more terrifying, one woman was trapped in her closet when a dresser mysteriously moved in front of the door while she was inside. Her roommate was not there, so she had to scream for help. Another student reported that her desk chair suddenly began to rock back and forth. And yet another woman awoke around 3 AM to see a shadowy figure going to and from her closet; in the morning, she discovered that her possessions had been tossed onto the floor.

The Phantom Fryer

There truly is no rest for the weary at Muchnic House on North Fourth Street in Atchison. Legend has it that a maid died in the building when she fell down the back stairs one Sunday morning. Her spirit has been known to turn lights on and off, and residents have also experienced the inexplicable scent of bacon frying. In 2005, a visitor who was taking a tour of the house—which is now an art gallery—saw a young woman dressed in a maid's uniform peering at the group from the top of the stairs. However, when the group arrived upstairs, no one was there.

Deal With the Devil

The Gargoyle Home on North Fourth Street is named for the menacing gargoyles that decorate the facade of the house, which is rumored to be cursed. The gargoyles were supposedly built to honor the original owner's pact with the devil; when a subsequent owner tried to remove the gargoyles in an attempt to make the house more pleasant, he fell to his death. In 2005, when the Travel Channel sent a paranormal investigation team to Atchison, the researchers equipment detected the presence of ghosts in the building.

A Really Friendly Ghost Can Be So Helpful

A beautiful two-story home on the corner of Fifth and Kearny Streets offers a great living space—as well as a helpful, friendly ghost. Once, a gentleman who lived in the house received help putting on his coat; he assumed that it was his wife, but when he turned around, nobody was there. Another time, while driving home from an event, the man's wife commented that she would love a cup of tea. The kindly spirit must have heard her because when the couple arrived at home, they discovered that hot water was in the kettle, and a cup, spoon, and tea bag were waiting for them. The couple also heard sounds coming from the attic when it was empty and experienced the mysterious scented of clover wafting through the house.

When Ghosts Don't Get Their Way... Watch Out!

Although every ghost story is unsettling in its own way, a restless spirit at Sallie's House might just be the most disturbing specter in a town full of them. This building on North Second Street once served as a doctor's office; the physician lived with his family upstairs and ran his practice on the ground floor. One night in the early 1900s, a girl named Sallie was brought to the office. It is unclear whether she had a severe respiratory infection or her appendix burst, but in any event, she died.

Sallie's spirit seems to have been reawakened in 1993, when a couple moved into the house with their young child. Sallie liked to rearrange the child's toys while the family was out, turn appliances on and off, and move pictures so that they hung upside down.

But Sallie was not the only spirit in the house: Allegedly, another ghost physically attacked the husband. A psychic told the couple that this spirit was in her thirties and that she had fallen in love with the husband. (Sallie told the medium that she did not like this other ghost.) The malevolent spirit tried to turn the man against his wife, but when that didn't work, the entity became violent. Just before the jealous spirit attacked the man of the house, the room grew very cold. Then, suddenly, scratches and welts appeared on his arms, back, and stomach. After the ghost tried to push the man down the stairs, the couple moved out. The malevolent haunting stopped, but in 2005, audio recordings picked up the sounds of children playing while the house was empty.

Take the Trolley and See Them All

These sites—and others—are all part of the popular Haunted Atchison Trolley Tour. The company that conducts this tour says the town has enough haunted sites to fill an itinerary of three full days, so it rotates its routes frequently.

Capitol Ghosts in Raleigh, North Carolina

Ghosts abound in North Carolina, but Raleigh—the state's capital since 1792—seems to be home to more than its share of playful poltergeists. The ghost of former governor Daniel Fowle haunts the North Carolina Executive Mansion, which has been the official residence of the state's governor since 1891. But whereas the governor's mansion holds just one ghost, the State Capitol is practically overflowing with spooks, almost all of whom prefer to make their presence known late at night.

✳   ✳   ✳   ✳

Weird Sounds

LONGTIME SECURITY GUARD Owen Jackson reported numerous encounters with the ghosts of the Capitol building. On several occasions, he heard the sound of books falling in the authentically restored state library on the third floor. But when he investigated the noises, no books were missing from the shelves or found on the floor.

Once in 1981, Jackson heard the sound of glass breaking on an upper floor; he fetched a broom to clean it up, but he found all of the windows intact and nothing else was broken. And on several occasions, Jackson heard mysterious footsteps and the sound of the building's elevator moving from floor to floor, as if transporting unseen visitors.

Another time, Jackson was sitting at the receptionist's desk preparing to make his rounds when he felt a hand rest on his shoulder. He quickly whirled around, but no one was there.

Watchful Wraiths

Jackson isn't the only person who has encountered the Capitol's ghosts. Late one evening, curator Raymond Beck felt the eerie sensation that someone was looking over his shoulder as he shelved some books in the building's library. After it happened a second time, Beck didn't wait around for it to happen again—he finished his chore and left as quickly as possible.

Later, Beck told Sam Townsend Sr., an administrator at the Capitol building, about his bizarre experiences. Townsend admitted that he, too, had heard and felt things there that he couldn't explain. One evening in 1976, for example, Townsend was finishing up some paperwork when he heard a key rattling in the lock of the Capitol's north entrance. He assumed that it was Secretary of State Thad Eure returning to his office to catch up on some work (as was his habit), but when Townsend went to say hello, Eure was nowhere to be found. As Townsend stood near the north entrance, he suddenly heard keys rattling at the south entrance. He searched the building from top to bottom but found no logical explanation for the mysterious noises.

On another occasion, Townsend was again working late when he heard footsteps approaching from elsewhere on the same floor. Thinking that it was Beck, Townsend went to Beck's office to let him know that he was there too, but the room was empty. Townsend heard the same phantom footsteps on several occasions and always at the same time—8:30 pm.

Seen and Heard

Townsend is one of the few people to see the Capitol ghosts as well as hear them. Once, Townsend walked by the Senate chamber on his way to his office and was startled to see someone standing just inside the chamber's doorway. But when he checked to make sure that his eyes weren't deceiving him, the figure had vanished.

Another time, Townsend almost bumped into a ghost that floated by him in the rotunda. Recalling the incident, Townsend said that he stepped aside quickly so as to "avoid a collision."

Owen Jackson also caught a glimpse of one of the spirits that dwells within the Capitol building. One night after he finished his rounds, he turned off all but the security lights, checked all the doors, and then exited the building and walked to his car. As he waited for his vehicle to warm up, Jackson glanced up and saw a man walk past an illuminated window on the second floor. According to Jackson, the figure was wearing the uniform of a Confederate soldier.

Rather than investigate, Jackson simply went home. As he later told a reporter, "I figured anybody [that's] been dead that long, I didn't want to tangle with him."

Who Founded the Mafia?

To be honest, we really didn't want to answer this question. But then our editors made us an offer we couldn't refuse.

✳ ✳ ✳ ✳

THIS IS LIKE asking, "Who founded England?" or "Who founded capitalism?" The Mafia is more of a phenomenon than an organization—it's a movement that rose from a complicated interaction of multiple factors, including history, economics, geography, and politics. Hundreds of thousands of pages have been written by historians, sociologists, novelists, screenwriters, and criminologists who have attempted to chart the history and origins of the Mafia, so it's doubtful that we'll be able to provide any real revelations in five hundred words. But we're a hardy bunch, and we'll do our best.

By all accounts, the Mafia came to prominence in Sicily during the mid-nineteenth century. Given Sicily's history, this makes sense—the island has repeatedly been invaded and occupied, and has generally been mired in poverty for thousands of years. By the mid-nineteenth century, Italy was in total chaos due to the abolition of feudalism and the lack of a central government or a semblance of a legitimate legal system.

As sociologists will confirm, people who live in areas that fall victim to such upheaval tend to rely on various forms of self-government. In Sicily, this took the form of what has become known as the Mafia. The fellowship, which originated in the rural areas of the Mediterranean island, is based on a complicated system of respect, violence, distrust of government, and the code of *omertà*—a word that is synonymous with the group's code of silence and refers to an unspoken agreement to never cooperate with authorities, under penalty of death. Just as there is no one person who founded the Mafia, there is no one person who runs it. The term "Mafia" refers to any group of organized criminals that follows the traditional Sicilian system of bosses, *capos* ("chiefs"), and soldiers. These groups are referred to as "families."

In the United States

Although the Mafia evolved in Sicily during the nineteenth century, most Americans equate it to the crime families that dominated the headlines in Chicago and New York for much of the twentieth century. The American Mafia developed as a result of the huge wave of Sicilian immigrants that arrived in the United States in the late nineteenth and early twentieth centuries. These newcomers brought with them the Mafia structure and the code of *omertà*.

These Sicilian immigrants often clustered together in poor urban areas, such as Park Slope in Brooklyn and the south side of Chicago. There, far from the eyes of authorities, disputes were handled by locals. By the 1920s, crime families had sprung up all over the United States and gang wars were prevalent. In the 1930s, Lucky Luciano—who is sometimes called the father of the American Mafia—organized "The Commission," a faux-judiciary system that oversaw the activities of the Mafia in the United States.

Though Mafia families have been involved in murder, kidnapping, extortion, racketeering, gambling, prostitution, drug dealing, weapons dealing, and other crimes over the years, the phenomenon still maintains the romantic appeal that it had when gangsters like Al Capone captivated the nation. Part of it, of course, is the result of the enormous success of the *Godfather* films, but it is also due, one presumes, to the allure of the principles that the Mafia supposedly was founded upon: self-reliance, loyalty, and *omertà*.

So there you have it: a summary of the founding of the Mafia. Of course, we could tell you more, but then we'd have to...well, you know.

Conneaut Lake Park

Would ghosts in an amusement park really be that amusing? It's no joke that guests at Conneaut Lake Park—a vintage entertainment complex and hotel in northwestern Pennsylvania—have reported a host of spirits that seem to be on an everlasting vacation at the historic resort.

✳ ✳ ✳ ✳

I T MAY SEEM odd that such a fun location would be haunted, but places where large numbers of people congregate naturally seem to accumulate ghosts. Conneaut Lake Park, which is located about 30 miles south of Lake Erie, opened in 1892 as Exposition Park on the western shore of the deep glacial lake that shares its name. The park became so popular that several hotels sprang up nearby to accommodate the crowds. The only one of those inns still operating today, the Hotel Conneaut, is famous for its lively ghosts. In fact, the hotel and park were featured on an episode of *Paranormal State* in 2009.

Conneaut Lake Park still features many quaint, refurbished old rides that evoke the laid-back atmosphere of the lakeside area's past. Its Blue Streak roller coaster is a retro rider's dream, and other attractions at the park bear equally colorful names such as Little Dipper, Witch's Stew, Roll-O-Plane, and Devil's Den. But it was on the wooden-tracked Blue Streak, which opened in 1937, where a rider allegedly died.

Only a few years after the roller coaster thrilled its first riders, legend has it that a tipsy sailor on shore leave made the foolish mistake of standing up just as the coaster made one of its trademark tight turns. The sailor went flying—in the opposite direction of the Blue Streak—and did not survive. The ride has reputedly been haunted ever since...but not by the sailor, by the ghost of a young girl wearing an old-fashioned dress.

The Burning Bride

In 1943, around the same time that the sailor was said to have met his end, a large section of the Hotel Conneaut burned and spawned the park's most famous ghost: "Elizabeth," the phantom bride. According to local lore, Elizabeth was a hotel guest who perished in the fire after her groom was unable to save her. Although historians have not found evidence that this actually happened, the spirit seems to remain in an eternal holding pattern, waiting to be rescued from the flames. A hint of jasmine-scented perfume is often the first clue that Elizabeth is near.

Many guests have reported seeing the apparition of a young woman wearing a 1940s-era dress gliding silently around the hotel. Sometimes she emerges from a solid wall that at one time was a hallway opening; she seems to be confused regarding her whereabouts. Occasionally, she is spotted waltzing with her groom on the front veranda.

Hotel Horrors

Another ghost at the hotel is the spirit of Angelina, a young girl who was allegedly killed in a fatal tricycle accident on the hotel's balcony or stairs. According to an article in the *Meadville Tribune*, spiritual medium Kitty Osborne saw the tiny trikester pedaling down a hallway just outside her room. Osborne told the *Tribune* that she was "flabbergasted" at the sight.

The *Tribune* also interviewed George Deshner, the park's general manager, who said that he and many other employees have had brushes with unknown forces in the hotel. On several occasions, staff members have checked to make sure that all of the hotel's windows are closed and locked for the night only to discover later that one had mysteriously reopened. Lights turn on and off by themselves, and the manager himself has felt unseen hands shove him against a wall.

Even the hotel restaurant harbors its own spook: a chef dressed in spotless whites with an old-fashioned bow tied around his neck. He is said to move brooms and garbage cans, and guests have reported seeing him staring at them through the restaurant's window after the eatery is locked up for the night. One group of women observed the otherworldly figure writing on a piece of paper. Perhaps he was planning the next day's dessert specials: booberry pie and sheet cake!

Conneaut Lake Park is unlike any other amusement park because it is also a town—its grounds include more than a hundred private residences, and it even had its own post office at one time.

The Maudlin Spirits of the Mounds Theater

In 1922, the Mounds Theatre opened on the east side of St. Paul, Minnesota, to showcase silent films. A few dramatic characters from that era are said to remain in the restored Art Deco building, but these entities are not confined to the silver screen.

✳ ✳ ✳ ✳

THE MOST FRIGHTENING spook at the Mounds is the spectral male figure that lurks in the dusty, antiquated projection room. Building director Raeann Ruth and three paranormal investigators who spent a night in the room all reported hearing a male voice alternately cry and swear up a storm. They also witnessed an angry male ghost staring at them with dark, sunken eyes. It certainly didn't help to alleviate any fears when the group discovered an antique Ouija board lying amid the old projection equipment.

Tragedies Spawn Terrors

A more benign ghost is dressed as an usher and seems to be crying. According to legend, he was a theater worker who found his beloved cuddling with someone else. It is believed that after death, he stayed attached to his life's greatest tragedy, looking for a way to make it right.

Tragic may also be the best way to describe another Mounds Theatre ghost—a young girl who skips around the stage bouncing a ball. During a recent renovation (2001-2003), a small dress and a child's shoe were found hidden in the theater. Some believe that these items could be linked to a possible child assault, which could explain why the girl's spirit still roams the theater.

New Life for Old Spirits

A nonprofit children's theater troupe now owns the building, thanks to the generosity of former owner George Hardenbergh, who bequeathed it to the group, Portage for Youth, in 2001, rather than see the grand old place demolished. Perhaps the influence of these happy young people will eventually banish the sad spirits lingering at the theater and help restore its original festive air.

The Paranormal at Paramount Studios

The studios of Paramount Pictures in Hollywood opened their doors in 1926. Since then, they've hosted everyone from early stars such as Rudolph Valentino and Clara Bow to modern mainstays such as Tom Cruise and Harrison Ford. Certainly, Paramount has been home to some of the greatest performers in Hollywood history—and a few have even stuck around even after death.

✳ ✳ ✳ ✳

Location, Location, Location

WHEN YOU CONSIDER the location of Paramount's studios, it's not surprising that they're haunted. After all, the back of the lot shares a border with the famous Hollywood Forever Cemetery. And just as not everyone interred at Hollywood Forever is famous, some of the ghostly residents of Paramount are relatively anonymous. One, a nondescript elderly woman, has been spotted roaming the halls of the Ball Building late at night. Certain that she's lost, several guards have tried to help her, but she always disappears before they can.

A ghost that seems to be afraid of the dark likes to wander around the second floor of the Chevalier Building. Guards say that the floor's lights mysteriously turn on at night after everyone has left the building; but when they investigate, nobody is there. Then there's the woman whose strong, flowery perfume can be smelled on the second floor of the Hart Building. She most often makes her presence known to men by throwing objects from desks onto the floor.

Next-Door Neighbors

Hollywood Forever Cemetery is a prominent neighbor of the studios, and guards working at the Lemon Grove Gate—the entrance closest to the graveyard—tell several spooky stories. One playful yet anonymous spirit seems to revel in getting the Paramount guards to chase it to the gate; then, just as the guards close in, it walks through the wall and into Hollywood Forever Cemetery.

One of Paramount's best-known visitors from next door was also one of its most famous stars. Rudolph Valentino was a heartthrob of the silent era whose most famous role was as the title character in *The Sheik* (1921). In 1926, when he died unexpectedly at age 31, fans the world over were devastated. A riot broke out at his funeral, and rumors persist that a few women took their own lives rather than live in a world without him. For decades, Paramount guards have reported seeing the original "Latin Lover" hanging out by the soundstages or leaving his tomb to visit the film studio that made him famous. According to some accounts, Valentino even dons his old costume from *The Sheik* from time to time.

She's Heeeeere

One of the youngest ghosts that haunts Paramount made her mark, ironically enough, in a movie about a haunted house. Heather O'Rourke began her film career with a role in *Poltergeist* (1982), and she quickly became a star. Soon after, she was on Stage 19 at Paramount shooting episodes of *Happy Days*. Sadly, in 1988, she died during surgery at age 12. Her friends and costars remembered fondly that she enjoyed running around the catwalks of Stage 19 between takes, filling the air with sweet laughter. In the 1990s, Stage 19 became home to a new sitcom called *Wings*, and the cast and crew of that show reportedly heard a child laughing and playing on those same catwalks. However, no child actors were cast as regulars on *Wings*, and the people who worked on the show were convinced that it was Heather.

Paramount is clearly a place where people are dying to get in, and the dead never want to leave.

The Lost Colony of Roanoke

Twenty years before England established its first successful colony in the New World, an entire village of English colonists disappeared in what would later be known as North Carolina. Did these pioneers all perish? Did Native Americans capture them? Did they join a friendly tribe? Could they have left descendants who live among us today?

❋   ❋   ❋   ❋

Timing Is Everything

TALK ABOUT BAD timing. As far as John White was concerned, England couldn't have picked a worse time to go to war. It was November 1587, and White had just arrived in England from the New World. He intended to gather relief supplies and immediately sail back to Roanoke Island, where he had left more than 100 colonists who were running short of food. Unfortunately, the English were gearing up to fight Spain. Every seaworthy ship, including White's, was pressed into naval service. Not a single one could be spared for his return voyage to America.

Nobody Home

When John White finally returned to North America three years later, he was dismayed to discover that the colonists he had left behind were nowhere to be found. Instead, he stumbled upon a mystery—one that has never been solved. The village that White and company had founded in 1587 on Roanoke Island lay completely deserted. Houses had been dismantled (as if someone planned to move them), but the pieces lay in the long grass along with iron tools and farming equipment. A stout stockade made of logs stood empty.

White found no sign of his daughter Eleanor, her husband Ananias, or their daughter Virginia Dare—the first English child born in America. None of the 87 men, 17 women, and 11 children remained. No bodies or obvious gravesites offered clues to their fate. The only clues that White could find were the letters CRO carved into a tree trunk and the word CROATOAN carved into a log of the abandoned fort.

No Forwarding Address

All White could do was hope that the colonists had been taken in by friendly natives. Croatoan—also spelled "Croatan"—was the name of a barrier island to the south and also the name of a tribe of Native Americans that lived on that island. Unlike other area tribes, the Croatoans had been friendly to English newcomers, and one of them, Manteo, had traveled to England with earlier explorers and returned to act as interpreter for the Roanoke colony. Had the colonists, with Manteo's help, moved to Croatoan? Were they safe among friends?

White tried to find out, but his timing was rotten once again. He had arrived on the Carolina coast as a hurricane bore down on the region. The storm hit before he could mount a search. His ship was blown past Croatoan Island and out to sea. Although the ship and crew survived the storm and made it back to England, White was stuck again. He tried repeatedly but failed to raise money for another search party.

No one has ever learned the fate of the Roanoke Island colonists, but there are no shortage of theories as to what happened to them. A small sailing vessel and other boats that White had left with them were gone when he returned. It's possible that the colonists used the vessels to travel to another island or to the mainland. White had talked with others before he left about possibly moving the settlement to a more secure location inland. It's even possible that the colonists tired of waiting for White's return and tried to sail back to England. If so, they would have perished at sea. Yet there are at least a few shreds of hearsay evidence that the colonists survived in America.

Rumors of Survivors

In 1607, Captain John Smith and company established the first successful English settlement in North America at Jamestown, Virginia. The colony's secretary, William Strachey, wrote four years later about hearing a report of four English men, two boys, and one young woman who had been sighted south of Jamestown at a settlement of the Eno tribe, where they were being used as slaves. If the report was true, who else could these English have been but Roanoke survivors?

For more than a century after the colonists' disappearance, stories emerged of gray-eyed Native Americans and English-speaking villages in North Carolina and Virginia. In 1709, an English surveyor said members of the Hatteras tribe living on North Carolina's Outer Banks—some of them with light-colored eyes—claimed to be descendants of white people. It's possible that the Hatteras were the same people that the 1587 colonists called Croatoan.

In the intervening centuries, many of the individual tribes of the region have disappeared. Some died out. Others were absorbed into larger groups such as the Tuscarora. One surviving group, the Lumbee, has also been called Croatoan. The Lumbee, who still live in North Carolina, often have Caucasian features. Could they be descendants of Roanoke colonists? Many among the Lumbee dismiss the notion as fanciful, but the tribe has long been thought to be of mixed heritage and has been speaking English so long that none among them know what language preceded it.

Sandstone Gateway to Heaven

For hundreds of years, rumors of the lost city of Angkor spread among Cambodian peasants. On a stifling day in 1860, Henri Mahout and his porters discovered that the ancient city was more than mere legend.

✳ ✳ ✳ ✳

FRENCH BOTANIST AND explorer Henri Mahout wiped his spectacles as he pushed into the Cambodian jungle clearing. Gasping for breath in the rain forest's thick mists, he gazed down weed-ridden avenues at massive towers and stone temples wreathed with carvings of gods, kings, and battles. The ruins before him were none other than the temples of Angkor Wat. Although often credited with the discovery of Angkor Wat, Mahout was not the first Westerner to encounter the site. He did, however, bring the "lost" city to the attention of the European public when his travel journals were published in 1868. He wrote: "One of these temples—a rival to that of Solomon, and erected by some ancient Michelangelo—might take an honorable place beside our most beautiful buildings."

Mahout's descriptions of this "new," massive, unexplored Hindu temple sent a jolt of lightning through Western academic circles. Explorers from western Europe combed the jungles of northern Cambodia to explain the origin of the mysterious lost shrine.

The Rise of the Khmer

Scholars first theorized that Angkor Wat and other ancient temples in present-day Cambodia were about 2,000 years old.

However, as they began to decipher the Sanskrit inscriptions, they found that the temples had been erected during the 9th through 12th centuries. While Europe languished in the Dark Ages, the Khmer Empire of Indochina was reaching its zenith.

The earliest records of the Khmer people date back to the middle of the 6th century. They migrated from southern China and nearby regions and settled in what is now Cambodia. The early Khmer retained many Indian influences from the West— they were Hindus, and their architecture evolved from Indian methods of building.

In the early 9th century, King Jayavarman II laid claim to an independent kingdom called Kambuja. He established his capital in the Angkor area some 190 miles north of the modern Cambodian capital of Phnom Penh. Jayavarman II also introduced the cult of devaraja, which claimed that the Khmer king was a representative of Shiva, the Hindu god of chaos, destruction, and rebirth. As such, in addition to the temples built to honor the Hindu gods, temples were also constructed to serve as tombs when kings died.

The Khmer built more than 100 stone temples spread out over about 40 miles. The temples were made from laterite and sandstone. The sandstone provided an open canvas for the statues and reliefs celebrating the Hindu gods that decorate the temples.

Home of the Gods

During the first half of the 12th century, Kambuja's King Suryavarman II decided to raise an enormous temple dedicated to the Hindu god Vishnu, a religious monument that would subdue the surrounding jungle and illustrate the power of the Khmer king. His masterpiece—the largest temple complex in the world—would be known to history by its Sanskrit name, "Angkor Wat," or "City of Temple."

Pilgrims visiting Angkor Wat in the 12th century would enter the temple complex by crossing a square, 600-foot-wide moat that ran some four miles in perimeter around the temple grounds. Approaching from the west, visitors would tread the moat's causeway to the main gateway. From there, they would follow a spiritual journey representing the path from the outside world through the Hindu universe and into Mount Meru, the home of the gods. They would pass a giant statue of an eight-armed Vishnu as they entered the western gopura, or gatehouse, known as the "Entrance of the Elephants." They would then follow a stone walkway decorated with nagas (mythical serpents) past sunken pools and column-studded buildings once believed to house sacred temple documents.

At the end of the stone walkway, a pilgrim would step up to a rectangular platform surrounded with galleries featuring six-foot-high bas-reliefs of gods and kings. One depicts the Churning of the Ocean of Milk, a Hindu story in which gods and demons churn a serpent in an ocean of milk to extract the elixir of life. Another illustrates the epic battle of monkey warriors against demons whose sovereign had kidnapped Sita, Rama's beautiful wife. Others depict the gruesome fates awaiting the wicked in the afterlife. A visitor to King Suryavarman's kingdom would next ascend the dangerously steep steps to the temple's second level, an enclosed area boasting a courtyard decorated with hundreds of dancing apsaras, female images ornamented with jewelry and elaborately dressed hair.

For kings and high priests, the journey would continue with a climb up more steep steps to a 126-foot-high central temple, the pinnacle of Khmer society. Spreading out some 145 feet on each side, the square temple includes a courtyard cornered by four high conical towers shaped to look like lotus buds. The center of the temple is dominated by a fifth conical tower soaring 180 feet above the main causeway; inside it holds a golden statue of the Khmer patron, Vishnu, riding a half-man, half-bird creature in the image of King Suryavarman.

Disuse and Destruction

With the decline of the Khmer Empire and the resurgence of Buddhism, Angkor Wat was occupied by Buddhist monks, who claimed it as their own for many years. A cruciform gallery leading to the temple's second level was decorated with 1,000 Buddhas; the Vishnu statue in the central tower was replaced by an image of Buddha. The temple fell into various states of disrepair over the centuries and is now the focus of international restoration efforts.

The Seven Wonders of the Ancient World

It was the ultimate destination guide—seven of the most spectacular hand-built wonders of the world. In fact, the Greek referred to these wonders as theamati, which translates roughly to "must-sees."

✳ ✳ ✳ ✳

THE FIRST COMPREHENSIVE listing of the Seven Wonders has been attributed to Herodotus, a Greek historian dating back to the 5th century BC. Other versions soon followed. Most of the earliest lists were lost; the oldest existing version known today was compiled by Antipater of Sidon in 140 BC. The items on his list are the ones that came to forever be known as the Seven Wonders of the Ancient World. Unfortunately, only one of the seven still exists today; all that remains of the other six are descriptions from writers.

So What's the Big Deal?

What makes the seven wonders of the world so wonderful? It's a combination of factors: the intricacies of the architecture, the scale of engineering, and the beauty of each project—not to mention the construction technology and available materials in use at the time. Religion often played a big role in the significance of these structures. Some were built to honor certain gods. Others were built to showcase important rulers, a number of whom had achieved a godlike following.

The Great Pyramid of Giza

Located on the west bank of the Nile river near Cairo, Egypt, this is the largest of ten pyramids built between 2600 and 2500 BC. Built for King Khufu, the Great Pyramid was constructed by thousands of workers toiling over the span of decades

The structure consists of more than two million 2.5-ton stones. If the stones were piled on top of each other, the resulting tower would be close to 50 stories high. The base covers an astonishing 13 acres.

It's not known exactly how the blocks were lifted. Theories include mud- and water-coated ramps or an intricate system of levers. Not only did the blocks have to be lifted, but they also had to be transported from the quarries. Even the experts can't say exactly how that was done. The mystery is part of the fascination. The pyramid originally stood 481 feet high but has been weathered down to about 450 feet. It was considered the tallest structure on the planet for 43 centuries.

The Great Pyramid is the only Wonder of the Ancient World still standing—a testament to one of the mightiest civilizations in history.

The Hanging Gardens of Babylon

Legend has it the Gardens were built by King Nebuchadnezzar II, ruler of Babylon (near modern Baghdad, Iraq), around 600 BC as a present for his wife, Amytis of Media. The gardens consisted of a series of terraces holding trees, exotic plants, and shady pools—all fed by water piped in from the Euphrates River and rising about 60 feet high. References to the Gardens appear as late as the first century BC, after which they disappear from contemporary accounts. There has been some speculation over whether or not the Gardens ever actually existed.

The Temple of Artemis at Ephesus

Constructed around 550 BC in what is now Turkey, the Temple was built in honor of Artemis (Diana), goddess of hunting and nature. The marble temple measured 377 by 180 feet and had a tile-covered roof held up by at least 106 columns between 40 and 60 feet high. The temple held priceless art and also functioned as the treasury of the city. It stood until 356 BC when it was purposely destroyed by an artist, known in infamy as Herostratus, who burned the Temple merely so his name would be remembered for ages. The outraged Ephesians rebuilt the temple, this time entirely of stone, but the new building was destroyed by invading Goths in AD 262. A few surviving sculptures are displayed at the British Museum.

The Statue of Zeus at Olympia

Even contemporary historians and archaeologists consider the Statue of Zeus at Olympia to be one of the best-known statues in the ancient world. The image, standing 40 feet high with a 20-foot base, was constructed by Phidias around 435 BC to honor Zeus, king of the gods. The statue depicted a seated Zeus (made of ivory, though his robes and sandals were made of gold) holding a golden figure of the goddess of victory in one hand and a staff topped with an eagle in the other. Atop his head was a wreath of olive branches.

In the lamplight of the temple, the statue seemed almost alive and attracted pilgrims from all over Greece for eight centuries. After the old gods were outlawed by Christian emperor Theodosius, the statue was taken as a prize to Constantinople, where it was destroyed by fire around AD 462.

The Mausoleum of Maussollos

This white marble tomb, built in what is today southwestern Turkey, was built around 353 BC for Maussollos, a Persian king. Around 45 stories tall, the building was covered in relief sculpture depicting scenes from mythology; gaps were filled in with bigger-than-life statues of famous heroes and gods. The very top was capped with a marble statue of Maussollos, pulled in a chariot by four horses. The structure was so impressive that the king's name has been lent to the present-day word mausoleum, now used to refer to an impressive burial place.

The tomb remained largely intact until the 13th century, when it was severely damaged by a series of earthquakes. In 1494, the Knights of Saint John raided its stonework to use as building materials for a castle being constructed nearby, and thus the Mausoleum was lost to history.

The Colossus of Rhodes

Standing nearly 110 feet tall—rivaling the modern Statue of Liberty, which tops out at 151 feet—the Colossus of Rhodes was a sight to behold. The bronze statue was built near the harbor of Rhodes in the Aegean Sea in honor of the sun god Helios. Construction took 12 years—from approximately 292 BC to 280 BC The exact pose of the statue is a matter of debate; records say that one arm was raised but are maddeningly silent on other details. The statue stood for only 56 years before it was toppled by an earthquake. It lay on the ground for another 800 years, still a tourist attraction. Accounts say a popular tourist game was to see if a person could encircle one of the fallen statue's thumbs with their arms. Finally, in AD 654, Rhodes was captured by Arab invaders who broke up the statue and melted it down for its bronze.

The Lighthouse of Alexandria

The youngest of the ancient wonders was a building with a civic, rather than a spiritual, purpose. The famed lighthouse of Alexandria was built around 250 BC to aid ships making the journey into that city's harbor. At 380 feet tall, it was a marvel of ancient engineering. Overshadowed only by two of the tallest Egyptian pyramids, a tower of greater height wouldn't be constructed for centuries. An interior ramp led up to a platform supporting a series of polished bronze mirrors, which would reflect sunlight during the day and firelight at night. The fuel source is uncertain but may have been oil or even animal dung. Some accounts claim the lighthouse could be seen 300 miles from the shore; this is almost certainly exaggerated, but more reasonable claims of 35 miles are impressive enough. It continued to impress travelers into the 1300s, when it was destroyed by an earthquake.

Legacy

It is a tribute to our ancestors that they were able to create works of architecture that capture our imagination even thousands of years after the structures themselves were destroyed. Several efforts are underway to name a definitive list of modern wonders, with such candidates as the Eiffel Tower and the Golden Gate Bridge. One such effort elicited votes from people all over the world via the internet. The finalists, in no particular order, were: Petra, Jordan; the Great Wall of China; the Christ Redeemer, Brazil; the Taj Majal, India; Chichen Itza, Mexico; the Colosseum, Italy; and Machu Picchu, Peru. Given the method of collecting votes, the validity of this list is disputed.

Coming to America

This land is your land, this land is my land....But who was here "first"? Although the Vikings (AD 1000) and 15th- and 16th-century Europeans claimed to be among the first to inhabit North America, this legacy actually belongs to the Native Americans. But where did THEY come from?

✳ ✳ ✳ ✳

Northeast Asia?

NATIVE AMERICANS AND Eastern Asians have several strong similarities—hair and skin color, little or no facial and body hair, and extremely distinctive dental shapes. Even sophisticated DNA studies show common links between the two groups. This evidence lends credence to the theory that a migration from Eastern Asia into North America (what is now Alaska and Canada) occurred via a land bridge. At the time of the last Ice Age—about 10,000 to 12,000 years ago—a large glacier formed across much of North America. The ice drew from the waters between Siberia and Alaska. The result was a dry ocean bed nearly 1,000 miles wide called Beringia. Small, nomadic bands of Asians—known as "hunter-gatherers"— began moving across Beringia in a constant search for food, such as small game animals, nuts, berries, and roots. Seasonal changes continued to push these visitors down the Pacific Coast and inland to what are now the Rocky Mountain states. As the ice melted, Beringia slowly began to shrink, returning to its watery origins within about 4,000 years.

According to anthropologist Paul Martin, the migration across the Americas continued at a rate of about eight miles per year. It took nearly 1,000 years to reach the southern tip of South America.

Japan or Southeast Asia?

Another theory of migration suggests that a small group of Japanese fishermen or sailors were caught in a mighty sea current some 3,000 to 4,000 years ago. They followed the tides from mainland Japan to the western coast of Ecuador in South America called Valdivia. Sound impossible? Consider the anthropological evidence: Ecuadorian pottery was found to be identical to the Jomon styles that existed in Japan at the very same time. Yet many experts suggest it is merely coincidence, and the source of the pottery is more likely Columbia than the Far East.

The famous finds of arrowheads near Clovis, New Mexico, in the 1930s showed that these Americans may have lived nearly 14,000 years ago—2,000 years earlier than those who crossed Beringia. More recent finds show that the early inhabitants from that area (and south, all the way to Brazil) resemble ancient Australian Aborigines. Other skeletal finds in contemporary times point to possible origins in Polynesia.

Europe or Africa?

Long before 1492, when Columbus sailed the ocean blue, plant forms known to be native to Europe and Africa somehow made their way onto North American soil. Cotton and the bottle gourd were already here in America when Columbus hit the beach in the Bahamas. What's more, the Topper archeological site in South Carolina offered artifacts that predate Clovis by as much as 35,000 years!

Though little hard evidence exists to suggest the origin of the Topper inhabitants, many doubt any connection to Asia or South America—leaving Europe and/or Africa as the possible homes of these early travelers to the New World.

Ghost Towns of the Ancients

It's hard to think of great cities like New York or London ever becoming the ghost towns of future centuries. But many New Yorks and Londons of the ancient world did just that—then kept archeologists and scientists busy for hundreds of years.

✳   ✳   ✳   ✳

A Wall, a Horse, and a Mystery

Most people have heard of the siege of Troy, that epic battle over a stolen princess that the blind poet Homer immortalized in the Iliad. The image of a "Trojan Horse" has made its way into film, literature, and even computer lingo. But the city that gave us the famed wooden horse faded into legend around 700 BC. For the next 25 centuries, the city of Troy was dismissed as a fable—an elusive ghost for archeologists and historians.

Details of the real Troy are fragmentary, handed down mostly through Greek myths and Homer's poetry. The city, on the Aegean coast of modern-day Turkey, lay along major trade routes from the Mediterranean to the Black Sea, and it steadily prospered since its Bronze Age founding around 3000 BC.

As Troy grew wealthy and powerful, its inhabitants protected themselves with massive stone walls. Homer's Troy boasted towers nearly 30 feet high and probably contained around 10,000 inhabitants at the time of the Trojan War. The city rose and fell several times (the last around the end of the 8th century BC), and it was rebuilt as a Roman outpost around the time of Christ.

The "Roman Troy" remained an important trading center until Constantinople became the capital of the Eastern Roman Empire and traders began to bypass the ancient town. Troy then began its final journey into decline and ruin. By the time Europe emerged from the Dark Ages, the city had been lost to the ages.

But in the 1870s, an eccentric German businessman named Heinrich Schliemann, who had been schooled on the Iliad as a boy, built a small fortune and began searching for the lost city. Over a 19-year period, Schliemann completed several amateur digs around a city that, in due course, yielded nine sites to bear the name "Troy." The seventh "Troy," a city from around 1200–1000 BC, appears to have been destroyed by fire and is the most likely candidate for the Troy of Homer's epic.

Go Tell the Whom?

Today we think of the ancient Greek city of Sparta as the "Spartan" (austere, militant, and culturally empty) counterpart to the more enlightened, democratic Athenian society. But in ancient times, Sparta lay at the "cutting edge" of political and military arts.

Sparta, the capital of the Lacedaemon kingdom on Greece's Ionic coast, inaugurated many idealistic traditions for which the Greek world became famous. It established a democratic assembly years before the Athenians adopted the practice; it allowed women broad rights to own property and attend schools; and it took its religion and art seriously.

After the Greek city-states combined to defeat the Persian invasion of 480 BC, a rivalry between Sparta and Athens led to the bitter Peloponnesian War (431–403 BC). The war ended in Spartan victory, but Sparta's defeat by Thebes 30 years later sent the city into a period of decline. It fell under Roman rule and succumbed to barbarian invasions, ultimately vanishing into ruin before AD 400.

In a passage from Thucydides's ancient work *The History of the Peloponnesian War*, the old chronicler muses: "Suppose the city of Sparta to be deserted, and nothing left but the temples and the ground-plan, distant ages would be very unwilling to believe that the power of the Lacodaemonians was at all equal to their fame."

Sure enough, the city left little of its original grandeur for later generations. It was not until some 1,500 years later that serious efforts were made to recover the home of the Spartans. In 1906, the British School at Athens did serious archeological work, discovering a theater, temples, and beautiful examples of early Spartan art, and opening the world's eyes to the cultural world that was Sparta.

Rome: Total War

One of the ancient world's greatest cities had the misfortune of bumping up against the most powerful military force of its time. Set on the North African coast near modern Tunisia's capital city, Tunis, the great city of Carthage was the hub of a Mediterranean trading empire that rivaled that of the later Italian upstarts. This rivalry with Rome produced three great wars of antiquity, called the Punic Wars.

By virtue of its location—south of Sicily on Africa's Mediterranean coast—Carthage, a trading empire founded by the seagoing Phoenician people around 814 BC, held a dominant position in Mediterranean trade from the 3rd and 2nd centuries BC. In 264 BC, Rome and Carthage got dragged by their allies into a war over Sicily. Round One went to the Romans. Two decades later, the Carthaginian general Hannibal led his elephants over the Alps into Italy on a legendary campaign of destruction, but the Romans eventually won that one, too.

A half century later, Rome goaded the Carthaginians into a third war. This time, the Roman general Scipio Africanus led a three-year siege of Carthage. After storming the walls and capturing the city, he burned the metropolis to the ground, destroyed Carthaginian ships in the harbor, and sold the populace into slavery. By 146 BC, the destruction of Carthage was complete.

In the 1st century AD, the Romans rebuilt the city as a shipping hub, and the "new" Carthage became a major food supplier for the Roman Empire. It remained a center of Roman Christianity until the end of the 7th century, when Arab invaders toppled the city and replicated Scipio's "complete destruction" formula. The city was supplanted by nearby Tunis, and today the ancient capital is a series of ruins in Tunis's suburbs, where archeologists are digging up statues, tombs, and other relics of one of the ancient world's lost empires.

George's Food & Drink: Serving Food, Wine, and Spirits

You won't find management denying that a ghost resides at George's Food & Drink in Boulder, Colorado; in fact, the place is named after him. Located just south of the Boulder Theater, the restaurant offers fare that it describes as "the next generation in comfort food." That begs the question: Just how much comforting are patrons going to need?

✳   ✳   ✳   ✳

GEORGE'S FOOD & Drink, which opened in 2008 near the Boulder Theater, was originally named The Lounge. The ownership's goal was to provide a place where concert- and theatergoers could have a quick meal or relax with an after-show drink. But it turns out that The Lounge attracts more than just patrons of the arts. One frequent visitor is George Paper, who managed the nearby theater in the 1920s, '30s, and '40s. So what's wrong with that? Well, nothing...except that George has been dead for decades.

George's spirit has been haunting the Boulder Theater ever since he suffered a fatal accident there in 1944. As manager, one of George's duties was to fix lighting problems. While performing a routine repair, George slipped and became tangled in the wiring, with tragic results—he accidentally hung himself.

At least George died doing a job that he loved. He loved it so much, in fact, that he stuck around: His friendly presence has been felt in the theater for years. Patrons and employees alike have reported feeling cold spots in the building, and some have even seen a ghostly man dressed in a 1920s-era suit. George's favorite trick is stealing perfectly good lightbulbs.

Owners of The Lounge renamed the establishment George's Food & Drink in his honor after they realized that he was appearing there quite often. Perhaps, like many other patrons, he's simply found a place to relax after taking in a show.

North Carolina's Train of Terror

North Carolina is rife with haunted houses. In fact, even the Governor's Mansion in Raleigh is said to contain a ghost or two. But one of the Tarheel State's most unusual paranormal events isn't housebound—it takes place on an isolated train trestle known as the Bostian Bridge near the town of Statesville.

* * * *

ON AUGUST 27, 1891, a passenger train jumped the tracks while crossing the Bostian Bridge, plunging seven rail-cars 60 to 75 feet to the ground below. Nearly 30 people perished. According to local legend, on the anniversary of the catastrophe, the sounds of screeching wheels, screaming passengers, and a thunderous crash can be heard near the Bostian Bridge. The ghostly specter of a uniformed man carrying a gold pocket watch has also been observed lingering nearby.

Another Victim Claimed

Sadly, on August 27, 2010, Christopher Kaiser, a Charlotte-based amateur ghost hunter, was struck and killed by a real-life train that surprised him on the Bostian Bridge.

According to police reports, Kaiser had brought a small group to the trestle in hopes of experiencing the eerie sounds that are said to occur on the anniversary of the 1891 crash. The group was standing on the span when a Norfolk-Southern train turned a corner and headed toward them. With the train rapidly approaching, Kaiser managed to push the woman in front of him off the tracks. His heroic action saved her life but cost him his own.

Other than witnessing this horrific accident, Kaiser's group saw nothing unusual that night. But many others claim to have seen strange phenomena on the Bostian Bridge. On the 50th anniversary of the 1891 tragedy, for example, one woman reportedly watched the wreck occur all over again. More than 150 people gathered near the trestle on the 100th anniversary of the crash in 1991, but nothing supernatural happened that night.

Did You Hear About What They Saw?

Who says that ghosts only show themselves to everyday people in out-of-the way locations? The following list just might convince you that when it comes to ghosts, not even the Hollywood elite is safe from a supernatural scare!

✳ ✳ ✳ ✳

Vincent Price

WHILE HE WAS alive, the great Vincent Price frightened the heck out of millions of moviegoers, but Price himself experienced a ghostly shock while he was on an L.A.-to-New York flight on November 15, 1958. Most of the trip was uneventful, but at one point, Price glanced out the window and was shocked to see giant letters that were "lit up with blinding light from within the clouds" spelling out "Tyrone Power is dead."

Price, who was a close friend of Power, was shocked by what he saw, but he was even more perplexed by the fact that no one else on the plane seemed to notice the words, even though some were looking out the windows. Before Price could speak, the words vanished as quickly as they had appeared.

Upon reaching New York, Price dashed to a phone and tried to call Power. That's when he learned that Power had just died of a heart attack in Madrid, Spain. Price originally thought that he'd had a psychic premonition, but as the years passed, he did not experience any similar events, which ultimately led him to believe that he'd been given an otherworldly message for his eyes only.

Paul McCartney

In 1995, Paul McCartney, George Harrison, and Ringo Starr entered a studio to record as The Beatles for the first time in decades. They had chosen to record the song "Free as a Bird," which was written by their dearly departed bandmate John Lennon, who had been gunned down in 1980. While recording the song, McCartney had the distinct feeling that Lennon's ghost was present for the session. McCartney said that they kept hearing strange noises coming from inside the studio and that the equipment malfunctioned from time to time. "There was just an overall feeling that John was around," McCartney said.

Sugar Ray Leonard

In 1982, after ruling the boxing world for several years, Olympic Gold Medalist and World Champion Sugar Ray Leonard found himself in a bad place. At age 25, he had been forced into an early retirement due to a detached retina. He wasn't happy with himself or with life. But all that changed when he and his wife were awakened one night by what sounded like children running in the attic above them. Leonard went to investigate, but his search came up empty. The next day, an exterminator was summoned, but he too found nothing.

The following night, Leonard woke up feeling as though he was being watched. Looking across the darkened bedroom, he saw the silhouette of a child, which he initially thought was one of his sons. But as the shape approached the bed, Leonard realized that it was a young girl. He was transfixed for several moments before he decided to reach out to touch the figure. When he did, the girl's image began to distort, taking on the look of someone who had been horribly burned. It was then that Leonard smelled gas.

Forgetting all about the ghost, Leonard woke his wife. She too smelled the gas, so the couple immediately grabbed their two sleeping children and fled to a relative's house. The following morning, Leonard called a repairman and asked him to check for a gas leak. Several hours later, the repairman called to tell Leonard that not only was there no leak, there weren't even any gas lines in or near the Leonard residence.

Leonard interpreted seeing the ghostly girl as a sign that he needed to recognize the importance of family. And although Leonard never saw the apparition again, he later discovered that a young girl had accidentally burned to death inside the home.

Anson Williams

Years before he would work his way into America's heart as the lovable Potsie Weber on *Happy Days*, Anson Williams had his own guardian angel. Both of Williams's parents told him that on many occasions, they would walk by his room at night and see the ghost of his grandmother standing watch over him as he slept. As he grew older, Williams would take comfort in that, especially since his grandmother had died before he was born and he never had the chance to meet her.

One night in 1971, Williams drove his car into an intersection and was broadsided by a car that had run a red light. Williams states that just as the cars collided, time suddenly began to move in slow motion, and as his head moved toward the windshield, he saw the face of his grandmother in the glass; he also heard her voice telling him, "Everything's fine." And although both cars were smashed beyond recognition, Williams walked away from the accident with only a scratch.

Marilyn Manson

You'd expect shock-rocker Marilyn Manson to have at least one creepy ghost story to tell, but you'd probably never guess that it happened to him at, of all places, a farm in Ohio.

As a teenager in 1986, Manson (then known simply as Brian Warner) befriended a classmate in rural Canton, Ohio. In an attempt to scare Manson, the boy took him to his family's barn, where the boy's older brother had created a sort of makeshift satanic altar, complete with strange symbols and rotting animal carcasses. The boy then picked up a book that was alleged to contain incantations intended to summon evil spirits and ordered Manson to read aloud from it. Before Manson could get very far, the older brother showed up, causing Manson and the other boy to flee into the woods with the book in tow.

After running for a while, the boys came to an old, abandoned house. They made their way to the building's basement, where

Manson was once again ordered to read aloud from the book. As he did, Manson became aware of strange symbols written on the cellar walls, along with what looked like handprints. As he continued to read, the boys began to hear people walking just outside the cellar door, followed by voices. Some of the voices were whispering, while others were clearly saying phrases such as, "Do you believe in Satan?" In a panic, Manson dropped the book and the two boys ran home.

The following day, Manson and his friend returned to the abandoned house to retrieve the book only to find no sign that a house was ever there. Manson called it "the most supernatural strange thing" that he ever experienced, which says a lot coming from him.

Michael Imperioli

Actor Michael Imperioli, who gained fame on *The Sopranos*, counts himself among those who have seen the mournful spirit of Mary, which haunts New York's Chelsea Hotel. Mary wasn't a poet or an artist like many of the Chelsea's guests; she was just a woman from Buffalo, New York, who was waiting for her husband's boat to arrive in New York City. Unfortunately, her husband was on the RMS *Titanic*, and when Mary received news of his fate that cold April night in 1912, she hanged herself in her room.

Typically, guests spot Mary on the eighth floor of the Chelsea; she is usually seen crying or staring longingly into the mirrors. While living on the eighth floor in 1996, Imperioli saw a woman weeping at the end of the hall. He approached her and noticed that she was wearing clothes from the early 1900s. When he asked if she needed help, he heard a lightbulb pop behind him and instinctively turned toward it. A second later, when he turned back around, the woman had vanished. Imperioli moved out of the hotel shortly after discovering that the woman he had encountered was Mary...and that she was a ghost.

The Last Run of the Montreal Express

At the site of a major New England train wreck, spirits move about restlessly. Are they searching for answers, looking for deliverance, or trying to prevent the disaster? Perhaps it is all of the above.

✳   ✳   ✳   ✳

SITES OF TRAGEDIES are hot spots for paranormal phenomena. In fact, such sites seem to feature a perfect amalgamation of the critical elements that are known to attract ghosts. First and foremost, they exemplify the "taken away too soon" factor; haven't we all heard of indignant souls that haunt this world primarily because their mortal stays were cut short? They also feature a distinct "if only I could have warned them" component. Spirits operating with this mindset feel that they could have prevented a particular tragedy if only their actions had been timelier or better orchestrated. Finally, consider the "why did you leave me?" aspect. This is the very sad question that ghosts and survivors alike ask when loved ones suddenly and unexpectedly die. The case of 13-year-old Joe McCabe falls into this category, but others who lost their lives during the ill-fated run of the *Montreal Express* on February 5, 1877, span all of the above.

Vermont's Worst Train Wreck

The accident occurred with the swiftness and brutality typical of such disasters. One moment, the *Montreal Express* was chugging through the night, passing over a wooden trestle at White River Junction, Vermont; the next, it was lying in a heap on solid river ice more than 40 feet below. Overturned gas lamps immediately burst into flames, but the situation went from bad to worse when the huge wooden bridge above the train caught fire. Many would-be rescuers were repelled by intense heat and smoke and could only listen to the plaintive wails of the unfortunate souls trapped in the wreckage. The horrors were unimaginable: Victims were burned to death, crushed, and, in a cruel twist of fate, slowly drowned as the fiery cars melted through the ice. Despite the valiant efforts of rescuers, 34 people perished.

It was later discovered that the train had passed over a defective piece of railway, which caused four of its cars to derail. But this knowledge hardly consoled survivors and grieving families: Their lives had been irrevocably altered the instant that the train left the tracks. The bridge was eventually rebuilt—this time out of steel—and life continued on as always. But the crash site wasn't quite ready to let go of its tragic past.

Ghosts in Training

The Paine House, which is located beside the 650-foot span, was used as a temporary hospital after the accident; it is one of the few structures in the vicinity that remains from the time of the crash. From a kitchen ceiling stained red with the crash victims' blood (which seeped through the floorboards from the room above, where the injured and dead were placed) to stories of livestock too frightened to enter the barn, the supernatural energy of this place is off the charts. Mysterious noises have also been heard coming from the long-abandoned house.

While unsettling, these bits of supernatural ephemera pale in comparison to happenings at the crash site itself. A man dressed in a railway uniform has often been spotted patrolling the empty tracks at night. Some suggest that this phantom may be the ghost of the train's conductor, Mr. Sturtevant. As the doomed *Montreal Express* made its way onto the wooden bridge, Sturtevant felt an unfamiliar grinding. Sensing trouble, he instinctively yanked the bell cord to signal the engineer to stop, but it was too late: Even with its brakes fully applied, the train derailed and tumbled onto the icy river below.

Perhaps the saddest tale from this incident involves young Joe McCabe. Just 13 years old at the time of the tragedy, the boy survived the wreck only to suffer the anguish of watching his father burn to death. Today, the spectral boy can sometimes be seen hovering just above the river, praying that his father will somehow survive. But it's an exercise in futility: McCabe's greatest desire shall never come to pass, and it appears that he's doomed to replay the most tragic event of his life over and over again.

The Glowing Coed

A tragic kitchen accident spawned a ghost that continues to haunt...and she's not alone.

* * * *

IN 1908, FUN-LOVING Condie Cunningham—a student at the Alabama Girls Industrial School (now known as the University of Montevallo), which is located south of Birmingham—was cooking fudge with friends in her dormitory's kitchen when flammable cleaning solvent accidentally spilled onto the stove. Condie's clothing caught on fire, burning her severely; she died in a hospital two days later.

More than a century later, Condie's tortured spirit still haunts Main Hall, where the terrible accident occurred. Witnesses report hearing her desperate cries for help, and a few people have even seen her ghost running through the building, glowing brightly as if on fire. Well, that's the assumption, anyway. In almost every account, witnesses said that they saw a flash of red—like fire—out of the corner of their eye, but when they turned, nothing was there.

College Spirit(s)

Several other spirits are said to haunt the hallowed halls of the University of Montevallo. In Reynolds Hall, one female student was reportedly kicked by an unseen force. Ghosts also haunt both of the school's theaters, where unexplained phenomena include doors swinging open by themselves, windows opening and closing on their own, and odd noises coming from the attic above one of the stages.

According to school historians, one of the theater's ghosts may be that of Henry Clay Reynolds, the college's first president. Another theater-bound specter is believed to be that of Walter H. Trumbauer, a well-respected drama instructor who—according to campus legend—often appears during College Night, an annual competition of student-performed musical theater. Supposedly, Trumbauer makes his presence known by causing a batten above the stage to sway over the performers who will win. After all, once a drama teacher, always a drama teacher—even in the afterlife.

Ghosts of Harpers Ferry

Harpers Ferry, West Virginia, is a picturesque town that has been at the center of a great deal of American history, most notably during the mid-19th century, when abolitionist John Brown staged a raid that proved to be a catalyst for the American Civil War. However, Harpers Ferry is also known for its ghosts. Here are a few of the many spirits that haunt this historic town:

✳ ✳ ✳ ✳

Rachael Harper

IN THE MID-18TH century, Robert Harper founded the town of Harpers Ferry. After he and his wife Rachael lost their first house in a flood, Harper began construction of a much grander home. But this was during the American Revolution, when laborers were hard to find, so the aging Harper did much of the work himself. He was quite concerned about lawlessness during this uncertain time, so legend has it that he instructed Rachael to bury their gold in a secret location and tell no one about it. Harper passed away in 1782, and after Rachael died unexpectedly following a fall from a ladder, the secret location of their gold was buried with her.

For many years, the Harper House has been considered haunted. People who pass it swear that they see a woman in old-fashioned clothes staring out from an upstairs window. Perhaps it's Rachael, remaining watchful over the family's gold.

18th-Century Soldiers

In the waning years of the 18th century, an army was sent to Harpers Ferry in preparation for a possible war between the United States and France. The army wound up waiting for a conflict that never happened, so to relieve their boredom, the soldiers paraded to fife and drum music. Unfortunately, a cholera epidemic struck the army while it sat idle, and many men died. Today, the spirits of the men seem to remain. Almost everyone in town has heard the faint sounds of feet marching, drums beating, and fifes playing as an invisible phantom army sweeps through town, doomed to repeat its nightly musical ritual for eternity.

John Brown

John Brown is probably the most noteworthy figure associated with the town of Harpers Ferry. Many people are familiar with his tall, gaunt, white-bearded image, so perhaps it's not surprising that many have seen someone looking exactly like him wandering around town. The resemblance to Brown is so uncanny that tourists have taken photos with the spirit; however, when the pictures are developed, "Brown" is not in them.

John Brown's ghost has also been spotted several miles outside of town at the Kennedy Farmhouse. It was there that Brown and his men stayed for several months while planning the raid. Even today, phantom footsteps, disembodied male voices, and snoring can be heard coming from the empty attic where the conspirators once stayed. It's no wonder that particular area of the house is largely shunned.

Dangerfield Newby

Another ghost seen at Harpers Ferry is that of Dangerfield Newby, a former slave who joined Brown's raid out of des-

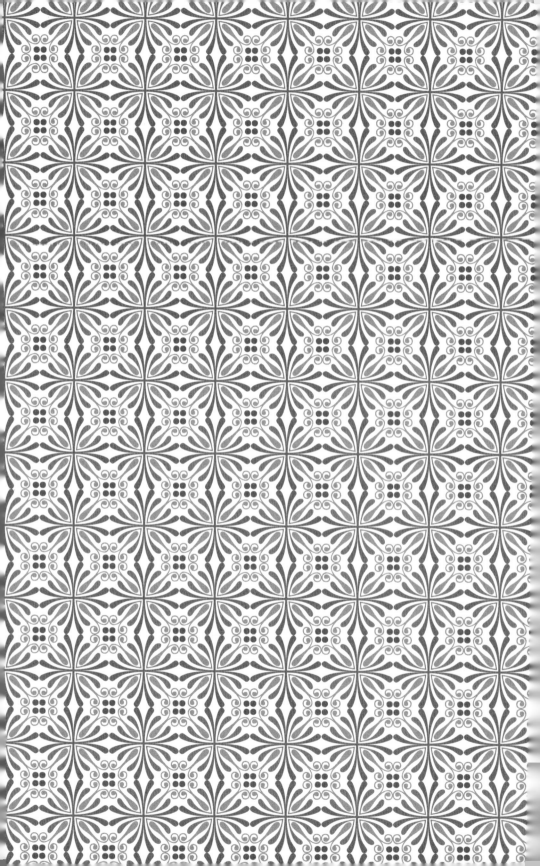